Labour is prior to and independent of capital. Capital is only the fruit of labour, and could never have existed if labour had not first existed. Labour is the superior of capital, and deserves much the higher consideration.

Abraham Lincoln,
first annual address to Congress, 1861

The behaviour of British Airways and its parent company towards its employees is a national disgrace. It falls well below the standards we would expect from any employer, especially in light of the scale of taxpayer subsidy, at this time of national crisis.

House of Commons Transport Select Committee,
The Guardian, 13 June 2020

We are fast approaching tipping points that will trigger escalating feedback loops of global heating. But investing in the net zero, climate resilient economy will create feedback loops of its own – virtuous circles of sustainable growth, jobs, and opportunity.

UN Secretary-General António Guterres,
COP26, Glasgow, 1 November 2021

Message to Students

Dear Student,

Thank you for buying *Human Resource Management: A Critical Approach*. This edition builds on six previous editions of Bratton and Gold's best-selling HRM textbook. This totally revised edition has been written in response to changing global events, new HRM research and feedback from students and lecturers around the world. This new edition provides an accessible but critical introduction to HRM that will equip you with a comprehensive knowledge and understanding of the latest relevant theories and practices of the subject.

The text is structured in five parts. Each chapter follows a similar structure in order to help you navigate easily through the text. At the beginning of each chapter, the **chapter outline** and **chapter objectives** summarise the key concepts that will be covered and the knowledge you will gain. The main text introduces you to the major HRM concepts and practices before finally offering critical comment and discussing alternative perspectives. **Reflective questions** encourage you to think critically about key issues and consider broader consequences of management decisions. The **HRM in practice** features illustrate current developments or practices in HRM so you can see the application (or non-application) of theory in the real world. The **Global HRM** features exemplify good (and poor) management practices in the global economy. **HRM web links** are also embedded in the chapters to help you research topics further and appreciate the application of HR practices in the contemporary workplace.

Red Globe Press subjected the manuscript to an extensive peer review process. In so doing, all the topics discussed have been updated (with over 400 post-2017 references); included are new sections on the gig economy, managing conflict, managing mental health, and sustainable HRM. This edition also contains new learning features such as: **Legal Focus, Ethical Insight, Digital Spotlight** and **Search & Watch**. At the end of each chapter, you will find a **summary** of the chapter content and some **review questions**. For international students, a **vocab checklist** feature on the companion website helps you to comprehend HRM-related terminology and other more sophisticated vocabulary for talking about the discipline, as well as language learning tips specially written by an ESL instructor for this book. We provide details of **further reading** sources to help you gain a higher mark for your HRM assignment, and there is a **case study** in each chapter to highlight the challenges of applying HRM theory in practice. Additional learning material including **practice HRM assignments**, which provide an opportunity to develop key professional and employability skills, can be found on the book's companion website. There is also a comprehensive searchable online **glossary**.

With rising tuition fees and many students experiencing virtual teaching, we endeavour to give value for money. When you buy this textbook, you can access the **companion website**, referred to above, at **www.bloomsbury.pub/bratton-hrm**. The companion website provides additional web links to further resources to help you research HRM topics, there is also access to summary lecture notes for each chapter and skill development exercises to improve your professional competencies, as well as the content mentioned above.

We hope our hands-on approach to learning helps you to make maximum use of the textbook and be successful in your HRM module and future career.

Good luck with your studies.
John Bratton
Edinburgh

HUMAN RESOURCE MANAGEMENT

A CRITICAL APPROACH

JOHN BRATTON AND JEFF GOLD
WITH
ANDREW BRATTON AND LAURA STEELE

BLOOMSBURY
NEW DELHI • LONDON • OXFORD • NEW YORK • SYDNEY

BLOOMSBURY INDIA
Bloomsbury Publishing India Pvt. Ltd.
Second Floor, LSC Building No.4, DDA Complex, Pocket C - 6& 7,
Vasant Kunj, New Delhi 110070

BLOOMSBURY, BLOOMSBURY ACADEMIC and the Diana logo are trademarks of Bloomsbury Publishing Plc

First published in Great Britain 1994
This edition published 2022

Cover design: eStudio Calamar
Cover image © Chaili Kwek/EyeEm

This edition published with permission from Bloomsbury Publishing Plc
50 Bedford Square, London, WC1B3DP, UK

A catalogue record for this book is available from the British Library.

A catalog record for this book is available from the Library of Congress.

ISBN: 9789356401297

10 9 8 7 6 5 4 3 2 1

Typeset by Straive
Printed and bound in india Gopsons Papers Pvt. Ltd.

This new edition is dedicated to front-line health-care workers who cared for us through the Covid-19 crisis, and to the families of those who lost their lives in doing so.

BRIEF CONTENTS

PART 1 Past as Prologue: The Ascendency of HRM

Introduction 2

PART 2 Human Resource Management as a Field of Study

Chapter 1 Contemporary Human Resource Management: The Role of Critique 18

Chapter 2 Corporate Strategy and Strategic HRM 50

PART 3 Fundamentals of HRM

Chapter 3 Job and Work Design 84

Chapter 4 Workforce Planning and Diversity 114

Chapter 5 Recruitment and Selection 142

Chapter 6 Performance Management 172

Chapter 7 Learning and Development 202

Chapter 8 Reward Management 232

PART 4 Managing the Employment Relationship

Chapter 9 Labour Relations and Collective Bargaining 264

Chapter 10 Employee Relations and Conflict Management 292

PART 5 Contemporary Issues

Chapter 11 HRM, Health and Well-Being 324

Chapter 12 Sustainable HRM and Environmental Sustainability 352

Chapter 13 International HRM in a Globalised Capitalism 378

Chapter 14 Back to the Future: Reimagining HRM in a Post-Pandemic Capitalism 408

Glossary *425*

References *426*

Name Index *482*

Subject Index *498*

LONG CONTENTS

Figures and Tables xviii
About the Author xxi
About the chapter contributors xxi
About the feature contributors xxi
Author's Acknowledgements xxiii
Message to Lecturers xxiv
Preface xxv
Tour of the Book xxviii
Search & Watch xxx
Digital Resources xxxii
Key Topics Grid xxxiii

PART 1 Past as Prologue: The Ascendency of HRM

Introduction 2
Work and employment relations in the age of neoliberalism 3
The ascendency of HRM 8
The context of management education 10
HRM: a discipline in crisis 12
The structure and content of the book 14

PART 2 Human Resource Management as a Field of Study

Chapter 1 Contemporary Human Resource Management: The Role of Critique 18
Introduction 19
Defining human resource management 19
Digital Spotlight: How digital technologies shape and direct HRM 23
The employment relationship 23
Ethical Insight: Is it ethical to insist workers should return to work during the Covid-19 crisis? 28
The scope and goals of HRM 29
The goals of HRM 31
Global HRM: Netflix: Line managers use 'keeper test' 31

Theorising HRM 32
- The Michigan model of HRM 33
- The Harvard model of HRM 34
- The Storey model of HRM 35
- The Ulrich Human Resource Business Partner model of HRM 37
- The Bath model of HRM 38

HRM in Practice: Managers as agents of the HRM function 40
HRM and the role of critique 41
- The effect of critique on work and people management 43

Summary 45
Review questions 45
Search & Watch 45
Legal Focus 46
Chapter case: Diversity at DigitalArt 46
Further reading 48

Chapter 2 Corporate Strategy and Strategic HRM 50

Introduction 51
Strategic management 51
HRM in Practice: 'Our people are our greatest asset'? 53
The five-step process of strategic management 54
Ethical Insight: Do ethics influence corporate strategy? 55
Hierarchy of strategy 56
Corporate-level strategy 57
- Business-level strategy 57
- Functional-level strategy 57

Strategic choice and corporate ideology 57
Building a sustainable strategy 58
Global HRM : Australian businesses urge green recovery from Covid-19 crisis 60
Strategy, ethics and corporate social responsibility 60
Strategic HRM 61
Defining strategic HRM 62
Theorising strategic HRM 63
- The 'best-fit' model 64
- The 'best-practice' model 64
- The 'resource-based' model 65

HR strategy and organisational dynamics 67
Line managers as agents of HR strategy 68
Digital Spotlight: Key metrics for aligning corporate strategy and HR strategy 69
HR strategy and performance 70
Critical perspectives and analysis 75
Summary 78

Review questions 78
Search & Watch 78
Legal Focus 79
Chapter case: Mandla Winery 79
Further reading 81

PART 3: Fundamentals of HRM

Chapter 3 Job and Work Design 84
Introduction 85
The nature of work 85
Global HRM: How could a four-day week work for Kiwis? 87
The meaning of job and work design 88
HRM in Practice: Teachers at breaking point 93
The development of work design 94
Ethical Insight: The ethics of zero-hours contracts 96
Classical work designs: scientific management 97
Post-bureaucratic design: the job characteristic model 100
Post-bureaucratic design: Japanese management 100
Digital Spotlight: Optimising the strengths of humans and machines 101
Contemporary design: process-centred and high-performance systems 102
Business process re-engineering 102
High-performance work systems 103
Critiquing job and work design 105
Summary 109
Review questions 109
Search & Watch 109
Legal Focus 110
Chapter case: Virtual teams at G&Q Manufacturing 110
Further reading 111
Chapter 4 Workforce Planning and Diversity 114
Introduction 115
The nature and scope of workforce planning 115
Ethical Insight: Diversity and inclusion: a question of economics or ethics? 117
The workforce planning process 118
Demand forecasting 118
Supply forecasting 120
Workforce action plans: organisational responses to forecasts 121
Global HRM: Domestic workers in Qatar and workforce planning 122
Workforce diversity 123
Diversity as lived experience 124

Digital Spotlight: Key metrics for workforce planning 125
Diversity management 126
Flexibility and precariousness 129
Zero-hours contracts 131
Teleworking 131
Outsourcing and offshoring 132
'Downsizing' or 'rightsizing' 133
HRM in Practice: Safeguarding the lives of BAME key workers 134
Critiquing workforce planning 135
Summary 137
Review questions 137
Search & Watch 137
Legal Focus 137
Chapter case: Køre (Part 1) 138
Further reading 140

Chapter 5 Recruitment and Selection 142

Introduction 143
The recruitment and selection process: overview 143
Workforce action plan 144
HRM in Practice: 'Princelings scandal': hired because of father's connections 145
Selection criteria 146
Measurement issues 148
Global HRM: Looks matter when hiring in Singapore 149
Perceptual biases 150
Reliability 151
Validity 151
Digital Spotlight: Algorithmic bias in recruitment and selection 153
Recruitment methods: attraction 153
Recruitment and selection paradigms 154
Recruitment channels 156
Selection: assessment 159
Ethical Insight : What behaviours are necessary for those seeking to conduct a job interview ethically? 159
CVs, application forms and biodata 160
Psychometric testing 160
Situational judgement tests 162
Selection interviewing 163
Assessment centres 164
Critiquing recruitment and selection 165
Summary 167
Review questions 167

Search & Watch 167
Legal Focus 168
Chapter case: Køre (Part 2) 168
Further reading 170

Chatper 6 Performance Management 172

Introduction 173
The nature and development of performance management 173
Ethical Insight: Does objective setting in performance management encourage unethical behaviour? 176
Performance management processes 177
Review performance plan 177
Planning future performance 179
Monitor performance 179
Performance appraisal 180
Antecedents of performance management 181
Digital Spotlight: Is online appraisal equitable? 181
Defining performance 182
Appraisal instruments for assessing performance 183
HRM in Practice: The benefits of mentorship during a crisis 185
Performance, judgements and feedback 186
Judgements and diversity 188
Appraiser bias 189
Types of appraisal 189
Dyadic relations and feedback 191
Performance appraisal as a strategic control 192
Performance and rewards 192
Performance and development 193
Global HRM: Culture of individualism and performance management in the US 194
Critiquing performance management 195
Summary 197
Review questions 197
Search & Watch 197
Legal Focus 197
Chapter case: Sustaintricity Co. 198
Further reading 200

Chapter 7 Learning and Development 202

Introduction 203
The context of strategic learning and development 203
Human capital theory 203
Learning and competitive advantage 205

Ethical Insight: Why does machine learning raise ethical concerns? 206
Workplace learning and knowledge creation 207
HRM in Practice: Is learning the key to tackling racism in the workplace? 209
Theoretical perspectives on adult learning 210
  Defining learning and development 211
  Learning theories 212
  Kolb's learning model 214
Global HRM: How Denmark became the home of the robotics industry 215
The strategic learning and development process 216
  Pre-L&D intervention stage 218
  L&D delivery stage 218
  Post-L&D intervention stage 218
Needs analysis: linking strategy to learning and development 219
  Organisational analysis 219
  Job analysis 220
  Individual analysis 220
Digital Spotlight: Reskilling workers for the age of AI 221
Evaluation of learning and development 222
Leadership development and coaching 223
  Coaching 225
Future challenges: machine learning and the Fourth Industrial Revolution 226
Critiquing the strategic learning and development discourse 227
Summary 228
Review questions 228
Search & Watch 228
Legal Focus 229
Chapter case: Diversity management at Køre (Part 3) 229
Further reading 230

Chapter 8 Reward Management 232

Introduction 233
The nature of reward 233
  Reward and the employment relationship 236
A strategic framework for reward 236
  Corporate strategy 237
  Reward objectives 237
  Reward choices 238
  Reward techniques 239
  Reward competitiveness 240
  Evaluation 240
HRM in Practice: Is the national living wage a departure from a deregulated labour market? 241

Job evaluation: internal equity 242
Gathering the job analysis data 243
Selecting compensable factors 243
Evaluating the job 244
Assigning pay to the job 245
Global HRM: What Iceland can teach the world about equal pay 246
Establishing pay levels: external equity 247
Digital Spotlight: Calculating unit labour costs (ULC) 250
The spirit of new pay 251
Individualising reward in the contemporary workplace 252
Inequality and the gender pay gap 252
Ethical Insight: Is it time for 'radical transparency' when it comes to pay? 253
The gender pay gap 255
Critiquing the strategic reward paradigm 258
Summary 260
Review questions 260
Search & Watch 260
Legal Focus 260
Chapter case: Basil Café 261
Further reading 262

PART 4 Managing the Employment Relationship

Chapter 9 Labour Relations and Collective Bargaining 264

Introduction 265
The nature of labour relations 265
Ethical Insight: Is a union-avoidance strategy unethical? 268
The legal context of labour relations 269
HRM in Practice: Unions and green groups call for a sustainable Covid-19 recovery 271
HRM and labour relations strategies 272
Global HRM: Do police unions lead to more violence? 276
Trade unions 277
Understanding why employees join trade unions 277
Trade unions in action 278
Union membership 278
Interpreting union decline 281
Trade union structure 282
Collective bargaining 283
Collective bargaining structure 283
The collective agreement: an overview 284
Digital Spotlight: Bargaining disruptive technological change: a case of mutual gains? 285

Critiquing labour relations 286
Summary 288
Review questions 288
Search & Watch 288
Legal Focus 289
Chapter case: Rajah Apparel Co. 289
Further reading 291

Chapter 10 Employee Relations and Conflict Management 292

Introduction 293
The nature of employee relations 293
Digital Spotlight: The surveillance of workers in a 'digital cage' 295
Understanding conflict and conflict management 296
- Types of conflict 297
- Causes of conflict 298
- Conflict management 299
- Disciplinary procedure 300

Employee grievance 301
- Sexual harassment as an employee relations issue 301

HRM in Practice: Online activism: how should HR respond? 303
Employee discipline 304
- Disciplinary concepts 304

Global HRM: International assignments can be tough for LGBTQ+ staff 305
Employee voice 306
- Forms of employee voice 309
- A general theory of employee voice 310
- Indirect employee voice 311
- Joint consultative committees 311
- European Works Councils 312

Employee communication 313
- Communication methods 314

Ethical Insight: Can we accord ethical legitimacy to 'pseudo-employee voice'? 316
Critiquing employee relations 316
Summary 318
Review questions 318
Search & Watch 318
Legal Focus 319
Chapter case: Rising tensions at Solas Resort and Spa 319
Further reading 321

PART 5 Contemporary Issues

Chapter 11 HRM, Health and Well-Being 324

Introduction 325
Sustainable health and safety and HRM 325
Ethical Insight: Employee genetic testing 327
The importance of health, safety and wellness 328
Economic considerations 328
Legal considerations 329
Psychological considerations 330
Ethical considerations 330
Global HRM: Supporting the mental health of Black employees 331
Workplace health and safety issues 332
Mental health at work 332
Workplace violence 336
Workplace bullying 337
Alcohol and drug abuse 340
Sick building syndrome 341
HRM in Practice: Employee perceptions of work-related stress 342
Workplace wellness 343
Digital Spotlight: OHS and well-being in Industry 4.0 344
Critiquing workplace health, safety and well-being 345
Summary 347
Review questions 347
Search & Watch 347
Legal Focus 348
Chapter case: Lagan Meadows Care Home – caring for the carers 348
Further reading 350

Chapter 12 Sustainable HRM and Environmental Sustainability 352

Introduction 353
The nature of environmental sustainability 353
HRM in Practice: Carney issues climate change warning to companies 356
Workers' pro-environmental behaviours 357
Environmental management systems 358
Ethical Insight: A just transition to a low-carbon economy: a question of ethics, economics or politics? 359
Motivators for embedding sustainability strategies 360
Global HRM: US and UK unions call for climate jobs and just transition 363

Environmental leadership and culture 364
- Environmental leadership 364
- Reframing organisational culture 365

Creating a low-carbon workplace through sustainable HRM 366
- Recruitment and selection 367
- Pro-environmental learning and development 368
- Performance management and sustainability 369
- Rewarding pro-environmental behaviours 369

Digital Spotlight: Key metrics for sustainability 370

Employee voice in environmental sustainability 371

Critiquing corporate-oriented sustainability 373

Summary 374

Review questions 374

Search & Watch 374

Legal focus 375

Chapter case: RailCo 375

Further reading 377

Chapter 13 International HRM in a Globalised Capitalism 378

Introduction 379

Globalisation and typologies of global business strategy 379
- Global business strategies 380
- The integration–responsiveness grid 382

Global HRM: Can quotas achieve gender equality? 384

The nature of international HRM 385
- MNCs and employment relations 385
- IHRM and SIHRM 386

A model of SIHRM 387
- (1) Exogenous factors 389
- (2) Endogenous factors 389
- (3) SIHRM 389
- (4) Pressures and goals 390
- (5) SIHRM orientation 390

HRM in Practice: 'We are expendable ...' 392

HR strategy in MNCs 393
- International staffing 394
- International reward 394
- International learning and development 395
- International performance appraisal 396
- Repatriation 397

Digital Spotlight: How technology drives the globalisation of work and employment 398

The convergence/divergence debate 399
Ethical Insight: Decarbonising the Global North at the expense of the Global South? 401
Critiquing international HRM 401
Summary 404
Review questions 404
Search & Watch 404
Legal Focus 405
Chapter case: IKAN 405
Further reading 407

Chapter 14 Back to the Future: Reimagining HRM in a Post-Pandemic Capitalism 408

Introduction 409
Past and present 409
Post-pandemic capitalism 411
Reimagining HRM 415
A final word 422
Further reading 424

Glossary 425
References 426
Name Index 482
Subject Index 498

FIGURES AND TABLES

Figures

1.1 The employment and psychological contract between workers and employers 27
1.2 HRM functions, contingencies and skills 30
1.3 The HRM cycle 33
1.4 The Harvard model of HRM 34
1.5 The Bath People and Performance model of HRM 39
2.1 The three traditional poles of a strategic plan 52
2.2 A conceptual overview of corporate-wide and HRM strategic decision-making 56
2.3 The four pillars of sustainability 59
2.4 The relationship between resources and capabilities, strategies and sustained competitive advantage 66
2.5 SHRM, employee well-being, the employment relationship and performance 72
2.6 A causal model of the HRM–performance relationship 73
3.1 A framework for analysing job design 88
3.2 The core dimensions of job design for individual employees 89
3.3 Alternative job designs for an employee 89
3.4 Mapping key developments in work design 95
3.5 An example of job rotation 99
3.6 An example of job enlargement 99
3.7 An example of job enrichment 99
3.8 The work design–human factor paradox 107
4.1 The workforce planning process 119
5.1 The stages of recruitment and selection process 144
5.2 Job description format 146
5.3 Rodger's seven-point plan 147
5.4 Munro-Fraser's fivefold grading system 147
5.5 An attraction–selection–attrition framework 155
6.1 The performance management cycle 178
6.2 Defining performance 183

6.3	BOS in a financial services company	184
6.4	Reactions to feedback on performance at work	187
6.5	Performance control in appraisal	192
6.6	Performance as a transformation process	193
7.1	Voluntarism versus interventionism in L&D	205
7.2	Kolb's experiential cycle of learning	215
7.3	The strategic learning and development process	217
7.4	A framework for the transfer of training	221
7.5	Levels of evaluation for training and learning	223
8.1	Behavioural outcomes of a reward system	234
8.2	A strategic framework for reward	237
8.3	The top 10 global gender gap index rankings (2020)	246
8.4	The construction of a pay level	249
8.5	Income inequality in selective countries	255
8.6	Gender pay gap in selected countries (2020)	256
9.1	UK trade union density, private sector collective bargaining and rising income inequality	287
10.1	Four important dimensions of employee relations	294
10.2	Manifestations of organisational conflict	297
10.3	The European code on sexual harassment	302
10.4	Framework for analysing employee voice	308
10.5	The engagement–commitment cycle	311
10.6	Key issues related to communication in the workplace	314
11.1	Typical symptoms of workplace stress	335
13.1	An integrated framework of SIHRM	388
13.2	Globalisation and HRM models	400

Tables

1.1	Selective HRM definitions: past and present	20
1.2	The Storey model of HRM	36
2.1	Strategy implementation and the four-task model of HRM	63
2.2	Pfeffer's (1998), Den Hartog and Verburg's (2004), Danford et al.'s (2008) and Guest's (2017) 'best' practices	65
2.3	Selective studies reporting an HRM–performance relationship	70
2.4	A framework for studying strategic HRM	74
3.1	Core elements of organisation structure	90
3.2	Key characteristics of bureaucratic, flat, matrix and boundaryless organisation structures	92
3.3	The traditional and process-centred work models	104

4.1 Key dimensions of flexible paid work 130
5.1 Competencies in a financial services organisation 148
5.2 Common misjudgements of others 150
5.3 Accuracy of a sample of selection methods 152
5.4 Reasons for poor results from selection interviewing 164
6.1 Selective definitions of performance management 174
6.2 Theories guiding performance management 180
7.1 Traditions of learning 212
7.2 Traditions of social learning 214
7.3 Assessment and analysis of training needs 220
8.1 Types of employee pay 239
8.2 Typical job ranking 244
8.3 Point system matrices 245
8.4 UK salaries for selective occupations and CEOs, 2019 247
8.5 Alignment of business strategy, work design and reward practices 251
9.1 Average trade union membership, union density and collective bargaining coverage in selective European countries, 2018 279
9.2 Average union membership in the UK, 1971–2019 280
9.3 UK average union density from 1996 to 2018, by broad sector 281
11.1 Differing approaches to well-being at work 326
12.1 Rank order of environmental managers' perceptions of drivers of sustainability initiatives 361
12.2 Different concepts of involvement and participation 371
13.1 MNCs IHRM orientation and global business strategies 390
13.2 Examples of learning and development interventions in MNCs 396

ABOUT THE AUTHOR

John Bratton grew up in Yorkshire, and now divides his time between Calgary, Alberta and Edinburgh, Scotland. He is Honorary Professor in the Management School at Queen's University Belfast, Northern Ireland. He holds a BSc in Economics from the University of Hull and a PhD in Sociology of Work from the University of Manchester, England. He has more than 30 years' experience of teaching a range of HRM, organisational behaviour and leadership courses, at both undergraduate and graduate levels mainly in the UK and Canada, but also in Finland and Singapore. His research interests traverse the sociology of work and management. John was the first Director of the Workplace Learning Research Unit at the University of Calgary, Canada, and has been a member of the editorial board of *Leadership*, the *Journal of Workplace Learning* and the *Canadian Journal for the Study of Adult Education*. In addition to writing this book, John is author of *Japanization at Work: Managerial Studies in the 1990s*; co-author of *Workplace Learning: A Critical Introduction* (2004); co-author of *Organizational Leadership* (with Keith Grint and Debra Nelson) (2005); co-author of *Capitalism and Classical Social Theory* (with David Denham) (2019), now in its third edition, editor of *Organizational Leadership* (2020) and author of *Work and Organizational Behaviour* (2021), now in its fourth edition.

About the chapter contributors

Andrew Bratton is a Lecturer in Human Resource Management at Edinburgh Napier University. He previously worked as a Knowledge Transfer Partnership (KTP) Associate in Innovation Management at the University of Strathclyde, in a Microsoft technology consultancy. Andrew's specialist interests include sustainable human resource management and the management of the employment relationship within the context of organisational change. His research and knowledge exchange work are focused on leadership, employee engagement, innovation, technology and action learning. His current research focuses on the application of sustainable practices in small and medium-sized enterprises.

Laura Steele is a Senior Lecturer in Business and Society at Queen's Management School, Belfast, where she also acts as Ethics, Responsibility and Sustainability Champion. Before joining the Management School, Laura worked predominantly in the public and voluntary sectors. Her teaching and research interests include ethics, social responsibility, and the impact of new technologies on business and society. She developed and hosts the 'QMS Good Business Podcast', which aims to go beyond the bottom line and explore the ethical, social and environmental responsibilities of organisations.

About the feature contributors

David Denham is an Honorary Research Fellow at Wolverhampton University, UK, where he taught a wide variety of sociology courses, including classical social theory, over a career of 35 years. He has published articles on the sociology of law, criminology and the sociology of sport. David is co-author of *Victimology: Victimization and Victims' Rights* (2008) and co-author (with John Bratton) of *Capitalism and Classical Social Theory* (3rd edn) (2019).

Alexis Evans is a Talent Acquisition analyst based in Berlin. She holds a double degree in Business Management from Northumbria University and Hochschule Heilbronn. Her bachelor thesis explored diversity hiring for technical roles in Berlin-based start-ups. Alexis is passionate about increasing diversity in entrepreneurship and co-leads the Berlin chapter of the SoGal Foundation.

Sarita Koendjbiharie is Assistant Professor of Management and Organization at the Faculty of Humanities at Leiden University in the Netherlands. She is course founder and leader and using a focused business school background has developed courses on organisational theory and behaviour as well as capstone consultancy and internship programmes. She teaches students to (self)reflect on socialisation by applying frameworks related to organisational culture, structure and leadership as outsider and insider to workplaces. Her research addresses theory-practice gaps, networks and early career formation. Sarita holds a PhD from the Rotterdam School of Management, Erasmus University.

Lori Rilkoff is a former Human Resources and Safety Director at the City of Kamloops in Canada. She has an MSc in HRM and Training and was an instructor in the Department of Business and Economics at Thompson Rivers University, Kamloops, Canada. Lori has been recognised by the City of Kamloops, Excellence Canada and by the Chartered Professionals in Human Resources of British Columbia for the encouragement and promotion of employer-based wellness programmes in the community. In 2020, she was awarded a Fellow of the Chartered Professionals in Human Resources (FCPHR) in recognition of her career contributions to the human resources profession.

AUTHOR'S ACKNOWLEDGEMENTS

In preparing for this seventh edition, I have endeavoured to meet the requests and suggestions from external reviewers. In this regard, I wish to thank the following:

Dr Douglas Martin, University of Central Lancashire, UK
Associate Professor Angela Knox, University of Sydney, Australia
Dr James Wallace, Swansea University, UK
Professor Geraint Harvey, Western University, Canada
Dr Samantha Evans, University of Kent, UK
Dr Yuanyuan Huo, University of Surrey, UK
Dr Nadia K. Kougiannou, Nottingham Trent University, UK

This edition contains video clips giving the personal views of business, trade union and HR professionals. Their contributions bring an invaluable insight into how HRM is operationalised in the workplace, and in this regard, I wish to give my special thanks to Gregor Karolus, Alison Blayney, Sarah Myers, Karen Jochelson, Keith Stopforth, Helen Tiffany, Ruth Altman, Ray Fletcher, Keith Hanlon-Smith, Lana Kularajah, Markus Hiemann and Lesley White.

I wish to thank Jeff Gold for permitting me to revise and update his chapters. Professor Gold has devoted over 20 years to the production of editions of this text and has decided to dedicate his academic interests in other directions. While not directly involved, his fingerprints remain on his revised chapters. It has been an enjoyable experience collaborating with Jeff. I would also like to thank the previous contributors to the book, Kirsteen Grant and Roselyn Larkin, and welcome new contributors Laura Steele, Alexis Evans and Sarita R. Koendjbiharie. Taken together, I believe they have considerably helped to enrich the chapters and to fulfil the purpose of this book. My greatest debt is to my partner, Carolyn Forshaw, who has given me unconditional support during the months over which this book and previous editions were written. Finally, I would like to acknowledge the support, creativity and hard work of the talented and dedicated editorial team at Bloomsbury, in particular Ursula Gavin, Sophiya Ali, Christian Ritter, Amy Brownbridge, Amanda Woolf, Anne Halliday and Sophie Dunbar.

John Bratton
Edinburgh

Message to Lecturers

Dear Lecturer,

Thank you for adopting *HRM: A Critical Approach*. Lecturers familiar with the previous six editions of the Bratton and Gold text may ask why the change to a slender edition. There are three reasons. The first is a change in personnel. Co-author and former colleague Jeff Gold has decided that the time has come to take a step back from contributing chapters and to devote his academic interests in other directions. I missed his close involvement in writing this edition. The chapters on recruitment and selection and learning and development still retain his fingerprints and much of his insights. The second reason for the change is to reflect on HRM policies and practices in the light of unprecedented contextual changes in which they are embedded. As we argued elsewhere, there is a strong case for what we call 'critical human resource management education' or 'CHRME'. This is even more important given the reverberations of the Covid-19 crisis. The effects of the pandemic, it is predicted, will persist for a generation. Nothing will ever be normal again. Overshadowing the public health crisis is the climate crisis and the deepening economic crisis as Britain withdraws from the European Union. That the triple crises entail change in the way work and people are managed is not merely advisable, it is necessary. That means much of the mainstream strategic HRM literature is inadequate for understanding contemporary business models and employment relations and we should be offering students a critical discussion of the core themes and debates around HRM in the post-Covid-19-Brexit era. It is therefore more appropriate than ever to emphasise 'critical' in the new subtitle.

The third reason for this slender edition is practical. Informal feedback suggested that most lecturers had insufficient time in a one-semester course to cover almost a third of the chapters in the expanded sixth edition. Since the first edition was published in 1994, successive reviewers have suggested additional new chapters, which resulted in the book expanding from its original 12 chapters to 17 in the 2017 edition. *HRM: A Critical Approach* reverts back to examining core HRM theories and practices while offering students a much-needed critical perspective on the HR function.

This new edition, however, continues to draw upon the pedagogical features developed in the previous six editions. Features which serve to highlight the frequent mismatch between the rhetoric and reality of HRM. The critical interrogation of HR practices and new additional pedagogical features appreciably set the book apart from the competition. We have tried to make the themes surrounding HRM relevant in the context of the triple crises, as well as intellectually rewarding.

Red Globe Press subjected the manuscript to an extensive peer review process, and I am extremely grateful to all the reviewers who made many valuable suggestions for revisions and additional material. The research and debate on all the topics discussed have been updated (with over 400 post-2017 references). Included also are new sections on the gig economy, managing conflict, managing mental health, and sustainable HRM. In addition, there are new or updated **Case studies, HRM in Practice** and **Global HRM**. In this edition, we provide new features to help your students: **Legal Focus, Ethical Insight, Digital Spotlight** and **Search & Watch**. More detail on these is provided in the Preface. Finally, as with previous editions, this book is supported by a **companion website**, located at www.bloomsbury.pub/bratton-hrm, which provides supplementary learning materials for you and your students.

As is inevitable, some high-quality articles and books may have inadvertently been omitted, so I would welcome suggestions of material to include and feedback to improve the next edition. Please contact me via the email address on the book's website.

John Bratton
Edinburgh

PREFACE

Welcome to *HRM: A Critical Approach*. It is only four years since we were writing the sixth edition of this text, but global events and, in Britain, Brexit, as well as my own thoughts on the HR function, have necessitated a major revision.

Who should use this book?

This book has been written specifically to provide a critical and engaging introduction to HRM. It is designed for undergraduate and post-graduate students and practising managers.

- Undergraduate students in Business Schools will find the book provides an engaging, accessible analysis of HRM theory and practice. It assumes some previous knowledge of organisational behaviour by the student, practitioner or general reader.
- MBA students will find the theories of job design, HR core practices, occupational health and wellness, and insight into sustainability HRM valuable.
- Postgraduate students on other management masters' programmes will find the critical comment and coverage, together with the background reading, provides a useful introduction to the field of HRM.
- Practising managers will find the theories and case materials contained in the book provide helpful insights into people management and the text covers major parts of the CIPD Leading, Managing and Developing People module.

Context

It is almost 30 years ago since Jeff Gold and I started collaborating on the first edition of *Human Resource Management: Theory and Practice*. As one would expect, the economic, political and social context has profoundly changed. In the 1990s, neoliberal ideology, privatisation, deregulation and European integration seemed to define the decade. Since the 2000s, in addition to ongoing wars and human catastrophes around the globe, modern-day capitalism has been shaken to its core three times. The global financial crisis of 2008, Britain's withdrawal from the European Union – Brexit – and, the most severe, the Covid-19 pandemic. When we started planning this new edition, Brexit had dominated UK political discourse for three years, so we assumed much of the analysis and examples would be driven by Brexit. In the sixth edition, we wrote that withdrawal from the EU is 'highly likely to affect the supply of labour and the HR planning and recruitment process'. We noted the uncertainty over whether an early casualty of Brexit would be the suspension of EU employment laws and regulations and the erosion of what remains of British worker and trade union rights and entitlements. Future research will show whether Britain outside the EU ushers in significant change to prevailing models of HRM.

It has been challenging to complete this new edition, and especially so when the process of writing was overshadowed by the coronavirus pandemic and the world passed through the 3 million mark for Covid-19 deaths. The pandemic has caused the worst public health crisis and economic shock in living memory. In the UK, at the time of writing, the unemployment rate is forecast to reach 10 per cent (Clark, 2020) following the closure of businesses due to national and local lockdowns, public health restrictions and social distancing measures. Of course, alongside the Covid-19-induced crisis is the climate crisis. On Thursday 27 July 2019 Britain recorded its highest temperature: 38.7 degrees. Large corporations are cited to be amongst the largest emitters of greenhouse gases. Given this indictment, a growing number of scholars argue that the collective knowledge and expertise residing in business schools can help mitigate climate change, and provide leadership for creating a more resilient, pro-environmental economy and workplaces (Robertson and Barling, 2015). Therefore, it seems a propitious moment to introduce pro-environmental issues into undergraduate modules. To meet this goal, we have included a chapter on sustainable HRM and, where it's relevant, examples of pro-environmental behaviours and practices to illustrate lessons from research and potential for future research endeavours. These extreme contextual changes suggest that a 'Global Britain' competing on the basis of deregulated labour market, job precarity and low wages would seriously undermine much of dominant theory of 'high-road' HRM. From a critical perspective, these developments have to be given serious consideration in Part 1 and throughout *HRM: A Critical Approach*, as context matters when studying HRM.

Critical approach

This text aims to provide students with a critical examination of the debates and themes surrounding HRM theories and the implementation of practices in the contemporary workplace. In so doing, we attempt to take the student into realms of people management not often explored in most undergraduate courses in management. We offer an intellectual journey that draws on Legge's (2005) tradition of exploring the 'rhetoric and reality' of HRM and Boxall et al.'s (2008) analytical approach to HRM, but we also take readers to unfamiliar paradigms and research from the realm of politics and sociology. Whether students perceive the world through an individual and psychological prism or a societal and sociological one has profound implications for how students understand organisational life, and how they understand the behaviour of workers and managers. We provide detailed critical discussion of diversity, inequality, well-being, sustainability and social power. In different ways, we ask: '*Cui bono*' – To whom is the benefit? If we want to understand how and why people are on precarious zero-hours contracts and experience inequality at work, we have to ask: who benefits from neoliberalism, the financialisation of the economy and the weakening of workers' bargaining power. This, we suggest constitutes and supports what we understand as a 'critical' approach to work and people management (Bratton and Gold, 2015). The intention is to draw upon both mainstream *and* critical perspectives, as a requirement for generating a more eclectic interdisciplinary dialogue on how work and people are managed in the third decade of the twenty-first century.

Textbooks are not neutral in the sense that they shape students' understanding of an academic field in particular ways by defining areas of theory and research (Ashcroft and Allen, 2003). In this sense, this book is not neutral, but will enable students to navigate through competing narratives and counter narratives on HRM, to engage with the failures and injustices of the neoliberal model, and to foster a more critical understanding of the theories that inform the practices that impact the management of work and people. It is the commitment to educate, not simply to 'train' employable skills, which differentiates *HRM: A Critical Approach* from mainstream textbooks.

New for the seventh edition

As we have already mentioned, this new edition was prepared during the Covid-19 crisis, a deep economic recession and on the eve of Britain's exit from the EU. Wherever possible, we have tried to make connections between the global and national crises, labour market and employment trends, and HRM in a way that we hope will be intellectually rewarding and relevant for students. Users of the previous editions will notice fewer differences between the chapters in this new edition because of a major rewrite primarily by a single author. The seventh edition incorporates new material and learning activities, including:

- 13 new or updated **Case studies** have been added, each written to strengthen the connection between theory and practice and to illustrate the practical application of the major concepts examined in the chapter.
- 13 new **HRM in Practice** provide thought-provoking examples of the interconnection between economic-social context and HRM.
- 13 new **Global HRM** explore employment-related practices outside Britain.
- 13 new **Legal Focus boxes** designed to encourage students to do online searches of employment law in their own jurisdiction, in a way that is thought-provoking and illustrates the dynamic nature of the employment relationship.
- 13 new **Ethical Insight boxes** written to explore critically areas of ethical concern in HR practices.
- 13 new **Digital Spotlight boxes** designed to illustrate the application of analytics and AI in HRM.
- 13 new **Search & Watch boxes** provide web links to online video clips on a theme covered in the chapter.
- An extensive reworking of all chapters to provide an accessible entry into the field and emphasise the link between theory and practice.
- The new Chapter 3 provides a critical overview of job design in the 'gig economy' resulting from increasing prevalence of on-demand, short-term work.
- The new Chapter 4 provides a critical discussion of diversity and diversity management.
- The new Chapter 11 examines issues related to employee well-being with an extended critical discussion on mental health and OHS in the wake of the Covid-19 pandemic.
- The companion website provides a learning platform with video clips with business and HR professionals, tests, web links and assignments to personalise the learning experience for each student. For lecturers, the companion website has resources that provide additional learning material to enhance their lectures and tutorials.

TOUR OF THE BOOK

Outlines guide you through the material in each chapter and allow your progress to be checked

Search & Watch features consist of video interviews with HR practitioners, accompanied by a summary of the interviewees' qualifications and experience, and questions to think about after watching the videos

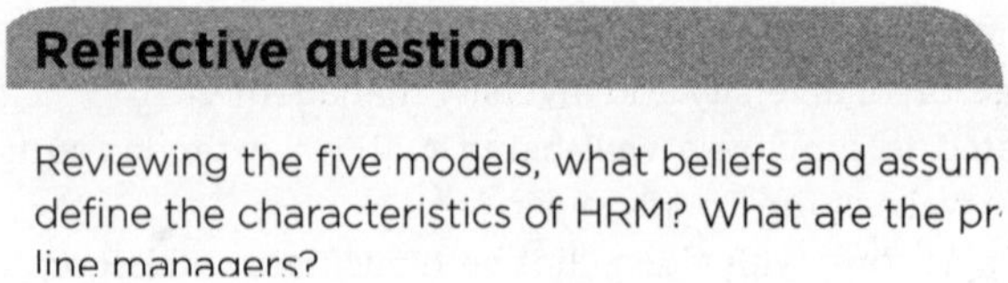

Reflective questions challenge and encourage you to think critically about the broader relationships and interactions between the topics under discussion

HRM web links enable you to download statistical information, follow current international developments in HRM practice and even monitor the job market in HRM

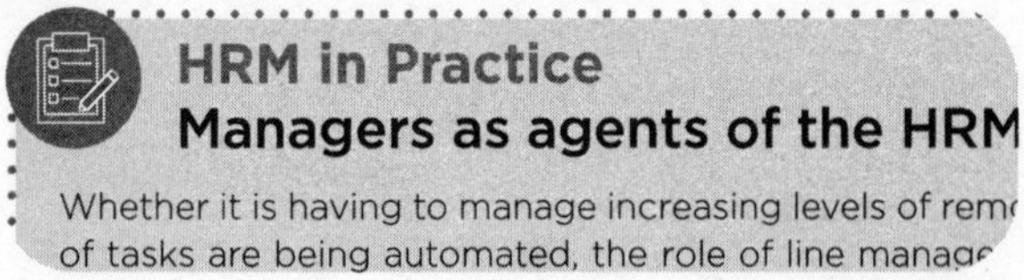

HRM in Practice features illustrate the link between HRM theory and practice in workplaces, covering contemporary themes and a diverse range of organisations in the UK and the EU

Global HRM features provide examples of employment practices and management in BRIC countries, as well as South Africa and North America, and problematise them

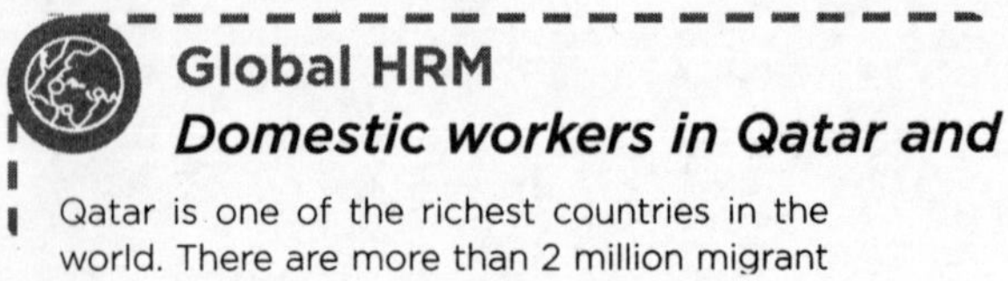

Legal Focus

Employment law, which is also called labour law, regulat
working people in the UK. Parliament and the courts ha

Legal Focus features give an insight into employment law and HRM

Ethical Insights examine ethical issues in HRM

Ethical Insight

Do ethics influence corporate strate

Over a decade ago, Behnam and Rasche (2009) asked, 'Are strategists from Mars and

Digital Spotlight

Key metrics for aligning corporate s

Effective strategic HRM is an analytical process and this entails th
supported by HR analytics (Armstrong and Brown, 2019). The

Digital Spotlights examine the application of analytics, AI and technology in HRM

Summaries provide an abbreviated version of the main concepts and theories, useful for your revision and checking understanding of the key points

Summary

In this introductory chapter, we have empha
emphasised that, since its introduction, the
has been subject to intense academic debate

Review questions

1. Explain the difference between the 'hard'
mental humanism' models of HRM. Which
and why?

Review questions test how much you have learned on completion of the chapter and useful for revision

Chapter cases offer references that provide an elaboration of the key topics discussed in the text and can be used to help gain a better mark in essays

Chapter case: Mandla Winery*

The setting

The South African wine industry's roots date back to 1659, wit

Further reading

Budd, J. W. (2020) The psychologisation of em
employment relationship, and the OB turn. *H*
83.

Further reading sections demonstrate the application of theoretical material from the text and facilitate an understanding and appreciation of the challenges of managing people at work

SEARCH & WATCH

This feature of the book, expanded for the seventh edition, enables self-directed learners to gain invaluable insights into the HR function and how practices are operationalised *in practice*. *YouTube* videos linked to chapter content appear throughout the textbook. In a series of filmed interviews, HR managers and directors from companies discuss their activities in the workplace, providing insights into the 'real world' of HRM. Emphasis is given to HRM's involvement in business strategy, in other words to how it shapes the future direction of organisations.

Each interview starts with a discussion of why the practitioners decided to work in HR and how they got to where they are now. This is followed by a consideration of selected key topics such as partnership, diversity, organisational culture, trade union relations and recruitment from their point of view, and ends with the HR practitioner giving their advice to those who wish to pursue a career in HR. Simply go to the companion website to watch the video. Then try and answer questions on the video that encourage you to think critically about what you have seen and relate it back to the topics under discussion in the chapter.

There are 14 interviews included in the book. Here is a list of the practitioners and which chapter you can find them in.

Introduction: Gregor Karolus, Chief HR officer, Springer Nature, talks in the first part of his interview, about the importance of ethics and compliance to a business and how these can be encouraged.

Chapter 1: Alison Blayney, HR Business Partner, TIGI Haircare, Unilever, talks in Part 1 of her interview about her role as HR Business Partner.

Chapter 2: Sarah Myers, Director of Talent Management at Sky, discusses how talent management operates in the company, how the recession has impacted on this, and how their approach is firmly tied to the business strategy.

Chapter 3: Gregor Karolus, Chief HR officer, Springer Nature, expands in the second part of his interview on high-performance workplace systems and how these are implemented in large multinational companies.

Chapter 4: Karen Jochelson, Director of Policy for Employment and the Economy, The Equality and Human Rights Commission, talks about the work of the Equality and Human Rights Commission on the issue of diversity and what methods can be used to encourage participation of women at board level, provide a better experience for women during pregnancy and maternity cover, and reduce the gender pay gap.

Chapter 4: Keith Stopforth, Head of Talent and Development at Bupa Health and Wellbeing, talks about the organisational culture at Bupa and how this is implemented, how talent management works in the company, and how Bupa views diversity in the workplace.

Chapter 5: Alison Blayney, HR Business Partner, TIGI Haircare, Unilever, talks in Part 2 of her interview, about the process of recruitment and selection and how these are conducted in the company.

Chapter 7: Helen Tiffany, Managing Director of HR consultancy firm Bec Development, talks about the importance of human resource development and coaching.

Chapter 8: Ruth Altman, an experienced freelance HR practitioner, discusses the challenges faced by HR departments in universities and how higher tuition fees will impact on the reward system at universities.

Chapter 9: Ray Fletcher, Director of Personnel and Development at Unite the Union, considers trade unions in the contemporary workplace, their contribution to workplace learning and possibilities for union–green coalitions.

Chapter 10: Keith Hanlon-Smith, Employee Relations Director at facilities maintenance company Norland Managed Services, discusses employee relations, the employment relationship and HR as a strategic partner (the Ulrich model).

Chapter 11: Lana Kularajah, Senior HR Business Partner, Transform Aid International/ Baptist World Aid Australia, speaks about mentoring programmes in leadership and management initiatives, particularly to encourage female progression to senior management positions.

Chapter 12: Markus Hiemann, Sustainability Manager for NHS National Services Scotland (NSS), discusses the issues surrounding sustainability and green HRM.

Chapter 13: Lesley White, Human Resources Director UK and Ireland for Huawei Technologies, discusses the challenges of working in a UK-based HR department for a company headquartered in China, cultural differences in working and management styles, and the place of HR in Huawei's business strategy.

DIGITAL RESOURCES

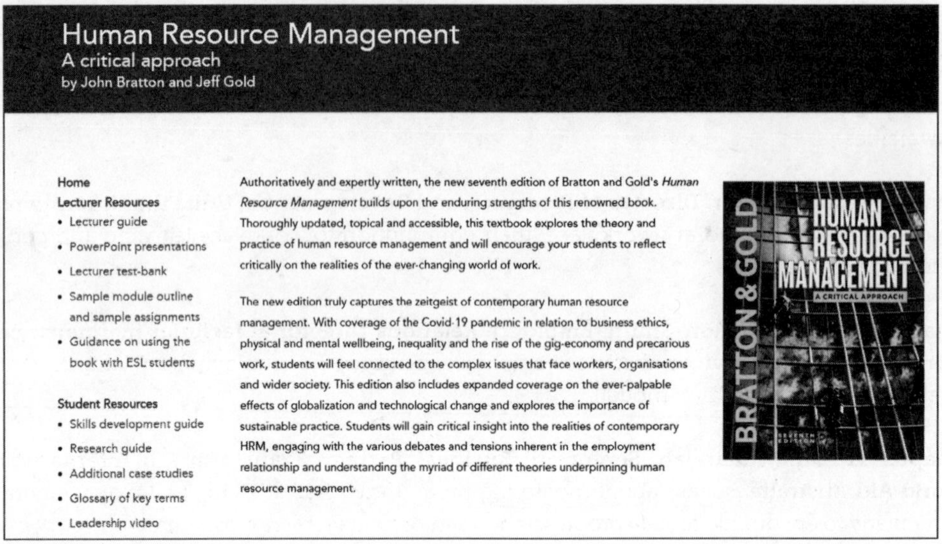

Student resources

For students a number of tools are provided to help you succeed in your HRM course:

- A *Skills Development Guide* offering detailed guidance on completing assignments and oral presentations
- A *Research Guide* offering tips on how to find information
- *Additional case studies and vignettes*
- *Chapter research questions*
- A *glossary* of key terms
- *HRM As I See It* video interviews
- *Learning tips* for ESL students
- *Vocab checklist* for ESL students

Lecturer resources

Lecturers who adopt the book on their course gain access to a selection of password protected resources to help plan and deliver their teaching:

- A *lecturer guide* including teaching ideas, guideline answers to chapter questions, and case study debriefs
- *Chapter research questions* to set as homework
- *PowerPoint presentations* including figures and tables for every chapter
- A *testbank* including over 400 multiple choice questions
- A *sample course outline* and sample final exam paper
- Guidance on using the book with ESL students

KEY TOPICS GRID

Chapters	CIPD New Professional Map[1]	Dimensions of Fair Work[2]	Sustainable Development Goals[3]
Chapter 1: Contemporary human resource management: the role of critique	• People practice	• Security • Fulfilment • Respect	• Decent work • Ethical values
Chapter 2: Corporate strategy and strategic HRM	• Business acumen	• Security • Fulfilment	• Sustainable growth • Environmental sustainability
Chapter 3: Job and work design	• Organisational development and design	• Fulfilment • Respect	• Decent work • Dialogue
Chapter 4: Workforce planning and diversity	• Diversity and inclusion	• Opportunity • Respect	• Gender equality
Chapter 5: Recruitment and selection	• Resourcing	• Opportunity • Respect	• Gender equality
Chapter 6: Performance management	• Organisational development and design	• Fulfilment • Effective voice	• Decent work and economic growth
Chapter 7: Learning and development	• Learning and development	• Opportunity • Fulfilment • Respect	• Quality education
Chapter 8: Reward management	• Reward	• Security • Respect • Effective voice	• Reduced inequalities
Chapter 9: Labour relations and collective bargaining	• Employee relations	• Effective voice • Security • Respect	• Peace, justice and strong institutions
Chapter 10: Employee relations and conflict management	• Employee relations	• Effective voice • Security • Respect	• Partnerships for the goals • Stakeholder approach
Chapter 11: HRM, health and well-being	• People experience	• Security • Respect	• Good health and well-being
Chapter 12: Sustainable HRM and environmental sustainability	• Ethical practice	• Fulfilment • Effective voice	• Climate action
Chapter 13: International HRM in a globalised capitalism	• Business acumen	• Opportunity • Fulfilment • Security	• Responsible consumption and production

1 The CIPD Profession Map sets the international benchmark for the people profession. Available online at: https://peopleprofession.cipd.org/profession-map#gref

2 The Fair Work Convention was established in 2015 following a recommendation of the Working Together Review. Its remit is to drive forward fair work in Scotland and its aspirational agenda is about fair work becoming a hallmark of Scotland's workplaces and economy. Available online at: https://www.fairworkconvention.scot/the-fair-work-framework

3 On 1 January 2016, the UN's 17 Sustainable Development Goals (SDGs) officially came into force. The Goals aim to end all forms of poverty. They are unique in that they call for action by all countries, poor, rich and middle-income to promote prosperity while protecting the planet. Available at: https://www.un.org/sustainabledevelopment/development-agenda-retired/

PART 1

PAST AS PROLOGUE

THE ASCENDENCY OF HRM

INTRODUCTION

During the time of writing this new edition, the world passed through the sombre milestone of 5 million Covid-19 deaths. As of November 2021, over 742,000 deaths were recorded in the US, more than the number of US troops killed during the Second World War and the Vietnam War (estimated at 463,915). In Europe there were 1,400,001 deaths, and in Britain 140,632 deaths were Covid-related. The UK figure far exceeds the total deaths from aerial bombing attacks during 1940–45 (estimated at 61,000 deaths) and the equivalent of wiping out every man, woman and child in Stirling or Southampton. Simultaneously, Britain's service-dominated economy recorded its deepest recession, more than any other country in the G7 group of prosperous economies (Rawnsley, 2021). In 2020, amid the turbulence caused by the coronavirus crisis, Britain's economy experienced its worst annual decline in more than 300 years. The official statistics showed that gross domestic product (GDP) fell by 9.9 per cent in 2020. It was the biggest contraction in annual GDP since the Great Frost in 1709, when the largely agrarian economy shrank by 13 per cent (Romei and Giles, 2021). The data suggests that the death rate is greater in those countries with deep systematic social inequalities and which most closely embrace the neoliberal troika of deregulation, privatisation and free-market globalisation – the 'Anglo-American' model of governance. Across Europe the coronavirus has caused the worst public health crisis and economic shock in living memory. Unable to consume, Britain's service-dominated economy sank into the deepest recession statistically on record. Amid record-high hospitalisation and Covid-19 deaths, national lockdown, bankruptcies and lost jobs, the virus is pulling health, income and educational opportunities and inequalities even wider (Johnson et al., 2021). The crisis turned the political economy upside down. Faced with record levels of pandemic-induced unemployment, the US and Europe have taken different approaches to tackling the economic crisis. The US largely relied on its unemployment insurance programme to deal with pandemic-induced unemployment. Many European countries, including the UK, adapted versions of the German '*Kurzarbeit*' (Rushe, 2019) – literally 'short work' – to allow businesses facing closure to apply for government subsidies to keep paying workers' salaries until the public health crisis was over. In a development unprecedented in British economic history, Britain's Conservative Chancellor undertook to pay 80 per cent of the wages of workers threatened by layoff because of Covid-19. As the country braced itself for a 'second wave' of Covid-19 infections, the Chancellor announced in October the expansion of the Job Support Scheme for local lockdown areas with required business closures to help protect jobs. As Macwhirter (2020) observed, in 2008, a Labour Chancellor, Gordon Brown, bailed out the banks: in 2020, a Tory Chancellor, Rishi Sunak, went some way to bail out most workers. The coronavirus crisis upended economic and political orthodoxies held for the past 40 years: Conservative politicians rediscovered the virtues of collectivism, solidarity and state intervention (Rawnsley, 2021).

While the Covid-19 pandemic has shaken modern-day capitalism to its core, the crisis should not deflect us from acknowledging that over the past 40 years, notably in the US and the UK, capitalism has systematically eroded the living standards of working people (Rubin, 2020). In the US and UK, employment is characterised by job insecurity, low rates of pay, with no benefits, and non-union forms of employment relations. Case and Deaton (2020, p. 9) observe, 'something is going on ... that is particularly toxic for the working class'. The message is that if we want to understand how and why a growing number of the working class are on precarious zero-hours contracts (ZHCs) and experience insecurity and extreme inequality, we need a dialogue between the present and the past, how ideas born in different historical periods and cultures transmit and endure as active ingredients in contemporary management thought and professional practice. As an academic discipline that informs professional practice, does human resource management (HRM) identify with the perspectives and sensibilities of the corporate elite? Has HRM contributed to the rise of job insecurity, non-union forms of employment and the general impoverishment of working-class living standards? Has HRM research impoverished the notion of 'critical' in the social sciences by privileging shareholder interests and neglecting worker well-being and wider societal concerns (Bratton and Gold, 2015; Dundon and Rafferty, 2018)?

This path of interrogation necessitates academics and HR professionals to start by asking, as the Ancient Romans did: '*Cui bono*?' 'Who benefits and how?' from pro-market neoliberalism, the ascendency of ideological individualism and the weakening of workers' wage-bargaining power. It also involves the application of Mills' (1959/2000) 'sociological imagination' to matters of HRM 'outcomes' that have 'wider social consequences' (Watson, 2010). This perspective constitutes and supports what we understand as a 'critical' approach to work and the management of workers (Bratton and Gold, 2015). To understand the past changes in work and employment relations, including the much less beneficial changes, we need to examine the antecedents of the rise of HRM. But, in doing this we should take heed of the words of historian E. H. Carr. In his acclaimed book, *What is History?* he advises the reader to 'study the historian before you begin to study the facts'. My own undergraduate learning of economic history was enhanced by Carr's advice. Today, his prescient warning that the value of facts depends on the analyst using them seems to resonate with public discourse on 'fake news' and the power of persuasive technology, such as Facebook. History is about interpretation. Thus, there are competing narratives of the changes that propelled the emergence of HRM, and different accounts will depend on the writer's selection and interpretation of the disruptive forces (Carr, 2019).

This introduction provides the context for the book. Specifically, it provides an overview of the social, political and economic changes over the last 50 years, setting an historical context for the ascendency of HRM. The ideas build on papers we wrote for *Human Resource Development International* and *Work, Employment and Society* under the 'Debates and controversies'. We conclude with an outline of the structure and content of this book.

Work and employment relations in the age of neoliberalism

> *Equality means dignity. And dignity demands a job and a paycheck that lasts through the week.* (Dr Martin Luther King, Jr)

The notion that work is at the centre of human activity pre-dates modernity. Work is a source of wealth; it affects the nature of day-to-day interaction in the workplace and the most personal aspects of our experience in the family and the community. As Case and Deaton (2020, p. 8) observe, 'Jobs are not just the source of money ... Destroy work and, in the end, working class life cannot survive'. For 30 years, following the Second World War, social and economic progress was remarkable in western Europe and the US. In the context of the US, manufacturing corporations, such as Ford, General Motors, Boeing, were a source of stability and job security. Companies producing automobiles, steel, or extracting coal paid good rates of pay, welfare benefits and had union forms of employment relations, particularly in the northern east-coast states. The rate of income growth reached its high in the 'golden era', the 30 years after 1945. Generally, American working-class parents were richer in 1975 than their grandparents, and their children had unparalleled opportunities to enter college. The political foibles of American capitalism, opposition to trade unions and the primacy of individualism, the latter encapsulated in the belief in being able to go from 'log cabin to the White House' – the 'American Dream' (Guest, 1990) – created more workplaces that favoured capital at the expense of workers. However, that period was arguably the years of the 'blue-collar aristocracy' (Case and Deaton, 2020, p. 20).

In Britain, and in other western European countries, similar improvements took place in health, education and living standards. The 1945–51 Labour government lead by Clement Atlee transformed the living standards and aspirations of the British working class. The Labour administration's macroeconomic policies were influenced by 'Keynesian economic doctrine' (Coates, 1975, p. 46), which resulted in relatively full employment and greater income equality. Growing incomes were buttressed by a massive expansion of the welfare state, a national health service, social housing and a raft of legislation giving protection to workers and their representative bodies, trade unions. The expansion was at least in some part a 'byproduct' of the Cold War and the associated political rivalry between capitalism and communism. In brief, British welfarism was a fashionable era-defining project that had cross-party support (Obinger and Schmitt, 2011). In 1979 around 50 per cent of workers in Britain were members of a trade union and total membership stood at over 12 million. Trade unions were considered to be 'one of the most powerful forces shaping our society' (Clegg, 1976, p. 1). This is not to argue that the years 1945—75 were paradise. Far from it. The post-war years saw a build-up of nuclear weapons, a protracted war in Vietnam, famine in emerging economies and ongoing stand-offs between capital and labour over the income distribution. Progress was not constant or linear, but, over 30 years, progress in living standards in the UK, western Europe and the US was prolonged enough that by the 1970s, people could reasonably expect it to continue.

By the turn of the new millennium, much of the optimism of the previous 50 years had faded. Towns in Britain and the US that used to produce automobiles, steel, glass, carpets or apparel had been hollowed out, their factories and mills closed. Income inequality is as extreme in 2020 in Britain and the US as it was at the beginning of the twentieth century. It is perhaps unsurprising that Thomas Piketty's *Capital in the Twenty-First Century* found its way onto the *New York Times* best sellers' list for four weeks. A reflection of the concern about global capitalism. From the 1980s, in marked contrast to the 'golden age' of Keynesian economics, the gap between rich and poor began to widen. In the 1970s, for example, CEOs of major American corporations were paid, on average, about 20 times as much as the average worker. By the 2000s, incomes had 'skewed' and CEOs were paid more than 300 times as much as the average worker (Krugman, 2020). Britain has a notably high level of income inequality compared to other European countries. After direct taxes and benefits, the poorest 10 per cent had an average disposable income of £9,644 (€10,608) in 2015–16 while the richest 10 per cent had nine times that at £83,875 (€92,262). While millions endured austerity, stagnant wages and the shrinkage of social support systems, households in the top 10 per cent of disposable income also had their income from property, interest and dividends double between 2010–11 and 2015–16, from an average of £19,000 (€20,900) each to more than £38,000 (€41,800) – well above the average household income of around £25,000 (€27,500) in 2015–16 (Jayanetti, 2019). The shift of the growing share of income to the top one per cent has meant that ordinary families have failed to share in economic progress, and, less tangibly, it has meant 'a loss of our sense of living in a shared society', Krugman (2020, p. 259), opines.

The 1945–51 Labour administration passed the Wages Councils Act 1945 to regulate pay, minimum hours of work and holidays for various sectors, particularly those employing low-skilled and low-paid workers. The Act was repealed by the Conservative government's Wages Act 1986, which decreased Wage Council power and scope. Prime Minister Margaret Thatcher promoted pay flexibility, profit-related pay and decentralised pay bargaining. John Major's Trade Union Reform and Employment Rights Act 1993 abolished most of the surviving Wage Councils (Hughes and Dundon, 2018). Since the abolition of Wage Councils, which attempted to rein in the excesses of a free labour market, there has been widespread income inequality. Further, the management of the employment relationships has changed for large sections of the working class. By the 2000s, precarious employment became a defining characteristic of many jobs globally and in Britain. 'Precarious work' has expanded in the so-called gig economy and platform work to include zero-hours contracts (ZHCs) workers with job insecurity, undefined working hours and volatile earnings. A zero-hours contract is an employment contract that disrupts traditional bilateral relations between capital and labour. The employer does not guarantee the individual any work, and, nominally, the individual is not obliged to accept any work offered (Wakeling, 2014). Some employment laws apply to workers on ZHCs, but others, which are costly to employers, do not, including redundancy pay, maternity leave and protection from unfair dismissal. In Britain, 896,000 people were on ZHCs in 2020, pre the Covid-19 emergency (Statista, 2020), Nearly 40 per cent of workers say their hours can vary from week to week (Butler, S., 2020a). Women, students in full-time education, young or older workers are more likely to be on ZHCs. Britain has an 'endemic low-pay culture'. It is telling that wages have become so low that human labour rather than automation is favoured: for instance, manual car washing. The Cambridge economist Ha-Joon Chang (2013) observes that the connections between work and well-being have been marginalised in public discourse stating, 'the crisis for British wage-earners is much more than the cost of living. It is a work crisis too'. An estimated eight million people in poverty now live in working households (Hughes and Dundon, 2018). After four decades of neoliberalism and recognition of the fact that the doctrine is increasingly deleterious to the natural world and the living standards of the many –or, as British Prime Minister Theresa May dubbed them, the 'just about managing' or 'JAMs' – critics describe Britain's economic model as 'broken' and radical critiques of neoliberal capitalism have acquired fashionable relevance.

Social scientists argue that a confluence of economic, social and political forces have slowly made working-class lives so much more precarious and difficult with far-reaching cultural and political repercussions beyond the economic. Perhaps the most significant of these forces is globalisation and technological change because combined they have reduced the value of unskilled wage-labour, substituting it with low-wage foreign labour or machines. Although globalisation is a contested concept, arguably, it is about the unfettered pursuit of profit and the primacy of multinational power over local power (Hertz, 2002). A significant body of literature connects globalisation to the decline of the US and UK's manufacturing competitiveness, particularly around themes such as the falling labour productivity, the global division of labour and power, and precarious employment. These trends, notably, Japanese and German firms' penetration into the US and UK markets, threatened US dominance, particularly in the automobile sector.

German firms posed a similar threat to UK manufacturers. The 'Search of Excellence' (Peters and Waterman, 1982) and 'Japanization' (Bratton, 1992; Elger and Smith, 2010) literature, which emphasised human capability as a competitive advantage, acted as a major impulse to increasing labour flexibility and the shift toward HRM models in organisations (Beardwell, 2001; Colville et al., 1999; Guest, 1990; Legge, 1995). The process of economic globalisation contributed to the transfer of manufacturing capacity from the US and UK to low-wage economies in Asia.

The Covid-19 crisis demonstrated the limits of 'deindustrialisation' and global just-in-time supply chains. Britain, once the 'workshop' of the world, could not produce adequate quantities of N95 face masks and other personnel protection equipment (PPE) for its venerated front-line health workers. US and UK companies still manufacture medical equipment, but the factories and the jobs are located somewhere else, many in China. The 'magic of just-in-time delivery ... doesn't work in an emergency' because the Chinese government controlled the world supply of the crucial commodities, observes Rubin (2020, p. xv). In the first wave of the pandemic, for hospitals and care homes desperate for PPE, global just-in-time supply was just too slow. In terms of understanding deep structural economic changes in the British economy, the shortage of PPE is a quintessential case of *rentier* capitalism. Economists Krugman (2012) and Christophers (2020) use the terms 'rentier regime' or 'rentier capitalism' to describe a business model which is an alloy of neoliberalism. Its essence is rent: income generated by virtue of exclusive ownership or control of a scarce asset. A rentier, either an individual or, more commonly, a corporation, controls the asset and is the recipient of the income flow. Rentier capitalism is an economic regime organised around income-generating assets – public sector contracts (e.g. PPE or the building and maintenance of hospitals or prisons), intellectual property, patents, copyright, data – in which overall income streams are dictated by rents and economic activity is dictated by the rentier class. Rentier capitalists are oriented to 'having' rather than 'doing' or profiteering from assets, without making anything of value to society; it is based on proprietorial rather than entrepreneurial ethos (Christophers, 2020; Thompson, 2013). The PPE case highlights a defining feature of rentier capitalism: the active role of the state. In this PPE case, the government's role was in creating and allocating the asset, the contract, just as in the 1980s and 1990s, when successive governments created income-generated assets by privatising utilities, rail networks and social housing.

Another significant structural change is the 'fourth industrial revolution' driven by artificial intelligence that has accelerated the demise of manual wage-labour, changed employment relationships and added fuel to the 'Future of Work' debate (see, for example, Skidelsky, 2020; Susskind, 2020). However, as Case and Deaton (2020) observe, other European countries and elsewhere face globalisation and technological change but, unlike the UK and US, have not experienced 'long-term stagnation of wages, nor an epidemic of deaths of despair' (p. 9).

Another interpretation of socio-cultural change focuses on the decline in traditional working-class values and the institutions of collectivism. There are several strands to this argument. An increasing number of working-class people abandoning collectivist values and pivoting towards more individualist ones; the most obvious examples would be the alleged disinterest in joining a trade union, the case of the sale of social housing in the 1980s and, perhaps more relevant in managing people, the rise of a new human 'spirit' changing the way people think and behave. Neoliberalism, it is argued, created a new archetype: a self-reliant autonomous individual, whose economic survival depends on flexibility, continuous upgrading of their own skills, and connectivity. Sociologists have labelled this new kind of person the 'neoliberal self' or 'entrepreneurial self' – a shift characterised as moving away from a 'culture of dependence' to one of self-reliance – in which workers become estranged not just from their labour, but also from others and their distinctive interests. So understood, in the Marxist intellectual tradition, an expression of 'self-alienation' which helps to perpetuate neoliberalism because it atomises workers while reinforcing antipathy to trade unions (see also Boltanski and Chiapello, 2018; Cullinane and Dundon, 2006; Godard, 2014). As a management function, HRM has been widely documented as playing a fundamental role in designing and bringing about the changes that have given rise to 'labour market flexibility', the individualisation of skills and pay, often associated with the HRM model of management, which many would argue has had a deleterious effect by tending to make wage-labourers exclusively responsible for their own success and failures. The new spirit allowed neoliberal capitalism and HRM to achieve contemporary legitimacy (Boltanski and Chiapello, 2018).

The rise of the HRM paradigm in Britain from the late 1980s is closely linked with another influential contextual development; the cognitive capture of the political elite of the neoliberal ideology that challenged post-war consensus around Keynesianism and attacked the institutions of collectivism. This ideological impulse saw the renaissance of 'market discipline', the shrinking of the state and a shift of the balance of economic power from labour to capital (Harvey, 2007). Graeber (2018) argues that the neoliberal ideology is 'really a political project dressed up as an economic one' (p. xxiv). While the doctrine of neoliberalism was always ostensibly about unleashing the power of the 'market', which is a euphemism for the power of private money, the overall effect of the free-market policies combined with economic globalisation, have neutered the power of trade unions, created an insecure, low-paid and overworked workforce, along with simultaneously shifting more wealth and power to the top 1 per cent of society. In the US, the Reagan administration embraced neoliberalism and 'Reaganomics' and the defeat of the air traffic controllers most visibly demonstrated the attack on the power of the trade unions. In the UK, under Thatcher's government, the 1984–85 mine workers' strike and defeat, along with the closure of much of the mining industry, had a similar political objective, which prompted employers to reorder employment relations.

This project to shift more power to employers was assisted by Thatcher's reform of the legal regulation of employment relations. Cumulatively, the changes to employment laws by the 1979–97 Conservative governments marked 'a radical shift from the consensus underlying "public policy" on labour relations during most of the past century' (Hyman, 1987, p. 93). The effect was to tilt the balance of power towards the employers and hinder union agency (see Brown et al., 1997). Combined with Thatcher's political assaults on the institutions of collectivism: the privatisation of publicly owned enterprises, the selling off of social housing and anti-union legislation, the most restrictive in western Europe, encouraged private and public sector organisations to initiate new employment practices (Hendry and Pettigrew, 1990). Economic globalisation and the neoliberal (deregulation) ideology that has dominated the world since the 1980s provides theoretical and empirical support for the thesis that postmodernity, in particular its association with globalisation, is not simply a quantitative extension of modernity but a qualitatively new phenomenon (Bratton and Denham, 2019). Neoliberal ideology, privatisation, deregulation and European integration defined the 1990s.

Since the 2000s, in addition to ongoing wars and human catastrophes around the globe, modern-day capitalism has been shaken to its core three times. The 2008 global financial crisis (GFC), Britain's withdrawal from the European Union – Brexit – and, the most severe, the Covid-19 pandemic. The 2008 GFC saw the Western banking sector put on life support by government bail-outs – to the tune of £737 billion in the case of the UK – and Fred Goodwin of the UK's Royal Bank of Scotland, as a token of public disapproval, was stripped of his knighthood. What started as a banking crisis morphed into a social crisis as the corporate and political elite implemented austerity economics in the form of wage and welfare cuts, spending cuts and tax rises and the privatisation of public assets. On 23 June 2016, 17.4 million Britons voted to sever the UK's 43-year membership of the European Union. The overall vote in June 2016 to leave the EU (Brexit) produced a margin of 52 per cent to 48 per cent (Scotland and Northern Ireland voted to remain). The result, reported by *The Times* as an 'earthquake' and by the *Telegraph* as the 'Birth of New Britain', has been interpreted as protest votes of mainly white manual working-class voters against unemployment, growing inequality and immigration. The country, dubbed 'Brexitland' by Sobolewska and Ford (2020), was fractured by class, race, income, ideology and geography. Economically depressed post-industrial towns in the north of England, Wales, rural England and seaside towns heavily voted 'Leave'; the political reaction of those most negatively affected by globalisation and the neoliberal ideology, the working class or the 'expendables' (Rubin, 2020).

The ascendency of HRM

The gathering pace of globalisation and neoliberal ideology in the 1980s provided the backcloth to the change towards individualised non-union employment relations and, in Britain, a burgeoning of academic interest in the study of the US import, HRM. Storey's (1989) seminal text generated the 'first wave' of debate on the nature and ideological significance of the HRM model. Early accounts compared the differences between the HRM model with personnel management. There is a general consensus that personnel management is largely conceived as an activity with little strategic integration between its various practices. The management guru, Peter Drucker (1961, p. 269) observed that the personnel function is 'a collection of incidental techniques with little internal cohesion'. That personnel management is conceived as having a piecemeal role, while that of HRM is more strategic, is a false dichotomy. Long- and medium-term labour costs and working practices are 'strategic' in a number of substantive ways. In Britain, personnel managers were primarily responsible for negotiating and administrating collective agreements on issues of pay and working practices (Gospel, 2013), which could directly impact a company's operating costs and productivity levels, and hence competitiveness. The provisions of the Health and Safety at Work (HASAW) Act 1974, which laid down general duties on employers, further suggests a more 'upstream' integrated approach in the traditional personnel function. The professed importance of collective bargaining to determine pay, negotiating with trade unions achieved a distinct identity; personnel roles were dominated by females while bargaining with 'militant unions' tended to be a male profession (Legge, 1986). The divide between 'personnel management' and 'labour relations' roles persisted in academia, with generally only labour relations research and university teaching having high stature. This engagement with trade unions point to another aspect of the debate on HRM's key characteristics; personnel management was embedded in a 'collectivist' or 'pluralist' frame of reference (Flanders, 1964), while a key distinguishing trait of HRM is its 'individualist' or 'unitary' frame of reference (Legge, 1995).

A further dimension of the early debate focused on 'hard' and 'soft' versions of HRM. The 'top down' 'hard' version gravitated towards the 'resource' concept to strategically managing work and the employment relationship. It was predicated on orthodox management theory that viewed workers as a cost that therefore must be controlled. The 'soft' HRM model, discussed in Walton's (1985) early and influential article 'From control to commitment in the workplace', focused more on the 'human' capacity aspects of securing competitive advantage and thus considered workers as an asset rather than as a disposable liability. It advocated high investment in workers' learning and development to secure high motivation, and the performance benefits of shifting from 'control' to 'commitment' strategies to enlist worker skills and loyalty. This socially consensual management model became known by various labels, such as the 'high-commitment workplace'. A determinate 'bundle' of HRM 'best practices' and 'lean' forms of work organisation facilitated the possibilities of synergies, which, it was argued, provided a distinctive basis for sustainable competitive advantage (Barney, 1991).

The imported HRM paradigm was heavily influenced by the 'strategy' concept (Porter, 1985) and both scholars and practising professionals conceived HRM as a strategic role. This acclaimed 'upstream' role generated the 'second wave' of debate on 'strategic HRM'. It was driven by two highly influential books on HRM: Fombrun et al., *Strategic Human Resource Management* (1984) and Beer et al., *Managing Human Assets* (1984). Fombrun and his colleagues produced the 'Michigan' or 'matching model' of HRM, which argued that for companies to 'survive' HRM must be 'integrated as a vital part of the planning system in organizations' (Devanna et al., 1984, p. 11). While underscoring a contingency approach – that a set of HR practices should be related to the context and situations of the organisation – the critical management task it was posited is to align the HR system with the strategic goals of the organisation (Baird and Meshoulam, 1988). This is the notion of 'vertical fit'. Beer and his colleagues produced the 'Harvard' model of HRM, which recommended that 'HRM policies need to fit with business strategy' (1984, p. 178). The authors also advocated that management concerns should go beyond shareholder interests and extend to all the organisation's stakeholders. This is the 'multi-stakeholder' approach. Therefore, in the early literature, strategic HRM as conceived is to develop an integrated and compatible set of HR practices to provide 'unifying frameworks which are at once broad, contingency-based and integrative', wrote Dyer and Holder (1998, p. 13). Similarly, they underscored a contingency approach in which the key management task was to align or 'fit' HR practices with corporate strategy. For some scholars, effective strategic HRM suggested a more holistic learning approach to strategy: 'Formulation and implementation merge into a fluid process of learning through which creative strategies evolve' (Mintzberg, 1987, p. 66). Strategic HRM as conceptualised by Storey (2001, p. 7), is premised on a human-oriented philosophy that committed and motivated workers give competitive advantage, that 'HRM decisions are of strategic importance and that therefore HRM policies should be integrated into the business strategy'. With its emphasis on strategy and the need to leverage human capability, it was regarded as a pivotal departure from orthodox personnel management.

In the 1990s, a 'third wave' of research and literature focused on the HRM–performance relationship. In the US, research on the HRM–performance relationship was conducted, for example, by Arthur (1994), Huselid (1995) and Ichniowski et al. (1996). In the UK, Guest et al. (2003), Purcell et al. (2003) and West et al. (2002) conducted studies with the object of demonstrating that sets of HR practice and organisational performance are positively correlated. Designing an integrated and compatible set of determinate HRM variables (or 'bundles' of practices) became *the* issue in the HRM academic field (Ichniowski et al., 1996).

The concept of vertical fit ignited a debate on the relative merits of what became known as 'best fit' and 'best practice' as a means of explaining the connection between a set of determinate HR practices specific to the organisation's situation and its performance. Huselid (1995) and Pfeffer (1994), and others, identified a list of key 'best' HR practices associated with high organisation performance. The ensuing HRM– performance debate has been intense and often inconclusive (Gerhart, 2008), not least due to the direction of causation in the relationship, thus, it is argued, making the 'performance goals' of the research an 'ill-fated project' (Delbridge and Keenoy, 2010, p. 804). For some academics, the HRM model was a distinctive approach that signalled the beginnings of a new theoretical sophistication for managing the employment relationship. Guest (1997, p. 269) considered an important distinguishing feature of HRM 'is its assumption that improved performance is achieved through the people', while detractors characterised HRM as 'old wine in a new bottle' (Keenoy, 1990, p. 367).

In Britain, the HRM paradigm came under critical scrutiny from three academic fields: labour relations (Godard, 1991; Guest, 1987; Hyman, 1987); critical management studies (Keenoy, 1990; Watson, 2004); and labour process theory (Thompson and Ackroyd, 1995). The antecedent of the labour relations critique is found in an early contribution from Guest (1987) in which he made comparisons between labour relations and HRM. Employment relations under 'old' style personnel management were categorised as pluralist, collectivist and low trust, whereas, in contrast, HRM regimes were characterised as unitarist, individualist and high trust. HRM was seen as a Trojan horse for union avoidance. Hyman (1987) offered a Marxian analysis arguing that employer commitment to workers is always conditional and both the control over and commitment from workers is the *leitmotiv* of the HRM model. As already noted, historically there is ample evidence of gender-based occupational segregation in personnel management and labour relations (LR) with men dominating 'masculine' labour relations negotiating positions, while 'soft' PM/HR practices, such as recruitment and training, was devolved to women (Legge, 1986). The academic discourse reflected the gendered perceptions of IR and HRM, with an agenda largely set by 'important men' in one discipline talking to other 'important men' in another (Townley, 1994, p. 16).

A coterie of critical management studies (CMS) scholars emphasised the need to understand the wider socioeconomic context that shapes – if not determines – management action (Delbridge and

Keenoy, 2010). Legge (1995) provided a ground-breaking critique of the HRM model, not least for the empirical mismatch between theory and actual HR practices, that has become an iconic description, the 'rhetoric' and 'reality' of HRM. Watson (2004) argued that HRM neglected the 'unintended consequences' and the 'collateral damage' to others resulting from the application of HRM practices. Scholars adopting a post-Braverman labour process theory (LPT) perspective unmasked the crucial role HRM techniques play in organising and controlling the workforce. One of the crucial propositions of LPT is the indeterminacy of the employment contract – the mismatch between the capacity for work and actual work effort – and, concomitantly, the persistence of worker resistance to management control strategies attempting to close the gap (Thompson and Ackroyd, 1995). In this view, HRM constitutes a nexus of control practices, a 'social technology' designed at making workers' behaviour and performance calculable and predictable (Townley, 1994). This summary of critical voices is inherently more sceptical about the 'progressive' nature of HRM and its capacity to reconcile the competing interests of capital and labour. Like HRM, these critical approaches do not speak with one voice, but they have provided a useful antidote to prescriptive, normative approaches to HRM.

The context of management education

An account of the precise antecedents of the ascendency of HRM needs to consider the changes in university management education. As HRM and neoliberal ideology began to enter mainstream thinking, there were discernible changes in British higher education. These changes include: the mainstream acceptance of HRM as an approach to managing the employment relationship at the expense of labour relations; the imposition and centrality of 'managerialist ideologies' and organising principles in British academic life (e.g. Callinicos, 2006; Lorenz, 2012; McCann et al., 2020; Smyth, 2017; Willmott, 1995a); and a growing emphasis in teaching 'employability' skills (Yorke, 2006). The eclipse of LR by HRM is illustrated by the closure of Keele University's department of labour relations. The university's rationale for closure was the claim that individual labour relations academics did not possess the 'appropriate skill sets' to teach HRM. The university's decision, however, was widely interpreted as an 'attack on the legitimacy of critical social science' (Darlington, 2009, p. 1). While not to diminish the significance of the closure of the department in Keele, those of us who started our career teaching trade union and labour relations studies have reached an accommodation with the teaching of HRM by adopting a critical approach derived from the employment relations tradition. However, individual accommodation does not lessen the significance of the rise of the so-called 'business-facing' university. With research and teaching priorities increasingly focused on what appears to be 'best *for* business, rather than to be best *for* society' (Godard, 2014, p. 13), these relatively new institutions are emblematic of the effects of competitive imperatives shaping university curricula and education.

Less obvious to those outside the university milieu is the systematic imposition of corporate 'managerialism' (Klikauer, 2013). Universities until the 1960s were administered on the old medieval principle that only academic staff, the 'producers of knowledge', had the right to organise their own affairs (Ginsberg, 2011). Increasingly, US and UK universities feature corporate cultures in which academic collegium has been replaced by career administrators. University 'efficiency' has come to mean devolving more power to non-academic administrators, so that academics have less autonomy. Academics have progressively become embedded in a nexus of managerialist procedures and mechanisms including budgeting and bidding, and performance measurements enveloped in the language of 'targets and terror' (McCann et al., 2020, p. 433). Critical accounts suggest these social technologies of power 'estrange' academics (Latimer and Skeggs, 2011, p. 393) and depict university cultures as 'toxic' (Smyth, 2017) and 'anxiety machines' (Hall and Bowles, 2016, p. 33). McCann and his colleagues (2020) provide a critical narrative of the encroachment of managerialism; arguing that Anglo-Saxon universities are metaphorically converging toward 'neo-Stalinist' governance regimes (p. 432). The testimony from 'Chloe', an Academic Dean at a prominent British university, describing her 'strategic leadership' role as a 'bullshit' job, so-called because she believed if she were not there, academic staff would be perfectly capable of carrying on by themselves, neatly summarised the impact of 'market discipline' on universities:

> It is not capitalism per se that produces the bullshit. It is managerial ideologies put into practice in complex organisations. As managerialism embeds itself, you get entire cadres of academic staff whose job it is just to keep the managerialist plates spinning – strategies, performance targets, audits, reviews, appraisals, renewed strategies, etc., etc. – which happen in an almost wholly and entirely disconnected fashion from the real lifeblood of universities: Teaching and education. (Cited by Graeber, 2018, p. 55)

Most of these 'managerialist plates' are formulated and implemented in university departments as part of the HR operating model, with HR professionals or 'business partners' aligned to and working closely with university leaders to enhance university performance. An awareness of the neoliberal context therefore is an important consideration in the debate on university management education and pedagogy. Not least because the perceived commodification of education and failure to problematise 'client power' can undermine efforts by academics to introduce critical management pedagogy (Sinclair, 2007). The Chartered Institute of Personnel and Development (CIPD) has had a direct effect on the university HRM curriculum by emphasising explicit 'what' and 'how' knowledge, with less attention to, at least until recently, its outcomes and the interests it serves (Watson, 2010). Amid narratives of agility, innovation and competition, the trend towards teaching applied knowledge is, in part, driven by professional bodies, such as the CIPD, and by research evincing that employers are looking to recruit graduates with 'employability skills', defined as 'a set of achievements, skills, understandings and personal attributes, that make graduates more likely to gain employment' (Yorke, 2006, p. 8).

The roots of the debate on the 'uses of the university' (Kerr, 1963/2001) in a liberal industrial democracy go back many decades. There is the liberal concept of a university as a centre of free thought where intellectuals can challenge beliefs and be a source of new thinking. Often, however, this concept is not realised. The French essayist, Julien Benda (1928/2006), argued that scholars had abandoned the classical ideal of 'disinterested judgement' and, in an age of rising antisemitism in Europe, had ignored 'flagrant injustices' in their own countries. In the 1960s, the German-American philosopher and sociologist, Herbert Marcuse, argued that universities could still function as a habitat for critical thought to develop but, ever more, in the 'real world' beyond the university, in order to sustain profitability, corporations utilise university research resources and an ever-growing supply of compliant graduates with advanced technical knowledge and skills (Marcuse, 1969, p. 62; cited in McCann et al., 2020, p. 435).

Benda's and Marcuse's views on university education exist within a wider analysis of corporate capitalism and provide a backcloth to recent debate on the struggles over the idea of business schools in Western democracies. Critical scholarship emphasises that what gets researched and taught at university business schools matters, in the sense that it influences students' world view and hence shapes the societies we live in (Parker, 2018). Today, business schools collectively are vulnerable to the accusation of intellectual betrayal. Far from acting as a catalyst for critiquing the dominant neoliberal agenda, business schools, collectively, have offered little intellectual opposition to free-market ideology. There are, of course, outstanding academics in Russell Group and post-1992 university business schools. The central argument, however, is that the majority has neglected critical social science. The abandonment of the panoply of intellectual ideals has had the effect of legitimising the neoliberal agenda (Currie et al., 2010). Discounting 'pious murmurings' about corporate social responsibility, critics argue that business schools focus too much on teaching one form of organising – market managerialism (Parker, 2018). That business schools largely failed to act as a counterweight to prevailing neoliberalism ideology is perhaps best illustrated by the pointed observation by US economist, Paul Krugman: 'economists have been part of the problem, not part of the solution' (2012, p. 92). Tett's (2009) searing narrative of the global financial crisis posits that the world of finance is only interested in mathematical equations and that its 'lack of interest in wider matters cuts to the very heart of what has gone wrong' (2009, p. 298). Politicians, financial regulators and bankers failed to employ 'holistic' thinking: the dynamics of neoliberalism and managerialism are closely entwined (Lorenz, 2012). The personal or local financial problems collectively are thus generally linked to wider macro and global structures. At an academic discipline level, a plausible argument is that most HRM scholars palpably failed to employ holistic thinking too. When HRM entered the mainstream in the 1990s, its willing handmaidens were the scholars who conducted the research and shaped the debate that purported to demonstrate the benefits of the HRM approach.

HRM: a discipline in crisis

The crisis in the academic discipline of HRM takes several forms. The first is that mainstream models of HRM are significantly out of sync with current employment practices. In 2020 multitudes of British and European workers are working remotely, coping with isolation or juggling jobs and families. Others are on insecure ZHCs, low pay, reduced hours, underemployment, in work poverty or unemployed. Extreme income inequality and seven-figure bonuses to 'super managers' (Piketty, 2014, p. 315) sit uncomfortably with the widely espoused rhetoric that 'people are an asset'. The second is the consensual HRM-inspired high-commitment workplace model. The 2008 GFC and the Covid-19-induced crisis have highlighted, at both an intellectual and practical level, the question of whether free-market globalisation and finance capitalism – the pre-eminence given to engineering financial assortments rather than production and product markets – can deliver on the promises of mutuality (Thompson, 2013). The high-commitment HRM model is built upon the presumption of enduring stability in the macroeconomic context in which companies operate and the use of profits to invest in technology and learning and development. However, the thesis put forward by Thompson and Harley (2008, p. 161) is that those organisations that have achieved performance gains through the appropriate HR practices are 'not immune from destructive effects of enhanced demand for shareholder value'. Further, mainstream studies of HRM obfuscate the significance of power structures to shape and reshape the ways in which organisations manage their workforces and, at firm level, how financialisation has had dysfunctional consequences for workers (Martin and Quick, 2020; Thompson, 2013). The interrogation of power can help contribute to our understanding of the realities of the employment relation as one of subordination, under material conditions of asymmetrical power and interest conflict (Godard, 2014).

A third consideration is the status of academic HRM. It is evident that its internal coherence has again become problematic. As an intellectual construct, 'carved out of the general managerial function' (Kaufman, 2008, p. 34), research provides compelling evidence that the boundaries and subject matter of HRM need to be redefined. The 2008 GFC was a reminder that capitalism is subject to economic forces, particularly those attached to profit-making, which involve constant change, restructuring and, from time to time, economic crises and recessions. Interesting, then, that mainstream HRM has paid only perfunctory attention to external macroeconomics that effect organisational performance. Instead, there has been an increasing tendency to obsess on knowledge areas pertaining to human 'talent' and its management as a core determinant of firm performance. While HRM–performance research conceptualises the HR 'black box' as a relational construct, which draws attention to the undeniable importance of leadership and organisational behaviour, as an academic discipline,

HRM has to encompass knowledge pertaining to the external context of organisations and consideration of the domains of political economy, labour markets and labour relations (Grimshaw and Rubery, 2008; Kaufman, 2012; Purcell and Kinnie, 2008). The presumption of instability of capitalism, then, suggests that the study of HRM has to pivot away from the over-reliance on knowledge areas pertaining to the 'psychologisation' of the employment relation (Godard, 2014). An analytical approach to HRM that is more integrated and better reflects the dynamics of capitalism advances studies of work and people management in two important respects. It draws on knowledge areas which are often on the periphery of HRM, including national macroeconomic policies, the sociology of work, trade union recognition and collective bargaining, labour markets, employment law and the like. An integrated approach helps us to better understand under what variety of capitalism assortments of HR practices are possible within organisations (Grimshaw and Rubery, 2008). Further, it offers a different perspective to studying the employment relationship. A contextualised multi-stakeholder approach founded on the long-term needs of *all* relevant stakeholders (Beer et al., 2015). Specifically, its consideration of structural power and conflict, the well-being of workers, society and the decarbonisation of work organisations is a paradigm shift from the mainstream dominant focus on shareholder interests and the HRM–performance relation.

The possibility of European and global economies fully returning to pre-pandemic norms seem improbable. The Covid-19 crisis has revealed glaring failures and cruelties in the current capitalist system and in the practice of HRM. The ideology of free markets has created two universes side by side – the wealthiest in society saw their fortunes reach record highs; while 60 per cent of the UK's poorest families turned to charity for food and clothing, and two-thirds went into personal debt merely to pay their rent and buy food (Butler, P., 2020). In the workplace, many employers have unilaterally cut wages, some through the brutal employment practice of 'fire and rehire' (Wall, 2021) or laid off their workers once the government's furlough ended, all the while coping with rapid digital transformation. At the societal level, global warming, extreme inequality and work poverty pose existential threats to businesses, society and the planet. Companies cannot survive if coastal towns are underwater, millions of people are unemployed or underemployed or working on ZHCs that pay less than the living wage. Organisational leaders need to embrace a prosocial purpose beyond profit maximisation and take responsibility for the well-being of their workers, society and ecological systems. The triple crises of climate change, Covid-19 and, for Britain, post-Brexit-defined economy, means the new normal will be very different. Take workers' rights: early indications are the Conservative government is favouring a deregulated approach to securing competitive advantage through low wages and fewer employment rights (Foster et al., 2021; Miliband, 2021), the so-called 'race to the bottom'. The changes will have huge implications for sectors such as hospitality and high street retail, which means a substantial rise in unemployment, especially for women and the young. The economic prognosis requires urgent robust solutions that free markets and charismatic leaders cannot provide. The post-pandemic landscape needs state intervention to build a sustainable low-carbon economy, a reformed social system, the regulation of markets (Rubin, 2020), stronger statutory protections for workers, including rootless digital gig workers, and to bring the power of capital and labour closer to balance. The enduring focus on maximising short-term profits and share price, especially in Britain, rather than risky new investment by 'ownerless corporations' (Hutton, 2014), provides a cogent case for critically examining management education.

Learners of management are not well served if the prescriptive HRM 'toolbox' approach bears little relation to a Covid-19-defined economy and organisational life. As a discipline, HRM has to pivot away from ideological individualism, the primacy of shareholder value, and give serious consideration to social justice and inequality theories. Challenging the status quo is not easy. But there is a body of work (e.g. Alvesson et al., 2009; Antonacopoulou, 2010; Bratton and Gold, 2015; Gold and Bratton, 2014; Godard, 2014; Parker, 2018; Watson, 2010) that acknowledges implicitly or explicitly the need for critical management pedagogy. Moreover, if business schools are to contribute to finding solutions to multiple concurrent crises that appear to be getting exponentially worse, they have to engage their students in a type of learning that will produce leaders who are able to make organisations effective in a variety of different ways: more efficient, more ecologically sustainable, more satisfying, more equitable and more democratic. The learning needs to incorporate four broad principles of critical pedagogy: questioning the taken-for-granted assumptions in the theory and practice of management; making explicit power relations in management practices; challenging leadership orthodoxy claims of rationality and objectivity; incorporating reflexivity and emancipatory models of governance (Reynolds, 1999; Sinclair, 2007).

Transformative changes to HRM theory and practices are occurring in parallel with potentially disruptive AI technology, global warming and a global pandemic that is likely to accelerate change in the nature of work and employment relationships. The Covid-19 pandemic represents both a crisis and an opportunity. A critical approach to studying HRM underscores the task of challenging the status quo as well as the opportunities facing students who, whether they know it or not, are actively designing the future of work organisations. Arguably, academic HRM has a responsibility for educating a new generation of leaders who can better address the competing demands for profit, social justice and environmental protection. In this project, students will be better served if HRM educators and professionals offer social leadership, subject existing and new business models to constant critical interrogation and expose structural inequalities, exploitation, domination and discrimination in work organisations.

This book aims to encourage students to adopt a more reflexive attitude to their HRM studies. Moreover, it is a call for reimagining HRM and in doing so it makes a small contribution to the broader, far more ambitious, project for 'reimagining capitalism'. This puts the onus on management educators to make the academic field of HRM less partisan and more critical by using a systematic set of principles to extend the analysis of HRM to largely excluded voices and cause–effect chains. Further, the scope of HRM inquiry should go beyond workplace-level analysis, which means a critical approach to HRM routinely investigates the well-being of the organisation with the well-being of workers, of the community and the planet. Anything less than these ambitious goals is 'to falsify and impoverish the notion of critical social science in the academic field of HRM and management generally' (Bratton and Gold, 2015, p. 503).

The structure and content of the book

This book is divided into four major parts, which are summarised below. While these parts are, of course, closely interconnected with the external and internal contexts, parts 2, 3 and 4 explore the core theories and HR policies and practices that are typically covered in a one-semester HRM module. Building upon critique, Part 5, retains updated and reworked chapters taken from the previous edition. It ends with a new chapter which considers the future of HRM in a post-Covid-19 world.

Part 2 introduces the arena of contemporary HRM. Chapter 1 discusses the nature and role of HRM and addresses some of the theoretical issues surrounding the debate on HRM. Chapter 2 examines strategic management and strategic HRM, a critical evaluation of studies of the HRM–performance relationship and the involvement of line managers in HRM. Chapters 1–2 provide the context of the theoretical and practical boundaries of HRM and prepare the groundwork for Parts 3, 4 and 5.

Part 3 covers the fundamentals of HRM from job and work design to reward management. Chapter 3 is a thoroughly reworked chapter to cover the major research on job and work design, high-performance work systems and its importance to HRM. Chapter 4 examines workforce planning and introduces concepts and practices associated with workplace diversity. Chapter 5 examines recruitment practices to enable organisations to attract a high-quality pool of job applicants, as well as the use of multiple methods of assessment, all designed to select workers. Chapter 6 examines the practice of performance appraisal and provides a critical review of some of the key developments in performance management and appraisal. Chapter 7 explains the link between corporate strategy and human resource development (HRD), discusses how HRD may be implemented and examines the favoured theories of adult learning and HR development practices. Chapter 8 presents a model of rewards to help the reader examine the complexities and practices associated with reward management. It provides evidence that variable pay systems are increasingly replacing traditional wage schemes, and that these new pay practices go hand in hand with a more precarious employment, the decline of union membership and collective bargaining.

Part 4 pivots towards a focus on managing the employment relationship. Chapter 9 highlights the major changes in labour relations, including the demise of collective bargaining and interest in partnership strategies. Chapter 10 examines worker 'voice' and considers the context in which worker voice has changed over time. It also discusses the nature of conflict in the workplace and various strategies to management conflict.

Part 5 looks at some contemporary HRM issues. Occupational health and safety have long been a neglected area of HRM. We seek to help to shift the balance in Chapter 11, which aims to explore why occupational health and safety is – or ought to be – a central pillar in HRM. In the context of the growing interest in a multi-stakeholder approach to strategic HRM and the pandemic, it also explores the issues of worker well-being and mental health. Chapter 12 examines the emerging literature on sustainable HRM and includes evidence from the author's own research. Chapter 13 has been reworked and updated to provide a critical examination of main themes covered in international HRM within the context of post-Covid-19 world. The final chapter of the book draws the critiques of HR practices together and examines the debate on how HRM, both as an academic discipline and as a form of professional practice, can be reimagined towards a new model for managing the employment relationship. Throughout the chapters, the intention is to draw upon both mainstream *and* critical perspectives, as a requirement for generating a more eclectic interdisciplinary dialogue on how work and people are managed in the third decade of the twenty-first century.

John Bratton
Edinburgh
November 2021

PART 2

HUMAN RESOURCE MANAGEMENT AS A FIELD OF STUDY

CHAPTER 1

Contemporary Human Resource Management: The Role of Critique

CHAPTER 2

Corporate Strategy and Strategic HRM

CHAPTER 1

CONTEMPORARY HUMAN RESOURCE MANAGEMENT

THE ROLE OF CRITIQUE

outline

- Introduction
- Defining human resource management
- The employment relationship
- The scope and goals of HRM
- Theorising HRM
- HRM and the role of critique
- Summary
- Further reading

Source: Scott Graham on Unsplash

objectives

After studying this chapter, you should be able to:

1. Define HRM and its relation to organisational management
2. Explain the central features and importance of the employment relationship
3. Summarise the scope and goals of HRM
4. Critically assess and discuss the theoretical and practical issues surrounding the HRM debate
5. Appreciate the importance of critique in studying HRM

Introduction

It was going to have been the economic event of 2020, but Britain's withdrawal from the European Union was overshadowed by the Covid-19 pandemic that swept across the globe. In Europe it caused an unprecedented public health crisis, disruption in global supply chains and a collapse in Britain's GDP triggering the deepest economic recession in 300 years (Partington, 2020a). A total of 8.9 million workers were temporarily laid-off under the furlough scheme with 80 per cent of their wages paid by the state. The International Labour Organization (ILO) predicted the equivalent of 195 million full-time job losses globally in the immediate aftermath of the pandemic (TUC, 2020f). The immediacy of these unprecedented events can easily distract us from the more persistent trends and features of work and organisations. Growth in digital technologies, the expansion of the so-called gig economy and platform work, zero-hours contracts, emasculated trade union power, extreme health and income inequalities, but side-by-side stratospheric levels of pay for CEOs. Managers continually seek order and predictability (Clegg, 2016), but the Covid-19 crisis is a trend accelerator. As a field of study, researchers have interrogated whether, and how, HR policies and practices might make worker behaviour more predictable, pro-environmental and performance less indeterminate.

This chapter begins your academic journey into the field by examining the long-running debate around the nature of HRM, its scope and its goals. We will examine the importance of the employment relationship before examining some influential frameworks for conceptualising models of HRM that help to assess its contribution to a work organisation. We conclude with an explanation of the role of critique in management studies. We begin, however, by looking at how academics have defined HRM.

Defining human resource management

Human resource management (HRM) is concerned with managing work and the employment relationship. As explained in the opening chapter, since its earliest inception the term HRM has been highly controversial and the antecedents facilitating its emergence include the renaissance of the free-market doctrine of neoliberalism. Legislation, most notably in the US and Britain, helped to dismantle the dominant post-war rule-based systems by undermining trade union membership and the *joint* regulation of pay (see van Wanrooy et al., 2013a). From the 1990s, HRM became widely accepted, particularly in the US and Britain, as an approach toward managing the employment relationship.

As personnel practices were eclipsed, US and British scholars attempted to define the intellectual boundaries of HRM by comparing it with personnel management, generating ever-more academic debate (Table 1.1).

There are significant differences between the two approaches to managing workers. The first two British definitions describe what the function of personnel management ideally should be. Analysing the statements, some common values and themes emerge. Evidently, personnel management is about '*working relationship*' and ensuring the '*agreement is fulfilled*'. The Institute of Personnel Management (IPM) goal reflects the pluralistic process of people management. The selective definitions perceive personnel management as occupying a neutral position, placed between the employer and the workers, and engaged in processes aiming to provide fair terms and conditions as well as having a responsibility to provide satisfying work. The personnel manager's role was described as the 'humane bureaucrat' and 'consensus negotiator' (Torrington, 1998, p. 58).

Early normative statements about HRM by US academics Fombrun et al. (1984) and Beer et al. (1984) arguably launched the academic study of HRM in Britain (Kaufman, 2015). While Fombrun et al. focused on the strategic role of HR practices in supporting organisational strategy, Beer et al. emphasise how HRM actions affect the nature of the employment relationship. Both US definitions assume a unitary frame of reference. The design of HR architecture is predicated on the belief in 'challenging,

Table 1.1 Selective HRM definitions: past and present

Personnel management is a series of activities which: first enable working people and their employing organizations to *agree* about the *objectives* and nature of their *working relationship* and, secondly, ensures that the *agreement is fulfilled* (Torrington and Hall, 1987, cited by Storey, 1989, p. 22, emphasis added).
Personnel management aims to achieve both *efficiency* and *justice*, neither of which can be pursued successfully without the other. It seeks to bring together and develop into an effective organization the men and women who make up the enterprise, enabling each to make his/her own best contribution to its success both as an individual and as a member of a working group. It seeks to provide *fair terms* and *conditions* of employment, and *satisfying work* for those employed (Institute of Personnel Management (IPM), cited by Hendry, 1994, p. 10, emphasis added).
The *strategic* human resource management function is activity engaged in attempts to *support the strategically oriented* organization as it struggles with the environmental trends (Fombrun et al., 1984, p. 12, emphasis added).
Human resource management (HRM) involves all management decisions and actions that affect the nature of the relationship between the organization and employees – its human resources (Beer et al., 1984, p. 1).
Human resource management is a distinctive approach to employment management which seeks to achieve competitive advantage through the *strategic deployment* of a *highly committed* and capable workforce using an array of cultural, structural and personnel techniques (Storey, 1995, p. 5).
HRM then is the process through which management builds the workforce and tries to create the human performances that the organization needs (Boxall and Purcell, 2016, p. 7).

meaningful work in return for loyal, committed service' as Fombrun and his colleagues (1984, p. 40) would put it. Performance is a product of all HR activities which should be aligned with the organisation's corporate strategy.

The definitions of HRM by British academics similarly underscore the importance of the 'strategic' dimension and worker development and 'commitment' in achieving competitive advantage. British scholarship theorised HRM as a contested arena, with divergent 'soft' and 'hard' approaches. The soft approach emphasises the 'H' and purports to place a high value on people as a creative asset and source of competitive advantage, and treats workers holistically, with attention to development, job satisfaction and well-being. In contrast, the hard approach puts the emphasis on the 'R' (Bolton and Houlihan, 2007). Its *leitmotiv* is minimising costs and profit maximisation and it views the worker as an atomised 'resource'. Hard HRM is associated with the Michigan model (Fombrun et al., 1984). Soft HRM is generally likened to the Harvard model (Beer et al., 1984). These divergent approaches have been identified as 'utilitarian-instrumentalism' and 'developmental humanism' models of HRM (Legge, 2005, p. xvi).

At a theoretical level, Boxall et al. (2008) advance the notion of 'analytical HRM' to emphasise that the primary task of HRM scholars is to build theory and gather empirical data in order to identify and explain 'the way management *actually behaves* in organising work and managing people' (Boxall et al., 2008, p. 4, emphasis added). This approach to conceptualising HRM has three interrelated analytical themes. First it is concerned with the '*what*' and '*why*' of HRM, that is, with understanding human behaviour in different contexts and with explaining motives. Second, it is concerned with the '*how*' of HRM, that is, the processes by which it is carried out. In this context, Blau's (1964) influential concept of social exchange theory (SET) is often referred to. SET emphasises instrumental human behaviour. People, it is said, will feel a sense of obligation to reciprocate when they perceive that they are being treated well by their employer (Gilbert et al., 2011a).

The 'what', 'why' and 'how' of HRM is likely to vary over time and space. Context is a crucial factor in explaining how employers manage their workers. Through the political economy perspective of 'varieties

SOPA Images/Getty Images

of capitalism' (Hall and Soskice, 2001), it is widely accepted that both 'soft' and 'hard' types of HRM are practised in different sectors, different organisations – large private or public sector organisations, small and medium-sized enterprises (SMEs), and among different occupations within the same organisation (Burawoy, 1979; Friedman, 1977; Wood, 2013). SMEs, for example, may lack the capability to develop sophisticated HRM practices (Bacon and Hoque, 2005). Financial performance data also suggests that soft/hard approaches produce divergent performance results. Retail giant Costco, defined by a 'soft' approach to HRM, has consistently outperformed Wal-mart, a retailer known for its 'hard' HRM (Cascio, 2006; Sisodia et al., 2014; Ton, 2014). The third analytical theme of analytical HRM is asking, '*Cui bono?*' – 'Who benefits and how well?' – when assessing HRM outcomes. This theme implies a critical objective and helps us to rediscover one of the prime objectives of the social sciences – that of asking tough questions about power and inequality (Watson, 2010).

We need a definition of the subject matter that distinguishes HRM from a set of 'neutral' functional practices, one that conceives it as embedded in a capitalist society and its associated ideologies and global structures, and envisions that HRM can positively affect the well-being of workers and contribute to decarbonising organisations. The following attempts to capture what HRM is about:

> Human resource management is a *strategic* approach to managing work and employment relations. It underscores that leveraging *people's* capabilities, commitment and cooperation is a prerequisite for realising desired *goals.* This is accomplished through a distinctive set of *integrated* employment practices and a *positive* employment relationship, *embedded* in an organisational, societal and ecological context.

Three important emphases can be identified in our definition as to what HRM aspires to be. First, HRM is considered as having a '*strategic*' role and hence it represents a confluence of both strategic management and HR management activities, so that the way work and jobs are designed, and effective worker[1] management, contributes to desired strategic '*goals*'. Second, and related, the primacy of *people* – only the 'human factor' has the inherent capacity to generate value. By their nature, other variables, such as technology, have inert potential that can only be leveraged by some human being. With this in mind, any adequate analytical conception of HRM should draw attention to the notion of *indeterminacy*: workers have a *potential* capacity to provide the added value desired by the employer. This emphasises that people are not passive inputs, but capable of potential agency and development.

The third area of focus in our definition is on the importance of the *integration* of the HR system with the organisation's goals. Recent HRM and leadership research have focused more on the argu-

1 In this text, as a rule, the term 'worker/s' is used rather than 'employee/s' as it is the most inclusive term for those in employment and for those who work in the gig economy without a traditional bilateral employment contract. The term includes all workers and employees at every occupational level but excludes the self-employed, except where specifically identified. In specific incidences, to comply with academic or legal convention, we use the term 'employee/s' when referring to 'employee relations' or citing employment-related statutes or case law.

ments and evidence that effective people management is associated with higher worker well-being and a *positive relationship* (Carter et al., 2013; Guest, 2017; Peccie et al., 2013). A high work-related well-being is associated with physical and mental health and dignity at work. A positive employment relationship is signified by high levels of trust, a perception of fairness, security and mutual respect (Guest, 2017). But an effective HR system does not exist in a vacuum. At the forefront is human agency that is socially constructed – shaped and reshaped by relationships, reflexivity, motivation, material resources, HR practices and effects (Lawrence and Phillips, 2019). The convulsions of the 2008 GFC and 2020 Covid-19 pandemic are events that remind us that HR practices are deeply embedded in the wider sociocultural and environmental context in which they operate.

The conception of critical HRM put forward here resonates with a perspective that economic-ecological-societal factors shape or direct HR policies and practices. In other words: context matters. The demand for dignity in the workplace and high worker well-being are key dimensions of a critical approach to HRM that emphasises the need to extend the analysis of HR outcomes beyond a narrow focus on financial or operational performance (see chapters 2, 11 and 12). During the coronavirus crisis, there was a belated recognition of the importance of people doing work often labelled as 'low skill', but which the national emergency showed to be essential for society to function. The effects of Covid-19 were shaped by multi-generational inequalities that define contemporary Britain (Jones, 2021). Data show that low-paid public-facing workers were among those likely to die from Covid-19 (ONS, 2020a). These workers, relentlessly squeezed to do more and exploited on low pay, the majority of whom are women (Robertson and Gebeloff, 2020), are too often over-looked in academic debate about normative HRM models and managing individual 'talent'. We need to beware that while people are critical for creating wealth and sustainability performance, and human dignity *in* and *at* work is, or *ought* to be, at the heart of HRM (Bolton, 2007), we do not deny fair reward, basic rights, security and dignities to *all* workers.

© John Bratton

Scottish economist and philosopher Adam Smith considered labour to be the ultimate source of economic wealth. People enter into a reciprocal relationship with employers to determine both the work performed and the exchange or wage to create economic wealth.

Reflective question

Reflect upon your own work experience or that of a family member or friend. Does the idea of 'hard/soft' approaches help explain the employer's logic underpinning choice of HR practices? To what extent, if at all, does the Covid-19 crisis justify a reassessment of employment practices?

Digital Spotlight
How digital technologies shape and direct HRM

Digital technologies are redefining the nature, structure and conditions of work and, as a result, have significant implications for HRM theory and practice (Meijerink et al., 2018). Many digital technologies are both driven by and contribute to increased datafication, automation and robotisation (Habraken and Bondarouk, 2017). Over four decades ago, Fox (1974) distinguished between material technology and social technology. The former consists of the physical device that can be 'seen, touched and heard', for example, a mobile phone, tablet or smart virtual assistant. In contrast, social technology encompasses the human processing arrangements that 'seek to order the behaviour and relationships of people' (Fox, 1974, p. 13). Social technology includes job classifications and boundaries, payment systems, decision-making procedures, appraisal processes and other workplace rules which 'seek to govern what work is done, how it is done, and the relationships that prevail between those doing it' (p. 1).

Digital technologies have both direct and indirect consequences for HRM (Meijerink et al., 2018). In regard to the former, configurations of digital hardware, software and electronic networking resources create e-HRM systems that enable intended HR practices to be implemented (Marler and Fisher, 2013). In addition, Artificial Intelligence (AI) and Machine Learning (ML) can be used to allocate tasks and automate feedback to workers without human input in what is termed algorithmic HR management (Chen et al., 2015). However, Meijerink et al. (2018, p. 2) notes that while 'these digital developments may make HRM more efficient and effective, they also raise concerns about worker privacy, the marginalisation of HRM professionals, worker resistance and perceptions of injustice'. In terms of the indirect implications of digital technologies on HRM, the rapid growth of online labour platforms, such as Amazon's Mechanical Turk, may fundamentally alter work relationships by crowdsourcing jobs to 'gig' or 'platform' workers on an 'on demand' basis (Meijerink et al., 2018; Nakatsu et al., 2014). According to Meijerink et al. (2018), these online platforms implement HRM practices in order to motivate, develop and retain workers. However, the authors suggest that such interventions are often designed by individuals from the fields of marketing, computing and data analytics, rather than HRM professionals. This arguably increases the risk of poorly thought-out policies and procedures being introduced.

Will HRM be able to rise to the technological challenges that lie ahead? Volini et al. (2017) argue that, as a field, HRM has already responded successfully to waves of disruption driven by technology. The 1980s, for example, saw advances in automation, particularly in regard to payroll processes and data administration (van den Heuvel and Bondarouk, 2017). In turn, the 1990s were associated with the creation of new performance management systems. Today, HRM professionals must be similarly poised to play a critical role in terms of understanding and integrating new technologies in order to help implement an organisation's strategic HRM.

Stop! How can HR analytics help improve decision-making in HRM?

Essential reading

Meijerink, J., Boons, M., Keegan, A. and Marler, J. (2018) Special issue of the *International Journal of Human Resource Management*: Digitization and the transformation of human resource management. *The International Journal of Human Resource Management*. DOI: 10.1080/09585192.2018.1503845

Note: This feature was contributed by Laura Steele.

The employment relationship

Work under capitalism has been studied for over two centuries. For Marx, work is central to our humanity. In a canonical text published in 1859, which serves as a 'guiding thread' for understanding the industrial capitalism, he wrote, 'men [sic] enter into definite relations that are indispensable and independent of their will' (quoted in Bratton and Denham, 2019, p. 101). Workers and capitalists enter into an employment relation or contract. The contract is characterised by two fundamental features: first, workers exchange their capacity to work, their 'labour power', as an object that is distinct from the person themself, and second, that capacity is regulated into uniform temporal units – hours, days, night shifts – using cash (see Edgell and Granter, 2020). The modern sense of time, work discipline and capitalist techniques of supervision to extract labour power from the person selling it is brilliantly documented by the social historian E. P. Thompson (1967). Marx's analysis of 'labour power' under capitalism came to dominate the sociology of work in the twentieth century.

Today, a deep understanding of HRM is not possible without appreciating the nature of the capitalist employment relationship (Budd and Bhave, 2013). As Marx pointed out: it describes an asymmetry of reciprocal relations between workers and their employer through which both the work performed (whether it is routine or creative) and the economic exchange (wage or salary) is contractually determined. Employment relationships vary: at one end of the scale, they can be a short-term, primarily but not exclusively economic exchange for a relatively well-defined set of duties and low commitment; at the other, they can be complex long-term relationships defined by a broad range of economic inducements and relative security of employment, given in return for a broad set of duties and a high commitment from the worker. HR practices have been identified as important antecedents of 'psychological' contracts (Guest et al., 2010; Rousseau, 1995; Rousseau and Greller, 1994). What, then, is the essence of the employment relationship? The literature identifies four key dimensions of the employment relationship: economic, social, legal and psychological.

The first dimension of the employment relationship is that it incorporates an *economic relationship*: the 'exchange of pay for work' (Brown, 1988). This 'exchange' is characterised by five other essential and interrelated features. First, *product market* conditions directly affect the employer's revenue, with potential changes to the terms and conditions of employment. Second, capitalism is subject to economic forces, particularly those attached to product markets and profit-making, which involves continuous change and restructuring and, periodically, economic crises and recessions (Fine, 1998). Third, and related, the *state* influences the economic relationship indirectly through fiscal and monetary policies which determine aggregate expenditure, investment, consumer spending and the general 'character' of the employer behaviour towards employment relations (Edwards, 2003b). Further the state effects the economic exchange directly through employment law on wages (for example, the statutory minimum wage). Fourth, the exchange is dependent upon a process of abstracting value in which work or effort level is *indeterminate*. Thus, the employer buys a *potential* level of physical or intellectual labour. When people enter into a work-wage bargain it places an obligation on both the employer and the worker: in exchange for a pay. The worker's time is not his own; it belongs to the employer who buys it. Insofar as a worker is working they are obligated to perform an amount of physical, intellectual or emotional labour. For the nineteenth-century historian Thomas Carlyle and philosopher Karl Marx, the phrase 'cash nexus' encapsulated the depersonalised nature of exchange between the employer and the worker. In customer-facing occupations found in tourism, hospitality and retail, 'work' or effort also includes workers' feelings and appearances, as well as the way they behave, so that as well as productive work there is 'emotional' and 'aesthetic labour' (Hochschild, 1983; 2012; Warhurst and Nickson, 2007).

Fifth, the work-wage bargain is structurally conflictual. In classical capitalism the 'wage' side of the bargain generates tension and conflict because wages are a cost to the employer, which affects profitability. As Brown (1988, p. 57) observes, 'Conflict is structured into employment relations' as wages or salaries to workers is a cost to the employer. The 'work' side of the contract also generates pressures and conflict because it is, as noted, the employer who buys a worker's time and the worker's labour power is inherently indeterminate. The function of management is, therefore, to transform this potential into *actual* value-added labour. HR practices are designed to narrow the divide between workers' potential and actual performance or, in Townley's (1994, p. 14) words:

> Personnel practices ... offer a technology which aims to render individuals and their behaviour predictable and calculable ... to bridge the gap between promise and performance, between labour power and labour, and organizes labour into a productive force or power.

Despite the interrelatedness of economics and HRM issues, HRM theorists have tended to neglect the former. An HRM perspective on the changing organisation of work and employment which neglects change in macroeconomic variables (e.g. Gross Domestic Product, aggregate investment), labour markets or globalisation lacks credibility (Grimshaw and Rubery, 2003). There is no single labour market (Fine, 1998), but labour markets are intimately connected to the employment relationship. Interestingly, then, analytical HRM has generally proved relatively immune to the influence of macroeconomics and consideration of the material and empirical realities of labour markets. This means that the socioeconomic relations (for example, the presence of trade unions and degree of collective bargaining to determine pay in a particular labour market) by which labour markets are structured occupy at best a secondary position in academic HRM, as divergences from the presumption of a harmonious system of developing and rewarding human capability. A consideration of macroeconomics and labour markets is an essential prerequisite for understanding the dynamics of the economic relationship on which different HRM models are built (see Grimshaw and Rubery, 2008).

PART 2

The second dimension of the employment relationship is that it incorporates *social relations* unique to a capitalist society. Workers and managers are not isolated individuals but members of a family, community and social groups, such as a trade union or professional association, who observe social norms and mores that influence their actions in the workplace. As Parker rightly observes, 'the family, the home, the school, leisure, social class, sexuality, the state are all domains of activity which are not routinely considered to be germane to explaining what people are like at work' (2018, p. 24). People enter organisations as the bearers of their own values, social norms, mores and histories that help to shape their individual beliefs and values about work. These observations suggest that employment relations are deeply textured and profoundly sociological (Bratton and Denham, 2019). People at work should not be viewed as atomised, unique individuals, but as the bearers of an objective structure of social relations shaped by life experiences, values, expectations and history (Clegg et al., 1999).

In the context of contemporary capitalist societies, the social context shapes the employment relation in other complex ways. As Solow opines:

> Wage rates and jobs are not exactly like other prices and quantities. They are much more involved in the way people see themselves, think about their social status, and evaluate whether they are getting a fair shake out of society. ... Buyers and sellers of labour might not accede to perceived injustice merely because of a little excess supply or demand. (Solow, 1990, pp. 21–2, cited by Grimshaw and Rubery, 2003, p. 45)

For Solow, pay and jobs are tied to social status, perceived self-identity, self-worth and social justice. His work underscores the role of trade unions as a social force within the labour market, and the associated development of workplace rules and practice to 'lubricate market mechanisms' (Grimshaw and Rubery, 2003, p. 45.) The work of Sennett (2012) insinuates that social factors shape and reshape employment relations. Workers forge informal bonds and friendships with co-workers including managers, and although these do not transform work into a 'conflict-free Garden of Eden', they do help to make work less soulless and to create civility in the organisation (2012, pp. 148–9).

A thorough interrogation of the social domain draws attention to the role of power in explaining the dynamics of the employment relationship. For unless the worker happens to be an international football celebrity, the employment relationship embodies an uneven balance of power between the parties. The dominant perspective defines power as the capacity or the potential to influence others in relation to their beliefs, attitudes or activities. This perspective is often associated with the well-known concept of social power (French and Raven, 1960). Through this theoretical prism, coercive, reward and legitimate power are predicated on a person's position in the formal hierarchy of the organisation. Warren (1969) argues that the most important source of power is coercion and reward. Coercive power is the primary force that keeps subordinates from retaliating when faced with abusive behaviour by a line manager (Lian et al., 2014). In contrast, subordinates comply because a manager can distribute rewards. An employer promising you a pay increase or promotion to act as she or he instructs is using reward power. Reward power is a function of dependence. The greater is worker B's dependence on manager A, the more power A has over B.

Critical scholars, on the other hand, contend that power is not simply something the powerful have and the powerless lack. Power is *exercised* through work organisations and society. As the French philosopher Michel Foucault (1998, p. 63) argues: 'Power is everywhere and comes from everywhere.' In Foucault's analysis, power is exercised many ways – 'economies of power', 'networks of power' and 'technologies of power' (Crane et al., 2008). Inequalities of power, in turn, structure the nature of work. Looking at the intersection of employment relation and power through a Foucauldian discourse analysis, what is clear is that the most astute understandings of power see it not as an individual phenomenon, but relational or interactive in nature (see Murphy and Bratton, 2020). Sennett's (2012) 'social triangle' concept – authority, mutual respect and cooperation – reminds us that people are different from other 'resources' because their cooperation and commitment always have to be won and sustained by management. Importantly, workers' agency potentially can resist management and engage in non-cooperation. The power–dependency relation is embedded and displayed within the unequal power dynamics of the employment relationship (see Budd and Bhave, 2013; Hyman, 1975). Looking at the development of the HRM canon over the last 30 years, it can be seen how little these inherent inequalities of power figure, despite the fact that they can be so readily observed in the contemporary workplace.

The third dimension of the employment relationship is that it involves a legal relationship: a network of contractual and statutory rights and obligations affecting both parties to the contract. Contractual rights are based upon case law (judicial precedent), and the basic rules of contract, insofar as they relate to the contract of employment, are fundamental to the legal relationship between the employer and the worker. It is outside the scope of this chapter to provide a discussion of the rules of contract. But, according to Kahn-Freund, the contract of employment, freely negotiated between an individual and their employer, can be considered to be the cornerstone of English employment law (Honeyball, 2010). Prior to the UK exiting the European Union, a large part of UK employment law was derived from EU law. For example, the EU Directive that mandated that fixed-term workers cannot be treated less favourably than comparable permanent workers in the same firm in terms of wages, benefits and training. In practice, however, workers' rights may not materialise because enforcement has largely been left to employers to decide which workers should qualify for employment rights. Further, few workers' rights are enforced by any state institution, leaving enforcement to employment tribunals and courts after individual workers or trade unions submit claims (Moyer-Lee, 2021). In February 2021, the Supreme Court ruling that Uber drivers are entitled to basic workers' rights illustrates the absence of basic protections such as minimum wage and paid holidays offered to workers in Britain (Croft and Venkataramakrishnan, 2021).

A fourth, less tangible dimension of the employment relationship is the *psychological contract*. The 'psychological contract' is a metaphor that captures a wide variety of largely unwritten expectations and understandings of the two parties about their mutual obligations. Guest and Conway (2002, p. 22) define it as 'the perceptions of both parties to the employment relationship – organization and individual – of the reciprocal promises and obligations implied in that relationship'. At the heart of the

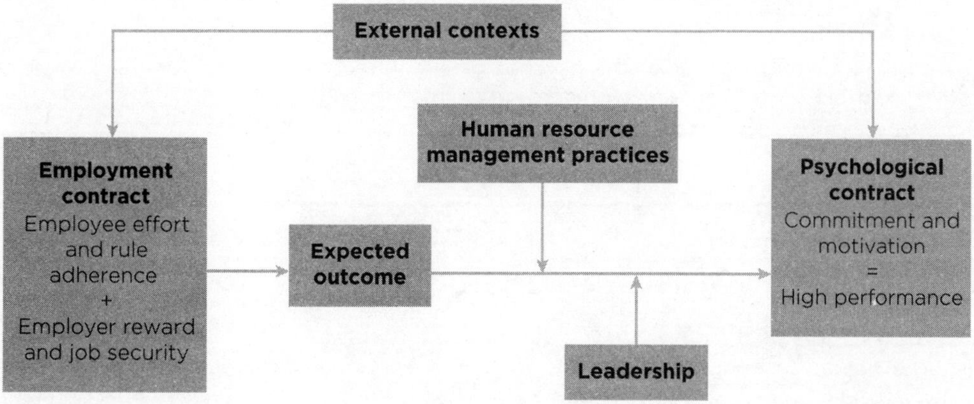

Figure 1.1 The employment and psychological contract between workers and employers

PART 2

concept of the psychological contract are levers for individual motivation (M) and task performance (O) beyond the 'expected outcomes' (Figure 1.1).

The psychological contract has important features that managers need to appreciate. First, HR practices may communicate different beliefs about the reciprocal promises and obligations that are present (Guest and Conway, 2002). Workers will have different perceptions of their psychological contract, even when the legal contract is identical. Managers will therefore be faced with a multitude of perceived psychological contracts (PPCs) within the same organisation (Bendal et al., 1998). A psychological contract breach (PCB) can affect both worker performance and retention, for example. Second, the PPC reaffirms the notion that the employment relationship is thought to be one of exchange – the promissory exchange of offers and the mutual obligation of the employer and worker to fulfil these offers. Third, PPCs are shaped in particular contexts, which includes national and organisational culture and climate. Cross-cultural studies suggest differences in the way workers perceive transactional (e.g. different expectations about workload) and relational (e.g. misunderstanding about reporting relationships) psychological contract breach (Balabanova et al., 2019). A study in the Netherlands found that the relationship between psychological contract fulfilment and work outcomes can be moderated by generational differences (Lub et al., 2016). Organisational-specific factors can influence PPC. In the context of non-union work regimes, gig working, zero-hours contracts and so-called 'downsizing', the psychological contract has become a fashionable framework for analysing changes to the employment relation (Saunders and Thornhill, 2006).

Although the PPC thesis offers important insights into the employment relationship, it does have major weaknesses. Godard (2014) is critical that the field of HRM has become increasingly dominated by psychological theorising: the 'psychologisation' of HRM. The essence of the PPC thesis is the idea that a workforce is a collection of atomised individuals, as though individual beliefs are fixed features of a worker's day-to-day behaviour. In doing this, in total contrast to critical paradigms, PPC neglects a well-established body of research grounded in sociology showing that people's beliefs and expectations about employment form *outside* the workplace. The idea that family members and peers can influence expectations about work and career opportunities is called 'orientation to work' (Bratton, 2021). The central importance of work and the four key dimensions of the employment relationship – economic, social, legal and psychological – means that the field of HRM needs to incorporate both multidisciplinary and multi-ideological perspectives (see also Budd, 2020).

Reflective question

What do you think of the concept of the psychological contract? How important is it to manage the psychological contract for (1) front-line workers, and (2) managers?

Ethical Insight

Is it ethical to insist workers should return to work during the Covid-19 crisis?

In August 2020, it was announced that the UK government intended to launch an advertising campaign encouraging individuals who had been working from home during the coronavirus pandemic to return to their offices the following month (BBC, 2020b). The initiative was reportedly motivated by concerns regarding the negative effect the situation was having on food and retail outlets in towns and city centres who depended on their custom. The campaign was to be focused on the social and productivity benefits of returning to the office, as well as the advantages of commuting by foot or bicycle (Rayner, 2020). In addition, the government also intended to ask employers to reassure their staff that premises were 'Covid-secure' by outlining measures that had been taken. The campaign was, however, postponed indefinitely (Rayner, 2020). First, due to reports that social-distancing guidelines were preventing companies from returning to their workplaces and, later, as the result of rising infection numbers. But, in the context of a global pandemic, is it ethical for employers (or, indeed, governments) to insist that employees return to the workplace?

Business ethics is, according to Crane et al. (2019, p. 5), the 'study of business situations, activities, and decisions where issues of right and wrong are addressed'. The authors stress that they mean *morally* right and wrong, as opposed to, for example, *financially* or *strategically* right or wrong. Morality 'is concerned with the norms, values, and beliefs embedded in social processes which decide right and wrong for an individual or a community' (Crane et al., 2019, p. 8). It is important to note that ethics is closely related to, but distinct from, the law. The law is frequently said to define the minimum acceptable standards of conduct, however, there are many domains that the law does not (and could not) cover (Crane et al., 2019, p. 8). Ethics, therefore, is frequently concerned with the 'grey areas', where 'values are in conflict' (Teviño and Nelson, 2014, p. 39).

The decision whether or not employees should be impelled to return to the workplace is one such 'grey area'. Ethical issues in HRM are often framed from the perspective of *employee rights* and *employee duties* (Crane et al., 2019). Workers are paid to do a job and, if they cannot do that job from home either at all or to an acceptable standard, then there is a strong argument that they have a duty to return to the workplace. However, the situation is complicated by the fact much is still unknown about the virus. In addition, each employee is dealing with their own particular set of circumstances (for example, they may have an underlying health condition), as well as a personal tolerance for risk shaped by complex social and cultural factors. As a result, the answer simply isn't black or white.

Stop! Do you think it is ethical to insist employees return to their place of work in the midst of a pandemic? Outline the reasons for your answer.

Essential reading

Jack, G., Greenwood, M. and Schapper, J. (2012) Frontiers, intersections, and engagement of ethics and HRM. *Journal of Business Ethics*, 111: 1–12.

Note: This feature was contributed by Laura Steele.

The scope and goals of HRM

In understanding the role of HRM it can be helpful to identify the major subdomains of HRM knowledge: micro, strategic and international (Boxall et al., 2008). The largest subdomain refers to *micro HRM* (MHRM), which is concerned with managing individual workers and small work groups. It covers activities such as workforce planning, job design, recruitment and selection, performance management, learning and development, and rewards. These HR subfunctions cover a myriad of evidence-based practices concerned with human behaviour, so many are informed by psychology and sociological-oriented studies of work (see, for example, Edgell and Granter, 2020; Warr, 2008). Human resource development (HRD) may be considered to be a subset of HRM. Stewart (2007, p. 66) defines HRD as 'planned interventions in organizational and individual learning processes'. Over the last 30 years HRD has grown rapidly, so much so, that it has become increasingly 'a movement in its own right' (Stewart et al., 2013, p. 5).

The second domain is *strategic HRM* (SHRM), which concerns itself with the processes of linking HR strategies with business strategies and measures the effects on organisational performance. *Strategic HRD*, which again may be considered as a subset of HRM or as a distinct field, has been defined as 'a coherent, vertically aligned and horizontally integrated set of learning and development activities which contribute to the achievement of strategic goals' (Garavan, 2007, p. 25). Strategic HRM and strategic HRD assumes hierarchy and is an endeavour undertaken by individuals with power (Parker, 2018). The third domain, *international HRM* (IHRM), focuses on the management of people in companies operating in more than one country.

Drawing on the work of Squires (2001), these three major subdomains help us address three basic questions:

- What do HR professionals do?
- What affects what they do?
- How do they do what they do?

To help us answer the first question – *What do HR professionals do?* – the literature identifies the key *MHRM* subfunctions performed by the HR department, but also the trend for some HR functions, such as recruitment and pay administration, to be outsourced to external specialist companies. Another development is for key HR functions to be devolved to line managers. For some observers these trends have been characterised as a 'crisis' as HR professionals struggle for relevance and status in cost-conscious times (Sparrow et al., 2011).

How the HR function is organised and how much power it has relative to that of other management functions is affected by both external and internal factors unique to the establishment. A rules-based, regulation-oriented national business system, with strong trade unions, employment laws on equity and affirmative action, elevates the status of the HR professional and strengthens the corporate HR function. In contrast, a market-oriented corporate culture, minimum investment in worker development and reliance on temporary workers, is associated with decentralisation of the HR function. As Lewin (2008) has observed, the main challenge in the third decade of the twenty-first century is for HR professionals to keep focused on a strategic role while also performing the essential operational role in their organisation.

To answer the second question – *What affects what managers and HR professionals do?* – necessitates an appreciation of contingencies influencing MHRM: the external context, strategy and organisation.

The *external context*, including globalised capitalism, the peculiarities of national employment systems and national culture, creates different tendencies in HR practice operating across national boundaries. The external context reinforces the notion that organisations are *embedded* within a particular capitalist society. Against an ever-changing contextual backdrop, Andolšek and Štebe (2005, p. 327) note the importance of employment law: 'the stronger the institutional framework ... the less [sic] options a company may have to impose its own approach to regulating its HRM'. The second contingency is *strategy*. Strategic HRM underscores the need for the HR strategy to be integrated with the organisation's strategy and highlights the responsibility of line managers (LM) for implementing HR policies and practices (see Figure 1.4 and Chapter 2). The third contingency is *organisation*, which covers a myriad of new working arrangements (see Chapter 3), such as work teams (Boltanski and Chiapello, 2018; Van Der Heijden et al., 2015). HR policies and practices are contingent upon external and internal contexts. Together, these changes create a wide variety of employment relationships, all of which demand the increasing sophistication of *micro* HRM (Farnham, 2015, p. 514), on the one hand, and leadership on the other (Bratton, 2020).

To answer the third question – *How do HR professionals and managers do what they do?* – requires us to identify key competencies. It is suggested that HR professionals should identify and master five competencies to fully contribute to organisational performance: strategic decision-making, personal credibility, delivery of foundational HR infrastructure (e.g. staffing), and business knowledge and HR technology. In high-performance work systems HR professionals and managers need to exhibit the competencies of change and culture management, effective communication, and coaching and mentoring (Agashae and Bratton, 2001; Brockbank and Ulrich, 2018; Ellinger, 2015).

Managing people is complex, and individual managers vary in terms of their capacity or inclination to master or use the core competencies of HR management. Given that HR management focuses on the human side of business, the quality of human relationships go some way to explaining different management styles and the distinction between a manager and a leader (Bratton, 2020). The micro and strategic domains of HRM/HRD, the contingencies influencing HR practices, and managerial skills are combined and diagrammatically shown in Figure 1.2.

The model implies not only that HRM is a multidimensional activity, but also that its analysis has to be multidirectional (Squires, 2001). We might, for that reason, examine the effect of artificial intelli-

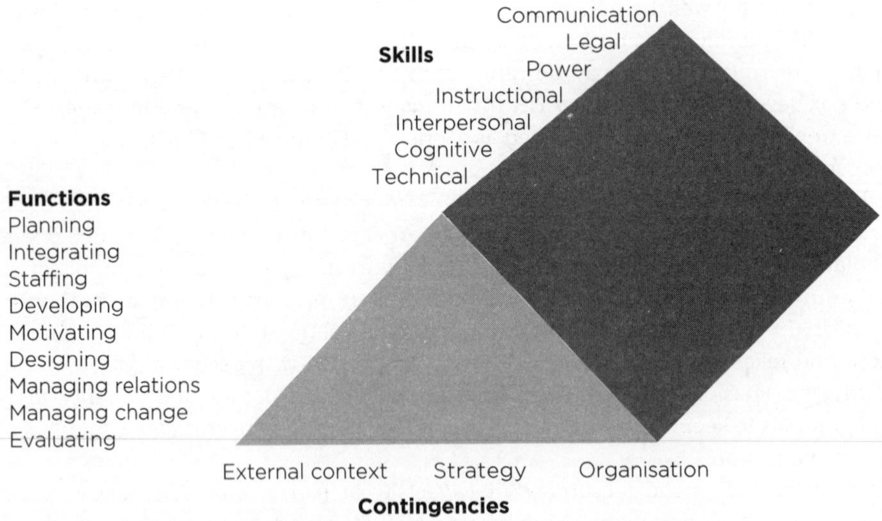

Figure 1.2 HRM functions, contingencies and skills

Source: Adapted from Squires (2001).

gence (AI) (a contingency) on HR functions, such as learning and development, and how HR functions are translated into action. The model is useful in other ways too: it serves to develop an 'analytical conception' of HRM by building theory and generating data based on managers' *intended* and *actual* actions in managing work and people across workplaces, sectors and market societies (Boxall et al., 2008) – the classic rhetoric–reality gap notably highlighted by Legge (2005). The multidimensional nature of the model offers managers a sense of professional 'identity' by detailing professional functions, processes and skills. Finally, it helps line managers to look beyond their immediate tasks and to be aware of the 'totality of management' (Squires, 2001, p. 482).

The goals of HRM

The diversity of HR policies and practices across public, private and not-for-profit organisations and the links to strategy raises another important question: *What are employer's goals in HRM?* In the mainstream HRM literature there is considerable academic debate addressing this question. The discussion suggests that the goal of HRM is to scaffold the organisation's desired objectives through stabilising a cost-effective and socially legitimate system of people management (Boxall, 2008). While recognising 'strategic tensions' within the organisation, Boxall and Purcell (2016) identify four key goals:

- *Cost-effectiveness* – maximising profits or minimising costs.
- *Flexibility* – short-run responsiveness and long-run agility in response to external pressures.
- *Social legitimacy* – how people are managed and led affects the ethical standing of the organisation in society.
- *Power* – managers aim to enhance their power as stakeholders.

The strategic HR goals may vary between private and public-sector organisations. They can also vary depending on whether organisational leaders demonstrate a commitment to an environmentally sustainable planet, by enacting policies and practices that will decarbonise the workplace. In terms of theoretical development, a fifth goal for HRM can relate to effective pro-environmental leadership (Bratton, 2020). It is suggested that none of these goals can be achieved without investment in worker learning and development (Poell et al., 2015). Few organisations have explicit goal statements. Even when they do, they should not be taken at face value. Leaders' aspirational rhetoric may mask powerful pragmatic and economic imperatives (Boxall, 2008; Wajcman, 1998).

Global HRM
Netflix: Line managers use 'keeper test'

The workplace 'culture' refers to an amorphous collection of interrelated values, understandings and behaviours that is shared by its workforce. For some, it refers to a 'binge-working culture' (Campbell, 2010) or a 'tick-box culture' (Travis, 2011) or one that 'engenders fear' (Krashinsky Robertson, 2020, p. B2). In the HRM canon, culture has been described as a 'key lever' and the 'holy grail' to release flexibility and commitment (Beer et al., 1984; Storey, 2007). The US company Netflix has revolutionised the home-entertainment landscape. In 1998 Netflix had 30 employees, in 2019 the company employed approximately 8,600. In 2019, Netflix had almost 193 million global subscribers, adding 26 million during the Covid-19 pandemic. In the same year, the company had US$1.87 billion in net income. According to Netflix's CEO Reed Hastings, the foundation of this growth is its culture and HR practices. Netflix's culture has been described as an 'undercurrent of dread'; while its HR practices prioritise 'hiring and keeping the best talent'.

One Netflix employee describes working through the night in a fruitless bid to allay her fear of the axe, and says pushing the elevator button at work every morning is like a 'trigger' for her anxiety. Another newly hired employee refused to unpack his boxes for months, unwilling to settle in when he could be fired at any time. Behind the workplace culture at Netflix is a principle that 'adequate performance gets a generous severance package'. Even good, hard workers are not safe if they are not exceptional; line managers are encouraged to use a 'keeper test' to fire anyone that they would not fight hard to keep if that person said they were leaving. Employees have to develop a tolerance for receiving constant feedback from co-workers. Reed Hastings acknowledges this is deeply uncomfortable but says 'we're not trying to do pain minimisation; we're trying to do growth maximisation'. On the flip side, employees are empowered to be innovative and make decisions such as when to take vacations, or to spend US$4.6 million for the documentary *Icarus* (Krashinsky Robertson, 2020, p. B2).

Companies such as Netflix and Amazon have been accused of having a high-pressure workplace culture with a 'hire and fire' management style. Coupled with high-pressure management, Netflix is able to extract the maximum productivity from its workforce. The idea that an employer would intentionally adopt practices that instil fear as a management strategy sits at odds with studies suggesting that the HRM-performance causal chain is predicated upon high-quality manager-subordinate relations and the rhetorical statements that the well-being of workers is of paramount importance.

Stop! Do you agree or disagree with the notion that fear of dismissal may be used as a management strategy? Why or why not? Can firms simultaneously be committed to their workers and create an office culture of fear?

Essential reading

Krashinsky Robertson, S. (2020) Why Netflix's uncomfortable office culture works. *The Globe and Mail*, Canada, p. B2; Hastings, R. and Meyer, E. (2020) *No Rules Rules: Netflix and the Culture of Reinvention.* London: Penguin. See also Kantor, J. and Streitfeld, D. (2015) Inside Amazon: wrestling big ideas in a bruising workplace. *New York Times*, 15 August; Spicer, A. (2015) The flaw in Amazon's management fad. *The Guardian*, 17 August.

Note: This feature was contributed by John Bratton.

Theorising HRM

Practice without theory is blind. (Hyman, 1989, p. xiv)

So far, we have explained that HRM varies across organisations and market societies depending upon a range of external and internal contingencies. In addition, we have identified the skills by which managers accomplish their HRM goals. We will now turn to an important part of the HRM discourse, the search for a theoretical model that demonstrates analytically the nature and goals of the discipline. Over the past 35 years, HRM scholars have produced multi-conceptual models. These models help to focus debate around such questions as 'What is the difference between HRM and personnel management?' and 'What outcomes are employers seeking when they implement an HRM approach?' Here, we identify five models developed by American and British academics. Each seeks to demonstrate, in analytical terms, the distinctiveness and goals of HRM.

These models fulfil several important intellectual functions for those studying HRM:

- They establish a cluster of variables and relationships between the dependent and independent variables to be researched. For example, 'Do pro-environmental green HR practices (*independent* variables) promote pro-environmental line manager and worker behaviours (*dependent* variables)?'
- They legitimise HRM. They demonstrate the distinctiveness of HRM practices: 'it is not the presence of selection or training but a *distinctive approach* to selection or training that matters. It is the use of high performance or high commitment HRM practices', writes Guest (1997, p. 273, emphasis added).
- They serve as a heuristic device by providing an analytical framework for studying HRM.

The Michigan model of HRM

As the name suggests, a group of academics at the Michigan Business School developed this model. Figure 1.3 shows four core HR activities: *selecting* people who are best able to perform defined jobs, *appraising* worker performance to facilitate 'equitable' distribution of *rewards*, by linking rewards to high levels of performance, and *developing* employees to enhance their work performance. The HR system is conceptualised as a 'cycle' that represents sequential managerial tasks (Devanna et al., 1984, p. 41). The authors suggest that performance is not only dependent on the HR system but strategy, structure and technology also influence organisational outcomes. Thus, this performance-oriented model emphasises the interrelatedness of the HR system, which is tightly aligned to the overall strategies of the business (see Chapter 2).

A *unitarist* perspective underpins this 'hard' model of HRM. Unitarism represents the standpoint that organisations are 'families' where employers and workers share common goals and dissent among workers is dysfunctional behaviour. The strengths of the Michigan model are that it expresses the coherence of the HR system and the importance of 'matching' internal HR policies and practices to the organisation's strategy. The notion of the 'HRM cycle' is useful as a heuristic framework for explaining key HR practices that make up the complex field of HRM. Its weaknesses include its prescriptive nature and its focus on just four HR practices. It also ignores multiple stakeholder interests, situational factors and the notion of management's strategic choice.

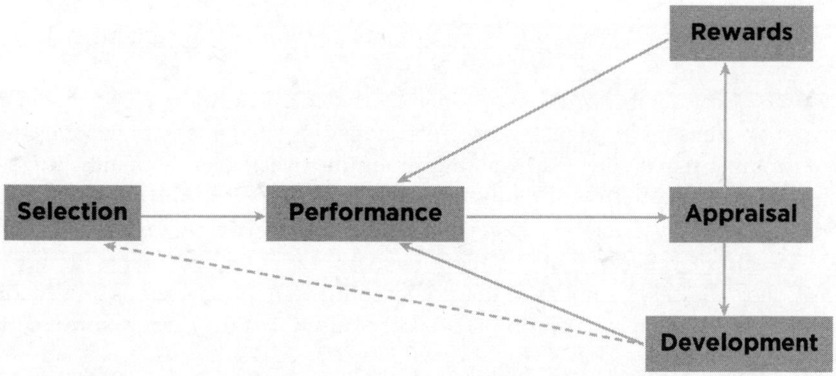

Figure 1.3 The HRM cycle

Source: Fombrun et al. (1984).

The Harvard model of HRM

As was widely acknowledged in the early HRM literature, the 'Harvard model' offered by Beer et al. (1984) provided one of the first comprehensive statements on the nature of HRM, the goals of employers and specific HR outcomes. The model (Figure 1.4) consists of six basic components: stakeholder interests, situational factors, HRM policy choices, HR outcomes, long-term consequences and feedback loop.

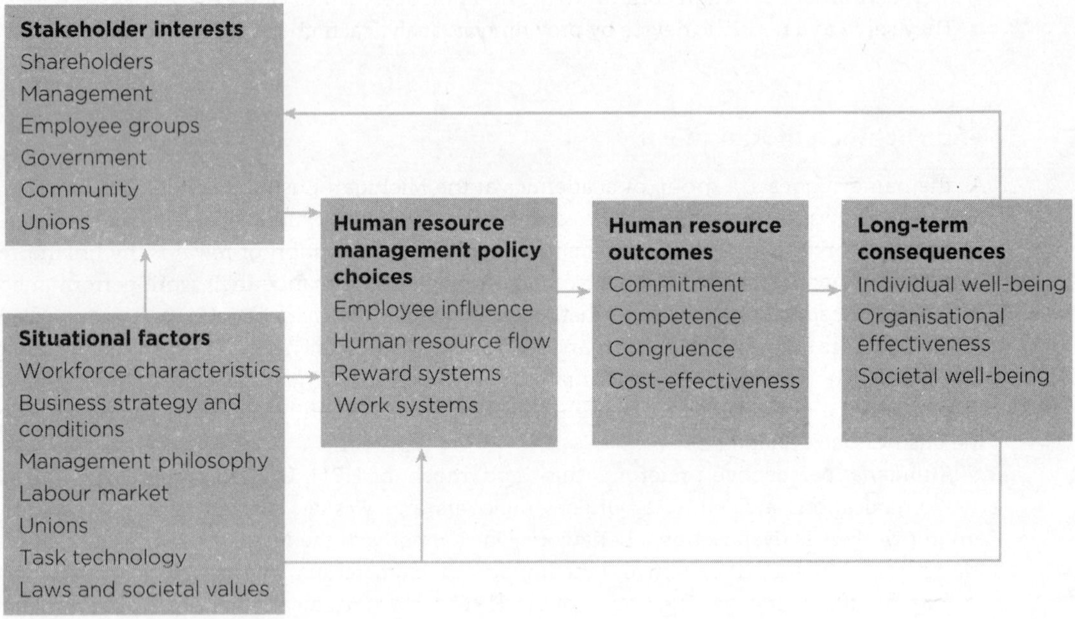

Figure 1.4 The Harvard model of HRM

Source: Beer et al. (1984).

1. *Stakeholder interests* – recognise the importance of 'trade-offs', either explicitly or implicitly, between the interests of employers and employees, shareholders, and trade unions. That organisations are made up of various interest groups, notably workers and unions, reflects more of a *pluralist* ideology.
2. *Situational factors* – influence management's choice of HR strategy. The model incorporates workforce characteristics (e.g. skilled or professional), management philosophy (e.g. neoliberalism), labour market regulations (e.g. working time directives), societal values (e.g. self-reliance versus collectivism) and patterns of unionisation (high or low trade union density). Analytically, the inclusion of contextual variables reflects social reality: 'the employment relationship entails a blending of business and societal expectations' (Boxall, 1992, p. 72).
3. *HRM policy choices* – emphasise that senior management's decisions and actions in HR management can be fully appreciated only if it is recognised that they result from an interaction between constraints and choices.
4. *HR outcomes* – identify the underpinning goals of employers. High employee commitment and competence are linked to longer-term effects on organisational effectiveness and societal well-being. HRM policies must 'fit' the business strategy (Beer et al., 1984, p. 178). A 'clan' HRM system

best fits a team-based, 'clan-oriented' organisation, which fosters 'a climate of interchangeability, enrichment, and group independence' (Beer et al., 1984, p. 182). This is what Legge (2005, p. xvi) calls the 'soft', or 'developmental humanism' model of HRM.

5. *Long-term consequences* – relate to three levels: individual, organisational and societal. At individual level, effects include psychological rewards that workers receive in exchange for their work. At organisational level, increased effectiveness ensures the survival of the firm. At societal level, by fully utilising people at work, some of society's goals (for example, employment) are attained.
6. *Feedback loop* – through which the outputs flow directly into the organisation and to the stakeholders. Situational factors influence HRM policy and choices. Conversely, long-term outputs can influence the situational factors, stakeholder interests and HR policies, and the feedback loop reflects this two-way relationship.

The strength of the Harvard model lies in its classification of inputs and outcomes at both the organisational and the societal level, creating the basis for a critique of comparative HRM. It contains elements that are analytical (situational factors, stakeholders, strategic choice) and prescriptive (commitment, competence), and therefore provides a useful analytical basis for the study of HRM. In their review of the HRM discipline, Beer et al. (2015), reaffirm that a core component of the Harvard model is it's contextual and multi-stakeholder approach, with particular attention being paid to the long-term needs of all relevant stakeholders. It has shortcomings, however. First, although the framework is more pluralist than is found in later models, it is still vulnerable to the charge of 'unitarism'. Second, is the absence of a coherent theoretical basis for measuring the relationship between HR inputs, outcomes and performance (Boxall, 1992; Guest, 1997; 2017). Third, it is open to the charge that scant attention is given to HR policies and practices that explicitly enhance individual well-being and address ecological interests.

The Storey model of HRM

The Storey (2007) model of HRM explicates the differences between 'personnel' and the HRM paradigm by proffering an 'ideal type'. We should note the usage of the 'ideal type' tool. Its originator Max Weber wrote, 'In its conceptual purity, this mental construct [*Gedankenbild*] cannot be found empirically anywhere in reality' (quoted by Bratton and Denham, 2019, p. 228). An ideal type therefore is not a description of reality. Its purpose is to act as a comparison with empirical reality in order to establish the differences or similarities between the two positions, and to understand and explain causal relationships. Developed by reconstructing 'implicit models' conveyed by managers during interviews, Storey posits that the model is 'an amalgam of description, prescription, and logical deduction' (Storey, 2001, p. 6). The four main elements in his HRM framework are: beliefs and assumptions, strategic qualities, the critical role of managers, and key levers (see Table 1.2).

1. *Beliefs and assumptions* – the most fundamental is that, ultimately, it is talented employees that distinguish successful organisations from mediocre ones. It follows logically from this that managers ought not simply to regard people as a cost, but to nurture employees as a *valued asset*.
2. *Strategic qualities* – seek to demonstrate that HRM is a matter of critical importance to strategic planning: 'Decisions about human resources policies should ... take their cue from an explicit alignment of the competitive environment, business strategy and HRM strategy' (Storey, 2001, p. 10).
3. *Role of managers* – emphasises the crucial role of line managers (LMs) in the effective delivery of HR policies and practices. Storey argues, 'If human resources really are so critical for business success, the HRM is too important to be left to operational personnel specialists' (2007, p. 10). Recent developments in HRM have seen increased devolution of HR function to LMs and HR professionals

Table 1.2 The Storey model of HRM

Personnel and industrial relations (IR) and human resource management (HRM): the differences		
Dimension	*Personnel and IR*	*HRM*
Beliefs and assumptions		
Contract	Careful delineation of written contracts	Aim to go 'beyond contract'
Rules	Importance of devising clear rules/mutuality	'Can do' outlook; impatience with 'rules'
Guide to management action	Procedures/consistency/control	'Business need'/flexibility/commitment
Behaviour referent	Norms/custom and practice	Values/mission
Managerial task vis-à-vis labour	Monitoring	Nurturing
Nature of relations	Pluralist	Unitarist
Conflict	Institutionalised	De-emphasised
Standardisation	High (for example, 'parity' an issue)	Low (for example, 'parity' not seen as relevant)
Strategic qualities		
Key relations	Labour–management	Business–customer
Initiatives	Piecemeal	Integrated
Corporate plan	Marginal to	Central to
Speed of decision	Slow	Fast
Critical role of management		
Management role	Transactional leadership	Transformational leadership
Key managers	Personnel/IR specialists	General/business/line managers
Prized management skills	Negotiation	Facilitation
Key levers		
Foci of attention for interventions	Personnel procedures	Wide-ranging cultural, structural and personnel strategies
Selection	Separate, marginal task	Integrated, key task
Pay	Job evaluation; multiple fixed grades	Performance-related; few if any grades
Conditions	Separately negotiated	Harmonisation
Labour–management	Collective bargaining contracts	Towards individual contracts
Thrust of relations with stewards	Regularised through facilities and training	Marginalised (with exception of some bargaining for change models)
Communication	Restricted flow/indirect	Increased flow/direct
Job design	Division of labour	Teamwork
Conflict handling	Reach temporary truces	Manage climate and culture
Training and development	Controlled access to courses	Learning companies

Source: Adapted from Storey (2007).

working more closely with LMs (CIPD, 2019g; Evans, 2015; Guest and King, 2004; Marchington and Wilkinson, 2008; McGuire and Kissack, 2015).

4. *Key levers* – focus on the techniques used to implement HR policies and practices, such as performance-related pay, harmonisation of conditions and investment in HRD. There is considerable unevenness in the adoption of these key levers. However, what is persuasive about the narrative is evidence of a shift away from rules as a basis of good practice, to the management of culture as a means of implementing transformational change.

The strength of Storey's model is the recognition of the critical role of front-line managers in enacting HR policies and practices. Further, it underscores the importance of organisational culture – assumptions, beliefs, values – and climate, that is, employees' perceptions of formal HR policies and the HR practices that act upon them. A weakness, perhaps for practitioners, is the absence of a more business-focused approach and a focus on cost-efficiencies.

The Ulrich Human Resource Business Partner model of HRM

The HRM profession has long sought to demonstrate the added value of HR activities in business terms. Such a position requires a transition from HR professionals focusing on the functional activities, such as recruitment and training, towards a partnership orientation, with HR professionals sitting 'at the top table' engaging in *strategic* decision-making (Francis and Keegan, 2006). A model most favoured to support such a transition from functional to strategic activities is David Ulrich's (1997) human resource business partner model (HRBPM).

Ulrich's original model highlights four key roles that HR leaders need to adopt to add the greatest value to the organisation:

- *Strategic partner* – future/strategic focus combined with business processes.
- *Change agent* – future/strategic focus combined with people.
- *Administrative expert* – operational focus combined with process.
- *Employee champion* – operational focus combined with people.

The HRBPM suggests that HR professionals must focus on both the strategic and the operational, in both the long and the short term. Activities range from managing business processes to managing people, suggesting that there are core competencies that HR professionals must secure and develop to help deliver value to the organisation. Central to Ulrich's model is the notion of *business partnering*. Business partners are HR professionals who work closely with leaders or line managers. A core HR competency, argue Ulrich et al. (2012), is that of being both credible (respected, listened to, trusted) and active (taking a position and challenging assumptions).

The strength of the HRBPM is its business-focused approach and affirmation of the strategic importance of HRM and HR leaders. Recent data found a joint effect of the strategic and operational roles on organisational performance, mediated by internal efficiency (Wach et al., 2021). One limitation relates to the assumption that HR 'business partners' have the business acumen to contribute to strategic formulation (Deloitte Consulting & Deloitte & Touche, 2000). The CIPD recommends HR professionals exercise caution when implementing the model, as there is a risk when the HR function is segmented of creating 'silos' (CIPD, 2015a).

HRM web links

Visit the companion website at **www.bloomsbury.pub/bratton-hrm** for more information on Ulrich's HRM model.

The Bath model of HRM

The Bath model is based on research undertaken at the University of Bath, England, commissioned by the CIPD. The focus is on the processes through which HR policies and practices affect employee motivation and performance (Purcell et al., 2003). The framework seeks to explain how people-added value is generated by the HR system – the 'black box' of worker behaviour – by incorporating wider contextual variables such as culture, climate and line-manager behaviour. It suggests that a performance-enhancing HR system alone is insufficient to create people-added value. The influence of LMs, for instance, shapes worker perceptions of the organisation's HR practices (Purcell and Kinnie, 2008). Figure 1.5 shows the six components of the model:

1. *HR system choices* – include job and work design, employee involvement in decision-making, learning and development, performance appraisal, teamworking, equitable rewards, job security, career opportunities, work-life balance. The model suggests that positive combination of determinate HR policies and practices will reinforce each other and will have greater effect than the sum of individual HR practices.
2. *Employee AMO* – for employees to perform beyond the minimum requirement of the job they must have **A**bility, be **M**otivated, and be given the **O**pportunity to deploy their knowledge and skills.
3. *Line management influence* – an employee's or group's performance is likely to be enhanced if their line manager (LM) is respectful, supportive, and facilitates the sharing of ideas and learning. LMs have discretion in the way they practice HR practices: it is they who 'bring policies to life' (Purcell et al., 2003, p. 8). LMs, therefore, strongly influence employee perceptions of HR practices.
4. *Employee responses* – HR policy and practice choice and LM behaviour affect the commitment of employees, work motivation and overall job satisfaction.
5. *Discretionary behaviour* – employees tend to engage in positive discretionary behaviours – working 'beyond contract' – when they learn new skills and participate in decision-making that affects their jobs. There is a culture of learning and they experience dignity *in* and *at* work.
6. *Performance outcomes* – long term, LMs striving to enhance employee responses will, it is argued, lead to favourable consequences for individual, group and organisational performance.

The Bath framework suggests that HR architecture indirectly affects performance through a causal chain of mediating human variables. The causal model draws on the AMO formula from Appelbaum et al. (2000) that performance is a function of workers' **A**bility + **M**otivation + **O**pportunity (i.e. AMO). The AMO theory has been adopted extensively by HRM scholars to potentially explain the HRM-performance relationship (Kellner et al., 2019). The AMO framework implies that a set or 'bundle' of associated HR variables strongly influence a worker's ability (A), motivation (M) and opportunity (O), which, in turn, causes performance-related outcomes (AMO = P). Worker ability, for instance, could possibly be improved via learning and development, motivation potentially develops through performance-based pay, and opportunity to participate in decision-making could be enhanced by worker voice mechanism (Boselie et al., 2005; Purcell et al., 2003).

The Bath model of HRM has multiple strengths. First, it takes a *process* approach to the study of HRM. It underscores that closing the gap between espoused HR policies and practices and their enactment is a complex transactional phenomenon that occurs between LMs and workers in different situations. Second, it is employee centred. Enhanced performance is a function of employee ability + motivation + opportunity. Third, its *leitmotiv* is the hoped-for-movement from behavioural compliance to worker commitment and increased performance via cultural change. HR scholars can use the model as a springboard to explore the process of 'followership', which elevates the importance of understanding the role and dimensions of employee-motivated capabilities (Bratton, 2020; Northouse, 2019).

The Bath model has several weaknesses. First, it is argued that there is insufficient evidence to test the model. Second, it recognises that culture and climate variables act both as an antecedent to the HR

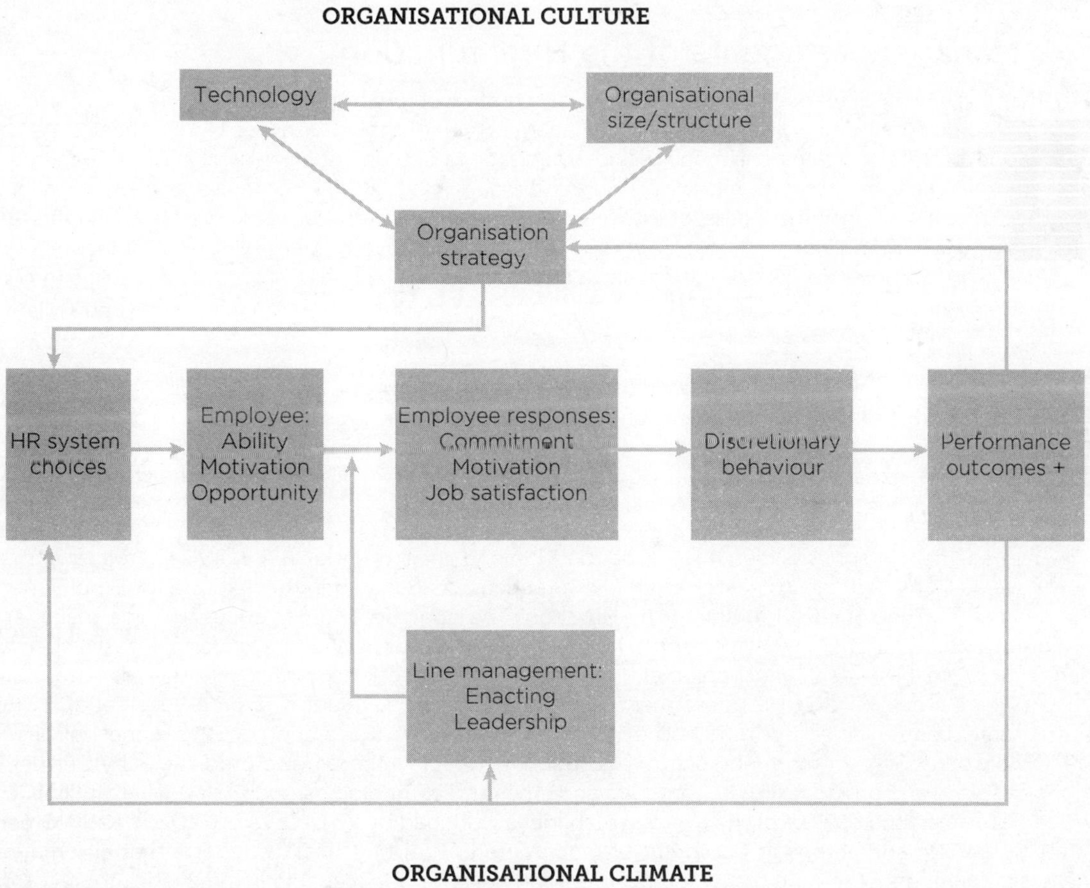

Figure 1.5 The Bath People and Performance model of HRM

Source: Created from the theories of Purcell et al. (2003); Purcell and Kinnie (2008).

system and as a mediator of its linkage to performance; but it does not explain how culture/climate influence the choice of HR practices or who actually benefits from these practices. Third, ability and motivational behaviour are viewed 'as a means rather than an end', principally focusing on performance with little consideration for worker well-being (Guest, 2017, p. 25).

Reflective question

Reviewing the five models, what beliefs and assumptions are implied in them? How well does each model define the characteristics of HRM? What are the pros and cons of devolving much of the HRM function to line managers?

HRM in Practice
Managers as agents of the HRM function

Whether it is having to manage increasing levels of remote workers or the fact that increasing numbers of tasks are being automated, the role of line managers is undergoing unprecedented change. As the Bath model of HRM illustrates, line managers in organisations play an important role in the management of the employment relationship and in ensuring and maintaining levels of organisational performance, yet their critical role in the process of HR practice delivery is often overlooked. Line managers are managers to whom individual teams report directly and who have responsibility to a higher level of management for those workers or teams, and correspondingly they have a key role in achieving core business objectives (Gilbert et al., 2011a). In the Engaging for Success report (MacLeod and Clarke, 2009, p. 31), Dame Carol Black said:

> If I could wave a magic wand, the one thing I would do is to improve the relationship between line managers and employees ... The nature and characteristics of the jobs that employees are required to do in terms of satisfaction, reward and esteem and degree of control are vitally important to them. The line manager has a key role. Good line management can promote better health and well-being and improved performance.

Line-management responsibilities have expanded beyond their traditional supervisory role and they now have an increased role in the delivery of HR practices. As outlined in the Institute for Employment Studies report 'The squeezed middle: Why HR should be hugging and not squeezing line managers' (Bajorek, 2020), there is now a widespread expectation that line managers undertake tasks such as performance management and implementing disciplinary procedures, previously the tasks formally undertaken by the specialist HR department, also known as 'HR devolution' (Op de Beeck et al., 2015). At the same time senior leaders require line managers to set targets and bring organisational policies to life, while workers expect more personal support and feedback. According to predictions by Gartner, a global research and advisory firm, automation and emerging technologies, such as artificial intelligence, will replace an estimated 69% of the average manager's workload by 2024 (Everett, 2020). Kevin Green, strategic advisor and author of *Competitive People Strategy*, optimistically suggests that automating increasing numbers of routine tasks 'sounds like good news' as it will enable line manages to 'focus on where they can add more value and extract value for the business' (Everett, 2020). How technology will shape the role of line manages in the future is still up for debate. However, recent research on the line managers' involvement in HRM highlights that, in practice, line managers are adaptive, wilful and agentic *human* actors whose differences in knowledge, skills and abilities (KSAs), including values, beliefs, personality and social standing within an organisation, shape organisational outcomes and the implementation of HR practices actually experienced by workers (Kehoe and Han, 2020). This suggests that while it may appear that technology will shape the narrative of how people are managed, it is up to managers and other employees to make decision on how much technology is part of the organisation and what they want to do with it.

Stop! If employee performance is founded upon high-quality manager-subordinate relationships, what can line managers actually do to improve employee relationships? Looking at Figure 1.5, how do line managers influence employee perceptions of workplace culture and HR practices?

Essential reading

Bajorek, Z. (2020) The squeezed middle. Institute for Employment Studies. February 2020; Everett, C. (2020) What will shape the managers of the future? *Personnel Today*, 16 July.

Note: This feature was contributed by Andrew Bratton.

HRM and the role of critique

Since Storey's (1989) landmark publication, the HRM canon has been subject to 'internal' and 'external' criticism (Delbridge and Keenoy, 2010). The principal 'internal' critics provide a sustained critique with respect to the divide between what can be described as the 'rhetoric and reality' of HRM (Legge, 2005). For some critics, however, the rhetoric *versus* reality focus is 'very sterile' and does not offer much critical insight into what is happening in organisations and with individuals when HRM is 'put into work' (Alvesson, 2018; Steyaert and Janssens, 1999). Other critics, such as Townley (1994), offer an absorbing analysis and critique of mainstream HRM using concepts drawn from the works of the French philosopher, Michel Foucault (1926–81). Bolton and Houlihan (2007) explored the ambiguity surrounding the term 'human resource management' itself, asking, 'Is the emphasis on the word "*human*" or on "*resource*" in management'? Boxall et al. (2008) significantly advanced the scholarship of HRM by integrating linkages to operational management decisions, organisational culture and the way workers experience the management process. For Boxall and his colleagues, 'analytical HRM' is concerned with the '*what*' and '*why*' of HRM; the '*how*' of HRM, in the chain of human capital processes that make models of HRM work well (or badly) – and who benefits if it does (2008, p. 7).

Notably, critical approaches to HRM start by asking, as the ancient Romans did, '*Cui bono?*' – '*Who benefits and how?*' For the past 30 years, critics point out, the dominant focus has been on the HRM–performance relationship at the expense of finding pathways to employee well-being (e.g. Guest, 2017; Kaufman, 2015; Marchington, 2015). Guest (2017) is critical of mainstream approaches to HRM and argues for the need to give less priority to the needs of shareholders and greater priority to employee well-being. Drawing upon research from the quality of working life (QWL) movement (Walton, 1974) and the job characteristic model (JCM) (Hackman and Oldham, 1980; Warr, 1987), Guest identifies five sets of HR practices – investing in employees, designing work that is engaging, prioritising physical and mental health and equitable rewards, building dialogic communications, scaffolding an organisational culture that is supportive and family-friendly – that potentially can promote employee well-being, create a 'strong' positive employment relationship and improve organisational performance. These HR practices support a stakeholder approach to work and people management, but are often missing in dominant HRM models, argues Guest (2017, p. 31). It is the absence of concern for employment-related well-being, job security and equitable rewards that has provided scope for a radical critique of HRM.

The external critique has come from academics within the broad field of critical management studies (CMS) and labour process theory (e.g. Alvesson, 2018; Godard, 1991; Thompson and McHugh, 2009; Watson, 2004). The intellectual roots of CMS are most obviously found in a Marxist, Weberian, feminist and post-colonial critique of capitalism. Karl Marx (1818–83) analysed the fundamental contradiction of capitalism that arose from structured tensions between capital (employers) and labour (employees). For Marx, economic imperatives compel employers and employees to cooperate, but also there are forces that simultaneously cause tension and conflict between the two groups. Importantly, workers experience alienation through the act of labour. Max Weber (1864–1920) pessimistically warns of creeping rationalisation and of the tendency of workers to experience debilitating disempowerment – an 'iron cage'. Weber also focused on the notion of '*paradox of consequences*' – two or more positions that each sound reasonable yet conflict or contradict each other. External critics in the Weberian tradition consider paradox theory to be a key analytical tool to investigate and critique contemporary work and management (Guerci and Carollo, 2016). For much of the twentieth century, critical scholars draw heavily on the works of Marx and Weber to explain management activities in terms of basic 'logic' underlying capitalism: profit (Baran and Sweezy, 1968).

A third and growing intellectual influence on CMS is the feminist paradigm. Its intellectual roots are to be found in the works of Mary Wollstonecraft (1792/2004), Charlotte Perkins Gilman (1892) and Betty Friedan (1963). Feminist writers provide a sophisticated understanding into pervasive gender-based injustices that women experience through 'entrenched social processes, such as patriarchal strategies and sexism' (Bratton and Denham, 2019, p. 19). Feminist scholarship constitutes what Alvesson calls 'a critique of critique' (2018, p. 52), in particular, CMS critiques that analyse work and how people are managed solely through a traditional Marxian class prism, oblivious to gender issues within the labour process. Theoretically, one of the most important consequences of gender analysis is its power to question mainstream research findings that segregate studies of HRM from those of gender divisions in the labour market, patriarchal power, gender inequality and work–life issues (Calás and Smircich, 1999; Cockburn, 1991; Knights and Willmott, 1986; Warhurst et al., 2008).

A fourth intellectual influence on CMS is post-colonial discourse and scholarship. Post-colonialist scholars have interrogated and challenged North American/European theorising about organisational life. Research into how HR policy and practice is diffused in multinational companies (MNCs) in 'emerging markets' underlines both the need and importance of post-colonial critique of management and organisational behaviour. Post-colonialists highlight, for example, that US/European theorising 'barely even begin to capture the diversity and complexity of myriad forms of action and experience across the multiplicity of cultures that populate the planet' (Prasad et al., 2018, p. 18). Interrogating underlying assumptions and values that inform Western disciplinary knowledge and garnering insights from indigenous voices is at the centre of the post-colonial critique (Bratton, 2021).

Intersectionality has become an important analytical and organising tool for critical workplace research. Intersectionality can be defined as an analytic tool that recognises that major axes of social division in a given society (e.g. class, race, gender, sexuality, age, disability) operate not as discrete entities, but build on each other and work together (Collins and Bilge, 2020). As feminists and critical race theorists have serially emphasised, a major problem with fixating upon class as a primary locus of difference, is that 'it tends to foster a blindness towards other various dimensions of difference that frequently intersect with class itself in significantly shaping a range of sociocultural ... and other dynamics' (Prasad et al., 2018, p. 18). Compared with the sociology of work discipline, it is plausible to argue that 'there is fairly little ambitious critical work within HRM' (Alvesson, 2018, p. 53). Intersectionality offers more ambitious critical research in investigating in more depth the complexity in human work experience. Moreover, it provides a more inclusive framework, one that has the potential to include 'positive work' of how HR practices impact the people who are deemed to be the 'recipients' of HRM.

The effect of critique on work and people management

The crises of climate change, global capitalism, the Covid-19 pandemic and social inequality are the drivers of social change. Critique is central to social change and to improving the management of work and people. Boltanski and Chiapello (2018, p. 27) explain the importance of critique like this:

> If capitalism cannot do without an orientation towards the common good, whence it derives reasons for committed engagement, its lack of concern for norms means that the spirit of capitalism cannot be generated exclusively out of its own resources. As a result, it needs its enemies, people whom it outrages and who are opposed to it, to find the moral supports it lacks and to incorporate mechanisms of justice whose relevance it would otherwise have no reason to acknowledge.

According to this perspective, critique serves to *improve* capitalism and, by extension, work organisations. The potential effect of critique on the management of work and people are of at least three kinds.

First, by testing various propositions about HRM, critique can delegitimise models of HRM and divest them of their effectiveness. Critique is akin to the premature lifting of the stage curtain at a theatre, exposing frenetic movement of the actors and off-stage attendants as they move the props. Critique unmasks the hypocrisy of moral pretentions – rhetorical assertions that *'our people are our greatest asset'* – that hide the reality of exploitation, alienation and domination. Critique from the margins offer re-evaluation of mainstream management theory and practice, or 're-imaginations' of the centre, in Clegg's (2016) words.

Second, evidence-based critique, in exposing inhuman or poor HR practices, can compel organisational leaders to justify those actions. And the more convincing the critique the more the justifications advanced in response will have to be combined with robust processes that guarantee a positive improvement in terms of well-being or social justice. For example, during the Covid-19 pandemic, policymakers and health executives were heavily criticised for failing to supply adequate PPE to health- and social-care staff (Campbell, 2020a; TUC, 2020d). When an organisation is obligated to respond positively to the points raised by critique, to maintain support of employees or customers, by the same gesture it incorporates some of the values shared by the critics.

Source: Li-An Lim on Unsplash

The third effect of critique is that it rests upon a less-optimistic analysis of the reactions of neoliberal capitalism. The old ways of doing business it condemns either change or perish. Thus, critique acts as a catalyst, hastening the transformation of new modes of work and management, which, in turn, create new tension because of labour-wage expectations shaped on their experience of previous HR architecture. At its heart, therefore, the dynamic effect of critique is to challenge, renegotiate, or even rescind prior to emerging anew (Boltanski and Chiapello, 2018).

There are growing demands for organisations to develop strategies which are environmentally sustainable and socially just, and therefore a reflexive, critical analysis of HRM is increasingly important to understanding organisational life (Bratton and Gold, 2015). In *HRM: A Critical Approach*, we are concerned with developing a context-sensitive understanding of work and HR practices. Throughout the book, we emphasise that paradox and antagonism are structured into the employment relationship; that different work regimes and HR strategies and practices can only be understood in the context of the wider cultural-political economy, and market factors that direct or influence work and employment. We aim to provide you with a more critical account of the realities of the workplace in capitalist societies, one that encourages a deeper understanding and sensitivity with respect to employment and HRM-related issues. In so doing, we hope the book captures the range of change evident in today's workplaces and will, moreover, lead to the kind of sensibilities that help you to sharpen your critical faculties, to question assumptions, and to seek multicausality when analysing both the theory and practice of twenty-first century HRM.

Summary

In this introductory chapter, we have emphasised the importance of managing people. We have also emphasised that, since its introduction, the way HRM has been conceptualised over the last 35 years has been subject to intense academic debate.

We have conceptualised HRM as a strategic approach, one that seeks to leverage people's capabilities and commitment with the goal of enhancing performance and dignity in and at work. These HRM goals are accomplished by a set of integrated employment policies, programmes and practices within an organisational and societal context. We suggest that the HRM approach as conceptualised here constitutes a critical approach to the discipline that extends the analysis of HRM outcomes beyond performance to include equality, dignity and social justice.

To show the multiple meanings of the term 'human resource management', we have examined five theoretical models. We have discussed whether HRM now represents a new orthodoxy; certainly, the language is different. We have explained that tensions are omnipresent. These include tensions between profitability and cost-effectiveness and employee security; between employer control and employee commitment; and between managerial autonomy and employee dignity. Throughout this book, you will gain insights into some of these tensions and inevitable paradoxes, which will provide you with a deeper understanding of HR-related issues.

Finally, we have examined the importance critique plays in management theory and practice. Humanity faces an existential crisis because of global warming and there are growing demands for organisations to develop and implement strategies which are environmentally sustainable and socially just. In this context, we have argued that a reflexive, critical analysis of HRM is increasingly important to understanding organisational life.

Review questions

1. Explain the difference between the 'hard' or 'utilitarian-instrumentalism' and 'soft' or 'developmental humanism' models of HRM. Which approach is likely to make organisations more efficient, and why?
2. What are the key elements of the employment relationship? How does an appreciation of the elements contribute to understanding the role of HRM in managing work and people?
3. What role can critique play in encouraging organisations to develop strategies which are environmentally sustainable and socially just?

Search & Watch

Visit YouTube and search for **Jack Welch: The Role of HR**. What HRM model, if any, examined in this chapter comes close to illustrating diagrammatically Welch's view of HRM?

Legal Focus

Employment law, which is also called labour law, regulates the rights and obligations of almost all working people in the UK. Parliament and the courts have long recognised the inequality between the powers of 'employer' and 'employee' and that women and people from ethnic minorities, LGBT+ people, disabled and older people have faced discrimination in securing employment. This acknowledgement has been an important factor in the legal regulation of the employment relationship. In the twentieth century, two parallel systems of legal regulation developed to address the imbalance of power between employers and employees, and the discrimination which some employees face. First, the role of trade unions as a way to counter the power of employers has evolved largely through legislation. The rights of trade unions have expanded and contracted under successive UK labour and conservative governments. The employment laws of the 1979–97 Conservative government sought to regulate the activities of trade unions. The employment laws of the 1997–2010 Labour government extended protection to individual employees. For example, the Work and Families Act 2006 gave additional protections in relation to pregnancy. EU law has had a major effect on UK labour law, particularly in the areas of equal pay and health and safety. The impact of EU law will decrease after Britain's exit.

Task Search online for government information in your jurisdiction on what legal provisions exist to address the following: (1) the relative inequality in power between employers and employees; and (2) the discrimination which some people face in securing employment or at work. (3) Then go to the companion website and look at Table 1.1 Selective Employment Statutes and Statutory Instruments, 1961–2020. Based on your online search, is the UK's regulation of the employment relationship a universal model emulated worldwide?

Reference

See Deborah Lockton and Tom Brown's *Employment Law* (2020), pp. 7–26, for a discussion on the sources and institutions of employment law.

Chapter case: Diversity at DigitalArt*

The setting

In her early career at Facebook, Google, Quora and Pinterest, Stanford graduate Tracy Chou noticed that the software engineering teams she was a part of consisted of mostly men, a few other Asians and the leadership was almost exclusively white males. As the lone female within most of these workplaces, Chou experienced unwanted flirtation, unease and differential treatment. While she loved coding, Chou felt that something was wrong with her and that she was not cut out for developing software. Blogging on being a woman in computing, however, connected her with other women and also people of colour who strongly related to her work experiences.

While such insights and personal observations indicated a lack of diversity, there existed no quantitative data on women or minorities across the overall industry. It seemed ironic to her how such a highly data-driven industry would track and measure basically everything except workforce diversity numbers. In the autumn of 2013 Chou wrote the blogpost 'Where are the numbers?' to call to action the technology industry to provide data on the number of women in engineering positions. Within several weeks Chou collected data on over 50 companies including several of Silicon Valley's largest companies such as Google, Apple and Facebook. When analysing the submitted data on the gender distribution (around 10–20%) Chou realised there actually was a systemic problem.

The problem

While the lack of diversity had been an open secret to IT industry participants, no public data existed prior to Chou's call for disclosure. While businesses had been communicating about their diversity initiatives there seemed to be a reluctance to share their workforce demographics. Among the reasons are the convenience of obscuring the problem and not having to addressing it actively with solutions, but also reputation and competition among companies in attracting female talent. However, without any benchmark, Chou argued, there can be no measured effectiveness of certain strategies for emulating across companies to make further progress on this pervasive issue.

However, there was evidence that a lack of diversity was an obstacle to change and often considered the cause of bad software design decisions. For example, the omission of a period tracker in the first launch in 2014 of the expansive Apple HealthKit (and its addition only in 2019), is being attributed by critics to the low representation of women in the company. Similarly, voice-activated digital assistants such as Amazon Echo need to take into account diverse living situations including abusive partners and also children. Before parental controls, a six-year-old girl was able to order a $160 (€141) doll's house and four pounds of sugar cookies via Amazon Echo Dot through an Alexa personal assistant.

PART 2

The assignment

DigitalArt is a small IT company located in Toronto, specialising in writing software programs for a range of companies in health care, food services and advertising. Dr Ryan Syed, the founder and current CEO, has plans to expand the business and double the workforce. DigitalArt currently employs ten software engineers, aged between 24 and 33 years; all are male. Two of the oldest engineers, Bob, 29, and Jaap, 33, both Caucasian, are team leaders and the staff work in an open-plan office.

You are a new consultant for Agenda Include, an IT consulting company based in San Francisco, California. You have been tasked with preparing an advisory report for Syed on a diversity and inclusion strategy. This is your first major project for Agenda Include and you are keen to do a really good report. Your report should draw upon current publications on the topic (see further readings below) and be sensitive to the rapidly changing world of work evolving because of the onset of the Covid-19 pandemic. In particular, your answer should address the following:

1. What barriers exist to increasing workforce diversity in IT companies and how may this relate to DigitalArt?
2. Explain the benefits of increasing diversity at DigitalArt from the point of view of [a] the employer, [b] employees and [c] the wider society? Where do their interests overlap?
3. Drawing on your understanding of the Storey and Bath models of HRM, how do you think the two team leaders can contribute (or hinder) to the HRM activities to pivot DigitalArt forward in fostering a more diverse and inclusive workplace?

Essential reading

Bartoletti, I. (2020) *An Artificial Revolution: On Power, Politics and AI*. Indigo Press.
Cain Miller, C. (2017) Tech's damaging myth of the loner genius nerd. *New York Times*, 12 August.
Chou, T. (2013) Where are the numbers? *Medium*, 11 October.
Silbermann, B. (2019) Building a more diverse Pinterest. *Pinterest Newsroom*, 14 January.

* DigitalArt is a fictitious company but draws from the experience and findings of Chou (2013). The names in the assignment are also fictitious.

Note: This case was contributed by Sarita R. Koendjbiharie, Leiden University.

Further reading

Budd, J. W. (2020) The psychologisation of employment relations, alternative models of the employment relationship, and the OB turn. *Human Resource Management Journal*, 30: 73–83.

Innocenti, L., Sammarra, A. and Profili, S. (2019) From control to commitment work systems: the role of HRM in the post-bureaucratic transition. In *Human Performance Technology: Concepts, Methodologies, Tools, and Applications* (pp. 1150–72). IGI Global. Available at: www.igi-global.com/chapter/from-control-to-commitment-work-systems/226611. Accessed 7 July 2020.

Norlander, P., Jukic, N., Arup Varma, A. & Nestorov, S. (2021) The effects of technological supervision on gig workers: organizational control and motivation of Uber, taxi, and limousine drivers. *The International Journal of Human Resource Management*. DOI: 10.1080/09585192.2020.1867614

Prasad, A., Prasad, P., Mills, A. J. and Mills, J. H (2015) Debating knowledge: rethinking critical management studies in a changing world. In Prasad, A., Prasad, P., Mills, A. J. and Mills, J. H. (eds) *The Routledge Companion to Critical Management Studies* (pp. 3–41). London: Routledge.

Shanahan, G. and Smith, M. (2021) Fair's fair: psychological contracts and power in platform work. *The International Journal of Human Resource Management*. DOI: 10.1080/09585192.2020.1867615

Vithana, K., Soobaroyen, T. and Ntim, C. G. (2021) Human resource disclosures in UK corporate annual reports: to what extent do these reflect organisational priorities towards labour? *Journal of Business Ethics*, 169: 475–97.

outline

- Introduction
- Strategic management
- The five-step process of strategic management
- Hierarchy of strategy
- Corporate-level strategy
- Strategic choice and corporate ideology
- Building a sustainable strategy
- Strategy, ethics and corporate social responsibility
- Strategic HRM
- Defining strategic HRM
- Theorising strategic HRM
- HR strategy and organisational dynamics
- Line managers as agents of HR strategy
- HR strategy and performance
- Critical perspectives and analysis
- Summary
- Further reading

CHAPTER 2

CORPORATE STRATEGY AND STRATEGIC HRM

Source: Photo by Sean Pollock on Unsplash

objectives

After studying this chapter, you should be able to:

1. Define what is meant by strategic management and explain how strategic organisational decisions impact employment practice choices
2. Describe how strategic priorities vary by level and critically comment on the links between strategic management and HRM
3. Explain and critique 'best-fit', 'best-practice' and 'resource-based' models of strategic HRM
4. Describe the positive contribution HRM can make to organisational performance and critique HRM–performance modelling
5. Critically assess and discuss the theories of strategic management concepts and HR practice choices, and the implications for stakeholders, society and the planet

Introduction

The triple crises of the coronavirus pandemic, global warming and, in Europe, Brexit combine to force leaders and HR professionals to look beyond traditional business models and micro-HR activities to focus on investing in the green transition, local supply chains and issues of strategic human resource management (Bailey et al. 2018; Butler, S., 2020b; Soper, 2020; Stiglitz, 2020).

The origins of SHRM are rooted in the concepts of strategic management and HRM. The word 'strategy' is derived from the Greek noun *strategos*, meaning 'commander in chief' and is associated with hierarchy and individuals with power (Parker, 2018). The concept of *strategic* HRM is concerned with formulating and implementing a set or 'bundle' of HR practices that will enable the organisation to achieve its strategic objectives. The concept of *HR strategy* describes a pattern of strategic choices that managers make to manage the employment relationship. The growth of interest in SHRM and HR strategy runs parallel with the increasing interest in leadership literature in '*followers*' and the central role followers play in the leadership process (Bratton, 2020; Uhl-Bien et al., 2014). SHRM represents an intersection between the literatures on strategic management, organisational behaviour and HRM. Running parallel is a stream of literature that explores the long-term performance effects of strategic human resource development (Garavan, 2007).

This chapter examines the strategic management process. It will then proceed to interrogate different 'models' of HR strategy before taking a critical look at studies of the HRM–performance relationship.

Strategic management

Conventional wisdom is that any credible business has a strategic plan. Management orthodoxy holds that strategy is a relatively orderly process undertaken by the upper echelon of the organisation to forecast discontinuities, develop an effective vision for the future and achieve superior performance relative to rivals. Hill et al. (2016) wrote, 'A strategy is a set of related actions that managers take to increase their company's performance' (p. 4). Henry (2018) described management strategy as 'doing well what your competitors cannot do or cannot easily do' (p 7) In for-profit organisations, if a strategy results in superior performance, it is said to have a competitive advantage. Mintzberg (1989) challenges the notion that strategy formulation is a relatively static, orderly process. His focus is on 'crafting' strategy: 'To manage strategy is to *craft* thought and action, control and learning, stability and change' (p. 38, emphasis added). Similarly, Macintosh and MacLean (2015) focus on the '*craft* of *collectively*' in strategy formulation which invokes sharing, learning and empowerment. A strategy can emerge collaboratively from business partnerships with suppliers and customers, non-profit and environmental agencies and groups. (Fishman, 2007).

Definitions of strategic management tell us as much about their underpinning assumptions and their context as they do about their subject. They implicitly contribute to the pervasiveness and dominance of the neoliberal ideology. In Britain, for example, a nexus of interrelated economic ideas, supported by corporate leaders (Salaman, 2016), has transformed private and public sector organisations through the doctrine of maximising shareholder value (MSV), financilisation, outsourcing or, in public sector organisations, by privatisation and the application of 'managerialism' (Klikauer, 2013; Thompson, 2013; van der Zwan, 2014).

For example, in public sector organisations, managerialist and business-oriented artefacts such as key performance indicators, numerical targets and use of precarious employment contracts have become a common feature of contemporary universities (see McCann et al., 2020 and the Introduction). New public management (NPM) theorists advocated quasi-market structures and for-profit models of corporate governance in public sector organisations such as local government, health care and schools (Ferlie and Ongaro, 2015). It should not surprise you that this is a contested approach, not least, because social scientists emphasise the diversity of cultural contexts (for example, England and Scotland) and the continuing distinctively democratic, value-driven nature of public administration. As Ferlie and Ongaro observe, 'The politico-administrative culture and societal contexts shape some of the very basic premises for the management of public service organizations' (2015, p. 221). NPM was predicated on neoliberal ideology that quasi-markets and competition eliminate waste and improve public services. The Covid-19 pandemic, however, has intensified the debate, in particular, with regard to the merits of 'in-house' versus outsourced services. NPM initiatives hollowed out public health services and expertise in England, which meant that the test-and-trace system had to be outsourced to private companies at an egregious cost. Contrary to neoliberal theory, evidence shows that England's £12 billion (€13.2 billion) centralised private for-profit test-and-trace system is a 'catastrophic failure' (Monbiot, 2020) and countries, such as Germany, that have retained test-and-trace in-house have fared far better in the emergency (Collington, 2020). The 2020 pandemic has given impetus to debate around corporate strategy and HRM that organisations need to orient themselves beyond the 'shareholder value' imperative and pivot toward a multi-stakeholder model of business, including improving employee well-being, societal well-being and sustainable pro-environmental performance (Houghton, 2019).

Whether in private- or public-sector organisations, a strategy is best understood as a pattern of decision-making based on a clear understanding of the 'craft' and a keen awareness of the environment and of the players who can contribute. While occasionally there is a significant discontinuity, when there is a *gestalt* shift in the environment, such as the Covid-19 pandemic, causing disruptive change, the real challenge in crafting strategy, argues Mintzberg, 'lies in detecting the subtle discontinuities that may undermine an organisation in the future' (1989, p. 40). The current strategic management opinion is that a successful strategy is consistent with an organisation's external environment and with its internal goals, resources, capabilities and shared values. Strategic management therefore requires ongoing adjustment of three major, interdependent poles: the environment, the resources available, and the values of senior management (Figure 2.1).

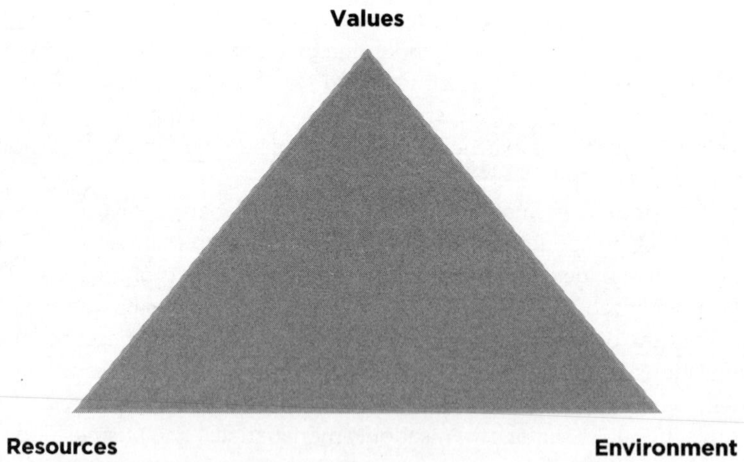

Figure 2.1 The three traditional poles of a strategic plan

PART 2

HRM in Practice
'Our people are our greatest asset'?

Source: Dan Gold on Unsplash

There is no legal definition of 'zero-hours contracts' but a government document states: 'A zero-hours contract is an employment contract in which the employer does not guarantee the individual any work, and the individual is not obliged to accept any work offered' (Wakeling, 2014). Zero-hours contracts contain no obligation to offer work or accept it. A person on a zero-hours contract is not legally an employee but is a 'worker'. Some employment laws apply to them, but others, which are costly to employers, do not, including redundancy pay, maternity leave and protection from unfair dismissal. Government figures (ONS, 2018b) show that the number of zero-hours contracts increased to 1.8m in the year to November, up from 1.7 in 2016; accounting for 6% of people in employment. Women, students in full-time education, young or older workers are more likely to be on zero-hours contracts.

During the 2020 Covid-19 lockdown, low earners were seven times more likely to work in sectors worst hit by shutdown such as retail, hotel and leisure, health and social care (Butler, S., 2020a). Commenting on the disproportionate impact on lower earners, Tim Roach of the GMB union, argued:

> This outbreak has shone a light on those left with more month than money. It's confirmed the damage done by the proliferation of zero hours agency work and bogus self-employment during the past decade. There can be no return to business as usual after this crisis. (Butler, S., 2020a)

Wakeling's analysis of zero-hours contracts reveals a contradiction between low commitment contracts and the performance of jobs over a long time which require a high sense of commitment and involvement, such as personal carers with the disabled or elderly: 'Two broad themes emerged. The first was to do with a lack of clarity over employment status, and a lack of awareness of employment rights … The second was to do with a disparity that often seems to arise between the emotional attachment many people form with their job or workplace and their contractual status' (Wakeling, 2014, p. 6). It also emerged that 'workers are often frightened to turn down work or look for other work in case their employer starts zeroing down their hours. These anxieties appear to reflect the imbalance of power between the worker and the employer' (Wakeling, 2014, p. 7). A general conclusion of the research was that contracts should be more transparent in terms of pay, possible working hours, holiday pay etc., which would contribute to an improved level of trust in the employment relationship.

Stop! Do you think that zero-hours contracts should be part of an organisation's corporate strategy? Do you think organisations simultaneously consider their people an asset and use zero-hours contracts?

Essential reading

Office for National Statistics (2018) Contracts that do not guarantee a minimum number of hours: April 2018; Butler, S. (2020) Coronavirus lockdown to hit low-paid, young and women hardest, warns IFS. London: *The Guardian*, 6 April.

Note: This feature was contributed by David Denham and updated by Andrew Bratton.

The five-step process of strategic management

There are no fewer than ten different schools of strategic management, most exhibiting different assumptions and theoretical perspectives (Mintzberg et al., cited by Ferlie and Ongaro, 2015, p. 2). What follows, therefore, is an introduction to the field. In the descriptive and prescriptive strategic management texts, strategy is depicted as a cycle in which several serially dependent steps follow and feed on one another. The strategy process has five serially dependent steps:

1. *Mission and identification of vision or goals* begins with leaders evaluating any discontinuities that may undermine the organisation in the future. The mission describes the organisation's *raison d'être* and indicates the direction senior managers, the so-called 'strategic apex' (Mintzberg, 1989, p. 98), are taking the organisation. A mission reflects a specific belief system or ideology that appeals to like-minded stakeholders (Lovelace et al., 2019).
2. *Environmental analysis* looks at the organisation's internal strengths and weaknesses and at the external environment for opportunities and threats. Strategists need a profound understanding of the competitive environment (Grant, 2016). Important considerations are referred to as 'strategic factors' summed by the acronym SWOT – **S**trengths, **W**eaknesses, **O**pportunities and **T**hreats or a variant acronym PRIMO-F – **P**eople, **R**esources, **I**nnovation, **M**arketing, **O**perations, **F**inance – framework (CIPD, 2018).
3. *Strategic formulation* involves senior managers evaluating the interaction between external and internal and strategic factors and decision-making that enable the organisation to meet its business goals. Crucial is the notion of 'strategic fit' (Grant, 2016, p. 10). The process, as described here, draws on the 'strategic choice' perspective, which emphasises the importance of asking such questions as who makes the decisions and why they are made (Child, 1972).
4. *Strategy implementation* focuses on the techniques used to implement the strategies. Fombrun et al. (1984, p. 26) observed that in many organisations much time and human energy is expended on strategic planning yet very little time into its implementation. Fast forward 30 years and strategy implementation is still reported to be problematic (Armstrong and Brown, 2019).
5. *Strategy evaluation* refers to the activities that determine to what extent the actual change and performance matches the desired change and performance.

The strategic management literature depicts the five steps as forming a rational and linear process. It is, however, important to note that it is a normative framework, that is, it shows how strategic management *should* be done rather than what is *actually* done by managers. Mintzberg (2009) believes that the model, uncritically taught to business students, tends to promote an 'excessively analytical, detached style of management' and underestimates the strategic role and contribution of HRM.

The literature tends to emphasise that strategic management is '*context-sensitive*', rather than 'context-free' (Ferlie and Ongaro, 2015, p. 221). It is a practice therefore *learned* in context. Divorcing the two helps to elucidate the Bank of England's monumental failure of management when 'the collective imagination of many bright people' failed to foresee the timing, extent and severity of the 2008 financial crisis (Elliot and Treanor, 2015). As we have already noted, the idea that strategic decision-making is a political process implies a potential significant gap between the mainstream classical model and social reality.

PART 2

Ethical Insight

Do ethics influence corporate strategy?

Source: Zbynek Burival on Unsplash

Over a decade ago, Behnam and Rasche (2009) asked, 'Are strategists from Mars and ethicists from Venus?'. Historically, strategy and ethics have been viewed as 'expressions of contrasting value-priorities' (Singer, 2010, p. 480). The former was concerned with concepts such as efficiency, utility and financial capital, the latter focused on justice, human rights and the avoidance of harms (Singer, 2010). However, over the last 40 years academics and practitioners have been striving to develop an ethics-strategy link, with each new corporate scandal providing fresh impetus for their work. In particular, there has been a focus on the role of ethics in terms of *strategy content* and *strategy context* (Behnam and Rasche, 2009). The discussion in relation to strategy content centres on the 'role of certain moral principles within strategic management' (Behnam and Rasche, 2009, p. 80). For organisations to be sustainable (financially and otherwise), it is suggested that they must integrate economic, social and environmental standards into their corporate strategy. Failure to do so may risk their 'social licence to operate' in some markets. There is evidence that an increasing number of businesses are taking this approach, articulating a commitment to, for example, Corporate Social Responsibility (CSR) or the Triple Bottom Line (TBL). However, we must be mindful of a gap between the values that an organisation espouses and those that it practices. 'There are many ways by which an organization can create a tension between espoused and practiced values. The two main ones relate to how it conducts its business and how it treats its employees' (Gopinath et al., 2018, p. 277). Therefore, it is essential to look beyond words and examine actions.

The strategy context perspective discusses 'the influence that morally sensitive circumstances of strategy-making have on strategic reasoning' (Behnam and Rasche, 2009, p. 80). Developing strategy, much like applying ethical guidelines, involves the development of a context-specific understanding of formerly generalised rules (Behnam and Rasche, 2009). For example, in the context of the coronavirus pandemic, corporate strategies may have to be rapidly reformulated and new ethical issues may come to the fore. In addition, Behnam and Rasche (2009) note that both strategy formulation and ethical reflection require considering others' ways of reasoning by demonstrating empathy. The consequences of an action, for example, the decision to treat workers as self-employed rather than employees, can be better understood by placing ourselves in their position. However, the authors point out that there are different motivations for such empathy: from a strategic perspective it is about creating sustainable competitive advantage, whereas from an ethical viewpoint it is about doing the 'right thing' morally.

Stop! Can you think of a decision that an HR professional may face that would be viewed differently from a strategic versus an ethical perspective?

Essential reading

Behnam, M. and Rasche, A. (2009) Are strategist from Mars and ethicists from Venus? – Strategizing as ethical reflection. *Journal of Business Ethics*, 84: 79–88.

Note: This feature was contributed by Laura Steele.

Hierarchy of strategy

Another aspect of strategic management in the multidivisional business organisation concerns the *level* to which strategic issues apply. Conventional wisdom identifies strategic formulation taking place at different vertical levels of organisational leadership; what is referred to as a hierarchy of strategy: corporate, business, functional. Figure 2.2 shows the hierarchy of strategy with key questions posed by each level of management when undertaking large-scale change (see Kotter, 2012).

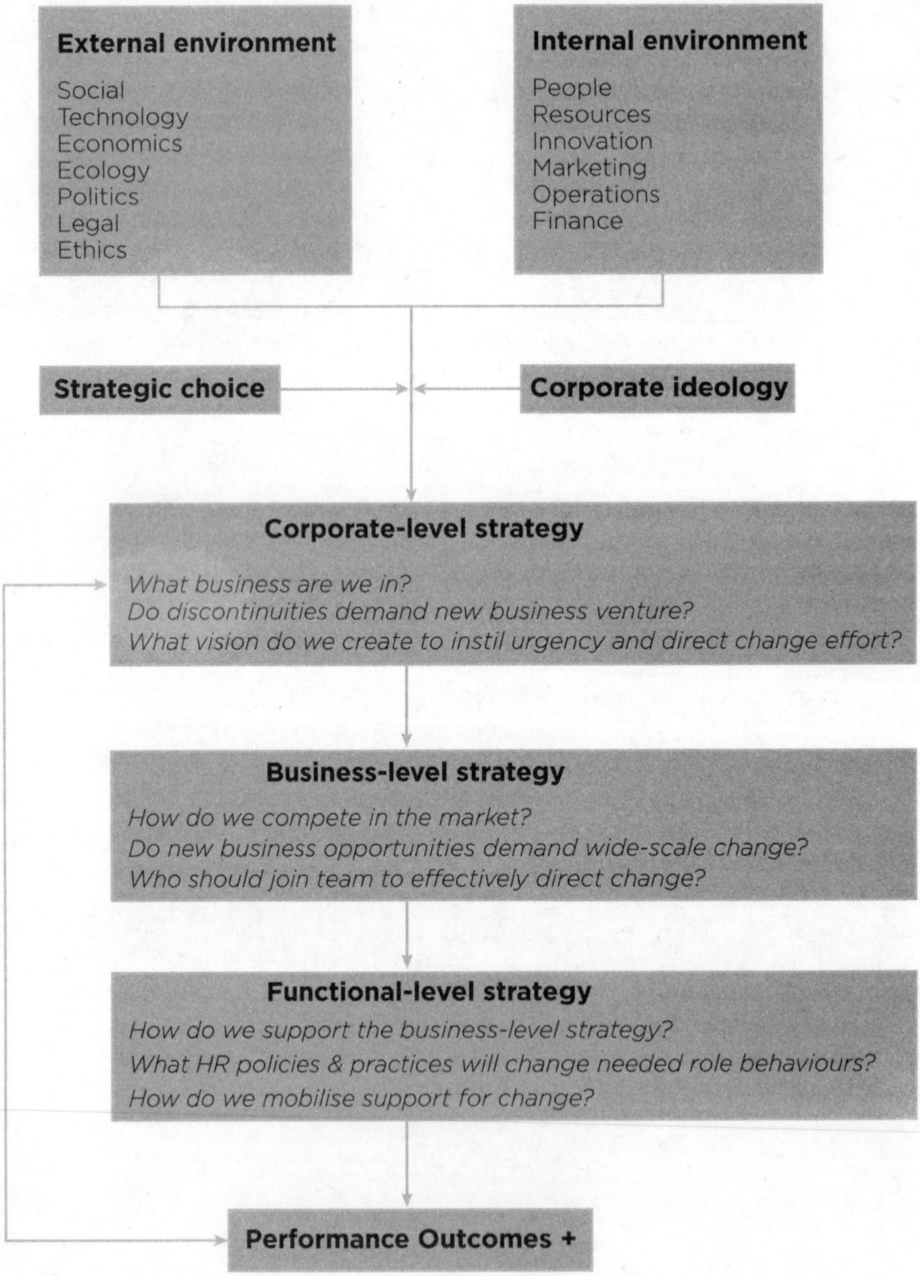

Figure 2.2 A conceptual overview of corporate-wide and HRM strategic decision-making

Corporate-level strategy

Corporate-level strategy describes an organisation's overall direction in terms of its general philosophy towards the growth and the management of its various operating units. The term 'corporate' is used in this book because the term 'corporate strategy' denotes the most general level of strategy in an organisation and in this sense embraces other levels of strategy in both large and small business enterprises, non-profit organisations and public services. Corporate strategies determine the types of business a corporation wants to be involved in, so address the question: '*What business are we in?*'

Business-level strategy

Business-level strategy deals with decisions and actions pertaining to each business unit. The principal objective of a business-level strategy is to make the unit more competitive in its marketplace. This level addresses the question: '*How do we compete?*' Porter (1980, 1985) made a significant contribution to our understanding of business strategy by formulating a framework that described three competitive strategies: cost leadership, differentiation and focus.

The *low-cost leadership* strategy attempts to increase the organisation's market share by having the lowest unit cost and price compared with those of competitors. In contrast, the *differentiation strategy* distinguishes an organisation's services and products from those of its competitors by providing such a distinctive high-quality service or product that the customer is prepared to pay a premium price. With the *focus strategy*, managers focus on a specific buyer group or regional market. This analysis suggests firms choose from four generic business-level strategies in order to establish and exploit a competitive advantage, for example:

- *Low-cost leadership*, e.g. Wal-Mart.
- *Differentiation*, e.g. Nudie Jeans.
- *Focused differentiation*, e.g. Mountain Equipment Co-operative.
- *Focused low-cost leadership*, e.g. Rent-A-Wreck Cars.

The different competitive strategies influence the 'downstream' functional strategies.

Functional-level strategy

Functional-level strategy pertains to the major functional operations within the business unit, including research and development, marketing, manufacturing, finance and HRM. This strategy level typically addresses the question: '*How do we support the business-level strategy?*' Consistent with this, key questions related to HRM policies and practices are highlighted in Figure 2.2.

In different organisations, the specific operation of the hierarchy of strategy might vary between 'top-down' and 'bottom-up' strategic planning. The top-down approach resembles a 'cascade' in which the 'downstream' strategic decisions are dependent on higher 'upstream' strategic decisions (Wheelen and Hunger, 2014). The bottom-up approach recognises that individuals 'deep' within the organisation might contribute to strategic planning. Mintzberg (1978) has incorporated this idea into a model of 'emergent strategies', which are unplanned responses to unforeseen circumstances by non-executive employees within the organisation.

Strategic choice and corporate ideology

Figure 2.2 shows corporate strategy being influenced by *strategic choice* and corporate ideology. Strategic choices are those that are considered 'fateful for a firm's survival or, ... explain major variations in its performance compared to its rivals' (Boxall and Purcell, 2016, p. 53). In terms of management theory, Child (1972) explains the significance of strategic choice like this:

> [When] incorporating strategic choice in a theory of organisations, one is recognising the operation of an essentially political process, in which constraints and opportunities are functions of the power exercised by decision-makers in the light of ideological values (Child, 1972, quoted in McLoughlin and Clark, 1988, p. 41).

The strategic choice perspective underscores the distribution of power within the organisation: 'where power lies, how it comes to be there, and how the outcome of competing power plays and coalitions within senior management are linked to employee relations' (Purcell and Ahlstrand, 1994, p. 45). The strategic choice perspective makes the discourse on strategy 'more concrete' and provides important insights into how the employment relationship is managed.

Corporate strategy will also be shaped by corporate leaders' political views or *ideologies*. As a sociological concept, ideology refers to the realm of ideas or culture in general, and that of political and economic ideas specifically. Numerous scholars have sought to investigate management and leadership through an ideological prism. Critical ideological and cultural analysis focuses on how neoliberalism has transformed business, ingrained the fabric of managerial decision-making, and fashioned the new individual neoliberal self (Boltanski and Chiapello, 2018; Schein and Schein, 2017) with attendant disregard for wider workers' and societal interests. Fundamental to understanding the behaviour of corporate leaders, it is argued, are the core ideas of neoliberalism, market fetishism and maximising shareholder value (Salaman, 2016).

Neoliberalism is a theory that believes in deregulation, privatisation and minimum state intervention in markets (Harvey, 2005). The idea of *market fetishism* holds that the markets, and market relationships, are the best way to achieve efficiency and should therefore act as a guide for all human activity. The doctrine of *maximising shareholder value* (MSV) is rooted in the work of the American economist, Milton Friedman (1977). He argued for a shift from 'stakeholder' capitalism – whereby CEOs running companies considered additional interests beyond the maximisation of profit, for instance, considering the interest of workers and the planet – to a more functional 'shareholder' capitalism. MSV implies that the ultimate measure of a company's performance is the extent to which it benefits shareholders through increases in profits or share price. Arguably, the doctrine encourages high-risk behaviour as evidenced by the 2008 global financial crisis (Martin, 2014). Martin Shkreli, CEO of a small American pharmaceutical company, captured the essence of shareholder value:

> This is a capitalist society, capitalist system and capitalist rules, and my investors expect me to maximise profits, not to minimise them, or go half, or go 70 percent, but to go to 100 percent of the profit curve that we're all taught in MBA class (cited by Henderson, 2020, p. 13).

These interlocking economic ideas and values find expression in strategic decision-making.

Building a sustainable strategy

The discussion about strategy formulation, so far, has given little consideration to whether strategic decision-making is sustainable or unsuitable. The crisis of climate change provides an opportunity for governments, investment funds and organisations to formulate plans for how to transition to a 'new

Source: Robert Nickelsberg/Getty Images

What role do you think HR plays in a sustainable business strategy?

normal' built around 'environmental sustainability'. In January 2021, Norway's sovereign wealth fund, which owns on average 1.4 per cent of every listed company in the world, boycotted four Canadian oil companies. 'We divest from companies where we no longer want to be a shareholder for ethical or sustainability reasons', the fund announced (Reguly, 2021). Sustainability can be defined as:

> A process of change in which the exploitation of resources, the direction of investments, the orientation of technological development, and institutional change are all in harmony and enhance both current and future potential to meet human needs and aspirations (Sumner, 2005, p. 81).

The concept of sustainability is elastic, and environmental critics warn that the omnipresence of the term in corporate discourse has come at 'the price of conceptual vagueness, fluidity and co-option' (Sumner, 2005, p. 84). The literature identifies four main approaches to studying sustainability: economic, environmental, social and cultural. The *economic* perspective can be divided into neo-classical and ecological schools of thought. The core premise of neo-classical economics is to maximise profits, increase output to further increase profits, ad infinitum. As far as the ecosystem is concerned, it is meant to serve that accumulation. Ecological economics acknowledges that orthodox growth models are responsible for the climate crisis. Adherents believe that sustainability involves 'handing down to future generations local and global ecosystems that largely resembles our own' (Goodstein, 1999, p. 109).

The *environmental* perspective defines sustainability in terms of 'the continued productivity and functioning of the ecosystem' (Brown et al., 1987, p. 716). The *social* perspective underscores the importance of 'improving the quality of human life' (Farrell and Hart, 1998, p. 7). The *cultural* perspective sees cultural enrichment as integral to sustainability (Brown et al., 1987). In terms of values, the environmental, social and cultural perspectives pivot away from orthodox monetary values towards *life* values. We can identify 'four interdependent pillars of sustainability': *sustainable economic activity*, *ecosystem protection*, *social equity* and *cultural vitality*, see Figure 2.3.

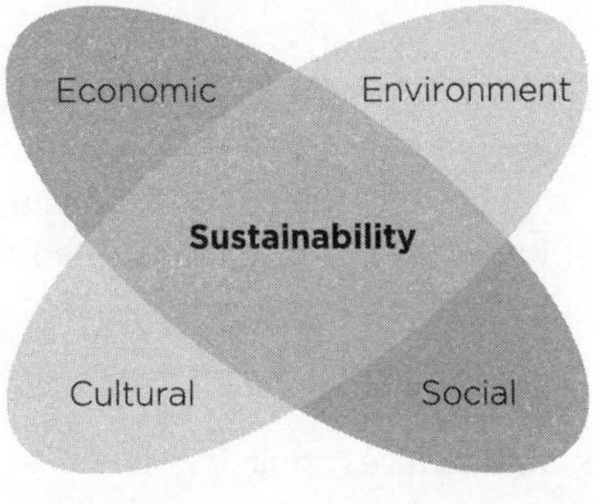

Figure 2.3 The four pillars of sustainability

Global HRM

Australian businesses urge green recovery from Covid-19 crisis

When companies make strategic decisions about what they can produce and at what price, they are acting as rational entities, motivated exclusively by profit. The more a company can drive its costs below those of its competitors, the greater the profits it stands to make. Take the example of US corporate giant McDonald's. The greenhouse gas footprint produced from the 550 million Big Macs sold in the USA every year is estimated to be equivalent to 2.66 billion pounds of carbon dioxide (Patel, 2009). And there are the hidden health costs of treating diet-related illnesses. These social costs are paid for, not by McDonald's, but by society through higher health costs. Thinking about food brings together the common valuation of the ecosystem, the need for responsive governments and the need for sustainable corporate strategies.

A leading Australian business group, representing over 60,000 businesses, is calling for the recovery from the Covid-19 pandemic and cutting greenhouse gas emissions to be tackled together, saying it would boost growth and support the transition to a sustainable, low-carbon economy. Innes Willox, chief executive of the Australian Industry Group, argues that economic recovery from the virus and the transition to a low-carbon economy are overlapping issues that need to be addressed together. As Morton (2020) reports: 'Covid-19 and climate are bigger than any economic challenge we've faced in the last century ... The path we choose in the coming months will have significant ramifications for our global economy and generations to come.'

The rationale and business strategy outlined by Industry Group was also articulated by John Grimes, chief of the Smart Energy Council: 'This is Australia's moment to modernise and grow the economy, create hundreds of thousands of new future-proof jobs and position Australia as a global renewable energy superpower.'

Stop! Using Figure 2.3 as a starting point, what kinds of corporate strategy should organisational leaders be developing? How do local and national attitudes about climate change influence business strategies and practices?

Essential reading

Morton, A. (2020) Australian businesses call for climate crisis and virus economic recovery to be tackled together. *The Guardian,* 4 May; Young, W., Davis, M., McNeill, I. M., Malhotra, B., Russell, S., Unsworth, K. and Clegg, C. W. (2015) Changing behaviour: successful environmental programmes in the workplace. *Business Strategy and the Environment*, *24*(8): 689–703.

Note: This feature was contributed by Andrew Bratton.

The 'four pillars of sustainability' can guide creative thinking and provide a framework for strategic planning for large organisations as well as SMEs. Foremost, these four streams of thinking suggest that a 'sustainable', low-carbon corporate strategy can be expressed as an axiom: the pursuit of *quadruple bottom line* performance – a balance of economic, environmental, social and cultural goals. The issue of sustainable low-carbon workplace strategy is examined in Chapter 12.

Strategy, ethics and corporate social responsibility

The formality of strategy formulation raises consideration as to whether strategic decision-making is ethical or unethical and how societal expectations impact on organisational strategies. These considerations are the province of business ethics and corporate social responsibility (CSR). *Ethics* are a set of moral principles and values that influence the decisions and actions of individuals within the organisation. A series of high-profile cases, including Tom Hayes, a former stellar trader at UBS and Citigroup, the phone-hacking scandal or 'Hackingate' at News International (UK) in 2011, and unlawful and unethical behaviour of prominent executives at Volkswagen involving alleged falsification of data on carbon emissions in 2015, have drawn public attention to business ethics and *white-collar crime*.

Ethics underscores the notion of *corporate social responsibility*, which is concerned with the ways in which managers' behaviour and actions exceed minimum compliance-based regulations. CSR concerns the ethical principle that an organisation should be accountable for how its corporate strategy might affect suppliers, local communities, society at large and the planet. Unsurprisingly, therefore, public attention has focused on the need for businesses to define their standards of ethical behaviour, for new CSR strategies and, moreover, for greater government regulation (see Ethical Insight, p. 55).

Strategic HRM

Since its inception, HRM has been deemed to be a strategic activity. In the 1980s, the exigencies of global competition and the popularity of Japanese management practices set the backdrop for strategic HRM. Initially, the focus of SHRM was on '*vertical integration*' and alignment between business strategy and HR strategy in order 'to support the strategically oriented organisation as it struggles with the environmental trends' (Fombrun, 1984, p. 12). This 'hard' HRM or 'top-down' approach was highlighted by Lorange and Murphy who emphasised the importance of 'bringing HR into strategic planning (1984, p. 275). In theory, designating HRM as strategic potentially elevates HR professionals to the top management decision-making cabal. But in practice, data suggests HR professionals rarely play a major role in formulating business strategies (Lawler, 2014; 2017).

Adopting an organisational behaviour perspective, alternative interpretations comprehend that strategic goal achievement hinges on 'micro-level' human synergy – ability, motivation, opportunity – the AMO model – and workers' perception of how and why HRM is delivered on the ground, in day-to-day social interactions and operations (Gilbert et al., 2011b; Purcell and Kinnie, 2008). The behavioural perspective of SHRM pivots attention towards the importance of '*horizontal integration*' of HR practices. This so-called 'soft' HRM approach appeared to be supported by many research studies finding positive linkages between an integrated 'bundle' of HR variables or practices and performance outcomes (Huselid, 1995). There is a managerial logic in focusing attention on how HR practices can harness people's assets to provide a competitive advantage when technological superiority, even once achieved, can soon erode it (Barney, 1991). Thus, many mainstream HRM writers go along with the view that, 'For a variety of reasons related to changing markets, demands for greater speed and flexibility, and the growing attention to "intangible assets", HR ... has the potential to influence firm performance in a way that was not possible 20 years ago' (Huselid and Becker, 2001, quoted in Guthrie et al., 2009, p. 112). Attaching the adjective 'strategic' to the acronym 'HRM' can only be justified if a coherent, mutually supporting set of HR practices is fully integrated with corporate strategy, and in doing so can 'contribute optimally to the organisation's goal achievement' (Alvesson, 2018, p. 52).

Source: Getty Images/gilaxia

Designating HRM as strategic potentially gives HR professionals a seat at the top management decision-making table.

Reflective question

Is there a strong business case for the strategic approach to HRM? If so, why?

Defining strategic HRM

The precise meaning of 'strategic HRM' remains problematic, not least because strategic HRM is sometimes, incorrectly, used interchangeably with HR strategy. It is unclear, for example, whether the acronym 'SHRM' relates to an outcome or a process. For Snell et al. (1996, p. 62), 'strategic HRM' is an outcome: 'as organizational systems designed to achieve sustainable competitive advantage through people'. For others, it is viewed as a process, 'the process of linking HR practices to business strategy' (Ulrich, 1997, p. 89). Similarly, Bamberger and Meshoulam (2000, p. 6) describe SHRM as: 'the process by which organizations seek to link the human, social, and intellectual capital of their members to the strategic needs of the firm'.

Some SHRM theorists have focused on the link between strategy formulation and strategic HRM formulation. A range of business–HRM links has been classified in terms of a proactive–reactive continuum (Purcell and Kinnie, 2008) and in terms of environment–HR-strategy–business-strategy linkages (Bamberger and Phillips, 1991). In the '*proactive*' orientation, the HR professional has a seat at the strategic table and is actively engaged in strategy formulation. In Figure 2.2 (p. 56), a proactive interpretation would suggest both a downward and an upward influence of HR professionals on organisation's business- and functional-level strategies.

At the other end of the continuum is the '*reactive*' orientation, which sees the HR function as being fully subservient to corporate-level and business-level strategy and ultimately determining HR strategy through a cluster of HR practices. This type of reactive orientation would be depicted in Figure 2.2 (p. 56) by a one-way downward influence from business-level to functional-level strategy. In this sense, an HR strategy is concerned with incentivising and reinforcing the different employee role behaviours appropriate for each competitive strategy. Schuler et al. (2001) emphasise the strategic 'reactive' role and the core contribution of the HR function, which is to ensure that:

- the organisation has the right number of qualified workers;
- workers have the right skills and knowledge to perform efficiently and effectively;
- workers exhibit the appropriate behaviours consistent with the organisation's culture and values;
- workers meet the organisation's motivational needs.

These four core activities can be seen as the *leitmotiv* of HRM and, according to Schuler et al. (2001), constitute the four-task model of HRM. This guides the organisation's pattern of strategic choices in HRM (Table 2.1).

The relationship between business strategy and HR strategy is said to be 'reactive' in the sense that HR strategy is subservient to 'product market logic' and corporate strategy; the latter is assumed to be the independent variable. As an observer put it, 'HRM cannot be conceptualized as a stand-alone corporate issue ... it must flow from and be dependent upon the organization's (market oriented) corporate strategy' (Miller, 1987, cited in Boxall, 1992, p. 66). There is some theorisation of the link between product markets and approaches to people management. Thus, for example, each of the Porterian 'generic strategies' involves a unique set of responses from workers and a particular HR strategy designed to develop and reinforce a unique pattern of expected behaviour.

Table 2.1 Strategy implementation and the four-task model of HRM

HR tasks	Major strategic decisions
Employee assignments and opportunities	• How many employees are needed? • What qualifications will the employees need? • What pay and conditions will attract people to the firm?
Employee competencies	• What competencies do employees have now? • What new competencies will be needed in the future? • How can new competencies be purchased or developed?
Employee behaviours	• What behaviours does the firm value? • What behaviours are detrimental to the strategy? • What behaviours need to be modified or eliminated?
Employee motivation	• How much more effort are employees able and willing to give? • What is the optimal length of time for employees to stay with the firm? • Can productivity be improved by reducing absence and tardiness?

There are many definitions of SHRM. The selected definitions below indicate HRM is 'strategic' by virtue of its alignment with business strategy and its internal consistency:

> The pattern of planned human resource deployments and activities intended to enable an organisation to achieve its goals. (Wright and McMahan, 1992, p. 298)
>
> All those activities affecting the behaviour of individuals in their efforts to formulate and implement the strategic needs of the business. (Schuler 1992, p, 30)
>
> An approach to management which encompasses those HR strategies designed to improve organisational performance and measures the impact of these strategies on organisational performance. (Boxall, 2008, p. 1)
>
> The choice, alignment, and integration of an organisation's HRM system so that its human capital resources most effectively contribute to strategic business objectives. (Kaufman, 2015, p. 404)

In their treatment of the field, Boxall and Purcell (2016) explain that strategic HRM is concerned with the role of HRM within management strategy to 'generate and protect competitive advantage' (p. 82). To sum up, SHRM is distinguishable from micro-level HRM in terms of its use of long-term planning of HRM activities and performance (Stewart, 2015), the 'systematic' linking of human capacity with the organisation's goals (Schuler and Jackson, 2014) and its tendency to be 'contingency-based and integrative' (Dyer and Holder, 1988, p. 13). The focus on the interface between strategic management and HRM emphasises that context should be paramount when examining the formulation and implementation of HR strategy.

Theorising strategic HRM

A key dimension of the academic and practitioner debate is over the *practice* of SHRM in terms of the ideal way to leverage organisation strategy and HR strategy relationships. The debate centres around the concepts: 'best fit', 'best practice' and the resource-based models.

The 'best-fit' model

In terms of the optimum way to leverage organisational strategy and HR strategy relationships, the best-fit school of thinking calls for the HR system to be *vertically* aligned with its corporate strategy and *horizontally* aligned so that each HR practice provides mutual reinforcement. In the Harvard model of HRM (see Figure 1.4, p. 34), leaders are encouraged to develop an internal HR strategy based on a consideration of stakeholder interests (e.g. shareholders) and situational factors (e.g. workforce characteristics): 'An organisation's HRM policies and practices must *fit* with its strategy in its competitive environment and with the immediate business conditions that it faces' (Beer et al., 1984, p. 25, emphasis added).

The notion of congruence or 'fit' between an external competitive strategy and an internal HR strategy is a central tenet of Beer et al.'s (1984) HRM model. In their words, there must be a 'fit between competitive strategy and internal HRM strategy and a fit among the elements of the HRM strategy' (1984, p. 13). The 'best-fit' model is predicated on *contingency theory*, that HR strategies should be related to the context and situations of the organisation. In the case of a subsidiary discount leisure airline (Jang, 2011), for example, consistent with the 'best-fit' model of SHRM, the airline would need to create a low-cost structure of employment relations, which would be quite different from that of the parent airline company. The two distinctive business models would therefore create two systems of employment relations: the so-called 'high road' and the 'low road' (Harvey and Turnbull, 2010).

The 'best-practice' model

The best-practice school of SHRM argues that all organisations will see performance improvements if managers identify and enact a universal set of 'best' HR practices (Delery and Doty, 1996). Proponents posit that top management should identify 'leading edge' best HR practices, communicate these best practices to line managers, commit long-term to these best practices, measure enactment of best practices and reward managers for implementing them consistently (Boxall and Purcell, 2016). Researchers have provided lists of best HR practices associated with a particular organisational culture (e.g. Pfeffer, 1998) or high-performance workplace systems (HPWSs) (e.g. Appelbaum et al., 2000; Danford et al., 2008; Den Hartog and Verburg, 2004). Whereas Pfeffer (1998) identified seven 'best practices' 'for building profits', both Den Hartog and Verburg (2004) and Danford et al. (2008) isolated eight and twelve HR practices respectively that feature in HPWS. In contrast, Guest (2017) singles out five sets of HR practices that are associated with high worker well-being, a positive employment relationship and performance, see Table 2.2.

A minority of organisations actually implement Pfeffer's seven practices (Kaufman, 2010). The study by Danford and his colleagues found a relatively high number of HPWS practices, such as teamworking, team flexibility and employee involvement in problem-solving (2008, p. 155). Deciding what constitutes 'best' HR practices and isolating the 'core' bundles remains a challenge for academics attempting to measure the HR–performance relationship (Purcell et al., 2009). Legge (1978) identified the problem of interest conflicts when she asked the familiar critical question: For *whom* is 'best practice' best? What if practice is good for shareholders and executives but bad for individual well-being? Where high performance is achieved through strategic 'best fit', is it at the expense of costly ethical standards (Winstanley and Woodall, 2000) or worker well-being? (Guest, 2017). And, what if the practice is good for CEOs but bad for workers? Arguably, this is the case with CEO remuneration in UK FTSE 100 and in US S&P 500 companies. In 2019 the CEO pay package was 117 times that of the average (median) UK full-time worker and 278 times more than the average US full-time worker (Rushe, 2019). Although it may be unrealistic to see a perfect alignment of interests, Boxall and Purcell (2016, p. 73, emphasis added) observe that: 'The most common implicit assumption in the best-practice literature is that "best

Table 2.2 Pfeffer's (1998), Den Hartog and Verburg's (2004), Danford et al.'s (2008) and Guest's (2017) 'best' practices

Pfeffer's 7 practices	Den Hartog & Verburg's 8 practices	Danford et al.'s 12 practices	Guest's 5 practices
Employment security	Employment skills	Self-directed teams	Investment in people
Selective hiring	Autonomy	Problem-solving groups	Engaging work
Self-managed teams	Pay-for-performance	Job rotation within teams	Positive work environment
Pay contingent on firm performance	Profit-sharing	Team briefings	Information sharing
Extensive training	Performance appraisal	Formal consultation	Supportive culture
Reduction in status differences	Teamworking	Works Council	
Information sharing	Job evaluation	Attitude surveys	
	Information sharing	Employee appraisal	
		Off-the-job training	
		On-the-job training	
		Harmonised conditions	
		Partnership	

Source: Compiled using concepts from Pfeffer (1998), Den Hartog and Verburg (2004), Danford et al. (2008) and Guest (2017).

practice" are those that *enhance shareholder value*.' Guest (2017) makes the case that any analysis of the HR strategy and performance relationship should shift the research focus away from shareholder interests and be more employee-centred and look at the kinds of HR practices that are explicitly designed to have a positive effect on worker well-being and employment relationship.

The 'resource-based' model

The resource-based view (RBV) is arguably one of the most popular models in mainstream management literature (Delery and Roumpi, 2017). Its genesis can be traced back to Selznick (1957), who wrote that companies possess 'distinctive competence' that enables them to outperform their competitors. Three decades later, Barney (1991, 1995), argued that 'sustained competitive advantage' is achieved through a careful analysis of its internal skills and capabilities, characteristics that competitors find themselves unable to imitate. Barney identified four characteristics of resources and capabilities – value, rarity, inimitability and non-substitutability – as being important for competitive advantage. Leonard-Barton (1992) similarly argues that the sum of people's 'core capabilities' or 'knowledge sets' has the potential to serve as a basis of competitive advantage. In terms of SWOT analysis, the RBV approach calls attention to the strategic importance of harnessing internal 'strengths' and neutralising internal 'weaknesses'. For Boxall and Purcell (2016, p. 96) resource-based SHRM can potentially produce a 'human resource advantage' and at the heart of the theory is identifying the most valuable human resources and safeguarding them with 'barriers to imitation'.

Teece's (2007; 2016) theory of 'dynamic capabilities' is an important development within the RBV School. This concept draws attention to the evolution of the organisation's competencies and capabilities over time. Such an evolution could enable the firm to respond to discontinuous market conditions or new regulations (e.g. new government policy on renewable energy) and to create new products, services or processes. The concept of dynamic capabilities acknowledges the criticisms that RBV is too static (Ferlie and Ongaro, 2015). Furthermore, the concept of dynamic capabilities emphasises that the management of people, knowledge and HRD become fundamental strategic issues (Teece et al., 1997, p. 514). Indeed, the capacity for organisations to explore and exploit new ideas and technology while simultaneously being adaptive to changes in the environment may go to the core of effective dynamic capabilities. Figure 2.4 summarises the relationship between resources and capabilities, strategies and sustained competitive advantage.

Closely related to RBV is *human capital theory* (HCT). Education economist Schultz (1972) argued that different levels of investment in human 'capital' were held to be a significant factor in explaining different rates of economic growth between Western and emerging economies. Human capital theory brings to the fore the unique nature of human capital as a 'resource' within the organisation to generate sustainable competitive advantage (Nyberg et al., 2014). However, human capital is different from other types of resources in that it is held by people, it is indeterminate and can easily be transferred to competitors if people leave (Delery and Roumpi, 2017, p. 9).

Both RBV and HCT emphasise the need to invest in learning and development and to create 'culture-oriented learning' (Rebelo and Gomes, 2011). The theories also underscore the value of distributed leadership (Teece, 2011) and understanding the process of *followership* (Bratton, 2020; Uhl-Bien et al., 2014). Similar to strategic management, the extent to which RBV and HCT enable organisations to outperform their rivals depends upon the predictability of, and knowledge about, the external contexts.

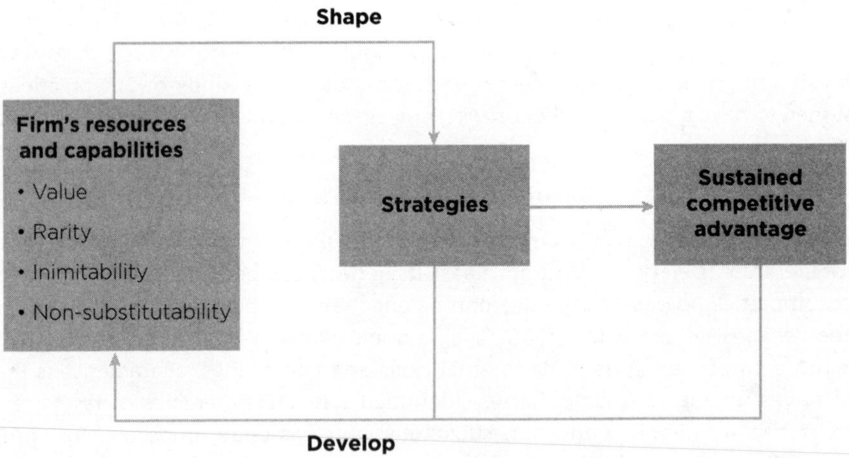

Figure 2.4 The relationship between resources and capabilities, strategies and sustained competitive advantage

HR strategy and organisational dynamics

The prime objective of HR strategy is 'to guide the process' by which organisations deploy and develop human potential and social relationships to improve their services or competitiveness (Morris and Snell, 2013). According to Bailey et al. (2018, p. 93) HRM scholars have devoted less attention to the concept of HR strategy. Bamberger and Meshoulam (2000) define HR strategy as:

> The pattern of decisions regarding the policies and practices associated with the HR system. (p. 5)

For Boxall and Purcell (2016) HR strategy is a pattern of strategic choices that managers make in managing work and people. They define HR strategy as:

> The critical set of economic and socio-political choices that managers make in building and managing a workforce. (p. 26)

Bamberger and Meshoulam (2000) make a useful distinction between top management's 'espoused' HR strategy and their 'emergent' strategy. The espoused HR strategy refers to the pattern of HR-related decisions made but not necessarily implemented, whereas the emergent HR strategy refers to the pattern of HR-related decisions that have been applied in the workplace. Thus, 'espoused HR strategy is the road map ... and emergent HR strategy is the road actually travelled' (2000, p. 6). In terms of process, an emergent HR strategy underscores the notion of the 'black box' of HRM, the complex set of worker attitudes and behaviours that make human non-substitutable capabilities inherently imprecise and indeterminate (see Chapter 1).

A recurrent theme in the literature is the variation in HR strategy, often explained by what political economists call 'varieties of capitalism' (Hall and Soskice, 2009), which acknowledges that economic institutions, levels of unionisation and legal systems vary across nations. HR strategy is therefore context sensitive. The choice of HR strategy is not random. It manifests two management logics. The first is the logic of direct, process-based control, in which the focus is on efficiency and cost containment (managers need to monitor and control workers' performance carefully). The second is the logic of indirect outcomes-based control, in which the focus is on actual results (managers need to engage workers' intellectual capital and cooperation). Thus, when managing people, control and cooperation coexist, and the extent to which there is any ebb and flow in intensity and direction between types of control will depend upon the 'multiple constituents' of the management process (Bamberger and Meshoulam, 2000). Differences in HR strategy provide the source of inevitable structural tensions between management and workers. Context as a determinant of HR strategy has been incorporated into some HRM models. For example, the Harvard model shows HR strategy choices to be influenced by contextual variables such as workforce characteristics, labour market, trade unions and societal values (Beer et al., 1984, see Figure 1.5).

Understanding the concept of HR strategy is further complicated when considering SHRM in multidivisional organisations operating across a variety of labour and product markets, and in multinational corporations (MNCs) operating across different cultures. Multidivisional analysis raises the question of whether local management should have the autonomy to adapt corporate HR strategy to the local context (Minbaeva and Andersen, 2012). Globalisation has given rise to 'societal analysis' (Maurice and Sorge, 2000) and the MNC has been widely theorised as being embedded in society. HR strategies are inescapably influenced by national cultural-legal factors and societal analysis has tended to discount universalistic HR strategies (Trompenaars and Hampden-Turner, 2012). It is argued that with global complexity organisations are no longer just looking to talented workers to implement their strategy, they are looking to people to also formulate their strategy. In the light of this, it is posited that the field of strategy and HR are 'converging' (Morris and Snell, 2013, p. 96).

Context and economic imperatives help explain variations in HR strategy. Given these exigencies: How do we reconcile the friction between a 'best-fit' or 'best-practice' approach to SHRM? It is tolerably clear: studies provide more support for the contextual 'best-fit' school (Boxall and Purcell, 2016). However, although context undeniably matters, the general principles underpinning ethical 'best-practice' prescriptions can inform and enhance the way work and people are managed.

Reflective question

What do you think of the argument that each type of competitive strategy requires a different HR strategy?

Line managers as agents of HR strategy

An HR strategy describes an organisation's pattern of strategic choices that managers make in managing people. But without effective implementation the best-laid HR strategy is of little use. Critical to enacting an HR strategy is the behaviours and actions of line managers (Purcell et al., 2003; Purcell and Kinnie, 2008). LMs are those employees who have 'responsibility for directly managing individual workers or teams [and] report to a higher level of management on the performance and well-being of the workers or teams they manage' (CIPD, 2015c). A far less generous description of the role of LMs is as 'taskmasters'. As Graeber (2018, p. 52) suggests, 'The entire job of middle management is to ensure the lower-level people hit their "productivity numbers" and they are "forced to supervise people who don't need supervision".' Increasingly, LMs have been given an enhanced role for enacting HR policies and practices. This development is partly explained by the notion that HRM is 'too important' to be left to HR specialists (Guest, 1987) and the influence of Ulrich's 'business partner' model (Ulrich et al., 2012). This interpretation, however, neglects other significant developments: the disempowerment of trade unionism in most workplaces, changes which, according to some observers, have empowered managers at all levels to 'near-imperial standing' (Hutton, 2015a, p. 182). The gig economy relies on low-paid workers often forced to experience abuse and bullying because they have no employment protection or trade union representative to act as a countervailing influence to LMs' power.

The Bath model of HRM (see Figure 1.5) emphasises that HR practices *per se* do not generate human-added value. A key mediating factor is the behaviour and actions of LMs. Often promoted on the basis of their individual performance, LMs are charged with both operational and HR responsibilities (McGuire and Kissack, 2015, p. 521). Evidence suggests that there are both pros and cons associated with delegating HR to LMs. On the positive side, it has been observed that LMs have a significant effect on 'employee commitment' (Hutchinson and Purcell, 2003); that LMs are 'enablers of learning' (Warhurst, 2013); and 'a critical lynchpin in delivering HRD' (McGuire and Kissack, 2015, p. 527). On the other hand, there are negative consequences, as evidenced by reports of interpersonal conflicts between HR specialists and LMs due to differences in the perception of 'red-tape', support and capability issues (Op de Beeck et al., 2015). Others report that some LMs lack competency and credibility in people management (Sanders and Frenkel, 2011), and lack of competency causes conflict in dyadic relationships, particularly in the area of performance appraisal (Redman,

Digital Spotlight

Key metrics for aligning corporate strategy and HR strategy

Effective strategic HRM is an analytical process and this entails the use of evidence-based management, supported by HR analytics (Armstrong and Brown, 2019). Therefore, it is vital for organisation leaders and HR professionals to identify, examine and understand the implications of key HR metrics. HR analytics (also referred to as 'people analytics' or 'workforce analytics') has been defined as: 'the synthesis of qualitative and quantitative data and information to bring predictive insight and decision-making support to the management of people in organisations' (KPMG, 2013, p. 4). HR analytics aims to improve operational and strategic decision-making and, ultimately, enhance performance (van den Heuvel and Bondarouk, 2017). While many organisations have long collected raw data, for example, in relation to turnover or sickness absence, this usually offers limited insight on its own. It generally only provides a snapshot of *what* happened in the past, not *why* it happened (or, indeed, what *may* happen in the future). In contrast, HR analytics can detect patterns within the data and even make predictions in relation to certain results or outcomes, for example, which workers are most likely to resign in the coming year. As a result of its potential, HR analytics now constitutes a core aspect of any sophisticated HR function (Edwards and Edwards, 2019). The information utilised for HR analytics purposes includes data related to:

- **Employee turnover:** regularly monitoring turnover can assist in identifying and addressing potential problems, such as workplace bullying or uncompetitive wages.
- **Employee mix:** most organisations employ a mix of full-time, part-time, permanent and temporary workers. By monitoring this and understanding how it relates to demand, businesses can attempt to establish the optimal ratio.
- **Overtime:** monitoring levels of overtime can help to identify patterns and understand fluctuations in workload. Overtime pay can significantly increase total labour costs; therefore, it may be necessary to readjust workplans to limit reliance on it.
- **Unplanned absences:** employee absenteeism can reduce productivity and increase costs. The more accurately unplanned absences are identified and, where possible, mitigated the better.

In addition, other sources, such as operational information or the results of customer satisfaction surveys, can be combined with people data and, when analysed using robust statistical techniques, may offer novel insights (Edwards and Edwards, 2019). Historically, however, two of the greatest challenges in terms of adopting HR analytics have been the complexity of the tools, particularly for those without a background in data analysis, and the difficulties associated with merging diverse data sets (Zielinski, 2019). However, cognisant of this, analytics platforms such as Visier and Workday have become increasingly user friendly. As a result, HR analytics seem set to become a key element of the modern HR professional's toolkit.

Stop! Identify *two* additional metrics that could prove useful in terms of aligning corporate strategy with HR strategy in addition to the four discussed above.

Essential reading

van den Heuvel, S. and Bondarouk, T. (2017) The rise (and fall?) of HR analytics: a study into the future application, value, structure, and system support. *Journal of Organizational Effectiveness: People and Performance*, *4*(2): 157–78.

Note: This feature was contributed by Laura Steele.

2001). It is the way HR practices are implemented by LMs that workers perceive and react to. Workers judge each HR practice and the way it is applied in terms of its usefulness or satisfaction to them, as well as whether it meets perceived ideas of fairness. Importantly, a set of tangible HR practices, as perceived by workers, constitutes an important element in the organisation's climate (Norton et al., 2015). These considerations can inform management practice on how organisations can respond to economic and socio-ecological choices.

HR strategy and performance

Do HR practices actually lead to superior worker and organisational performance? And if so, how? Much of the research in SHRM over the last three decades has concentrated on interrogating what happens in the 'black box' between HR strategy and organisation performance. Purcell and Kinnie (2008, p. 533) noted that the quest to establish an unambiguous causal link between strategic HRM and performance became 'the HRM Holy Grail'. Studies demonstrate that 'bundles' or sets of 'best' HR practices, rather than a single HR practice, deliver improvements in performance (Huselid, 1995; Ichniowski et al., 1997; Katz et al., 1987). Serious interrogation of the HRM–performance linkage therefore involves a series of interrelated choices that support the analysis. First, researchers have to choose a set of HR variables or practices and, second, they must choose a performance benchmark for the organisation under scrutiny. The best-known list of 'best-practice' HR variables is Pfeffer's 7 practices (see Table 2.2). Table 2.3 shows selective studies that propose particular combinations of HR variables can lead to quantifiable enhancement of organisational performance.

Table 2.3 Selective studies reporting an HRM–performance relationship

Researchers	Country	Sector	HR practices & performance findings
Arthur (1994)	US	Steel	Higher productivity, lower waste rates and employee turnover.
Huselid (1995)	US	Multiple	HR practices around AMO model. Lower turnover, higher productivity and financial results.
Ahmad & Schroeder (2003)	Multiple	Manufacturing	Investigated 107 plants in four countries. Data from 107 plants validated Pfeffer's 7 HR practices; increased operational effectiveness, mediated by employee commitment.
West et al. (2006)	England	Health care	HR practices (e.g. training, performance management, participation, teams) linked to patient mortality ratio.
Purcell et al. (2009)	England	Finance	Combination of HR practices and perception of CSR positively associated with employee commitment, and turnover linked to improved financial output, mortgages.
Heffernan et al. (2009)	Ireland	Multiple	Combination of HR practices positively associated with climate, creativity, learning, collaboration, innovation and organisational performance.

Jones (2010)	Finland	Retail	Participatory HR practices positively correlated with business performance.
Chand (2010)	India	Hospitality	HR 'best practice' positively correlated with improved service quality, customer satisfaction and business performance.
Elorza et al. (2011)	Spain	Multiple SMEs	HR practices addressing AMO formula resulted in higher employee commitment, lower absenteeism and enhanced productivity.
Delery & Gupta (2016)	US	Motor Carriers	'Systems' of HR practices that ensure selectivity in staffing, performance-based pay and employee participation in decision-making correlated with higher levels of organisational effectiveness.

The selected HRM–performance studies, and others besides, point to a positive association between an organisation's HR architecture and performance. However, they also illustrate the diversity in the choice of HR practices and performance variables, and even in the same study the effect of HR practices differs across performance outcomes. For example, Arthur's (1994) study included job empowerment but it is excluded in Huselid's (1995) study, and West et al.'s (2006) study investigated the effect of six practices which are associated with HPWS. Reviewing some of the seminal HRM–performance studies, both Ichniowski et al. (1996) and Coombs et al. (2006) conclude that complementary combinations of HR practices gave rise to superior output and quality performances, and that the magnitude of these performance effects was 'large'. But they do emphasise that '*whole systems* need to be changed' in order to enhance performance (Ichniowski et al., 1996, p. 32, emphasis added). However, HPWS can produce a negative effect on employees' interests and well-being (Peccie, 2004, and cited by Armstrong and Brown, 2019, p. 29). This is because high-performance team-based regimes tend to lead to an intensification of work and a more efficient exploitation of wage-labour (see Chapter 3).

Early researchers such as Schuler and Jackson (1987) concentrated principally on the 'top-down' managerial approach to SHRM, examining the link between HR strategy and financial performance, inferring that only shareholder interests matter. More recent research, in contrast, concentrates more on the arguments for and evidence of a *multi-stakeholder* approach to SHRM. A multi-stakeholder approach to SHRM, one that gives due attention to the interests and needs of other stakeholders including workers, is found in the 'balanced scorecard' (Kaplan and Norton, 1992). The balance scorecard is predicated on the premise that for an organisation to be successful it must satisfy the needs of all stakeholders. Four performance indicators are suggested: *financial*, e.g. profitability; *customer relations*, e.g. customer loyalty; *internal processes*, e.g. knowledge-sharing; and *learning and growth*, e.g. worker flexibility.

In the aftermath of the 2008 GFC and 'austerity' macroeconomic management when, arguably, precarious employment strategies became more common, more attention has been paid to the well-being of workers (Guest, 2017; Marchington, 2015; Peccie and Van De Voorde, 2019). As Paauwe et al. (2013, p. 75) attest, 'little attention has been paid to the meaning of performance from the perspective of other stakeholders'. Guest (2017) draws upon well-established research from the quality of working life (QWL) movement (Walton, 1974) and the job characteristic model (Warr, 1987) to support his thesis that five sets of worker-oriented HR practices explicitly designed to promote well-being and a positive employment relationship can affect both individual and organisational performance, thus producing mutual gains for employers and workers. A model of this relationship is shown in Figure 2.5.

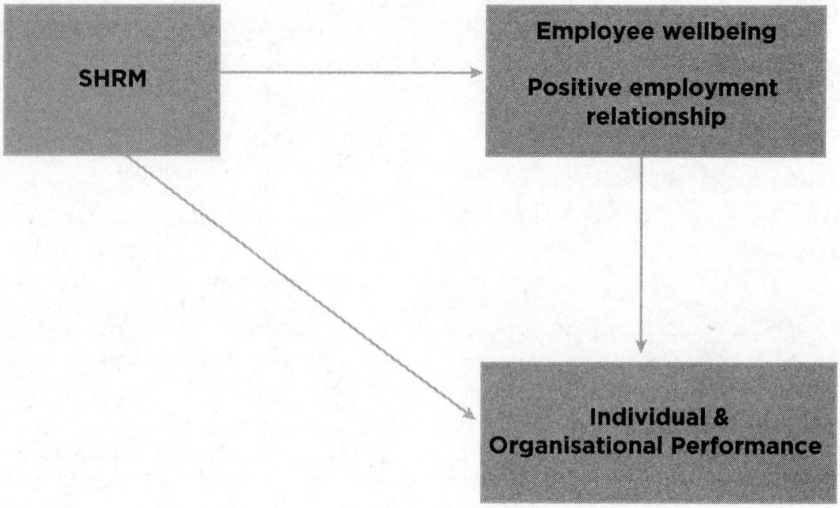

Figure 2.5 SHRM, employee well-being, the employment relationship and performance

Source: Based on the theories of Peccei et al. (2013) and Guest (2017).

Although mainstream HRM–performance studies claim to have found a positive association between sets of HR variables and performance, the methodological challenges of demonstrating the causal links between the two measures are formidable (Bou-Llusar et al., 2016). The challenges were summarised by Wright and Gardner (2003, p. 312) who wrote:

> Methodologically, there is no consensus regarding which practices constitute a theoretical complete set of HR practices; how to conceptually categorize these practices; the relevance to business strategy; the appropriate level of analysis; or how HR-performance and firm performance are to be measured ... Theoretically, no consensus exists regarding the mechanism by which HR practices might impact on firm outcomes.

There are two kinds of challenges researchers face: those dealing with *research design*, and those concerned with *causality*. With regard to research design, the first challenge is deciding the *independent* variable, *HR practices*. There is no agreement on what constitutes core 'HR practices', and ambiguity surrounds which appropriate bundles or sets of practices should be scrutinised. The analysis of Boxall and Purcell (2016) and others suggest that the AMO framework (see Figure 1.5) is the established starting point to explain the HRM–performance relationship. The implication is that any HR strategy ought to enhance worker ability (A), motivation (M) and opportunity (O) to perform, 'each of which will add value to performance in a particular context' (p. 155). However, other management practices, such as just-in-time, total quality control, and lean production, all closely associated with Japanese management methods (e.g. Bratton, 1992), or the synergistic relationship between these and HR practices might have positive outcomes for performance (Wood, 2019). Second, there are differences in terms of who or what should be studied, that is, the *unit of analysis*.

Third, with regard to the *dependent* variable performance, the studies differ in their foci. Performance variables focus almost exclusively on financial measures (Boselie et al., 2005). However, researchers often have little choice but to use 'intermediate' indicators to measure performance such as quality or labour productivity (Betcherman et al., 1994). Fourth, there are differences regarding the

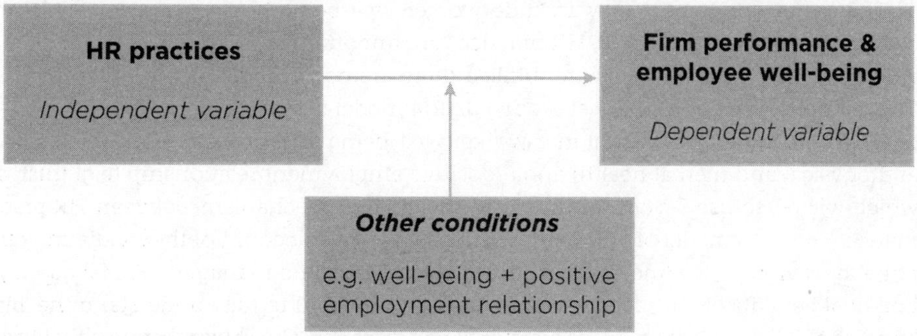

Figure 2.6 A causal model of the HRM–performance relationship

Source: Based on the theory of Sayer (2000).

selection of key informants in survey studies. When only a single respondent (typically an HR manager) is selected it raises the question of competence, whether the informant can provide accurate information about all the variables relevant to measuring performance (Gerhart, 2008). It is recommended that data collection should be from multiple key-informants (Bou-Llusar et al., 2016).

The studies have a second major weakness related to the concept of *causality*. *How* exactly do HR systems increase performance? A key element of a theory is a causal mechanism, that is, some notion of how the independent and dependent variables are related, see Figure 2.6.

Reflective question

Revisit Figure 2.6. What factors or 'other conditions' mediate the causal effect of HR practices?

The causal mechanism can also be considered as the process, or chain of cause-and-effect linkages, that mediates the causal effect (Remler and Van Ryzin, 2011). There is no consensus regarding the precise cause-and-effect linkages through which strategic HR practices generate long-term value (Wright and Gardner, 2003). The analysis of Danford and his colleagues argue that studies may lack robust evidence 'governing *direction* of causation' (2008, p. 152, emphasis added). It could be that only high-performing firms introduce best-practice HRM, for example.

Explaining the process by which a particular set of HR practices might enhance organisational performance comes down to understanding the logic of causation in social research. Sayer (2000) explains that the 'linking mechanism' between HR practices and performance is complex and messy, therefore researchers have to rely on careful conceptualisation of multiple practices and 'other conditions', the *mediating* effects of other key variables (Boselie et al., 2005). The *internal* causal 'mechanism' could, for example, be that workers' motivation increases performance, or that the organisation's culture and climate enhances workers' commitment and flexibility.

HRM web links

Visit the companion website at **www.bloomsbury.pub/bratton-hrm** for more information on the logic of causality and the positivist and critical realist view of causation.

The 'other conditions' may include worker well-being and a positive employment relationship (Guest, 2017). As already noted, HR practices are important antecedents of psychological contracts and when psychological contracts are fulfilled there are positive well-being outcomes (Guest et al., 2010). The central proposition of Guest's (2017) SHRM model is that the presence of the five sets of HR practices will be associated with higher worker well-being (e.g. positive work-related social relationships and physical and mental health) and a positive employment relationship (e.g. trust, security, fairness) which will be, to use Sayer's terminology, the 'linking mechanism' between HR practices and performance. The Bath model of HRM also reminds us to take account of the mediating effects of organisational behaviour including the significant role of first-line managers (FLMs) agency in attaining the potential benefits of HR practices (Yang and Arthur, 2021) to fully understand the 'black box' between bundles of HR practices and organisational performance. Guest (2017) argues that the quest to demonstrate a positive relationship between HR variables and performance has been at the expense of a concern for the well-being of workers. Above all, in the context of a spike in work-related mental health associated partly with the coronavirus pandemic, changes in the nature and context of work – for example, homeworking, greater isolation, fear about job insecurity – support the case for HR practices that can at least partly ameliorate the threats to employee well-being. The SHRM literature identify significant gaps between HR practices that organisations report using and workers experiences of those practices, raising a question about the extent to which planned HR practices are effectively implemented within the organization (Yang and Arthur, 2021). Recent empirical studies remind us that we should be cautious about generalising from the HRM-performance findings because the results are not directly applicable in all contexts (Purcell et al., 2009).

Table 2.4 A framework for studying strategic HRM

SHRM concepts	SHRM approaches	SHRM practice
Resource-based view Barney (1991) Barney & Wright (1998)	**Multi-stakeholder** Beer et al. (1984; 2015)	**Vertical and horizontal fit** Fombrun et al. (1984) Baird & Meshoulam (1988)
Ability Motivation Opportunity theory Appelbaum et al. (2000)	**Employee well-being** Peccie et al. (2013) Guest (2017)	**Best fit v. best practice** Purcell (1999)
Human capital theory Schultz (1972) Nyberg et al. (2016)		**Performance** Huselid (1995) Purcell & Kinnie (2008)

Source: Inspired by Armstrong and Brown (2019).

A literature review by Armstrong and Brown (2019) led to the conclusion that SHRM is not an easy concept to define or to deliver and that numerous concepts have emerged concurrently, which helps to explain the continuing controversy about its aims and effect. A framework for studying the evolution of SHRM as discussed above is shown in Table 2.4. The key *concepts* associated with SHRM include the RBV, the AMO model, human capital theory, and strategic choice. Two broad *approaches* to SHRM can be identified, the multi-stakeholder and worker well-being, with the latter receiving more attention from academics. SHRM *practice* focuses on three sets of activities, namely, vertical and horizontal fit, best fit versus best practice and SHRM-performance. Although Boxall (2018, p. 27) observes that generally SHRM has become 'a more balanced subject' because it is embracing both sides of the employment relationship, worker well-being and organisational performance, Armstrong and Brown

(2019) argue the subject has been too oriented towards shareholder interests (maximising firm performance) and much less concerned with the interests of the other stakeholders, especially wage-labour. This provides latitude for critique from those writing from a critical management studies (CMS) perspective.

Critical perspectives and analysis

Existing conceptualisations of SHRM are based upon the mainstream rational perspective of managerial decision-making – definable and coherent acts of linear planning, choice and action. Critical scholarship has challenged the assumption that a firm's business-level strategy and HR system have a logical, linear relationship. On the contrary, strategy formulation is often informal, politically charged and subject to contingency factors, and key decision-makers often lack information, time and 'cognitive capacity' (Bamberger and Meshoulam, 2000). As Mabey et al. (1998b, p. 520) observe: 'Much SHRM literature assumes a naive, over-rationalist view of organizational decision-making.' Globalization, deregulation of markets and financialization have combined to 'upend' the business environment and create a potential strategy disconnect (Reeves and Deimler, 2011; van der Zwan, 2014). Critical scholars repudiate the image of the corporate leader as a reflective strategist. In most cases strategic actions are more likely to be frenetic and ad hoc (Hales, 1986; Powell and Wakeley, 2003) and strategic HRM actions are often reactive and short-term oriented (Paauwe and Boon, 2019).

Another area of critique is the focus on aligning the HR function with business strategies – the best-fit approach. It is argued that contingency analysis relies exclusively on external marketing strategies (how the firm competes) and disregards the internal operational strategies (how the firm is managed) that influence HR practices (Purcell, 1999). The best-fit model privileges only one step in the full circuit of industrial capital (Kelly, 1985). In coping with internal contradictions, the organisation not only has to 'fit' HR practices to competitive strategy but must also integrate business and worker needs. To put it another way, the best-fit model places the emphasis on the realisation of profitability within product markets rather than at the complex contingent variables that constitute the full labour process or the 'black box' between HR practices and performance, where managers and workers together are engaged in creating added value the organisation needs. Worker motivation and commitment are, as ever, central to managing employment relations, but strategising about 'best-fit' disregards 'employee interests' and ignores important psychological aspects of the employment contract.

Financialisation is a term used to describe the role and pre-eminence of finance to the working of the economy, and daily life. Krippner (2005, p. 174) defines financialisation as 'a pattern of accumulation in which profits accrue primarily through financial channels rather than through trade and commodity production'. At organisation level, financialisation manifests itself in the form of a stronger emphasis on maximising shareholder value (MSV). Critical scholars of MSV focus on the resulting changes in corporate strategies and organisational structures that have encouraged 'strategic alliances' (Hoogvelt, 2001), greater emphasis on non-production activities, outsourcing and 'disaggregation' through global supply chains (Davis and Kim, 2015). MSV companies aim to be as small as feasible with minimal assets and employment. 'Whereas the conglomerate firms of the 1960s and 1970s sought to straddle the Earth, the contemporary share-priced-oriented firm seeks to dance on the head of a pin', observes Davis and Kim (2015, p. 211). The primary allegiance of executive leaders in MSV-oriented companies is to their shareholders, not the workforce. Corporations are profit seekers and the demand for an HR strategy is fashioned by MSV as well as specific economic contingencies of firms (Kaufman and Miller, 2011). In contemporary firms, a variety of HR strategies exist not only between, but also within, companies. The most robust critique of the best-practice HRM model is economic-social-oriented with a focus on the implications of financialisation on economic outcomes for workers and trade unions (see Chapter 9), patterns of inequality and social change. This suggests that the impulse behind managerial choices in HR strategy is primarily economic rather than opting for as many 'best practices' as possible (Boxall and Purcell, 2016).

Within the context of neoliberal economic globalisation, global just-in-time supply networks, financialisation (Epstein, 2015; Thompson, 2013) and technological advancement encourage 'strategic alliances' between rival giants. These contingencies can result in an unpredictable variety of HR strategies not only between, but also within, organisations (Storey, 2001). In such contexts, it is implausible that the best-practice model can apply across all organisational situations at all times. The most robust critique of the best-practice model is economic-oriented. Private sector organisations are profit seekers and the demand for an HR strategy is fashioned by specific economic contingencies of firms (Kaufman and Miller, 2011). Therefore, the impulse behind managerial choices in HR strategy is primarily economic rather than opting for as many 'best practices' as possible (Boxall and Purcell, 2016).

The RBV model has been part of mainstream strategic management theory for 30 years, during which time it has been subjected to considerable mainstream criticism (Paauwe and Boselie, 2003). Not least, that 'strategic' learning calls for weighty investment in learning and development (Guest, 2017; Poell et al., 2015). More ambitious critical work has come from Jacoby (2005), for example, who observes that investment in HRD varies between employers depending on whether or not top management are insulated from shareholder pressure demanding a short-term growth in shareholder value. The more they are insulated from shareholder pressure, the higher the likelihood that they will invest in their workforce. Hutton (2015b) makes a similar point about 'quarterly capitalism' that allegedly puts the short-term interest of shareholders in a position of primacy at the expense of long-term investment, including investment in employee training, which would appear to undermine RBV theory. Contrary to rhetorical claims that 'people are out most valued asset' there is a paucity of interest in most organisations in ambitious high-commitment HRM, characterised by caring, and long-term positive relationships and worker development (Alvesson, 2018). An increasing number of HRM scholars appear to be repudiating mainstream interpretations and asking, '*Qui bono?*' – who benefits from SHRM? The focus of most SHRM research is on the interests of shareholders. Put in more colloquial language, the nucleus of SHRM is the financial 'bottom line', but often also failing to protect the well-being of the workforce reflected in physical and mental ill-health, insecurity and inequitable rewards (Cascio, 2015; Guest, 2017; Kaye, 1999).

Consistent with our focus on paradox, management's actions create potential 'strategic tensions' (Thompson and McHugh, 2009; Watson, 1999). Thus, one strategic action might undermine another strategic goal. Acceding to the imperatives of a global free market, there is, for example, a tendency in a recession for corporate management to strive for profits by mass redundancies – so-called 'downsizing' – and by applying more intensive performance outcomes to those remaining at unit level. This pattern of action constitutes an HR strategy even though it manifests a disjunction between organisational design and employment relations. As Purcell (1989, 1995) points out, an organisation pursuing a strategy of downsizing might 'logically' adopt an HR strategy that includes the compulsory lay-off of non-core workers and, for the identifiable core of workers with relatively rare attributes, a compensation system based on performance results. In such a case, the business strategy and HR strategy might 'fit', but, as Legge (2005, p. 128) points

Source: © Andrew Bratton

Critics contend that the nucleus of SHRM is the financial 'bottom line' at the expense of failing to protect the well-being of the workforce.

out, these HR practices are unlikely to engender employee commitment and will cause a misfit with 'development-humanist' values. The goal of 'external fit' of business and HR strategy can contradict the goal of employee commitment and cooperation. The lessons of the Covid-19 pandemic are that ethical and fair treatment of all workers, including those previously considered 'unskilled', ought to push people issues to the forefront of today's business models. It would be reassuring to think so.

As you have read through this text so far, however committed managers might be to a particular HR strategy; there are external economic forces and internal 'structural contradictions' at work that will constrain their action. Interesting, then, that much of the SHRM literature focuses on internal consideration of 'fit' between business strategy and HR practices and generally treats the external economic context in which organisations operate as fundamentally stable. This presumption of macroeconomic stability, however, could be considered a precondition for the long-term policies of a developmental-high-commitment HR strategy (Rubery and Johnson, 2019). Extending the disconnected capitalism thesis (DCT) put forward by Thompson's (2013) analysis of the effects of the 2008 economic crisis on HR models, the unprecedented collapse of businesses and the disruption of global supply chains during the 2020 pandemic were not connected to any failures of HR strategy or to any problems of worker performance or commitment. The failure to supply personal protective equipment (PPE) to front-line workers was a consequence of four decades of globalisation, deindustrialisation and finance capitalism. Financialisation is profit-making through financial instruments rather than engaging in productive activities in the real economy (see Martin and Quick, 2020; Thompson, 2013; and 'Search & Watch' below).

Critics argue that financialisation accelerates the trend towards outsourcing and off-sourcing. The use of 'creative' financial practices – buying back the firm's shares, maximising shareholder value (MSV), loading the company with debt – not only disincentivises investment in the workforce and has dysfunctional outcomes for trade unions (see Chapter 9) but often undermines the viability of the whole organisation (Wylie, 2020). Thus, failure to connect the workplace and developments of financial capitalism directly put in question the presumptions underpinning SHRM. Further, as hopefully you understand by now, all organisations are embedded in national cultures, and HR strategy will therefore be shaped by socio-political factors. Within national boundaries organisations often have more than one HR system. The kind of analysis is nicely summed up by Hyman's pronouncement that 'there is no "one best way" of managing these contradictions, only different routes to partial failure' (1987, cited by Thompson and McHugh, 2009, p. 110). Reflecting on the SHRM discourse, the leader-centric view of the corporate leader as a reflective 'strategist' is no longer fashionable in leadership discourse (Bratton 2020; Thompson and McHugh, 2009, p. 113). Critical work on constructions of HR strategy may expose the possible consequences of an organisation's pattern of strategic choices for legitimising hierarchy, differentiation and the continued treatment of workers as a commodity (Alvesson, 2018).

Summary

This chapter has examined different levels of strategic management. Strategic management plans provide the context within which HR plans are developed and implemented. We have drawn attention to the more critical literature that recognises that HR strategic options are, at any given time, partially constrained by the outcomes of corporate and business decisions, the current distribution of power within the organisation and the ideological values of the key decision-makers.

The dominant message of SHRM is misleadingly straightforward: if an organisation's HR strategies are aligned with business strategy there will be positive outcomes. But, in reality alignment is not easy. In no work organisation does a one-size-fits-all approach apply to SHRM. We critiqued here the 'best-fit', 'best-practice' and RBV models of SHRM. We explained that, in the globalised economy with market turbulence, the 'fit' metaphor might not be appropriate when organisations need to learn more quickly to compete with their rivals or to meet ecological goals. The 'best-practice' model may serve shareholder or executive interests but may be bad for workers' and society interests. The RBV model underscores the importance of an organisation's human endowments. But, in the gig economy, there is little evidence to suggest that the 'developmental humanist' approach has been implemented consistently or on a scale commensurate with the SHRM rhetoric.

We examined the empowerment and the crucial role of LMs in enacting and delivering an organisation's HR strategy. Finally, we critically examined the methodological and theoretical concerns relating to HR–performance research. Critics argue that the effectiveness of strategic choices in HR is difficult to measure due to the problem of quantifying the HR and performance variables and meeting the criteria of causality.

Review questions

1. Can society and organisations achieve 'a quadruple bottom line' and if so, what, if anything has to change?
2. Explain the difference between 'strategic HRM and HR strategy? Do some aspects of corporate strategy have the potential to render the ideals of HRM unobtainable?
3. How can the effect of an HR strategy on organisational performance be explained?

Search & Watch

Visit YouTube for **Noam Chomsky** (2016) **Financialisation of the Economy**. Explain the importance of financialisation for business strategy and HR strategy. Does financialisation at the level of the firm undermine the developmental humanist HRM model?

Go to the video hub at www.bloomsbury.pub/bratton-hrm and view the interview with **Sarah Myers, Director of Talent Management, Sky** (www.sky.com). Sky entertains more than 10.1 million homes through the most comprehensive multichannel, multiplatform television service in the UK and Ireland. Sarah joined Sky in 2003. She is a Fellow of the Chartered Institute of Personnel and Development and has an MSc in Human Resources from the London School of Economics. She is also a member of the HR Leadership Alliance for the Heads of Talent Management, an alumna of the School of Coaching and a member of the Editorial Board of *People Management* magazine.

Click on Sarah's picture to watch her talking about business strategy and how it related to her work at Sky. Once you have watched the video try and answer the following questions: (1) What does Sarah mean by looking 'end to end' in talent management? (2) How is development related to talent groups at Sky? (3) In Sarah's view, how is talent linked to succession?

Legal Focus

Historically in the UK, employment relationships were contractual relationships like any other, governed by the common law of contract. In the private sector, the status of working people was usually clear: most people were employees, self-employed or partners. In the private sector, the status of worker, as a category of working person distinct from employees and self-employed has emerged over time and grown in significance. The effects of technology, outsourcing of work and the use of zero-hours contracts have affected how people work and their relationships with organisations. An employee has greater rights than a worker, who in turn has greater rights than an independent contractor, so it is important to determine the status of the parties in the employment relationship. While complex, the courts consider multiple factors, including the degree of control exercised by the employer, to determine whether a person is an employee. For example, homeworkers were classified as employees because the employer provided work on a regular basis and decided how, at what time and place of performance.

Task Search online for government information in your jurisdiction on how an employee is legally defined and compare and contrast it with another country, such as Australia or Canada. Address the following questions: (1) What are the differences between an employee, a worker and an independent contractor? (2) What are the implications of these differences for the HR function?

Reference

See Deborah Lockton and Tom Brown's *Employment Law* (2020), pp. 29–50, for an extended legal analysis of the nature of the employment relationship.

Chapter case: Mandla Winery*

The setting

The South African wine industry's roots date back to 1659, with the first bottle produced in Cape Town that year. However, it wasn't until the 1990s, when international boycotts were removed with the end of Apartheid, when the industry flourished. South African winemakers' quick adoption of viticulture and winemaking technologies resulted in high-quality products for the new export markets. By 2019, South Africa was producing 974 million litres of wine with export revenues of £852 million.

The rapid growth of the industry raised concerns by conservationists about the country's most vulnerable natural habitats being targeted in the quest for vineyard expansion. One such area is the Cape Floral Kingdom, located in the Cape Province of South Africa, where nearly 95% of the country's wine production occurs. As one of the richest plant areas on earth, it has earned international recognition as a global biodiversity hotspot.

In 2004, with Cape Flower Kingdom's unique vegetation and ecosystems under threat, the wine industry and the conservation sector embarked on a pioneering partnership to create the Biodiversity and Wine Initiative (BWI). The programme aims to promote changes in farming practices that enhance the suitability of vineyards as a habitat for biodiversity. Since 80% of the Cape Floral Kingdom is privately owned, landowner participation in conservation efforts is essential. The BWI lays out specific criteria for wine producers to participate in the programme and they must have plans and schedules in place to ensure continual improvement. In addition, programme participants must be compliant with industry-prescribed environmental responsibilities.

The problem

South Africa's wine industry directly employs nearly 290,000 workers, with 58% of employees considered unskilled, 29% semi-skilled and 13% skilled. While most employees receive fair and competitive compensation, training and skills development programmes are lacking, and more than half the wineries in South Africa do not have any dedicated HR resources.

Jabulani Dlamini, the head of Mandla Winery, is one of the landowners in the Cape Floral Kingdom that the BWI has targeted for participation in their programme. Jabulani is interested in sustainability as a long-term strategy, but he is struggling with recent events that have devastated the local wine industry. He had just recovered from the 2018 drought in the region when the government's ban on domestic and export alcohol sales during the Covid-19 pandemic further eroded his profit margins. Jabulani realises that in order to comply with the BWI's environmental standards, he will need to have employees with current technical knowledge and skills related to sustainable farming practices. He must now make the decision either to invest in the development of their skills or to recruit qualified external help, although these new employees might demand higher wages. Jabulani wants to be sure that the business strategy he is about to embark on will result in growth for his winery to cover his expected increased costs and an ability to survive changing market conditions.

The assignment

Working either alone or in a study group, prepare a sustainable green business plan drawing on this chapter and other recommended material that addresses the following:

1. How do the 'four pillars of sustainability' discussed in this chapter fit with Mandla Winery's participation in the BWI programme?
2. For employees to be committed to the corporate strategy, they need to understand the business case for sustainable wine production. Why is sustainability important to Mandla Winery and what can Jabulani do to pursue sustainability for the company's and the community's good?
3. Which HR strategy (commitment, collaborative, paternalistic or traditional) would be the most effective in helping Jabulani with the challenges he will face in pursuing a sustainable approach to wine production in the current market conditions? Why?

Essential reading

Evans, S., Vladimirova, D., Holgado, M., Van Fossen, K., Yang, M., Silva, E. A. and Barlow, C. Y. (2017) Business model innovation for sustainability: towards a unified perspective for creation of sustainable business models. *Business Strategy and the Environment*, *26*(5): 597–608.

Gillinsky, A., Newton, S. K. and Vega, R. F. (2016) Sustainability in the global wine industry: concepts and cases. *Agriculture and Agricultural Science Procedia*, 8: 37–49.

Lopez-Cabrales, A. and Valle-Cabrera, R. (2020) Sustainable HRM strategies and employment relationships as drivers of the triple bottom line. *Human Resource Management Review, 30*(3): 100689.

For more on the Cape Floral Kingdom and the BWI programme, go to https://wine.co.za/page/page.aspx?PAGEID=2666

Note: This case was contributed by Lori Rilkoff.

*The name of the company is fictitious but is based on South African data and research.

Further reading

Armstrong, M. and Brown, D. (2019) Strategic human resource management: back to the future. Available at: www.employment-studies.co.uk/system/files/resources/files/517_Strategic-Human-Resource-Management-Back-to-the-future-IES-CIPD-2019. pdf.

Boxall, P. and Purcell, J. (2016) *Strategy and Human Resource Management* (4th edn). London: Palgrave Macmillan.

Cook, H., Mackenzie, R. and Forde, C. (2016) HRM and performance: the vulnerability of soft HRM practices during recession and retrenchment. *Human Resource Management Journal, 26*(4): 557–71.

Epstein, G. (2015) *Financialization: There's Something Happening Here*. Political Economy Research Institute. Amherst, MA: University of Massachusetts. Available at: https://www.peri.umass.edu/publication/item/684-financialization-there-s-something-happening-here.

Mintzberg, H. and Waters, J. A. (1985) Of strategies, deliberate and emergent. *Strategic Management Journal, 6*(3), 257–72. Available at: https://doi.org/10.2307/2486186.

Thompson, P. (2013) Financialization and the workplace: extending and applying the disconnected capitalism thesis. *Work, Employment and Society, 27*(3), 472–88.

Yang, J. and Arthur, J. B. (2021) Implementing commitment HR practices: line manager attributions and employee reactions. *The International Journal of Human Resource Management, 32*(16), 3339–3369, DOI: 10.1080/09585192.2019.1629986.

PART 2

PART 3

FUNDAMENTALS OF HRM

CHAPTER 3

Job and Work Design

CHAPTER 4

Workforce Planning and Diversity

CHAPTER 5

Recruitment and Selection

CHAPTER 6

Performance Management

CHAPTER 7

Learning and Development

CHAPTER 8

Reward Management

CHAPTER 3

JOB AND WORK DESIGN

outline

- > Introduction
- > The nature of work
- > The meaning of job and work design
- > The development of work design
- > Classical work designs: scientific management
- > Post-bureaucratic design: the job characteristic model
- > Post-bureaucratic design: Japanese management
- > Contemporary design: process-centred and high-performance work systems
- > Critiquing job and work design
- > Summary
- > Further reading

Source: Photo by Maxime on Unsplash

objectives

After studying this chapter, you should be able to:

1. Explain the nature of work and the core dimensions of job and organisational design
2. Understand how management decisions concerning job and work design affect employee commitment, well-being, performance, and organisational and societal outcomes
3. Define job design and describe specific work organisation strategies
4. Understand the relationship between different job and work designs and HR strategies
5. Understand the theoretical arguments underpinning process-centred and high-performance work systems

Introduction

The way jobs are designed, and work organised is a critical internal contingency affecting HRM. Management is the chief architect of job and work design, and different strategic choices have created contrasting job structures and work systems. For example, there are jobs that provide workers with no variation in the tasks performed, their work activities being closely supervised. In contrast, jobs may be structured that require workers to perform a wider range of tasks within a self-managing team. A well-established body of research traversing organisational behaviour, leadership and HRM explores how different work design systems have important consequences for workers' motivation, work-related stress and individual performance. Purcell et al. (2009) on their part, associate job design with outcomes that motivate workers and produce in them the ability and opportunity (the AMO formula) that will eventually lead to performance-related outcomes. This premise, which has its intellectual roots in Douglas McGregor's *The Human Side of Enterprise* (1960) and Fredrick Herzberg's (1968) Job Satisfaction model, proposes that the 'opportunity to succeed' is contingent upon the way jobs and work are designed. The way work is designed has also influenced the theory and practice of leadership (Grint, 2011). The academic work known as labour process theory emphasises the continuity and limited effects of new work design configurations.

In this chapter, we define work and explain existing knowledge on how strategic choices in the design of jobs affect attitudes and behaviour in the workplace. We take an historical perspective to demonstrate the link between job design theories and management practice. We draw on the contributions of psychology, sociology and labour process to examine the implications of different configurations for managing work and people. We conclude with a critique of mainstream theories and studies that provide the foundations of our current understanding of emerging trends in job and organisational design.

The nature of work

When we refer to the term 'work', what do we mean? Usually, we see it as the opposite of play. The notion that work is central to human activity and transformative is rooted in North European theology, specifically Calvinism (see, for example, Bratton and Denham, 2019; Edgell and Granter, 2020). A body of research has found what might be called 'the paradox of modern work' – that is, most people's sense of dignity and self-worth is found in work, but most people hate their jobs (Graeber, 2018). The discipline of the sociology of work, not to mention HRM, has devoted much research agency to trying to understand how both these emotions can be true simultaneously. The challenge of defining work is illustrated by two similar tasks. Completing the forms to apply for a student loan is not seen as work but when form filling is part of a clerical worker's job it is. Similarly, when a mature student looks after their own child, this is not seen as work, but if they employ a child-minder, it is, for the minder, work. These examples illustrate that work cannot be defined simply by the content of the activity. Work is not just an activity, something one *does*, but something a person *has* (Gorz, 1982). We can begin to understand the complexity of work and its social ramifications by exploring the following definition:

> Work refers to physical and mental activity that is carried out to produce or achieve something of value at a particular place and time; it involves a degree of obligation and explicit or implicit instructions, in return for a wage or reward. (Bratton, 2020, p. 31)

This definition draws attention to some central features of work. First, the most obvious observation is that work involves 'physical and mental' activity for the purpose of adding 'value', which suggests that the activities of both a construction worker and a computer systems analyst can be considered to be work. 'Mental activity' also includes the commercialisation of human feeling, or what, in her classic study of Delta Airlines flight attendants, sociologist Arlie Hochschild called 'emotional work' (Hochschild, 1983; 2012). Others have focused on aesthetical labour which highlights the servility of routine work performed by service workers within the customer–employee interface (Warhurst and Nickson, 2007). The fact that the service sector provides the most employment in Britain (Nixon, 2009) emphasises how important it is to analyse the full array of emotional and aesthetic work that takes place in the workplace, as well as the processes by which emotional and aesthetical labour is extracted and exploited (Bolton, 2009).

Second, work is structured spatially – geographically – and, by time and people's spatial embedding, shapes work and management practices (Herod et al., 2007). Throughout most of the twentieth century, work was typically carried out away from home and at set periods of the day or night. In the twentieth century the mass timetable of the '8 to 5' factory world, and the '9 to 5' office world, has given way to a complex flexi-place, flexi-time world, the iPhone symbolising the 'work anywhere' culture of our times (Donkin, 2010). The first lesson the Covid-19 pandemic has taught us is that there is greater scope for working away from formal organisations, and that this has ecological and health benefits. Thus, 'place and time' locates work within a social and ecological context.

Reflective question

How has the Covid-19 pandemic transformed the way we think about work and the skills required?

Third, work always involves social relations between people: between employer and employee, between first-line manager and other employees, between co-workers and, in some workplaces, between manager and trade union representatives. Social relations in the workplace can be cooperative or conflictual, hierarchical or egalitarian. Thus, to be 'in work' is to have a definite relationship with some other who has control of the time, place and activity.

Source: Joel Muniz on Unsplash

The fourth element of work is a payment. Pay is typically of two types: *extrinsic* and *intrinsic*. The employee provides physical effort and/or mental application and accepts fatigue and the loss of control over their time. In return, the extrinsic work rewards that they usually receive consist of (primarily) a wage or salary and possibly bonuses. The intrinsic rewards the worker might get from the job include status and peer recognition.

We should note that not all work, either physical or mental, is remunerated. Some of it is household-based work – cooking, child-rearing, cleaning and so on – and some of it is done voluntarily, for the good of society, for instance working for a food bank. These activities are unpaid yet are identical to those in some paid jobs, such as working in a nursery or a warehouse. Here we concentrate on paid work, and as a consequence we largely omit the critically important area of unpaid work, although that is not to suggest that we see it as unimportant.

Global HRM

How could a four-day week work for Kiwis?

Source: Getty Images/Nazar Abbas Photography

How would you like a four-day workweek? It may sound like a trick question, but it could become increasingly common as employers and governments look for alternative ways to increase productivity and boost worker well-being. For example, New Zealand's prime minister Jacinda Ardern has suggested employers in a post Covid-19 economy should consider a four-day working week and other flexible working options to boost the country's domestic tourism industry. Speaking on a Facebook Live video after her first post-lockdown visit to the tourist hotspot of Rotorua, Ardern said:

> I heard lots of people suggesting we should have a four-day week. Ultimately that really sits between employers and employees ... There's lots of things we've learned about Covid and that flexibility of people working from home, the productivity that can be driven out of that ... (Roy, *The Guardian*, 2020)

New Zealand's tourism industry is an important part of its economy and the four-day week is a way in which New Zealand's economy can recover from the Covid-19 crisis. Andrew Barnes is the founder of the New Zealand financial services firm Perpetual Guardian, a business of more than 200 people that transitioned to a four-day workweek in 2018. He found that the change to a four-day week resulted in an increase in worker productivity by 20% and lower stress levels and better job satisfaction. Other reported benefits of a four-day work week include improved worker mental and physical health, family and social lives, and reduced carbon emissions. The mental health benefits of a shorter working week could also be crucial to help economies recover post-Covid-19 crisis, said Barnes: 'The 4 Day Week is a tool to protect the health of workers in every respect, making this model all the more relevant to the new world we find ourselves in' (Whiting, 2020b). Similarly, Aidan Harper, from the 4 Day Week Campaign, said: 'Work has changed for ever as a result of this crisis and we want to make sure we have a better model of work emerging from it as we had going in' (Murray, *The Guardian*, 2020). The amount of time people spend in work is not inevitable. Work time has varied dramatically throughout history and continues to vary widely between countries. Reductions in working hours have always been the result of conscious action and collective effort – the eight-hour workday, the weekend, the right to paid holidays and rights for those who work part-time were won by campaigners, trade unions, progressive employers and eventually government legislation.

Stop! What are the benefits and potential drawbacks of implementing a four-day work week? Can the four-day working week work for everyone?

PART 3

Essential reading

Roy, E. (2020) Jacinda Ardern flags four-day working week as way to rebuild New Zealand after Covid-19. *The Guardian*, 20 May; Whiting, K. (2020) New Zealand Prime Minister opens door to 4-day working week. World Economic Forum, 20 May. You can read more about the work of the 4 Day Week Campaign at, https://www.4dayweek.co.uk/

Note: This feature was contributed by Andrew Bratton.

The meaning of job and work design

The term 'job design' is used here to signify a narrower focus and 'work design' to denote a broader conceptualisation that links the job to its wider context or work system (Parker and Wall, 1998). A job is a combination of tasks assigned to a worker. From this perspective, Parker and her colleagues define job design as the content and organisation of tasks (Parker et al., 2017, p. 404), and Bratton (2021, p. 36) defines it as 'the process of assigning tasks to a job, including the interdependency of those tasks with other jobs'. A related concept is job analysis which refers to the systematic process of collecting and evaluating information about the tasks, responsibilities and context of a specific job. This information is used for developing a job description, a summary of the duties and responsibilities, and reporting relationships that pertain to a particular job. Derived from the job descriptions are the job specifications, which are the individual qualifications deemed necessary to successfully perform the tasks involved with the job. Job descriptions and specifications are used in a variety of HR activities, including workforce planning (Chapter 4), recruitment and selection (Chapter 5), performance management (Chapter 6), learning and training (Chapter 7), and reward management (Chapter 8). As illustrated in Figure 3.1, job design and the information from job analysis is the foundation for an HR strategy.

Job design focuses directly on work-related tasks or activities that employees undertake to produce and deliver a good or service for the organisation. To begin, we need to understand the core dimensions of job design. A job comprises one or more *tasks* a worker performs, it involves identifiable *skills*, and it has defined areas of responsibility or *autonomy*. Job design can result in the fragmenting of tasks into repetitive, routine and unskilled work. But it can also lead to multiple tasks and skilled work.

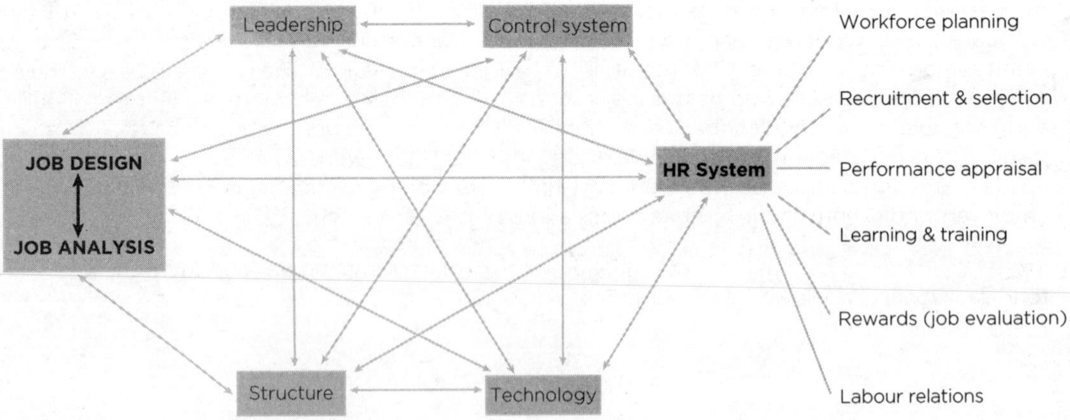

Figure 3.1 A framework for analysing job design

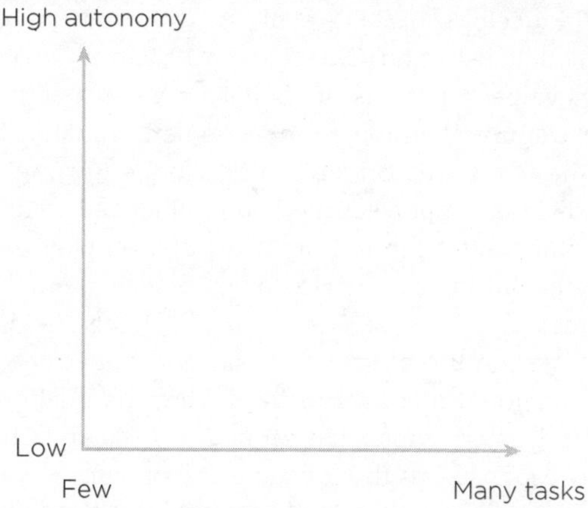

Figure 3.2 The core dimensions of job design for individual employees

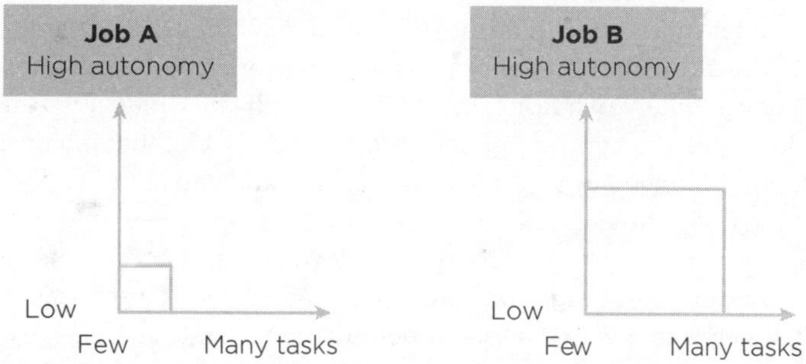

Figure 3.3 Alternative job designs for an employee

Managers face strategic choices in designing a job. At its most basic level, job design decisions produce low or high levels of horizontal and vertical job-related tasks. The core dimensions of job design are shown in Figure 3.2.

The horizontal axis in Figure 3.2 represents the functional or technical tasks that are required to produce a product or service. Job design choices can entail only one simple task or a series of tasks combined in one job, depicted as a movement along the horizontal axis. Horizontal job enlargement has the effect of increasing cycle times and creating more complete and, hopefully, more meaningful jobs. The technical dimension, then, is concerned with the range of tasks undertaken by employees and raises issues of multiskilling and functional flexibility. The vertical axis, on the other hand, represents the decision-making aspects of work activities, and shows the extent of employees' autonomy in the job. The extent to which the job allows workers to exercise choice and discretion in their work runs from low to high.

The two core dimensions enable us to contrast two jobs, shown as A and B in Figure 3.3. The characteristics of job A limit the content or scope of the job, giving minimal, if any, discretion over how work-related tasks are performed. The focus is on a rapid completion of tasks and close supervision.

In contrast, job B is designed with more tasks and offers the employee more autonomy over how those tasks are performed. The focus is on improving job satisfaction by allowing the worker to complete several tasks with some self-supervision. European and US research underscores the fact that most workers prefer jobs in which they can exercise some influence over decisions on how they do the tasks (Boxall and Purcell, 2016; Gallie et al., 2013). Job design has been linked to specific epochs or crises in capitalism (Boltanski and Chiapello, 2018; Grint, 2011; Wall et al., 2004). During the last millennium, there have been periods of capitalism when traditional job design, which emphasised minimum skills and training, dominated management thinking and practice, which contrasted with other times when the focus was on 'enriching' and 'enlarging' individual jobs. Contemporary job design theory for individual employees has been influenced, and explained by, the *Zeitgeist* of the day – the 'spirit of the times' – for job redesign to foster employee engagement or 'voice' in decisions affecting work, with the objective of increasing employee commitment, job satisfaction and improved performance outcomes.

The critical literature, on the other hand, has questioned the view that job redesign is primarily motivated by a management ideology of improving the quality of work (Thompson and McHugh, 2009). From the 1980s, Western capitalism, argue Boltanski and Chiapello (2018), faces a crisis in falling profitability and one response was the restructuring of work. Key to the new strategy was a critique of job specialisation or Taylorism (see below) and enhancement of flexibility and worker autonomy to elicit workers' knowledge and capabilities. As Parker and Wall (1998), and others, attest, individual workers not only execute assigned tasks, but they also engage in emergent tasks, and sometimes self-initiated activities. Much of management thinking and practice in the 1980s was to encourage workers to enact flexible work. In terms of job design: 'It breaks down into internal *flexibility*, based on the profound transformation in the organization of work and the techniques employed (multitasking, self-control, development of autonomy, etc.)' (Boltanski and Chiapello, 2018, p. 218). The analysis of the transformation of work over the last 40 years affirms the fact that job design does not exist in a vacuum. Job design is derived from, and is embedded within, an organisational structure.

Organisational structure as defined by Bratton (2021, pp. 286–7) is 'the means by which senior management divides work activities such as task allocation, and coordinates and controls these activities toward the achievement of organizational goals'. An effective organisation structure needs to do two things. First, it needs to *divide* the total function and task into manageable subfunctions and subtasks – sometimes known as 'differentiation'. Second, it needs to *coordinate* the completion of these tasks so that they fit together to accomplish the total task of the organisation – sometimes known as 'integration'. The way managers design organisation structure reflects well-documented contextual changes, including accelerating globalisation, complex supply chains, new technologies, increasing requirements for environmental sustainability, including carbon footprint savings, and growing demands to do more with less (UN, 2018).

A variety of dimensions can be used to conceptualise organisation structure. While definitions are elastic, here we examine structure by listing and explaining the seven core elements mainstream organisation theorists consider managers should address: work specialisation, departmentalisation, hierarchy, span of control, chain of command, centralisation and formalisation (Daft, 2015), see Table 3.1.

Table 3.1 Core elements of organisation structure

Element	Decisions
1. **Work specialisation**	How should work tasks be divided?
2. **Departmentalisation**	What jobs should be grouped together?
3. **Hierarchy**	How many levels of management should there be?
4. **Span of control**	How many employees can a manager effectively supervise?
5. **Chain of command**	To whom should individuals and groups report?
6. **Centralisation**	Where should decision-making authority be located?
7. **Formalisation**	How many rules are needed for efficient functioning?

- *Work specialisation* describes the degree to which work in the organisation is divided and allocated to different categories of employees or groups. Also known as division of labour. Management has to decide whether employees do a single task (high specialisation) or several different tasks (low specialisation).
- *Departmentalisation* refers to the way jobs in the organisation are grouped together. Decisions have to be made on whether jobs should be grouped within departments whose employees share a common expertise (function) or according to the type of service or product the organisation produces.
- *Hierarchy* describes the levels of management, whether there are many (tall hierarchy) or few (low or 'flat' hierarchy) between the top CEO and the front-line workers. The extent to which an organisation has many layers of management will affect reporting relationships, internal communication and styles of leadership.
- *Span of control* defines the number of subordinates that a single manager can supervise effectively. If this span is narrow, managers have few subordinates reporting to them. If it is wide, managers are responsible for many subordinates. The larger the span, the less potential for control by direct supervision.
- *Chain of command* is the uninterrupted line of authority that extends from the top of the organisation to the lowest level and clarifies who reports to whom with respect to their work.
- *Centralisation* refers to the degree to which decision-making is concentrated at a single point in the organisation. A *centralised* organisation is one in which the CEO makes all the decisions, and line managers just carry out their directives. A *decentralised* organisation is one in which top managers solicit input from line managers.
- *Formalisation* describes the degree to which organisations standardise organisational behaviour through written rules, procedures and related mechanisms. The more rules there are about what is to be done, when it is to be done and how it should be done, the greater the degree of formalisation.

PART 3

Reflective question

Using the concepts in Table 3.1, consider the organisational design of your university. Evaluate its specialisation, departmentalisation, hierarchy, span of control, etc. Is your university excessively bureaucratic or 'flat'? What are the strengths and weaknesses of its current structure?

As you have hopefully realised through our discussion of the elements of organisation structure, decisions of organisation structure within an organisational design process involve far more than deciding the degree of job fragmentation, the grouping of jobs and the extent of rules. Organisation design decisions focus on a basic problem for management: 'How much organisation and control of behaviour is necessary for efficient functioning?' It is around this dilemma that the study of work design takes place.

Parker (2014, p. 663) defines *work design* as, 'the content and organisation of one's work tasks, activities, relationships, and responsibilities', and Morgeson and Humphrey (2008, p. 47) defined it as 'the study, creation, and modification of the composition, content, structure, and environment within which jobs and roles are enacted'. Job design itself is at the core of work design. Work design matters. Indeed, job and work design can affect the survival of the organisation and therefore be part of a strategic approach to managing people (Daniels et al., 2017).

Management choices about work design (sometimes known as 'work systems') affect the coordination between functions and tasks, the quality of the decisions managers and workers make, the extent to which people's knowledge, experience and capabilities are utilised, the extent to which employees are committed to organisational goals, and the extent to which people's needs for development and quality of work life are met (Beer et al., 1984, p. 10). Scholars have recently argued that management choices about work design affect employee well-being, positive work attitudes, and individual, group, and organisational performance (Parker et al., 2017).

Work design is embedded in the organisation's structure, which can take many forms ranging from hierarchical *bureaucratic* to decentralised team-based forms. Table 3.2 shows the key characteristics of four types of organisational structure: bureaucratic, flat, matrix and boundaryless.

Bureaucracy has existed for centuries, for example, in the hierarchical nature of the Catholic Church and in the ranks of armies. Western capitalist economies, in the early 1900s, saw the widespread development of mass-production and organisational architecture based on rules, procedures and narrow spans of direct control. The *bureaucratic* structure created a particularly efficient form of rationalisation (Bratton and Denham, 2019), ideal for mass-production and use in fast-food (Ritzer, 2014). However, in the 1980s, scholars and managers deemed bureaucratic structures to be ill-equipped to meet the demands of global capitalism (Du Gay, 2000).

The *flat* and *matrix* structures are less hierarchical and more flexible, and designed to overcome the dysfunctions of bureaucracy. The matrix structure combines a traditional functional hierarchy with separately managed project teams that draw workers from across different functional departments. As a business student, you are likely to experience a matrix structure. Your university course is taught by lecturers from a number of different departments, for example, Accounting, Economics or Management. Your HRM lecturer likely reports to two managers. One responsible for the function (Management), the other manager or course coordinator responsible for the delivery and qual-

Table 3.2 Key characteristics of bureaucratic, flat, matrix and boundaryless organisation structures

Structure	Characteristics
Bureaucratic	Top-down management decision-making
	Many levels and top-down communication channels
	Highly specialised jobs with narrowly defined job descriptions
	Focus on individual performance targets
Flat	Decentralised decision-making
	Few levels and multidirectional communications
	Broadly defined jobs requiring multiple skills
	Team working and product development
Matrix	Each job has two elements: functional & service/product
	HR personnel for service A are responsible to both the HR director and the service A director.
Boundaryless	Decentralised decision-making with wide span of control
	Broadly defined jobs requiring multiple skills
	Team working and product development
	Employees communicate using social media, e.g. Zoom
	Non-essential jobs or functions to core business outsourced

ity of the course (the product). Although it allows for easier collaborative working, cultural issues can make matrix structures less efficient (Katzenbach and Smith, 2015).

The *boundaryless* structure is a relatively recent phenomenon, which continues to this day (Anand and Daft, 2007). A boundaryless structure as defined by Bratton (2020, p. 304) is an organisational configuration designed to remove vertical, horizontal and external barriers so that employees, managers, customers and suppliers can work together and share ideas to their mutual benefit. It is conceived as substituting a hierarchical model of structure for permeable boundaries, through both *internal flexibility* and *external flexibility*. The latter by partnerships with two or more outside organisations and by *outsourcing* to firms with lower costs within the country or *offshoring* work to a different country (Davis-Blake and Broschak, 2009). A business model known as 'Nikefication', in recognition of the US company that pioneered manufacturing its products offshore in Vietnam (Davis and Kim, 2015), the outsourcing and offshoring of previously internally provided processes (e.g. apparel making) or services (e.g. IT servicing or training) 'hollows out' the organisation, reducing its boundaries, workforce and intellectual know-how (Child, 2015). According to Boltanski and Chiapello (2018, p. 218), external flexibility presumes:

> A so-called network organization of work, wherein 'lean' firms seek the resources they lack from a profusion of subcontractors, as well as a labour force that is malleable in terms of employment (casual jobs, temping, self-employed workers), working hours, or the duration of work (part-timers, variable hours).

The network organisation of work is a feature of the so-called gig economy which accounts for 4.7 million workers in Britain. For gig workers, network configuration has re-forged the employment relationship. Historically, interest in work design began in response to the wide-scale adoption of mass production and scientific management principles in the design at the beginning of the twentieth-century. The theory underpinning these innovations in work redesigns is discussed next.

HRM in Practice
Teachers at breaking point

Source: Matthew Horwood/Getty Images

According to official figures, more than half a million workers in Britain suffer from workplace stress. The single highest cause is high workload, with the consequence that workers are repeatedly having to meet tight deadlines, operate at high speeds or generally work intensively with few breaks (Green et al., 2018). Although evidence of rising work intensification has been reported in many British workplaces, teachers have experienced especially high levels of required work intensification. According to a recent study, teachers in England work 47 hours a week on average during term time, including marking and administration, increasing to about 50 hours in the summer during exam time (Weale, 2019). This is eight hours more than teachers in comparable industrialised countries. Consequently, nearly three-quarters of teacher now describe themselves as 'stressed', and more than a third of education professionals have experienced a mental health issue in the past academic year. Sinéad Mc Breart, chief executive of Education Support, a charity that gives mental health help to education professionals, said the sector was now at breaking point:

> 'We are beyond "crisis". We are in a state of distress.' If the situation continued, she argued, it would result in 'burnt-out leaders on an industrial scale' and schools would face problems recruiting and retaining teachers. 'We know that [the] performance of anyone in any job is compromised by stress and poor wellbeing. We are going to see that in our classrooms. As it is, 10 million children are spending a significant amount of time every year in high-stress environments - and that is going to affect them. (Ferguson, 2019)

Research suggests that work-related stress, burnout and dissatisfaction many employees are experiencing is a result of poorly designed work (Parker et al., 2019). Work design refers to the nature and organisation of tasks, activities and responsibilities within a job or work role. From a psychological perspective, when work is well-designed, workers have interesting tasks, autonomy over those tasks and a reasonable level of task demands: reasonable workloads, clear responsibilities and manageable emotional pressures. For employees, the benefits of well-designed work include job satisfaction, improved work-life balance, lower job stress and better well-being. For employers, good work design means opportunities to fully harness the skills and creativity of workers by providing more job autonomy, one of the strongest drivers of employee creativity and innovation in the workplace. Despite the benefits of well-designed work, poor work design is common in many work organisations. Studies point towards both macro-level factors, such as the decline in unions and inadequate employment legislation (Parker et al., 2017), and micro-level factors such as managers and organisational leaders usually viewing work design from a process perspective (for example, introducing lean principles) and paying insufficient attention to skills utilisation and employee well-being.

Stop! Managers and HR professional have an important role when it comes to designing quality work. How do HR professionals design more meaningful work? What role should employees and their representatives play in the process?

Essential reading

Ferguson, D. (2019) Record levels of stress 'put teachers at breaking point'. *The Guardian*, 10 November; Parker, S. K., Andrei, D. and Van den Broeck, A. (2019) Why managers design jobs to be more boring than they need to be. *Harvard Business Review*, 5 June; Weale, S. (2019) 25% of teachers in England work more than 60 hours a week - study. *The Guardian*, 18 September.

Note: This feature was contributed by David Denham and updated by Andrew Bratton.

The development of work design

Work design research has had a long history. Since the epoch of the Industrial Revolution, the design and transformation of work has been studied. The factory system was investigated by Adam Smith in the eighteenth century, and by Karl Marx in the nineteenth century. From the second decade of the twentieth century, the interpretation of business crisis as a crisis of bureaucracy spurred multiple research on work design. Figure 3.4 shows four key approaches to organising work – (1) scientific management; (2) job characteristic model; (3) Japanese management theories; and (4) integrated contemporary process-centred theories – that map onto distinct historical developments.

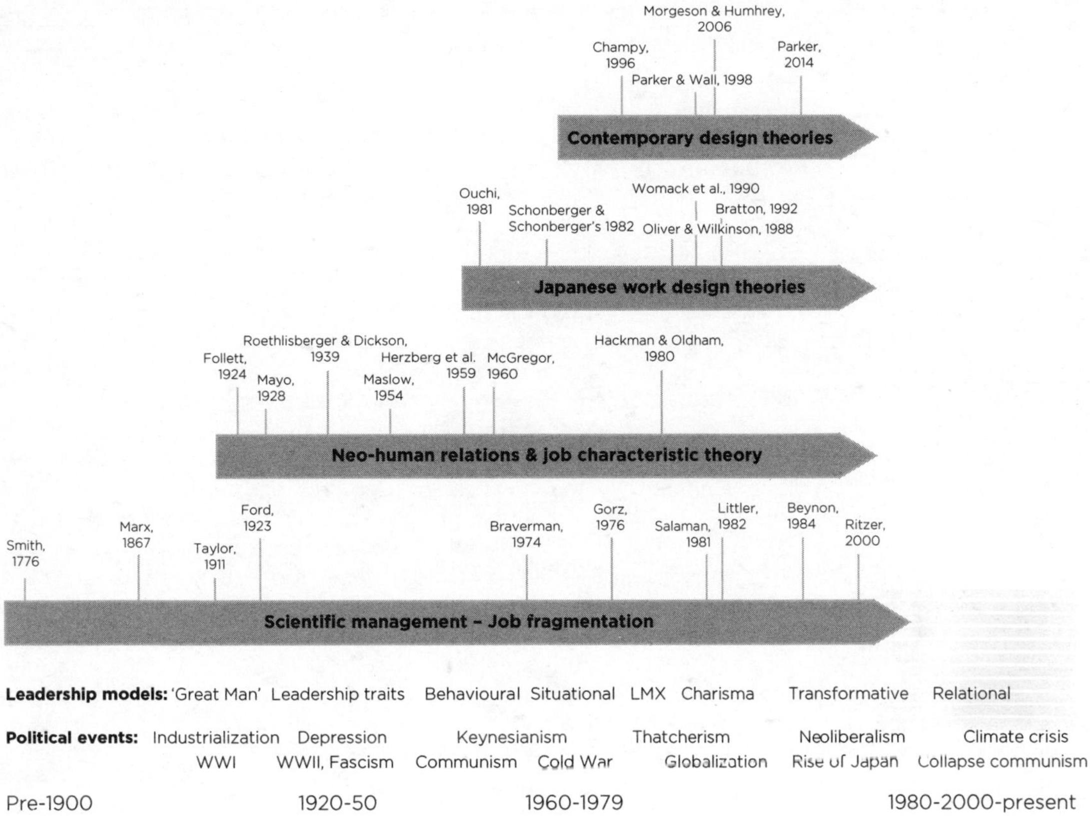

Figure 3.4 Mapping key developments in work design

Source: Created from the theories of Grint (2011) and Parker et al. (2017).

Source: Rob Kim/Stringer/Getty Images

Leader-centric theories focus on traits and charisma. Sir Richard Branson, who allegedly possesses superior attributes compared with non-leaders, has used public relations to create an image of 'a maverick underdog' and 'bureaucracy-buster' starting companies under the Virgin brand.

In mapping developments in work design theory over the last 100 years, it is important to understand that scholars necessarily take their view of their research, in part, from their academic field of study informed by the changing context of capitalism. Work design theories, therefore, have a theoretical inheritance, largely drawn from psychology and sociology, but also are informed in different epochs by multiple theorising on leadership and contextual forces influencing organisational strategy. Importantly, the development of work design is not linear, but, rather, swings between different business models informed by periodic crises in profitability and new thinking on corporate strategy and leadership. The trajectory of leadership theory, for example, has oscillated between *leader-centric* (e.g. 'Great Man', Trait, Situational) to more *follower-centric* (e.g. leader member exchange (LMX), Relational, Distributive) models, as managers wrestle both with competitive advantage and labour challenges. When scientific management dominated

Ethical Insight
The ethics of zero-hours contracts

In August 2020, the Office for National Statistics (ONS) reported that 3.2% of people in employment in the UK were on a 'zero-hours' contract (ZHC), compared to just 0.8% in 2000. (Farina et al. (2019), however, suggest the true figure may be significantly higher if other, similar, work arrangements were included in the statistics). According to ACAS (2020), a person is considered to be on a zero-hours contract if their employer does not have to give them a minimum number of working hours and they do not have to take any work offered. Zero-hours contracts are particularly common within the domains of health and social care, delivery driving, hospitality work and the gig economy (ACAS, 2020). Lack of agreement as to a definition of ZHCs makes international comparison difficult, however, similar arrangements can be observed in countries such as Ireland, Australia, Canada and the United States (Datta et al., 2019).

By law in the UK, an employee on a zero-hours contract has the same rights as those on a standard contract, including the national minimum wage and holiday pay (ACAS, 2020). However, if they do not work a sufficient number of hours, they may not be entitled to sick pay or pension contributions (Howlett, 2020a). Proponents of ZHCs argue that they provide much-needed flexibility, particularly in industries that experience erratic and unpredictable demand. In turn, it has been suggested that, as a result of their personal circumstances, certain workers, such as students or semi-retired people, might prefer to be on a highly flexible contract. In addition, some may view a ZHC as a way to get their 'foot in the door' of an organisation.

Many workers, unions, politicians and other key stakeholders, however, argue that ZHCs are unethical. It has been suggested that the balance of power is heavily tilted towards employers and 'flexibility' could be more accurately described as 'exploitation' (Elliott, 2016). Farina et al. (2019, p. 507) note that, while ZHC jobs and workers are heterogeneous, they 'have become increasingly concentrated amongst young workers, full-time students, migrants, black and minority ethnic workers'. There is also growing evidence that ZHCs may have a negative impact on career progression (Gheyoh Ndzi, 2019). Johnston (2015), however, argues that ZHCs are not inherently immoral, instead 'it is the abuse, as opposed to the use, of these types of contracts which raise issues of fairness'. Such concerns can be situated within the broader debate regarding the gap between the 'rhetoric' and the 'reality' of HRM (Legge, 1998). As Crane et al. (2019) note, for example, 'new working patterns' often equate to temporary and part-time roles instead of permanent, full-time positions and precarious working arrangements. 'Empowerment' may involve forcing someone else to take risk and responsibility beyond their pay and position (Crane et al., 2019).

Stop! What is your view on the issue of ZHCs: are they ethical or do they result in exploitation?

Essential reading

Farina, E., Green, C. and McVicar, D. (2019) Zero hours contracts and their growth. *British Journal of Industrial Relations*, *58*(3): 507–31.

Note: This feature was contributed by Laura Steele.

work design, leadership shifted from heroic individuals to focus on individual traits (e.g. intelligence), with leaders as repositories of knowledge of mass production (Grint, 2011, p. 8).

The ascendency of different ideologies accompanied the transformation of work design – from Keynesian economics and collectivist thinking to neoliberalism and the primacy of the market (Boltanski and Chiapello, 2018). Therefore, overlaying the four clusters of work design theories shown in Figure 3.4 are econ-political and cultural factors and different perceptions of effective leadership that are inseparably intertwined (Bratton, 2020; Grint, 2011). As others have opined, when change in leadership and work design theories are situated within the machinations of the wider econ-cultural context, 'what seems 'normal' only appears so when framed by the political ideologies of the day (Grint, 2011, p. 12).

Classical work designs: scientific management

The 'classical' approaches to designing jobs and work systems are considered classical partly because they identify ideas and issues that keep occurring in contemporary literature, albeit using a different vocabulary (Grey, 2005). An early contributor was Adam Smith (1723–90). Smith observed that the division of labour or job simplification leads to productivity (output per worker) increases because of enhanced dexterity, and specialisation stimulates the invention of new machinery. Smith's early example of job design was taken from the production of nails. He wrote (1776/1982, p. 109):

> Man draws out the wire; another straightens it; a third cuts it; a fourth points it; a fifth grinds it at the top for receiving the head ... the important business of making a pin is, in this manner, divided into eighteen distinct operations.

In the nineteenth century, Charles Babbage pointed out that by simplifying tasks and allocating fragmented tasks to unskilled workers, the employer could pay a lower wage, and thus 'dividing the craft cheapens its individual parts' (Braverman, 1974, p. 80). Karl Marx (1818–83) argued that job simplification also stultified human creativity and that, as such, it 'alienated labour' (Bratton and Denham, 2019, p. 98). The influence of Smith's and Babbage's theories on work design and management can be found in Frederick W. Taylor's book *The Principles of Scientific Management*, published in 1911.

Frederick W. Taylor (1856–1915) pioneered the scientific management movement often referred to as *Taylorism*. This form of job and work design, it is argued, is 'both a system of ideological assertions and a set of management practices' (Littler, 1982, p. 51). Taylor was appalled by what he regarded as inefficient working practices. His approach to job design was based on five main principles:

- maximum job fragmentation;
- the divorce of planning and doing;
- the divorce of 'direct' and 'indirect' labour;
- the minimisation of skill requirements and time for learning the job;
- the reduction of material-handling to a minimum.

The centrepiece of scientific management was the separation of tasks into their simplest constituent elements, and as such 'Taylorism embodies a dynamic of deskilling' (Littler, 1982, p. 52). Some writers argue that Taylorism was a relatively short-lived phenomenon, while others have argued that, in the late twentieth century, the direct and indirect influence of Taylorism was extensive (Littler and Salaman, 1984, p. 73).

Reflective question

Can you think of jobs in the hospitality sector that support the charge that the way work is organised continues to be imbued with neo-Taylorism?

The American car-maker Henry Ford (1863–1947) applied the major principles of Taylorism, but also installed specialised machines and perfected the flow-line principle of assembly work; this kind of work design has, not surprisingly, come to be called Fordism. This classical work system is characterised by two essential features: first, a system of conveyor lines that feed components to different work stations to be worked on; and second, the standardisation of parts to gain economies of scale and lower unit costs. Management's control over the work system was enhanced by detailed time and motion studies that attempted to discover the shortest possible task-cycle time. Ford's concept of people management was simple: 'The idea is that man [sic]... must have every second necessary but not a single unnecessary second' (Ford, 1922, quoted in Beynon, 1984, p. 33). Recording job times meant that line managers could closely monitor their subordinates' performance. Ford's production system was, however, not without its problems. Workers found the repetitive work boring and unchallenging, often expressed in high rates of absenteeism and labour turnover. Taylor-style work design techniques also carried control and coordination costs. Job simplification needed extensive planning and direct supervision of workers. Despite these limits, Taylorism and Fordism became the predominant approach to job design in vehicle production in the USA and Europe.

In the 1920s, Harvard Business School professor Elton Mayo (1880–1949) applied the insights of social psychology to the design of work and to management practice. He criticised F. W. Taylor for focusing solely on the engineering aspects of work and for believing that employees were solely motivated by extrinsic (monetary) rewards. Mayo's research at the Hawthorne Works of the Western Electric Company in the USA found that not only economic incentives, but also the working environment and social relations motivated workers. The message for management was quite clear: rather than depending on management controls and extrinsic rewards, management needed to influence the work group by cultivating an organisational climate that met the social needs of workers. Mayo's findings ushered in what became known as the *human relations movement*, which advocated worker participation and non-authoritarian first-line managers to promote a climate of good human relations, in which both the quantity and quality of the service or the goods demanded by the organisation could be met.

From the 1950s, Abraham Maslow (1908–70) along with Frederick Herzberg (1923–2000) introduced the *Neo-Human Relations School*, which challenged the core principles of Taylorism and focused on the psychological needs of employees. Human relations emphasised five core principles:

- The principle of closure, whereby the scope of the job is such that it includes all the tasks to complete a product or process, thus satisfying the social need of achievement.
- A good design incorporating control and monitoring tasks, by which the individual or group assumes responsibility for quality control.
- Task variety, whereby the worker acquires a range of different skills so that job flexibility is possible.
- Self-regulation of the speed of work.
- That the design should encompass a job structure allowing some social interaction and a degree of cooperation between workers (Littler and Salaman, 1984).

Competitive pressures in the 1970s compelled an increasing number of Western companies to redesign jobs. The earliest antidote to Taylorism was the use of *job rotation*, which simply involves the periodic shifting of a worker from one work-simplified task to another (Figure 3.5). The advantage of job rotation is, it was argued, that it reduces the boredom and monotony of doing one simplified task by diversifying a worker's activities. Another shift away from Taylorism was provided by the concept of *job enrichment* popularised by Herzberg (1968, p. 83), who referred to it as 'vertical job loading'. Herzberg's approach involved the horizontal expansion of work tasks (Figure 3.6). Instead of only grilling hamburgers, for example, a griller's job could be enlarged to include mixing the meat for the burger or preparing a side salad to accompany the order. With a larger number of tasks per worker, the time-cycle of work increases, thus reducing repetition and monotony. According to Herzberg's theory, designing and managing work provided the opportunity to release workers' energy, creativity and motivation. In contemporary HRM literature, the theory finds expression in the AMO formula (Appelbaum et al., 2000; Kellner et al., 2019). As explained in Chapter 1, the AMO framework suggests that HR practices, such as job design, will influence a worker's ability (A), motivation (M) and opportunity (O), which, in turn, leads to

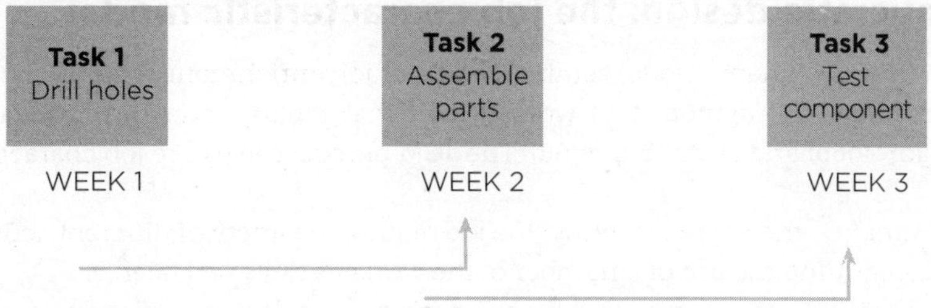

Figure 3.5 An example of job rotation

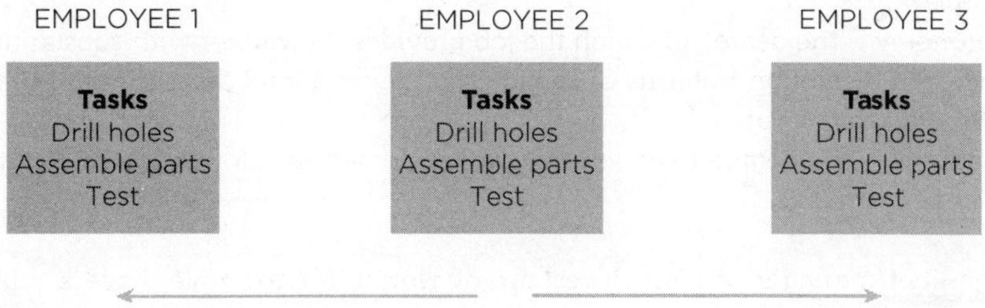

Figure 3.6 An example of job enlargement

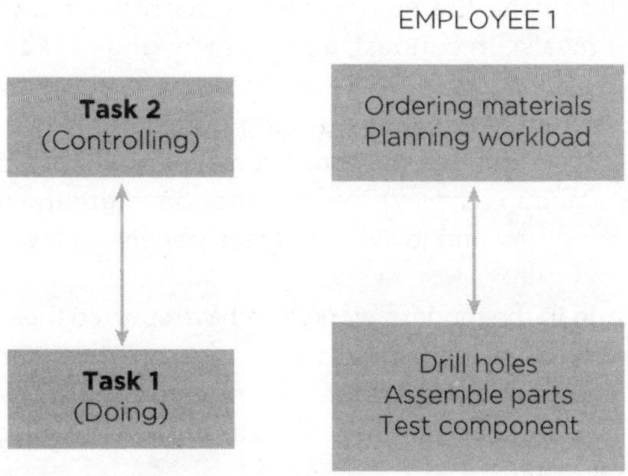

Figure 3.7 An example of job enrichment

improved performance (AMO = P). In terms of job design principles, worker ability, for instance, could be improved via workplace learning or training, motivation potentially develops through engaging in a larger number of complex and interesting tasks, and opportunity to participate in decision-making could be influenced by empowering workers. Thus, performance-related outcomes are a function of workers' **A**bility + **M**otivation + **O**pportunity (see Figure 1.5).

A later and more sophisticated effort to overcome some of the major shortcomings of Taylorism was the vertical expansion of jobs, often referred to as *job enrichment*. This approach takes some authority from the immediate supervisors and adds it to the job (Figure 3.7). Increased vertical scope gives the worker additional responsibilities, including planning and quality control. For example, the fast-food worker from our previous example might be expected not only to grill the burgers and prepare the salad, but also to order the produce from the wholesaler and inspect the food on delivery for its quality.

Post-bureaucratic design: the job characteristic model

Hackman and Oldham's (1980) seminal model of job enrichment – the *job characteristic model* (JCM) – is an influential approach to work design that builds upon the foundational work of Douglas McGregor (1960) and Hertzberg (1968). The JCM proposes five core job characteristics:

- *Skill variety* – the degree to which the job requires a variety of different activities in carrying out the work, requiring the use of a number of the worker's skills and talents.
- *Task identity* – the degree to which the job requires the completion of a 'whole' and identifiable piece of work.
- *Task significance* – the degree to which the job has a substantial impact on the lives or work of other people.
- *Autonomy* – the degree to which the job provides the worker with substantial freedom, independence and discretion in terms of scheduling the work and determining the procedures to be used when carrying it out.
- *Feedback* – the degree to which the worker possesses information related to the actual results of their performance.

The chef/manager of a small restaurant would, for example, have a job high on skill variety (requiring all the skills of cooking plus the business skills of keeping accounts, and so on), high on task identity (starting with raw ingredients and ending with appetising meals), high on task significance (feeling that the meals have brought pleasure to the customers), high on autonomy (deciding the suppliers and the menus) and high on feedback (visiting the customers after they have finished their meals). In contrast, a person working for a fast-food chain grilling hamburgers would probably have a job low on skill variety (doing nothing but grilling hamburgers throughout the shift), low on task identity (simply grilling burgers and seldom preparing other food), low on task significance (not feeling that the cooking makes much of a difference when the burger is to be covered in tomato ketchup anyway), low on autonomy (grilling the burgers according to a routine, highly specified procedure) and low on feedback (receiving few comments from either co-workers or customers).

Changes occurring in the modern workplace have spurred theories that extend the JCM (Morgeson and Humphrey, 2008) to include social work characteristics (Karasek and Theorell, 1990), emotion work (Zapf, 2002) and electronic performance monitoring (Nebeker and Tatum, 1993). A significant extension of JCM is to work design that can help support the effectiveness and well-being of knowledge workers (Parker, 2014).

Contemporary, post-bureaucratic approaches to job design have drawn upon, and have sometimes reacted against, classical approaches to work practices (Grey, 2005). For many scholars, the paradigm shift in work redesign that has occurred over the past three decades revolves around variants of team-based working, including 'Japanese work systems' and high-performance work systems (HPWS).

Post-bureaucratic design: Japanese management

Three decades ago, influential management consultants proclaimed the need for Western companies to embrace the 'art of Japanese management' (Grey, 2005). The 'Japanese way of work' set off a process of job and work redesign, and concomitant changes in managing the employment relationship (Bratton, 1992; Thompson and McHugh, 2009).

Schonberger and Schonberger's (1982) analysis of the Japanese work system highlighted both horizontal and vertical job enlargement. Machines are arranged in a group or 'cell' – cellular technology – and multiskilled workers have flexible job boundaries including self-inspection, which means that the team completes a whole component from start to finish. The Japanese management work design was also based on total-quality control and the practice of zero or low inventory known as just-in-time. In the USA, these practices were studied and implemented as part of the *'lean production'* movement (Womack et al., 1990). The work team makes production and quality-improvement decisions. In other words, the form of job design resembles job B shown in Figure 3.3 earlier in this chapter.

Academics differ over whether or not the Japanese model constitutes a significant departure from traditional job design principles. While some argue that 'Japanisation of work' is distinctive because it creates a complex web of *dependency relationships* that calls for adroit management (Oliver and Wilkinson, 1988), others emphasise that the Japanese model is predicated on computer-controlled autonomy (Bratton, 1992) and constitutes a sophisticated mode of behavioural control designed to encourage a 'clan' culture that reproduces the conditions of workers' own subordination (Wells, 1993).

Digital Spotlight
Optimising the strengths of humans and machines

Source: Getty Images/Image Source/ Monty Rakusen

Over the last decade, newspaper headlines warning of substantial job losses resulting from increased automation have become commonplace. In 2019, for example, the BBC reported that up to 20 million manufacturing jobs around the world could be replaced by robots by 2030. There is little doubt that new technologies have begun 'encroaching into human skills in a way that was completely unprecedented' (Brynjolfsson and McAfee, 2014). However, it is important to note that, first, automation typically eliminates *activities*, rather than entire occupations and, secondly, that there are many areas in which humans outperform machines and will likely continue to do so (Chui et al., 2016). As a result, it is vital that organisational leaders carefully consider job and work design in the digital age in order to optimise the strengths of both.

Job design has significant implications in terms of employee commitment, satisfaction, productivity and performance. In regard to the latter, Wilson and Daugherty (2018) found that firms achieved the greatest performance improvements when they harnessed the benefits of machines *and* humans working in harmony. Machines in the form of AI possess speed, scalability and unparalleled quantitative capabilities. In contrast, human strengths include leadership, teamwork, creativity and social skills. Together they can yield 'collaborative intelligence'.

According to Wilson and Daugherty (2018), humans must assist machines in three ways: they must *train* the machines to perform certain tasks; *explain* the outcomes of those tasks, particularly when the results are counterintuitive or controversial; and *sustain* the responsible use of machines. In turn, the authors state that smart machines can *amplify* the cognitive strengths of humans; *interact* with customers and employees, for example, in the form of a chatbot, to free employees to engage in higher-level tasks; and *embody* human skills to extend physical capabilities (for example, a 'cobot' arm controlled by human workers that can lift and install heavy components). Wilson and Daugherty (2018) argue that, in addition to rethinking business processes to take advantage of the benefits of automation, managers and HR professionals will need to develop employees with 'fusion skills' that enable them work to effectively at the human-machine interface. This includes, for example, the capacity to know when (and, equally importantly, when not) to delegate to machines.

Stop! Thinking of a health-care environment, what tasks do you think could be successfully delegated to machines and which do you think should always be performed by humans?

Essential reading

Wilson, H. J. and Daugherty, P. R. (2018) Collaborative intelligence: humans and AI are joining forces. *Harvard Business Review*, July–August.

Note: This feature was contributed by Laura Steele.

Contemporary design: process-centred and high-performance systems

The Japanese model is no longer avant-garde, but numerous US and European studies show that team-based work systems in various forms have become the dominant reality (see, for example, Fröbel and Marchington, 2005). The alternatives have been numerous, some with significant overlap, and organisational theorists use a multitude of new acronyms such as BPR and HPWS to describe work regimes designed to encourage workers to collaborate in finding improvements in the way their work is organised and coordinated.

Business process re-engineering

Business process re-engineering (BPR) falls within the post-bureaucratic genre (Albizu and Olazaran, 2006). According to the re-engineering guru James Champy (1996, p. 3), BPR is 'about changing our managerial work, the way we think about, organize, inspire, deploy, enable, measure, and reward the value-adding operational work. It is about changing management itself.' Central to re-engineered work systems, argues Willmott (1995b), is the 'reconceptualization of core employees' from being considered a variable cost to being represented as a valuable asset capable of serving the customer without the need for a command-and-control style of leadership. With the primacy of 'customer value', workers are encouraged to exercise initiative in creating value for customers and thereby profits for the company. According to Hammer (1997, pp. 158–9):

> Obedience and diligence are now irrelevant. Following orders is no guarantee of success. Working hard at the wrong thing is no virtue. When customers are kings, mere hard work – work without understanding, flexibility, and enthusiasm – leads nowhere. Work must be smart, appropriately targeted, and adapted to the particular circumstances of the process and the customer ... Loyalty and hard work are by themselves quaint relics ... organizations must now urge employees to put loyalty to the customer over loyalty to the company – because that is the only way the company will survive.

This passage is most revealing. It presents the debate on employee commitment, shared commitment and reciprocity in a different light. Furthermore, in the re-engineered organisation, responsibility for the fate of workers shifts from managers to the marketplace – customers. In Hammer's (1997, p. 157) opinion, 'The company does not close plants or lay off workers – customers do, by their actions or inactions.'

Re-engineering is therefore market-driven. In essence, it views the management of people through an economic prism focusing on the relationship between the buyer and the seller of services or goods rather than between the employer and employee. In contrast to Beer et al.'s (1984, p. 153) 'four Cs' – commitment, competence, cost-effectiveness, congruence – Hammer and Champy (1993) emphasise only 'three Cs' – customers, competition and change. Moreover, reflecting the rhetoric of 'free markets', they emphasise that a government policy of 'tough love' towards business has created the need for BPR. For Champy (1996, p. 19), using a mixture of language discarded by the political 'old Left' and terminology of the 'new Right', 'a dictatorship of the customariat or ... a market democracy ... is the cause of a total revolution within the traditional, machine-like corporation'. According to proponents of BPR, the HRM implications include changing the criteria for selection, training and rewards. As Hammer (1996, p. xiii) points out, for HRM, 'everything must be rethought: the kinds of work people do, the jobs they hold, the skills they need, the ways in which their performance is measured and rewarded ... the roles managers play'. Moreover, HRM plays a crucial role in constituting an atomised self as line managers and workers are required to deal directly with external suppliers.

HRM web links

Visit the online resource centre at **www.bloomsbury.pub/bratton-hrm** for an introductory guide to BPR.

High-performance work systems

High-performance and agile work systems are concepts that currently dominate the work design literature. An agile work system as defined by Holbeche (2018, p. 9) is 'an organization's ability to develop and quickly apply flexible, nimble and dynamic capabilities'. It's a complex construct taking multiple forms which can apply to a number of post-bureaucratic organisational forms. A high-performance work system can be conceptualised as a strategic and holistic approach to managing people and work, through the successful implementation of a set of HR practices that contribute, at an operational level, to the totality of high-performance working.

The fundamental assumptions underpinning high-performance work (HPW) configurations are neither new nor radical. This approach combines a cluster of HPW practices that can (hopefully) lead to superior performance. The inference is that the achievement of HPW requires a deliberate and sustained focus on not only ensuring effectiveness in how people are managed and developed strategically in their workplace, but, importantly, in how work and jobs are organised and designed operationally to enable higher levels of workplace skills utilisation (Grant et al., 2014). Indeed, Belt and Giles (2009, p. 3) suggest that HPW is 'a general approach to managing organisations that aims to stimulate more effective employee involvement and commitment in order to achieve high levels of performance'. Perhaps the most important defining characteristic of an HPW system is that it 'possesses autonomy in the performance of its daily work activities' (Nijholt and Benders, 2010, p. 381).

Therefore, by organisation, Table 3.3 compares key characteristics of the HPW paradigm with bureaucratic work design model. The process-centred and HPW focus places much greater emphasis on human capability/value and on fostering a work environment in which workers are encouraged to

Table 3.3 The traditional and process-centred work models

Work design characteristic	Traditional focus	Process-centred/HPW focus
Structural design	Hierarchical	Flattened, boundaryless, network
Work organisation	Specialised and individual	Flexible and teams
Leadership	Autocratic	Distribution/multi-level
Focal point	Profit	Customer
Competitive advantage	Minimising costs	High-quality
Control	Centralised	Decentralised/team
Resources	Capital (e.g. technology)	People and information
Labour	Homogeneous	Culturally diverse
Quality	What is affordable	No compromise
Communications	Monologic mode (top-down)	Dialogic mode (exchange of views)

collaborate in action learning projects to seek improvements in the way their work is distributed and coordinated.

High-performance working is generally enacted through mutual employer–employee reciprocation: employers develop high-commitment and trust-building work practices, and, in return, employees experience higher levels of job autonomy and involvement (Thompson, 2003). The approaches most commonly attributed to high-performance working are high-involvement or 'radical decentralization' (Lee and Edmondson, 2017) and high-commitment management (Boxall and Macky, 2009) and high-engagement management (Bridger, 2015). Indeed, it may be argued that where intrinsically motivating high-involvement practices are used, mutually reinforcing extrinsic high-commitment (for example, benefit and reward) practices are also required. This implies a causal path, in that through, for example, effective job design, continuous development practices, relational leadership workers experience (or perceive) higher levels of participation and involvement and may subsequently be more inclined to experience higher levels of job commitment and organisational engagement.

Sustainable high-performance working is not generally achievable solely by upskilling workers; instead, high performance is some kind of function of an employee's ability, motivation, and the opportunity to deploy skills (Bloom et al., 2004, p. 40). In other words, the AMO formula examined in the Bath model of HRM. Macky and Boxall (2007) suggest that improved organisational performance is realised via three causal routes:

- employee capability setting the upper limit of performance;
- motivation influencing the extent to which that capability is applied;
- opportunity for employees to participate and apply their skills effectively.

A variant of sustainable high-performance working is the notion of 'smart working'. The CIPD (2008, p. 4) defines smart working as: 'An approach to organising work that aims to drive greater efficiency and effectiveness in achieving job outcomes through a combination of flexibility, autonomy and collaboration, in parallel with optimizing tools and working environments for employees'. Smart working has been the subject of extensive research conducted by the CIPD (2008). The Fair Work Framework (FWF) reflects a more radical approach to designing work. The Fair Work Convention report (2016, p. 5) defines fair work as: 'Work that offers effective voice, opportunity, security, fulfilment and respect; that balances the rights and responsibilities of employers and workers and that can generate benefits for individuals, organisations and society'. The FWF, which forms an important element of our discussion on 'reimagining HRM' – see Chapter 14 – extends work and job design into the domain of workplace governance and employment relations.

Workers' reactions to high-performance work practices or 'smart working' are likely to be shaped by their past experiences and perceptions of formal HR policies and the HR practices that translate policies into action (Messersmith et al., 2011; Olson et al., 2020). See Figure 1.5 and look at the potential impact of employee perception in influencing the effectiveness of high-performance work practices. Acknowledging the theoretical challenges of statistical causality, it suggests that between the actual implemented work practices and the subsequent behavioural change lies the imponderable 'black box' of HRM: how workers will perceive, react to and experience new work practices.

The degree of conceptual ambiguity enveloping the high-performance causal chain is fuelled by the lack of an agreed list of determinant internal high-performance HR practices, a challenge we explored in Chapter 2. The problem is compounded by a 'failure to operationalise HPWS sufficiently ... or the lack of evidence governing the direction of causation' (Danford et al., 2008). Other commentators have highlighted the difficulty for employers to know which particular HPW practices are best suited to their organisation and, crucially, how these should be configured, aligned and measured (Hughes, 2008). It is in part for this reason that the rhetoric of optimism surrounding enriched work designs in general, and HPWS in particular, is in direct conflict with the actual number of organisations implementing such practices (Parker and Ohly, 2013; Warhurst and Findlay, 2012).

Critiquing job and work design

We started this chapter by examining the meaning of work in contemporary Western society and then went on to evaluate four contrasting and significant work design approaches that map onto distinct historical developments: (1) classical Taylorism; (2) the job characteristic model; (3) Japanese management; and (4) contemporary high-performance models. The dominant narratives of work design are predicated upon the rational perspective of managerial decision-making – coherent acts of planning, choice and action. Graeber (2018) provocatively argues that perhaps a significant factor influencing work and job design is the process of 'bullshitization' – the growth of 'bullshit' jobs that are 'so completely pointless, unnecessary, or pernicious that even the employee cannot justify its existence' (pp. 9–10). According to Graeber, 'bullshit' jobs proliferate in large part because of the 'peculiar nature of managerial feudalism' (2018, p. 243). A 2016 US survey found that only 39 per cent of office workers' time was devoted to their designed work duties, owing to a rise in time dealing with emails, 'wasteful' meetings, 'ticking boxes' to satisfy superiors, and administrative tasks, such as writing up reports justifying what they do, and less and less time actually doing assigned duties.

Bolton's (2007) work reminds us of the centrality of job and work design to human dignity *in* and *at* work. The ways in which work is organised and managed can all operate to promote or deny dignity. According to Bolton, the notion of dignified work is about much more than escaping routine and mundane work or attaining a state of 'self-actualization'. But neither is it an individual thing. Instead, it is a multifaceted phenomenon that embodies both objective factors (for example, job security) and subjective factors (for example, respect). As such, job and work designs that offer a degree of responsible autonomy and social esteem and respect provide 'dignity *in* work'; work configurations that offer, among other things, 'voice' and safe and healthy working conditions, afford 'dignity *at* work' (Bolton, 2007).

We complete this chapter by critiquing job and work redesign and by identifying tension and paradox. With regard to classical work designs, some scholars suggest that Taylorism did not appeal to most employers (Rose, 1988). But this interpretation represents a woeful misreading of the actual development of work design. The direct and indirect influence of Taylorism on manual and non-manual jobs has been extensive (Littler and Salaman, 1984). Contemporary work design is imbued with neo-Taylorism.

Ritzer's (2004) 'McDonaldization of society' illustrates the adoption of neo-Taylorism to the fast-food industry:

> Bureaucracies emphasize control over people through the replacement of human judgment with the dictates of rules, regulations, and structures. Employees are controlled by the division of labor, which allocates to each office a limited number of well-defined tasks. Incumbents must do the tasks, and no others, in a manner prescribed by the organization. They may not, in most cases, devise idiosyncratic ways of doing those tasks. Furthermore, by making few, if any, judgments, people begin to resemble human robots or computers. Having reduced people to this status, leaders of bureaucracies can think about actually replacing human beings with machines. (Ritzer, 2000, p. 24)

Interactive service fast-food work is characterised as low-paid, low-skilled, low-autonomy and poor career prospects. The term 'McJob' (Etzioni, 1988) embodies the worst elements of service sector employment. In spite of the research indicating that 'McJobs' are boring, unchallenging and controlling, some mainstream scholars have suggested that fast-food work and HR practices are a more nuanced phenomenon that allows for unambiguously negative outcomes, but also offers positive outcomes as a potential 'stepping-stone' to a rewarding career (Daniels, 2004) and 'job security' to younger and older employees (Gould, 2010, p. 799).

The 'call-centre discourse' was part of the dominant rhetoric of the so-called 'new economy' in the 2000s. Critical researchers have drawn attention to contemporary Taylorist-type surveillance in call centres. Various metaphors have been used to capture call-centre work: 'electronic sweatshops' or the 'electronic panopticon', the 'assembly-line in the head' and the often-quoted 'electronic Taylorism' (for example, Callaghan and Thompson, 2001; Sewell, 1998; Taylor, 2010; Taylor and Bain, 1998; Thompson and McHugh, 2009). Such arguments echo earlier debates on deskilling in manual and routine clerical work. Job specialisation has also been linked to class, gender and race inequality within the context of the organisation. Class hierarchies are organised through job tasks and responsibilities – typically skills performed by minority individuals are devalued in the workplace, which are, in turn, linked to organisational hierarchies and pay (Acker, 2016). When jobs are redesigned to increase job specialisation, they reduce the variety of tasks performed by some workers; other co-workers then 'capture' the learning and discretion associated with performing the vacated tasks. Job specialisation can thus erode pay for some workers while advantaging other co-workers undertaking the extra tasks. Therefore, without fixed job hierarchies and pay rates, generally associated with non-unionised workplaces, interdependencies in organisational task allocation yield unequal pay premiums among co-workers (Wilmers, 2020).

Critical workplace scholars offer a more disparaging and ideological evaluation of the JCM and job enrichment theory (Thompson and van den Broek, 2010). Friedman's (1977) early, but influential, study argues that although job enrichment techniques may increase job satisfaction and commitment, the key focus remains on managerial control. Thompson offers one of the most penetrating early critiques of job redesign. He argues that many job enrichment arrangements 'offer little or nothing that is new and are often disguised forms of intensified [managerial] control' (1989, p. 141). The application of JCM principles is prescriptive but the potential of AMO for understanding the so-called HRM 'black box' remains elusive (Kellner et al., 2019). Contemporary work design such as business process re-engineering (BPR) has come under scrutiny by workplace scholars. Grint and Willcocks (1995), for example, offer a scathing review of BPR, arguing that it is not new and pointing out that it is essentially political in its rhetorical and practical manifestations. Willmott is similarly disparaging of BPR, emphasising that re-engineering is 'heavily top-down' and pointing out that the re-engineered organisation, using information technology while creating fewer hierarchical structures, also produces 'a fist-full of dynamic processes ... notably, the primacy of hierarchical control and the continuing treatment of employees as cogs in the machine' (Willmott, 1995b, p. 91). As Storey observes, workers fear BPR initiatives mean brutal job losses aimed only at enhanced profits: 'They are usually correct on both counts' (2018, p. 97). BPR does not obviate the inherent conflict of interest between employers and employees. When examined in the context of employee relations, BPR can be interpreted 'as the latest wave in a series of initiatives ... to increase the cooperation/productivity/adaptability of staff' (Willmott, 1995b, p. 96).

The antecedents of high-performance work systems (HPWS) can be found in the neo-human relations and Japanese team-based movements developed over the last four decades. High-performance work designs are most often presented as being positive for workers in that they provide for more skills and autonomy and thereby contribute to increased job satisfaction and commitment (Boxall et al., 2015). However, it has been argued to the contrary that rather than being about working 'smarter', HPWSs have been associated with job losses and increased work intensification (Ramsay et al., 2000) and forms of 'controlled participation' (Danford et al., 2008; Edwards et al., 2002, p. 36; Godard, 2004). Bratton's (1992) study of teams also reminds us of the need to develop a context-sensitive understanding of self-managed teams. These critical accounts suggest that high-performance work design may not necessarily have universally 'positive' or 'negative' outcomes for workers. Rather, outcomes can vary depending on contingencies such as hierarchy and social relations within the workplace, and the presence and power of trade unions (see Edwards et al., 2002).

Paradox is evident in work system design, and there are a number of ways in which to think about and conceptualise this paradox. Here we use a simple model presented by Jaffee (2001) and illustrated in Figure 3.8. The model shows that paradox stems from what is called 'differentiation–integration tension'. This refers to the inherent tension between management strategies for achieving a rational division of economic activities and, simultaneously, for ensuring that these activities are coordinated and integrated. Differentiation and job specialisation are fundamental management principles that underscore organisational goals to control costs. As organisations increase in size and complexity, integration becomes an issue: the coordination and integration of interdependent activities.

The tension between differentiation and integration can be illustrated by a familiar manufacturing strategy: that management initially redesigns work involving a rigid division of labour and highly specialised tasks. The intended consequence is to rationalise operations and make workers more produc-

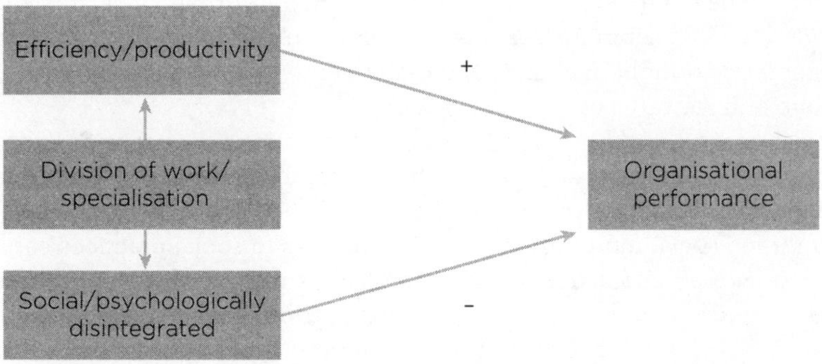

Figure 3.8 The work design–human factor paradox

Source: Adapted from Jaffee (2001).

tive. The unintended consequence, however, is a work experience that produces low levels of job satisfaction, motivation and commitment. This, as we discussed earlier, can limit the positive contribution made by job specialisation. Topcic et al.'s (2016) study suggests that different high-performance work designs are more strongly associated with negative pressures on employees than others. Comparing a 'challenge demand' HPW model – focusing on performance evaluation and ongoing learning – with a 'job resource' model, centred around flexible working hours and participation in decision-making, the study found a positive relationship between the challenge demand model and increased employee stress. The pressures associated with 'challenge demand' work design may, therefore, 'drive out HR support activities ... needed to sustain employee motivation and morale' (Scarbrough, 2000, p. 16).

The tension between management control and worker empowerment 'ties managers up in knots' (Gulati, 2018). Management are left with a conundrum: how to control the labour process without creating the conditions that inhibit the enlistment of workers' knowledge, creativity and discretionary efforts. As Geary and Dobbins (2001, p. 5) remind us:

> Management remains caught between two opposing imperatives: attempts at regulating employees too tightly run the risk of endangering the employees' creativity and commitment to management goals, while empowering employees runs the risk of reducing management control.

This fundamental paradox at the heart of the employment relationship becomes even more acute when managers introduce internal and *external* flexibility. In terms of the latter, Legge's (2007) analysis of the flexible networked organisational configuration identifies the tension that occurs when employers strive for both control *and* commitment. Organisational flexibility resulting from global just-in-time supply chains and interorganisational business arrangements are, she deftly observes, likely to 'inhibit the development of commitment to a common organizational culture and often involve the disruption of the psychological contract' (Legge, 2007, p. 53).

The notion of tension and paradox is apparent in contemporary process-centred BPR and team-based work designs. While new work design forms appear to present a strategic 'developmental' opportunity, other structural developments such as strategic outsourcing, the doctrine of short-term shareholder value, are 'highly inimical to a strategic approach' to HRM (Storey, 2018, p. 103). Some scholars (e.g. Piore and Sabel, 1984) consider that self-managed teams reverse Taylorism, others make a compelling case that new post-bureaucratic designs have, paradoxically, revitalised Weber's typology of bureaucracy. New performance-related incentives, for example, have generated behavioural rules that reinforce bureaucratic control: 'Thus, intriguingly, the use of bureaucratic control emerges as the main element of labour control in this type of workplace' (Pulignano and Stewart, 2006, p. 104).

Physical spaces structure social life in organisations. Gonsalves's (2020) recent study draws attention to another form of paradox, the 'flexibility paradox'. He suggests a reconfiguration of physical space intended to reduce costs can have the unintended consequence of disrupting taken-for-granted social mores and practices. Changes to social practices can result in workers feeling less concerned about trait inferences of dependability and commitment arising from their physical presence. Covid-19 has intensified precarious forms of paid work and, at the same time, forced many employers and permanent core employees to start working from home, spurring more long-term questions about virtual work policies. Therefore, these findings contribute to understanding the significance of the relationship between flexible work policies, temporal flexibility and physical space.

Summary

This chapter defined work as a physical and mental activity performed to produce or achieve something of value at a particular place and time, under explicit or implicit instructions, in return for a reward. Since the epoch of the Industrial Revolution scholars have studied job and work design. We explained that job and work design is embedded in the organisation's structure, and these can range from hierarchical bureaucratic to decentralised network/virtual forms.

The chapter examined alternative work designs. Contemporary organisational scholars provide evidence in abundance of internal and external 'flexibility' designed to minimise costs and increase profitability. In many cases, 'new' work regimes embody neo-Taylorist principles and a technical mode of managerial control. The research on non-standard employment and the 'McDonaldization of work' suggests both change and continuation in work design.

Critical analysis of HPWSs show that the design is a complex 'interlocking' arrangement of technical, behavioural and cultural dimensions. The literature is couched in the language of 'high-involvement' or 'employee empowerment' but the evidence on investment in high-quality training convincingly suggests, in most cases, the reality does not match the rhetoric, and 'non-educative work is systemic' (Bratton, 1999, p. 491). BPR and HPWS practices provide an ideological platform to legitimise and gain support from workers for the new work designs. In the context of capitalist employment relationships, tension and unintended consequences will arise with each new work system, making it imperative to understand how new forms of work can change employees' perceptions of the content of the psychological contract.

Finally, we have cautioned against conceptualising new work systems as a smooth transition from one ideal-type model to another. The tendency to compress the specific into categories of general trends not only compresses variations in work design, but also attaches a false coherence to emerging work forms. Change has to be situated within the machinations of the wider context, which is sporadic, and subject to constant renegotiation.

PART 3

Review questions

1. Why define 'work' by its social context rather than by the content of the activity itself? What do writers mean when they say job and work design has to be situated within the machinations of the wider context?
2. 'Job enrichment work design is simply an attempt by managers to control individuals at work.' Do you agree or disagree? Discuss.
3. 'McJobs' is a term often used by critics of the 'gig economy' to capture the realities of workplace life confronting young people today. How do the job design concepts discussed in this chapter help you to understand the term 'McJobs'? Is it an accurate description of employment today?

Search & Watch

Visit YouTube and search for **Matthew Taylor, James Manyika: Seeking autonomous and flexible work**. What are the implications of flexible work designs for HRM?

Then go to the video hub at www.bloomsbury.pub/bratton-hrm and watch the interview with **Gregor Karolus Chief HR Officer, Springer Nature** (Part 2). Watch Gregor speak about implementing HPWSs, and then think about the following questions: (1) Why did Gregor move to HR? (2) How can HR play a positive role in creating a high-performance workplace? (3) Why does Gregor believe that trust is important in an HPWS?

Legal Focus

Redesigning work may lead to the organisation reducing its workforce – this is sometimes referred to as 'downsizing'. In the UK, a legal definition of 'redundancy' is found in section 139 (1) of the Employment Rights Act (ERA) 1996. This states that a redundancy occurs in three situations: the employer has ceased, or intends to cease, business, the employer is relocating or is reducing his workforce. Compensation for redundancy was one of the first protection rights introduced into British labour law. The aim of a redundancy payment is to recognise an employee's stake in their job. This means that the employee's stake increases the longer s/he has worked for the employer.

Task Search online for government information in your jurisdiction about redundancy. (1) What is meant by 'redundancy'? (2) To what extent is there a statutory duty on an employer to consult with the union or employee representatives when making a certain number of employees redundant?

Reference
See Deborah Lockton and Tom Brown's *Employment Law* (2020), pp. 379-98, for a discussion on the Employment Rights Act (ERA) 1996, covering statutory provisions and case law related to redundancy.

Chapter case: Virtual teams at G&Q Manufacturing

The setting

According to Statistics Canada, 40% of Canada's workers found themselves working from home in 2020 due to the Covid-19 pandemic, a far cry from the less than 10% who worked remotely in 2018. This will likely be a permanent change for many. One of the reasons employers were hesitant about implementing such work arrangements in the past was the fear that without in-person oversight, workers would not be as productive. However, the necessity for social distancing and self-isolation during the global pandemic forced employers to continue operations without the physical presence of line managers. While the experience showed employers that remote employees are more likely to overwork when the boundaries between their personal and work lives become blurred at home, it also presented new challenges in managing work relationships integral to surviving in the post-pandemic marketplace.

The problem

When G&Q Manufacturing, a large agricultural machinery manufacturer located in Manitoba, announced that all its administrative staff were to work from home due to the COVID-19 pandemic, Finance Manager Ryan Cheng was not overly concerned about his department. Although he knew there would be challenges, he also had confidence that they would continue to be a highly functioning team. There had been few conflicts between team members in the office and they were often seen together socialising outside of the workplace.

Ryan arranged for weekly team video conference calls and for the first couple of weeks, he saw little change in the team's approach to their work and their colleagues. They did express some concerns about how their demanding workloads might take up more of their personal time at home, but overall everyone seemed upbeat and pleased about not having to commute to the workplace every day.

However, as the company continued to require employees to work remotely with no end in sight, Ryan began to notice a difference in the tone and demeanour of his staff. When one employee made a humorous comment about Finance Clerk Liam sitting in his kitchen during a conference call, the normally talkative Liam fell silent and did not participate any further in the meeting. Jia, a single mother with two small children, became visibly upset when two employees made remarks about her children crying in the background and the fact she wasn't wearing her 'usual make-up'. A recent hire, Aamir, was not invited to an online meeting and he later angrily called Ryan to complain about 'discriminatory treatment'.

When the team failed to meet an important budgetary deadline, Ryan was finally forced to take action. He sought help from Dylan Lee, another manager in the organisation whose team seemed to be thriving. 'When your staff are at work their personal home lives are not visible, but now they are all in different places and situations,' he told Ryan. 'They are isolated from their team and the actions of their colleagues may be more readily misinterpreted. Your new virtual team needs to develop communication and collaboration skills for this different way of working.'

PART 3

The assignment

Working either alone or in a study group, write a report to *Finance Manager Ryan Cheng* answer the following:

1. What do you see as the advantages to a company like G&Q Manufacturing of its employees working from home? What would be the disadvantages?
2. How does the work of Bolton (2007) regarding work design and human dignity apply to the situation at G&Q Manufacturing?
3. What ideas do you have that could help improve the virtual team's collaboration and communication skills as Dylan has suggested?

Essential reading

Connelly, C. E. and Turel, O. (2016) Effects of team emotional authenticity on virtual team performance. *Frontiers in Psychology, 7*: 1336.

Felstead, A. and Henseke, G. (2017) Assessing the growth of remote working and its consequences for effort, well-being and work-life balance. *New Technology, Work and Employment*, *32*(3): 195–212.

Gallacher, G. and Hossain, I. (2020) Remote work and employment dynamics under COVID-19: evidence from Canada. *Canadian Public Policy*, *46*(S1): S44–S54.

Kramer, A. and Kramer, K.Z. (2020) The potential impact of the COVID-19 pandemic on occupational status, work from home, and occupational mobility. *Journal of Vocational Behavior*, *119*, 1034422.

Maes, J. D. and Weldy, T. G. (2018) Building effective virtual teams: expanding OD research and practice. *Organisation Development Journal*, *36*(3): 83–90.

Note: This case was contributed by Lori Rilkoff.

Further reading

Bakker, A. B. and van Wingerden, J. (2021) Rumination about COVID-19 and employee well-being: the role of playful work design. *Canadian Psychology, 62*(1): 73–9.

Donnelly, R. and Johns, J. (2021) Recontextualising remote working and its HRM in the digital economy: an integrated framework for theory and practice. *International Journal of Human Resource Management, 32*(1): 84–105.

Edgell, S. and Granter, E. (2020) *The Sociology of Work* (3nd edn). London: Sage.

Godard, J. (2004) A critical assessment of the high-performance paradigm. *British Journal of Industrial Relations*, *42*(2): 349–78.

Graeber, D. (2018) *Bullshit Jobs: A Theory*. New York: Simon & Schuster.

Holbeche, L. (2018) *The Agile Organization: How to Build an Engaged, Innovative and Resilient Business* (2nd edn). London: Kogan Page Publishers.

Lehdonvirta, V. (2018) Flexibility in the gig economy: managing time on three online piecework platforms. *New Technology, Work and Employment*, *33*: 13–29.

Parker, S. K., Morgeson, F. P. and Johns, G. (2017) One hundred years of work design research: looking back and looking forward. *Journal of Applied Psychology*, *102*(3): 403–20.

Storey, J. (2018) New organizational structures and forms. In J. Storey, P. M. Wright and D. Ulrich (eds) *The Routledge Companion to Strategic Management*, (pp. 90–105). London: Routledge.

Yavorsky, J. E., Ruggs, E. and Dill, J. (2021) Gendered skills and unemployed men's resistance to 'women's work'. *Gender, Work and Organization*. DOI:10.1111/gwao.12694

CHAPTER 4

WORKFORCE PLANNING AND DIVERSITY

outline

- Introduction
- The nature and scope of workforce planning
- The workforce planning process
- Workforce diversity
- Flexibility and precariousness
- Critiquing workforce planning
- Summary
- Further reading

Source: iStock.com/Prostock-Studio

objectives

After studying this chapter, you should be able to:

1 Explain the meaning of workforce planning and its importance for strategic HRM

2 Explain the workforce planning process by which organisations can forecast their current and future workforce requirements

3 Understand and critically evaluate diversity management

4 Critically evaluate the various approaches to flexible working and explain how some HR practices have a disproportionate effect on diverse social groups, specifically by class, gender and age

Introduction

How certain are you that you can make a plan for the future? The Covid-19 pandemic and global warming pose an existential threat to humanity. The coronavirus has severely disrupted globalisation, national economies and workplaces. In Britain, Brexit will have wide-scale implications for companies and organisations across sectors of the economy – manufacturing, hospitality, food processing and agriculture. In all likelihood, when you graduate you will face a very different workplace and labour markets (Coates, 2018). Climate change threatens livelihoods across the planet and to pivot to emissions-reducing goals, proactive state-led economic activity will need to build new, locally suitable infrastructure and practices (Järvensivu et al., 2019). Will efforts to reduce carbon emissions impact your employment goals? Are you more or less confident of making a plan now that Britain has exited the European Union? Managers too plan for the future in order to ensure that their organisation has the right number of people at the right time, with the right kind of attributes and skills, which are aligned with the strategic objectives of the organisation (Baron et al., 2010). A plan that achieves this is called a *workforce plan*, and its purpose is to provide some degree of certainty and control over future HR-related events. However, in addition to the Covid-19, global warming and Brexit crises, two other converging crises – artificial intelligence (AI) and disruption of European and global supply chains – make the process of workforce planning increasingly challenging. The crises have increased the need for planning to become both an analytical process for predictability and a creative process for working with unpredictability. As you will recall from reading Chapter 2, it is important to understand HR practices within their strategic context and the ability of HRM professionals to participate in strategic decision-making has been enabled by their use of HR 'analytics' (Hesketh, 2014).

PART 3

In this chapter we examine the processes involved in developing a workforce plan and explain why organisations undertake such HR activity. We then address diversity in organisations and explain that it is multifaceted and not without controversy. In addition to being more diverse, the contemporary workforce is more flexible, and we detail this development. We conclude with a critique of workforce planning, highlighting the disproportionate implications on social groups by gender, age and class. We begin, however, by looking at the nature, scope and importance of workforce planning.

The nature and scope of workforce planning

What we now call workforce planning was originally referred to *as 'manpower planning'*. During the twentieth century, this represented a response by personnel and HR managers to ensure that the necessary supply of people was forthcoming to allow targets to be met. In theory at least, a 'manpower' plan attempted to balance both the demand and supply of people within an organisational context. The notion of a balance between demand and supply reflects the influence of classical labour economics, in which movement towards an 'equilibrium' serves as an ideal. Traditionally, *Manpower planning* was concerned primarily with numbers; that is, with the number of persons available – or potentially available – to specific labour markets (Psacharopoulos, 1991). But beyond the literate accuracy of the word, there are deeper conceptual objections to the use of 'manpower'. Stainer (1971) criticised traditional approaches as being too detached from the organisation's strategic objectives. Because the interaction between the demand and supply of people was highly complex within a context that included aims of optimisation and overall equilibrium, manpower planning attracted operational research and the application of statistical techniques (Bartholomew, 1971). Manpower planning was also associated with more centralised, sophisticated computer modelling and became probably beyond the comprehension of most managers (Parker and Caine, 1996). Hence, during the 1980s, manpower planning acquired a poor reputation as a system with few benefits and only a few examples of when 'comprehensive and systematic manpower planning [was] fully integrated into strategic planning' (Cowling and Walters, 1990, p. 6). More user-friendly PC-based personnel information systems enabled personnel departments to build up a 'toolkit' of analytics consisting of key labour measures relating to, for example, worker turnover, retention and absenteeism. All of which could be relatively easily expressed graphically to reveal trends and future paths.

During the 1990s, there was increasing acknowledgement that manpower planning did not address some important workforce behavioural issues, such as work motivation. Moreover, HRM academics and professionals sought to make an explicit link between strategy, structure and people. The process to bring this about was increasingly referred to as *human resource planning* (HRP). In addition to being a more acceptable gender-neutral term, HRP, for some scholars, symbolised the intention to link HR practices to superior organisational performance (see Chapter 2). Importantly, HRP was seen to encompass not just 'hard' statistical forecasting of labour demand and supply, but also embracing plans across the whole range of HR activity, including such apparently 'soft' issues as employee motivation, commitment and organisational culture, so key HR practices could meet the needs of its workers, enhance their potential and meet the performance needs of the business strategy. In the 1990s, as with HRM in general, there emerged 'hard' and 'soft' versions of HRP (Iles, 2001, p. 140).

In the late 2000s more varied approaches and methods relating to planning emerged. Modern *workforce planning* (WP) has its roots in 'manpower' planning, 'succession' planning and 'human resource' planning (Turner, 2010). Workforce planning centres on the premise that an organisation's corporate strategy should fashion its HR strategy (Chapter 2). According to the CIPD, workforce planning is 'a core business process to align changing organisational needs with people strategy' (CIPD, 2018).

Workforce planning, however, is far from a standardised activity. It covers a wide range of activities. It is defined by Reilly (1996) as 'a process in which an organisation attempts to estimate the demand for labour and evaluate the size, nature and sources of supply which will be required to meet the demand'. Mathis et al. (2014, p. 44) posit that its objective is: 'to ensure that the organisation has the *right number of people* with the *right capabilities*, at the *right times*, and in the *right places*.' Drawing on Curson et al. (2010), we define workforce planning as:

> The process of forecasting the demand and supply of skills against the requirements of future services delivery or production in a context of uncertainty and change. It is a process that must be set in a particular organisational context and can cover many different activities, including analytics, and the diagnostic and strategic understanding of HRP.

Workforce planning can be supported through the use of human resource information systems (HRISs) which can provide a more systemic consideration of skill requirements and their linkage with the organisation's strategy (Bhuiyan et al., 2014). Indeed, HRISs can generate, capture, track and disseminate organisational knowledge, in all its manifestations in software packages and online, can be a key feature of knowledge management and organisational learning, and both can be facilitated by an HRIS. Indeed, HRISs can generate, capture, track and disseminate organisational knowledge, in all its manifestations in software packages and algorithms. Both knowledge management and organisational learning, for example, can be facilitated by an HRIS; what has been described as a form of 'organisational intelligence' (Nagendra and Deshpande, 2014).

WP can be broader in scope than forecasting the demand and supply of skills or use of analytics; it can include 'intelligent' planning which takes into account not only strategic management plans but also considers worker behaviours and organisational culture in relation to skill procurement. Leeds Teaching Hospitals NHS Trust, for example, expanded conventional WP activity to include a multidisciplinary group within the Trust in order to maximise the value of insight from business units and achieve consistency across finance, workforce, activity and to ensure all business cases are robust and comprehensive (LTHT, 2019). Studies of 'best practice' WP emphasise it is an ongoing process. As Curson et al., (2010, p.117) observe, workforce planning should be 'a continuous and iterative process with regular, preferably annual, cycles to supply skill needs'.

Organisations and some scholars argue that a turbulent business environment and the inherently 'political nature of managerial decision-making' renders WP redundant (Iles, 2001, p. 140). While recognising the important criticism of WP, others suggest four broad reasons for the continued importance of planning:

- It provides the information on the quantity and quality of people needed to achieve the organisation's strategic objectives.
- It can identify potential deficits or surpluses of people, enabling organisations to make more informed decisions about any gaps, and the best use of its people.
- It enables better control over numbers employed and labour costs.
- It provides a profile of current workforce, which informs diversity management decisions.

WP helps to make sense of the socially constructed nature of organisations, but points to a process that extends beyond the collection and analysis of labour market data. The next section examines the WP process.

Reflective question

How do you think the Covid-19 pandemic affects workforce planning?

Ethical Insight
Diversity and inclusion: a question of economics or ethics?

Over the past four decades, numerous academic and practitioner publications have set out the economic arguments in favour of diversity and inclusion (D&I). Business in the Community (2020), for example, recently reported that the 'business case for diversity is clear: diverse organisations perform better, have higher worker satisfaction and better financial returns, and are more innovative'. Indeed, McKinsey & Company (2015) found that companies with strong gender and ethnic diversity are 15% and 35% respectively more likely to outperform their competitors. In addition, a survey by PwC (2017) revealed that 54% of women and 45% of men stated that they researched whether a company had D&I policies in place before deciding whether to accept a position.

There are, however, a growing number of voices calling for individuals and organisations to stop relying upon the business case for D&I. Naima McCloskey (2020), for example, argues that studies such as those outlined above 'become the fodder that those from marginalised backgrounds are compelled to compile and cite to "convince" their executives to engage in even superficial "inclusion" initiatives'. She continues that inclusion efforts that focus on how people already leading businesses 'can reap *further* material rewards seems decidedly ill-suited for anything other than vacuous press releases, ineffective committees and events where the canapé budget far outweighs resources allocated for anything more meaningful'.

In addition, Naima McCloskey (2020) cautions that if an individual from a marginalised group within society is hired, they may come to the workplace with the weight of expectation that their status will (or at least should) boost the organisation's performance. It is a heavy burden for anyone to be required to carry. Also, focusing on the business case may serve to create the impression that D&I initiatives are an 'optional extra' that can be abandoned during times of economic hardship (an argument that is supported by evidence that unemployment is rising faster for women and people of colour in the United States in the wake of the coronavirus pandemic (Kalev, 2020)). Finally, despite all the attention given to it, the business case does not actually seem to have been particularly convincing: progress towards equality within the workplace has been slow and stilted.

Subjecting D&I – or, indeed, any other ethics or social justice concern – to a financial cost benefit analysis is arguably at best degrading and at worst dangerous. (There was, after all, once a compelling 'business case' for slavery). Instead, Wang (2020) argues that 'it's time to try a new framing: firms need to view D&I as an important part of a broader movement to bring more equitable economic opportunities and enshrine human dignity to those who have been historically marginalized'.

Stop! What is your view: should we cease making the business case for diversity and inclusion or will some people always need to see the economic evidence?

Essential reading

Eswaran, V. (2019) The business case for diversity in the workplace is now overwhelming. *World Economic Forum*, 29 April.

Note: This feature was contributed by Laura Steele.

The workforce planning process

The literature makes it clear that workforce planning is far from a homogeneous activity (Curson et al., 2010, p. 112). It covers a wide range of activities and these can be dissimilar in different organisational contexts. There is general consensus, however, that recognises the demand for skills is derived demand and that effective WP entails planners having the strategic understanding and nuances associated with strategic management. In broad terms, the workforce planning process has three stages:

- forecasting future demand for human resources;
- forecasting the internal and external supply of human resources;
- formulating and implementing an action plan.

Figure 4.1 summarises the workforce planning process.

Demand forecasting

Internal demand forecasting aims to determine the future workforce in terms of numbers and skills or competencies, to meet the organisation's strategic goals (Cappelli, 2009). The forecasts are typically associated with particular job categories and skill sets. The process is informed by a SWOT analysis. Demand forecasting may be undertaken using either quantitative or qualitative methods.

Assessing demand – quantitative approaches

- *Time series analysis* studies the organisation's past and present employment levels in various departments, job categories or skills areas to predict future staffing needs. Trend analysis is useful as an initial estimate only, since given constant contextual change it is unlikely that previous trends will determine future trends.
- *Ratio analysis* involves making predictions of staffing needs based on the ratio between some variable (e.g. sales volume) and the number of staff required to deliver the service (e.g. number of salespeople). Ratio analysis assumes that productivity remains about the same, but it is more useful than time series analysis if there are significant changes between past and future expectations.

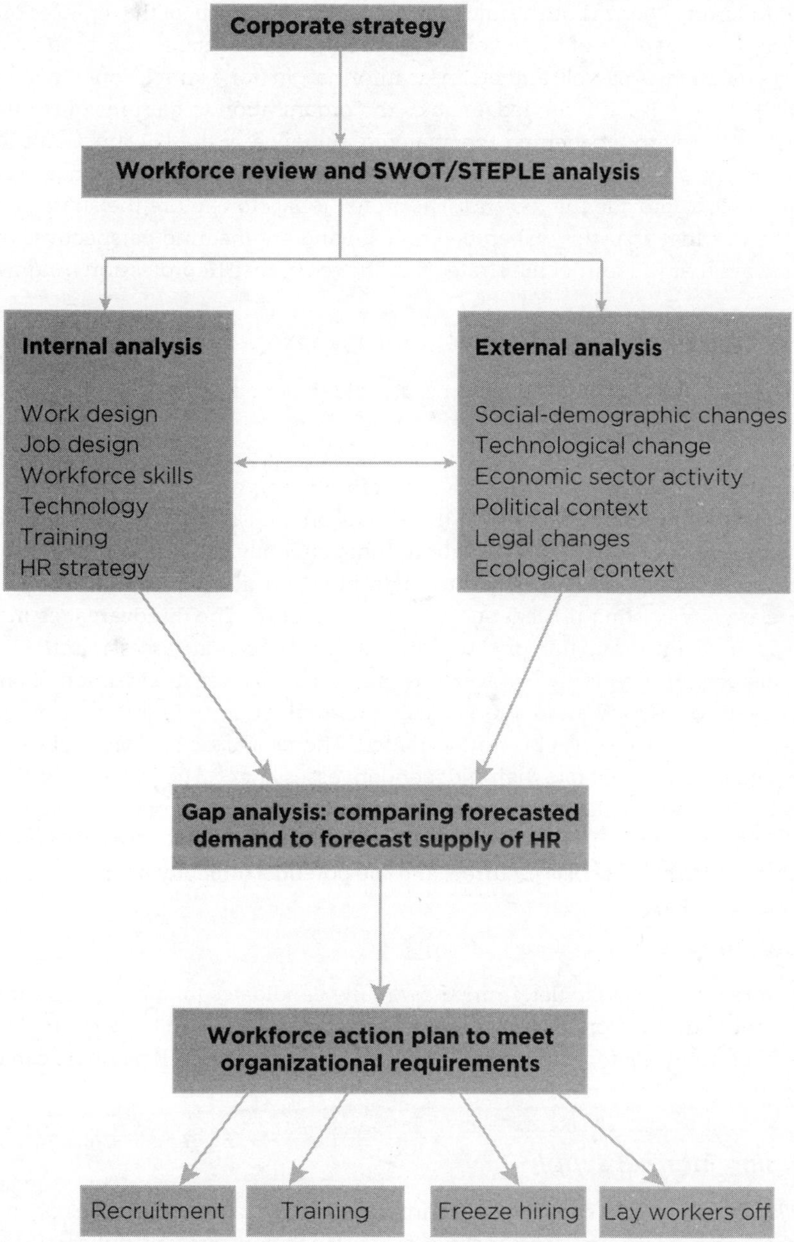

Figure 4.1 The workforce planning process

- *Multiple regression* is a more sophisticated statistical method to determine the effect of one variable (e.g. number of acute-care beds in a hospital) on another variable (e.g. number of required nurses) as a predictor of staffing needs. The accuracy of multiple regression is dependent on the availability of the data and the size of the sample.

Workforce planning is helped by HR analytics, which enables HR professionals to gain insights into their workforce. Described as a 'must have' capability for the HR profession, HR analytics, also known as workforce analytics, is both a strategic and operational concept that enables organisations to understand important aspects of their workforce through using data. It uses both people-data, collected by HR systems (such as payroll) and business information (for example, operations performance data). At its core, HR analytics, it is argued, enables the organisation to gain insights into their workforce and can be a pathway to broadening the strategic influence of the HR function (CIPD, 2019d). However, there are some potential negative effects of HR analytics for HR professionals. The HR analytics industry often fails to provide the tools for HR professionals to capture the strategic value of HR data and there is a risk that analytics will embed finance and engineering perspectives on HRM at boardroom level in ways that will restrict the strategic influence of the HR profession (Angrave et al., 2016).

Assessing demand – qualitative approaches

The qualitative methods rely on expert stakeholder judgement. Two methods are used to collect data: nominal group and Delphi techniques.

- *Nominal group technique* draws on expert informants and asks each questions on workforce planning. Each informant writes down their ideas on the issue or problem, clarification is then sought, followed by discussion and evaluation. Independently, each informant is then asked to rank the ideas. A key advantage is the involvement of expert informants and it is a useful approach when there are few existing precedents on how to proceed. The disadvantages include subjectivity and the potential for 'group thinking' which leads to less accurate assessment.
- *Delphi technique* typically involves external experts as well as key internal employees. Participants are asked to respond anonymously using a survey questionnaire to a problem on HR planning. Direct face-to-face contact is not permitted. The results are collated and each group member uses the feedback to recalibrate their independent assessment. The process continues until a consensus has been obtained (Rothwell, 1995). As with the *nominal group technique*, an advantage of the *Delphi technique* is the involvement of expert informants and a focus on the future. Disadvantages include the time and costs incurred, and the potential difficulty in synthesising diverse opinions.

Supply forecasting

Supply forecasting aims to determine how many candidates for a projected vacant position will likely come from within the organisation and how many positions will have to be filled by external candidates. To project the supply of internal and outside candidates, HR planners can use different analytics and sources of information.

Assessing internal supply

- *Skills inventories* can supply detailed information about the capabilities of current employees. Data gathered on each employee include current position, present duties and responsibilities, skills, qualifications and training undertaken over time in the organisation. To be useful, skills inventories must be updated regularly.
- *Employee flow analysis* involves examining employee turnover and wastage analysis. Morrell et al. (2001) have suggested that explanations of voluntary employee turnover fall into two categories: labour market and psychological motives. Research on employee turnover has focused on the latter, seeking to explore more closely why voluntary turnover occurs, which is particularly important given the costs of replacing and recruiting new staff, as well as the pressure on the remaining staff to cover the work. Morrell et al. (2004) suggested the use of surveys, career guidance and exit interviews to minimise turnover.

$$\text{Wastage analysis is: } \frac{\text{the number of employees leaving in a specific period}}{\text{the average number employed in the same period}} \times 100$$

As a general rule, waste declines within different age groups, when unemployment is high and within different categories of employees, such as gender (Gallagher, 2000).

- *Succession planning* is the process of identifying and developing potential future leaders or senior managers, as well as individuals to fill other business-critical positions, either in the short term or the long term (CIPD, 2020j). According to the CIPD, succession planning is important to both large blue-chip companies and SMEs, but the practice has declined because of flatter and boundaryless organisational structures and rapid change in the business environment. Succession planning is complicated because it has emerged that, despite expectations, not all baby boomers retire, either because they are in good health or the 2008 GFC significantly reduced retirement savings and they cannot afford to retire (Friedberg, 2020).
- *Markov modelling* is derived from probability theory. The technique aims to track the overall pattern of employee movement between positions inside the organisation and an outward movement from the organisation and develop a transitional probability matrix for forecasting internal supply by specific categories, such as position and gender. The modelling is done by a computer, but the underlying logic is straightforward: when an employee moves from one position to another they have to be replaced and this replacement typically comes from the position below the incumbent who is moving on (Parker and Caine, 1996). From this information, success plans and replacement charts can be developed.

Assessing external supply

An organisation has access to external statistics to help project the supply of potential new employees. Examples include: graduates from schools/university/college; skill levels, population density; age profile; local unemployment rates.

The WP process extends beyond the notion of an 'equilibrium' between demand and supply which is more a theoretical concept. The more probable situation is one of continuous imbalance as a result of the dynamic conditions facing any organisation, people's behaviour and the imperfections of mathematical models. The 'diagnostic approach' (Fyfe, 1986) builds on and broadens the demand and supply approach to identify problem areas and understand why they were occurring. A diagnostic approach involves using the above techniques, such as employee turnover and wastage, as well as by obtaining qualitative data from interviewing workers. Such interviews might reveal concerns with job satisfaction and the career paths open to workers, or breaches of the psychological contract (discussed in Chapter 1). The loss of talented workers has important cost implications, and a diagnostic approach to retention can provide a significant pay-off.

Workforce action plans: organisational responses to forecasts

The end result of the forecasting process is an estimate of the short-term and long-term labour requirements. The organisation can respond in multiple ways to demand and supply forecasts. Figure 4.1 only shows four options when faced with managing shortages or surpluses: recruit new permanent or part-time employees (Chapter 5), invest in training existing employees, apply a freeze on hiring or lay workers off. Other options might be to redesign jobs (discussed in Chapter 3). Mello (2005) provides more detailed analysis of the options.

According to Apedoe-Dzidza et al., (2008), workforce planning secures 'the organisation of qualified candidates for vacancies that may occur in key positions' (p. 70). However, as you have hopefully seen through reading so far, organisational responses to demand and supply forecasts are subject to a number of constraints, not least, in Britain, labour shortages caused by Brexit. The coronavirus pandemic has put a spotlight on health care. Workforce planners in the sector face significant challenges due to the large variety of skill classifications, needs and availability of qualified staff. Curson (2006) sees medical workforce planning as analogous to crystal-ball gazing, and Parsons (2010) views it as both a science and an art because predictions for the future, based on the analysis of trends, can hardly be relied upon when future requirements based on need rather than demand are likely to change so rapidly. Van Greuningen et al. (2012) have identified weaknesses in the very sophisticated Dutch health workers planning model, in which the importance of interdisciplinary teams is becoming an increasingly vital part of providing holistic health care.

Global HRM

Domestic workers in Qatar and workforce planning

Qatar is one of the richest countries in the world. There are more than 2 million migrant workers in Qatar – a significant number given the country's overall population is 2.6 million. In recent years, the foreign labourer population has grown significantly as the country has undergone a construction boom ahead of the 2022 Fédération Internationale de Football Association (FIFA) World Cup. Many of these workers come from across South Asia and Africa including 175,000 domestic workers – over half of whom are women. These workers arrive in Qatar and are employed under the *kafala* visa sponsorship system, which ties migrant workers to their employer, which some critics argue is a twenty-first-century form of indentured servitude.

Source: Yancy Min on Unsplash

Qatar has a long history of migrant worker abuse and exploitation, which has received widespread international condemnation in recent years. Such issues are not unique to Qatar. Some 35 million migrants are employed in the six Gulf Cooperation Council countries, in Jordan, and in Lebanon, and incidences of worker exploitation are well documented (Cousins, 2020). As international pressure mounts on Qatar to tackle labour exploitation ahead of the 2022 World Cup, it announced on 16 January 2020 that most migrant workers previously prevented from leaving the country without their employer's permission, including domestic workers, will no longer need an exit permit. Nicholas McGeehan, director of Fair/Square, a human rights research advocacy organisation, explained that the new requirement is problematic for domestic workers because those who wish to leave must first seek permission from their employer:

> 'It's a serious problem because this has been really well documented how appalling the abuses of domestic workers are ... we're talking about in some cases serious physical, psychological, sexual abuses in Qatar', he said. 'And you're talking about relationships of extreme control and

domination. The idea that a domestic worker is going to be happy to simply inform their employer that they're leaving completely neglects the relationships there and the seriousness of the abuses'. (Dehghan, 2020)

Despite these reforms, critics argue that Qatar's controversial *kafala* system remains intact for domestic workers, which means that many domestic workers may be trapped in their employer's household because leaving without permission is not allowed. However, Houtan Homayounpour, head of the International Labour Organization project office in Qatar, had a more optimistic view of the new reforms: 'Domestic workers now simply have to inform their employer that they will be leaving and do not have to ask for their approval ... the removal of exit permits and the introduction of free labour market mobility [in the coming weeks] will practically mark the end of the kafala system in the State of Qatar' (Dehghan, 2020). This highlights that it is difficult to disentangle employment regulation from other forms of state regulation. For example, the availability of migrant workers to Qatari employers is controlled by state immigration policies. The employment policies operating in Qatar (which enable employers to access migrant workers but deny those workers basic workplace rights) also suggest that the state is not necessarily a neutral actor and is colluding with employers to exploit workers.

Stop! Can you identify ways in which state regulation of employment has affected workforce planning in an organisation you are familiar with? Do you think the state should be intervening in the operation of the labour market in these ways? Why or why not?

Essential reading

Dehghan, S.K. (2020) Qatar eases exit rules but concerns linger over abuse of domestic workers. *The Guardian*, 23 January; Cousins, S. (2020) Migrant workers can't afford a lockdown. *Foreign Policy*, 8 April.

Note: This feature was updated by Andrew Bratton.

PART 3

Reflective question

Given the triple crises facing Britain, is statistical modelling a 'solution' for all workforce planning issues?

Workforce diversity

In recent years an important topic in all kinds of organisations has been diversity management (DM) (Bendl et al., 2017). An understanding of diversity as a strategic imperative, and their unintended consequences, provide a foundation for effective diversity initiatives (Leslie, 2019). Organisations in different cultural contexts, however, interpret diversity and its management in various different ways. Mainstream DM literature has focused on organising different diversity categories, such as gender, class, race, ethnicity, religion, age and (dis)ability. However, diversity strategies often tend to neglect the management of inclusion of sexual orientation, or 'sexuality', or people with visible and invisible disability. Queer theoretical thinking has entered into organisational studies focusing on the experience of people who were excluded from society and organisations due to their gender identity, and/or their sexual identity. Queer theory starts from the premise that dual categorisation like 'sex' (man/woman), 'gender' (male/female) and 'sexuality' (heterosexuality/homosexuality) are not 'naturally' given characteristics of a human being but results of social and cultural processes (Bendle and Hofmann, 2017). BAME (Black, Asian and minority ethnic) and LGBT+ (lesbian, gay, bisexual, transgender and more) are categories found in the literature and, as it will become apparent, make the dimensions of diversity nuanced and not without controversy. While visible disability may be apparent, invisible disability, or hidden disability, captures a whole spectrum of hidden disabilities or challenges that are not immediately apparent. For example, some people with visual or auditory disabilities who do not wear glasses or hearing aids, or discreet hearing aids, may not be obviously disabled (Jones, 2016).

Diversity as lived experience

European societies have never been static, and transformation continues in the 47 members: from Iceland in the North Atlantic to Eurasian Russia and Turkey in the east. Migrations have also transformed North American, Australian and New Zealand societies. The movement of people has created societies that are rich in ethnic, linguistic and cultural diversity. Diversity therefore defines modernity.

In Britain, for example, social surveys show that 8 million people, or 14 per cent of the UK population, are currently from ethno-racial minorities. By 2051, the size of the visible minority population is estimated to double to 16 million and make up 20 per cent of the population. The presence of visible minorities, however, began well before the migration to Britain of Black Caribbean workers in the 1950s. The sugar and slave trades were the most lucrative industries in the British Empire and inevitably involved the movements of thousands of Black people back and forth between Britain, Africa and the Caribbean. Workers from BAME communities tend to be over-represented in the lowest positions and under-represented in the upper hierarchy in organisations (McGregor-Smith, 2017). Research shows that, for many workers from ethno-racial minorities, ethnicity shapes their lived experience (Gillborn, 2015) . Studies suggest that the disability wage gap is robust and progress towards pay equity for people with disabilities in full-time employment is slow (Hallock et al., 2014; Jones, 2016; Yin et al., 2014). Two other social trends over the last 30 years also highlight diversity in the workplace: the growth in the number of women entering paid work and, partly due to demographic factors, health improvements and changes in pension legislation, the increasing numbers of older workers who are delaying retirement and remaining in employment.

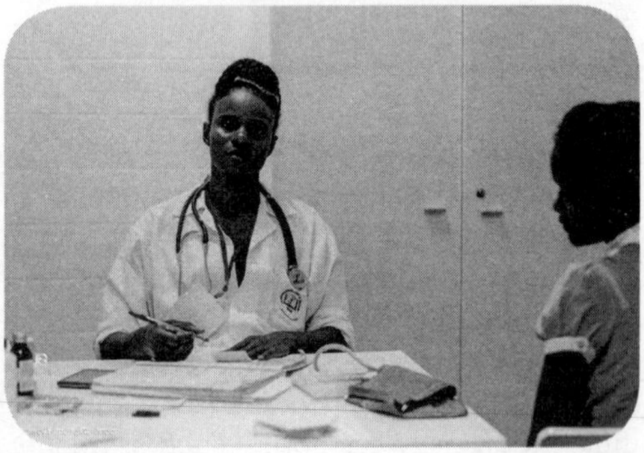

Source: Francisco Venancio on Unsplash

Workers from Black, Asian or minority ethnic backgrounds have unequal access to resources and receive less favourable treatment on a range of measures related to pay, job performance and promotion opportunities.

Diversity architecture challenges many traditional stereotypes. Social stereotypes are a form of schema containing generalised ideas about the characteristics or attributes of a group (Judd and Park, 1993). For example, we may say that Japanese men and women are better at mathematics than creative thinking, that differing traits and abilities make women particularly well suited to nursing occupations, and that older workers are less likely to accept change than their younger co-workers. These are all examples of stereotypical beliefs about groups of people that are related to ethno-racial factors, gender and age because they make assumptions that the characteristics in question will be true of all or most of the individuals in these categories.

Digital Spotlight
Key metrics for workforce planning

'Strategic workforce planning is about getting the right people with the right skills in place at the right time in order to fulfil an organization's mission and goals' (Tucker, 2019, p. 15). Over the last two decades, strategic workforce planning (SWP) has evolved from an annual headcount of employees, to a formal, year-round business process that is aligned with the wider corporate strategy (Tucker, 2019). Technology can be used to enhance SWP and, in turn, SWP can aid in identifying and addressing the technological skills gaps many organisations are currently contending with. It has been reported that, since 2015, the time it takes to close a skills gap has increased tenfold (La Prade et al., 2019), and 60% of executives have admitted that they struggle to keep their workforce current (McKinsey, 2017). As a result, companies such as IBM are using advanced analytics, artificial intelligence, machine learning and market-based skills data in order to gain actionable, predictive insights for SWP (Moore and Bokelberg, 2019). However, in order to optimise SWP, high-quality data on a range of factors is required, for example:

What?	Why?
Headcount	Headcount is the most fundamental SWP metric and is essential for completing many other calculations, for example, rate of turnover, average salary, etc.
Job type	Awareness of job types across the organisation is vital for workforce planning, for example, identifying if there is a shortage of staff within a particular department.
Age	An overview of the age ratio is useful for a variety of purposes, including planning for retirement and succession.
Gender	Understanding the gender balance within the organisation is useful in terms of identifying under-representation.
Ethnicity	Data on the ethnic diversity ratio within the organisation can help leaders to determine whether minorities are appropriately represented.
Tenure	Information on tenure can help to create a picture about employee satisfaction, entitlement to benefits based on length of service, etc.
Performance	Performance is easier to measure for some roles than others, however, providing appropriate metrics are used, it can help managers and HR professionals to gauge the employee's performance against organisational, departmental and individual targets.
Turnover	Data on turnover levels is vital for assessing management effectiveness and overall organisational health.
Skills	Understanding the types and levels of skills possessed by employees is vital for planning for the future and addressing key gaps.

IBM's state-of-the-art SWP system has been designed to infer employee skills and proficiency levels based on the digital footprint of each individual within the organisation (Moore and Bokelberg, 2019). This information is then used to offer personalised learning recommendations, which employees are encouraged to pursue with the assistance of a 'cognitive career coach'. IBM reports that this approach has increased employee engagement by 20% (Moore and Bokelberg, 2019).

PART 3

Stop! Think of two additional metrics that could prove useful in terms of SWP in addition to those discussed above. What insights might these offer to managers and HR professionals?

Essential reading

Tucker, E. (2019) How to modernize workforce planning. *People & Strategy*, *42*(4): 14–19.

Note: This feature was contributed by Laura Steele.

Stereotypical beliefs still exist, particularly with regard to gender differences (Bordalo et al., 2019) and age (Hanappi-Egger and Ortlieb, 2017; Mencl and Lester, 2014). Gopal (2019) makes the important point that racism is not a matter of subjective 'experiences' but has objective structural outcomes. That is, for people of colour in largely white organisations, racism can be identified not just in discriminatory practices but in unequal access to resources, representation, opportunities and differing entitlements. Studies comparing the work experiences of white and ethno-racial minority employees found that women and men from visible minority groups received less favourable treatment on a range of measures related to pay, job performance and promotion opportunities (Noon and Hoque, 2001), and that there is a correlation between pay penalty and multiple disadvantages in terms of gender, race, age and disability (Woodhams et al., 2015).

Diversity management

The BBC was only the latest organisation to discover the importance of diversity and equality policy, after the corporation's handling of viewer complaints about BBC Breakfast presenter Naga Munchetty. The BBC initially ruled that Munchetty had breached editorial guidelines in a conversation with her co-host Dan Walker about US President Donald Trump. The BBC, however, had to defend itself against complaints that only a woman of colour had been disciplined and not her white, male co-host (Waterson, 2019a).

Historically, HR practices supporting diversity can be seen as part of a strategy to comply with *equal opportunities legislation*: that people should be treated equally regardless of race, ethnic origin, gender, sexual orientation and other social categorisations, so that 'individuals are enabled freely and equally to compete for social rewards' (Jewson and Mason, 1986, p. 307). The European Union (EU), Australian, Canadian, New Zealand and US laws mandate equal opportunities (EO). The EU has been highly influential in promoting EO initiatives among member states, for example, the UK Equality Act 2010. In this context, HR policies and practices help to prevent discriminatory behaviour, are drivers of diversity and central to managing diversity in organisations (Downey et al., 2015).

Jewson and Mason set equal opportunities within a free-market tradition, and point to a liberal approach based on 'positive action' to ensure fair and meritocratic procedures in organisations, underpinned by anti-discrimination legislation. They contrast this with a more radical view, highlighting the embedded nature of discrimination, of 'positive discrimination' to achieve fairness, although this still remains unlawful in Britain. It is argued, however, that EO legislation fails to mitigate inequalities partly because disadvantaged groups are treated as homogeneous (Ashley et al., 2015). Many organisational theories affirm that people are not homogeneous (Bratton, 2020). Diversity focuses on the facets that make each of us unique as individuals.

The concept of *diversity* is a more sophisticated extension of minimum standards set by EO legislation. It is based upon intersectional analysis, which highlights the important reality of the different experiences of disadvantage that can occur between and even within social groups (Bagilhole, 2009). For example, experiences of racism and racial discrimination differ in important ways for Black

Caribbean women and Black Caribbean men. Equal opportunities and diversity focus attention on 'multiple disadvantage', so that ensuring different treatment for different groups and managing equal opportunity and diversity are not alternatives, but are interdependent (Bagilhole, 2009; CIPD, 2010b). Diversity management is a concept and process that acknowledges the value of differences and the promotion of equity among the workforce, to create added value and enhance performance. The CIPD considers diversity management to be part of an HR strategy: 'An effective diversity and inclusion strategy goes beyond legal compliance and seeks to add value to an organisation, contributing to employee well-being and engagement' (CIPD, 2020c, p. 1).

Increasingly, the support for diversity in the workforce has moved from a 'liberal' moral concern to comply with equal opportunities legislation and increase the representation of minority groups in organisations, to a focus on how diversity can be a valuable asset, improve the quality of decision-making and provide a competitive advantage to the organisation. Downey et al.'s (2015) study, for example, concludes that 'diversity practices with employee engagement, [are] a vital ingredient in overall workplace well-being' (Downey et al., 2015, p. 35). According to the CIPD (2020a), there are three important reasons why organisations should go beyond legal compliance on EO: people issues, market competitiveness and organisational reputation:

- *People issues* – an inclusive workplace helps to recruit and retain talented people.
- *Market competitiveness* – a diverse workforce can help enhance creativity and innovation.
- *Organisational reputation* – a diverse workforce enhances its image and can attract customers.

This contemporary approach is 'concurrent with the broader rise of neoliberalism' (Baker and Kelan, 2019, p. 119). The notion of leveraging difference is found in Schneider's (2001, p. 27, emphasis added) definition of diversity, which is 'about creating a working culture that seeks, respects, values and *harnesses* difference'. In contrast to the focus on equal opportunities, there is an acceptance that there are differences between people, that such differences can be valued and that they are the source of human potential that can be utilised: a valuable 'resource' in competing both locally and globally. Dijk et al. (2012) make a similar argument that diversity and inclusiveness is a strategic imperative to improve organisational performance. By valuing individual differences, workers' attitude (e.g. commitment), behaviour (e.g. turnover) and performance (e.g. creativity) will increase, it is argued. For example, in Britain, Barclays Bank declared:

> Building diverse teams made up of people with different backgrounds, experiences, attitudes, values and opinions creates greater opportunities for learning, innovation and creativity. These in turn should fuel performance and return on investment. (Barclays, 2020)

According to Liff (1997), there are four approaches to managing diversity based on the degree of commitment to social group equality as an organisational objective, and on the perceived relevance of differentiation between social groups for policy-making:

- The first approach might be to *dissolve differences* in order to 'stress individualism' (Liff, 1997, p. 13) so that everyone's needs and desires for effective working are recognised. This tends to minimise differences, giving little recognition to the value of difference – rather like traditional equal opportunities approaches.
- In contrast, a second approach is to *value differences*. Crucial here is the recognition that past practices have reinforced inequalities and led to under-representation and disadvantage. This may

mean that there needs to be a change in practice to create a culture reinforcing the fact that everyone has a valued role in an organisation.

- The third approach of *accommodating differences* seeks not to waste talent but to ensure that everyone has an equal chance. This could mean, for example, targeting recruitment for under-represented groups that have the necessary qualifications.
- A fourth approach is to *utilise differences*, recognising their usefulness and developing policies that value them. Liff uses the example of a career track for 'family' women with career breaks, gradual promotion and part-time work. The crucial feature of the policy would be that this track would be valued in the same way as the traditional track.

Probably the most important feature in recent diversity literature is the recognition that organisational leaders should consider diversity and inclusion to have strategic value (Celik et al., 2012; Greene and Kirton, 2011), and be embedded in a cultural change process (Dijk et al., 2012).

Best diversity practices emphasise that while recruiting a diverse workforce is necessary, it is insufficient. Diversity goals require organisations to recruit workers from different social groups, inclusion goals require commitment of senior management to build a culture where all employees, irrespective of the demographics, are socially accepted and treated equally. In other words, 'individuals within the workforce need to feel they belong' (Barclays, 2020). For diversity to be taken seriously, the general argument is that it has to be more than checking possible prejudice in the recruitment literature or expecting line managers to take responsibility for implementing HR policy (Celik et al., 2012). Greater attention needs to be given to developing a culture of tolerance and inclusiveness (Nguyen, 2014; Wallace et al., 2014).

Individual interpretations of diversity management affect employee perception and understanding. Olsen et al. (2016), for example, found that women define gender diversity management as meaning the management of male to female employee ratio and that is standardised to the local demographics – a compliance approach. Conversely, in France, women identified gender diversity management as the need to recognise that different management techniques were required in order to ensure effective management or a business benefit approach.

The CIPD (2010b) found a range of barriers to building a diverse workforce, such as unsuccessful previous experiences, an exclusive orientation towards talent and a lack of boardroom diversity. Britain's technology sector, for example, has a lack of diversity amongst its senior leadership, according to a recent survey (Hern, 2018). Just 12.6 per cent of women in technology are board members, compared to 30 per cent of female representation now achieved by FTSE 100 businesses. The survey also found that just 8.5 per cent of senior leaders in technology come from a Black, Asian or minority ethnic (BAME) background. Technology companies often argue that diversity is difficult to achieve because of 'the lack of a "pipeline" of talent' (Hern, 2018, p. 35). Nguyen (2014) suggests that diversity management needs tailoring to the specific needs and culture within three levels of an organisation – the strategic (culture, vision, mission and business strategy), tactical (staffing and training) and operational (flexible employment and work–life balance) – and at each of these levels line managers or team leaders need to be involved (Ashikali and Groeneveld, 2015).

In a world where diversity is not simply about race, disability or gender but is now concerned with issues such as transgender individuals (Ozturk and Tatli, 2015), the inclusion of HIV-positive employees in hospitality industries around the world (Yap and Ineson, 2012), and the impact of both legal and illegal immigration (Brunow, 2014), there is a distinct broadening of the HRM remit. The shift in focus from legal compliance to harnessing diversity for strategic organisational performance places greater emphasis on HRM to find ways to maximise the benefits of diversity within a sustainable and inclusive working environment, and by highlighting the strategic role of diversity management (Ehrke et al., 2014).

Another challenge for HRM scholars is that although diversity management has become an established field of research, there is a need for an agreed definition of diversity (Kapoor, 2011). In practical terms, the definition adopted affects the understanding of 'what' diversity is for a particular organisation, 'why' an organisation is implementing diversity management and 'how' diversity becomes part of the business strategy (Van Ewijk, 2011).

Reflective question

The message from scholars and professional bodies is that diversity is a 'strategic' advantage for organisations. How can it be, then, that many organisations seem unable to plan for a diverse workforce?

Flexibility and precariousness

In planning how to respond to global competition, rapid technological and social change, and customer demands, many organisations significantly increased what from the 1980s onwards was called 'flexibility'. Boltanski and Chiapello (2018, p. 218) argue that flexibility makes it possible to transfer the burden of market uncertainty onto wage-earners. There are two types: internal flexibility, based upon redesigning work, and external flexibility, involving malleable organisational structures (discussed in Chapter 3). In the 1980s, an influential model was developed by Atkinson and Meager (1985) of a 'flexible firm', which identified four types of flexibility that could be implemented:

- *Functional* – the ability of a firm to match staff skills to tasks as workloads, work methods and technology change.
- *Numerical* – a firm's ability to adjust the level of labour inputs to meet fluctuations in output.
- *Distancing strategies* – the replacement of internal workers with external subcontractors, that is, putting some work, such as running the firm's canteen, out to contract (now referred to as 'outsourcing').
- *Financial* – support for the achievement of flexibility through the pay and reward structure.

These flexibilities are achieved through a division of workers into the core and the peripheral workforce. Flexibility here is something done *to* the workforce (Alis et al., 2006). The core group is composed of those employees expected to deliver functional flexibility and includes those with company-specific skills and perhaps high discretionary elements in their work. The peripheral group, on the other hand, is composed of a number of different workers, such as those directly employed by an organisation as secondary workers to perform work with a low discretionary element, or those employed as required on a variety of contracts, for example part-time, temporary, casual workers, or the self-employed. This category of employee might involve highly specialised workers such as consultants or, increasingly, junior academics, as well as those deemed to be low-skill, such as health and home care workers who put their lives at risk by going into work without adequate personal protection during the Covid-19 emergency. Casual or temporary kinds of employment are not new; the concern is about the growth in such contracts in recent years (Pennycook et al., 2013; Standing, 2011).

Another feature of employment in the neoliberal era is the demise of the regulated and collectively negotiated contract of employment. Employers have alleviated market uncertainty by using flexible or non-standard contracts such as:

- *Annualised hours* – working time is organised on the basis of the number of hours to be worked over a year rather than a week; it is usually used to fit in with peaks and troughs of work.
- *Compressed hours* – allows individuals to work their total number of agreed hours over a shorter period. For example, workers might work their full weekly hours over four rather than five days.
- *Flexi-time* – workers have a choice about their actual working hours, usually outside certain agreed core times.
- *Home-working* – either on a full-time basis or on a part-time basis where workers divide their time between home and office.
- *Job-sharing* – involves two people employed on a part-time basis but working together to cover a full-time post.
- *Shift-working* – gives employers the scope to have their business open for longer periods than an eight hour day.
- *Staggered hours* – workers can start and finish their day at different times.
- *Term-time working* – workers can take unpaid leave of absence during the school holidays.

The increasing trend towards internal and external flexibility has been accompanied by 'precarious' forms of employment, a development known as the 'destandardization of work' thesis (Edgell and Granter, 2020). This theory is built around three key dimensions of employment model: the employment contract, the work site and working hours. Comparing the differences between the standard and non-standard models of employment, the latter is deregulated and individually negotiated, spatially variable involving multiple sites, and variable time (Beck et al., 1992; Castells, 2001). Table 4.1 shows some key dimensions of flexible models of paid work.

Table 4.1 Key dimensions of flexible paid work

Dimensions	Flexible and gig work
Contractual	Deregulated, individually negotiated, unpaid internships, freelancing, zero-hours contracts
Spatial	Spatially variable, multi-sites, teleworking, global, offshoring, e.g. call centres, digital platforms
Temporal	Variable time, zero-hours contracts, outsourcing, e.g. Uber, Deliveroo

Source: Inspired by theories of Edgell and Granter (2020).

More recently, the notion of 'neo-villeiny' has emerged. Essentially, this refers to a form of hyper-flexible and precarious work. Neo-villeiny departs from the traditional bilateral employment contract in four distinct ways: no guarantee of any income; extensive unpaid and speculative work that is highly beneficial to the organisation; bondage to the organisation; and payment of rent to the organisation. Harvey et al.'s (2017) study found all these features of neo-villeiny in self-employed personal trainers working at gyms or fitness centres. There are positive and negative aspects of flexible work. For workers, flexible work offers choice and is associated with individual control, autonomy and work–life balance (Bal and Dorenbosch, 2015; Kelliher and Anderson, 2008). But flexible and precarious work can disproportionately impact negatively on particular groups of workers by gender, race and class (Baker and Kelan, 2019; De Stefano, 2015; Friedman, 2014) and can be seen as the 'best of bad options' because permanent, better-paid and more secure jobs have become uncommon (Kessler, 2018, p. 27–43). Flexible and precarious employment has been linked to the related concept of *precarity*. The philosopher and gender theorist Judith Butler (2009) describe precarity as a state of existence in which the material provision and psychological wellness of a worker are adversely affected by a lack of regular or secure income. An insidious form of precariousness was revealed during the Covid-19 emergency. The Institute for Fiscal Studies (IFS) found that women were more likely to be furloughed and at risk of losing their jobs (Griffiths and Calver, 2020). Thus, it is argued, diverse vulnerable groups, specifically working-class women, are at greater risk of precarity as a result of neoliberal, deregulated labour markets and employment practices.

Flexibility and precarity have profound implications for HRM in both theoretical and practical ways. Mainstream studies of strategic HRM and performance tend to assume, albeit implicitly, that competitive advantage is predicated on the firm's recruitment and control of human potential or 'talent' – labour that is rare, inimitable, non-substitutable – that is, above all, skilled, stable and motivated, rather than competing through the use of highly flexible, common, substitutional labour (Harvey and Turnbull, 2020; Marchington et al., 2013). Therefore, flexibility has implications for modelling the HRM–performance relationship as well as for workforce planning and other HR practices, such as learning and development and rewards.

Reflective question

Looking at these key dimensions of flexible work, what implications do they have for skills, work motivation, the psychological contract and workforce planning?

Over the last 30 years, Britain's labour market has become widely known for its flexibility. A detailed analysis is beyond the scope of this chapter (see Edgell and Granter, 2020), but here we explain some key concepts relevant to workforce planning.

Zero-hours contracts

Zero-hours contracts is one of the most discussed areas in the de-standardisation of work thesis. A form of temporal flexibility, a worker does not have a contract for a fixed number of work hours but is paid only for the hours actually worked (van Wanrooy et al., 2013a). In Britain, the number of people on a zero-hours contract has mushroomed in recent years, from 585,000 in 2013 to around 900,000 in early 2020 (TUC, 2020g). The HR practice of zero-hours contracts is embedded in neoliberal ideologies that collude in inequality (Baker and Kelan, 2019). By 2018 the incidence of zero-hours contracts in Britain was up from 1.7 million in 2016 to 1.8 million in 2018 (Partington, 2018).

People on zero-hours contracts are more like to be women, young, students or those in part-time employment. There is particular concern over the fairness of zero-hours contracts and the abuse with which such systems are used. As with all flexible working arrangements, those who voluntarily choose to work in this way are provided with the flexibility to enable particular lifestyle choices. However, for those who involuntarily find themselves working within these contracts, they can cause financial hardship as there is no regularity of work, the worker has very few rights, including no paid leave, and faces insecurity and poverty (Bell and Blanchflower, 2013; Standing, 2014).

Teleworking

A form of spatial flexibility, teleworking, telecommuting and/or home-working is 'performed by individuals who are employed by an organization but who work at home or at a telecentre for some portion of their working time during regular business hours' (Duxbury and Higgins, 2002, p. 157). Huws (1997) has identified five main types of teleworking:

- *Multi-site* – an alternation between working on an employer's premises and working elsewhere, usually at home, but also in a telecottage or telecentre.
- *Tele-home-working* – work based at home, usually for a single employer and involving low-skilled work performed by people tied to their homes.
- *Freelancing* – work for a variety of different clients.
- *Mobile* – work carried out using communication technology such as mobile phones, fax machines and PC connections via the Internet, often by professional, commercial, technical and managerial staff who work 'on the road'.
- *Relocated back functions (call centres)* – specialist centres carrying out activities such as data entry, airline bookings, telephone banking, telephone sales and helpline services.

The trend towards greater home-working and teleworking is being driven by a variety of factors: faster ICT media; new virtual platforms such as Zoom and Micro Teams; people expecting more flexibility and a better work–life balance; and employer initiatives to use home-working to reduce costs (Dwelly and Bennion, 2003). A variety of benefits are claimed for teleworking, including a reduction or elimination of travelling to work accompanied by a reduction of stress and fewer interruptions, which can in turn increase productivity (Vesala and Tuomivaara, 2015). In addition, working at home can also mean a reduction in carbon emissions and improvements in air quality as carbon-fuelled commuting is reduced (Monbiot, 2017). The Covid-19 crisis witnessed a phenomenal boost in this form of spatial flexibility and post-crisis that experience may permanently change demand for teleworking.

Source: iStock.com/shironosov

Outsourcing and offshoring

As you will recall, outsourcing and offshoring was examined in Chapter 3 as part of the discussion on work design. Organisations can increase external flexibility by dividing up or 'disaggregating' their value chains by outsourcing (Boltanski and Chiapello, 2018; Contractor et al., 2010; Johnson et al., 2019). Through a network organisation of suppliers, 'lean' organisations can *outsource*, that is, buy resources they lack from a profusion of external providers, often in emerging markets paying low wages. This allows an organisation to focus on its core capability. According to Harland et al. (2005), in addition to focusing on core activities, the principal drivers for outsourcing are freeing up assets, reducing costs and the potential benefits of working with a supplier or partner who is able to exploit advanced technologies. For example, in the pharmaceutical industry, specialist contract research organisations provide outsourced services in areas such as data management, medical coding and marketing, allowing companies to focus on high-value activities. An organisation using outsourced supply chain networks is said to be particularly suited to the contingencies arising from an increasingly globalised, uncertain and competitive world (Antai, 2011; Johnson et al., 2019).

It is argued that *offshoring* is another option for reducing costs and increasing profits. For example, Farrell (2005, p. 68) argues that the 'price' of an organisation's ability to cut costs and create new markets is 'continuous change and higher turnover for workers', which can cause 'pain and dislocation'. Offshoring has, therefore, become linked to neoliberal claims of increasing productivity arising from economic globalisation (Amiti and Wei, 2009). There are commercial and strategic risks associated with both outsourcing and offshoring. Both are susceptible to disruptions in the supply chain, as witnessed during the Covid-19 crisis when there was a breakdown in the supply of personal protective equipment (PPE) for health-care workers (EU, 2020).

There are also dangers in disaggregating work, in which parts of skilled work are allocated to less-skilled and cheaper workers. Such a process has the potential to continue until the skilled work has been lost (Norlander et al., 2015). Glaister (2014) examined the growth of HR outsourcing, finding that its role becomes limited, with a loss of strategic influence and less skill development. Interestingly, research by Woodall et al. (2009) found that the decision to outsource HR was usually taken because of the success of outsourcing other activities., rather than a full understanding of the costs and benefits. It was also found that reductions in core HR staff meant significant challenges in providing a high-quality service in other HR activities, partly because there was insufficient expertise among HR practitioners.

'Downsizing' or 'rightsizing'

Workforce planning is always a contingent process, and one of the contingent factors is clearly economic conditions. Laying off workers is one organisational response to demand and supply forecasts, as shown in Figure 4.1. The decade following the 2008 financial crisis has been characterised by job losses in all sectors, the emphasis shifting from the private to the public sector in Britain following a decade of 'austerity economics' (Toynbee and Walker, 2020). However, making workers redundant, or 'downsizing' as it is sometimes referred to, has also been a feature of many economies in the face of global pressures and cost competition. As Datta et al. (2010, p. 282) argue, it has 'become the norm' in many countries. One theory is that other organisations benefit from the redundancy because highly skilled workers enter the labour market. Research suggests this may not work and that highly skilled workers may become underemployed in work not matching their skills (Dobbins et al., 2014). Indeed, a feature of work following the GFC is how workers made redundant had to move into lower-level work based on lower pay and fewer hours (Warren, 2015).

Laying off workers has negative consequences for the remaining workforce and the organisation, as well as for those who have been made unemployed. First, and perhaps most obviously, redundancy is a violation of the psychological contract based on a build-up of mutual expectations and obligations between employees and the organisation, in which the greater the degree of workers' involvement in their work, the greater their feeling of violation (Stoner and Gallagher, 2010). Second, there is a loss of skill, knowledge and social capital – the talent that employees accumulate over years of practice at work (Yu and Park, 2006). Third, there is an effect on those workers who remain untouched by downsizing. If they respond sympathetically towards those made redundant, they may experience effects such as guilt, lower motivation and commitment, mistrust and insecurity (Thornhill et al., 1997); this is referred to as 'survivor syndrome'. Fourth, redundancy is stressful for those made unemployed, possibly due to the process of being made redundant itself and then through the experience of unemployment (Sennett, 1998).

In their wide-ranging review of research, Datta et al. (2010) found that the negative outcomes of redundancy have as much to do with the manner of implementation as with the fact of having been made redundant itself. Forde et al. (2008) explored the idea of 'socially responsible restructuring' during a period of mass lay-offs in the UK steel industry. This idea is based on the need to engage with the interests of all stakeholders during the process of restructuring and redundancy as part of an organisation's corporate social responsibility agenda, as suggested by the European Union (European Commission, 2008). It is suggested that HR has a key role to play to ensure 'ethical stewardship' (Forde et al., 2008, p. 22) in situations such as redundancies. There is also a need to understand the psychological aspects of the 'grief' that often besets individuals and the human phenomenon of the emotional 'grief cycle' during downsizing (Davey et al., 2013). Ultimately, however, during periods of recession, cost-reducing strategies such as redundancies produce conflict; within the constraints of neoliberal capitalism, there are no easy answers.

HRM in Practice
Safeguarding the lives of BAME key workers

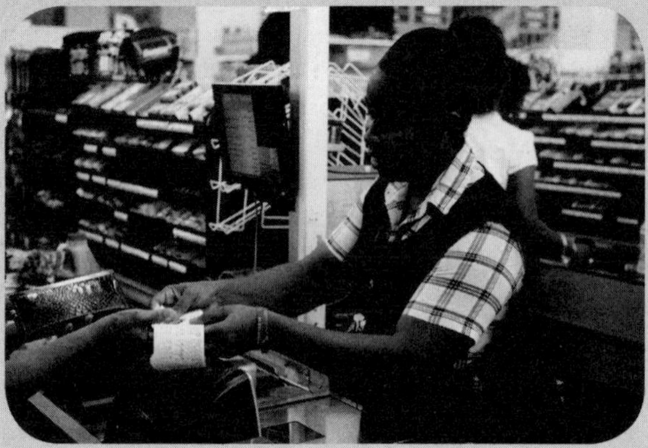

Source: Natalie Dawkins/Macmillan Education

Britain's lowest-paid workers, women, young adults and specifically Black, Asian and minority ethnic (BAME) groups have jobs with the biggest health and economic risks during the coronavirus lockdown.

According to a study by the Resolution Foundation on the uneven impact of the Covid-19 pandemic on workers, the health risks from Covid-19 and the negative economic impact would be far greater for some than others. Identifying 8.6 million key workers putting their health at risk to keep the country running, the study found that women were more than twice as likely than men to occupy roles in health and social care, as well as education, food and retail, with parents more likely to be key workers, including as many as two in five working mothers (Partington, 2020c). Employees of non-white ethnicity are more likely to work in jobs that are at risk from Covid-19-related furloughs and lay-offs in the short term, and certain at-risk occupations tend to be disproportionally filled by BAME workers. Examples include:

> Taxi drivers and chauffeurs, where black, Asian and minority ethnic groups make up 13 percent, 5 percent, and 4 percent of employment, respectively. People of Asian ethnicity, who account for 7 percent of the UK's total workforce, make up 13 percent of cooks, chefs, catering, and bar managers and driving instructors. Black workers, whose share of employment overall is 3 percent, make up 6 percent of such vulnerable jobs as dental nurses, workers in the apparel trade, and cleaning occupations. (Allas et al., 2020)

As outlined in the Public Health England commissioned report *Disparities in the risk and outcomes of COVID-19*, death rates from Covid-19 were highest among people of Black and Asian ethnic groups. In a previously unpublished section of the review of the disease's disproportionate impact on BAME workers, it reports: 'Racism and discrimination experienced by BAME key workers [is] a root cause effecting health and exposure risk' (Campbell, 2020b). This highlights the complex relationship between race, class and health inequality in the workforce in Britain. It also emphasises that health inequalities are further exacerbated by the material and psychological effects of racism. These dynamics mean that the uneven distribution and effects of Covid-19 cannot be explained by biomedical factors alone, but are questions of political economy (Gore, 2020). A key question is, to what extent do workforce planning practices contribute to safeguarding the lives and livelihoods of vulnerable workers during a public health emergency?

Stop! Can you think of two ways the government or employers could better protect workers' health during a pandemic? What role do HR professionals play in ensuring workforce planning processes take account issues of diversity, inclusion and health inequality?

Essential reading

Allas, T., Canal, M. and Hunt, V. (2020). COVID-19 in the United Kingdom: assessing jobs at risk and the impact on people and places. McKinsey & Company, 11 May; Partington, R. (2020) UK's lowest paid most at risk during Covid-19 crisis, report finds. *The Guardian*, April.

Note: This feature was contributed by Andrew Bratton.

Critiquing workforce planning

Despite the apparent logic of rational workforce planning, there is evidence that external and internal scanning and planning is not always formally developed and implemented, even in large organisations. Organisations adopt a variety of WP practices in a pragmatic way to deal with economic exigencies and the changing environment. Huselid (1995) and Rothwell (1995) established that environmental volatility had an important effect on the adoption of WP approaches. The rate of environmental change renders WP so problematic that it becomes impractical. Workforce plans are developed but not implemented because external or internal changes invalidate the proposed initiatives. For example, in 2008, the British bank Northern Rock was nationalised during the financial crisis. Within two years over 2,000 jobs were lost at the bank. The experience of Northern Rock illustrates that accurately forecasting the 'right people, right skills, right place and right time' is fraught with difficulty in a globalised neoliberal world. High levels of volatility, as the Covid-19 crisis illustrated, may make WP futile, whereas low levels of volatility make it superfluous (Huselid, 1995).

Neoliberalism and economic globalisation have given rise to HR practices that impact WP, including the demise of the standard employment model in which workers have full-time work and a secure wage or salary, the growth of informal short-term work contracts, and global supply chain networks, all of which increases interdependency, risk and complexity, which confounds an organisation's ability to formulate strategic plans (Johnson et al., 2019; Torres et al., 2015). Over the next decade, planners face the Brexit-related challenge of recruiting EU nationals for the care and agricultural sectors (CIPD, 2019a). Consistent with Huselid (1995) and Rothwell (1995), the argument is made that the so-called gig economy and platform working renders WP redundant. The non-standard employment model reduces fixed costs associated with a regular workforce, and the organisation benefits also by being able to rapidly respond to changes in demand for services or products. Gig working means that workers with the right skills can be resourced from the external labour market at the right time when needed (Kispal-Vitai and Wood, 2019).

Organisations making large-scale use of gig working may experience reputational damage by 'being named and shamed as exploitative' (Kispal-Vitai and Wood, 2019, p. 257). Gig workers are compelled to work long hours, without benefits, and receive low wages that hardly cover subsistence. Consistent with research on the psychological contract (see Chapter 1), an ad hoc approach to resourcing driven by cost reduction may produce improved short-term financial results but are highly likely to have a negative impact on worker commitment to the organisation. Gig working therefore undermines research-based evidence that commitment is closely tied to the psychological contract (Battisti et al., 2007). Thus, in WP, as in other HR activities, organisations face a strategic choice. Although the use of gig workers may have positive results, a consistent finding in the research is that, *ceteris paribus* (other things being equal), high-performance HR practices lead to a positive psychological contract and positive organisational outcomes (Boxall and Purcell, 2016; Kehoe and Wright, 2013).

Neoliberal ideologies obscure HR practices, such as resourcing, that have given rise to precarious working and precarity. The rise of gig work and precarious forms of employment impact disproportionately on minority groups, class, age and gender. Although precarious work started in low-skill manual occupations, it has become ubiquitous in professional occupations such as consulting, design and academia (Jarvis and Pratt, 2006; Standing, 2014). One key objective to diversity management has been training minority groups with the skills they need for 'success'. The aim is to give women, for example, the skills they need to empower themselves in the organisation. Underpinning diversity management is an assumption that everyone is endowed with equal opportunities and disparities in achievement are perceived as individual success/failure. However, Baker and Kelan (2019) observe that 'women are blamed for their own lack of success rather than the structures and cultures that perpetuate misogynistic models of the ideal employer' (p. 121).

Critics argue that DM has focused only on practices that help individuals to achieve success and has neglected 'deeper' socioeconomic inequality. It is argued that the focus away from equal opportunities to DM can lead to 'identity-blind' policies and procedures, which ultimately maintain unequal power relationships between dominant and minority groups and neglect structural inequalities (Choi and Rainey, 2014; Richardson and Monro, 2013). Consistent with this argument, Ashley et al. (2015) found a lack of social mobility of university graduates into elite law and accountancy firms in London: this can be described as a 'class ceiling'. Social studies affirm that entry into 'blue-chip' companies is largely determined by the wealth and social class of one's parents (Hinsliff, 2017).

Baker and Kelan (2019) suggest that effective diversity management must entail a deeper understanding of lived experiences of diverse individuals and social groups in the workplace. This would therefore require 'HRM to understand diversity as intersectional' (p. 128). There is a paucity of intersectional research, and critics contend that management scholars need to practise intersectionality as part of their research design. Why? Because it's contended that the intersectionality of class, ethnicity and age shows the different ways that other social groups are perceived and treated in organisations. Importantly, management scholars and practising managers should avoid treating minority social groups as internally homogeneous. A study by Corritore et al. (2020), for example, highlights interpersonal and intrapersonal cultural heterogeneity; the notion that diversity can exist within persons when individuals hold multiple cultural beliefs about the organisation. We should also note that BAME workers are, in terms of work motivation, as inspirationally divided as white workers. Therefore, research is needed into the processes by which HR interventions '(re)inforce or mitigate inequalities associated with the intersections age, ethnicity, and class' (Hanappi-Egger and Ortlieb, 2017, p. 465).

Summary

We began this chapter by explaining that environmental shocks and disturbances have increased the need for workforce planning to become both an analytical process for predictability and a creative process for working with unpredictability, unknowable shocks and complexity. Workforce planning is a process of forecasting the demand and supply for skills against the requirements of future services delivered and production in a situation of volatility and change. Workforce planning is a process supported by the use of ICT, enabling the production of people analytics that can be used to produce various forecasts and scenarios relating to future possibilities and unexpected shocks. Such systems can also be provided as a feature of e-HR.

We also examined in detail different forms of flexibility – internal and external – which then led us to analyse the decline of standard forms of employment in which workers have a dependent relationship with employers; full-time work and a regular wage or salary has become less dominant. This development of precariousness, we suggested, coincided with the rise of neoliberal ideologies.

We examined the concept of equal opportunities and contrasted EO with diversity management. Diversity management is, in theory, a means of creating heterogeneity in the workforce; a variety of experiences and networks enhancing the ability of individuals to succeed in the workplace. Best HR practice emphasises the need for diversity to be embedded in organisational culture and processes of change. Effective diversity management requires a deeper understanding of diverse individuals and, importantly, how diversity intersects with class, gender and race.

Review questions

1. Some argue workforce planning is central to strategic planning, but others contend that environmental volatility and gig working has made workforce planning ineffective and unnecessary. What is your view – and why?
2. How effective are the various approaches to managing diversity in organisations at reducing inequalities?
3. How does flexibility transfer the burden of market risk and uncertainty onto individual workers? To what extent, if at all, has the Covid-19 pandemic triggered new thinking on how and where we work?

Search & Watch

Visit YouTube and watch the **Financial Times** video titled: **Poor worker conditions power gig economy.** How does gig working change the traditional relationship between an employer and employee? With the development of the gig economy, is workforce planning changing – and how?

Legal Focus

In the UK's gig economy, there has been an increase in the use of zero-hours contracts, in which employers are under no obligation to provide work and employees are either under an obligation to do the work that is offered or, if not obligated to do it, unlikely to be offered additional work if they do not accept it. Another development complicating the legal status of employer and employee is the increase of app-based services offering food delivery or taxi rides. App developers have sought to avoid creating direct contractual relationships with those providing the work and to characterise these workers as self-employed. Thus, a business 'offloads' its risk for managing its workforce. In 2017, Matthew Taylor proposed a 'fair balance of rights and responsibilities for people whatever their status'. The recommendations of the Taylor review have yet to be implemented. The classic feature of a zero-hours employment contract is that it gives an employee no right to a particular number of working hours each week or month, but when the person is working, they are an employee (that is, there is a contract). The issue is about the duration of the contract, see *Halawi v WDFG UK Ltd* [2015] 3 All ER 543.

Task Search online for the ***Taylor Review of Modern Working Practices* [2017]** and the case of ***Halawi v WDFG UK Ltd* [2015] 3 All ER 543**. Also search for government information in your jurisdiction on protection for employees on zero-hours contracts and compare and contrast it with another country, such as Australia or Canada. (1) How can statute law help to bring a fairer balance of rights for people working in the gig economy? (2) What are the arguments for and against banning zero-hours contracts?

Reference

See Deborah Lockton and Tom Brown's *Employment Law* (2020), pp. 33–9, for a legal discussion on tests for determining employment status of gig workers.

Chapter case: Køre (Part 1)

The setting

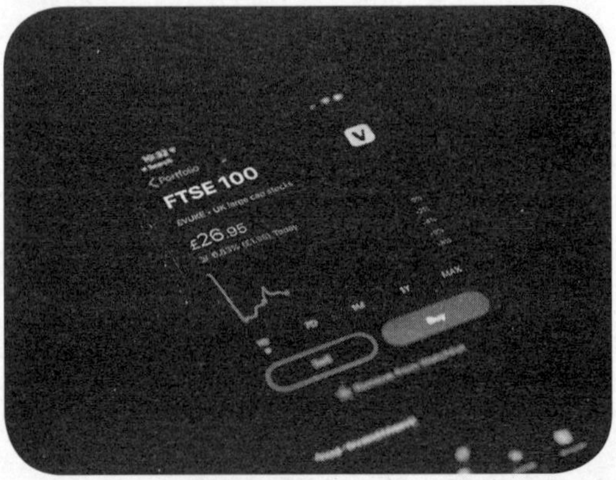

Source: Jamie Street on Unsplash

The financial technology (FinTech) sector is dynamic, innovative and hyper-responsive to new industry trends. The average Global Adoption Rate is 64%, showing FinTechs to be part of the Global mainstream. Køre is a FinTech company based in Copenhagen, Denmark. Their mobile-first platform allows consumers to make payments, track their expenses and invest small amounts in the stock market through an app. A Series C funding round has raised $26 million to expand Køre into the US market. The expectation of rapid growth has led the company to hire a dedicated Human Resources department to alleviate HR responsibilities from the managers and team leads. Until now, HR topics in the company have been covered to a varying degree by the managers and team leads. These activities have mainly focused on recruitment, promotion and ad hoc training. Køre's company values are: (1) Be an Entrepreneur: Move fast and take risks to respond to emerging FinTech trends; (2) Seek Excellence: Go the extra mile to push for success in your projects; and (3) Work Hard, Play Hard: Set challenging goals and celebrate success with a young, dynamic team.

The problem

The demographic of the employees at Køre is mostly young, white men. The founders, Lucas Jensen and Victor Pedersen, have explained this by stating that finance and technology are historically male-dominated sectors, but it is beginning to appear online that the organisational culture has gained a reputation for being 'toxic'. The lack of diversity is not a concern for Lucas and Victor. They expect the new HR department to continue the current practices used by the managers and team leads, while also implementing operational processes such as payroll and leave management. A few members of staff have voiced their concerns over groupthink and hurtful 'banter', the most vocal of which is Hanne Larsen who works in the Data Science team.

Hanne noted:

> Sometimes, I feel like I'm trapped in a frat house. The men in my team joke around with the managers and they go out drinking together until 2am. I feel left out because they make important project decisions while they're together.

Lucas countered:

> At Køre, we have different personalities, approaches to work and communication styles. This helps us to respond to trends and grow rapidly. During this international expansion, speed and efficiency are our highest priority.

Hanne disagrees:

> Everybody else in my team seems to communicate in the same way, and my ideas are constantly belittled because I'm not included in the 'banter'. I feel like I'm not being taken seriously because I'm a woman of east-Asian descent, and the team see me through their own stereotype of a 'submissive Asian woman'. This is a company-wide issue that must be addressed.

The investors are concerned that this discrepancy could damage the reputation of the venture capital (VC) firm, and devalue Køre. They request that the HR department devises a diversity and inclusion strategy that they can show to the public to preserve the image of the VC firm and improve the image of Køre.

The assignment

You have joined Køre's new HR department as an HR specialist. Work as part of a small group to create a ten-minute presentation highlighting steps that can be taken by the company to improve the organisational culture through diversity and inclusion. The presentation should be targeted towards the investors, Hanne, and Lucas and Victor. You must consider:

1. Both the business case and the social justice case for diversity.
2. How the steps respond to the company values at Køre.
3. How to implement the steps in the USA during the expansion.

Essential reading

Mensi-Klarbach, H. and Risberg, A. (2019) *Diversity in Organisations – Concepts and Practices* (2nd edn). London: Red Globe Press.

Chartered Institute of Personnel and Development (2019) *Diversity Management that Works: An Evidence-based View*. London: CIPD.

Note: This feature was contributed by Alexis Evans.

Further reading

Chartered Institute of Personnel and Development (2019) *Diversity Management that Works: An Evidence-based View*. London: CIPD. Available at: https://www.cipd.co.uk/knowledge/fundamentals/relations/diversity/management-recommendations.

Curson, J. A., Dell, M. E., Wilson, R. A. Bosworth, D. L. and Baldauf, B. (2010) Who does workforce planning well?: Workforce review team rapid review summary. *International Journal of Health Care Quality Assurance, 23*(1): 110–19.

Eaton, A. and Heckscher, C. (2021) COVID's impacts on the field of labour and employment relations. *Journal of Management Studies, 58*(1): 275–9.

Ford, J., Atkinson, C. and Harding, N. (2021) 'You Just Had to Get on with It': Exploring the Persistence of Gender Inequality through Women's Career Histories. *Work, Employment and Society, 35*(1): 78–96.

Kessler, S. (2018) *Gigged: The End of the Job and the Future of Work*. New York: Macmillan.

Lavelle, J. (2007) On workforce architecture, employment relationships and lifecycles: expanding the purview of workforce planning and management. *Public Personnel Management, 36*(4): 374–85.

Mensi-Klarbach, H. and Risberg, A. (2019) *Diversity in Organisations – Concepts and Practices* (2nd edn). London: Red Globe Press.

Schwab, A., Werbel, J.D., Hofmann, H. and Henriques, P. (2016) Managerial gender diversity and firm performance: an integration of different theoretical perspectives. *Group Organization Management, 41*(1): 5–31

Standing, G. (2014) Understanding the Precariat through labour and work. *Development and Change, 45*(5): 963–80.

CHAPTER 5

RECRUITMENT AND SELECTION

outline

- Introduction
- The recruitment and selection process: overview
- Workforce action plan
- Selection criteria
- Measurement issues
- Recruitment methods: attraction
- Selection: assessment
- Critiquing recruitment and selection
- Summary
- Further reading

Source: wocintechchat on Unsplash

objectives

After studying this chapter, you should be able to:

1. Understand the importance of recruitment and selection for organisational performance and in the formation of the employment relationship
2. Understand the key features of recruitment and selection process, and methods used to attract and assess applicants
3. Explain the importance of perceptual sets, reliability and validity in the selection process
4. Explain the effectiveness of various selection methods
5. Appreciate the importance of ethics and legal requirements in the recruitment and selection processes

Introduction

In December 2014, Harry Clarke was at the wheel of a refuse lorry when it went out of control killing six pedestrians in Glasgow city centre. At the fatal accident inquiry, it emerged that there were no references on Mr Clarke's employment record with Glasgow City Council, and that Clarke had been suspended from his former job as a bus driver in 2010. The lawyer referred to 'a grossly incompetent employment process'. Organisations with robust selection processes, however, can have unintended consequences. For example, the use of digital interviews can result in negative perceptions of the organisation, which might cause applicants to self-withdraw from the selection process (Langer et al., 2017). Recruitment and selection hinge around two core processes, namely attraction and assessment. Both processes are typically the first encounter applicants have with the organisation, and, as the opening example illustrates, their effect can be huge not only in terms of who is selected for employment, but also for shaping the psychological contract (Chapter 1) and subsequent worker performance and retention (Searle, 2003).

In this chapter, we define recruitment and selection and explain various methods used to attract and assess people for employment. We provide a common framework that views recruitment and selection as a sequential process with distinct interconnected stages. We explain the importance of perceptual biases, reliability and validity, and critically explain the effectiveness of selection methods. We conclude with a critique of the social technologies used in selection, which unmasks seemingly apolitical HR practices for eliciting knowledge of applicants and the selection of people to work in the organisation.

The recruitment and selection process: overview

Recruitment and selection have always been considered a critical stage in the HRM cycle (Devanna et al., 1984, see Figure 1.4). Both are often conflated but there are important differences between them, which may be performed by different HR professionals. Recruitment is the process of attracting a pool of capable people for a vacancy within the organisation. Selection is the process of choosing future workers from within that pool of applicants, the most qualified person to carry out the role, using valid assessment methods. The recruitment process may be outsourced to an agency, whereas, typically the final selection activity and decision is undertaken internally.

Scholars and practitioners argue that recruitment and selection should be aligned with strategy, that there are multiple systems of recruitment and selection procedures that would be appropriate for attracting and selecting people with the right mix of knowledge, skills and abilities (KSAs) that match the organisation's strategy. There is no one best practice. Drawing on contingency theory, a perspective which argues that, to be effective, managers must adjust their practices to take account of contextual factors (e.g. size, organisational structure, technology, its environment), different systems of recruitment and selection practices are necessary to create a workforce with the requisite level of KSAs congruent to the different levels of job complexity and uncertainty faced by the subunits of workers (Collings and Kehoe, 2018). As we go on to explain, recruitment and selection practices should be analysed through this strategy-contextual prism. Figure 5.1 shows a framework of five stages of recruitment and selection, starting with a workforce action plan. The diagram shows that decisions over the assessment methods used to evaluate applicants are influenced by the criteria for selection and measurement issues.

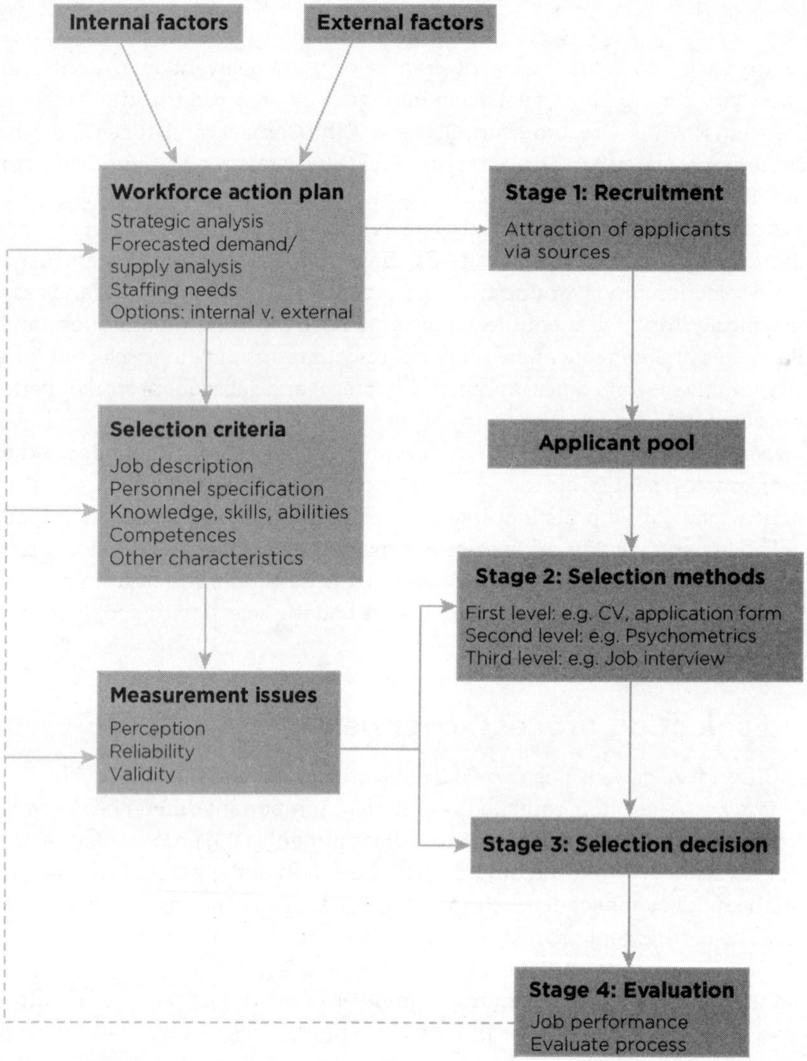

Figure 5.1 The stages of recruitment and selection process

Workforce action plan

The process begins with the *workforce action plan* that is formulated with due attention to the organisation's corporate and HR strategy. As we discussed in the previous chapter, a key part in enacting a workforce plan is addressing any identifiable imbalances in labour and ensuring that the workforce has the relevant skills and abilities for the organisation's current and future needs (CIPD, 2020i). Decisions about recruitment and selection, however, are influenced, if not determined, by the effect of unplanned macro-level and global events.

After almost a decade of austerity, the CIPD reported in 2015 that UK employers were operating in the most buoyant labour market experienced since the GFC. The majority of employers reported that

HRM in Practice

'Princelings scandal': hired because of father's connections

It is often said that it is not what you know but who you know. In the world of international finance and banking, that might be truer than you think. In 2016, JPMorgan Chase, an American investment bank, agreed to pay $264 million to settle a United States federal government investigation into its practice of hiring well-connected Chinese 'princelings' to win business. Princelings describes the children of prominent senior Communist party officials, but the term is often applied more generally to the descendants of China's elite. Beginning in 2006, senior Hong Kong-based JPMorgan bankers set up and used a 'client referral programme', also referred to as the 'Sons and Daughters Programme', to hire candidates referred by key clients and government officials. It is reported that JPMorgan bankers even created 'referral hires vs revenue' spreadsheets to track the hiring of Chinese officials' relatives, 'which has an almost linear relationship' with new business in China (Lynch et al., 2016):

> Most of those offered jobs through the programme lacked the education and experience of other new hires. The son of one Chinese official who was given a JPMorgan job in New York was kept on for 10 months despite sending an email that 'contained some inappropriate sexual remarks' and being seen as 'immature, irresponsible and unreliable', according to internal emails quoted in the agreement ... One internal bank email in 2009 referred to a princeling as 'an intern doing nothing'; the following year, a supervisor warned a colleague about 'his napping habit'.

JPMorgan engaged in a systematic bribery scheme by hiring children of government officials who were often unqualified. Senior managers knew that the firm was potentially violating the Foreign Corrupt Practices Act, a United States federal law that prohibits US companies from bribing foreign government officials. The three-year investigation revealed that the 'firm's internal controls were so weak that not a single referral hire request was denied' (Rushe, 2016). This high-profile scandal highlights that even in highly regulated multinational organisations, internal HR processes can be ignored as workers may be incentivised to overlook improper hiring practices to access lucrative business deals in the pursuit of increased profits. As discussed in this chapter, this scandal illustrates that the nature of recruitment and selection practices are shaped by an organisation's business strategy and overall philosophy towards people management.

Stop! Can you think of other high-profile examples of unfair hiring practices in the private or public sector? What practical steps can HR professional take to mitigate against corrupt hiring practices?

Essential reading

Rushe, D. (2016) JP Morgan Chase to pay $264m over Chinese 'princelings' bribery scheme. *The Guardian*, 17 November; Lynch, D., Hughes, J. and Arnold, M (2016) JPMorgan to pay $264m penalty for hiring 'princelings'. *Financial Times*, 17 November.

Note: This feature was contributed by Andrew Bratton.

PART 3

the competition for well-qualified 'talent' had increased, that talent management was being given a higher priority for organisations with an increased focus on talent development and retention, and that 78 per cent of employers surveyed had experienced difficulties in recruiting skilled workers, mainly in the private sector (CIPD 2015d). Fast forward five years, and the CIPD *Labour Market Outlook* reported a sharp fall in recruitment activity among employers, the lowest level of activity since 2005, due to the Covid-19 pandemic (CIPD 2020e). The net employment balance – the difference between the proportion of employers expecting to increase or decrease employee levels – decreased 25 points from +21 to -4, its lowest point since this measure was first introduced in the 2012/13 report. The 2020 report noted that the employment forecast is particularly dire in hospitality, business services and manufacturing. The economic consequences of coronavirus are illustrated by the planned cutting of 9,000 jobs, 20 per cent of the workforce, the majority at UK sites, at the iconic British company Rolls-Royce, which in May 2020 had its debt marked down from investment grade to junk status by credit ratings agency Standard & Poor (Business Leader, 2020).

In addition to the environment, workforce recruitment and selection is inseparably entwined with corporate strategy, as illustrated by HSBC's recent planned shedding of staff. HSBC, which has 235,000 employees in 64 countries, was under pressure to increase returns. Its shares had fallen 38 per cent, their lowest in two decades. In response, HSBC announced a strategy to pivot more of its business deeper into China and Asia in search of higher returns while cutting 35,000 jobs in early 2020 (Dunkley, 2020). The high levels of volatility render the forecasting of demand and supply of labour and recruitment activity among employers decidedly problematic. Convulsions in the labour market over the last decade also epitomise the close connection between recruitment and selection and the wider socioeconomic, and political context.

Selection criteria

The ultimate objective of the selection process is to hire people with the right mix of attributes so as to maximise the likelihood of high performance. Traditionally, *job analysis* provides the basis for recruitment and selection decisions and performance criteria. A job description specifies the tasks and responsibilities that make up the job. Against each job description, there is normally a specification of the standards of performance (Smith, 2015). A typical format for a job description is given in Figure 5.2.

JOB DESCRIPTION

Job title

Department

Responsible to ...

Relationships

Purpose of job/overall objectives

Specific duties and responsibilities

Physical and economic conditions

Figure 5.2 Job description format

PERSONNEL SPECIFICATION

Physical characteristics
Attainment
General intelligence
Specific aptitudes
Interests
Disposition
Circumstances

Figure 5.3 Rodger's seven-point plan

PERSONNEL SPECIFICATION

Impact on other people
Qualification and experience
Innate abilities
Motivation
Adjustment

Figure 5.4 Munro-Fraser's fivefold grading system

In addition to a job description, there is, in the form of a *person specification*, some attempt to profile the 'ideal' person, with regard to knowledge, skills and abilities (KSAs), and other characteristics, to fill the job. Traditionally, a format for a personnel specification has been the seven-point plan, based on the work of Rodger (1970) and shown in Figure 5.3. An alternative is Munro-Fraser's (1971) fivefold grading system, as in Figure 5.4. In both forms of personnel specification, it is usual to indicate the importance of different requirements. Thus, certain requirements might be expressed as essential and others as desirable.

Both a job description and person specification have been key elements in the traditional repertoire of HR managers. In recent years, information derived from the analysis of work performance has been utilised to create a taxonomy of either criterion-related behaviours or standards of performance referred to as *competencies* or 'worker-oriented attributes' (Searle, 2003, p. 28). According to the CIPD (2010d, p. 1), competencies are 'the behaviours that employees must have, or must acquire, to input into a situation in order to achieve high levels of performance'. Competencies help align the organisation's strategic direction and the internal skills and behaviours (Chouhan and Srivastava, 2014).

Table 5.1 shows how one large financial services organisation sets out its competencies. Each is defined and described by a range of indicators that enables assessment and measurement.

The definition of competencies should allow the identification and isolation of dimensions of behaviour that are distinct and are associated with effective performance. Often, competence indica-

Table 5.1 Competencies in a financial services organisation

Personal focus	Self-control Self-development Personal organisation Positive approach
Customer focus	Creating customer service Delivering customer service Continuous improvement
Future focus	Delivering the vision Change and creativity
Business focus	Delivering results Providing solutions Systemic thinking Attention to detail
People focus	Developing people Working with others Influencing Leading

tors are clustered into groups, for example, problem-solving, administrative, leadership, and so on. The assessment of competencies is one means of selecting employees and also helps in developing the 'employer brand' which may initially attract prospective recruits (Das and Ahmed, 2014; Jain and Bhatt, 2015).

Data-driven algorithms may be deployed at one or more stages of the recruitment process, for example, to navigate a large pool of potential job candidates. These software systems can in some cases be so efficient at screening CVs that 72 per cent are rejected before a human ever sees them (Mann and O'Neil, 2016). But there are disadvantages to this level of efficiency. To be eligible for consideration, the applicant must present a CV incorporating all the phraseology and competencies contained in the job advertisement so that the software can recognise the applicant's qualifications. Only those applicants identified by the computer algorithm can be considered for employment. Computer algorithms are, in part, people's opinions embedded in code and, as such, may inadvertently reinforce discrimination in hiring practices (see Digital Spotlight, p. 153).

Measurement issues

Once a job description, person specification and competencies for the job have been produced, assessment techniques can be chosen to evaluate applicants for the position for the purpose of predicting their future job performance. The psychology of work literature provides rich data about the effectiveness of selection techniques (Woods and West, 2020). The concept of perceptual biases and two statistical concepts – reliability and validity – are of particular importance in selection.

Global HRM
Looks matter when hiring in Singapore

Source: Li Yang on Unsplash

Marina Bay Sands, Singapore

The hospitality industry is a major contributor to the Singapore economy. In 2018, Singapore was the fifth most-visited city in the world, and second most-visited in Southeast Asia. In the hospitality industry, front-line workers are the medium through which companies interact with customers and they are often seen as a source of service differentiation. In the process of service delivery, managers rely on workers to maintain the quality of service provided (Nickson et al., 2005). For example, the appearance and the speaking voice of front-line workers when servicing customers conveys an aesthetic expression that is beneficial to provide customers with the experience of high quality and service and to enhance corporate image. This phenomenon demonstrates the importance of front-line workers and aesthetic labour to the hospitality industry. Aesthetic labour refers to the concrete abilities and attributes expressed by an individual upon entering the workplace. As Tsaur and Tang (2013, p. 19) explain:

> Through the process of recruitment, selection, and training business owners modify, develop, and commoditize these abilities and attributes, converting them into aesthetic abilities or skills to create a new service style, whereas employees perform aesthetic labour throughout the three stages: recruitment and selection, training, and service delivery.

Organisations require workers' aesthetic labour in three stages. In the recruitment stage, employers look for employees with an attractive appearance including a pleasing smile, pretty teeth, neat hair and good body proportions. In the process of selection, the importance of appearance is also emphasised. By serving customers, workers engage in aesthetic labour. Aesthetic labour is essential to the hospitality industry. The burden of aesthetic labour has the potential to create perceptual biases associated with subjective judgements about potential employees. For example, research on tattoos and perceptions of employment suitability in the hospitality industry has demonstrated a negative tattoo bias (Tews and Stafford, 2020). In Singapore, no federal legislation currently exists that specifically bans employers from making employment decisions based on criteria that include physical attractiveness or personal appearance. Recent research in Singapore suggests that having a tattoo could harm a worker's chance of getting hired. According to a recent YouGov survey (Ho, 2019), almost half (47%) of respondents reported that they would be less likely to hire someone with a tattoo, even if they were qualified for the position. Older Singaporeans are more likely than younger ones to hold this view. While almost six in ten (59%) of those aged 55 and over report that they would be less likely to hire someone if they had a tattoo, this figure falls to one in three (33%) among 18–24-year-olds. Although one in ten (10%) of Singaporeans have a tattoo and they are becoming more mainstream, they appear to negatively affect employability and are largely unwelcomed in most workplaces and especially in front-line roles in the hospitality industry.

PART 3

Stop! Unconscious racism, ageism, sexism and appearance discrimination play in big role in who gets hired. What are the practical ways of reducing bias in the recruitment and selection process?

Essential reading

Ho, K. (2019) Half of Singaporeans would be less likely to hire a candidate with a tattoo. YouGov, 29 May; Roepe, L. (2017) How your appearance impacts hiring decisions. *Forbes*, 1 November; Tews, M. J. and Stafford, K. (2020) Tattoos and perceptions of employment suitability in the hospitality industry. *Journal of Human Resources in Hospitality & Tourism, 19*(2), 148–67; Tsaur, S. H. and Tang, W. H. (2013) The burden of esthetic labor on front-line employees in hospitality industry. *International Journal of Hospitality Management, 35*, 19–27.

Note: This feature was contributed by Andrew Bratton.

Perceptual biases

Evidence-based selection aims to increase the objectivity of a selection method, by reducing the effect of a number of *perceptual biases* associated with subjective judgements about potential employees. Perception, the process of selecting, organising and interpreting information in order to make sense of the world around us, shapes human action (Bratton, 2020). The concept of perceptual bias describes a replicable pattern in erroneous judgement, illogical interpretation, or what is broadly called irrationality. Table 5.2 shows the most common misjudgements of others are the halo effect, the primacy effect, the regency effect, the beautyism effect and the similarity effect (Galin and Benoliel, 1990).

Table 5.2 Common misjudgements of others

Bias	Descriptor
The halo effect	The tendency for a recruiter to draw a negative or positive impression about a candidate based on a single observation, such as a visible body tattoo or because the individual attended Eton, the elite private British school.
The primacy effect	The tendency to pay too much attention to our first perceptions about a candidate. The adage, 'don't judge a book by its cover' illustrates the primacy effect. People can find it surprisingly difficult to change their initial perceptions.
The recency effect	The tendency for assessors to overemphasise the last perception about a candidate.
The beautyism effect	The tendency for assessors to rate a candidate they perceive to be physically attractive more highly than those they do not.
The similarity effect	The tendency for decision-makers to rate candidates whom they perceive to be similar to them more highly than those they do not. This similarity can be based on overt characteristics such class, sex, ethnicity or age, or can be based on perceived similarity in more covert terms, such as similarity in political interests, sport or personality traits.

These combined effects – called idiosyncratic rating tendencies – are perceptual biases that all humans possess and, conjoined, can account for about 62 per cent of the variation in assessors' subjective ratings of job applicants (Scullen et al., 2000). Therefore, making decisions to include (or exclude) a candidate for future employment is inherently problematic. HR professionals choose a particular assessment method on primarily the method's reliability and validity.

Reliability

In the abstract, the term *reliability* refers to the extent to which a particular selection method, applied repeatedly to the same object, yields the same result each time. If, for example, you were being interviewed by two managers for a job in two separate interviews, you would hope that the interview method would provide data such that the interviewers agreed with each other about you as an individual. Alternatively, if a number of candidates were given the same selection test, you would want to have some confidence that the test would provide consistent results concerning the individual differences between candidates. Reliability is represented by a coefficient, a number between 0 and 1 that represents the degree to which measurements of the identical thing using the same assessment method will agree with one another. A value of 1 representing perfect agreement between measurements, while a value of 0 represents no agreement. The statistical analysis of selection methods provides a *reliability coefficient*, and the higher the coefficient (that is, the closer it is to 1.0), the more dependable the method.

Validity

In statistical usage, the term *validity* refers to the extent to which a selection method actually measures what it sets out to measure. There are different forms of validity, but the most important in selection is *criterion-related validity*, sometimes called *predictive validity*, based on some external criterion. For example, the predictive validity of a written driver's test is determined by the relationship between the scores people achieve on the test and their subsequent driving records. Thus, in this example, the driving record is the external criterion. In selection, criterion-related validity measures the results of a method (e.g. personality test) against a set criterion (e.g. future job performance) of a candidate.

Validation is in practice a complex process, and studies involving a large number of candidates are required in order to allow a robust correlation coefficient to be calculated. Criterion-related validity is represented by correlational data, taking coefficients between 0 and 1 (with 1 representing perfect prediction and 0 representing no predictive power). Table 5.3 shows a summary of the predictive validity of selection methods.

Assessment methods with a criterion-related validity value of 0.5 and above are considered strong predictors of job performance. However, selection instruments with validities as low as 0.20 can represent meaningful predictive effects for job per-

While validity should be the prime factor in deciding selection methods, in practice, the choice of which selection methods to adopt, including which will be cost-effective, ethical and legally defensible, is grounded in a specific workplace situation.

Source: iStock.com/NickyLloyd

Table 5.3 Accuracy of a sample of selection methods

Method	Criterion-related validity (where 1.0 is certain prediction)
General mental ability tests	0.65
Structured interviews	0.58
Unstructured interviews	0.58
Assessment centres	0.36
Biodata	0.35
Work sample tests	0.33
Situation judgement tests	0.26
Reference check	0.26
CV/application form data	0.18
Years of experience	0.16
Years of education	0.10
Personality questionnaires	0.04
Graphology	0.02

Source: Schmidt et al. (2016).

formance and, besides, different selection techniques can be assessed in relation to each other according to their validity coefficient results. Validity is related to the particular situation in which performance is carried out. However, such problems have not stopped many organisations using tests and other selection methods that have been validated by the test designers in a range of organisations or situations.

Obviously, selection methods should be both reliable and valid. However, social scientists are aware that there is often a tension between the criteria of reliability and validity, forcing a trade-off between the two. For example, if a doctor is seeking to hire a new receptionist for a busy general practice serving a diverse inner-city community, talking to applicants would seem to provide a more valid measure of future job performance than gaining a high score on an IQ test. To some extent, this dilemma explains two distinct approaches to social research: quantitative versus qualitative. Therefore, although workplace psychology scholars recommend that validity should be the prime factor in deciding selection methods, in practice, the choice of which selection methods to adopt, including which will be cost-effective, ethical and legally defensible, is grounded in a specific situation. A small-scale enterprise may legitimately decide to conduct the oft-criticised interview for hiring a customer-facing receptionist rather than adopt an alternative valid but less-nuanced selection method.

Reflective question

Why would an SME legitimately decide to conduct the oft-criticised interview for hiring a new employee?

Digital Spotlight
Algorithmic bias in recruitment and selection

Increasing use of algorithms in the recruitment and selection process has raised questions as to whether they are helping to reduce bias or, in fact, reinforcing it (Bogen, 2019). Computer algorithms are, simply put, a set of rules or instructions for the machine to follow when attempting to solve a problem or complete a calculation. Algorithms may be deployed at one or more stages of the recruitment process, for example, to target job advertisements towards particular groups or identify potential candidates from recruitment websites. They can also be utilised to read and rank CVs and assist recruiters in assessing the competencies of candidates. The latter can be particularly useful when there are a large number of applicants, as is frequently the case for major multinationals or during times of economic recession. As discussed in this chapter, the potential for bias, both conscious and unconscious, amongst human decision-makers is well documented (Agarwal, 2018). It was hoped that algorithms could help to eliminate the potential for bias and thereby create a level playing field for candidates. However, algorithms present problems of their own.

Algorithmic decision-making can replicate historical or institutional biases, serving to further entrench disadvantages. Perhaps the most infamous case of algorithmic bias in the recruitment process involved Amazon (Gershgorn, 2018). Between 2014 and 2017, the company attempted to build an automated system to analyse résumés (CVs) and identify optimal candidates. The algorithm was trained on a decade of Amazon's own hiring data. The results were alarming: the algorithm reportedly developed a bias against female applicants. The presence of the word 'women' (for example, 'women's soccer captain') on an application would lead the algorithm to rank the candidate lower. This situation likely stemmed from the high proportion of men within the tech industry, causing the algorithm to believe that being male was one of the defining characteristics of a desirable employee. Despite efforts by the company's engineers, the problem could not be adequately resolved, and the project was ultimately abandoned.

While the results may be unintentional, and the intent to eliminate bias, the fact that discrimination is perpetrated by a machine rather than a human will likely not be a defence against allegations of discrimination. Companies are generally responsible for their hiring decisions, regardless of how and by whom (or what) they are made. As a result, it is critical that any algorithms developed, as well as the data they are trained upon, are thoroughly tested to ensure that they are fit for purpose.

Stop! When it comes to developing algorithms for recruitment and selection, what particular concerns should managers be aware of?

Essential reading

Bogen, M. (2019) All the ways hiring algorithms can introduce bias. *Harvard Business Review*, 6 May.

Note: This feature was contributed by Laura Steele.

PART 3

Recruitment methods: attraction

In systematic approaches to recruitment and selection, stage two of the process comes after the formulation of the workforce plan, which guides decisions about selection criteria, and ultimately the choice of selection assessment methods (Figure 5.1). There are wide variations in practices, reflecting an organisation's strategy and its philosophy of people management. In large multinational organisations, for example, there is a distinction between policies to attract those destined for international careers and practices suited to local conditions (Mahmood, 2015).

Where indicated by the workforce plan, an organisation will seek ways of attracting a large pool of capable applicants and then differentiating between them, in order to hire the 'right' people (Nabi et al.,

2015). The process highlights three crucial issues. First, there is a need to attract people's interest in applying for employment. Under different labour market conditions, power in the recruitment process will swing between the buyers or sellers of labour – the employers and employees, respectively. Prior to the Covid-19 pandemic, employers both in Europe and globally noted that there is mounting competition for 'talented' employees (CIPD, 2015d; Gager et al., 2015). Second, people may be capable of fulfilling a role in employment, but the extent to which this will be realised is not totally predictable. Third, the choice of selection method sends signals about the organisation that make the employer more or less attractive for some groups (Carless, 2006). Take, for example, the group known as Generation Y (those born between around 1977 and 1994), as a contrast to Generation X (born between around 1965 and 1976). Generation Y are said to be confident and thrive on challenging but flexible work, expecting quick feedback and reward while maintaining a balanced lifestyle (Broadbridge et al., 2009; Gager et al., 2015; Kultalahti and Viitala, 2015). Similarly, applicant attraction is influenced by 'employer branding' (Das and Ahmed, 2014). Employer branding plays an important part in, first, attracting the right pool of applicants, and second, ensuring there is a good person-employer match ((Jain and Bhatt, 2015; Mostafa and Gould-Williams, 2014; Yu, 2014). Therefore, when making choices about recruitment and selection methods recruiters need to be cognizant of generational differences in values and work expectations as well as 'employer branding'.

Before we examine recruitment and selection processes in depth, it is important to step back and briefly delve into the different theoretical approaches to these activities. By being forewarned, you will be effectively forearmed against inevitable tensions researchers and practitioners face, which help us understand why there may be a gap between empirical research and HR practice.

Recruitment and selection paradigms

There is usually more than one way to make sense of the social world. Different points of view usually yield different explanations. Underlying these different explanations, or theories, are paradigms; models or frames of reference we use for observing and understanding, which shape both what we see and how we understand it. Workplace theorists have developed three distinct paradigms for understanding recruitment and selection processes: psychometric, person organisation fit and social process.

Psychometric paradigm

The *psychometric paradigm* is the most well-established approach to recruitment and selection (Al-Sharif et al., 2019). Psychometrics are 'standardized assessments of psychological attributes' (Saville, 2016, p. 5). There are two types: the 'can do' assessments of maximal performance and the 'will do' assessments of typical performance. In terms of employment selection, this usually involves assessment tests where there are right and wrong responses (e.g. IQ tests) and those without explicit 'correct' answers (e.g. personality tests). This paradigm shares many features of positivism, an epistemological position that advocates the application of the research methods of the natural sciences to the study of social reality. Positivism is generally taken to entail empirical testing and the generation of hypotheses that can be tested (Bryman, 2015). In this approach to studying recruitment and selection, the role of the organisation is dominant. Managers are able to identify, measure and select the applicant with the necessary relevant knowledge, skills and abilities (KSAs) for the job. Implicit in this approach is the belief that job roles can be performed one best way and can be objectively captured and measured to create a criterion space, and, despite much being known about the cognitive limitation of managers, especially in a selection situation (Simon, 1960; Zedeck, 1986), organisations and their agents engage in rational decision-making. An applicant plays a passive role; they provide data by completing tests to assess their KSAs and thus their suitability. The advantage of this approach is its use in high-volume multiple vacancy positions, such as military or government agencies. A foremost critique of the effectiveness and validity of this model is the stability of the job role criterion. As already discussed, flexibility, gig working and the fast-changing global job market seriously undermine the stability of the criterion space used to identify applicants (Anderson et al., 2004).

Person organisation (PO) fit paradigm

An alternative paradigm, one that highlights the multidimensionality of the recruitment and selection process, is the *person organisation (PO) fit paradigm* (Schneider, 1987). The focus of this model is on the interaction between an individual and their surroundings. Projected images (e.g. 'branding'), values and information on espoused goals will have meaning to potential applicants in the external labour market. Interactional psychology posits that the interaction of an individual and situational factors shapes individual behaviours (Krahé, 1992). In the context of recruitment and selection, the interaction between an individual and their environment provides the basis for a compatible PO fit. Parkes et al. (2001), Schneider (1987) and Schneider et al., (1995) proposed an attraction–selection–attrition framework to explain the workings of this process and the differences between organisations that are caused by the attraction of people to the organisation's goals, their interaction with those goals, and the fact that 'if they don't fit, they leave' (p. 437) (Figure 5.5).

Schneider argued that people are attracted to an organisation on the basis of their own interests and personality. Thus, people of a similar type will be attracted to the same place and the attraction of similar types will begin to determine the place. Following selection, people who do not fit, because of either an error or a misunderstanding of the reality of an organisation, will leave, resulting in attrition from that organisation (Phillips et al., 2014).

Central to this theory are the organisation's goals and culture, and out of these emerge the HR architecture and processes that will form the basis of decisions related to attraction. Though there are multiple definitions, organisational culture can be defined in a sentence short enough to tweet: 'it is a social construct made up of values, patterns of relationships and ways of doing things in a par-

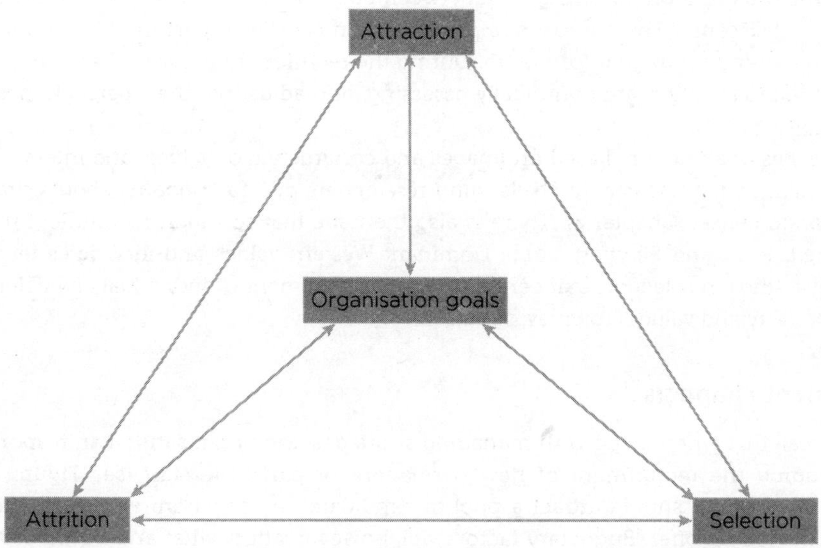

Figure 5.5 An attraction–selection–attrition framework
Source: Schneider (1987). Reproduced with permission of John Wiley & Sons, Inc.

ticular organisation' (Denham and Bratton, 2020, p. 83). Defined in this way, it is not surprising that a growing body of cultural literature is contributing to our understanding of decisions related to attraction.

Judge and Cable (1997) found support for the attraction–selection–attrition model. They report that applicants seek PO fit, attempting to match their values with the reputation surrounding an organisation's culture. McCulloch and Turban's (2007) study of attrition at US and Canadian companies showed that taking PO fit into account during selection played a key role in preventing high attrition. PO fit can be enhanced by an attention to socialisation processes once new employees have been selected (Das and Ahmed, 2014). There is also research interest in the extent to which there is a match between an individual's KSAs and the requirements of a job, referred to as the *person–job fit* (PJ). Carless (2005) found that both PO and PJ fit were positively linked to attraction – the perception that an organisation was a desirable place to work. Others have investigated *person–team fit* (De Cooman et al., 2016), which focuses on the issue of team perception and person fit, requiring all team members to perceive both supplementary fit – similar characteristics such as values, abilities and goals. Bringing these concepts together, there is an indication that the person–environment fit includes a PO fit, PJ fit, person–group fit and person–supervisor fit (Chuang et al., 2015).

Social process paradigm

The third paradigm, which is garnering increased support in a more globalised world in which labour scarcity is emerging in senior professional roles, is the *social process paradigm* (Herriot, 1987; Walker et al., 2015). In this paradigm, the role of the organisation and of an applicant are both proactive, in that the focus is on the social interaction between the two principal parties: the applicant and the recruiting organisation. Potential employees become co-constructers and active negotiators of any recruitment and selection process. Moreover, applicants are regarded as having multiple skills and abilities that they bring to the job role, not only potentially changing how their role is performed but also effecting the jobs of others as 'a result of their distinctive enactment of the role' (Searle and Al-Sharif, 2019, p. 218). Therefore, attention is on building relationships between the applicant and others in the organisation, fostering trust between both parties and thus the quantity and quality of information disclosure. The approach is predicated on each new person with whom the applicant interacts, providing accurate information. During the recruitment process, therefore, both the applicant and the organisation are continually assessing, and adjusting, their perceptions of each other (Bangerter et al., 2012).

The analysis of attraction, based on images and congruence of values, and interactions and relationship building, is increasingly challenging researchers due to concerns about attracting a more diverse workforce (see Chapter 4). There is also the issue that so much recruitment theory is Western-oriented (Ryan and Ployhart, 2014). Dominant Western values and ideologies tend to adopt an individualist ethos in selection that centre on the measurement of individual characteristics such as skills, personality and values (Townley, 2014).

Recruitment channels

You will recall that when faced with managing shortages, the organisation can respond in multiple ways including the recruitment of new permanent or part-time staff (see Figure 4.1). Effective recruitment channels should attract a pool of candidates, all of whom will be interested to some degree in the job on offer. Budgetary factors will, however, affect what and how recruitment channels are used, with more use of e-recruitment, as we will consider below. Generally, the HR literature advocates the intelligent use of recruitment channels in all circumstances. For example, the ageing profile of the workforce around the world requires an adjustment of recruitment policies (Connell et al., 2015). The appropriate use of technology is a consideration. Henkens et al. (2005) found that the use of the Internet for recruitment reflected a bias towards younger applicants (Finkelstein, 2015). Since the 2000s, employers have pivoted from using traditional processes, such as CVs, to the increased use of the Internet and social networking to attract applicants. The main channels for attracting applicants include:

- employee referrals;
- advertising;
- recruitment agencies;
- Internet and social networking;
- internships.

Employee referrals

Employee referrals, sometimes known as word-of-mouth, are one of the most enduring sources for attracting potential applicants, especially when focused on the organisation (Van Hoye, 2013). Providing individuals are given realistic information about the organisation and the reliability of the source, employee referrals are a means of discerning organisational attractiveness and enabling insight into PO fit. The realistic information hypothesis suggests that individuals recruited via employee referrals have a more accurate understanding of the organisation and the job requirements (Zottoli and Wanous, 2000). It is plausibly argued that employee referrals have several advantages; low-cost, pre-screening by employees, and the strengthening of the relationship with current employees. Organisations with successful equality and diversity programmes in place are in a more advantageous position to attract and retain the best staff of scarce skills (Öztürk et al., 2017). Thus, a potential disadvantage of employee referrals is that potentially they may undermine efforts to increase workforce diversity.

Advertising

Advertising and other recruitment literature comprise a common means by which the organisation's values, ethos and desired image are made manifest, often in the form of glossy brochures or, increasingly, websites. The utilitarian approach that focused on specifying job details, terms and conditions has been superseded by advertising that attempts to communicate a message about the company image aiming to raise the degree of attractiveness for potential recruits (Baum et al., 2016).

Recruitment agencies

Employment agencies are one source of lower level, non-managerial employees. Executive recruitment firms, or 'headhunters' are an alternative source for managerial positions. Outsourcing recruitment is not problem free. First, the agency's recruiter may misrepresent the organisation by giving unrealistic information to the individual if their priority is only with a fast placement. Second, the agency might inundate the organisation with CVs without careful screening. Universities and colleges are another source of potential applicants with specialised skills for professional or skilled positions. People who perceived a recruiter as having certain attributes, such as trustworthiness, competence and being personable, were more attracted to a job suggested by the recruiters or with the recruiter's organisation (Chapman et al., 2005).

Internet and social networking

There has been a rapid growth in e-recruitment (Ahmed et al., 2015). Consequently, organisations are advised to consider the design of their websites and the terms that applicants might use to carry out job and vacancy searches (Yang et al., 2014). According to the CIPD (2015d), 65 per cent of organisations have improved their company website. It has also been shown that the usability of an organisation's website affects an applicant's perception of a job, with a focus on hyperlinks and text rather than graphic images and navigation links (Allen et al., 2013), E-recruiting offers a portal for organisations to provide relevant and up-to-date job information in a far more consistent manner than in the past (Pisano et al., 2017). There are, however, issues with e-recruitment, including the one-way communication system, the fact that it is impersonal and passive, and the fact that it creates an artificial distance between the individual and the organisation (Stone et al., 2015). As e-recruitment has developed, it has been accompanied by the use of tools for filtering applicants (Parry and Tyson, 2008), probably much valued by employers during a Covid-19-induced recession when the ratio of applications to positions available is high.

Since the 2000s, social networking sites such as LinkedIn and Facebook, and social media such as Twitter, have grown in popularity, and all of these allow information about vacancies in organisations to be shared. LinkedIn enables recruiters to access a vast number of suitably qualified applicants, so how a potential applicant develops their online persona becomes important (Zide et al., 2014). A survey of recruiters found that 73 per cent of respondents had previously used social media for recruitment (Acikgoz and Bergman, 2016). While employees can quickly, through social media, refer their friends towards vacancies (Uen et al., 2015), it is also possible for organisations to search the public pages of social network sites to glean information about a person's links to different bodies, e.g. gym or political parties. Acikgoz and Bergman (2016) found that 93 per cent had the intention of reviewing candidates' social media profiles for the purposes of informing their hiring decisions.

Source: Photo by helloimnik on Unsplash

Reflective question

How does the use of social networking increase risks for (a) applicants and (b) organisations?

There are risks associated with the use of social media in recruitment and selection. First, social media provides a platform for negative comments about companies, with a global reach, damaging the employer branding (Iddekige et al., 2013; Kuhl, 2014). Second, selection decisions may be taken on the basis of data or personal information, such as images, which is often viewed out of context, that is not job-relevant and introduces perceptual biases. Third, information on social networking platforms is obviously not structured, which means that potential applicants are treated differently in terms of the information used to assess them, therefore issues of reliability and validity come to the fore (Brown and Vaughn, 2011). Despite these risks, we can confidently predict that the use of social networking platforms will remain an important source for recruitment and selection.

Internships

One method of attracting applicants is through internships or placements. These are often used by students for work-based research as part of their programmes (Hynie et al., 2011). In that internships provide an opportunity for students and graduates to gain experience and develop a relationship with the organisation, this method reflects the *social process paradigm* approach to recruitment and selection. If students then take up positions within the organisation, the organisation gains both through the motivation of students to work and in terms of savings on training and induction. Because internships offer employers an advanced opportunity to assess potential applicants, a late-stage assessment method, such as an employment interview, is increasingly used, which we consider below.

Selection: assessment

The methods chosen to select new employees must treat candidates fairly, without discrimination or bias, and throughout the process decisions are made based on the candidate's ability to perform the role and contribute to the organisation, and their potential for development (CIPD, 2019i). It is also important to consider applicants' reactions because it is during the selection process that the psychological contract begins to form (Rousseau, 2004). Different selection methods are used at different stages of the process: early *shortlisting* and middle and final *assessment*.

Ethical Insight
What behaviours are necessary for those seeking to conduct a job interview ethically?

In 2019, a tweet detailing a candidate's 'brutal' experience during a two-hour-long job interview went viral. Olivia Bland claimed that the CEO of Tech Applications UK, Craig Dean, 'tried his best to intimidate' and 'assert power' during the interaction (BBC, 2019). Bland reported that the interview began in an 'utterly bizarre' fashion, with Dean asking 'a lot of personal questions', before 'tearing apart, line by line' everything she had submitted in the written part of the application process. After telling her everything she did wrong during the interview, Dean allegedly offered Bland the position. She declined. The company denied that any bullying had occurred but stated that they would take the 'opportunity to reflect carefully on our recruitment process and HR policies' (BBC, 2019). So how should organisations wishing to conduct an ethical interview (and avoid being the subject of online outrage) approach the process?

Practical steps that organisations can take to minimise the risk of ethical failings within the recruitment process include the training of all staff members, especially those involved in hiring, in relation to ethics, equality and diversity. It may also be beneficial to provide succinct written guidance that outlines key aspects of relevant legislation and reiterates the organisation's values. In addition, many organisations now standardise their interview process, for example, by asking all candidates the same set of questions and scoring them according to a points-based system. Finally, it is important to note that the interview can also represent an opportunity to gauge the applicant's ethical standards and ascertain whether these align with those of the organisation. However, there would be little benefit in directly asking the individual if they strive to be ethical (few people are likely to say 'no'!). Instead, it is better to ask broader questions, for example, 'Tell me about a time where you faced an ethical challenge in the workplace and how you responded'.

Stop! If asked to offer guidance to line managers on conducting an 'ethical' interview, what key recommendation(s) would you make?

Essential reading
CIPD (2019) *Ethics at Work: An Employer's Guide*. London: CIPD.

Note: This feature was contributed by Laura Steele.

CVs, application forms and biodata

A *CV* (a curriculum vitae, also called a résumé) is normally the preliminary first-stage *screening* device used to create a pool of potential candidates in order to move to later stages of assessment. A CV enables employers to consider the individual in a particular way, constructing profiles around education, employment history, qualifications and achievements. These are then ranked in order of importance. However, there is a lack of standardisation of the layout or information provided. Reading and sorting through CVs in high numbers is relatively resource-intensive. As they collect a diverse range of data about an applicant, there has been interest in how selectors make decisions on the basis of data submitted, and whether such decisions are informed by the criteria set out in the job descriptions and specifications or are subject to personal bias. For example, would an applicant who attended a particular university be more likely to be selected on the basis of their CV? Studies have revealed some interesting contradictions between the use of objective knowledge and criteria, as set out in the formal documentation, and more implicit knowledge and emotion (Proença and de Oliveira, 2009). *Application forms* compel applicants to present information in a standardised structure. By using an application form an organisation can control the information that applicants submit. Both CVs and application forms remain popular methods to include (or exclude) applicants from the early stage of the selection process, but they are poor predictors of job performance, showing predictive validity coefficients of 0.16 (Schmidt et al., 2016).

In the 1990's *biodata* became popular for screening candidates. The notion that individuals are the summation of their behaviour and experience along with the widely held view that the best predictor of future behaviour is past behaviour, is the central premise of biodata (Parker, 2007). Its origins go back to the US when, in the 1890s, it was used to select life insurance agents. The algorithm is similar to credit scoring used by financial bodies. The predictive validity coefficient of biodata is 0.35 (Schmidt et al., 2016). It is claimed that biodata does not have any adverse impacts in terms of gender or ethnicity (Breaugh et al., 2014).

Psychometric testing

Research on *mid-stage assessment* techniques has long been dominated by the psychometric paradigm (Searle and Al-Sharif, 2019). This dominance is reflected in widespread use of psychometric tools designed to assess inner aspects of an applicant, such as intelligence and personality traits, that often cannot be observed or measured directly. Psychometric informed literature affirms that intelligence testing is the best predictor of job performance, above that of personality assessment (Schmidt and Hunter, 1998).

We can make the following distinctions between different kinds of test:

- *Ability tests* – these are designed to assess the maximum performance an applicant can currently achieve; as such, they focus on cognitive abilities such as comprehension and numerical skills, but also include physical skills testing such as keyboard speeds.

- *Inventories* – these are usually self-report questionnaires about personality, indicating traits, intelligence, values, interests, attitudes and preferences.

Ability tests may be of a general kind, for example those relating to general mental ability or abilities such as verbal fluency, numerical ability, aptitude (Toplis et al., 2005). For example, a recent study found that more than 50 per cent of university graduates failed the verbal (53.5 per cent) and numerical reasoning (83.5 per cent) tests (Bradley et al., 2020). The job performance validity of cognitive ability tests is high at between 0.51 (Schmidt and Hunter, 1998) to 0.65 (Schmidt et al., 2016). Test developers have produced an array of different instruments designed for distinct job levels, such as craft apprentices, clerical, managerial or graduate. Bertua et al. (2005) investigated whether general mental ability (GMA) tests were valid predictors of job performance and training success across a range of occupations, including senior managers. The authors claimed that the results provided 'unequivocal evidence for the continued and expanded use of GMA tests for employee selection in UK organizations' (Bertua et al., 2005, p. 403). The CIPD reported that around 45–47 per cent of companies in Britain use GMA tests (CIPD, 2019i).

PART 3

Limitations on the value of intelligence as a predictor have led to a growing interest in the assessment of another kind of intelligence based on feelings, sensing others' feelings and the ability to perform at one's best in relationships with others. This is referred to as *emotional intelligence* (Dulewicz and Higgs, 2000), and there is mounting evidence that employers are attempting to utilise this view of intelligence in their competency frameworks (Miller et al., 2001). Goleman (2006) popularised the concept of emotional intelligence and efforts have been made to develop a test with valid and reliable psychometric properties (Akerjordet and Severinsson, 2009).

Personality testing has been increasingly used to assess applicants' dispositions and behaviourial styles that are considered desirable for some job positions (Wiggins, 1996). For our purpose, personality refers to 'a relatively enduring pattern of thinking, feeling and acting that characterises a person's unique response to her or his environment' (Bratton, 2021, p. 117). Personality questionnaires often are based upon the ubiquitous Big Five Model, which proposes that five core dimensions underlie all others and encompass most of the significant variation in human personality (John et al., 2008). The five dimensions are:

HRM web links

Visit the companion website at **www.bloomsbury.pub/bratton-hrm** to find out more about emotional intelligence tests.

- *Emotional stability (neuroticism)* – adjustment versus anxiety, level of emotional stability, dependence versus independence.
- *Extroversion* – sociable versus misanthropic, outgoing versus introverted, confident versus timid.
- *Openness to experience* – reflection of an enquiring intellect, flexibility versus conformity, rebelliousness versus subduedness.
- *Agreeableness* – friendliness versus indifference to others, a docile versus a hostile nature, compliance versus hostile non-compliance.
- *Conscientiousness* – the most ambiguous factor, seen as educational achievement, or as will or volition.

Salgado (1997) sought to explore the predictive validity of the Big Five Model in relation to job performance and found conscientiousness and emotional stability to be the main predictors of job performance. However, others expressed concern about an over-reliance on personality tests with respect to their use in predicting future performance, especially in relation to complex tasks such as management. Robertson et al. (2000) attempted to test the link between conscientiousness and the performance of 453 managers in five different companies. The results showed no overall statistical relationship. The finding supports the view that suitability for complex managerial work cannot be assessed on the basis of a narrow measurement of a psychological profile. Other studies have found that the job performance validity of personality tests is low at 0.04 (Schmidt et al., 2016). However, it would seem that academic debates on predictive validity are not particularly significant for HR practitioners, who tend to choose tests because they are well-known (Furnham, 2008).

Online testing reduces the number of unsuitable applicants (Czerny, 2004), although such an assessment tool may also reject well-qualified applicants. The banking organisation Lloyds TSB, for example, had an online application form based on its competency framework. This acted as the early-stage assessment of applicants. The second stage involved an online 20-minute numerical reasoning test (Pollitt, 2005). It is claimed that online testing provides organisations with the ability to assess applicants at any time and any place in the world (Lievens and Harris, 2003). One difficulty, however, is that there is a loss of control over the administration of the assessment. Thus, while candidates can take a test at any time and in any location, there are cases of candidates being helped by a third party to complete the test (Toplis et al., 2005).

Psychometric testing offers organisations a cost-effective assessment process in their search for the right people to match the company's needs. Although evidence does confirm that psychometric testing can differentiate between individual applicants, concerns have been identified as to the extent to which a test might discriminate unfavourably against BAME groups (Gonzales et al., 2002; Holtz et al., 2005), which can lead to legal challenges. In this context, some organisations have introduced name-blind applications in an effort to avoid discrimination where an applicant's name might lead to bias against people from ethnic and religious minorities (Davies, 2015). Concerns that online tests serve to further advantage young middle-class white males have also been investigated (Lin et al., 2015; Sanchiz et al., 2017). As Searle and Al-Sharif (2019) warn, decision-makers must ensure they select the best candidate, and that 'built-in biases do not continue to result in the false-rejection of otherwise effective candidates' (p. 223).

Situational judgement tests

Situational judgement tests (SJT) are a mid-stage mode of assessment that leans towards the *PO fit paradigm* approach to recruitment and selection. It is premised on fitting the individual to the organisation, finding the 'right' person for the job (Corstjens et al., 2017). It is 'the psychological calculation of suitability' (Townley, 1994, p. 94). SJTs make a job more visible through the illumination of job action, thereby necessarily making the applicant 'known' to the assessor. That is, 'the one functions to produce knowledge of the other' (Townley, 1994, p. 93). SJTs can take two forms – behaviourial-based or knowledge-based – in which candidates respond in a manner that they judge would be most appropriate. For example, candidates are given a hypothetical work-related scenario describing a problem, and are asked to choose a response from a list of alternatives (Lievens et al., 2008). SJTs often focus on testing attitudes and ethical values rather than knowledge. An example of the former would be a candidate demonstrating, perhaps through role play, how they would handle a case of workplace bullying by a co-worker. A knowledge-based scenario may involve giving health and safety advice to a line manager within legislative guidelines.

SJTs provide a more complex assessment that homes in on candidates' judgements, abilities and behaviours. Research suggests that SJTs are reliable and have been demonstrated to be a good predictor of future job performance, showing a predictive validity coefficient of 0.33 (Schmidt et al., 2016).

Interestingly, SJTs have also predicted organisational citizenship behaviours (Rockstuhl et al., 2015). There are disadvantages with using SJTs, however. Such assessment methods may demand more in-depth job knowledge, which may be problematic for graduates with limited work experience, and they are resource-intensive (Nguyen et al., 2005).

Selection interviewing

Although there is a growing use of psychometrics and assessment centres, the interview remains dominant and is a widely used *late-stage* assessment method. The interview, together with application forms and letters of reference, make up 'the classic trio' of assessment tools (Cook, 1994, p. 15). In the post-Covid-19-pandemic workplace, with access to secure media platforms such as Zoom or Microsoft Teams, the virtual interview is likely to emerge as a popular means of assessment. Different categories of selection interviews have developed:

- *Information elicited* – interviews have a specific focus and require information at different levels: a focus on facts, subjective opinion, attitudes or values.
- *Structure* – interviews may vary from the completely structured, with planned questions, to the unstructured, allowing spontaneity for the applicant but little control for the interviewer. A compromise between the two extremes is most likely.
- *Order and involvement* – the need to obtain different kinds of information may mean applicants are interviewed serially or by a panel.

Over 70 years ago, research showed the interview deficient in terms of both reliability and validity. Its reliability ranged from having a correlation coefficient (r) of 0.23 to 0.97, with a median value of r = 0.57 (Wagner, 1949). The received wisdom of work psychologists was that selection decision-makers should find an alternative assessment method (Ulrich and Trumbo, 1965). However, contrary to the accepted wisdom, recent research has revealed that the predictive power of unstructured interviews may be close to that of structured formats (see Table 5.3).

There have been two lines of research to examine the reasons behind such poor results for the selection interview (Table 5.4). The first focuses on how interviewers process information that leads to a decision on acceptance or rejection. The second focuses on the skills of effective interviewing.

Arvey and Campion (1982) reported improved reliability and validity when interviews were based on job analysis information, and adopted a *situational* approach (Latham et al., 1980), in which questions focus on what an applicant would do in a series of situations (Chapman and Zweig, 2005). Barclay (1999) reported on an extension of the structured approach using behavioural interviewing combined with a competency 'SAR' framework. This format involves asking the candidate to give an example of a *situation* they had deal with at work (e.g. repeat absenteeism of an employee), explain their *actions* and the *result*. Behavioural interviewing is also defined as *competency-based interviewing* (Barclay, 2001), which seeks to determine behavioural patterns present in the most talented group of applicants. These behavioural patterns are labelled 'differentiator competencies', and the whole premise of the process is based on the accurate definition of the criteria most critical for job success. Recently, there has been an interest in *values-based interviewing,* in which questions focus on a candidate's behaviour in situations but are then followed by probing questions to reveal values based on what a candidate considers important and why (Francis, 2013).

These approaches to interviewing have not been without controversy or criticism. The interviewer is faced with a choice: establish a good rapport with a candidate to elicit a positive reaction or use probing questioning that theoretically will have a higher predictive validity. Evidently interviewers had mixed preferences (Chapman and Zweig, 2005). Further, the competency-based interview assumes that behav-

Table 5.4 Reasons for poor results from selection interviewing

Processing of information	
Pre-interview	Use of application forms to reject the applicant on grounds of sex, academic standing or physical attractiveness.
First impressions	Decisions made quickly lead to a search during the rest of the interview for information to support those decisions.
Stereotypes	Interviewers may hold stereotyped images of a 'good' worker against which applicants are judged. Such images may be based on prejudice.
Contrast	Interviewers may compare applicants against each other rather than against objective criteria, e.g. an average applicant who follows one below-average may be rated as above average.
Attraction	Interviewers may be biased towards applicants they 'like'. This attraction may develop where interviewers hold opinions and attitudes similar to those of the applicant.
Skills of interviewing	
Structure	Variations in interview structure affect reliability, low scores being gained for unstructured interviews.
Questions	Interviewers may use multiple, leading and unlawful questions.
Listening	Interviewers may talk more than listen, especially if they view the applicant favourably.
Retention and interpretation	Interviewers may have a poor recall of information unless guides are used and notes made. Interviewers may have difficulty in interpreting the information.

iour is consistent over time, but this premise can be challenged on the basis that people do learn from their mistakes and can learn new ways of behaving (Martin and Pope, 2008). While a structured approach provides a degree of control over the interview, it is likely that candidates prepare their answers in advance or distort their responses to create a desirable impression (Levashina and Campion, 2006).

HRM web links

Visit the companion website at **www.bloomsbury.pub/bratton-hrm** for particular guidance on competency-based interviews.

Assessment centres

Assessment centres (ACs) use more elaborate versions of assessment drawing upon both the psychometric and PO fit models, a recognition of the weakness of single measures to assess candidates. Originally established for the selection of military officers during the Second World War, an assessment centre is a *late-stage* evaluation process lasting for one to three days. The episode provides for an in-depth standardised assessment of mental capability and behaviour based on multiple selection tools, including psychometric tests, work sample type exercises, group exercises, role plays and interviews. It is claimed that ACs are particularly suited for high-level managerial and graduate vacancies in dynamic complex work environments (Wilk and Cappelli, 2003). Lloyds Bank, for example, used attendance at an assessment centre, lasting 24 hours, in their last stage of the selection process (Pollitt, 2005).

Assessment centres offer many advantages, allowing the recruiter to observe and assess candidates undertaking a number of work-related activities, thereby providing a fuller picture of an applicant's strengths and weaknesses. Assessment centres have been demonstrated to be good predictors of future job performance, showing predictive validity coefficients of 0.36 (Table 5.3). However, ACs only measure situation-specific performance rather than cross-situational managerial and leadership skills (Bycoi et al., 1987). Research has also highlighted that the context and composition of the group attending may influence the predictive scores (Becker et al., 2011).

Critiquing recruitment and selection

As you have hopefully recognised through this book so far, the practice of HR management can only be understood in the context of the wider economic-political and cultural factors which shape those practices. And, of course, in Britain, Europe and North America, of significance here is class, gender and race. Following the brutal killing of the African American, George Floyd, there have been national conversations about European and US history and statues of white Europeans, and organisation after organisation has publicly affirmed their support for the Black Lives Matter movement. There has been a positive shift in public attitudes: the rejection of racism (Malik, 2020). While ostensibly employers' selection methods must treat candidates fairly, without discrimination or bias, in Britain class and race undoubtedly play a part in recruitment and selection, with many top professions inaccessible to graduates from a BAME or working-class background (Doward and Munro, 2017; Muir, 2017; Savage, 2015). In 2020 Britain, explicit racism is unlawful, but the pandemic has held up a 'mirror to the structural racism' in the labour market (Parveen, 2021). And studies have found that employers are still refusing to consider applicants because of their race or ethnicity (Heath, 2019). Minority ethnic applicants have to send in around 60 per cent more CVs to get a job interview. Name-blind CVs have been suggested to eschew discrimination at the applicant screening stage, but these are only moderately effective, given evidence of extensive discrimination in late-stage selection interviews. Eliminating inequalities, whether race, class or gender, it is argued, cannot be reduced to iconoclastic discourse about statues of slave traders because their heirs retain power and political influence (Bennett, 2020) and structural injustice endures unchallenged. As Malik (2020, p. 35) rightly argues, 'the heart of the problem lies in warped social relations and deformed institutional structures'. As society and organisations search for new ways to eliminate social inequalities, a good starting point is to put a spotlight on recruitment and selection processes.

In post-Brexit Britain, despite the talk of meritocracy, 'social mobility in Britain has stalled' (Bratton and Denham, 2019, p. 373). Closely related to the issue of class and social mobility is power. For the French philosopher Michel Foucault (1926–84), power operates within all social institutions, at all levels of social interaction and through all individuals. Importantly, moreover, 'power does not intrude from powerful individuals; it *exudes from within*' (Murphy and Bratton, 2020, p. 63). From Foucault's conception of an all-pervasive disciplinary power, Townley (1994) plausibly argues that HR practices, such as those used in the recruitment and selection process, constitute invisible power. Selection methods, or what Townley calls 'social technologies', often seem to be neutral, benign and objective, but the criteria built into such procedures make up a knowledge portfolio that provides the organisation and its agents with power to influence and control individual employees.

Within the positivist tradition, the goal of the recruiter is to identify individual differences (e.g. mental ability, work experience, qualifications) and behavioural differences (e.g. attitudes and values) using various assessment tools. Recruitment and selection tools therefore make individual differences and capabilities visible to the recruiter. As such, these technologies provide an important means of 'knowing' and, subsequently, managing people. For example, the use of psychometric tools 'individualises' the applicant in terms of their particular psychological profile and human foibles. The act of enumerating attributes, values and human interactions to others in a codified manner permits for the amount of a particular psychological attribute to be measured and thereafter compared with other candidates or employees. It is through these assessment technologies 'individuals are rendered observable, measurable and quantifiable' (Townley, 1994, p. 95). In so doing, 'the minutiae of the human soul' become the managed domain for HR managers (Rose, 1990, p. 72).

Critics also contend that psychometrics provide a 'cocktail of "scientific" measurement' about candidates (Hollway, 1991, p. 57 and cited by Townley, 1994, p. 88). For some, these 'pseudoscientific' tools have an ideological dimension of *individualism* – in which individual characteristics and past behaviour are claimed to predict future job performance; *managerialism* – in which managers define the criteria for performance against a hierarchical evaluation of success or failure; and *utility* – in which the costs and benefits, in monetary terms, of using different selection techniques are assessed within a hierarchy of power (Iles and Salaman, 1995; Townley, 1994).

The structured selection interview is another example of a social technology. A form of 'confessional device', which, while appearing as an innocuous encounter between interviewer and interviewee, is designed to obtain first-hand information about past behaviour and values as it relates to specific job roles and enables the interviewer to interpret the 'inner meaning of the outward sign' of the interviewee (Townley, 1994, p. 115). Moreover, studying recruitment and selection methods for predicting managerial talent from a critical perspective reveals experiences that fall outside mainstream literature: that candidates are inherently assessed not only in an image of management, but also one that is a gender-specific model of what constitutes managerial activity (Calás and Smircich, 1990; Wajcman, 1998). Despite the evidence of a strong positive relationship between ethnic minority presence in the boardroom and positive firm performance (Öztürk and Calás, 2017), the absence of diversity among organisational leaders has implications for what is understood and measured as managerial characteristics (Morouney, 1991).

Debates on the theories of difference, hegemonic masculinities and intersectionality can be related to debates around class, gender, race, and the choice of recruitment and selection tools and practices (Hearn and Louvrier, 2017). Considered within the context of the globalisation of recruitment and selection, the dominant practices constitute a nexus of interrelated Anglo-Saxon theories, knowledge and values (Ryan and Ployhart, 2014) that, arguably, support a defective and unsustainable model of capitalism (Salaman, 2016). In particular, psychometric tools are inherently biased towards a Western view of intelligence 'imbued with a mono-cultural attitude towards assessment and using a particular linguistic repertoire which may be at odds with culturally diverse populations' (Searle, 2003, p. 276). In MNCs, where often traditional Western HR practices are advocated, it is highly likely that local cultural factors will produce variations in recruitment and selection methods (see, for example, Zhu et al., 2013). The Covid-19 pandemic draws further attention to the issues concerning the role of social networking, globalisation and the changing nature and place of work, and their influence on recruitment and selection.

Reflective question

Do some selection tools tend to be skewed against female or BAME applicants? Why or why not?

Summary

This chapter has examined the nature of recruitment and selection. The attraction and subsequent retention of employees is seen as crucial to performance and the employment relationship. It is essential that organisations see that, whatever the state of the labour market and their power within it, contact with potential recruits is made through the projection of an 'image' that will impact on and reinforce the expectations of potential recruits. Theorists have identified three distinct paradigms for understanding recruitment and selection processes: psychometric, person organisation fit and social process. We have examined selection criteria and measurement issues and discussed various methods used to attract applicants, noting the growth of social media as a form of e-recruitment.

We have explained that recruitment and selection should be aligned with strategy; that there are multiple ways of attracting and selecting workers with the right KSAs that match the strategy of a particular organisation. There is no one best practice. Selection methods are chosen on the basis of their consistency in measurement over time – reliability – and the extent to which they measure what they are supposed to measure – validity. Psychometric-based testing is used by organisations to assess applicants' inner constructs, such as personality traits and to screen applicants more quickly. They may, however, filter out good applicants as well as unsuitable ones. We critically examined a range of assessment methods. The interview is the most common and, unsurprisingly, has been the subject of much research. Recent years have witnessed the growth of competency-based interviewing. The use of assessment centres is the most comprehensive form of evaluation used in selection, comprising a range of psychometric tests, situational judgement tests and structured interviews.

Review questions

1. Do you consider social media and online recruitment methods more effective in attracting applicants than traditional methods? Why or why not?
2. How can the validity of an employment interview be improved? To what extent do some selection methods disadvantage BAME groups?
3. Should employers refuse to hire people without Covid-19 vaccine? Why or why not? [Hint: see Legal Focus.]

Search & Watch

Visit YouTube and search the video titled: **Short man, or overweight woman? Your size could make you poorer.** Research suggests that women who were 6.3 kilos heavier than average were likely to have an income £1,500 (€1,680) less per year than their slimmer colleagues. Men who were 7.5 centimetres shorter than the national average, were also likely to have an income that was £1,500 (€1,680) less per year than their taller colleagues (Tyrrell et al., 2016). Appearance bias leads to discrimination on the basis of weight and height and other physical characteristics. Think about the following: (1) What other forms of bias can influence the recruiter? (2) Why is it important to be aware of perceptual biases?

Then go to the video hub at www.bloomsbury.pub/bratton-hrm and watch **Alison Blayney's (HR Business Partner, TIGI Haircare, Unilever)** interview discussing recruitment and selection. Answer the following: (1) How does Alison claim she is proactive in recruiting? What does she mean by 'going beyond normal sourcing strategies' to build talent pools? (2) Is LinkedIn effective for Alison? How does she use the employee referral scheme and who benefits from it? (3) How does Generation Y differ from Generation X? Explain how the employee brand is 'leveraged' to attract Generation Y.

Legal Focus

Under UK common law, the employer can employ or refuse to employ anyone whom the employer chooses for whatever reason, including sex, marital status, race, age or sexual orientation. Unsurprisingly, therefore, over the last 50 years, statute law has increasingly sought to restrict an employer from exercising their common-law rights. The Race Relations Act 1965 and the Disability Discrimination Act 1995 prohibited direct discrimination in employment on grounds of race and disabilities. Pre-Brexit, an important influence on UK legislation has been Article 157 of the Treaty of Rome, and Council Directive EEC 76/207 strengthens the principle of equality, requiring equal treatment for men and women in all aspects of employment. To comply with its EU obligations, the UK Equality Act 2010 provides protection against discrimination on the basis of nine protected characteristics.

The Covid-19 vaccine raises the controversial question of mandatory immunisation for hiring new or existing employees in certain fields. Requiring Covid-19 immunisation as a condition of employment cuts through myriad ethical and legal areas, including employees' religious beliefs, personal privacy, bodily integrity, human rights and health and safety. Employers are looking to draw up 'no jab, no job' contracts for employees. Some companies, ranging from care-home operators to large multinational groups, are considering employment contracts requiring new and existing staff to have the Covid-19 vaccination. At the time of writing the law is unclear. Generally, the law recognises the need to balance the competing interests of personal privacy and public and employee safety. In Canada, for example, front-line health-care workers must be immunised against rubella. Those employees refusing to be vaccinated against Covid-19 may face consequences, such as being moved to another workstation or placed on leave or required to wear extra PPE (Mahoney and Fine, 2020).

Task Search online for government information in your jurisdiction prohibiting direct discrimination and compare and contrast it with another country, for example, Australia or Canada. (1) What is meant by direct discrimination? (2) What characteristics are protected against discrimination in the UK's Equality Act 2010? (3) What companies are considering or have implemented 'no jab, no job' employment contracts for new or existing employees?

Reference

See Deborah Lockton and Tom Brown's *Employment Law* (2020), pp. 153–77, for a discussion on the Equality Act 2010, covering direct discrimination in the workplace. See also Beioley, K., Parker, G., Strauss, D., Hancock, A. and Venkataramakrishnan (2021) UK companies look to make Covid-19 vaccinations mandatory. *The Financial Times*, 16 February, for a discussion on mandatory immunisation for workers.

Chapter case: Køre (Part 2)

The setting

Køre is a FinTech company based in Copenhagen, Denmark, which we introduced in the previous chapter on workforce planning. In preparation for international expansion to the USA, $26 million has been raised in a Series C funding round. Køre has hired a designated HR department to alleviate recruitment, promotion and training tasks from the managers and team leads. Currently, the employees at Køre are mostly young, white men. Reports of a 'toxic' work environment have been published online, and a small group of employees have voiced their concerns and experiences to the founders. The investors requested that the newly hired HR department create a diversity and inclusion strategy to preserve their image and the valuation of Køre. The founders, Lucas Jensen and Victor Pedersen, have agreed to the strategy that was created by the HR specialists but still prioritise speed and efficiency over any other metric. The current key performance indicators (KPIs) of the recruitment team are:

1. Time to hire: the amount of time taken to hire an employee since the role was first opened.
2. Cost of hire: the amount of recruitment budget that was spent on hiring the new employee.

The problem

The diversity and inclusion strategy created by the HR specialists includes increasing the number of diverse employees through recruitment efforts. Due to the expansion, ten roles have been opened in the technical team, including data scientists, machine learning engineers and software engineers. Prior to the introduction of an HR department to the company, technical hiring was the responsibility of the VP Engineering, Jan Madsen.

In a short email to the recruitment team, Jan warns:

> There is a competitive market at the moment for technical talent. Hiring junior data scientists is easier because applicants come from a variety of physics and mathematics backgrounds, but there is a long time-to-hire for senior roles. We need employees at Køre who can deal with the fast-paced environment, go the extra mile in their projects, and fit within the current team. You can focus on the diversity strategy in your own time, but we need these roles filled quickly.

The recruitment process suggested by Jan comprises five stages:

1. CV screening by recruiters.
2. Introductory call with a recruiter for 15 minutes, making an initial assessment of the person organisation fit and answering questions about the company.
3. Technical challenge that must be completed within 24 hours to measure the job-specific skills of the candidate.
4. Interview with Jan for an hour to discuss experience and person–job fit.
5. Contract negotiation and agreement call with a recruiter.

Jan prefers an unstructured interviewing style, as he will be working closely with the new employees and wants to have the freedom to get to know the candidate in a relaxed atmosphere. He takes pride in the camaraderie within the technical team and believes that the new employees should fit into the current 'work hard, play hard' dynamic. The HR team have received training on how to assist in visa applications and organise relocation if necessary. Køre also allows employees to work remotely. The job descriptions have been reworked to make them more inclusive, and a diversity statement has been added. Finally, a small budget has been allocated to improve the image of Køre through employer branding.

The assignment

You are part of the recruitment team at Køre, focusing on technical roles. Create an infographic of a recruitment process, and highlight how each stage would best enable diverse applicants. Draw on the recruitment methods discussed in this chapter. You should also consider how the change in the recruitment process affects the KPIs.

Essential reading

Brown, J. N. (2011) *The Complete Guide to Recruitment: A Step-by-step Approach to Selecting, Assessing and Hiring the Right People*. London: Kogan Page Publishers.

Chartered Institute of Personnel and Development (2019) *Diversity Management that Works: An Evidence-based View.* London: CIPD.

Rijamampianina, R. and Carmichael, T. (2005) A pragmatic and holistic approach to managing diversity. *Problems and Perspectives in Management*, *3*(1): 109–17.

Note: This case was contributed by Alexis Evans.

Further reading

Anderson, N. and C. Witvliet (2008) Fairness reactions to personnel selection methods: an international comparison between the Netherlands, the United States, France, Spain, Portugal, and Singapore. *International Journal of Selection and Assessment, 16*(1): 1–13.

Burnton, H., Daugherty, B., Dickins, D. and Schisler, D. (2016) Dominant personality types in public accounting: selection bias or indoctrinated? *Accounting Education*. DOI: 10.1080/09639284.2015.1127768

Hedenus, A., Backman, C. and Håkansson, P. (2021) Whom do you know? Recruiters' motives for assessing jobseekers' online networks. *The International Journal of Human Resource Management, 32*(8): 1754–77. DOI: 10.1080/09585192.2019.1579245

Pan, Y., Froese, F., Liu, N., Hu, Y. and Ye, M. (2021) The adoption of artificial intelligence in employee recruitment: the influence of contextual factors. *The International Journal of Human Resource Management*. DOI: 10.1080/09585192.2021.1879206

Schmidt, F. L., Oh, I. S. and Shaffer, J. A. (2016) *The Validity and Utility of Selection Methods in Personnel Psychology: Practical and Theoretical Implications of 100 Years of Research Findings*. Philadelphia, PA: Temple University, Fox School of Business Research Paper. Available at: http://home.ubalt.edu/tmitch/645/session%204/Schmidt%20&%20Oh%20MKUP%20validity%20and%20util%20100%20yrs%20of%20research%20Wk%20PPR%202016.pdf.

Searle, R.H. (2003) *Selection and Recruitment: A Critical Text*. Milton Keynes: Open University/ Palgrave Macmillan.

CHAPTER 6

PERFORMANCE MANAGEMENT

outline

- Introduction
- The nature and development of performance management
- Performance management processes
- Defining performance
- Performance, judgements and feedback
- Critiquing performance management
- Summary
- Further reading

Source: Photo by fotographierende on Unsplash

objectives

After studying this chapter, you should be able to:

1. Explain the key elements and purpose of an effective performance management system
2. Critically evaluate the assumptions that underpin performance appraisal
3. Understand the relationship between performance, motivation, reward and development
4. Explain why context matters when contrasting different approaches to performance management
5. Explain why critics posit that performance management and appraisal is a control technology

Introduction

As a student, you will be familiar with being assessed by your tutor. Whether in the form of assignments, group presentations, examinations and so on, you have had the chance to demonstrate your academic capabilities. Any information you receive about your performance scores, the feedback, will, in turn, affect your own self-appraisal. Consider for a moment your reactions to the feedback you received on your last assignment. Did you regard the assessment of your work to be fair? Did the feedback provide specifics on what you did well and how you could improve? Establishing academic standards, evaluating your academic performance and providing feedback are processes that share much in common with performance management in the workplace. Performance management (PM) entails job-related goal setting, evaluation of performance, feedback, and worker rewards and development. Performance appraisal is part of this process which evaluates individual performance based on the judgement of line managers or others. Both performance management and appraisal address the indeterminate nature of the employment relationship (see Chapter 1) by providing clarity about effort-reward employer expectations (Brown and Lim, 2013). Mainstream HRM literature posits performance management and appraisal as a strategic HR process central to improving both individual and organisational performance against pre-defined business strategies.

In this chapter, we provide a diagrammatic overview of performance management and critically explore its nature, evolution and diffusion in organisations. We consider recent developments which consider PM as a process of continuous dialogue or 'performance conversations' between leaders and followers. When it is reported that an increasing number of employers appear to be questioning the value and relevance of traditional performance appraisal, we seek to explain some of its contentious features. We conclude by offering a critique of performance management and appraisal.

The nature and development of performance management

For Fombrun and his colleagues (1984), performance is a function of all HRM components: selecting the most capable people, appraising their performance to facilitate the equitable distribution of rewards and developing workers to enhance their current performance (see Figure 1.1). They asserted that 'the performance appraisal process is the key to an effective human resource system' (1984, p. 46). Indeed, performance and leveraging human potential are *leitmotivs* running through modern HRM literature. Rather than performance appraisal being seen as 'technical' readjustment prompted by immediate concerns with productivity and global competition, appraisal is 'integral' to the HRM model (Townley, 1989, p. 92). The recent converging of digital technologies and people analytics has offered new possibilities for monitoring worker performance (Findlay and Thompson, 2017). From a management point of view, performance provides the main thrust of both day-to-day and strategic people management (CIPD, 2016). Performance management is posited as a strategic management activity in that its aim is to maximise worker capabilities and potential and ensure that worker contribution is aligned with pre-defined organisational strategy (Fombrun et al., 1984; Williams, 2008).

The origins of performance management can be found in Peter Drucker's (1961) management by objective (MBO) approach to management. MBO was posited as a 'scientific' mechanism that measured work against stated targets. Greenwood (1981, p. 225) defined MBO as:

> A process whereby the superior and subordinate managers of an organization *jointly* identify its common goals, define each individual's major areas of responsibility in terms of results expected of him [sic], and use these measures as guides for operating the unit and assessing the contribution of each of its members.

Analysing this definition, several key themes emerge. First, MBO tended to be only applied to those employees holding management positions. Second, subordinate managers played a major role in setting their own targets and not in merely receiving objectives from above. Third, measurements provide a guide for future behaviour and action. The measurement of performance is at the core of MBO. As Drucker espoused: '[The] task can be identified. It can be defined. Goals can be set. And performance can be measured. And then business can perform' (1961 p. 347). The broad thrust of traditional MBO, in particular the emphasis on 'jointly' identifying common objectives, is replicated in models of performance management.

Reflective question

What are the potential problems associated with measuring performance of knowledge workers or professionals where there may be no clear-cut measurable output?

There is no conclusive definition of performance management, but as Table 6.1 shows, researchers around the English-speaking world have conceptualised performance management as a process, and as a matter of a particular behaviours, such as objective setting, measurement and feedback.

Table 6.1 Selective definitions of performance management

The process through which the critical job behaviors of the management are identified, the specific objectives of each individual manager are set, and the steps or resources needed to attain each of them are agreed upon (Latham, 1984, p. 87).
A process for establishing a shared understanding about what is to be achieved, and how it is to be achieved; an approach to managing people which increases the probability of achieving job-related success (Weiss and Hartle, 1997, p. 77).
A philosophy for managing the behaviour of people within a context that facilitates and supports the alignment of individual goals with organizational goals in order to achieve organizational and financial performance (Whitford and Coetsee, 2006, p. 65).
An activity that establishes objectives through which individuals and teams can see their part in the organisation's mission and strategy, improves performance among employees, teams and ultimately organisations and holds people to account for their performance by linking it to reward, career progression and termination of contracts (CIPD, 2016, p. 5).
The process of goal setting, performance monitoring for feedback and development, and performance appraisal for evaluation as input to compensation and other administrative decisions (London and Mone, 2018, p. 245).

These definitions define the dimensions of performance management in similar ways. First, the concept of process features in most definitions of performance management. The activity is perceived as a systematic and holistic process in which the participants influence each other to understand and agree on 'shared understandings' about what needs to be done and how to do it and the process of facilitating individual development effort to improve future performance. Second, and related, notions of 'shared understanding' reflect a unitary view of the organisations: seeing the organisation as a single entity with one goal and claiming that individual employees, managers and organisational interests are one and the same. The different ways performance management is defined places emphasis on day-to-day observable individual behaviours that meet pre-determined targets or objectives.

A fourth dimension is the focus on strategy – concerned with the broader issues facing the organisation – and, as such, is a significant departure from traditional MBO. It is a strategic focus on organisational objectives that gives performance management its distinctive position in HRM (Baron, 2009). Performance management is considered strategic for two key reasons: first, because it is an important element in the distribution of rewards and to the perception on the part of employees that the decisions around their distribution is equitable. Second, data generated through the performance management process give focus to employees' training and development needs (Devanna et al., 1984, p. 47). However, the degree to which strategic aims and a performance management system (PMS) are integrated is open for discussion, creating a gap between the familiar rhetoric and the reality claims for the contribution of performance management to organisational performance (Stanton and Nankervis, 2011).

Early methods used for evaluating an employee's performance were referred to as performance appraisal systems (PAS) which typically centred around the completion of an annual interview and report. Interestingly, all but one definition avoids the use of the term 'performance appraisal' (PA), which has connotations with the negative aspects of traditional appraisal systems (Armstrong and Taylor, 2014, p. 334). Performance management has developed from appraisal schemes with a narrow operational focus to a more strategic-oriented concept (Brown and Lim, 2013). As a process, performance management is not a single annual event, but is best conceptualised as an integrated series of reciprocal interactions and conversations about setting goals and performance appraisal, as well as learning, development and reward decisions.

Performance management systems (PMSs) have changed over the last 50 years. Whereas MBO and early PA schemes utilised quantitative scales and formats for evaluating performance, in contrast, PMSs are more likely to include both quantitative and qualitative measures. In the academic arena, this change has shifted the focus of research. Whereas early research emphasised validity, reliability and absence of bias, contemporary research tends to focus on the social context and on employee reactions to the performance process (Brown and Lim, 2013). Probably the most significant change over the last 30 years has been the diffusion of PMS to non-managerial workers. Influenced by new public management (NPM) thinking, an increasing number of public-sector employers have imported PMS from the private sector into public organisations (Whitfield, 2012).

All OECD economies, with few exceptions, have performance management systems in place (Farnham, 2015). Survey evidence collated from more than 1,000 organisations in more than 50 countries reported most organisations use formal performance and appraisal management systems (Gunnigle et al., 2014; Mercer, 2013). In Britain, by the turn of the millennium, survey data indicated a high level of agreement among respondents regarding the importance of performance management and the inclusion of regular review meetings (90 per cent), objective setting (82.5 per cent), regular feedback to individuals (83 per cent), performance appraisals (82.8 per cent) and assessment of development needs (75.1 per cent). However, in reality such activities were not always completed – for example, only 62.7 per cent completed regular review meetings to assess their progress against targets and only 75.3 per cent set objectives or targets. Performance appraisal was more likely, at 81.3 per cent (CIPD, 2009). Six years later, another CIPD survey of a small sample of senior HR leaders found that 49 per cent of the leaders' organisations used performance management (CIPD, 2016, p. 8). An extensive employment relations survey of workplaces in Britain indicated that a significant proportion of non-managerial workers were undergoing formal performance appraisal of one kind or the other. UK-based data covering 2004 to 2011 shows the proportion of non-managerial workers being appraised increased from 51 per cent to 87 per cent (van Wanrooy et al., 2013b, p. 99).

As discussed in previous chapters, the choice of which HR practices to adopt, including performance and appraisal management practices, is grounded in a specific situation, not least size and organisational culture considerations. Data on PMS in SMEs, usually understood as any enterprise with between 10 and 249 staff (along with microenterprises with fewer than ten staff), are generally inconsistent. But survey evidence suggests 'a relatively low take-up' of formal appraisal practices in SMEs (Farnham, 2015, p. 518). Most SMEs have little time for an analysis of performance, and measurement activity, if it does occur, is mostly undertaken in response to problems as they emerge (Garengo et al., 2005; Gold and Thorpe, 2008).

The strategic decision to adopt PMS in public service organisations has been influenced by the wider economic-political context. Mainstream accounts emphasise NPM efforts to reconfigure the 'value-drivers' through more measurement against targets. In the 1990s, therefore, there was a shift towards a more 'customer-oriented' approach to performance measurement, referred to as 'new managerialism' (Mwita, 2000). The pivot towards 'customer-oriented' has obvious parallels with the ascendency of 'customer democracy' found in business process re-engineering (Hammer, 1997, see Chapter 3). The clear intent of new management is market-driven. Policy-makers saw such management practices as important drivers of public sector improvements in productivity (Boxall and Purcell, 2016).

Ethical Insight
Does objective setting in performance management encourage unethical behaviour?

In 2020, Wells Fargo, a leading US-based multinational financial services company, was fined US$3 billion by federal authorities as the result of a 'staggering' fake accounts scandal (Egan, 2020). Employees at the institution opened as many as 3.5 million fraudulent accounts over a 15-year period (Mehrotra and Keller, 2017). Such activity is known as 'gaming', which is defined in the *Wells Fargo Code of Ethics* as, 'the manipulation and/or misrepresentation of sales or referrals ... in an attempt to receive compensation or to meet sales goals' (McClean, 2017). The firm stated that it did not tolerate gaming and fired approximately 5,300 staff members between 2011 and 2016 as a result (Egan, 2016). However, it has been suggested that the misconduct was in fact driven by Wells Fargo's business model, which 'imposed unreasonable sales goals on its employees along with unreasonable pressure to meet these goals' (Jaeger, 2020). There were longstanding concerns regarding the culture within Wells Fargo. In 2013, the *Los Angeles Times* reported that a 'pressure cooker' sales environment 'battered' employee morale and led to 'ethical breaches, customer complaints and labor lawsuits' (Reckard, 2013). Employees were reputedly sacked for calling the company's ethics hotline about improper sales tactics, with one former HR official claiming Wells Fargo would find ways to fire workers 'in retaliation for shining light' on sales issues (Egan, 2016). Authorities said that senior executives at the community bank 'minimized the problems' by shifting the blame to 'individual misconduct instead of the sales model itself' (Egan, 2020).

'Setting goals is one of the established tools that managers have to increase staff motivation and performance' (Healy and Niven, 2016, p. 3). However, as the Wells Fargo case serves to illustrate, they may be a catalyst for unethical behaviour. It has been suggested that personality differences may explain, at least in part, why some people act unethically when given a performance goal and others do not. Research conducted by Healy and Niven (2016) suggests that some individuals have 'high moral justification', meaning that they possess a tendency to portray an unethical act as being in service of some valued or moral purpose. In addition, the authors found that the more specific a goal was (for example, a numerical target versus a vague exhortation that you should 'do your best'), the more likely subjects were to overstate their performance. In order to mitigate against misconduct, the Institute of

Business Ethics (IBE) (2020) stresses that performance management should be central to embedding ethical values into business practice, with careful attention paid to '*what* is accomplished and rewarded so that only goals which support an organisation's ethical commitments are put forward'. In addition, the IBE suggests that it is vital that employees are assessed and rewarded based on *how* they achieve the goals set (IBE, 2020).

Stop! If asked to offer guidance to line managers on setting appropriate performance goals, what key recommendation(s) could you make?

Essential reading

Healy, C. and Niven, K. (2016) When tough performance goals lead to cheating. *Harvard Business Review*, 8 September.

Note: This feature was contributed by Laura Steele.

Performance management processes

Classic models of performance management are conceptualised as a set of interconnected activities. The CIPD (2019h, p. 2) suggests that performance management involves activities that:

- establish objectives through which individuals and teams can see their part in the organisation's mission and strategy;
- improve performance among employees, teams and, ultimately, organisations;
- hold people to account for their performance by linking it to reward, career progression and termination of contracts.

At an operational level, models depict a four-stage process or cycle, Figure 6.1. The cycle helps us to understand PM as an ongoing process, with multiple and overlapping parts. Objectives are jointly established, revised as expectations and context change, feedback is received, learning and support is experienced. Performance appraisal is just one part of the PM process, designed to assess individual vis-à-vis pre-determined objectives.

Review performance plan

Most PMS models attempt to show a strategic integration of the organisation's HR strategy, which can together be linked to the goals and direction of an organisation. The first stage of the cycle assumes that all work performance is derived and driven by organisational strategic objectives, which in turn determines departmental or functional objectives. Individual performance objectives and standards derive from these strategic considerations. Examples of organisation strategies shaping performance objectives and measurement include: increasing return on investment, pivoting from global supply chains to local and interventions to create low-carbon organisational culture (Norton et al., 2015).

The process of reviewing current performance might incorporate, especially for managers, development centres. Similar to assessment centres (see Chapter 5), development centres focus more on individual or team-analysis diagnostic activities, designed to enable managers to consider the extent of their employees' or teams' skills utilisation, and identify areas of strength and areas for development

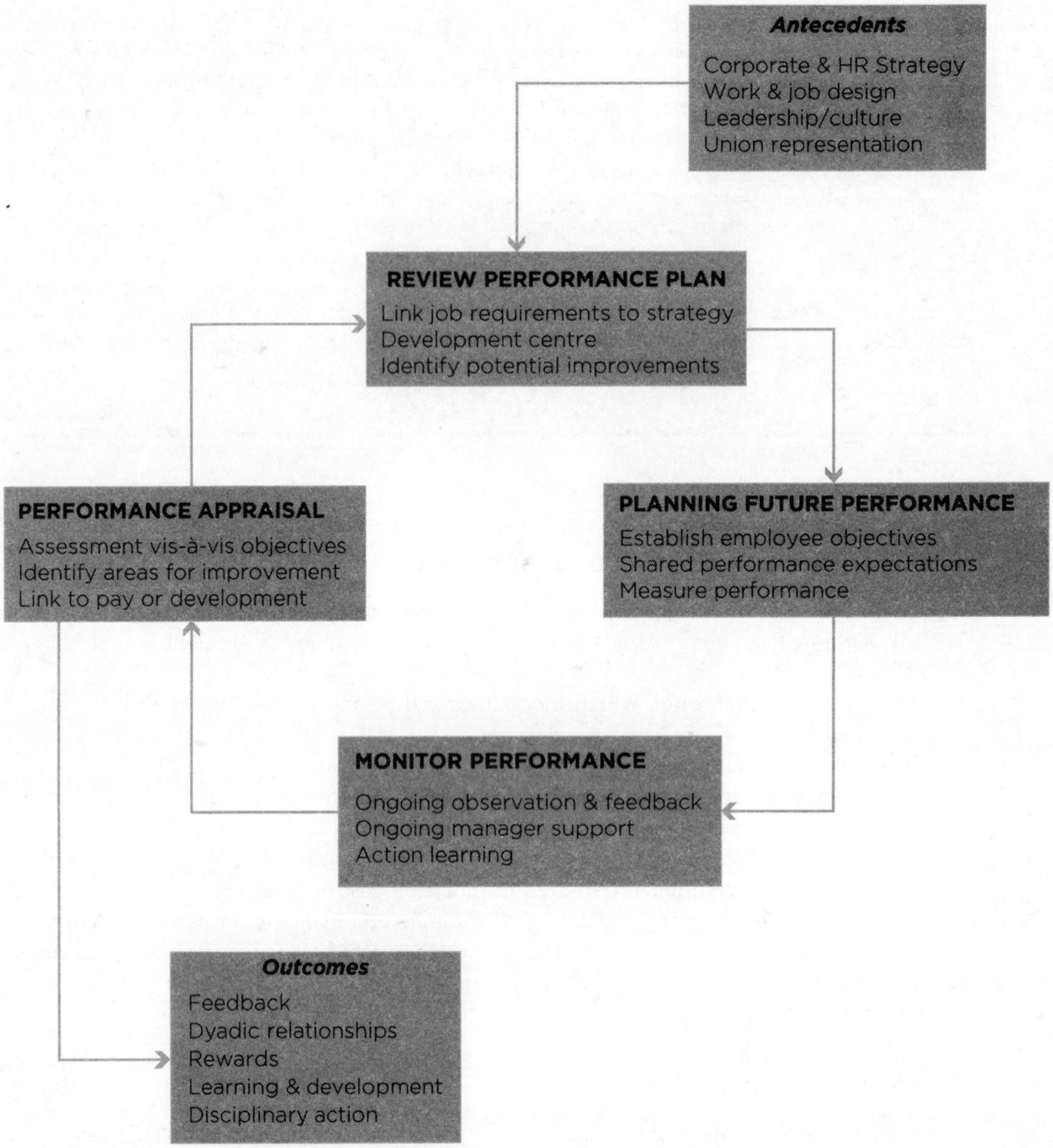

Figure 6.1 The performance management cycle

(Ballantyne and Povah, 2004). PMS relies heavily on line managers for their effective operation, and this cannot always be assured (Rashidi, 2015; see also Figure 1.4). It is for this reason that effective PMS appears to be associated with increased employee engagement (Mone et al., 2011). There is a body of HRD research that has examined the value of action learning, whereby a small group of managers and other employees come together to work and learn simultaneously in pursuit of practical solutions to pressing real individual or team-owned problems, through reflection, questioning and dialogue (Claxton and Gold, 2013, p. 276). In a Covid-19 world, one that requires mature discussion, without the *faux* certainty, on how organisations navigate unprecedented change, 'a pragmatic co-creation of knowing, *with,* not *about*, people' (Bradbury, 2015, p. 1), can help organisations deal with change. A critical analysis of action learning generally makes more explicit the tensions and power dynamics which naturally arise from such interactions (Trehan and Pedler, 2009).

Planning future performance

Stage two of the cycle involves establishing and agreeing future performance objectives between managers and employees together with establishing performance standards. PMS is based on an understanding of what constitutes 'performance'. There are two broad approaches to defining performance in PMS (Armstrong and Taylor, 2014). The first is focused on outputs or *results* where performance can be measured (for example, immunisation targets for GPs) and metrics used to determine the achievement of objectives. The legacy of MBO and the 'scientific' management maxim of 'what gets measured gets done', is highly influential in this quantitative approach, requiring consideration of both *what* to measure to assess performance results and *how* to quantify it. The second approach is focused on inputs or *behaviour* where performance cannot be readily quantified in absolute terms. This relates to the assessment of attitudes, behaviours, commitment, emotion or competencies employers want their staff to demonstrate. The assessment of behavioural performance or emotional performance is probably more important in service-providing organisations (see Chapter 3). The different approaches to rating performance are examined in more detail later in this chapter.

PART 3

Expectations about performance objectives are typically defined by the acronym 'SMART' – *Specific, Measurable, Attainable, Realistic* and *Time-related*. Finally, the most influential models of PM are those that have argued that objectives should be *agreed* between manager and employee and, in a nod to contingency theory, *flexible* to permit for renegotiation the behavioural implications of unforeseen circumstances. A fundamental criticism of objective setting is that it is overtly normative, that it inadequately captures the nuances of contemporary knowledge and service work, and, more worrying, that it may give rise to unethical behaviour (Ordonez et al., 2009).

Monitor performance

Performance management is 'a natural process of management' (Armstrong and Taylor, 2014, p. 336) – management's *reason d'être*. The third stage of the cycle focuses on monitoring employee performance. In that the process entails ongoing observation, feedback, conversations on performance and manager support, it is arguably the most important feature of PMS that differentiates it from traditional PM systems, which were usually built around the 'dreaded annual appraisal' interview (CIPD, 2019i, p. 3). Coaching has become a key activity line managers can use to improve individual performance and support organisational change. Such is the belief in the value of coaching that many organisations seek to develop a 'coaching culture' (Garvey et al., 2009).

In its current guise, performance management is viewed as a holistic set of both formal and informal processes and research suggests that effective performance management relies on ongoing 'performance conversations' (CIPD, 2019i), particularly when linked to action learning or participatory inquiry. In Storey's model of HRM (see Table 1.2), one key lever for energising individual performance is the organisation's culture and climate. We have a sizeable body of research which shows that organisations use their core values, which, as cultural theorists remind us, shape the form of human behaviour (Bratton, 2021). For example, senior managers, the sponsors of PMSs, are far more likely to report that PMSs 'enshrine their vision and cardinal values' (Nankervis et al., 2012, p. 49). Table 6.2 lists five theories that underpin core elements of PMS, briefly describes implications for practice and provides seminal references.

Table 6.2 Theories guiding performance management

Theories	Practice	Key contributors
Goal theory	Help set specific and achievable goals.	Latham and Locke (1979)
Expectancy theory	A motivation theory based on the idea that performance effort is directed towards behaviours that employees believe will lead to a desired outcome.	Vroom (1964); Lawler (1973)
Equity theory	A theory that explains work motivation based on how people develop perceptions of fairness in the distribution of resources.	Adams (1965); Giles et al. (1997)
Social cognitive theory	Core concept is self-efficacy – what people believe they can or cannot do powerfully affects their performance. Training, coaching and setting challenging but realistic and achievable goals reinforces self-efficacy.	Bandura (1986); Bandura and Locke (2003)
Feedback-oriented theories	Examines the effects on individual characteristics on reactions to performance appraisal, including how personal attributes can be changed and developed.	VandeWalle et al. (1999); Dweck (1999)

Reflective question

Looking at the motivation theories in Table 6.2, which theory best suggests that job motivation improves when employees link job performance and rewards? What motivates you to work, extrinsic or intrinsic rewards? What demotivates you?

Performance appraisal

A joint review of performance leads to the completion of the PM cycle. Performance appraisal provides a formal opportunity for the joint analysis of an employee's performance against agreed objectives and, importantly, to map out a plan for improvements in individual performance. It is recommended that the review is 'concrete, not abstract' and managers and individuals should together identify areas for performance improvement in the future (Armstrong and Taylor, 2014, p. 338). A long-held HRM opinion is that the most effective way for dealing with poor performance is to 'focus on the future rather than the past' (Latham, 1984, p. 97), because focusing on the past is likely to cause negativity due to the different perceptions of past events by the appraiser and subordinate. Where appropriate, performance appraisal of employee performance is used to determine resource decisions such as pay, and learning and development. The common practices in PM examined so far have remained broadly stable for over three decades, but recently there has been a proliferation of popular articles challenging the received wisdom on PA, which we examine below. Before explaining PA, we need to complete our examination of the PM cycle and to pause and give an overview of the antecedents of performance management.

Source: Getty Images/Thomas Barwick

Antecedents of performance management

A critical analysis of any social phenomenon needs to interrogate its antecedents, or more simply put, something existing or behaviours that potentially cause an outcome. An important group of antecedents that have been studied relate to those contextual factors that influence the performance management cycle and direct the purpose of the performance appraisal including: corporate strategy, the HR strategy, structure, job design, leadership, national and organisational culture, and the presence (or not) of trade unions, for example (Milliman et al., 2002; Pun and White, 2005). Context and choice are important when designing and enacting a PMS. But, 'There is no single best approach. Each organisation should develop practices that are relevant to their specific context and their actual (or desired) organizational culture' (CIPD, 2019h, p. 3).

The role of leadership is considered crucial in implementing an effective PMS. This means that leaders have the ability to employ 'complex inter-personal constructs' in order to adapt leadership style or behaviours to the required contexts (Scott, 2020, p. 258). The recent focus on 'performance conversations' in PMS suggests that effective leadership is best conceptualised, not so much as a set of personality traits or charisma, but 'as the readiness of leaders to engage, listen and to learn from followers' (Bratton, 2020, p. 2). Cultural theorists believe that culture is central to 'all aspects of organisational life' (Alvesson and Sveningsson, 2016, p. 26), including the design and enactment of PMS (Tziner et al., 2005). Evidence abounds of organisations having a 'box ticking' or 'alpha male' culture (Denham and Bratton, 2020, p. 80). In the public sector, with multiple professional occupations and high trade union density, if performance management is perceived to be more punitive than developmental – dubbed 'targets and terror' (Bevan and Hood, 2006) – the lofty goals associated with strategic-oriented PMS may be difficult to achieve (Boxall and Purcell, 2016).

Traditionally, performance measurement has been based on accountancy models, with embedded assumptions relating to costs and profit – the bottom line. This is the rationale for a 'control approach' performance management and appraisal. It is argued that the control approach is an outcome of the doctrine of 'shareholder value' (Salaman, 2016). Hence, influenced by this doctrine, managers base operational decisions and practices around efficiency and short-term financial performance. In a Covid-19 world, perhaps, especially in small and medium-sized enterprises, the control approach may become part of a set of taken-for-granted assumptions that dominate organisational life.

PART 3

Digital Spotlight
Is online appraisal equitable?

Performance appraisal is a core, though frequently criticised, aspect of HRM. As highlighted in this chapter, performance-related information can be utilised for a variety of important organisational purposes, including making administrative decisions (for example, in relation to pay rises or promotions) and providing feedback to employees in regard to their strengths or areas for further development. In addition, it can serve as criteria for the assessment of other HR systems, including the effectiveness of selection procedures (Farr et al., 2014). Over the last two decades, there has been a gradual shift away from traditional 'paper-and-pencil' (P&P) performance appraisals to online software platforms (Thompson et al., 2003). However, despite the plethora of packages now available, adoption has not been as swift as once predicted. One recent survey, for example, revealed that 42% of performance reviews in the UK are still documented in printed form (Gentle, 2019). Online appraisal systems began as an electronic version of the traditional P&P appraisal document. However, many are now vastly more sophisticated and can 'pull' relevant data from other sources within the organisation, for example, an employee's sickness absence record.

Several potential benefits of online appraisal systems have been identified. For example, they can enhance organisational efficiency and decision-making by centralising several HR functions and making information available to employees, managers and HR professionals on a 24/7 basis (Farr et al., 2014). This may be particularly useful in the context of multinational organisations which operate across several time zones. There is also some evidence that they can be more cost effective than traditional appraisals, though the initial investment required may be substantial (Bondarouk et al., 2017). In addition, online appraisal can make it easier to facilitate multisource or 360-degree feedback (Summers, 2001).

It is important, however, to also acknowledge the concerns that have been raised in relation to online performance appraisal systems. Miller (2003), for example, notes that technology can be utilised to quantify an employee's performance. However, this is more likely to happen in relation to jobs that are highly repetitive and leave little scope for personal judgement and discretion. Monitoring of this nature may erode trust and lead the worker to believe that the intention is to control, rather than coach or develop. In addition, there may be a failure to account for system factors (for example, an employee in a call centre may handle a smaller number of customer complaints but these may be of a significantly more complex nature) (Miller, 2003). Further, certain workers may find online performance appraisal dehumanising or struggle with computer literacy (Miller, 2003). As a result, it can be argued that, even as we move inexorably towards a future dominated by technology, there will always be a need for the 'human element' when it comes to HRM.

Stop! What issues should managers and HR professionals be mindful of when moving from traditional to online performance appraisal systems?

Essential reading

Bondarouk, T., Parry, E. and Furtmueller, E. (2017) Electronic HRM: four decades of research on adoption and consequences. *The International Journal of Human Resource Management, 28*(1): 98–131.

Note: This feature was contributed by Laura Steele.

Defining performance

In order to manage performance, it has to be defined and measured. However, the concept is subjective in nature which is why there is no universal, unambiguous definition of performance. Brumbach (1988, p. 387) offers this definition: 'Performance means both behavior and results. Behaviors emanate from the performer and transform performance from abstraction to action. Not just the instruments for results, behaviours are also outcomes in their own right – the product of mental and physical effort applied to tasks – and can be judged apart from results.' This definition infers that when assessing employees' performance both *inputs* (behaviour) and *outputs* (results) should be considered.

For Wholey (1996), performance is not an objective reality waiting to be measured and judged, but a socially constructed reality that exists in people's minds and is open to interpretation. Thus, performance may include outcomes, e.g. products, but can also embody notions of efficiency and cost effectiveness. Elena-Iuliana and Maria (2016) argue that organisations are challenged to meet by performance the values and expectations of wider society, particularly in the light of new pro-environmental standards on sustainable development. Therefore, performance can be conceptualised as a triangular relationship between organisational and societal objectives, resources and results, and the maelstrom of efficiency, effectiveness and budget allocation.

Precisely what performance should be measured depends upon the nature of the organisation's business, the values, interests and expectations of the society at large, and the jobs of the people within it. It is the extended consideration outside the dualism of behaviour and results that provokes

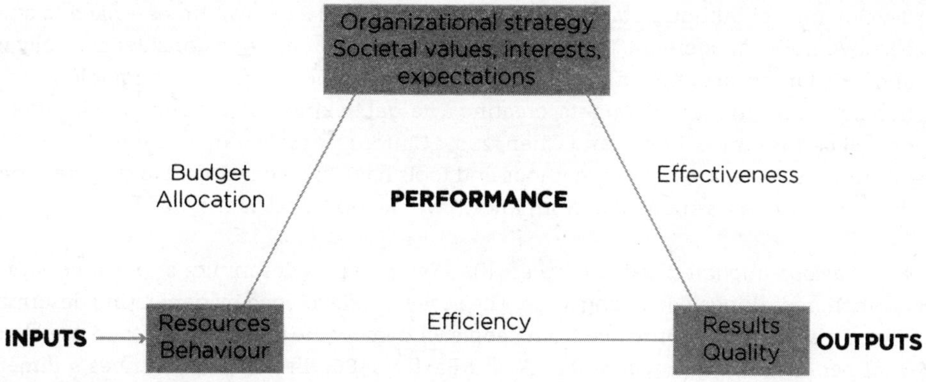

Figure 6.2 Defining performance

Source: Adapted from Elena-Iuliana and Maria (2016).

Elena-Iuliana and Maria (2016, p. 183) to conclude an organisation's objectives can be 'volatile, controversial and contradictory', which makes performance a subjective phenomenon. While the question '*how* is performance defined?' is important, a second is '*who* within the organisation defines performance standards?' Performance requirements typically cascade top-down through the organisation's hierarchy, but, depending upon organisational leadership, a bottom-up approach, where workers are allowed to set their own performance objectives, or a combined top-down and bottom-up approach may exist (Nonaka and Takeuchi, 1995). Whether it is predominantly top-down or bottom-up, the process of determining performance standards is intertwined with power. Murphy and Bratton (2020) contend power is omnipresent because it constitutes the very way we talk and think about ourselves and implies that managers and workers are deeply enmeshed in their own subordination, not least in the processes of performance management.

Appraisal instruments for assessing performance

Figure 6.2 suggests two principal approaches to rating performance: those oriented towards *inputs* and those oriented towards *results*. *Inputs-oriented appraisal*, also referred to as *competency-oriented* appraisal, is based on the visible demonstration of specific essential skills and behaviours thought to be related to high performance. Hochschild's (1983) pioneering work on emotion management, and the possible consequences of its commercialisation, has extended the scope for managers to judge employees' behaviour in terms of displayed emotion in customer-facing work (Bolton, 2005).

Results-oriented appraisal is based on setting measurable, achievable and time-bounded objectives or outcomes, most often agreed between manager and subordinate, and aligned towards achieving department or organisational objectives. Typical measurements might be sales, the number of satisfied customers or number of publications or research funding. When available, measurements can be taken at different points in time and comparisons made with objectives. It is not surprising that most measurements are quantifiable, although many organisations will attempt to combine both competency and results-based approaches in order to have the dual benefits of scaffolding long-term workforce learning and development and achieving short-term performance goals.

There is a relatively large number of studies that have examined whether inputs-oriented and results-oriented modes of appraisal reflect performance control or development approaches. Factors for consideration will relate to how objectives and targets are set, how managers and workers interact towards their achievement, and whether workers use the measurements as feedback in order to develop further. Although targets, for example, hospital A&E wait times, linked to strategic goals can be 'powerful' management 'tools', too many targets and failure to consider carefully *what* is targeted, and *who* targets are applied to, can lead to the phenomenon termed 'targetology' to describe a fixation of organisations with targets, creating a 'target ticking' culture and thereby affecting morale and overall performance (Boyne and Chen, 2007; Clifford, 2016; Doran et al., 2008).

Over the years, a variety of methods and tools have been developed to help develop PMSs that produce accurate assessment of performance. Two methods will be covered:

- *Behaviour-anchored rating scales* (BARSs) provide descriptions of important job behaviour 'anchored' alongside a rating scale. The scales are developed by generating descriptions of effective and ineffective performance from people who know the job; these are then used to develop clusters of performance and scales (Rarick and Baxter, 1986). Each scale describes a dimension of performance that can be used in appraisal. For example, in a scale developed for the behaviour of 'planning', the performance scale can vary between 'Excellent' and 'Unacceptable', and in between would lie a range of possible behaviours with varying degrees of effectiveness.
- *Behavioural observation scales* (BOSs) were developed as an improvement to BARSs (Latham and Wexley, 1994). This method involves the people doing the rating assessing the frequency of specific job-related behaviours that are observable. Figure 6.3, for example, shows BOSs that have been derived from a financial services company.

Developing people

a Gives praise where it is due to others in the team

1----------2----------3----------4----------5

Never *Always*

b Provides constructive feedback to colleagues

1----------2----------3----------4----------5

Never *Always*

c Shares best practice with others

1----------2----------3----------4----------5

Never *Always*

Figure 6.3 BOS in a financial services company

Both BARSs and BOSs are based on specific performance and on the descriptions of workers involved in a particular job. Research by Tziner et al. (2000) provided a comparison between BARSs and BOSs with respect to the satisfaction of those being rated with their appraisal and with the setting of goals to improve performance. It was found that goals developed using BOSs were more specific than those set using a BARS since they were based on what a 'rater' actually observed rather than on evaluation. Furthermore, since BOSs require a rating of several behaviours, rather than the identification of a single 'anchor', as in BARSs, this reduces bias and allows more specific feedback, with the formation of clearer goals. What is particularly interesting is the potential for such tools to enhance self-appraisal and allow a dialogue between workers, line managers and others based on more objective criteria (see below).

HRM in Practice
The benefits of mentorship during a crisis

Source: iStock.com/monkeybusinessimages

During the Covid-19 pandemic, UK employees working from home reported increased pressure to be available and found themselves less able to switch off, with excess workloads and fear of redundancies driving presenteeism. According to a study of UK workplaces, almost half (46%) of workers carrying out their jobs remotely during lockdown reported feeling more pressure to be 'present' for their employer and colleagues, with more than a third (35%) saying they had continued to work despite feeling unwell (Palmer, 2020). Of those who had worked through illness, more than a quarter (26%) also reported workload as a reason for not taking a day off, and 16% cited fear of redundancy. Jonny Gifford, research adviser at the CIPD, argued even before the pandemic work was becoming worse for our physical and mental health (Howlett, 2020b):

> 'As the full scale of the economic crisis unfolds, the outlook looks even bleaker,' he said. 'We'll likely see employers trying to do more with less, which will only increase people's workload and the pressure they are already under. Many people will also be worried about losing their job or living on a reduced income.'

Similarly, Paul Avis at Canada Life investments, reported that the lockdown had worsened the 'always on' culture that had been creeping into workplaces over recent years (Palmer, 2020):

> 'As the physical and mental wellbeing of UK employees is stretched to the limit, productivity could be significantly hit,' he warned. 'But with so many people frightened they might lose their jobs as a result of the coronavirus pandemic, it's no surprise they're working through sickness and worried about the implications of taking time off.'

As millions of workers struggled to carry out their jobs remotely during the pandemic, managers unaccustomed to supervising employees from afar also faced challenges in evaluating performance and providing good feedback. To help adjust to the significant challenges that have been imposed on work-life balance during the pandemic, multinational companies like Unilever have invested in mentorship programmes as one strategy to help support workers' professional growth and well-being (Sharma, 2020). In theory, relationships like that of a 'mentee-mentor' can be mutually beneficial because they provide an opportunity for mentors to 'reflect' about themselves and their profession, while their mentees can expand their knowledge and skills and gain valuable advice from a more experienced colleague. For example, mentoring can be part of an ongoing performance conversation at work and could be integrated into a formal performance management strategy. Sharma (2020) argues that mentoring is beneficial during periods of crisis because workers perform better and experience more work-life satisfaction. However, in practice some studies suggest that mentoring has the potential to create negative career outcomes for mentees and mentors and, in some cases, benefits women's career advancement more than men's (Tharenou, 2005).

Stop! Does mentoring have the potential to help workers perform better and improve work-life satisfaction? What are the characteristics of successful and failed mentoring relationships? Can you identify practical steps that can be taken to ensure mentorship relationships are mutually beneficial?

Essential reading

Howlett, E. (2020) Work is detrimental to employee wellbeing, CIPD survey finds. *People Management*, 4 June; Palmer, S. (2020) Excess workloads and fear of redundancy driving presenteeism during lockdown, study finds. *People Management*, 2 June; Sharma, S. (2020) The importance of mentoring through a crisis. *People Management*, 9 June.

Note: This feature was contributed by Andrew Bratton.

Performance, judgements and feedback

Judgements about an employee's performance usually lead to decisions about their contribution, value, worth, capability and potential. Decisions will be interpreted by an employee as feedback, defined as 'actions taken by (an) external agent(s) to provide information regarding some aspect(s) of one's task performance' (Kluger and DeNisi, 1996, p. 254). A sizeable body of research has examined the effect of feedback on employees. Indeed, employees' reactions to feedback are a critical feature of PA. The PA process can increase job satisfaction (Taylor and Pierce, 1999) and build trust in the organisation (Mayer and Davis, 1999), but can also result in burnout and stress (Gabris and Ihrke, 2001), less job satisfaction and lower commitment (Brown et al., 2010).

Reactions to performance appraisal are influenced by an employee's personality (for example their self-esteem) and how they perceive (e.g. as fair) the appraisal system (CIPD, 2019h, p. 3). Employees' perceptions of fairness are influenced, in part, by the capacity for the appraisee to participate in its processes (Brown and Lim, 2013). Employees' reactions to feedback or how they perceive the accuracy of the feedback received, referred to by Anseel and Lievens (2009) as 'feedback acceptance', is determined also by the extent to which feedback confirms how people see themselves: their self-esteem. An employee's self-esteem is affected by PA feedback because studies show that employees usually rate themselves higher than their evaluators do, whatever their performance (Brown and Lim, 2013). The desire to see oneself in a positive way Jordan and Audia (2012) call, 'the self-enhancement motive'. Employee reactions to feedback have been associated with a range of outcomes and there is no simple formula for how feedback can be used to motivate people, even though managers may be quite convinced, in their own minds, that there is. However, we do know that feedback has a definite influence in terms of demotivation (Coens and Jenkins, 2002). Figure 6.4 shows the range of employee reactions to feedback on their performance at work.

Reflective question

Why do researchers suggest that performance appraisal can impact negatively on organisational culture? Why might PA not 'transfer well' to companies operating outside North America and Europe?

As suggested, the response to feedback can result in two possibilities: validation if there is agreement with the judgement made, or a defensive posture when there is disagreement. The latter is especially likely when feedback is negative or critical, and the impact on subsequent performance can also be negative.

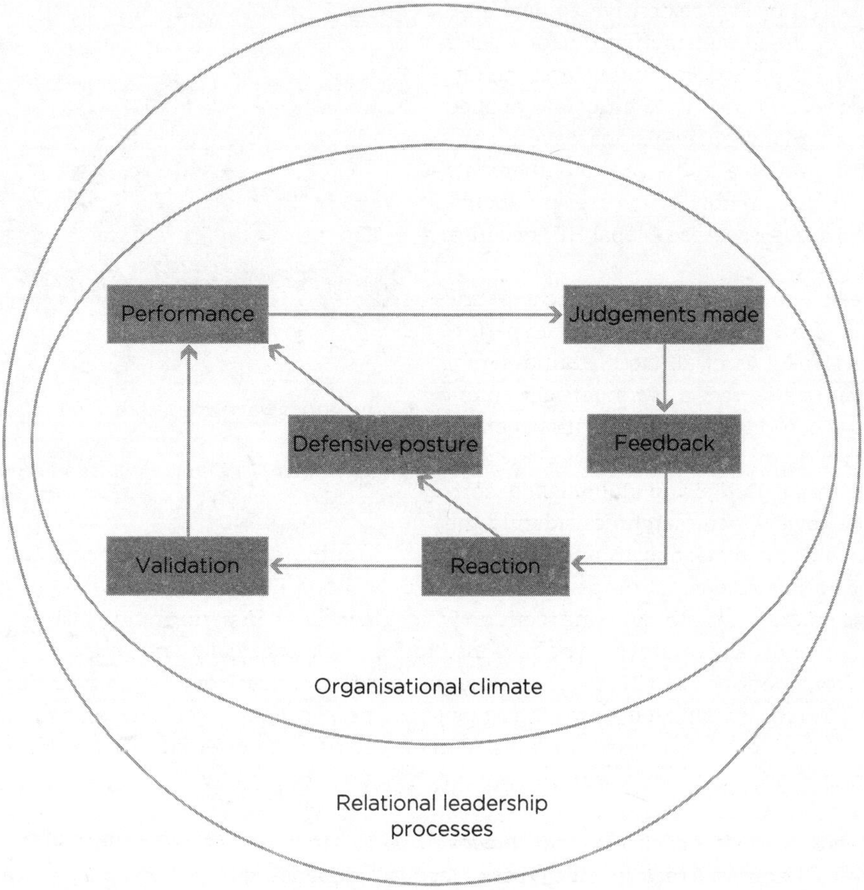

Figure 6.4 Reactions to feedback on performance at work

Reactions to performance feedback can act to demotivate employees. The seminal study by Meyer et al. (1965) at the General Electric Company found that although PA allowed for general praise, criticism was more specific and prompted defensive reactions. Defensive behaviour was partly caused by most appraisees rating themselves as above average, but employee reactions could also be partly explained by underperformers being dismissed. In 2015, it was reported that GE abolished its 'rank and yank' PA system, which assigned workers a performance score relative to their peers and resulted in the lowest percentile getting dismissed (Duggan, 2015).

Researchers have long searched to find a way of evaluating workers that avoids high levels of negativity and discomfort. Studies have found that feedback is likely to be accepted when employees perceive it is fair, sincere and not designed as an excuse to punish (Varma et al., 2020). Managers are likely to provide lenient ratings to avoid negativity and unpleasantness that are potentially associated with lower ratings (Brown and Lim, 2013). Echoing the problem of errors in judgement caused by perception, a manager's positive opinion for an employee often results in leniency and 'halo' mis-judgements, and less inclination to address under-performance (Lefkowitz, 2000). Self-efficacy and feedback discomfort have been found to change through training interventions (Bernadin and Villanova, 2005). Generally, appraisal as an informal and continuous process will make the formal appraisal less isolated and less prone to discomfort and negativity.

There is, however, extensive evidence on problems in implementing formalised appraisal. Few appraisees understand the rating process and how the ratings are applied and, while many organisations devote considerable resources to the practice, there is a paucity of data on how it increases productivity (Jacobs, 2016; see also Global HRM feature, p. 194).

Researchers have searched for a causal link between PMS and organisational performance. Nankervis et al. (2012) found senior managers perceived a stronger alignment with respect to PMS and organisational effectiveness but line managers were 'less than effusive' (p. 49). DeNisi and Kluger (2000) conducted a review of research considering the relationship between feedback and performance. The authors found that, in one-third of cases, feedback had a negative effect on performance. As DeNisi and Kluger highlighted, when feedback does have the potential to help someone focus on what is to be done in performing a task or learning details, performance usually improves. The response to feedback, especially critical feedback, is likely to be affective or emotional, which can be detrimental to performance. However, to avoid high levels of discomfort, Kluger and Nir (2009) propose a positive approach, called *feedforward*. By focusing on positive stories of experience from work that can look forward to offer support so that the employee's performance can improve, a win-win approach will be adopted that avoids a retreat into defensive emotions.

Source: LinkedIn Sales Navigator on Unsplash

Some critics have argued that appraisal attempts to simplify a relationship between managers and employees that is ambiguous, complex and dynamic.

Acceptance of feedback may not, however, be as simple as first thought. Studies suggest that employees themselves seek specific types of feedback depending on the goal that is directing the need for feedback. For example, if an employee seeks feedback related to a learning orientation, they may be more likely to accept feedback that is self-negative, in contrast, a performance orientation will likely prompt the desire for feedback that is self-positive. It is suggested that questions from managers or team leaders such as 'How do I impede your success?', will create a safe environment for employees to seek negative feedback (Gong et al., 2014, p. 23). Buckingham (2016) suggests a similar positive approach by suggesting that the appraiser should focus not on the appraisee's past performance or skills, but rather on their '*own future actions*' with respect to each employee. As well as feedback provided to employees on their performance, some might prefer to take a more proactive stance, seeking feedback themselves. Such behaviour may be undertaken in pursuit of a goal, as well as to provide protection for a person's image or ego (Anderson et al., 2003).

Judgements and diversity

PMSs are used for many purposes, including helping in decision-making regarding people's careers, the development they will undertake and their future promotion in the organisation. Well-documented patterns in organisations suggest that BAME groups suffer disadvantages in these areas (see Chapter 4). For example, in Britain and the US, despite many companies signalling their support for Black Lives Matter after the killing of George Floyd in 2020, most companies do not 'walk the talk'. In 2020, the British company Gate Ventures is led by a six-person board of directors with three BAME directors, one of whom is female. But Gate Ventures is the exception when it comes to diversity across

British boardrooms (Makortoff, 2020). The Black ethnic community in Britain had the lowest percentage, just 5 per cent, of workers in 'manager, director or senior official' jobs (ONS, 2020b). Almost 60 per cent of companies in the FTSE 350 do not have any BAME directors. It is a similar story in the US. In 2004, non-white men held 11.9 per cent of the board seats of the Fortune 100, America's top companies. In 2018, that figure had inched up to 13.7 per cent (Fortson, 2020). Women face a 'glass ceiling', suggesting that there are limits on their progress in organisations.

Appraiser bias

There are many reasons for the lack of diversity in organisations. One reason, which we have examined in a previous chapter, relates to bias and stereotyped judgements about other people. Evaluators all have their own biases. As in selection decisions (see Table 5.2), distortions occur in how people and their performance are rated (Grote, 1996), such as when managers make judgements based on stereotypes and generalisations, demonstrate similarity bias (rating people who are similar to them more highly) and relying on first impressions or comparisons with others to make judgements.

One explanation for the occurrence of these distortions in judgement during PMS is provided by social role theory (Eagly, 1987). This suggests that social structures influence the roles that people can adopt and the behaviours expected. For example, if it is expected that women will become mothers, this will affect how the different genders are viewed in a PMS. As women leave work to care for children, this reinforces the consistent expectation of the social role of women (Diekma and Eagly, 2000), and even when women return to work, it is expected that there will be conflicts between family and work (Benschop and Doorewaard, 1998). The PA process requires evaluators to make a judgement about the value of an employee both in the present and in the future, and this may cause some tension and discomfort in employee relations. It is a tension that has never been resolved and lies at the heart of most debates on performance management generally, and appraisal interviews in particular, as we explain below.

Types of appraisal

It is important that appraisal is perceived to be fair and ethical (Ilgen et al., 1979; Sillup and Klimberg, 2010), particularly with respect to what is called 'procedural justice', which concerns perceptions of *how* appraisal is conducted and completed rather than the outcomes of appraisal (Cawley et al., 1998). Research completed in China by Chen et al. (2011), for example, found that perceptions of procedural justice moderated employees' reactions to appraisals. They found that if procedural justice was high, this increased employees' acceptance of performance goals, even if the appraisal was negative. There is still, however, a tendency to associate feedback with criticism even though most people do their work well most of the time (Swinburne, 2001). One way to mitigate the negative perceptions of PA is to widen the sources of feedback to include:

- self-appraisal;
- peer-appraisal;
- multisource feedback.

Self-appraisal

The facility to employees to evaluate their own performance has become routine practice in some organisations. As already noted, all employees have an opinion on how well they are performing, the rewards they desire and deserve, and the training they require. Ashford et al. (2003) found that self-appraisal offered the positive qualities of self-trust, reliability, availability and trustworthiness. Not surprising, perhaps, there is evidence that self-appraisal produces differences in ratings obtained by an individual's assessment and that of their superior, particularly when the PMS focuses on evaluation and control (Eichinger and Lombardo, 2003). In uncertain times, self-appraisal allows the emergence of data and ideas for use in a discussion about performance, especially where the work is complex or knowledge-intensive (Ryan and Tipu, 2009). Employees can learn to appraise themselves and will treat this as part of their own development if they can see its value for themselves rather than viewing it as a manipulative management tool.

HRM web links

How good are you at seeking feedback? What are the skills needed for giving and receiving effective feedback? The following website may help you: https://uwaterloo.ca/centre-for-teaching-excellence/teaching-resources/teaching-tips/assessing-student-work/grading-and-feedback/receiving-and-giving-effective-feedback.

Peer-appraisal

Peer-appraisal gives a more accurate assessment because peers work in close proximity to appraisees (Borman, 1994). Research suggests that this is particularly the case in self-managed work teams. There is evidence that peers tend to be less forgiving about their peer's performance (Bratton, 1992) and give punitive evaluations (Saavedra and Kwun, 1995). Peer-appraisal appears to be especially suitable for professional and knowledge-based workers such as doctors, teachers and academics. The responses can be unpredictable, but research suggests that some will undertake further learning as a consequence (Colthart et al., 2008), and that peer-led discussions about learning and development are more acceptable than other alternatives (Main et al., 2009). There are, however, some possible tensions, since peers in managerial roles are usually connected with each other through their work or more informal relationships and may be unwilling to offer formal feedback or make comparisons between their peers. Within teams, peer feedback can lead to resistance and avoidance of blame if the team is not performing well (Peiperl, 2001). Payne et al. (2009) compared employee reactions between those who completed online appraisals and those who used a more traditional approach. The results indicated greater participation in the process, in terms of completing self-ratings, by the online appraisees, but there was also a perception that the online process was of lower quality. Self- and peer-appraisal for development will not occur unless it is set in an organisational culture and climate that facilitates and encourages such a process.

Multisource feedback

The process of multisource feedback (MSF) provides more data about an employee's behaviours by gathering feedback from different people, including self, peers, supervisor or team leader, subordinate staff and customers. When feedback is received from 'all round' a job, this is referred to as 360-degree appraisal or feedback. The value of 360-degree appraisal will depend on how the process is positioned in an organisation, on how a climate of support is established and facilitated for its implementation, on amelioration of the negative effects and on training interventions (McCarthy and Garavan, 2001).

As with all approaches to appraisal, there can be both positive and negative reactions to 360-degree appraisal. There is evidence that the upward appraisal for managers leads to performance improvement where managers start from a low or moderate rating and the feedback process is sustained over time; there is less effect, however, on managers who already have a high performance rating (Reilly et al., 1995). Perhaps one of the most valued features of upward appraisal is the opportunity for staff to express their views in a constructive manner, which adds to their sense of being included (Howe et al., 2011).

Source: Tumisu/Pixabay

Customer feedback can be incorporated into multi-source feedback.

Reflective question

Have you ever felt your work performance to be judged unfairly against a social stereotype?

Dyadic relations and feedback

Previous studies of performance management have tended to neglect the role played by the quality of the relationship between the appraiser and appraisee (Wang and Varma, 2019). While a close scrutiny of leadership theories is outside the scope of this chapter, researchers have long recognised the 'dynamics of the interconnections' between leaders, line managers, the enactment of HR practices and outcomes (Purcell and Kinnie, 2008). Within the wider context of the organisational behaviour, leader-member exchange (LMX) theory emphasises the importance of the quality of the dyadic relationship between, for example, a team leader and an individual member. Leadership researchers have found that 'not all relationships are created equal' (Epitropaki et al., 2018, p. 121). There are two types of relationships, the 'in-group', those with expanded role responsibilities, and the 'out-group', with restricted role responsibilities (Uhl-Bien, 2003). Workers in the in-group receive more information, support and attention from their manager than do out-group members. Less-privileged workers who perceive themselves outside the in-group can be de-motivated and have lower job satisfaction. The creation of differentiated LMX relationships might also be unlawful, especially if those cast into the out-group are mostly BAME workers. LMX research suggests that because people are uniquely different, people in a leadership role should establish a special relationship with 'each of his or her followers, rather than treating followers as a homogeneous group' (Bratton, 2020, p. 177). Thus, the appraiser and appraisee together can create a positive environment for acceptance of feedback, and without this nuanced understanding of the process of 'following', our grasp of PMS is imperfect (Bratton and Francis, 2020; Uhl-Bien et al., 2014).

HRM web links

Because of the difficult nature of appraisal, a plethora of resources and training programmes is available. For basic advice on appraisal interviewing, check the Advisory, Conciliation and Arbitration Service (ACAS) at www.acas.org.uk. ACAS also publishes a booklet on appraisal-related pay available on their website.

Performance appraisal as a strategic control

Performance appraisal (PA) is the 'cornerstone of an effective human resource system' (Devanna, 1984, p. 109). PA is the process that brings about and sustains effective and/or efficient worker performance (Latham, 1984). Performance appraisal is central to improving performance (Aguinis, 2009) and, therefore, despite obvious pitfalls, it is an accepted part of management orthodoxy. Not least, because the process serves to demonstrate that the performance of employees is under control, or at least to give the appearance of it being so. As Barlow (1989, p. 500) has stated, 'Institutionally elaborated systems of management appraisal and development are significant rhetoric in the apparatus of bureaucratic control.' It is not surprising therefore that most appraisal schemes are underpinned by a 'performance control approach' (Randell, 1994, p. 235). Figure 6.5 show the links in the performance management chain, with a focus on setting measurable objectives or key performance indicators linking individuals to an organisation's strategic direction and future outcomes.

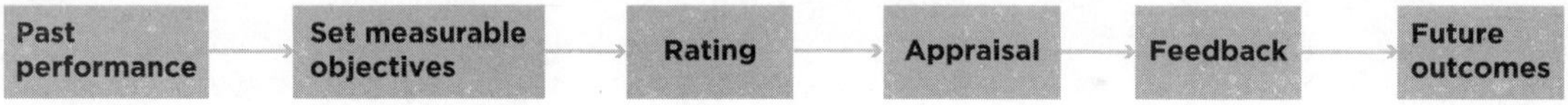

Figure 6.5 Performance control in appraisal

Source: Based on Randell (1994) and CIPD (2019i).

The idea of control, arguably, is at the heart of performance appraisal, and this stems from the key points we raised above about judgements and feedback. We have already examined some important unintended outcomes from performance appraisal (negative reactions of employees and dyadic relationships); next we examine two dominant areas of research looking at strategic outcomes: rewards and employee learning and development.

Performance and rewards

The principal purpose of a PMS is to make managerial decisions concerning pay and promotions – the *control* purpose – and to enhance human capital and help organisations change through strategic training and development initiatives – the *development* purpose. With regard to rewards, Devanna et al. (1984) posit, the function of performance appraisal is to 'facilitate the equitable distribution of rewards, motivating employees by linking rewards to high levels of performance' (p. 41). Work rewards often are conceptualised as being of two types: extrinsic and intrinsic. *Extrinsic rewards* claim to satisfy basic needs for human survival, as well as needs for social recognition. They derive from the *job context*, such as pay. *Intrinsic rewards* derive from factors inherent in the work itself, the *job content*, such as the degree of autonomy. We examine rewards in Chapter 8.

Although there exists considerable debate and controversy surrounding the extent to which financial rewards affect worker motivation (see, for example, Aguinis et al., 2013), research suggests pay is utilised to influence behaviour. In some organisations, it remains common practice to use the appraisal process as a method for differentiating between low and high performers and the compensation link provides a 'logical way' of distributing financial awards (Laud, 1984, p. 122). It has become fashionable to de-emphasise the link between PA and financial rewards, while emphasising the need for 'developing people and rewarding them in the broadest sense' (Armstrong and Taylor, 2014, p. 348). Van Wanrooy and her colleagues (2013), however, provide copious evidence that, in Britain at least, over the last two decades, an increasing number of employers are linking individual performance or output to financial rewards. In 2011, 20 per cent of workers received performance-related pay (PRP) in addition to their fixed wages. There is substantial variation across sectors – 7 per cent of employees were in receipt of performance-related pay in the public sector compared with 28 per cent of private sector workers (Van Wanrooy et al., 2013, Table 5.9, p. 98). This growth of individual PRP mirrors the 'hollowing out' of union influence in the workplace in Britain, a theme we examine in Chapter 9. Workers for whom PRP is a motivator will self-select to work in organisations which do link pay and performance (Fang and Gerhart, 2012). The indeterminate nature of the typical employment contract makes 'motivation (working harder) a running theme in management' (Bratton, 2021, p. 174). Pay is only one, albeit important, determinate factor. In making decisions about linking individual performance to pay, due consideration should be given to the many unintended consequences, therefore, it is important to know how and when rewards will affect behaviour and improve performance.

Performance and development

It is highly unlikely that the pressure for rationality, efficiency and control in organisations will disappear as it is a powerful force that underlies any organised activity. However, for a PMS to be seen as a driver of innovation and organisational performance, one of its planned outcomes has to include an alignment with the organisation's training and development policies (Baron, 2009). This perspective supports the 'developmental humanism' model of HRM (Legge, 2005, p. xvi), and, of course, provides a contrast to the control orientation of a PMS. The contrast between control and developmental approaches could not be greater for managers: the former involves a concentration on methods and tools, the latter a shift towards attitudes, values and beliefs (Wilson and Western, 2000). A developmental PMS that attempts to harness human potential would, for many organisations, mean a more inclusive approach to people management (Iles and Preece, 2010).

PART 3

Researchers advocate a shift towards a future-oriented and development process that actively involves employees in continuously developing ways of improving performance in line with needs: the 'feedforward' appraisal process (Kluger and Nir, 2009). Pivoting to such a direction requires a more flexible approach on the part of managers. Of necessity, there has to be a shift in attention towards the *future* performance. This will demonstrate the value of a PMS as a means of recognising employees' growth potentials, via feedback on what they have done, and engaging in a dialogue about improving future performance. The hallmarks of Deloitte's PA system, for example, are agility, one-size-fits-one and *constant learning* (Buckingham, 2016).

Future performance can be presented as a relationship between means and outcomes (Ouchi, 1979). The *means* take the form of the attributes, skills, knowledge and attitudes (competencies) of individual employees that are applied to a task in a specific context. The *outcomes* take the form of results achieved, which may be measurable either quantitatively or qualitatively against an explicit or implicit standard or target. Between means and outcomes lies the behaviour of the individual in a transformation process, as shown in Figure 6.6.

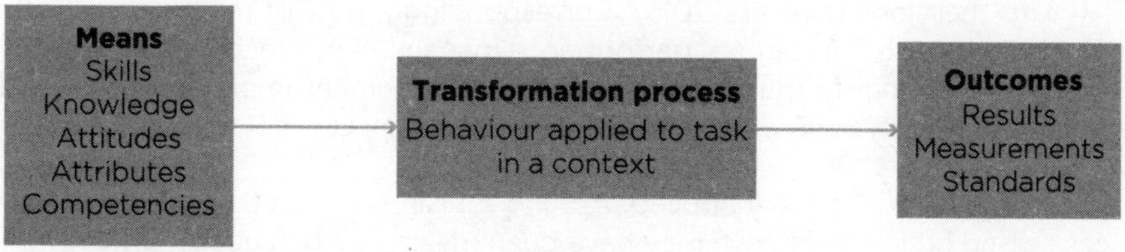

Figure 6.6 Performance as a transformation process

Although all phases of this process can form the focus of performance management, particular attention to behaviour in the transformation process will reveal how an individual has applied knowledge and skills carrying out a job task; this will include taking account of all aspects of the context, including time and place, technology and other circumstances. There is significant interest in this part of the transformation process, because it is in praxis that creative thinking and innovation happens (Crossan and Apaydin, 2010). Senior organisational leaders can influence innovation by constructing cultures in which people feel encouraged and enabled to innovate, as well as setting goals and directing resources and activities (Denti and Hemlin, 2012). Workplace learning researchers have focused on the knowledge that people learn informally in practice, which is acquired intuitively and implicitly, often without intention (Bratton et al., 2004; Spencer and Kelly, 2013). Such knowledge is often referred to as 'tacit knowledge', a rather ambiguous term but one that is seen as key in knowledge creation as it emerges from practice (Nonaka et al., 2000), and as a key feature of workplace learning (see Gold et al., 2010).

The focus on learning-oriented practice as the starting point for PMS processes is brought into greater prominence when we consider that many workers now perform tasks that are knowledge-intensive within what is recognised as a knowledge or information economy (Webster, 2014). Much of the management rhetoric is about highly skilled jobs requiring significant and ongoing learning, or life-long learning. Chapter 7 examines learning and development in detail, but here we highlight the role of continuous learning in the transformation process, which can, among other things, generate data for a whole gamut of developmental decisions over time, starting with adjustments to reach minimum standards and moving on to career changes and progression.

Global HRM

Culture of individualism and performance management in the US

In the 1980s, former General Electric CEO Jack Welch popularised the 'rank-and-yank' practice of rating workers and firing the bottom 10%. While this may have improved company performance in the short term, critics argue that it had a negative impact on organisational culture and eventually forced managers to get rid of talented employees (Meinert, 2015). In the modern workplace, employee performance is always managed through a variety of control strategies shaped by market, regulatory, organisational, technological, labour supply and labour value considerations (Thompson and Findlay, 2017). The use of computer and telecommunications technologies has offered new possibilities for monitoring employee performance, with more emphasis on people analytics and 'smart' metrics. These trends create a workplace environment in which employee performance can be monitored, measured and compared in more intensive and advanced ways. As a result, research suggests that employees strongly dislike performance evaluations. According to the Corporate Executive Board (CEB) survey of Fortune 1000 companies, 66% of employees were strongly dissatisfied with the performance evaluations they received in their organisation. Furthermore, about 66% of employees say the performance review process interferes with their productivity, and 65% of the employees believed that performance evaluations were not even relevant to their jobs (Meinert, 2015). Correspondingly, 95% of managers reported that they were not satisfied with their organisations' performance management process either. Interestingly, there is little empirical evidence that formalised performance management improves productivity. However, there is extensive evidence on the problems in its implementation. One HR manager put it this way:

> No one knew how the ratings were applied. Around four in five said they didn't understand the rating process ... and I think one in five may have been making it up. (Jacobs, 2016)

This illustrates some of the challenges of a mainstream performance management approach. This is concerning considering the amount of resources that organisations devote to conducting performance evaluations. The CEB research suggests that when we take into account how much money organisations are investing in their performance appraisal technology and how much time managers are spending to evaluate workers, on average US organisations spend $3,000 per year, per employee. This suggests that billions of dollars are spent every year because more than 90% of American companies provide performance evaluations at least once a year (Chun et al., 2018). Managing performance is, arguably, the core concern of management, which in turn influences the nature and experience of work. Workers have a legitimate interest in how their performance is managed, but also in the nature of that performance given that job performance is linked to job quality and job satisfaction (Thompson and Findlay, 2017).

Stop! What impact does the performance review process have on the employees HR is trying to motivate, engage and retain? What impact does the process have on the organisation's performance?

Essential reading

Chun, J., Brocker, J. and De Cremer, D. (2018) People don't want to be compared with others in performance reviews. They want to be compared with themselves. *Harvard Business Review*, 22 March; Findlay, P. and Thompson, P. (2017) Contemporary work: its meanings and demands. *Journal of Industrial Relations*, *59*(2), 122–38; Jacobs, K. (2016) CIFF's fresh approach to performance management. *HR Magazine*, 17 March.

Note: This feature was contributed by Andrew Bratton.

Critiquing performance management

Performance management and appraisal can be critiqued at several levels: from within the academic discipline of HRM, from the stance of critical management studies (CMS), and from the work of Michel Foucault and critical discourse analysis (CDA). Analytical HRM is highly sceptical about claims of universal applicability for particular HR practices (Boxall et al., 2008). From this perspective, researchers have argued that facets of the PM cycle are not readily transferable across cultural settings (Dowling et al., 2017; Tziner et al., 1998). Detractors have also drawn upon the Weberian notion of a 'paradox of consequences' that can arise from HR practices (Weber, 1922/1968). Through this prism of criticism, scholars point out that strategic objectives can conflict with one another. For example, adopting a total-quality-control (TQC) system is a manufacturing strategy designed to achieve 'zero defects' (Bratton, 1992, p. 26), which conflicts with a development-oriented PMS model and, concomitantly, an organisational culture that is tolerant of mistakes providing they are seen as a learning opportunity and not repeated.

Another focus of criticism within mainstream HRM is the predilection to establish the connection between individual performance measurement and organisational performance. Serial research on the HR–performance relationship, however, suggests that there is no one 'magic bullet' that is *the* practice, including a PMS, that will enhance worker and organisational performance (Ichniowski et al., 1996, p. 32, emphasis added). Despite widespread adoption, the effectiveness of PA is disputed with many organisations reporting that managers go through the motions of performance management, but do not provide the continuous attention required of ongoing evaluation to ensure relevance and success (Scott, 2020).

CMS scholars have argued that the growth in usage of performance appraisal among non-managerial workers reflects the neoliberal penchant for individualising contracts that explicitly link performance to pay. Closely related, is the phenomenon of de-unionisation that can be observed in the US, Britain and parts of the European Union (see Chapter 9). In their in-depth analysis of the restructuring of work and the rise of 'neo-management' in the 1990s, Boltanski and Chiapello (2018, p. 284) observe:

> The individualization of wages took the form of an enhanced role for immediate superiors ... in appraising wage-earners. Once or twice a year, each wage-earner 'reviews their situation' with their superior, leading to a 'general appraisal'. For firms, this method of determining wages has the advantage of engaging the maximum number of wage-earners in situations where they have to make judgements about colleagues and also, in a sense, about themselves. But wage-earners obligated to appraise one another can also find it *more difficult to forge a common front against central management.* (emphasis added)

This critical interpretation suggests that, as a management tool, PM is integral to the individualistic-oriented HRM model, which can be characterised as the atomisation of employment relations.

The wave of PMS in the public sector originated because of expenditure and budgetary problems (Farnham, 2015). Performance-related pay schemes fuelled the ideological stance that the performance of public-sector wage-earners should be regularly evaluated by their managers (Derlien and Peters, 2008). Therefore, it can be plausibly argued that the surge in PMS is, at least in part, ideologically driven and linked to the decline of collectivism and the rise of individualist HR practices. The gender dimension is also a focus for critics. Bryan and Bryson (2016) found that performance-related pay is more prevalent for men. Women may also be given poor evaluations or precluded from promotion because of the perceived 'gender hierarchical threat' (Inesi and Cable, 2014). This phenomenon is observed when male evaluators see behaviour or competency signals as a threat to the traditional gender hierarchy, which leads to a negative bias when appraising women's on-the-job performance.

Critical analysis of PM and PA indicates that processes are used to bring more certainty in the otherwise indeterminate employment contract, to impose organisational politics (Holzer et al., 2019) and 'invisible' forms of control using opaque algorithmic performance evaluations (Rahman, 2021). Further, routine managerial bias in the measurement of employee performance, it is argued, means that PM/PA approaches to managing the employment relationship are far from neutral, both in intention and scope. This shadows the entire rationale for maintaining PMSs, which are potentially open to corruption because they can ultimately undermine both workers and an organisation's manager-subordinate relations (Scott, 2020; Townley, 1993). Townley's (1993; 1994) pioneering Foucauldian-inspired analysis conceptualises PM/PA as an enabling tool to permit individuals to be compared to each other, 'to render them known', and in this sense PA 'operate[s] to individualise and standardize' both the worker and work (1994, p. 45). It is the control-oriented PMS that supplies a 'disciplinary matrix' for underperforming workers which, Townley speculates, is perhaps another reason why PAs are 'part of best management practice' (1994, p. 46).

Finally, critique of PM/PA can draw on critical discourse analysis (CDA) which studies how societal power relations are established and reinforced through language (Fairclough, 2013). Words are how we express the meaning of life, but words can be corrupted to the point that they disguise, rather than describe, social reality. From this perspective, all the talk about performance appraisal as the 'objective' measurement of worker performance, functioning to close the performance 'gap', obviates the real nature of management parlance. PMS serves to minimise opportunities for collective action because individuals are encouraged to make decisions based solely on their own self-interest (Whitfield, 2012) and, relatedly, they serve to 'communicate organizational norms or culture' and reinforce this process (Townley, 1989, p. 103). Work habits, attitudes, values and other personal attributes are learned, while bad habits and dissenting voices are expunged through performance appraisal (McKinlay and Starkey, 1998). PMSs define human talent in narrow quantitative terms of those employees displaying enthusiasm, cooperation and emotional labour that further the goals of the organisation.

Summary

In this chapter, we have explained the idea of PMS, that the principal dimensions of an employee's work can be defined in performance terms, allowing measurement over agreed periods of time, and taking account of particular constraints within an organisational context. In models of strategic HRM, performance management forms the nub of the strategic link between HR inputs and practices and organisational performance. Through its link to measurement, it is claimed that performance management provides evidence that management is rationally, efficiently and effectively controlling an organisation. There are, however, measurement models that take a wider view, perhaps more strategic and long term, which encompass a range of values (not just financial) and can stimulate continuous improvement.

We explained the notion of a performance management cycle, which integrates various HR processes, including development centres, objective setting and personal development planning, feedback and reviews. Further, we explained that performance management has a 'control' purpose to aid decisions about rewards, and a 'development' purpose designed to improve individual or team performance by identifying training opportunities and action learning. A PMS integrates many complex variables and performance goals that may not be achievable.

The chapter also explained that performance can be rated in different ways: inputs and outputs. Rating behaviour within performance permits the use of such techniques as BARSs and BOSs. Performance might be appraised using a variety of sources, also known as 360-degree appraisal. We explored the role managers play in providing feedback, both formally as part of a PMS and informally as a series of performance conversations. The acceptance of feedback will depend on its frequency as part of high-quality dyadic relationships and on how well managers have a nuanced understanding of their staff's work motivations.

Review questions

1. What is the strategic purpose of performance management and appraisal?
2. How does national culture change the nature of performance appraisal?
3. To what extent, if at all, can leader subordinate relationships effect subordinate performance appraisal? Do you think that students should have more say in appraising and assessing themselves and each other?

Search & Watch

There are many training videos on the Do's and Don'ts when conducting an appraisal interview. As an example, visit YouTube and watch the video titled: **Good performance appraisal role play**. For a light-hearted look at the appraisal interview, look at **Big Keith's Appraisal** for the BBC's *The Office*. What is considered 'good' and 'bad' interview practice? What is considered to be an effective appraisal interview and why?

Legal Focus

UK statute law has sought to restrict an employer from exercising their common-law rights to employ or refuse to employ anyone whom the employer chooses for whatever reason they wish, including reasons relating to sex, religion or age. The Equality Act 2010 provides protection against direct and indirect discrimination on the basis of protected characteristics (See Legal Focus, Chapter 5). Indirect discrimination is treating people indiscriminately, in a way which particularly disadvantages people by reference to a protected characteristic, e.g. sexual orientation. Whereas direct discrimination aims to achieve equality of treatment, indirect discrimination assumes equality of treatment, and aims to achieve a 'level playing field', where people sharing a particular protected characteristic are not subjected to requirements which many of them cannot meet but which cannot be shown to be justified. For example, in *Price v CSC* [1978] IRLR 3, the requirement to be between the ages of 17 and 28 for promotion to executive officer was held to be indirect discrimination, as more women than men would be out of the labour market having children between those ages. Sections 20 and 21 of the UK Equality Act 2010 outlines the duty of an employer to make 'reasonable adjustments' in favour of disabled persons.

Task Search online for government information in your jurisdiction prohibiting indirect discrimination and compare and contrast it with another country, for example, Australia or Canada. (1) What is meant by indirect discrimination? (2) Give three examples of indirect discrimination that may arise in the recruitment and selection process? (3) In performance appraisal, can any provision, criterion or practice (PCP) put a disabled employee at a substantial disadvantage compared with a non-disabled employee?

Reference

See Deborah Lockton and Tom Brown's *Employment Law* (2020), pp. 177–93, for a discussion on the Equality Act 2010, covering indirect discrimination.

Chapter case: Sustaintricity Co.

The setting

Sustaintricity Co. is a large energy company which upholds its competitive position in the market thanks to a diverse energy mix. It prides itself on its investment in renewable energy and is one of the major players in this area. The company produces and supplies both electricity and gas, and also offers contracting services. Sustaintricity has expanded its workforce significantly over the last few years and now has a large workforce based across multiple sites, a significant percentage of which is unionised. At a strategic level, sustainability is considered a priority and its importance is communicated to all employees. Internal communications, such as newsletters and electronic notifications, and training workshops all highlight the company's sustainability principles. These principles are also demonstrated through Sustaintricity's employee and community projects, and of course through the investment in renewable energy and energy efficiency at sites. The International Energy Agency (IEA) estimates emissions will decline by 8% in 2020 and energy use will decline by 6%. This presents significant challenges for Sustaintricity to invest in renewable energy and the creation of low-carbon jobs while responding to the wider socio-political context of putting emissions into structural decline and increasing energy sector resiliency.

Source: Ricardo Gomez Angel on Unsplash

The problem

Performance measurement and appraisal are often seen as key features of an organisation's strategic drive to achieving a low-carbon workplace (LCW). In terms of environmental management, performance appraisal aims to guide employees' actions toward desired environmental performance outcomes. Mainstream 'sustainable' or green HRM (GHRM) scholars suggest that, without performance appraisal employee environmental improvement efforts may falter.

However, integrating performance appraisal with sustainability objectives presents many challenges, particularly the *measurement* of environmental performance across the organisation. At Sustaintricity, environmental performance is an aspect of work that is formally evaluated for the majority of employees. The formal link between employee environmental performance and pay is established in the performance appraisal system (PAS), first introduced in 2013. At least in theory, PAS has the potential to influence Sustaintricity's employees' performance rating and annual incremental pay.

In practice, however, managers and workers have expressed concern that the introduction of the PAS had led to an increase in their workload. At a meeting held to discuss some of the issues, one Sustaintricity manager said: 'the PAS system has intensified our work by "squeezing" complex jobs into standardised measures' and she questioned the assumption that there was 'a link between individual effort and reward'. Another manager at the meeting expressed concern that PAS could 'potentially have a negative impact on line-manager and employment relations'. The manager explained:

> [The PAS] is a distraction. You are obviously the guys' managers, but at the same time because you are spending so much time with them you need to get along with them as well.

Tomi Aanu, the HR Director, who was chairing the meeting, summarised the main concerns of the managers and added that their experiences mirror published evidence drawing attention to the added pressure on line managers when pay is linked to performance. She promised to take a second look at the present PAS system to see how it could be improved. Tomi Aanu prides herself on her use of evidence-based HR management to design policies.

The assignment

Working as a group or on your own, prepare a report for Tomi Aanu drawing on the material from this chapter. Address the following:

1. How can performance appraisal activities help this organisation meet its sustainability objectives? What role, if any, should line managers play in implementing sustainability initiatives?
2. What are the challenges associated with integrating performance appraisal with sustainability objectives?
3. What changes would you suggest to Sustaintricity's PAS?

Essential reading

Haddock-Millar, J., Sanyal, C. and Müller-Camen, M. (2016) Green human resource management: a comparative qualitative case study of a United States multinational corporation. *International Journal of Human Resource Management*, *27*(2): 192–211.

Jabbour, C. J. C. (2011) How green are HRM practices, organisational culture, learning and teamwork? A Brazilian study. *Industrial and Commercial Training*, *43*(2): 98–105.

Gordon, M. (2020) Covid-19 and the campaign against climate change and a just transition. *Scottish Left Review*, *118*, 14.

Govindarajulu, N. and Daily, B. F. (2004) Motivating employees for environmental improvement. *Industrial Management and Data Systems*, *104*: 364–72.

Note: This case was contributed by Andrew Bratton.

Further reading

Bacouel-Jentjens, S. and Brandl, J. (2015) Cross-cultural responses to performance appraisals in Germany and France: a refinement of the picture. *International Journal of Cross Cultural Management*, *15*(3): 285–304.

Buckingham, M. and Goodall, A. (2015) Reinventing performance management, *Harvard Business Review*, April.

DeNisi, A. S. and Murphy, K. R. (2017) Performance appraisal and performance management: 100 years of progress? *Journal of Applied Psychology*, *102*(3): 421–33.

Findlay, P. and Thompson, P. (2017) Contemporary work: its meanings and demands. *Journal of Industrial Relations*, *59*(2): 122–38.

Holzer, M., Ballard, A., Kim, M., Peng, S. and Deat, F. (2019) Obstacles and opportunities for sustaining performance management systems. *International Journal of Public Administration*, *42*(2): 132–43.

Rahman, H. A. (2021) The invisible cage: workers' reactivity to opaque algorithmic evaluations. Administrative Science Quarterly. Available at: https://doi.org/10.1177/00018392211010118.

Scott, B. (2020) Performance management and leadership. In J. Bratton (ed.) *Organizational Leadership* (pp. 245–65). London: Sage.

Townley, B. (1993) Performance appraisal and the emergence of management. *Journal of Management Studies*, *30*(2): 221–38.

CHAPTER 7

LEARNING AND DEVELOPMENT

outline

- Introduction
- The context of strategic learning and development
- Workplace learning and knowledge creation
- Theoretical perspectives on adult learning
- The strategic learning and development process
- Needs analysis: linking strategy to learning and development
- Evaluation of learning and development
- Leadership development and coaching
- Future challenges: machine learning and the Fourth Industrial Revolution
- Critiquing the strategic learning and development discourse
- Summary
- Further reading

Source: heylagostechie on Unsplash

objectives

After studying this chapter, you should be able to:

1. Define and explain terms relating to learning and development in the workplace
2. Explain key adult learning theories that influence the design and delivery of learning and development interventions
3. Discuss what constitutes a strategic approach to learning and development and identify key issues that need to be considered in planning, designing, executing and evaluating a learning and development intervention in the workplace
4. Discuss emerging issues that will affect learning and development in the future

Introduction

The Covid-19 crisis has had profound effects on the way in which we live, work and learn. To keep in touch, grandparents were coached by their grandchildren to use Zoom, health-care professionals learned that low-cost dexamethasone reduces death by up to one-third in hospitalised patients with respiratory complications of the virus, agile restauranteurs introduced home-delivery services during the lockdown, and colleges identified the conditions necessary to enable a skills-led recovery (Little, 2020). Few relationships, commented Drucker (1999), are as important to organisational leaders as the relationship to government. It is no surprise, therefore, that both business and government share a significant interest in the relationship between education and skills development, economic growth and competitiveness (Barnett, 2018). There is evidence of connections between high skill levels, high worker autonomy and engagement, and measurable improvement in organisational performance (Noe and Tews, 2018). For workers, acquiring skills, upskilling and reskilling are considered a prerequisite for employability and social mobility (Becket and Hager, 2013), and are associated with well-being (Wilkinson and Pickett, 2018).

PART 3

This chapter begins by briefly explaining the context of learning and development with particular focus on human capital theory and its role in strategic HRM. Next, we provide a conceptualisation of strategic learning and development, a process which emphasises sequential planning and action, and which also integrates workplace learning and organisational strategy. We identify key issues such as adult theories of learning, the evaluation and transfer of learning, coaching and leadership development. The chapter concludes with a critique of learning and development.

The context of strategic learning and development

Since the 1950s, economists have argued that investment in education can have positive effects on both economic performance and social well-being. Schultz (1961), for example, posited that different levels of investment in human 'capital' were held to be a significant factor in explaining different rates of economic growth between Western and emerging economies. The United Nations Development Index (HDI) provides a broad measure of national and societal well-being, incorporating a range of economic, social and environment indicators, such as income, life expectancy and educational attainment. In 2011, the top-ranked country was Norway; the UK was ranked 28th (Fiscal Commission, 2013, p. 59).

Human capital theory

The contribution of education and training to a nation's economic development and growth is known as human capital theory. Proponents of the theory argued that education could be divided into 'consumption' and 'investment' activities and that the state should primarily fund investment in 'human capital'. State investment in education and the skilling and technical education of 16- to 24-year-olds is predicated on the assumptions that training, learning and development (L&D) will increase labour productivity. This discourse involves thinking in terms of human value (and performance) as a return on investment (ROI) and assessed in terms of costs and benefits (Garrick, 1999).

At a national level, most governments consider a skilled workforce a key factor in promoting economic growth and improving living standards. McLean (2004) suggested that national interest in HRD arises from the need to alleviate poverty, improve the quality of people's lives, globalisation and labour shortages. Alagaraja and Wang (2012) echo these issues when they point out the need to consider the societal context and the differences between developed and emerging economies when considering a national HRD strategy. Analysing Canada's approach to training, for example, Hughes and Grant (2007) observe:

> Canada's productivity is lagging behind that of its competitors. One strategy Canadian organizations are using to meet these challenges is the renewal and upgrading of their workers' skills. By spending on TLD to build workers' skills, organizations seek to create enough additional human capital to make themselves more competitive. (p. 1 and cited by Spencer and Kelly, 2013, p. 10)

This thinking encouraged national governments to justify educational expenditure in economic terms, 'essentially in service of capitalist production', as opposed to traditional liberal education motives (Spencer and Kelly, 2013, p. 11). In the 1990s, it also encouraged the imposition of 'market discipline' in UK university education (Callinicos, 2006; Willmott, 1995a) and a growing emphasis in teaching 'employability' skills in business programmes (Yorke, 2006). Employability means that students can distinguish, acquire, modify and continually enhance the competencies, skills and personal attributes that make them more likely to find meaningful paid work. The concept of *work-integrated learning* (WIL) has been trending in recent years and during the Covid-19 crisis as a means to boost graduate employability with a focus on competencies and skills. Oliver (2015) suggests that WIL includes a range of learning activities that resemble tasks expected of employed graduates in their early careers, or proximal to the workplaces or spaces, physical or digital, where professional work occurs (Oliver, 2015). With teaching priorities designed to meet the employability criterion and the needs of business, 'business-facing' universities are emblematic of the effects of competitive imperatives shaping university curricula and education (Bratton and Gold, 2015).

A national system for L&D is created by an architecture of learning development policies, programmes, practices and investment choices of the state. In understanding the debate, however, it is important to do what we have tried to do throughout this text, and that is to develop a knowledge base of competing ideological perspectives or paradigms. The choices and actions national governments make regarding L&D will be influenced, if not determined, by ideology and the macro-political contexts. Two broad approaches to L&D can be identified: voluntarist and interventionist. In the US, Canada and Britain, for example, decisions about L&D are taken principally by employers in what is referred to as a *voluntarist* or market-oriented approach. The government's role is to encourage employers to take responsibility for their own training and development and for financing it. In Britain, the dominant voluntarist approach relies heavily on market forces for training and skills development. However, in 2015, the UK government announced an interventionist programme, an 'apprenticeship levy', for companies that had a turnover of more than £3 million (€3.33 million), which was to be equal to 0.5 per cent of the wage bill. The purpose of this was to raise revenue for apprenticeship training. There were concerns, however, about the levy with some employers seeing the programme as a 'payroll tax' (Johnson, 2015).

Britain's voluntarist approach can be contrasted to many European Union member states adopting an *interventionist* strategy in which the government or its agents seek to influence decision-making in organisations and make decisions in the interests of the economy as a whole. For example, in France, Belgium, Denmark, Spain, Italy, the Netherlands and the Nordic countries, relations between capital, labour and the state are different and tend to be cooperative rather than adversarial (Thelen, 2004). Employer-union-state collaboration encourages a national system of skills development and often leads to respected qualifications (see, for example, Rubery et al., 2003). These two approaches are often combined, albeit usually with a preference for one against the other, as shown in Figure 7.1.

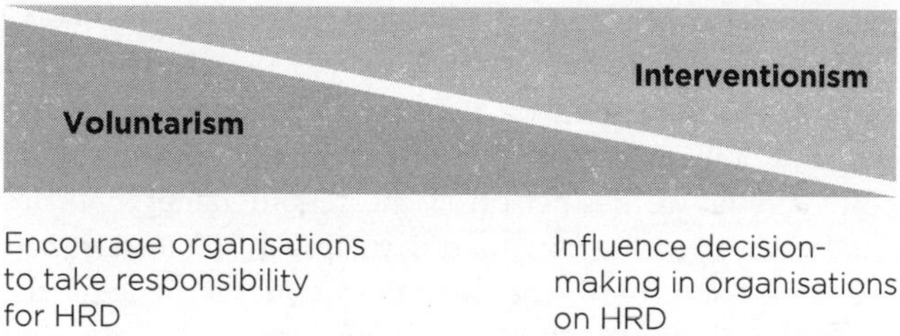

Figure 7.1 Voluntarism versus interventionism in L&D

Reflective question

What are the pros and cons of the voluntarist and interventionist approaches? To what extent do the above features of human capital theory influence the learning programme in which you are involved?

Learning and competitive advantage

Human capital theory had an important message for organisations and workers. The lesson for organisations is that if workers learn at work and contribute to organisational learning, the organisation's human capital will grow. Garrick (1999) argues that human capital theory 'fuelled a very powerful discourse of workplace learning' that 'ultimately serves capital interest' (p. 218). The following two quotes provide an insight into the learning discourse:

> More of the effect [improved performance] undoubtedly comes from individuals 'working smarter' – in part by being able to actually implement their wisdom and knowledge in the actual work process and in part because of the training and job rotation practices that enhance the opportunity to learn. (Pfeffer, 1998, p. 60)

> A company that gets an early start in accumulating knowledge, and then continues to learn faster than its rivals, can build an almost insurmountable lead. (Hamel, 2000, p. 101)

The discernment that competitive advantage relies upon managers enlisting workers' tacit knowledge and skills is not new. As just noted, it is embodied in the economic theory of human capital (Schultz, 1981) and contemporary theorising about L&D is also rooted in the resource-based view of the firm (Barney, 1991). What is new, however, is that, in the past three decades or so, largely in response to global competitive pressures, the linkage of L&D interventions and competitiveness has become incorporated into mainstream management thinking (Bratton et al., 2004).

For employers and management theorists alike, training, learning and development has come to represent a key 'lever' that can act as the engine for sustainable competitive advantage. As Beer et al. (1984, p. 85) muse, 'employee development is a key strategy for organisational survival and growth'. Although Hall (1984, p. 159) observed that in most US organisations 'the strategic *development* of human resources is virtually non-existent', he echoed other HRM scholars and considered, 'Focused goal-centred development is an integral part of any effective strategic human resource management process (1984, p. 181).

Others came to a similar conclusion that investing in L&D has become a 'litmus test' of whether or not employers have adopted the normative model of HRM as identified as 'soft' or 'developmental humanism' of the Harvard School (Keep, 1989; see also Chapter 1). A *developmental humanistic* approach, based on the personal empowerment of the workforce through learning, highlights how individuals are most productive when they feel that their work is personally meaningful rather than simply a means to an end (Gold and Bratton, 2014). However, for learning and development professionals, the purpose of strategic L&D should always be a 'double focus – the needs of the learners *and* the needs of the organization' (Beevers and Rea, 2016, p. 27). According to the CIPD (2020f), strategic learning and development, 'sets out the workforce capabilities, skills and competencies the organization needs, and how they can be developed to ensure a sustainable, successful organization' (2020, p. 1).

Reflective question

People respond to learning interventions in different ways. Thinking back on your own learning experiences, what learning activities went (a) really well and (b) awfully amiss?

Ethical Insight
Why does machine learning raise ethical concerns?

'Decision-making on numerous aspects of our daily lives is being outsourced to machine-learning (ML) algorithms and artificial intelligence (AI), motivated by speed and efficiency in the decision process' (Lo Piano, 2020, p. 1). HR is no exception to this. Simply put, ML is the science of getting computers to learn and act like humans. In the HR context, ML has already been deployed in recruitment and selection, performance management, and compliance and reporting. In addition, there is growing interest in the use of ML for (human) learning and development. For example, ML can be utilised to create personalised learning pathways and conversational interfaces that mimic chat with a real human coach (Biswas, 2019).

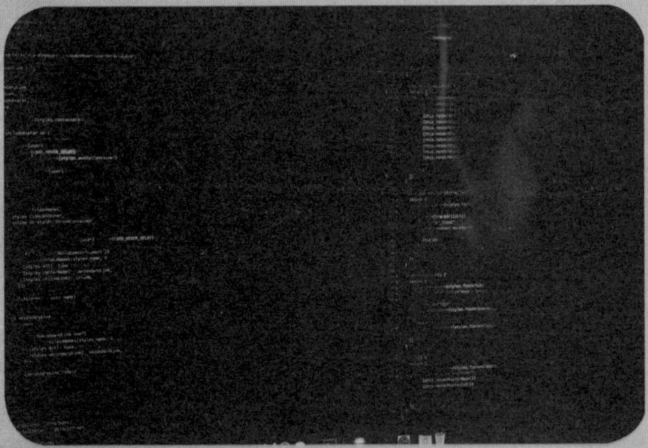

Source: Charles Deluvio on Unsplash

There are, however, some significant ethical concerns in relation to ML. These relate to three broad areas: the data, the algorithm and the outcome. Reflecting first on data, for an ML system to be effective, it is generally considered to need access to a large volume of data. This may be obtained from inside or outside the organisation. The former may involve the mining of information held on employees, while the latter typically entails either locating open-source data sets or purchasing them 'off the shelf' from a third party. Each option has its own advantages and limitations. Data collated internally, for example, may be more relevant and cost effective. However, depending on the nature of what is captured and how it is obtained (for example, covertly versus overtly), employees may find the process intrusive.

Algorithms – the set of rules or instructions for the machine to follow when attempting to solve a problem or complete a calculation – are value-laden (Brey and Soraker, 2009). The developers who create them and the users who configure them have a desired outcome in mind and, as a result, tend to prioritise some values and interests over others (Mittelstadt et al., 2016). In addition, the algorithm may be working with incomplete or flawed data. As a result, bias can creep in and, for reasons outlined below, may go unnoticed.

Finally, in terms of outcomes, ML models typically operate as 'black boxes': data goes in, decisions come out, but what happens in between is murky. Indeed, it has been argued that ML models 'that exhibit the best predictive accuracy, and therefore, the most powerful ones, are, paradoxically, those with the most opaque black-box architectures' (Carabantes, 2020, p. 309). As a result, it may not be possible to discern *how* or *why* a particular outcome was reached. This has enormous implications in the HR context: if, for example, a person is turned down for a training scheme or promotion opportunity there is arguably a moral imperative (and sometimes a legal requirement) that they be able to ascertain the rationale behind the decision.

Stop! If you were asked to advise on the ethical issues arising from the use of ML in HR, what would be the key points you would make?

Essential reading

Mittelstadt, B. D., Allo, P., Taddeo, M., Wacher, S. and Floridi, L. (2016) The ethics of algorithms: mapping the debate. *Big Data and Society*, July–December: 1–21.

Note: This feature was contributed by Laura Steele.

PART 3

Workplace learning and knowledge creation

As an area of research, scholarship and practice, workplace learning encompasses a range of modes of enquiry and theoretical frameworks (Munby, 2003). It has become an established metaphor for capturing formal, nonformal, self-directed, collective and even tacit informal learning activities in the workplace (Solomon, 1999). Ever more sophisticated conceptualisations of workplace learning suggest multiple approaches for understanding the phenomenon. Central to the theorising is an openness to expand our understanding of both work and learning (Bratton and Sawchuk, 2001).

In terms of expanding the notion of 'work', it expands beyond the boundaries of 'paid work' undertaken in organisations to consideration of 'unpaid work', in the home and the community (Livingstone, 1999; Spencer, 1998; Waring, 1999). Understanding *how* 'learning' in the workplace is accomplished expands beyond behavioural psychology ('stimulus-response') and cognitive psychology ('information processing') to incorporate awareness of sociocultural factors, including communities of practice, relationships and the role of social participation. Sociocultural perspectives understand learning is intertwined with the culture, economics, power and social dynamics of particular groups and contexts (Fenwick, 2001).

In considering work-related learning and knowledge creation, scholars distinguish between 'knowing-that' and 'knowing-how'. The former is concerned with knowledge about facts and explanations for facts that are explicit and communicable, whereas the latter refers to the ability to do something in a particular situation. Knowing-that is based on knowledge that has been *codified*, for example written into books, journals or on the Internet, and therefore becomes communicable. It is this knowledge that lies at the heart of the digital revolution. Knowing-how, in contrast, is personal knowledge, based on the requirements of the situation and the understanding of the person carrying out the performance. This is referred to as *tacit knowledge*; it is the ability to deal with different situations, known and unknown, often responding spontaneously to surprise through improvisation and without thought (Schön, 1983). Knowing-how is particularly important in the performance of high-skilled work and when dealing with a new or unexpected situation, which 'cannot be accomplished by procedural knowledge alone or by following a manual' (Eraut, 2000a, p. 128). However, there are different interpretations of tacit knowledge. Collins (2001) suggests it could mean 'concealed knowledge' or 'the tricks of the trade', which is deliberately concealed. Gourlay (2006) argues that the term 'tacit knowledge' is used where people cannot 'give an account' (p. 67) of an action or behaviour. While different interpretations exist the sharing of tacit knowledge is recognised as beneficial for innovation and effectiveness (Arnett and Wittman, 2014).

Tacit knowing by employees is a starting point for a range of ideas concerning how learning by individuals can become shared by teams and organisations as a whole. For example, Crossan et al. (1999, p. 525) present four processes:

- *Intuiting* – individuals see patterns in their experience that provide new insights, which they translate into metaphors for possible communication to others.
- *Interpreting* – individuals explain their insights to themselves and then others through talk, and these then become possible ideas for application.
- *Integrating* – the group shares in the understanding and takes action as a consequence.
- *Institutionalising* –the learning at individual and group levels becomes organisational through 'systems, structures, procedures and strategy'.

Recognising that power is a ubiquitous feature of organisational life (Miller et al., 1999) and managers and non-managers are 'in a web of power' (Hardy and Clegg, 1999, p. 383) they have helped to create, Crossan et al. (1999) suggest that these processes are unlikely to flow without difficulty. For example, power and politics are likely to play a role in the way in which ideas are accepted, rewarded or rejected. These perspectives acknowledge the importance of context in learning and knowledge creation. It is a key feature of workplace learning that it is an everyday process where people become enmeshed in a 'web of relations' composed of actions that they complete with others, based on a set of values that are socially formed. Workplace learning can be helped or hindered by such values (Fenwick, 2008).

The cultural view of workplace learning supports the idea of a community of practice (CoP) (Lave and Wenger, 1991). As originally developed, learning within a CoP is strongly related to becoming a practitioner within a CoP, with its own norms, stories and views about what is effective. This makes the task of achieving the benefits of strategic learning or organisational learning (OL) even more complex, suggesting that organisations need to be conceived as a 'community-of-communities' (Brown and Duguid, 1991, p. 53). Nevertheless, CoPs provide a powerful image for the creation of knowledge that can be used for strategic advantage (Saint-Onge and Wallace, 2012).

Learning at work is the norm for most workers. They exchange information and share ideas to solve problems and improve ways of working, either one-to-one or in groups or teams. The notion of a '*learning organisation*' (LO) extends that simple idea to include a concept of collective or organisational-wide learning that results from individual, CoP or group learning (Spencer and Kelly, 2013). The LO was popularised by Senge (1990) and Pedler et al. (1988; 1991). Senge made the claim, 'If teams learn, they become a microcosm for learning throughout the organization' (1990, p. 236). In Britain, Pedler et al. (1988) conceptualised an LO as an organisation that facilitates the learning of all its members and continuously transforms itself. Pedler et al. (1991) went on to provide a list of dimensions of an LO, such as strategically oriented towards learning and development, engagement in decision-making and reward flexibility. Although there is enthusiasm for OL, it is difficult to implement (Garavan, 1997) and overly bureaucratic organisational structures pose particular difficulties for enactment (Örtenblad, 2004). Potentially, greater attention to workplace learning allows for a more reciprocal and proactive influence on organisational strategy (Slocum et al., 2014).

Field (2004) provides a more critical assessment of OL: 'whole organizations rarely learn ... what is referred to as "organizational learning" is actually learning by shared-interest groups within the organization' (p. 216). Schied and his colleagues (1997) also point out that workplace learning can morph into a culture of 'control'. Karlsson (2012) also observed that workers doing boring repetitive work learned to 'make time' by extending their tea breaks. Challenging the fashionable OL rhetoric, Bratton et al. (2004), note management control issues and argue that workers learn that work organisations are a rich source of learning. Through direct experience and agency, workers' 'learn collectivist values as opposed to individualist values' and that improvements in the terms and conditions of employment can be better accomplished by collective action (p. 67).

It should be obvious by now that, as a field of study, learning and development can be explored and interpreted from different perspectives. In mainstream literature, workplace learning is often presented as unproblematic: learning is a 'win-win' situation benefiting everyone. However, this brief excursion into the field has highlighted tensions between human capital theory and the developmental humanist perspective. The different perspectives and diverse research findings strengthen the case for a more critical approach to strategic learning and development (Bierema and Callahan, 2014). As in other areas of HRM, the catastrophic effects of Covid-19, climate change and disruptive technologies (Susskind, 2020) are bound to raise difficult questions and choices for governments, organisations and individuals in terms of upskilling and reskilling, continuous learning and development. Now that we have examined *why* learning is important to organisations and people, we go on to address a central question: *how* do individuals learn?

HRM in Practice

Is learning the key to tackling racism in the workplace?

Source: Getty Images/skynesher

In the summer of 2020, spurred into action by the US Black Lives Matter movement and the resulting global wave of protests condemning police brutality and systemic racism, many organisational leaders have chosen to respond by making public statements to tackle racial discrimination. But the same racialised violence that many are waking up to as unjust and unacceptable is happening within the walls of our workplaces. According to Banks and Harvey (2020) the key difference between 'police brutality' and 'corporate brutality' is the means. The former is primarily focusing on the physical and the latter is more systemic and covert. To respond to increased calls for racial equality organisational leaders must first acknowledge the experiences of Black and ethnic minority workers. John Amaechi, an organisational psychologist who specialises in issues of race in the UK, argues that learning is the key to addressing issues of racism in the workplace:

> We need to stop looking at this as a deficit model - black people aren't broken, women aren't broken, people with disabilities and impairments aren't broken. The environment they are in is toxic,' Amaechi said. 'That's the model that we need to approach our learning with. And when you do that you suddenly realise who needs learning.

This suggests that instead of trying to upskill minorities the focus should be on training designed to address the organisational cultures that are holding minority workers back. It is also important to acknowledge there are teaching challenges inherent in teaching about racism. Nonetheless, research shows that experiential learning can be an effective approach to teach about racism. For example, the following excerpt describes an experiential learning activity designed to teach about racism (Loya and Cueavas, 2010, p. 239):

> Students were lined up, evenly, and then asked to step forward or backward depending on their answers to certain questions. Sample questions include 'If you were ever called names because of your race or culture, take one step back,' and 'If most of your teachers were from the same racial or ethnic background as you, take one step forward' ... Some students quickly moved forward, while several students had to step backward and ended up, literally, with their backs against the wall. One participant in the exercise began crying - tears silently streaming down her face - as the reality of literally having her 'back against a wall' sunk in.

Learning is crucial to shaping how people view themselves and their views on racism. Critical scholars have argued that organisational leaders could be more successful if they have the resources to properly identify the harm being done to Black and ethnic minority workers, to identify organisational-and industry-specific actions that could remedy the harm, and to hold themselves accountable (Banks and Harvey, 2020). Investing in anti-racist training for all workers is one way to make progress to eliminate racism and racial discrimination in the workplace.

Stop! What is the role of HR professionals in addressing issues of race and racial discrimination at work? What are some of the challenges of teaching about racism in the workplace?

Essential reading

Banks, K. and Harvey, R. (2020) Is your company actually fighting racism, or just talking about it? *Harvard Business Review*, 11 June; Bunglawala, Z. (2019) Please, don't call me BAME or BME. Civil Service Blog, 8 July; Churchill, F. (2020) Learning is key to addressing racism, Amaechi tells Festival of Work. *People Management*, 11 June.

Note: This feature was contributed by Andrew Bratton.

Theoretical perspectives on adult learning

The terms learning and development can cover a myriad of activities, and it is important to define the meaning of these terms. How we understand and explain how adults learn in organisations is, of course, crucial to any attempt to design and implement effective L&D activities. For the purposes of this book, we use the following definition of learning:

> A process of acquiring new knowledge and behaviours as a result of practice, study, or experience. It involves a relatively permanent change in cognition, behaviour, and affect. (Salas et al., 2012, p. 77)

> A relatively permanent change of behaviour or human capabilities resulting from processing new knowledge, practice or experience. (Bratton, 2021, p. 202)

> The process of learning in the workplace 'is always there in all workplaces at all times'. (Poell, 2014, p. 23)

Workers inevitably learn how to perform their jobs through sharing ideas and information. Learning is a desired outcome of training (Billett, 2006; Bratton et al., 2004).

Although training and learning are related, they are not equivalent terms. As we have noted, a great deal of learning at work occurs informally outside of formal training, and training does not always produce learning (Antonacopoulou, 1999). Before examining learning theories, we need to distinguish between training, development and education. According to Armstrong and Taylor (2014, p. 284):

- *Training* – the systematic application of formal processes to impart knowledge and help people to acquire the skills necessary for them to perform their jobs satisfactorily.
- *Development* – the growth or realisation of a person's ability and potential through the provision of learning and educational experiences.
- *Education* – the development of the knowledge, values and understanding required in all aspects of life rather than the knowledge and skills relating to particular areas of activity.

Training is the planned and systematic activities designed to promote the acquisition of new knowledge (i.e. need to know), behaviours (i.e. need to do) and attitudes (i.e. need to feel) (Salas et al., 2012, p. 77). As Armstrong and Taylor (2014, p. 284) remark, 'learning is what individuals do; training is what organisations do to individuals'. The notion of development is coupled with training but is more holistic in that it extends to changing the behaviour and capabilities of the whole individual by facilitating their growth (Gibb, 2003).

Defining learning and development

Over the last 30 years, numerous definitions of human resource development (HRD) have been developed to incorporate the dimensions of learning, training and development. Nadler and Nadler (1989, p. 4) define HRD as:

> Organized learning experiences provided by employers, within a specified period of time, to bring about the possibility of performance improvement and/or personal growth.

The 'and/or' proviso in the definition has been subject to critical treatment in which the 'performative' focus is seen to dominate over a more empowering 'learning' focus (see Rigg et al., 2007). The term 'human resource development' (HRD), while extensively used in academia, has, in recent years, lost favour and has largely been replaced by the term 'learning and development' (L&D) to avoid its reference to people as a resource, which is considered 'demeaning' (Harrison, 2009), and to tilt the focus more towards learning. Harrison (2009, p. 8) offers the following definition of learning and development:

> The primary purpose of learning and development as an organizational process is to aid collective progress through the collaborative, expert and ethical stimulation and

> facilitation of learning and knowledge that support business goals, develop individual potential, and respect and build on diversity.

Other writers, such as Armstrong and Taylor (2014), include the methods to facilitate learning in their definition:

> The process of ensuring that the organization has the knowledgeable, skilled and engaged workforce it needs. It involves facilitating the acquisition by individuals and teams of knowledge and skills through experience, learning events and programmes provided by the organization, guidance and coaching provided by line managers and others, and self-directed learning activities carried out by individuals. (2014, p. 284)

As others have suggested, some learning processes are not planned at all but emerge informally through everyday work-related activities in organisations. Recognising such phenomena, we suggest our own definition of learning and development to be:

> A process that facilitates the acquisition of knowledge, skills and attitudes that enables and results in learning at and through work.

Learning and development (L&D) is not a discrete 'event', but a *process* which opens up our thinking by conceptualising L&D as a social construct, relational – meaning it involves ongoing relationships with others – dynamic and interwoven within a specific organisational context. It does not limit L&D to 'performative' considerations but focuses on empowerment through learning. In a Covid-19 world, our definition also recognises that L&D is practised by more than employers and it can be boundaryless, that is, outside the formal organisational structure. The notion of learning 'through work' makes the key linkage between job design and learning opportunities (Bratton, 1999; 2001). The way work and jobs are designed – the number of tasks involved and the degree of autonomy (see Chapter 3) have an effect on skills that workers can learn and develop.

Learning theories

Contemporary workplace L&D is grounded in the science of learning (Salas et al., 2012) and there exists a substantial body of ideas and research examining adult learning (see Beckett and Hager, 2002). We begin our review of the science by examining what can be called the 'classical' theories of learning: behavioural and cognitive. These theories are considered classical partly because they represent the early contributions to our understanding of how people learn, and also because some of the ideas recur in modern adult learning theories. The main differences between the two classical approaches are summarised in Table 7.1.

Table 7.1 Traditions of learning

Associative learning or behaviourism	Cognitive learning
Learning in terms of responses to stimuli: 'automatic' learning	Insightful learning
Classical conditioning (Pavlov's dogs)	Thinking, discovering, understanding, seeing relationships and meaning
Operant or instrumental conditioning	New arrangements of previously learned concepts and principles

The best-known *behavioural* psychologists, Ivan Pavlov (1849–1936) and B.F. Skinner (1904–90), explained learning in terms of the interaction of the human being with their environment. Pavlov held that animal and human learning could be explained by the phenomenon of classical conditioning (Chance, 2009). Pavlov trained dogs to salivate in response to a variety of stimuli, such as the sound of a bell. This reaction was achieved by pairing the sound of the bell with food. For Pavlov, learning was nothing more than 'a long chain of conditioned reflexes' (Walker, 1996, p. 20). Skinner explained human learning in terms of the phenomenon of instrumental or operant conditioning, and he held that reinforcement (either positive or negative) was a necessary part of the process (Skinner, 1954). An operant is a response that has some effect on the environment. For example, when a child cries and is then fed, the child has made an operant response that influences when food will be served. Skinner believed that learning at work was also influenced by what he called 'continuous reinforcement', that is, every desired response is followed by a reward.

The origins of the *cognitive* approach to learning can be traced to research by Wolfgang Köhler (1887–1967). In contrast to behaviourists, Köhler argued that animals' problem-solving did not have to develop incrementally through stimulus-response associations. Through observations of chimpanzees, Köhler concluded that 'learning involves insight into the problem as a whole, occurs suddenly, is retained and is transferred readily to new situations' (Bratton, 2021, p. 210). More recent interpretations, however, suggest that 'insightful learning' might occur after a mental 'trial and error' process in which individuals envisage a course of action, and choose the option that is most likely to aid decision-making (Bernstein et al., 1999).

Beckett and Hager (2002, p. 98) view behaviourist and cognitive theories as representing a 'standard paradigm of learning'. The assumption of both approaches is that the 'human mind' is viewed as a 'stock room' that is at first empty but gradually becomes filled with knowledge. Both theories have value in L&D. For example, behaviourist theories underpin the importance of reinforcement and feedback in learning, including the opportunity to practise new skills. Cognitive theories focus on how learners process information through thinking and memory, organised into patterns or schema to attend to what is happening (Sadler-Smith, 2006). People process information somewhere between two preferences:

- *Analytical* – a preference for step-by-step models and structured decision-making.
- *Intuitive* – a preference for less structure and more openness and creativity.

Research suggests, however, that it is possible to consider both analytical and intuitive processing together. For example, a high preference for both would indicate versatility and openness but also structured thinking (Hodgkinson and Clarke, 2007). There has been a growing interest in the use of cognitive styles in organisations, and a review by Armstrong et al. (2012) recommends a need to extend research into the use of and effect of measuring cognitive styles in such areas as team leadership, group problem-solving and conflict, particularly in the context of social interactions, for example collaboration in teams.

Following the work of Albert Bandura (1925–2021), sociocultural learning scholars explain human learning as the interaction between internal processes and their social context. Learning is characterised as a reciprocal process that happens through direct observation and modelling. Individuals learn by observing others whom they believe are credible and knowledgeable (so they can act as 'models'). What is learned is then encoded into memory to serve as a guide for later behaviour. Further, adult learning is influenced by an individual's 'self-efficacy', that is, a person's judgement about whether they can successfully learn new knowledge and skills (Bandura, 1977). Two theories that we have cho-

Table 7.2 Traditions of social learning

Self-directed learning	Experiential learning
A self-initiated process of learning	Emphasises centrality of experience
Individual empowerment	Learning 'cycle' contains elements of cognitive, behaviouralist and andragogical concepts
Organising material that allows for learner autonomy	Holistic – learning is both concrete and abstract, active and reflective

sen to focus on here – *self-directed* and *experiential* – draw upon social-learning theory and have been influential in the design of adult learning activities.

The literature on *self-directed* learning has helped to define the unique characteristics of adult learning. The concept emphasises the need for and ability of adults to control and manage their own learning, that individuals should be empowered to control their own learning, and learning material should allow for greater learner autonomy and control over the learning process. Thus, the person is expected to assume primary responsibility for their own learning, and the process focuses on self-development. Further, the learner's life experience is central to the learning process (Caffarella, 1993). Parallels can be drawn with the humanistic psychology of Maslow (1954) and with the North American philosophical orientation of individualism (Bratton, 2021). In terms of workplace practice, the approach emphasises the importance of specifying learning objectives, much like performance management objectives, often in the form of learning contracts.

Kolb's learning model

The *experiential* learning approach, often referred to as Kolb's (1984) learning cycle, focuses on the interaction of learners with their context. The learning cycle is popular in the HRD canon, possibility because it contains elements of cognitive, behaviourist and andragogical concepts that can potentially encourage creativity and innovation. Andragogy views learning as the construction of meaning through experience (Knowles, 1998). Figure 7.1 shows Kolb's experiential learning cycle, which suggests that for learning to occur, all the stages of the cycle should be completed.

Kolb's learning model has been very influential for many HRD practitioners and has also heightened awareness of the factors that contribute to learning or prevent learning at work. Learning activities at work could thus be designed on the basis of individual and group learning preferences. Learners might also attempt to overcome their blocks to learning. Individuals might, for example, lack the belief that they can take action in certain situations, or they might have negative feelings about certain activities. Kolb's theory of learning fostered an interest in adult self-development, and the importance of reflection to examine behaviour and assumptions about learning (Mezirow, 1991). Within the social-learning genre is the work of Vygotsky (1978) and his sociocultural theory of human development (Bratton et al., 2004; Wells, 1999). Vygotsky (1978) suggested that learning occurs through participation in actions and interaction with others, mediated through the use of 'tools' such as language. Drawing on the work of Vygotsky (1978) and Bakhtin's (1981) philosophy of language, Gold and Yeo (2013) set up an integrated experiential learning approach that brings together social context, cognition and action.

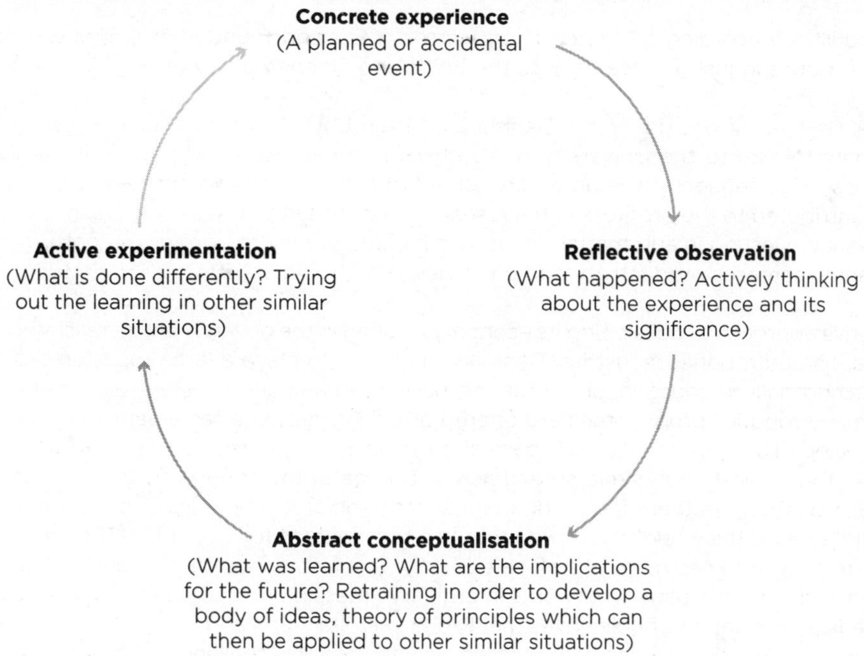

Figure 7.2 Kolb's experiential cycle of learning

Global HRM

How Denmark became the home of the robotics industry

Source: Yancy Cameron Venti on Unsplash

Denmark is quickly becoming one of the world's most successful countries for robotics innovation. Denmark is a small country with a population of less than six million, which has meant it has often 'worried' about its manufacturing industry. According to its official website, Denmark values trust, openness and 'an almost total lack of corruption', which makes it a good place for business (Waterfield, 2019). Its 'flexicurity' model means it is easy to hire from its small pool of workers but also let them go if business conditions change. The population is supported by an education system that is free for students. The Danish robotics industry is currently booming. The 2019 annual survey from trade association Odense Robotics shows that 8,500 people now work for Danish robotics companies, 3,900 of them in and around Odense, Denmark's third largest city (Odense Robotics, 2020). If the industry follows growth forecasts, the Danish robot industry will employ 25,000 employees in 2025. In terms of market growth, Danish robotics companies' total revenue rose by 18% in 2018, reaching $995 million with exports increasing 26%. These figures are particularly significant because just 15 years ago Denmark did not have any robotics industry. According to Enrico Krog Iversen, CEO and founder of OnRobot, the success of Denmark's robotics industry dates back to the 1980s and Odense, a city of 180,000. Iversen explained:

> In the 1980s, Maersk was the first in Denmark to use robots for welding, painting and processing, and donated €10m to the University of Southern Denmark to allow it to continue its research in robotics ... Subsequently, the university attracted extremely competent and bright professors, which contributed to the progress in the research ... Importantly, as a nation, Denmark understood early on that investing in automation not only mitigates against the growing employment gap but significantly increases productivity and efficiency. (Waterfield, 2019)

This innovative approach to developing its economy resulted in the government increasing investment into the automation and robotics industries. Denmark continues to place a large focus on teaching robotics and engineering skills in educational institutions, basic programming skills are taught at primary school level, and many robotics programmes are offered at universities. In a testament to its success, Odense recently developed a 'swab robot' in the space of only four weeks, which could transform the fight against Covid-19. As the Covid-19 pandemic spread across Europe in the spring of 2020, a robotics professor from the University of Southern Denmark and a doctor from a local hospital posed the question: 'What if they could develop the world's first swab robot to test patients for Covid-19?' The robot would enable large-scale testing, and keep medical staff safe. This type of fast innovation demonstrates the importance of nurturing such interdisciplinary networks in ordinary times, in order to be ready when disaster strikes. Years of dedicated work and public investment to attract start-ups and researchers to Odense paid off when the talent on the ground decided to collectively take on this challenge.

Stop! The triple helix model of innovation refers to collaborative arrangements between government, business and academia. What is the role of national and local governments in supporting robotics innovation in Denmark? Would this model work in other countries?

Essential reading

Waterfield, S. (2019) How Denmark became the unlikely home of the robotics industry. *Institution of Mechanical Engineers*, 7 August; Odense Robotics (2020) Global robotics footprint made in Odense. Odense Robotics Insight Report; Callesen, J. (2020) Here's what the first coronavirus 'swab robot' can teach us about fast innovation. *World Economic Forum*, 24 June.

Note: This feature was contributed by Andrew Bratton.

The strategic learning and development process

Traditional perspectives viewed training as an on-off activity that occurred when a new employee joined the organisation or following a performance appraisal. A trainer-centred activity that is 'done to' an employee (Sloman, 2005). Traditional training centred on the four-stage systematic training cycle (STC), which promoted the systematic use of training needs analysis, training design, delivery and evaluation. The STC model emphasises 'logical and sequential planning and action' and was widely adopted, becoming ingrained in the thinking of most training practitioners (Buckley and Caple, 2007, p. 24). It was also criticised for being slow and unresponsive to change (Rayner and Adam-Smith, 2009).

Contemporary approaches, in contrast, put the emphasis on the learner and the opportunities for them to learn *through* work, not just *at* work. Contemporary L&D models seek to be both systematic and integrated. An approach that highlights key interdependencies within organisations, such as the linkage to strategy, the role of line managers, the importance of organisational culture and knowledge transfer (Hirsh and Tamkin, 2005). For L&D professionals, the emphasis on linking organisational strategy with learning and development interventions means that they have to engage with managers and non-managers at both the strategic and the operational level in order to provide value and enhance their credibility. The image is closer to that of what is called a 'business partner', in which L&D practitioners work alongside business units as agents or facilitators of change (see Chapter 1 and Ulrich et al., 2009).

Following Ulrich (1997), it is posited that professionals responsible for L&D have three options:

- To provide routine transactional services such as traditional training programmes, as part of a *shared service* provision with other HRM professionals;
- To become more specialist by providing leading and complex L&D processes that are valued by others within a *centre of excellence*, perhaps by using the latest research in collaboration with universities;
- To become strategic *business partners*, working with business leaders on the organisation's agenda for the future.

In most cases, but especially as strategic business partners, this means L&D becoming what the CIPD (2010b; 2020a) calls an insight- and business-driven discipline, possibly in contrast to a people-driven discipline. Others, however, warn that such prioritisation has the potential to expunge concerns for people and their development and well-being (Keegan and Francis, 2010).

Despite widespread criticism of the four-stage systematic training cycle, contemporary models that add the word 'strategy', thereby enhancing the prestige of HRD, continue to incorporate the principles of the STC. An example of this are the models provided by Tannenbaum (2002) and Salas et al. (2012), which provide the 'most comprehensive' framework of the strategic learning and development process (Noe and Tews, 2018). All L&D activities are not only planned, designed and evaluated, but are aligned with strategic goals and objectives. Thus, strategic learning and development cannot be differentiated. Salas et al. (2012) provide evidence-based activities for strategic learning, which are undertaken before, during and after training, shown in Figure 7.3.

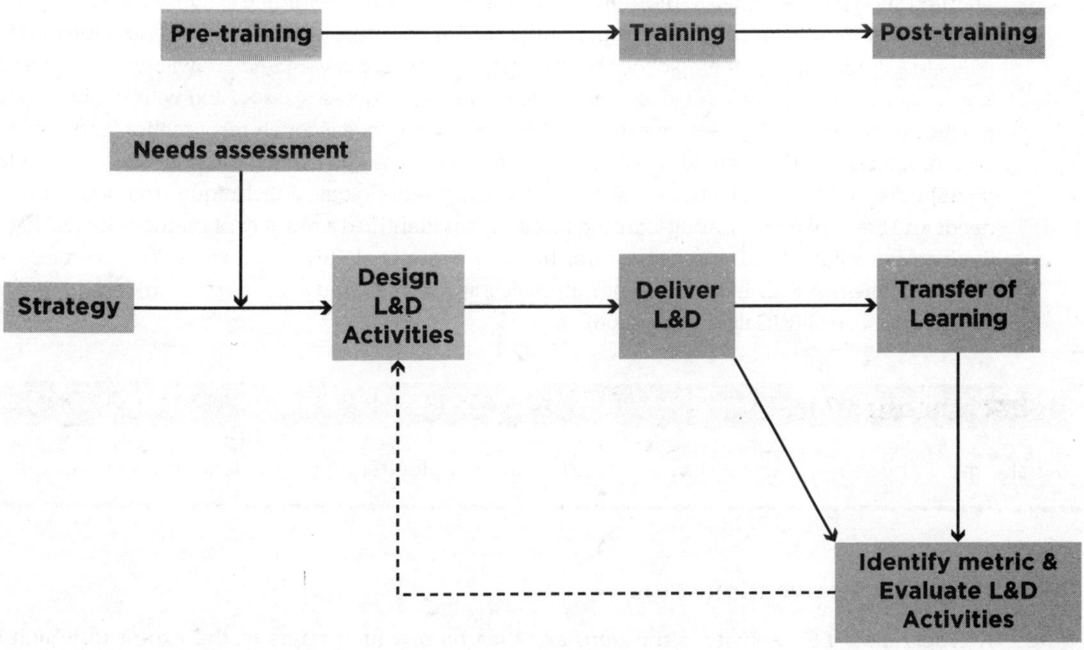

Figure 7.3 The strategic learning and development process
Source: Based on the theories of Tannenbaum (2002) and Salas et al. (2012).

Pre-L&D intervention stage

In the pre-L&D intervention stage, long- and short-term strategic learning goals are identified, leaders prepare a learning culture, and a training and learning needs analysis (TLNA) is conducted. While a consideration of the future is an essential feature of human existence (Bell, 2001), when considering long-term learning goals, there is increased interest in the benefit of Futures and Foresight Learning (FFL), defined as a consideration of predictable, possible, plausible, probable, preferable and creatable futures. The notion of prediction is possible due to advancements in AI and predictive models in daily life. Since humans can develop and hold onto false assumptions about the future – such as the impact of a global pandemic – it is suggested that counter-factual FFL can give strategic direction to learning and development by provoking organisations to consider improbable or nonpreferred scenarios (Gordon and Todorova, 2019).

Training and learning needs analysis (TLNA) identify what needs to be learned and by whom (see below). The *design of L&D processes* should be driven by the results of the TLNA exercise and theories of adult learning. In addition, learning activities should be designed to enable transfer by, for example, including features of the work situation (Grossman and Salas, 2011). Therefore, the learning processes that take place away from the work setting need to be sensitive to practices as within work. This will enhance the trainees' perceptions of the value of and potential to use what is being learned (van der Locht et al., 2013).

L&D delivery stage

A number of key considerations and activities take place during L&D delivery stage. Adult education scholars have noted that adults bring to the learning environment individual characteristics, such as self-efficacy, motivation, experience, that influence the learning outcomes. *Self-efficacy* – a person's belief that they are capable of performing a task or activity – influences the learning process and outcomes. Training should be designed to promote self-efficacy and then to reinforce it afterwards. Research suggests that *motivation to learn* can be an important predictor of actual learning in training. Motivation to learn refers to a condition when employees believe that training is relevant and are willing to exert effort in the learning environment (Salas et al., 2012). Andragogy – the processes associated with the organisation and practice of teaching adults – suggest that a learner's *experience* is a rich resource for learning. Therefore, L&D processes should include problem-solving, discussion and simulation exercises. As Bratton (2021, p. 216) notes 'learning practitioners should embrace methodological techniques that focus on an adult's needs and life experiences. Adult learning research has identified a number of methodologies that enhance the learning value of L&D strategies: error training (Frese et al., 1991), role-modelling exercises (Bandura, 1977), self-directed learning (Jarvis, 1991; Knowles, 1998), and simulation or the working representation of organisational reality (Galvao et al., 2000).

Reflective question

What is meant by self-efficacy and why is it important in understanding adult learning and L&D outcomes?

Post-L&D intervention stage

A crucial *post-L&D* activity is the *transfer of learning*, which refers to the extent to which learning accrued during training is subsequently applied on the job or affects learners' performances. From a management point of view, transfer is critical because, without it, an organisation is less likely to receive any demonstrable benefits for its L&D investments (see more on learning transfer below).

A learning culture and support from managers has a direct effect on trainees' motivation for the transfer of learning (Chiaburu and Tekleab, 2005). In addition, the concept of 'transfer climate' appears to be important. That is, the extent to which learners perceive the post-training environment (including line managers and peers) as supportive of the learner's newly acquired knowledge and skills and whether those skills are practised and maintained (Rouiller and Goldstein, 1993). *Line managers' support* activities can include goal setting, reinforcement activities, encouragement to attend and modelling of behaviours, all part of their role as coaches to motivate their staff to transfer learning to work (Gegenfurtner et al., 2009). *Evaluation* is the final stage of the strategic learning and development process (see below).

Needs analysis: linking strategy to learning and development

For Salas et al. (2012, p. 83), a learning and development needs analysis (LDNA) is 'the first and probably the most important step toward the design and delivery of any training'. The purpose of needs analysis from a strategic perspective is to align training, learning and development with the strategic goals of the organisation (Noe and Tew, 2018). A critical issue here, one we examined in Chapter 2, is organisational 'fit' (also known as 'vertical' or 'external' fit). Boxall and Purcell (2016) argue that HR strategies should fit in with an organisation's wider strategy and other critical features, including its structural features. In this line of thinking, the wider organisation strategy informs and directs the learning and development strategy. The outcome of the LDNA process is fivefold:

- Align learning and development intervention to organisation's strategy
- Expected learning outcomes
- Guidance for training and learning design and delivery
- Ideas for evaluating training and learning
- Information about organisational factors that will likely hinder or facilitate training and learning effectiveness.

The literature outlines a variety of needs analysis models to explicitly align learning and development to specific organisational contexts. Noe and Tews (2018) reviewed a variety of frameworks and observed that 'models that link training and development needs to what organizations *use*, *do*, *produce*, and *deliver* are best suited for strategic training and development purposes' (p. 265, emphasis added). The most well-known model identifies three levels of analysis:

- Organisational analysis
- Job analysis
- Individual analysis, shown in Table 7.3.

Organisational analysis

Organisational analysis examines strategic priorities, organisational culture, resources and support for L&D. The strategic focus necessitates examining key organisational objectives and challenges, identifying the functions and jobs that most influence organisational success, clarifying the most critical competencies and establishing overall strategic learning imperatives (Tannenbaum, 2002).

Table 7.3 Assessment and analysis of training needs

Organisational analysis	Job analysis	Individual analysis
Culture audit and diagnosis Skills audit Development of competency framework Workforce plan Analysis of performance management data Critical incidents External research Benchmarking External assessment, e.g. the Investors in People awards in the UK and worldwide.	Job analysis Job documents – description, specifications Problem-centred analysis Key task analysis Competency analysis Job or occupation standards (defined within vocational qualifications)	Performance management and appraisal data including multisource feedback Direct observation Performance standards measurement Development centre results Completion of psychological tests Self-appraisal

Job analysis

Job analysis is 'the blue-print' (Salas et al., 2012, p. 81) for the learning and development. TLNA reveals what skills are needed to complete the job. Understanding skills and how skills are defined is central in debates about L&D. Felstead et al. (2002) propose that 'skill' can mean:

- competence to carry out a task;
- a hierarchy of skill levels that are dependent on the complexities and discretions involved;
- a variety of types, including generic skills applied in diverse situations, and specific skills suitable for particular contexts.

Source: CDC on Unsplash

Most decisions on the definition of skills take place in organisations, exposed to factors such as the structure of domestic markets, short-term financial pressure, models of competitive advantage, cost containment and standardisation (Wilson and Hogarth, 2003). These all combine to design tasks to a low specification, requiring low skills and providing low value added (Bloom et al., 2004). Even if an organisation reports a deficiency in skills, these can easily be defined in low skills terms, in what Bloom et al. (2004, p. 12) call a 'latent skills gap', where organisations can accept and adjust to low skill requirements, losing awareness of the restriction that this imposes.

Individual analysis

Individual analysis determines who has (and who lacks) the perquisite knowledge and skills, data that can be derived from PM/PA (see Chapter 6). As Devanna and her colleagues (1983, p. 41) note, appraisal facilitates '*developing* employees to enhance their current performance'. Managers and HRD professionals have to determine who will most likely benefit from learning and development activities and whether the content matter or pedagogy is aligned with particular learners' needs (Salas et al., 2012).

Based on the work of Baldwin and Ford (1988, p. 65), Figure 7.4 shows a model of learning transfer. The framework specifies six crucial linkages, indicated by the arrows. We can, for example, see that new skills can be learned and retained, but support and opportunity to use the learning must be provided in the work environment. The influence of the framework can be seen in the work of Holton et al. (2007), who have developed a Learning Transfer System Inventory that allows an organisation to diagnose the factors affecting or preventing the transfer of learning. The items in the inventory relate to:

- motivational factors relating to the expectations that people have about applying new skills;
- secondary influences concerning the degree of preparedness of learners, and their belief or conviction in their ability to use their skills;
- environmental elements such as supervisor support or sanctions, and peer support;
- ability elements relating to the opportunity to apply new skills, the energy and workload of learners, and the way in which training is designed to link to work performance.

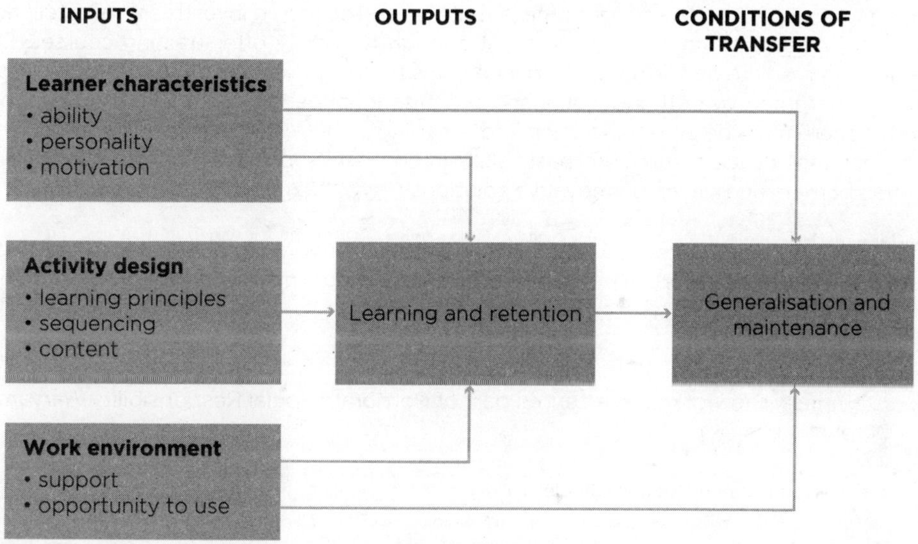

Figure 7.4 A framework for the transfer of training

Source: Baldwin et al. (1988). Reproduced with permission.

Digital Spotlight
Reskilling workers for the age of AI

Pre-Covid-19, some organisations were struggling to recruit employees with the technical skills they require while, at the same time, pondering how to redeploy workers whose roles are at risk of becoming obsolete due to technological advancements. In such cases, reskilling or upskilling represents a potential solution.

A survey by consulting firm PwC (2019a) revealed that 79% of CEOs believe a lack of key skills is threatening the future growth of their organisation. This is a particular issue within the energy industry, where major multinationals including Royal Dutch Shell, BP and ExxonMobil are seeking to harness the potential of artificial intelligence (AI) (Castellanos 2020). AI can be used for a variety of purposes within the sector, including deep-water drilling, predictive analysis and the locating of faults within complex systems. However, suitably qualified staff are proving difficult to recruit. It has been suggested that this is due, at least in part, to some younger people being reluctant to apply because they believe the work is dangerous and physically demanding (McFarland, 2020). Compounding the problem, energy companies increasingly find themselves competing for talent against the likes of tech giants such as Amazon, Facebook, Google and Netflix (McFarland, 2020).

In April 2020, Shell announced that it was addressing the issue by collaborating with educational company Udacity to upskill their employees in AI (Caminiti, 2020). Shell revealed that around 2,000 of their 82,000 workers worldwide had either expressed an interest in AI training or had been approached by their managers to participate in courses on the likes of Python and R. Those selected complete an online programme, referred to as a 'nanodegree', at their own pace during working hours. The course typically takes four to six months to complete, based on an average of 10 to 15 hours engagement per week (Caminiti, 2020). Participants come from a diverse range of backgrounds, including petroleum engineers, chemists and geophysicists. Shell's general manager of data science, Dan Jeavons, said, 'Technology is moving so quickly that if you're not continually training your people, you're going to get out of date'. He considers the money spent on the programme 'a material and strategic investment' (Castellanos, 2020).

Industry experts, however, caution that it is not enough to simply offer training courses. Employees need to be given immediate opportunities and incentives to apply their learning, so that it translates into real-world skills that improve both individual and organisational performance (PwC, 2020). In addition, they argue that there must be an emphasis on 'cross-skilling', where specialists in one area (for example, chemical engineering) develop sufficient basic skills in another (such as AI) to be able to break down communication barriers and develop innovative solutions (PwC, 2020).

Stop! In the light of developments in AI and changes in the way we work due to the Covid-19 pandemic, how can HR professionals support managers and employees in terms of preparing for and engaging in upskilling/reskilling?

Essential reading

Medros, A. (2019) Reskilling workers is a central part of Corporate Social Responsibility. *Harvard Business Review*, 1 October.

Note: This feature was contributed by Laura Steele.

Evaluation of learning and development

Evaluation serves to provide feedback to the L&D facilitator, so that improvements may be made to activities. It can also provide data to demonstrate that the L&D activities have accomplished the set learning objectives, that these objectives resulted in enhanced performance on the job and that investment in human capital can be justified. Kirkpatrick's (1998) framework is widely used in organisations for evaluating learning. It consists of four measurements to be taken at four stages, in sequence, to show a chain of causality, shown in Figure 7.5. Level 1 – learners' reactions (how well trainees liked the L&D activities); Level 2 – learning (principles, facts, skills learned); Level 3 – behaviour (resulting changes in behaviour on the job); and Level 4 – results (quantifiable outcomes of L&D, e.g. fewer errors).

Proving the worth of L&D by producing an acceptable ROI is certainly important to organisations. However, there are persistent doubts about the efficacy and value of such an exercise, especially in

Level 1: Reaction
of the learners following an activity

Level 2: Learning
skills and knowledge gained as a result of the activity

Level 3: Behaviour
the effect on the performance of the learner within the workplace

Level 4: Results
the effect of changes in performance on measurable results at work for example production/service figures, costs, and so on

Figure 7.5 Levels of evaluation for training and learning
Source: Inspired by Kirkpatrick (1998).

terms of the idea that learning outcomes can be quantified and measured as if in a chain of causality (Guba and Lincoln, 1989). Anderson (2007), for example, points to the need for any method of evaluation to include the values of those receiving the learning and development.

The alignment of L&D learning to the organisation's strategy and beyond represents a pivot from the traditional linear reasoning of mechanistic models because establishing the metrics strategically allows them to become part of the overall evaluation process, providing meaning to managers and those participating in L&D. In this way, it is posited that an organisation engages in what Preskill (2008) calls 'evaluation capacity-building', so evaluation becomes purposeful and useful not only in improving the effects of L&D but on enhancing the learning climate and learning in the workplace. Finally, the integrated model shown in Figure 7.5 gives greater consideration to contextual factors such as the motivation, interests of learners, the support from line managers and leaders, and the learning culture. In essence, it encourages leaders to become 'systemic' in their thinking about the learning processes at work (Chiaburu and Tekleab, 2005).

Reflective question

To what extent does the model shown in Figure 7.5 retain some of the features of the STC and offer a 'strategic approach to learning and development'?

Leadership development and coaching

The training and learning principles examined in Figure 7.2 can be applied to the challenge of developing effective leaders (Salas et al., 2012). Leadership development generally differs from training in that its learning objectives are 'higher order' (more complex) and are less connected to individual jobs. Typically, trainees have more discretion in personalising development content and incorporate a variety of both formal and informal learning activities, including one-to-one mentoring, coaching and action learning. As others have cautioned, however, it is difficult to generalise about developing leaders because of the variations in the contexts faced (Burgoyne et al., 2004). Gold et al. (2010) suggest two possible definitions of leadership development (LD). The first is applicable where it is believed possible to specify a 'best way' to lead or manage:

> A planned and deliberate process to help leaders and managers become more effective. (p. 19)

Planning and deliberation are based on the existence of specified ideas, models and theories that leaders need to learn in order to practise. Such a definition underpins many leadership development programmes available, including those that provide accreditation. In contrast, Gold et al. (2010) offer a definition that gives more prominence to how leaders and managers really work and learn in the workplace:

> A process of learning for leaders and managers through recognized opportunities. (p. 19)

This definition acknowledges how leadership development might occur informally without planning and deliberation. A key issue for researchers, however, is how leaders might recognise learning opportunities as part of their work. Writers such as Vince and Reynolds (2010) point to the importance of reflection in capturing learning from work, allowing sense-making and changes in communities of practice to be considered. In contrast to individual leader development, 'leader*ship* development' expands the *collective capacity* of organisational members to engage in leadership roles and processes (McCauley and Brutus, 1998). From this perspective, those in leadership positions work with others in meaningful ways – 'to learn' their way out of problems (Day, 2000, p. 582).

Theories of 'followership' provide a nuanced explanation of how leaders and followers '*together* co-produce the leadership relationship' (Bratton and Francis, 2020, p. 311, emphasis added) and how learners can engage, listen and learn from others. Part of this process involves leaders and followers reflecting on events and critiquing common assumptions (Seijts et al., 2017).

In many organisations, models of leadership are expressed as competencies. In the context of leadership, Armstrong (2012) suggests three facets to competency:

- *Input* – knowledge, skills and personal attributes;
- *Process* – the behaviour required to convert the input into outputs;
- *Output* – the outcomes achieved.

Thus, competence or competency are concerned not only with the inputs and processes of behaviour but also with the outcomes of leader's behaviours (Gold et at., 2012, p. 135). Competencies alone do not explain a leader's performance: context matters (Boyatzis, 1982). This echoes Boak and Crabbe's (2019) observation that the development of leadership competencies can arise informally from interactions and reflection in the workplace, rather than through formal training

There is a relatively large body of literature on leadership development. Most of the literature concentrates on 'how to' develop leadership while a few authors offer a more nuanced perspective focusing on experiential learning as a crucible for leadership development and on the importance of reflectivity. Moreover, the need to recognise that, 'leadership, learning and development are becoming more intimately linked' as organisations seek to navigate differently through economic turmoil and change that require managers and workers to keep 'learning together in order to recalibrate with changing contexts' (Carroll, 2015, p. 103). We will conclude our brief sojourn into the field by pointing to Watt et al.'s (2020) observation, that leadership development, while taking many forms, to be effective must contain activities that reflect two principles: first, the activities must contain critical reflection to allow the articulation of assumptions about a leader's work. This requires an openness on the leader's part to listen, to be challenged and to learn. Second, those activities must be designed to encourage learners to embrace suitable learning methods to leadership development through activities such as mentoring and coaching. This dual path for leadership development is the minimum prerequisite for those in senior management positions in a disruptive post-Covid-19 world.

Coaching

Coaching has become a significant activity in the strategic learning and development process. Coaching is concerned with performance and development issues, between a coach and an employee, and structured around specific goals (CIPD, 2015d; Sikora and Ferris, 2014). In the workplace, it has been conceptualised as the art of facilitating the learning and performance of another person (Downey, 1999). Coaching can also be framed as supporting 'natural learning processes' and as an 'intervention' to facilitate the experiential learning cycle (Watt et al., 2020, p. 278). It can be contrasted with *mentoring*, which tends to focus on long-term issues such as careers and leadership development.

Gold et al. (2012) have suggested that coaching provides two benefits for an organisation: first, managers who are coached are more likely to improve their own performance, and second, managers who coach are more likely to learn about their subordinates and improve their performance. Other benefits include the relief of stress, and by experiencing how to show compassion to others, there is increased leadership sustainability through restoration of the body's natural healing and growth processes (Boyatzis et al., 2006). There is also a view that coaching success during the performance appraisal process is mediated by the perception of the manager's trustworthiness and ability to have honest conversations (Godfrey et al., 2014; Kim et al., 2015).

Studies indicate an interest in developing a coaching culture (Garvey et al., 2014). Knight and Poppleton's (2008) research found three approaches to developing a coaching culture:

- *Centralised* and *structured* – senior managers provide high support and formal structures to ensure consistency.
- *Organic* and *emergent* – based on informality and networks, coaching evolves with practice.
- *Tailored middle ground* – this involves a blend of the previous two approaches, with some degree of direction for consistency but also a response to the particulars of the context.

For a coaching culture to emerge, there needs at some stage in all cases to be momentum based on good practice, training for coaches and support from senior managers who see the value of coaching (Garvey et al., 2009). There are a number of 'how to' models for best coaching practice (see, for example, Whitmore, 2002), but, as other researchers have pointed out, coaches are often required to respond spontaneously to the person they are coaching, with little time for deliberating or specifying a model. At such moments, coaches have to respond with what they have available – their experience and wisdom derived from experience (Gold et al., 2012).

Future challenges: machine learning and the Fourth Industrial Revolution

For more than 20 years there has been a growth of various technologies that has provided new products and services for consumers based on increased efficiency of business, sometimes at the expense of reduced numbers of humans. Such technologies include artificial intelligence, machine learning, robots and deep learning, usually referred to as the Fourth Industrial Revolution (4IR) (Schwab, 2017). Even before the Covid-19 era, there were debates about the extent to which 4IR will replace human skill (Fry, 2018) and its potential to disrupt human lives (Mason, 2016). During the pandemic, many businesses adopted e-technologies, such as Zoom and Microsoft Teams and undertook virtual training events (EY, 2020), so in the Covid-19 era, it is highly likely that 4IR technologies will be extended.

In the wake of Covid-19 it is likely that the trend toward homeworking, paid work at home, will accelerate and be a typical spatial location in modern societies (Edgell and Granter, 2020). Homeworking by definition suggests that organisations will need less space. During the emergency the CEO of Barclays bank, which operates from a tower block in London's Canary Wharf, stated, with some prescience, 'the notion of putting 7,000 people in the building may be a thing of the past' (Jolly, 2020, p. 54). As a student, you are probably all too aware, the Internet and intelligent mobile devices overcome the restrictions on time and space and become a ubiquitous learning tool (Lin and Chen, 2017). Digital Learning (DL) refers to any teaching practice that effectively uses technology to strengthen a learner's learning experience. Indeed, designing activity for digital learning has come to the fore during the coronavirus pandemic.

Machine learning (ML) is a far more sophisticated use of computers for learning. It refers to technology that 'allows computers to learn directly from examples and experience in the form of data' (Royal Society, 2017, p. 19). In other words, ML seeks to emulate how humans learn. To achieve the machine-like status, a computer is 'trained' with data that is relevant to a particular problem, for example, who are the best candidates to recruit, from which an algorithm is developed to analyse data to form patterns to calculate answers. As this process is constructed, the machine forms and develops its own understanding or artificial intelligence (AI). ML can augment its intelligence by working through databases automatically, referred to as Data Mining, and build new or higher-level concepts, referred to as 'Deep Learning' (Goodfellow et al., 2016). Machine learning, together with data science and infrastructure development, can develop capabilities into business opportunities (McAllister, 2020).

Whereas the assembly-line and 'systematic training' symbolised modernity in the 1960s, 4IR technologies, Digital Learning and Machine Learning (ML) are likely to do so in the 2020s. Deloitte (2018) estimated that employment in 44 per cent of professions was falling in the UK due to displacement by 4IR technologies. There are three possibilities: replacement of human skill, complement to human skill and advancement of human skill. Morgan (2019) argues that there is a gap in involvement and participation in how ML and AI are shaped. Although ML and AI can improve organisational decision-making (Eubanks, 2019), ML is capable, as are humans, of learning bias (Cheatham et al., 2019). For example, Amazon used ML in its recruitment process only to find the algorithm was biased in favour of males because it had been trained on data which came mainly from men. Amazon postponed this process (Mujtaba and Mahapatra, 2019). The training of ML raises important ethical issues of fairness and social justice. Harrison et al. (2020) found that while some HRM practitioners were aware of ML and AI, it remained something of a 'black box'. Most HRM L&D practitioners had little involvement in the formation of ML or experience of working with the designers of algorithms to identify how ML could provide tangible HRM opportunities that address stakeholder needs. Gold and his colleagues (2020) advocate the need for 'hybrid professionals' that is, active participants in developing ML. As argued by Schwab and Davis (2018), to maximise the opportunities and avoid the negative effects of ML and AI, there is a need for stakeholder collaboration and the embedding of human values within algorithms so that they can be 'shaped to enhance the common good, environmental stewardship and human dignity' (p. 2).

Critiquing the strategic learning and development discourse

Scholars have critiqued human capital theory. Critics argue individuals are socialised into acceptance of the 'need' to 'invest' in their own education and development, simultaneously with the acceptance of the state abdicating responsibility and funding. As the OECD point out, with organisations increasing skill requirements, 'persons with low levels of educational attainment may find themselves at a distinct disadvantage in the labour market' (OECD, 1996, p. 34). The argument is that if students want high-paying jobs they have to 'invest' and increase their 'human capital' (Spencer and Kelly, 2013). The cost of education and development is transferred from the state to the individual along with increased uncertainty, risk and insecurity in the employment relationship, which further brings to the surface ethical considerations (Woodall and Douglas, 2000). This echoes an interpretation suggested in other chapters so far, the atomisation of the employment relationship. The human capital theory, as it relates to learning and development, is predicated on the idea that high-skill levels will increase performance and profits, yet in the gig economy, there are many employers which profitably operate on the basis of minimal or zero skills and learning.

Taylor (1991) argues that the systematic training model is based on flawed assumptions and is merely a 'legitimizing myth' (Taylor, 1991, p. 270) to establish the role of the trainer and allow management's right to define skill within the employment relationship. It is often assumed, for example, that training is in everyone's best interest. In times of change, however, the definition of skill and the redesign of work may lead to a divergence of interest between workers and employers, and may unbalance the employment relationship between them. Although systematic models might have helped to professionalise HRD and provide a simple and easily understood explanation of training and learning procedures, such models are incomplete and only suitable for organisations operating in stable environments where strategic goals can be clearly set, outcomes measured and compliance is obtained from workers. Continued adherence towards what is still essentially a mechanistic procedure may well prevent employers tapping into a more nebulous but powerful force such as human creativity (Taylor, 1991).

An analysis of workplace learning is incomplete without taking into account the milieu of asymmetrical power relationships which exist in the workplace, rooted from the societal configuration of class, gender and race/ethnic relations. As Grugulis (2019, p. 303) rightly observes, we have to consider the social context of skill and learning. There is evidence that gender, race or age can be 'used as a proxy for judgements on ability, capacity and achievement'. A gendered analysis of paid work, in particular, the distinction between full-time and part-time work, and workplace learning can lead to women workers being defined as 'relatively uninterested in opportunities for such learning, be they formal or informal' (Probert, 1999, p. 111). Further, women's domestic and care roles can influence social judgements and lead to their exclusion from equal learning opportunities. A more inclusive and nuanced understanding of learning and development needs to acknowledge the general nature of finance capitalism. The logic of maximising shareholder value (MSV) means there is less investment in human capital (Martin and Quick, 2020; Thompson, 2013). HRD scholars and practitioners need to acknowledge the dynamics and tensions in capitalist employment relations, the tension between managerial control and work-based learning, and the effects of complex interconnecting levels of domination stemming from class, gender and race relations in society (Bratton et al., 2004). Workers are both active and acted upon, argues Usher (2000) and the notion of *the* 'flexible learner', a key metaphor in HRD, through learning flexibility, can be simultaneously empowering and disempowering. Finally, diversity training can target a wide variety of groups. But scholars have critiqued the 'discrimination and fairness' approach to training for not addressing power differences and conveying an image of harmonious differences (Benschop et al., 2017).

Summary

We started the chapter by explaining the widely held assumption that education and training contributes to a nation's economic development and growth, known as human capital theory. This theory is central to understanding the enthusiasm for, and role of, strategic learning and development in many large organisations. In the mainstream literature, most attempts to define strategic learning and development suggest that it has three purposes: first, to align all L&D activities with the organisation's strategic goals; second, to improve the performance of people; and third, to help people learn and develop their full human potential in terms of job-related work.

We explained that learning is a desired outcome of training and noted that, while related, training and learning are not the same. We defined learning and development as a process that facilitates the acquisition of knowledge, skills and attitudes that enables and results in learning at and through work.

Learning and development are grounded in learning theories and we chose four influential theories to examine and contrast: classical behavioural and cognitive, and self-directed and experiential learning.

We provided an overview of traditional training which was viewed as a one-off activity. This was contrasted with contemporary approaches that put the focus on the learner and the opportunities for her or him to learn through work, not just at work, and attempts to be both systematic and integrated, an approach that highlights key interdependencies within organisations, such as the linkage to strategy, the importance of culture and knowledge transfer. We presented a model showing these key interdependencies. We then examined emerging developments in machine learning and finished with a critique of learning and development, paying particular attention to issues of diversity, race and power.

Review questions

1. Explain how training, learning and development play a strategic role in organisations.
2. What are the three main levels at which training needs are assessed and *who* could assist in the process?
3. How have learning theories influenced the design and delivery of L&D interventions?

Search & Watch

How can managers ensure they improve the skills of their workforce and how do they ensure the next generation of workers has the skills needed? Visit YouTube and watch **Jan Hills: How can neuroscience help us to understand how we learn in organisations?** What is the significance of the premise put forward by the presenter that learning is a process?

Go to the video hub at **www.bloomsbury.pub/bratton-hrm** and watch the interview with **Helen Tiffany, Managing Director, Bec Development** (www.becdevelopment.co.uk). Bec Development is a people development consultancy firm, working with clients to implement growth in their organisations. It specialises in learning and development. Helen and her team work closely with each of their clients to help implement change through staff development, in line with the strategic aims of their clients' organisations. She is a Fellow of the CIPD, sits on the Council for the Association for Coaching and is a member of the executive board for Mentoring Digital Minds.

Watch Helen talk specifically about coaching, and then think about the following questions: (1) What is 'unique' about the sector in which Helen works? Does this affect the approach to learning and development? (2) How does Helen's view of HR relate to business strategy? How can this be achieved? (3) According to Helen, why has coaching become so important? Why is it having such a large impact?

Legal Focus

The right to be treated fairly and equitably is fundamental to people management. As we have explained in previous chapters, the UK Equality Act 2010 prohibits acts of discrimination by an employer during the recruitment and selection process. The Act 2010 also prohibits unlawful acts in the area of learning and development. Section 111, for example, makes it unlawful for a person to instruct, cause or induce someone to discriminate against or harass or victimise another, or attempt to do so. Section 63A of the Employment Rights Act 1996 gives an employee who is 16 or 17 years old and who is not receiving full-time or further education the right to time off with pay, during working hours, in order to undertake study or training leading to a relevant qualification. The Health & Safety Act (HASAWA) 1974 provides that an employer shall allow an employee who is a safety representative time off with pay during normal working hours to undergo training. Section 43 of the Employment Act 2002 introduced a new type of trade union representative called a 'union learning representative' (ULR). The role of a ULR is to analyse learning or training needs of their members.

Task Search online for government information in your jurisdiction about provisions related to learning and development and compare and contrast it with another country, such as Australia or Canada. (1) How does the legislation effect employee's rights related to training? (2) What are the differences, if any, between these two countries' approaches to statutory employment protection?

Reference

See Deborah Lockton and Tom Brown's *Employment Law* (2020), pp. 203–4; pp. 270–3, for a discussion on legislation covering learning-training-related issues in the workplace.

PART 3

Chapter case: Diversity management at Køre (Part 3)

The setting

Køre is a FinTech company based in Copenhagen, Denmark, which we introduced in Chapter 4 on workforce planning and used also to examine the recruitment process in Chapter 5. Following a successful Series C funding round, the firm recently expanded into the US market, opening a satellite office in Silicon Valley. In order to meet growing demand, Køre hired ten new employees, including data scientists, machine learning specialists and software engineers. The company had been marred by claims of a toxic work environment, dominated by young, white men. However, due to efforts by the HR department, combined with input from the founders, Lucas Jensen and Victor Pedersen, there was evidence of a positive shift in the organisational culture. The new recruits, which included four women and three people from Black, Asian, or minority ethnic (BAME) backgrounds, had integrated well with the existing staff and the atmosphere at the company's headquarters on Vingårdstræde was invigorating.

The problem

Just two months after the new staff joined, the coronavirus pandemic began, impacting all aspects of Danish society. Where possible, employees were encouraged to work from home. This was relatively easily achieved at Køre given the existing policy facilitating remote working. The Head of HR, Anja Dall, was keen to ensure that progress in regard to diversity and inclusion was not lost due to the crisis. She sent an email to Jan Madsen, the VP of Engineering, to this effect:

> Jan, as you know, over the last several months we have developed and implemented a new diversity and inclusion strategy, as well as recruited ten talented new employees from a range of different backgrounds. The months ahead are likely to be challenging, but I think it is essential

that we try to keep on track. As a result, I am proposing that the HR department develop a short online course on diversity and inclusion for all staff. Would you be supportive of this?

The following morning, Anja received a reply from Jan:

> Anja, I appreciate the efforts of the HR department in relation to diversity and inclusion. However, given current pressures, unless there is a clear rationale for what will be addressed in the course and why it matters, I just don't think we can make it a priority. Can we schedule a quick online meeting tomorrow to discuss the issue in more detail?

You have recently joined Køre as an HR specialist. You receive an email from Anja containing Jan's view that the diversity course should be postponed. Anja has asked you to prepare a response.

The assignment

Working in a group or on your own, design a short deck of slides, as well as one page of notes, outlining the rationale for developing the course on diversity and inclusion, as well as some suggestions for indicative content. Drawing upon the material covered in this chapter, you might consider the following questions:

1. What are the most important factors to take into consideration when trying to convince line managers and team leaders of the value of diversity and inclusion within Køre?
2. What would be the learning outcomes for the course?
3. Drawing upon Kolb's experiential learning theory, what learning activities would be most appropriate for Køre, and why?

Essential reading

CIPD (2019) *Diversity Management that Works: An Evidence-Based Review*. London: CIPD.

Note: This case was contributed by Laura Steele.

Further reading

Alfonso, J., Gil, J., García-Alcaraz, L. and Mataveli, M. (2021) The effect of learning culture on training transfer: empirical evidence in Spanish teachers. *The International Journal of Human Resource Management*, *32*(5): 1038–61. DOI: 10.1080/09585192.2018.1505763

Collins, C. J. (2021) Expanding the resource based view model of strategic human resource management. *International Journal of Human Resource Management*, *32*(2): 331–58.

Garavan, T. (2007) A strategic perspective on human resource development. *Advances in Developing Human Resources*, *1*: 11–30.

Gedro, J., Collins, J. C. and Rocco, T.S. (2014) The 'critical' turn: an important imperative for human resource development. *Advances in Developing Human Resources*, *16*(4): 529–35.

Gold, J., Nichol, L. and Harrison, P. (2020) L&D must be a participant not a bystander in machine learning. *People Management*, 10 September. Available at: https://www.peoplemanagement.co.uk/voices/comment/ld-must-be-participants-not-bystanders-in-machine-learning.

Haynes, R. and Alagaraja, M. (2016) On the discourse of affirmative action and reservation in the United States and India: clarifying HRD's role in fostering global diversity. *Advances in Developing Human Resources*, *18*: 69–87.

Noe, R.A. and Tews, M.J. (2018) Strategic training and development. In J. Storey, P. M. Wright and D. Ulrich (eds) *The Routledge Companion to Strategic Human Resource Management* (pp. 262–84). London: Routledge.

Watt, P., Boak, G. and Gold, J. (2020) 'Leadership development' in J. Bratton (ed.) *Organisational Leadership*, (pp. 267–85). London: Sage.

CHAPTER 8

REWARD MANAGEMENT

outline

- Introduction
- The nature of reward
- A strategic framework for reward
- Job evaluation: internal equity
- Establishing pay levels: external equity
- The spirit of new pay
- Inequality and the gender pay gap
- Critiquing the strategic reward paradigm
- Summary
- Further reading

Source: iStock.com/martin-dm

objectives

After studying this chapter, you should be able to:

1. Explain the key objectives of reward systems
2. Evaluate different approaches to reward that seek to align pay systems with an organisation's business strategy
3. Explain the manner and extent to which pay influences workers' attitudes and behaviour
4. Describe and evaluate job evaluation as a method for developing a pay system
5. Explain how governments and trade unions intervene in the pay determination process
6. Explain the importance of inequality in understanding the inherent tensions in managing the employment relationship

Introduction

During the coronavirus crisis, governments in Denmark and elsewhere in the European Union announced lockdowns and agreed to pay a significant proportion of furloughed workers' wages, with conditions that employers committed to no redundancies for 12 months. In Britain, the government's Coronavirus Job Retention Scheme (CJRS) paid up to 80 per cent of the wages of 9.4 million workers, but the wage subsidy was not accompanied by any stipulation about redundancies (Sikka, 2020). Amidst the crisis, research reported that permanent starting salaries dropped at the quickest rate on record (Cameron, 2020). Sixty-three of Britain's super-rich, including 20 billionaires, sought to furlough their workforce under the taxpayer-backed scheme (Watts, 2020). Despite the crisis, easyJet paid £60 million (€66.6 million) in final dividend to its co-founder, Sir Stelios Haji-Ioannou, while putting its staff on unpaid leave. The debate around the devastating effects of the Covid-19 crisis on workers' pay alongside stratospheric levels of CEO executive pay is a reminder that HRM operates in an arena of continuous tension that is inherent in the generation of added value, and of society's values related to employment and disquiet about growing inequality. Moreover, the crisis starkly demonstrated the links between income inequality and public health. Low-paid workers avoided the Covid-19 testing system because they cannot afford to self-isolate and lose pay if they become infected (Tapper, 2021). Pay is one of the most prominent and regularly discussed features of the employment relationship. The underlying assumption in HRM is that effective reward design can be a key contributor to strategy execution and the effectiveness of the organisation (Gerhart, 2018). However, from the point of view of workers, reward or pay is imperative to their economic and physical survival (Edgell and Granter, 2020).

This chapter provides a conceptual framework for examining and understanding strategic reward. It considers issues of internal equity and the legal and collective determination of reward packages. It concludes with a critical look at income inequality and a critique of reward management.

PART 3

The nature of reward

In reward literature, the term 'compensation' is used as an alternative to 'reward' (Martocchio, 2019). Although both terms are problematic, we consider that the new vocabulary of 'reward management' best captures the new individualisation of wages, which focuses on the worker's market worth, flexibility and performance (Boltanski and Chiapello, 2018). Managers typically defined reward as the package of financial or *monetary* rewards (wages, salaries and benefits) and non-financial or *non-monetary* rewards that a worker receives, but workers generally define it even more narrowly as just the wage or salary received from the employer for their work. Reward is one of the key sources of tension and conflicts in the employment relationship which means that the choice of reward design impacts other HR policies and practices and can be a major factor in successfully effecting an organisation's strategy (Martocchio, 2019). Therefore, to understand the crucial role that reward plays in managing the employment relationship, it is necessary to conceptualise it in its broadest sense.

An organisation can provide two broad types of reward:

- *Extrinsic rewards,* which satisfy a worker's basic needs for survival, security and recognition, and derive from factors associated with the job context. This includes financial rewards other than a wage or salary, such as benefits covering health care, working conditions and managerial behaviour.
- *Intrinsic rewards* refer to psychological 'enjoyment' and the satisfaction of 'challenge' (Bratton, 2021), sometimes called 'psychic income', that a worker derives from their paid work. These rewards derive from factors inherent in the way in which the work is designed, that is, the job content.

Armstrong and Brown (2019, p. 1) define reward as:

> The recognition of the contribution or achievement of individuals or groups by a financial payment or by some form of non-financial recognition.

It can also include an intangible payment and here we define reward as:

> A package of monetary, non-monetary and psychological payments that an organisation provides for its employees in exchange for the work they perform.

This definition draws attention to the multifaceted nature of the employment relationship, which involves complex, multiple exchanges. Reward is primarily, but not exclusively, the exchange of pay and other tangible monetary benefits but can include other intangible benefits such as a positive emotion (Kessler, 2007). The mix of extrinsic and intrinsic rewards provided by the employer is termed its *reward system*. The monetary element can be divided into pay, consisting of the workers' wages or salary, and non-pay benefits, including, for example, medical insurance and a pension. The notion of 'total reward' includes a wide range of both direct (e.g. salary) and indirect (e.g. benefits) financial rewards and non-monetary compensation on offer which are complementary and compatible with the organisation's culture (Azasu, 2009). Combined pay and non-pay benefits constitute the *payment system*.

Source: PhotoDisc/Getty Images

Reward is one of the key sources of tension and conflicts in the employment relationship.

However, it is pay that has traditionally been the centrepiece of the reward system and is unique for several reasons. First, a pay rate is the most tangible aspect of a job and is easy to quantify. Second, the pay rate is instrumental in satisfying an array of human needs, including self-esteem and status. Third, unlike some other job characteristics, for example, greater job responsibility, most workers prefer higher pay to less (Gerhart, 2018). An effective reward system should promote desirable employee and organisational behaviours (Latham, 1984; Long and Singh, 2017), shown in Figure 8.1.

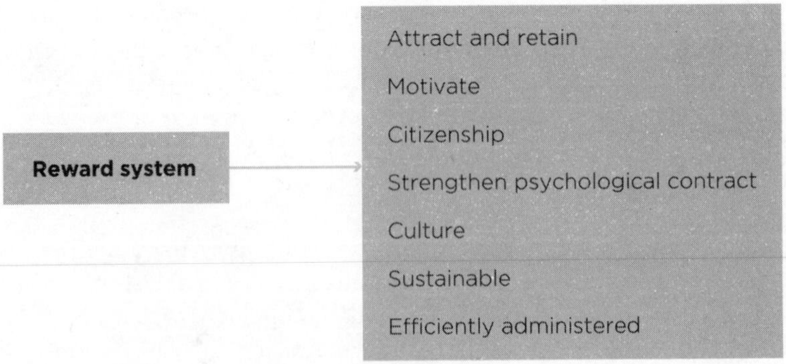

Figure 8.1 Behavioural outcomes of a reward system

In summary, a reward system needs to attract and retain qualified people to the organisation; it should motivate an employee's desire to perform her or his job duties well, encourage employees to voluntarily undertake special behaviour beneficial to the organisation, strengthen the psychological contract, influence organisational culture that is desired, for example, innovative or learning or output-oriented, be sustainable within the financial means of the organisation and be efficiently administered.

A reward system consists of the integrated policies, processes, practices and administrative procedures for implementing the system within the framework of the HR strategy. A reward strategy comprises an organisation's plan and actions pertaining to the mix and total amount of direct pay (for example, salary) and indirect monetary payments (e.g. shares) paid to various categories of employees. Research has focused on reward strategy alignment or 'fit' with the context:

- vertical alignment with organisational strategy;
- horizontal alignment between reward strategy and other dimensions of HR practices.

The principal focus of the strategic reward literature has been on vertical alignment, which we examine below (for more detail, see Gerhart, 2007; 2018; Lawler, 1984). A number of key questions pertain to any reward strategy: How should monetary payments be paid? How should profits or improvements in costs be distributed: to employees or only to shareholders? How should pay be used: to reward individual or group behaviour? How much should be paid? The optimal choice ultimately depends on the objectives of management. As Beer et al. (1984, p. 9) observe, 'Rewards, both financial and otherwise, send a powerful message ... as to what kind of organisation management seeks to create and maintain, and what kind of behaviour and attitudes management seeks from its employees.'

Reward for many front-line workers may include, at one extreme, direct pay only; the organisation paying a pay rate in line with statutory minimum wage or as little as the labour market will tolerate (Richbell and Wood, 2019). Since the 2000s, the expansion of the gig economy has been matched by a growing proportion of workers being employed on minimum wage. At the other extreme an organisation may offer no pay whatsoever. It is easy to think, 'Who works for nothing?', but an increasing number of companies are using unpaid internships (Boffey, 2012) and many voluntary organisations, such as Oxfam, Médicins Sans Frontières and food banks, rely upon unpaid volunteers. Organisations employing diverse groups of employees in terms of skills and professional qualifications are more likely to adopt a more sophisticated reward strategy. The point here is that the amount of pay (extrinsic) reward needed to hire people will vary depending upon the availability of other (intrinsic) rewards that the organisation offers (Long and Singh, 2017).

Source: Danielle Cerullo on Unsplash

What forms of intangible or non-financial reward might contribute to employee commitment to the organisation?

Reward and the employment relationship

To fully understand rewards within an HR strategy, it is necessary to recall the nature of the employment relationship we discussed in Chapter 1. We noted there that the employment contract is an indeterminate exchange (Hyman, 1989), whereby labour receives a cash (or other) payment in exchange for their physical and/or mental effort. All pay systems contain two elements that are in contradiction with each other:

- *Cooperation* between employee and employer or manager is an essential ingredient of the employment relationship if anything is to be produced. Cooperation is fostered through the logic of financial gain for the worker.
- *Conflict* is engendered through the logic that makes the 'buying' of labour the reward for one group and the cost for the other.

These two features of the employment contract mean that employees and those responsible for reward management have different objectives when it comes to monetary rewards. For employees, the pay cheque is typically the major source of personal income and hence a critical determinant of an individual's standard of living and social well-being. In classical capitalism, employees constantly seek to maximise their pay because of inflation and rising expectations. The employer, on the other hand, is interested in the absolute cost of the rewards because of its bearing on profitability or cost-effectiveness. The importance of this varies with the type of organisation. The relative labour costs in a petroleum refinery, for example, are minimal, whereas in health care or hospitality they are substantial.

This fundamental tension underpinning the exchange makes the employment relationship unstable, which, in the context of global capitalism, is constantly being adjusted. Furthermore, the employees' contribution, or 'effort' itself, is 'a highly unstable phenomenon', and a payment system forms part of an array of managerial strategies to control the contribution or 'effort' of people (Baldamus, 1961; Watson, 2008). Unsurprisingly therefore, it has been conceded that the satisfactory management of reward is an essential, although not sufficient, condition of the satisfactory management of people (Brown, 1989).

Reflective question

Think about the reward system at your most recent job. Did it cause conflict or tension among the workforce? If so, why?

A strategic framework for reward

Strategic rewards focus on the design and implementation of reward systems that reinforce employee behaviours that support the successful formulation and execution of an organisation's competitive strategy. It is generally agreed that to act strategically there would be a need for reward professionals to engage widely and fully in strategy formulation (Storey et al., 2018). To help us examine the complexities and principles underpinning strategic reward, the 'new pay agenda' – we provide a comprehensive model for analysing the different components of a reward system and to act as a guide for the chapter, which is presented in Figure 8.2. The model contains six basic elements: corporate strategy, reward objectives, reward choices, reward techniques, reward competitiveness and outcomes.

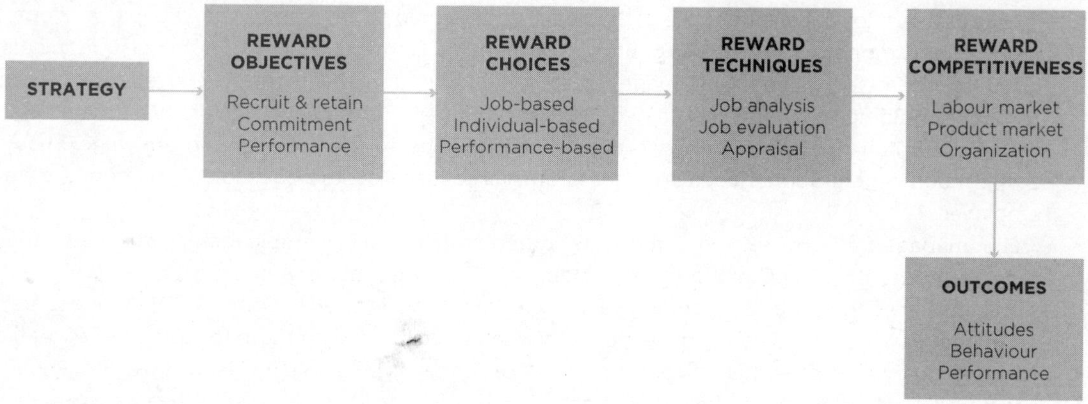

Figure 8.2 A strategic framework for reward

PART 3

Corporate strategy

First, the strategic process begins with identifying the organisational strategy. As with other key HR practices, a reward system is linked to an organisation's overarching strategic goals. *Strategy* focuses on those reward choices that support the organisation's strategic goals. Going back to our discussion on corporate strategy (see Chapter 2), this means that each business strategy – and in this example we used Porter's (1980; 1985) typology of cost leadership (achieving lowest unit costs in the sector), differentiation (e.g. based on superior service or quality) or focus (a 'niche play' in cost or differentiation) – should be supported by a different HR strategy, including a package of rewards; the principle of *strategic reward*.

Reward objectives

Second, *reward objectives* to support the strategy are identified. Schuler and Jackson (1987) argue that different competitive strategies imply different kinds of employee attitudes and behaviours. Three principal behavioural objectives are desired by management: *membership* behaviour, *commitment* behaviour and *performance* behaviour.

Motivation theories suggest that the reward system can play an essential role in eliciting all three (Long and Singh, 2017). The general assumption is that rewards can stimulate desirable employee behaviours (e.g. performance) and discourage unfavourable ones, such as absenteeism. For example, if an organisation chooses a competitive strategy of differentiation through continuous product innovation, this will call for a learning culture and high-engagement and cooperative behaviour. The organisation's reward practices would therefore need to emphasise extrinsic rewards focusing on group or organisational performance pay (e.g. profit-sharing) for knowledge, and intrinsic rewards for the job itself. Research suggests that rewards can have positive connotations for potential applicants and influence membership behaviour or recruitment (Kuhn, 2009, p. 1,646). Commitment behaviour is an elusive construct and, depending on the writer's perspective, is discussed in terms of 'organisational citizenship behaviour' (Long and Singh, 2017) or 'compliance' and 'control of meaning', that is, psychosocial factors subject to manipulation by management (Thompson and McHugh, 2009).

Research on reward outcomes has two major shortcomings. First, the focus has traditionally been on financial rewards, whereas scholars have recently highlighted the added value of focusing on non-financial rewards (Hofmans et al., 2013). Second, reward theorists have traditionally attempted to unravel the reward–satisfaction relationship for the 'average' employee, thereby neglecting potential individual employee differences in this relationship (De Gieter and Hofmans, 2015).

Pay and employee behaviours lie at the heart of the employment relationship. People seek employment to earn money to live. In this context, pay theorists Gomez-Mejia et al. assert that 'money is the quintessence of all business language' (2010, p. 5). Although the incentivising effect of extrinsic rewards should never be underestimated (Boxall and Purcell, 2016), especially for an estimated 439,000 workers in Britain, mainly affecting women, illegally paid below the hourly minimum wage (Busby, M., 2019), much organisational behaviour research has focused on the question 'Can money motivate employees?'

For managers, discovering what motivates different categories of employees is of the same magnitude as finding the Holy Grail (Bratton, 2021, p. 173). The different answers reflect a fundamental tension between economic and psychological theories of motivation. On the one hand, labour economists argue that pay incentives can achieve performance targets by paying more to spur extra effort ('tournament theory'). On the other hand, the primacy of money is challenged by social psychologists who have drawn attention to employees' 'hierarchy of needs' (Maslow, 1954), cognitive choices (Adams, 1965; Locke, 1968; Vroom, 1964) and the importance of 'self-concept' (Fairholm, 1996; Leonard et al., 1999) as inner sources of energy that motivate 'non-calculative-based' workplace behaviour.

Sisodia et al. (2014) go as far as to assert that employees crave 'psychic income' as well as financial income: 'people want work that engages them wholly, that fulfils their emotional and social needs, that is meaningful – in short, work that is psychologically rewarding' (p. 62). Thus, the message for practitioners is that it is inappropriate to assume that all rewards have the same influence on the attitudes and behaviours of every individual employee. Studies demonstrate that financial rewards stimulate extrinsic, but not intrinsic motivation (Deci and Ryan, 2000). De Gieter and Hofmans's (2015) study is individual-sensitive, finding support for the presence of individual differences in the relationship between satisfaction with different reward types and turnover intentions, but, importantly, not task performance. Given the different schools of thought, it is not surprising that reward theorists disagree over the strength of the pay–performance link. Caruth and Handlogten (2001, p. 4) express the received wisdom of the reward–performance relationship thus:

> A compensation system that rewards employees fairly according to efforts expended and results produced creates a motivating work environment.

The research on performance behaviour highlights the importance of relationships between line managers and employees: what LMs do and how well they do it (Purcell and Kinnie, 2008). Blinder's (1990, quoted by Kessler, 1995, p. 261) insightful conclusion is particularly helpful: 'Changing the way workers are treated may boost productivity more than changing the way they are paid.' Put another way, creating dignity *at* work (Bolton, 2007) may improve performance behaviour more than money does.

Reward choices

Third, the strategic reward imperatives are translated into specific reward options. Three *reward choices* are shown: job, individual and performance. *Job-based* reward is a system whereby the level of pay, expressed in either hourly (waged) or fixed (salary), is assigned to the jobs that employees perform. Jobs of similar value to the organisation are assigned to the same pay grades: the higher the value of the job, the higher the pay grade. In establishing the internal value of its jobs, an organisation has to consider both external and internal labour market equity (Kessler, 2007). Job-based pay systems are considered to reinforce bureaucratic hierarchical structures, encourage a 'command and control' style of management and be less compatible with team-based work systems (Guthrie, 2008).

Individual-based pay is a system whereby pay is assigned to the breadth and/or depth of knowledge, formal qualifications, skills or competencies possessed by an individual employee. Under this type of pay regime, pay enhancements are awarded when employees are certified as having acquired additional knowledge, qualifications or skills that are of value to the organisation. Research suggests that person-based pay systems are a 'better fit' with high-involvement work systems (Guthrie, 2008; Lawler, 2000).

Performance-based pay is a system tied to an employee's 'effort' or performance. The performance might derive from the contributions of the individual or a team (Table 8.1). *Individual* pay is directly related to the individual's commitment of time, performance or a combination of both. *Team* pay systems have become more prevalent in Europe and North America with the popularity of high-performance work systems. *Organisational* pay, such as profit-sharing, is seen by managers as a way of increasing organisational performance through employee involvement in decision-making (Pendleton, 1997) and by encouraging stronger employee identification with the business (Long and Singh, 2017).

Table 8.1 Types of employee pay

Type of reward	Examples	Type of behaviour
Individual rewards	Basic wage Overtime Payments by results Commission Merit pay or performance-related pay Benefits	*Time*: maintaining work attendance *Energy*: performing tasks *Competence and performance*: completing tasks without errors
Team rewards	Team or group bonus Gain-sharing	*Cooperation*: with co-workers
Organisational rewards	Profit-sharing Profit-related Employee share incentive plan	*Commitment*: to strategic goals

Reward techniques

Fourth, strategic reward process is associated with three *reward techniques*. Job analysis and job evaluation highlight the importance attached to *internal equity*, that is, the pay relationships between jobs within a single organisation. *Job analysis* refers to the systematic process of collecting and evaluating information about the tasks, responsibilities and context of a specific job. The basic premise underlying job analysis is that jobs are more likely to be described, differentiated and equitably evaluated if accurate information is available to decision-makers (Newman et al., 2016). *Job evaluation* involves systematically comparing jobs in terms of their relative contributions to the organisation's goals. We will examine job evaluation in more detail below. *Performance appraisal* (PA) is used to evaluate a person's overall capabilities and potential, enabling informed decisions to be made for the purpose of performance. As noted, the practice has come under much critical scrutiny in recent years. PA is examined in more detail in Chapter 6.

Reward competitiveness

Fifth, the strategic imperative focuses on *reward competitiveness*. This draws attention to the importance of *external equity* and, by implication, why the organisation needs to pay 'competitive' labour market rates for a given occupation. The organisation has three options: to be a pay leader, to match the market rate or to lag behind what competitive organisations are paying. Kessler (2007, p. 167) argues that external equity is an 'imperative' if it is going to 'win the talent war' of attracting and retaining talented people. Research suggests that pay sends 'signals' to prospective applicants regarding the organisation's values and culture (Barber and Bretz, 2000; Guthrie, 2008). Reward competitiveness has typically been analysed in terms of three contingencies: labour market, product market and organisational.

Labour market

The study of pay requires a context. For example, in the ongoing equal pay dispute involving the supermarket Asda, a management spokesperson said, 'Pay rates in stores differ from pay rates in distribution centres because ... they operate in different market sectors and we pay the market rate in those sectors, regardless of gender' (Iqbal, 2020). In neo-classical economic theory, pay is the outcome of the forces of the demand for and supply of labour. But government actions affect both the demand and the supply of labour, and consequently pay. Legislation can, for example, restrict the supply of labour – a law setting minimum age limits would restrict the supply of young people. Government action can also affect the demand for labour because the government and its agencies are a major employer and therefore a dominant force in determining pay in and beyond the public sector, and government expenditure can affect consumer demand for goods and services and hence indirectly the labour market.

Product market

The degree of competition between producers and the level of the demand for products or services are two key product market factors affecting the ability of the firm to change the prices of its products and services. If prices cannot be changed without negative effects on revenue, the ability of the organisation to pay higher rates is constrained. The product market factors thus set the limits within which the pay level can be established.

Organisational

Doeringer and Piore's (1971) classic study of internal labour markets explained that job evaluation and organisational culture and practice took precedence over external labour market information in shaping internal reward systems (Grimshaw and Rubery, 2008). One important critique, however, is that they neglected to consider 'societal effects' on reward systems. Kessler (2007, p. 175) argues that 'real societal pressures ... have propelled external and internal equity to the centre of the pay agenda'. In Britain, the 'collapse of collective bargaining' (Brown et al., 2009, p. 354), as well as performance management systems (PMS), strongly influence reward design (Corby et al., 2009).

Evaluation

The final step involves evaluating whether the chosen reward package helps to motivate the right kind of performance, attract the right kind of people, and create the right sort of culture consistent with performance goals. Studies on vertical alignment have shown that alignment of reward strategy with business strategy may have performance outcomes (e.g. Rajagopalan, 1997). Organisations having more financial risk tend to have less risk sharing in their reward for executives (e.g. Bloom and Milkovich, 1998). Research on horizontal alignment is problematic because of the difficulty of isolating reward from other HR strategy elements, 'making it difficult to draw robust conclusions' about what other HR variables work best with a particular pay system (Gerhart, 2018, p. 235). A team-based pay system may facilitate the sharing and creation of tacit knowledge and informal learning among team members (Kim and Gong, 2009). The evidence, however, is far from conclusive.

HRM in Practice

Is the national living wage a departure from a deregulated labour market?

Source: Waqas Saeed on Unsplash

Neoliberal theories assume that economies are more successful if employers can take decisions free from the constraints of government intervention such as employment protection legislation and the power of trade unions to negotiate wages and working conditions. The New Labour government elected in 1997 halted the momentum of deregulation through the minimum wage, the strengthening of some trade union rights and the adoption of European directives that limited the length of the working week. The Coalition government of 2010–15 continued to attack regulations on the free market, such as restricting the scope of employment protection laws (Noon et al., 2013, p. 28). The Boris Johnson Conservative government elected in 2019 has fuelled fears that workers' rights and protections could be weakened with post-Brexit employment legislation.

Collective bargaining declined from 60% of UK workplaces in the 1980s to 23% in 2017 (ONS, 2019). The reasons for this change are partly the product of anti-union laws but also the decline of manufacturing, which reduced the membership and influence of trade unions. Globalisation, increased competition and the privatisation of many state-controlled industries further contributed to the decline in the influence of trade unions.

In April 2013, 5.2 million, or 22%, of employees were low paid (£7.69 an hour) – when measured in terms of hourly wages, this was below two-thirds of the gross median hourly pay of all employees (Corlett and Whittaker, 2014). Alongside a national minimum wage, a strategy to improve employees' living standards was to supplement low wages with tax credits. However, as the number in low-paid jobs increased, welfare payments became burdensome and the payment of a supplementary income to the low paid was seen as a subsidy to employers who pay low wages. Large numbers of low-paid workers provide a problem for capitalism as they depress both tax revenue and the demand for goods.

In December 2019, in a surprise announcement designed to gain support with low-paid workers after Boris Johnson's election victory, the government said the national living wage for over-25s would increase from £8.21 an hour to £8.72 from the start of April 2020. Johnson said that the increase was the 'biggest ever cash boost' to the legal pay floor (Partington, 2019, courtesy of Guardian News & Media Ltd), and TUC general secretary, Frances O'Grady, said the rise was long overdue:

> Workers are still not getting a fair share of the wealth they create, and in-work poverty is soaring as millions of families struggle to make ends meet ... No more excuses, working families need £10 minimum wage now, not in four years' time.

Against the backdrop of the UK facing the deepest recession in 300 years and uncertainty over Brexit (Giles, 2020), critics suggest that the link between work and making ends meet has become increasingly frayed in twenty-first-century Britain. The Joseph Rowntree Foundation report that while paid employment reduces the risk of poverty, about 56% of people living in poverty in 2018 were in a household where at least one person had a job, compared to 39% 20 years ago (Inman, 2020).

Stop! HRM has been seen as bypassing collective bargaining, and remuneration policy has been part of the HRM function to secure employee commitment. Do you think the government should play an active role in shaping pay policy?

Essential reading

Inman, P. (2020) Number of people in poverty in working families hits record high. *The Guardian*, 7 February; Office for National Statistics (2019) Labour market economic commentary: February 2019; You can read more about the work of the Joseph Rowntree Foundation at www.jrf.org.uk.

Note: This feature was contributed by David Denham and updated by Andrew Bratton.

Job evaluation: internal equity

Advice on the design of reward systems emphasises the importance of establishing pay differentials which are felt to be fair (e.g. Armstrong and Murlis, 2007). Equity theory explains how workers develop perceptions of fairness in the distribution of resources (Adams and Freedman, 1976). Perceptions of pay unfairness have been related to a range of negative effects for organisations and individuals, including job dissatisfaction, reduced organisational commitment, loss of trust in the organisation, depression and somatic symptoms such as headaches and stomach aches (e.g. Shaw and Gupta, 2001). There is evidence of high levels of support for pay differentials 'to reflect differences in responsibility, knowledge, skills and abilities and performance', but this may be due to employees' attitudes to pay simply mirroring widely shared social norms about the way that pay should be determined (Dickinson, 2006, p. 179). Pay equity legislation requires that equal pay be paid for jobs of equal 'worth' or value to the organisation (Gomez-Mejia et al., 2010, p. 5). Thus, traditional reward models emphasise the importance of *internal equity*, and the method most often used to establish and maintain internal constancies is job evaluation. Formal job evaluation is a generic label for a variety of processes used to establish pay structures by systematically comparing jobs in terms of their relative contributions to the organisation's overarching goals (Newman et al., 2016). It can be defined as:

> A systematic process designed to determine the relative worth of jobs within a single work organisation.

The goal of job evaluation is to achieve internal equity by determining a hierarchy of jobs that is based on the relative contribution of each job to the organisation. This hierarchy is then used to allocate rates of pay to jobs regardless of the employee working in that role. The importance to managers of job evaluation has increased because of equal pay legislation, which requires, either implicitly or explicitly, that gender-neutral job evaluation schemes be adopted and used to determine and compare the value of jobs within the organisation.

Job evaluation is often misunderstood, so the following three characteristics of all formal job evaluation methods need to be emphasised:

- The technique is systematic rather than scientific: it depends on a series of subjective judgements.
- The premise that job evaluation is based on the worth of the job rather than on the worth of the employee in that particular job is fundamental (Welbourne and Trevor, 2000).
- The validity of the job evaluation process, or how accurately the method assesses job worth, is suspect (Collins and Muchinsky, 1993).

It is important to emphasise that job evaluation is not scientific but is based on a sort of tacit theory of value: an idea of what is a worthwhile job, and therefore what is not. It is notoriously difficult to tease out exactly what that theory is in any given organisation or industry, let alone come up with any reliable, objective system of measurement that would make it possible to say that job X is more valuable to an organisation or society than job Y. This has not deterred HR practitioners from trying, however. As Graeber (2018) likes to point out, there is an inverse relation between social value and the level of pay. This is, the more social value job X creates or benefits others, the less one is likely to be paid for doing it. Intersectional thinking and analysis expose gender-bias. A higher weighting is given to physical demands and continuous service, which tend to favour men, and by the gender association of job titles. For example, an evaluator assigning significantly lower ratings, that is, an estimated 'value', to jobs with a female-stereotyped title, such as 'secretary', than to the same job with a more gender-neutral title, such as 'assistant' (McShane, 1990). Such a non-analytical approach would be open to legal challenges. Further, job evaluation involves discretionary decision-making and therefore 'departmental power' can affect the assessment (Welbourne and Trevor, 2000).

Although it is difficult to develop a subject-free measure of value, most organisations use what is described as 'analytical' job evaluation – in which jobs are broken down into individual elements (Egan, 2004) – involving four steps:

1. Gathering the job analysis data
2. Selecting compensable factors
3. Evaluating the job
4. Assigning pay to the job.

Let's look at each of these in turn.

Gathering the job analysis data

Information must be collected via a method of job analysis, and validity should be a guiding principle in this first step. The job analyser must accurately capture all the job's content because ambiguous, incomplete or inaccurate job descriptions can result in jobs being incorrectly evaluated.

Selecting compensable factors

Compensable factors are the factors the organisation chooses to reward through differential pay. The most typical compensable factors are skill, effort, knowledge, responsibility and working conditions.

Evaluating the job

There are different ways to evaluate jobs, but the point method is the most commonly used technique. For comparison purposes, we will provide here a description of the ranking method.

Source: National Cancer Institute on Unsplash

In a typical job ranking system like the one in Table 8.2 this forklift driver is neither the most valued nor the least valued employee. How fair do you think this ranking method is?

In *ranking*, jobs are ordered from the least to the most valued in the organisation, this rank order or hierarchy of jobs being based on a subjective evaluation of relative value. In a typical factory, we might finish up with the rank order shown in Table 8.2; in this example, the evaluators have agreed that the job of inspector is the most valued of the six jobs listed. Rates of pay will then reflect this simple hierarchy. This method has a number of advantages: it is simple, fast and inexpensive. The ranking method will be attractive for small organisations and for those with a limited number of jobs. Obvious disadvantages are that it is crude and entirely subjective; the results are therefore difficult to defend, and legal challenges might make the approach costly.

The *point method* evaluates jobs on the basis of a set of compensable factors in order to establish a hierarchy of jobs. Internal jobs are compared with each other across several factors, such as skill, mental effort, responsibility, physical effort and working conditions. For each job, the compensable factors are ranked according to their relative importance in each job. Once each benchmark job has been ranked on each factor, the decision-maker allocates points to each factor. Each job's relative value, and hence its location in the pay structure, is determined by adding up the points assigned to each compensable factor. A variation of the point system is the widely used 'Hay plan', which employs a standard point matrix applicable across organisational and national boundaries.

The exercise starts with the allocation of a range of points to each compensable factor. Any number between 1 and 100 points might be assigned to each factor. Next, each of the factors is given a weighting, which is an assessment of how important one factor is in relation to another. In the case of the machinist, for example, if skill is felt to be twice as important as working conditions, it is assigned

Table 8.2 Typical job ranking

Job title	Rank
	Most valued
1. Forklift driver	1. Inspector
2. Machinist	2. Machinist
3. Inspector	3. Secretary
4. Secretary	4. Forklift driver
5. File clerk	5. Labourer
6. Labourer	6. File clerk
	Least valued

twice as many points (20 versus 10). The results of the evaluation might look like those displayed in Table 8.3. The point values allocated to each compensable factor are then added up across factors, allowing jobs to be placed in a hierarchy according to their total point value. In our example in Table 8.3, this would mean that the machinist's wage rate would be twice that of the labourer. Such a differential might be unacceptable, but this difficulty can be overcome by tailoring the job evaluation scheme to the organisation's pay policy and practical objectives.

The advantage of the point system is that it is relatively stable over time and, because of its comprehensiveness, is more acceptable to the parties involved. Its shortcomings include a high administrative cost, which might be too high to justify its use in a small workplace. However, as noted above, job evaluation is not an objective system of measurement and it is difficult to determine whether, in this case, the job of inspector is more valuable to the organisation than the job of forklift driver, because the process involves subjective judgement.

PART 3

Table 8.3 Point system matrices

Job title	Factor					
	Skill	Mental effort	Respon-sibility	Physical effort	Working conditions	Total
Forklift driver	10	10	10	10	5	45
Machinist	20	15	17	8	10	70
Inspector	20	20	40	5	5	90
Secretary	20	20	35	5	5	85
File clerk	10	5	5	5	5	30
Labourer	5	2	2	17	9	35

Reflective question

Thinking about measures of value, does the economy undervalue childcare or nursing jobs and overvalue a telemarketer or corporate lawyer, for example? If some position went unfilled in an organisation, e.g. the CEO or President of a university, would there be a noticeable effect on the organisation? Has the Covid-19 pandemic caused society to reflect on the value and pay of some jobs? If so, why?

Assigning pay to the job

The final outcome of the evaluation exercise is a hierarchy of jobs in terms of their relative value to the organisation. Assigning pay to this hierarchy of jobs is referred to as 'pricing the pay structure' and requires a policy decision on the pay structure in the organisation. Despite its reported demise, job evaluation is 'alive and kicking in the public sector, driven in large part by concern about pay for work of equal value' (Corby et al., 2009, p. 8).

Global HRM

What Iceland can teach the world about equal pay

Iceland, a country of over 364,000 people, has been ranked by the World Economic Forum (WEF) as the global leader in reducing gender inequality. On 1 January 2018 the country passed the world's first equal pay law. The law requires companies and government agencies with 25 or more workers to analyse their salary structures every three years to ensure that men and women are being paid the same for doing the same jobs. Then they must report back to the government for certification or face penalties that include fines (Bjarnason and Hauser, 2018). These recent legislative measures have positioned Iceland at the forefront of global efforts to minimise gender inequality and, in 2020, it ranked first in the world for its progress towards gender parity. This legislation can be better understood within the context of Iceland's history around gender equality. For instance, three key historical moments include the general women's strike in 1975 where 90% of women participated, electing Vigdís Finnbogadóttir in 1980 as the world's first democratically elected female president, and the election of the women's party into parliament in 1983 (Tarr, 2018). The ten top countries for gender parity are outlined in the figure below.

Figure 8.3 The top 10 global gender gap index rankings (2020)

Source: Compiled using data from the World Economic Forum (2019).

The Global Gender Report 2020 benchmarks 153 countries on their progress towards gender parity in four dimensions: economic participation and opportunity, education attainment, health and survival, and political empowerment. In addition, it also examines gender gap prospects in the professions of the future (World Economic Forum, 2019, p. 9). At a global level, the report presents a mixed picture. Overall, gender parity has improved because of greater political representation of women. However, women's participation in the wider labour market has stalled and financial disparities are increasing. For example, in economic participation and opportunity, progress has regressed forcing gender parity to a poor 58%, which in time represents 257 years before gender parity can be achieved. Research suggests the three primary reasons for this are: (1) women have greater representation in roles that are being automated; (2) not enough women are entering professions where wage growth is most pronounced (for example, technology); and (3) women face perennial problems of insufficient household and care infrastructure and access to financial capital (World Economic Forum, 2019). Early feminist theorists such as Mary Wollstonecraft (1759–97) focused on the relationship between the family and work inequality (Bratton and Denham, 2019). Critical scholars continue to highlight that the gender equality gap will only be narrowed by a fundamental altering, not just of organisational practices, but of cultural assumptions about the respective roles of women and men in the workplace and home (Fine et al., 2020).

Stop! What barriers would prevent your government from introducing these policies? How do you promote gender equality in the workplace?

Essential reading

Bjarnason, E. and Hauser, C. (2018) Iceland makes companies prove they're not paying women less. *The New York Times*, 3 January; Fine, C., Sojo, V. and Lawford-Smith, H. (2020) Why does workplace gender diversity matter? Justice, organisational benefits, and policy. *Social Issues and Policy Review, 14*(1), 36–72; Tarr, T. (2018) How Icelandic women really feel about the new equal pay law. Forbes, 8 January; World Economic Forum (2019) Global gender gap report 2020. World Economic Forum, 16 December.

Note: This feature was contributed by Andrew Bratton.

Establishing pay levels: external equity

This section examines two aspects of pay structure: *pay dispersion* and the *basis of the pay level*. Pay structures can range from a relatively flat or 'egalitarian' pay distribution, with limited differences across levels and jobs or positions, to pay distributions that are 'hierarchical', displaying wide differences across levels and positions. Pay survey data appear to show a trend towards pay structures that are hierarchical and 'tournament-like' – high pay for a few at the top of the pay structure and low pay for the vast majority at the bottom (Hutton, 2015a; Piketty, 2014; Stiglitz, 2015). UK earnings statistics show that, in 2019, prior to the Covid-19 pandemic, the average UK salary for full-time workers was £36, 611 but the gender gap in Britain is 13.7 per cent, which means that, on average, men earn 13.7 per cent more than women. For example, in the age category 22–29, the average salary is £28,386 (men) and £24,715 (women), a gap of £3,671. We look at executive pay in more detail when we examine income inequality below.

With respect to the basis of the pay level, any job reflects its relative and absolute worth. A job's relative worth to the organisation is determined by its ranking through the job evaluation process, whereas its absolute worth is influenced by what the labour market pays for similar jobs. Both globally and nationally, labour market rates differ considerably, a factor that has encouraged the offshoring of work from high-wage economies to those where local wage rates that are much lower. In most developed economies, pay rates may be determined through bilateral negotiations between the employer and trade union(s) over pay and conditions of employment, see Chapter 9. In Britain, during the Covid-19 crisis, the issue of pay and the value we assign to it has become particularly divisive.

Table 8.4 UK salaries for selective occupations and CEOs, 2019

Über-salary earners	James 'Jes' Staley, Barclays Bank	£5.9 million
	Willie Walsh, BA	£3.2 million
	Sharon White, John Lewis	£990,000
Over £40,000	Air traffic controller	£85,714
	Medical practitioner	£79,157
	Police officer	£41, 017
£31,000 – £40,000	Business sales executive	£37,720
	Office manager	£33,458
	Nurse	£32,338

£20,000 – £30,000	Probation officer	£27,129
	Administrative occupation	£25, 388
	Refuse collector	£20,316
Under £20,000	Sales assistant	£18,655
	Care worker	£18,413
	Shelf-filler	£17,233

Source: Office for National Statistics (2019).

Reflective question

Looking at the selective occupations, what do the various salaries suggest about the value we assign to jobs? Is gender important in valuing jobs?

Table 8.4 shows the value we assign to a range of occupations. To answer the question 'How do organisations assign a pay rate?', most organisations rely on pay surveys of 'benchmark' jobs. The data from these are used to anchor the organisation's pay scale, other jobs then being slotted in on the basis of their relative worth to the organisation.

In determining the pay level, an organisation will have to combine the results of the job evaluation process (internal equity criteria) and labour market data (external competitiveness criteria) on a graph, as depicted in Figure 8.4. The horizontal axis depicts an internally consistent job structure based on job evaluation; each grade being made up of a number of jobs (A–O) within the organisation. The jobs in each category are considered equal for pay purposes – they have about the same number of points. Each grade has its own pay range defining the lower and upper limits of pay for jobs in that grade, and all the jobs within the grade have the same range. Jobs in grade 1 (that is, jobs A, B and C), for example, have lower points and pay range than jobs in grade 2 (D, E and F). The actual minimum and maximum pay rates paid by the organisation's competitors are established by survey data. Individual levels of pay within the range may reflect differences in performance or seniority. As depicted, organisations can structure their rate ranges to overlap a little with adjacent ranges so that an employee with experience or seniority might earn more than an entry-level person in the pay grade above.

Each dot on the graph in Figure 8.4 represents the intersection of the going pay rate (the vertical axis), as determined by the pay survey, and the point value (horizontal axis) for a particular benchmark job. Key jobs B, E and L are, for example, worth 100, 375 and 750 points respectively and are paid £7.50, £9.00 and £11.80 an hour. A pay trend line is drawn through the dots, as close to as many points as possible, using a statistical technique called the least squares method. The pay trend line serves as a reference line around which pay structures and rates are established for non-benchmark jobs in the organisation.

There are two steps in this process. The first step is to locate the point value for the non-benchmark job on the horizontal axis; the second is to trace the line vertically to the pay trend line and then horizontally to the pay scale. The amount on the vertical axis is then the appropriate pay rate for the non-benchmark job. Non-benchmark job H is, for example, worth 500 points. By tracing a vertical line up to the pay trend line and then horizontally to the vertical pay scale in Figure 8.3, it can be seen that

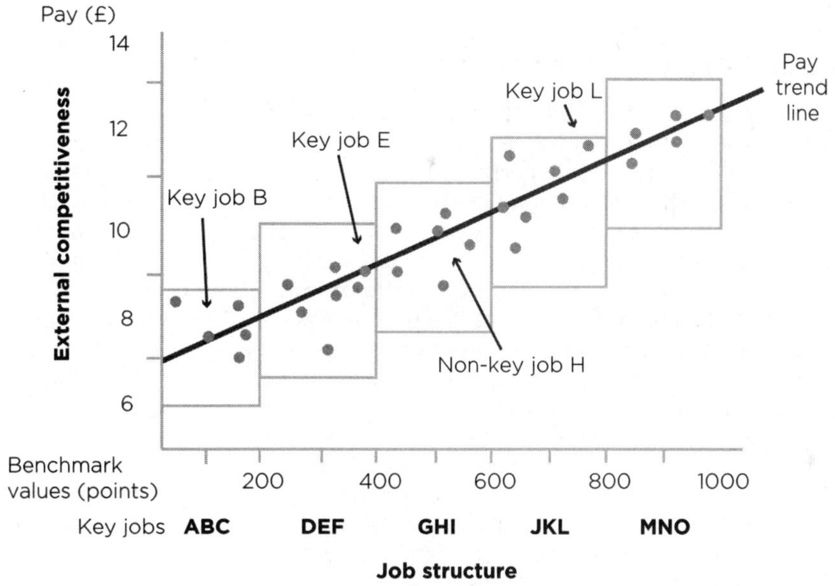

Figure 8.4 The construction of a pay level

the appropriate pay rate for job H is £10.00 per hour. Thus, both market survey information and job evaluation translate the concepts of external competitiveness and internal equity into pay practices.

Once a pay trend line has been established, management has three choices: to *lead* the competition, to *match* what other organisations are paying or to *lag* behind what competitors are paying their employees – establishing a lag or lead policy by shifting the pay trend line down or up. The least-risk approach is to set the pay level to match that of the competition, although some organisations may set different pay policies for different categories of employee with different skill sets. An organisation could, for example, adopt a 'lead' policy for critical skills, such as computer design engineers, a 'match' policy for less critical skill sets and a 'lag' policy for jobs that could be easily filled in the local labour market.

The construction of a pay structure, as depicted in Figure 8.3, using both equity (job evaluation) and labour market data (pay surveys) presents a largely deterministic view of reward management (Gomez-Mejia et al., 2010, p. 13). This prescriptive approach has been questioned in a number of related ways. First, research avers considerable divergent pay practices between and within organisations. Gomez-Mejia et al. (2010) report that it is not unusual to find 3 to 1 difference in pay level for identical job titles in the same labour market. Second, external and internal equity considerations are 'largely inappropriate' in terms of upper management pay and scientific professionals (Gomez-Mejia et al., 2010, p. 14). Third, the pay issues and challenges found in each organisation are typically unique and less structured than traditional models suggest. Thus, while guided by external and internal equity considerations, pay rates will be influenced by many factors, including HR strategy, organisational culture and collective bargaining. Finally, prescriptive reward models neglect 'societal effects' and wider socioeconomic, political and cultural factors, which shape – if not determine – pay practices.

Digital Spotlight
Calculating unit labour costs (ULC)

HR analytics has been described as 'data mining' - collecting HR-related data and finding linkages between different sets of the data and HR practices - to provide the basis for assessing the effect of HR practices on employee and organisational performance. As others have explained, the value of HR data is realised by utilising it to analyse strategic questions about how people create value for the organisation (Angrave et al., 2016). HR analytics can provide guidance on strategic reward management. It can help to control labour costs or what is technically called unit labour costs (ULC), which is the average cost of labour per unit of output and is calculated as the **ratio of total labour costs to actual output.**

To illustrate the application of HR analytics in reward management, assume an employer produces 200 widgets per day. The total number of widgets produced every week is 1,000, which we call total output 'Q'. The employer has a total workforce of 50 employees, which we call 'L'. Therefore, labour productivity (the output per employee) for the employer will be Q/L, which is 1,000/50 = 20. As this chapter explains, typically reward includes a basic wage, sometimes referred to as direct pay, plus additional non-payment items that nonetheless have a cost to the employer and thus are called indirect pay or benefits. Examples of benefits include an occupational pension, health insurance or childcare facilities. Further, assume therefore that the employer pays a base wage of €525 per employee per week, which we call 'W'. In addition, to the basic wage, the employer also incurs additional labour costs of €100 per week per employee on benefits, which we call 'B'.

The unit labour cost (ULC) can help to measure how people create value for the organisation. In this example, the total weekly labour cost will be the wage cost (W) plus the cost of additional benefits (B) multiplied by the number of employees (E), which in this simple example will be: [€525 +€100] x 50 = €31,250. Unit labour costs (ULC), that is the labour cost of producing one widget, will be €31,250/1,000 (Q) = €31.25. ULC can be calculated using the formula: ULC = E [W + B]/Q.

Although the ULC formula is simple, an added complication is whether *all* employees are counted? In calculating the ULC does the employer only count *direct* labour, that is, those actually labouring to produce the 1,000 widgets or are the firm's administrative assistant, receptionist or portfolio coordinator counted in the total wage cost (W)? Jobs that the late David Graeber (2018) provocatively calls 'bullshit' jobs, those that are so completely pointless, unnecessary, that even the employee cannot justify, and add nothing to producing the widgets.

To be more competitive strategic reward management may involve various options to reduce ULC. From a labour economics perspective, the options include: (1) Increase the value of Q by getting employees to work faster, longer, smarter (e.g. teamworking, see Chapter 3) or a combination of all three. (2) Introduce technology to reduce the number of employees (E). (3) Reduce total pay by introducing an element of variable pay based on performance-related pay (PRP). (4) Reduce total pay by unilaterally cutting wage rates. The important point to stress here is that HR analytics enables managers to demonstrate the effect that reward policies and practices have on employee performance, but these various options to reduce wage costs have unintended consequences and risks attached. The priorities for reward policy, and the role of HR analytics in decision-making therein, will depend on what the organisation and HR strategy is seeking to achieve in the context of the competitive environment in which it is operating and what the organisation can afford.

Stop! What actions might an employer take to influence Q, E and W? What would this mean in terms of managing work and people? What difficulties might you face as a manager? (Hint: look again at the book's opening vignette on British Airways).

Essential reading

Arnold, J. (2017) How to calculate the total cost of your workforce, *HR Magazine*, 23 May; Ahmad, R. and Scott, N. (2019) Technology innovations towards reducing hospitality human resource costs in Langkawi, Malaysia, *Tourism Review*, 74(3): 547–62.

Note: This feature was written by John Bratton.

The spirit of new pay

The 'new pay agenda', with its focus on aligning reward with corporate strategy, while no longer so new, caught the *zeitgeist* (Corby et al., 2009). The espoused theory of strategic reward is predicated on the notion of 'strategic choice', which involves managers choosing a reward system that is judged to be closely aligned with the organisation's strategy. Lawler (1984, pp. 146–7) articulates its essence:

> The design of an effective reward system demands not only a close articulation between the business strategy of an organisation and the reward system, but also a clear fit between the reward system and the other design features of the organisation.

Latham (1984) and Lawler's work (1971; 1973; 2000; 2011) has been highly influential in shaping research on strategic reward. The model draws upon four neoliberal principles: a strategic orientation to reward; flexible pay that is responsive to product and labour market conditions; individualisation of the employment contract, and, in particular, pay related to performance; and unitarism, a perspective that assumes management and employees share a common set of interests or goals in the pursuit of mutual gain and which thus regards organisational conflict harmful and to be avoided.

The strategic approach has been used as an analytical tool for explaining developments in, and factors influencing, the choice of reward systems over the last three decades. The multiple neoliberal imperatives, for example deregulation, global cost pressures and flexible work methods, explain why managers may choose a PBR (payment by results) pay scheme based on individual performance. In contrast, where the product market requires a high-quality manufacturing strategy, they may choose a pay-for-knowledge and profit sharing scheme. The contemporary literature on the 'new pay agenda' has emphasised the need for organisations to adopt reward practices that encourage a constellation of attitudes and behaviours meeting the perceived needs of the organisation, as illustrated in Table 8.5.

Table 8.5 Alignment of business strategy, work design and reward practices

Bureaucratic 'old' job-based pay model	Post-bureaucratic 'strategic' pay model
Base wage or salary	Variable pay
Based on cost of living and labour market	Based on organisational performance
Evenly distributed between employees	Differentiated
Correlated with seniority	Based on individual performance
Based on individual performance	Based on team (unit) and organisational performance
Viewed as a result of behaviour values	Used as a means of communicating

Source: Adapted from Pfeffer (1998).

Since the 2000s, diversity and its management has become a feature of modern organisations (Bendl et al., 2017) and Lawler (2011) has argued for diverse reward options. A reward strategy that takes cognizance of diversity and adopts a more individualised approach to pay will, it is argued, find it easier to identify and retain well-qualified and creative people. He opines, 'when individualisation is well executed and well managed it is the best way to develop a superior relationship with an organisation's most important source of competitive advantage, its talent' (2011, p. 32). Brown (2014) takes the individual productivity concepts associated with 'smart teams' (Beatty and Barker-Scott, 2004) and applies them to reward strategy. He argues that the concept of 'total rewards' is too generic and is outdated, and proposes the notion of 'smart rewards'. Brown differentiates four elements of this emerging reward strategy: a focus on a few core values; a stronger basis in evidence and measurement; greater worker voice through rewards; and a dialogic mode of communication. Brown posits that such employee-engaging reward practices are more likely to be performance-enhancing. This suggests that an effective reward system should 'reward employees for the right things, in the right way, and for the right reasons' (Cotton, 2020, p. xvi).

Individualising reward in the contemporary workplace

The individualisation of rewards has made it possible to control wage-earners individually, and thus to make workers more compliant (Boltanski and Chiapello, 2018). A variable pay scheme is a widely used method to individualise pay. Despite the simplicity of the title 'variable pay scheme' (VPS), this reward option has been defined in different ways and comes in many guises. Lazear (2000, p. 410) defines variable pay as 'pay that is tied to some measure of worker output'. Historically, the most typical form of variable pay was merit pay or *performance-related pay* (PRP). The principle of PRP can be characterised by the linking of an individual employee's pay increase to an appraisal process. As part of the new pay agenda, PRP has moved away from subjective assessments based on individual behavioural traits (individual inputs) towards those assessed against an objective criterion (that is, individual outputs). PRP has also been extended from managerial and professional occupations downwards to other job categories in general. The contemporary PRP scheme, it is claimed, is based solely on performance and tied more closely to the overall objectives of the organisation.

Kessler and Purcell (1992) characterise PRP as a means of translating and signalling market-based organisational goals into personalised performance criteria. PRP is not to be confused with PBR pay schemes. Van Wanrooy et al. (2013a) explain the difference between these two similar pay schemes. Whereas PRP is determined through a *subjective* assessment of individual performance by a manager (see Chapter 6), PBR is measured according to *objective* criteria – the amount done or its value, rather than the hours worked (2013a, p. 95). Another pay incentive scheme is profit-related pay, which links part or the whole of employees' pay to the profit levels of all or part of the organisation. VPSs can therefore take several forms: PRP or merit pay, PBR and profit-related pay. The Workplace Employment Relations Survey (WERS) found that 55 per cent of all UK workplaces used at least one form of VPS in 2011, compared with 54 per cent in 2004. However, there was substantial variation across sectors, with private sector workplaces almost three times as likely as public sector workplaces to use at least one VPS, at 59 per cent and 21 per cent respectively. In the private sector, 28 per cent of workers received PRP compared with only 7 per cent of public sector employees (Van Wanrooy et al., 2013a).

Inequality and the gender pay gap

Income inequalities are extremely high and have been rapidly increasing over the last three decades (Savage, 2015). Following the 2008-9 recession, average wages fell almost consistently in real terms until mid-2014. From 2014 to 2016, wages increased, though not back to their pre-recession levels. It is probably not a huge surprise that survey evidence suggests during the Covid-19 crisis, despite government support, financial well-being of workers in the bottom wage quartile deteriorated drastically (Leslie and McCurdy, 2020). Yet, by contrast, the world's billionaires increased their already-huge fortunes during the coronavirus crisis to a record high of £7.8 trillion ($10.2 trillion) (Neate, 2020). If equality is judged in terms of equality of income, equality of opportunity, equality of health or equality of education, then inequality is a persistent feature of the human condition, or, to use Owen Jones's simile, inequality runs through Britain like letters in 'a stick of rock' (Jones, 2016, p. 33). Inequalities

Ethical Insight

Is it time for 'radical transparency' when it comes to pay?

The variation in remuneration between people with different characteristics doing the same job is referred to as the 'pay gap' (Amadxarif et al., 2020). The collection and analysis of data on pay gaps can help to shed light on inequality within workplace rewards. Areas of particular focus (and subsequent concern) have included gender, ethnicity and disability. In regard to gender, on average, women in OECD member countries are paid 13.5% less than their male counterparts (World Economic Forum, 2020). (The figure for lower-income, non-OECD countries is likely higher.) Obtaining an accurate picture of the ethnicity pay gap globally is more difficult. A recent report by the Office for National Statistics (ONS) in the UK suggests that the ethnicity pay gap is closing. However, ethnic minorities are around twice as likely to be unemployed as their white peers (Begum, 2020). The disability pay gap may be the widest of all, standing at 15.5% in the UK (TUC, 2019a).

Increased transparency regarding pay has been suggested as a means of closing the 'gaps'. In many countries, however, discussion around salaries remains taboo. It has been argued that disclosing their salary to a colleague is one of the 'most subversive acts' an employee can undertake (Jacobs, 2019). Many organisations work 'very hard' to make pay opaque, because they would struggle to justify differences (Jacobs, 2019). Not only does such secrecy place workers at a disadvantage in terms of negotiating a salary, it makes it difficult to identify disparities by gender, ethnicity or disability. A combination of technology, legislation and the actions of some organisations means that this is slowly changing. Jacobs (2019) notes that websites such as Glass Door and Salary Expert are helping workers find information about pay that would previously have been unavailable. From a legislative perspective, a number of countries, including ten within the EU, have introduced at least one core pay transparency measure, such as a right for employees to obtain salary information or a pay reporting duty (Veldman, 2017). In addition, an increasing number of organisations, including the software company Buffer, are practising 'radical transparency' by revealing every employee's salary.

Those who oppose pay transparency – or at least caution that it is not a panacea for addressing inequality – argue that it is exceedingly difficult for individuals to accurately assess their own performance, which may be the reason for pay disparity in some cases. Zenger (2016), for example, questioned a group of 700 engineers about their performance in relation to their peers. 'The results were startling. Nearly 40% felt they were in the top 5%. About 92% felt they were in the top quarter' (Zenger, 2016). As a result, he suggests that publicising pay may lead employees – many of whom overestimate their own performance – to believe they are underpaid and respond by deliberately reducing their productivity or leaving the organisation.

Stop! What is your view: is there an ethical argument for 'radical transparency' when it comes to pay? What issues might organisations who decide to introduce pay transparency need to be mindful of?

Essential reading

Baker, M., Halberstam, Y., Kroft, K., Mas, A. and Messacar, D. (2020) Can transparency laws fix the gender wage gap? *Harvard Business Review*, 26 February.

Note: This feature was contributed by Laura Steele.

exist in all aspects of life – access to education, health care, the legal system – and not just in income (Wilkinson and Pickett, 2018). There is compelling evidence too that extreme inequality damages economies (Hutton, 2015a; Piketty, 2014; Rubin, 2020; Stiglitz, 2013). Here, the aim is to understand how inequality affects employees' commitment, trust and behaviours.

Reflective question

How does extreme inequality impact on the employment relationship?

Equality can be defined as the state of being equal, especially in status, rights or opportunities. For our purposes, perhaps the most important point to be taken from the debate surrounding the concept is that equality is socially constructed. It concerns practices, policies and the organisational structures that shape them and is typically understood to be subjective (Colquitt et al., 2001). The concept of 'social equality' will serve as the starting point for discussing the connection between capital and inequality in the context of the contemporary work organisation.

Pay inequality has been a universal feature of capitalist societies, even if the degree of inequality has varied enormously. Wilkinson and Pickett's work, *The Spirit Level* (2010), identifies three ways of measuring pay inequality.

- Compare the *ratio of household income* – after taxes and benefits and adjusted for the number of people in each household – that is received by the top and the bottom 20 per cent of the population.

Typically, the richest half of the population receive approximately 75 or 80 per cent of all income, and the poorest half get the remaining 25 or 20 per cent. For example, in the highest ranked countries of Finland, Norway and Sweden, the richest 20 per cent are less than four times as rich as the poorest 20 per cent. In contrast, in Singapore, the USA, Portugal and Britain, the richest 20 per cent get about nine times as much as the poorest. Figure 8.5 shows the sizes of income inequalities across selective countries. At the top are the most unequal, and the bottom are the more equal.

Research has found that in past epidemics, poverty and inequality can exacerbate rates of transmission and mortality. The Corvid-19 pandemic has exposed, fed off and increased existing inequalities of health, wealth, gender and race (Berkhout et al., 2021; Bibby, 2020). Berkhout et al.'s report for Oxfam International published on the first day of the World Economic Forum – the 'Davos Agenda' – provides stark evidence that the gap between rich and poor is widening. The combined wealth of the world's ten richest men increased by $540 billion during the pandemic, as incomes deteriorated for billions of people. During the pandemic, digital titans Mark Zuckerman of Facebook, Jeff Bezos of Amazon and Elon Musk of Tesla added to their collective wealth. According to the Bloomberg billionaires index, Elon Musk has overtaken Jeff Bezos to become the world's richest person. Musk's net worth reached $186 billion (£136 billion) in January 2021, making him $1.5 billion (£1.1 billion) richer than Bezos, who had held the top spot since October 2017 (Neate, 2021). Based on Bezos's 2019 earnings, it was estimated that an Amazon warehouse worker would take 293 hours, or over eight weeks, to earn what Bezos makes in a second (TUC, 2020b).

- *The Gini coefficient* which measures income inequality across a whole society rather than just comparing its extremes.

The Gini coefficient would be equal to 100 if one person received all the income and everyone else received nothing (maximum inequality). The Gini coefficient would equal 0 if everyone received exactly the same amount of income (perfect equality). The Gini coefficient of inequality in personal income and wealth fell steadily in the second half of the twentieth century; in recent decades, in step with the rise of neoliberalism, it has risen sharply. In other words, the world is getting less equal (Jenkins, 2021).

Figure 8.5 Income inequality in selective countries

- *Compare the pay rates of the top 1 per cent* with the other 99 per cent of society, typically the pay of corporate CEOs and average workers in the same organisation.

CEO's pay is notoriously complex, with separate components paying off on different timescales. In 2019, the median pay of a FTSE 100 CEO is 144 times higher than the UK median of £24,006 for all workers (CIPD, 2019h). A similar trend of average CEO pay has been recorded in the USA. In 2019, the average chief executive of an S&P 500 company earned 287 times more than their median worker (Fernandez Campbell, 2019).

Great men, great pay? It has been argued that CEOs' performance bears little relation to the high salaries they command.

Source: Ludovic Marin/Getty Images

The gender pay gap

The gap between the earnings of men and women is another dimension of income inequality. The gap can be calculated in various ways. The OECD calculates the gender pay gap (GPG) by measuring the difference between the average (median) earnings of

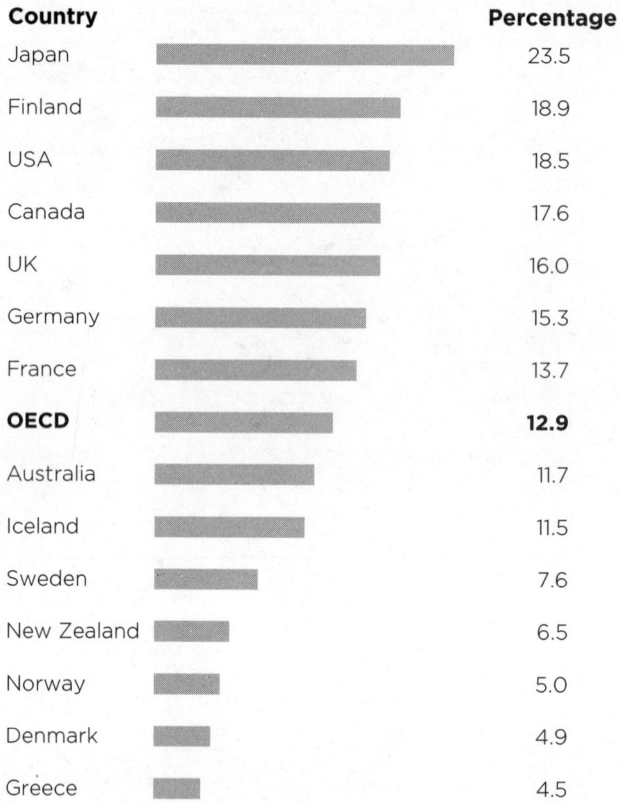

Figure 8.6 Gender pay gap in selected countries (2020)

Source: OECD (2020b).

men and women relative to the median earnings of men. Figure 8.6 shows that gender pay gap levels vary significantly across economies.

How much less do women earn than men? In 2020, women's hourly earnings were on average 23.5 per cent below those of men in Japan, compared to an average of 4.9 per cent in Denmark. Intersectional analysis can provide insights into inequality regimes (Healy et al., 2019); the gender pay gap in relation to age and ethnicity, for example. The GPG is generally much lower for new labour market entrants (up to 24 years old) and tends to widen with age. Limited data on the ethnicity pay gap – the difference in median pay between white and BAME workers – shows an ethnicity pay gap in favour of workers who disclose as white (see, e.g. University of Bristol, 2020). Further, GPG tends to be higher in the private sector than in the public sector. Since 2017, in an attempt to increase transparency and address the structural forces of pay inequalities, large UK employers who have a headcount of 250 or more must report any gender pay gap. The BBC, as an example of the effects of this transparency, has been engulfed in controversy over the pay gap between men and women journalist (see Siddique, 2020). A growing body of literature is analysing the unequal effects of the pandemic on the gender pay and career gap. Covid-19 has negatively affected in a substantial way the earnings of working-class women. Moreover, the pandemic has also highlighted the various ways gendered labour in the care sector, eldercare, has suffered an exogenous shock, exposing the way in which society is dependent on gendered labour that is generally low-status, low-paid or unpaid (Özkazanç-Pan and Pullen, 2020). Even for many professional women who have not lost their jobs, the crisis could affect the trajectory of their careers, with consequences for long-term earnings, as many have been forced to take on additional care responsibilities (Doolittle and Wang, 2021). Extant gender inequalities in academia, for instance, could widen as Covid-19 disrupts research productivity due to changed caring or schooling responsibilities (Pereira, 2021). As critical economists have pointed out, unpaid 'caring labour' is an old inequality that is not factored into the accounts of 'the economy' (Ferrant et al., 2014).

A growing body of international literature suggests that the rate of income inequality is greater in those countries that most closely embrace the neoliberal troika of deregulation, privatisation and flexible labour markets (Bratton and Denham, 2019). French economist Thomas Piketty's economic tome *Capital* offers detailed evidence on the structured pattern of income inequality with a focus on the USA, the UK and France. He observes:

> Since the 1970s, income inequality has increased significantly in the rich countries, especially the United States, where the concentration of income in the first decade of the twenty-first century regained – indeed, slightly exceeded – the level attained in the second decade of the previous century. (2014, p. 15)

Arguably, the most significant insight of Piketty's work is that it shows that, if unregulated, capitalism can be expected to produce rates of return on investment that are so much higher than overall rates of economic growth that the only possible outcome is an even greater inequality in income (Graeber, 2014).

There are many reasons for the dramatic rise of income inequality, and space only permits a mention of a few. These include the decline in union membership (see Figure 9.1, for example), the growth in precarious employment and zero-hour contracts, the erosion of workers' protections, the process used to set CEOs' pay and the ideology of 'meritocratic extremism'. The 'stratospheric' pay of CEOs has also been explained by Piketty as a form of 'meritocratic extremism', by which he means the apparent social norm in some modern societies, especially those of the US and UK, 'to designate certain individuals as "winners" and to reward them all the more generously if they seem to have been selected on the basis of their intrinsic merits' (Piketty, 2014, p. 334). Hutton (2015b), observes that British CEO pay, once adjusted for the size of the corporation under management, is the 'highest in the world' and much higher than in EU member states and Japan (p. 95). Moreover, many CEOs of FTSE 100 companies are unexceptional, and 'for every appointment of a CEO, another 100 people could have filled the role just as ably, and ... many chosen for the top jobs were "mediocre"' (Boffey, 2016a, p. 1).

Reflective question

How much more than the average worker *should* CEOs make? Hint: in the 1970s, management guru Peter Drucker suggested a cap on the ratio of CEO to average worker salary of 25:1. In 2013, the Swiss electorate voted in a referendum against a ratio between CEOs' and employees' pay of 12:1. What criteria should be used to justify CEO pay?

But what is the relevance of inequality, in all its dimensions, to HRM? Evidence suggests that employees' motivation is influenced by relative, rather than absolute, rewards. Employees compare their pay with that of comparable co-workers or 'referent others' (Corby et al., 2009, p. 12). These are typically their own co-workers (internal equity), but this may extend to those doing comparable jobs in other organisations (external equity). Although the evidence is mixed, some studies suggest that a more 'egalitarian' pay structure enhances employees' cooperation and satisfaction (Guthrie, 2008, p. 355). The extravagant CEO pay phenomenon can have a malign organisational effect, inviting scepticism and resentment from low-paid workers, which can deplete commitment. Collectively, if the perception of negative inequity is strong and is shared by a sufficient number of workers, unionisation and conflict can occur.

Critiquing the strategic reward paradigm

As in other areas of HRM, at both practical and theoretical levels, reward has an interlocking set of tensions and paradoxes. In capitalism, reward is a cost for employers, but for employees it is typically their only source of income. Each party attempts to secure a pay outcome that, from their position, is more satisfactory. During the pandemic, for example, many companies cut workers' rewards by introducing the practice of 'fire and rehire'. Workers were dismissed and then immediately rehired on a contract offering a lower wage and worse employment conditions. Over two-thirds of companies accused of initiating 'fire-and-rehire' were reported to be making a profit and half had claimed government support during the pandemic (Wall, 2021). Thus, conflict is structured into reward management. Labour market data affirm that there is an inverse relation between social value and the level of pay (Graeber, 2018; Özkazanç-Pan and Pullen, 2020). Financialization has not only exposed the limitations of mainstream strategic compensation theories but also highlighted the various ways in which it has increased economic inequality. The gross pay inequality in corporate America and Britain can be explained by the development of the doctrine of maximisation of shareholder value (MSV). How does MSV change behaviour? The behaviour of top corporate executives was changed by making a substantial proportion of their salaries and bonuses directly linked to the company's share price. When share options are added on top of these rewards, MSV becomes the principal motivation in every boardroom: share price is sacrosanct. MSV is a key factor in explaining the trend towards 'tournament-like' pay – that is, high pay for a few at the top and low pay for the vast majority at the bottom (Henderson, 2020; Piketty, 2017; Rubin, 2020). From the early 1990s, MSV was the irrefutable doctrine of corporate capitalism (Blakeley, 2019; Martin and Quick, 2020; Wylie, 2020). Arguably, MSV encourages high-risk behaviour, as evidenced by the 2008-9 global financial crisis and the collapse of UK construction giant Carillion (Martin, 2014; Wylie, 2020).

At the bottom end of the pay scale, the individualisation of pay seeks to increase employees' commitment, motivation and flexibility. However, performance-related pay (PRP) in team-based work regimes may be counterproductive. In team-based regimes pay-based individual performance risks fuelling dissatisfaction delineated in Adams' equity theory. PRP is prone to the 'twin vices' of subjectivity and inconsistency (Guthrie, 2008; Kessler, 1994) and might become discredited because of perceived 'procedural injustices' caused by inconsistent performance appraisals (see Chapter 6). Further, attempts to change workers' commitment through PRP arrangements might be undermined if pay to superior performers cannot be fulfilled due to the company's poor financial performance. Disappointment might cause a breach of the psychological contract. With regard to the concept of strategic reward, the principle of 'fit' commonly cited in the literature is fraught with difficulties. The causal relationship between pay and organisational performance is a hypothesis based on the assumption that reward practices change employees' attitudes and employees' behaviour in ways that advance organisational goals. This is somewhat at odds with the expanded multicausational approach, which privilege social relations between line managers and other employees and 'bundles' of HR practices as the key levers (Purcell and Kinnie, 2008).

A critical analysis of the strategic reward paradigm has to take cognizance of the relationship between power and reward options. The choice of a reward system is shaped, if not dictated, by perceptions of power on the part of both management and labour. The balance of power is a strategic factor that helps to explain not only the choice of reward arrangements within any HR strategy but the dominance of the doctrine of MSV. The British corporate class have been able to pursue MSV unchallenged due to the shift in the balance of power between capital and labour caused by the decisive decline of trade unions (Blakeley, 2019). As others have noted, a major goal of the 'new pay' paradigm is the individualisation of pay and to shift more risk onto workers, an objective that fits with a wider social agenda to undermine union power and collectivist values (Boltanski and Chiapello, 2018; Corby et al., 2009; Fieschi, 2019). Finally, every crisis is a trend accelerator. The future of post-pandemic labour markets is likely to see even more young people across Europe occupy their hours with low-paid, unskilled jobs with little security (De Stefano, 2015; Edgell and Ganter, 2020; Mason, 2016). The coronavirus pandemic will almost certainly be the most catastrophic historical event which will overwhelm the working poor of the US and Britain. Certainly, for HRM, with its rhetorical strategic goal of harnessing human potential, the reward system has to address issues of pay inequality.

Summary

This chapter has emphasised that reward is central to the effective management of the employment relationship. The strategic pay model we have developed shows that reward is multidimensional and emphasises two fundamental policy issues: *internal* and *external equity*. The underlying assumption is that the strategic choices made by managers on the reward system can influence each step of the strategy process and are a key contributor to the effectiveness of the organisation. Although this view has been contested, we explained that the current new pay literature stresses that an 'effective' pay system is one that is aligned with the organisation's business strategy.

We discussed why no single best reward system exists. A reward system that may seem highly appropriate in one period, with a particular organisation and work design supporting a management strategy, or with a particular group or individual employees, can be highly inappropriate in the next, when the business strategy and organisational design or individual employees change.

We explained that changes in reward systems reflect shifts in management thinking. The adoption of more variable pay systems is ideologically driven to encourage labour flexibility, although the literature on organisational behaviour and reward management is replete with evidence-based examples of incentivising (and disincentivising) reward systems, so there is no consensus on the type of pay system that might encourage behavioural change.

Finally, we examined how government intervenes *directly* in the pay determination and explored the issue of wage inequality. Under the logic of political economy, reward systems cannot remove the contradictory tensions that bedevil the capitalist employment relationship.

Review questions

1. Explain the statement 'The design of a reward system is contingent upon the organisational context in which it must operate.'
2. What are the advantages and disadvantages of rewarding employee behaviour versus rewarding outcomes? In what circumstances would an incentive-pay scheme have a motivational or a demotivational effect on employees?
3. Do job evaluation schemes hinder or promote gender pay equality? Has the pandemic exposed the way society is dependent on gendered labour? How can job evaluation schemes build greater fairness into the ratings of job characteristics?

Search & Watch

Visit the video hub at www.bloomsbury.pub/bratton-hrm and view the interview with **Ruth Altman, Freelance HR practitioner,** talking about the challenges of working in a HR department at a university, and how higher university fees will impact on the reward system in universities. Then think about the following questions: (1) How does Ruth explain the development of the psychological contract at work? (2) How are changes in universities affecting HR in general, and reward management in particular?

Legal Focus

Pay equity legislation is defined as those laws that are intended to eliminate established inequalities in pay received by women and (often specifically identified) members of minority groups working for a given employer. In 2020, despite the UK government passing the Equal Pay Act (EPA) 1970, there is still a gap between men's and women's hourly pay. In 2019, the gender pay gap was 8.9 % among full-time employees and 17.3% among all employees, according to data compiled by the Office for National Statistics. Each year, a day can be identified from which, because of the gender pay gap, women in effect work without pay for the rest of the year. In 2019, that day was 14 November when the average woman is essentially working unpaid until the end of the year. The Equality Act 2010 repealed the Equal Pay Act (EPA) 1970. Along with Article 157 of the Treaty of Rome and EU Equal Pay Directives, the UK Equality Act (EA) 2010 creates an independent right to equal pay. The EA 2010 provides three bases of claiming equal pay: (1) like work; (2) work rated as equivalent; and (3) work of equal value. Section 66 of the EA 2010 deems that all contracts of employment include a 'sex equality clause'. This means that to claim equal pay, the female employee needs a contract with which to compare terms.

Task Search online for government information in your jurisdiction on equal pay and compare and contrast it with another country, such as Australia or Canada. (1) On what basis can an employee claim equal pay? (2) What is the significance of a 'comparator' when a female employee claims equal pay? (3) What is meant by (a) 'like work' and (b) what role does a job evaluation system (JES) play in claiming equal pay?

Reference

See Deborah Lockton and Tom Brown's *Employment Law* (2020), pp. 225-48, for a detailed discussion and analysis of equality of terms in the employment contract.

PART 2

Chapter case: Basil Café*

The setting

Prior to the economic recession caused by the 2020 Covid-19 pandemic, the UK foodservice market was set for a healthy expansion in growth with a predicted value of £160 billion by 2030. This was based on an estimated 10% growth in the UK population, as well as the impact of a significant increase in the millions of annual tourists expected to arrive on its shores every year, nearly as many as the UK population itself. The industry was braced to develop novel foodservice offerings to meet the needs of this broader customer base. At the same time, there was a growing consumer demand for an enhanced 'dining experience', with higher quality food and drink. As a result, it was anticipated that skill shortages would worsen, with restaurants racing to take advantage of the new opportunities and hoping to find workers capable of meeting the challenges these fresh prospects would bring.

The problem

In the spring of 2019, Basil, a specialty food shop located in Morningside, Edinburgh, was expanded to include a high-end evening café which would highlight international ingredients found in the deli portion of its business. While her steady customers for the deli were residents from the surrounding area, owner Sara McCorkell felt confident the café would be an attractive dining venue for the growing number of international tourists who visited the city throughout the year. Sara was eager to set an opening date before the first summer tourists arrived in June.

With her business already bringing in over £750,000 in sales every year, Sara was poised to add to the 20 staff she currently employed to run the deli. However, she wanted to ensure her staff working in the café would have sufficient skills to deal with the international tourists she hoped to attract and questions they might ask about her unique menu offerings. Sara had never experienced any difficulty in recruiting, but retaining employees proved difficult during the peak summer season when local eateries enticed them with higher hourly rates.

Sara thought that maybe a different approach to compensating her staff would be prudent now that she was to start a restaurant business of her own. She approached her son Brodie, who had graduated from a business programme a few months earlier, for advice. 'I don't want to get into a "hourly wage war" with the other restaurants,' she told him. 'I can't afford to compete with them on pay when I'm just opening mine.' Brodie agreed. 'Why not consider an incentive-pay system that would link the worker's pay to the cafe's performance?' he suggested. Sara thought this was an interesting idea. She asked Brodie to provide more details on what the appropriate pay system would look like and the basis for his recommendation.

The assignment

As Brodie, drawing on the material in this chapter, prepare PowerPoint slides with notes for Sara including answers to the following:

1. How do the higher skills of the café workers Sara would like to recruit play a part in the 'fit' between her business model for the café and the pay system she chooses?
2. What are the advantages and disadvantages of variable payment schemes?
3. Of the three variable payment schemes (performance-related pay, profit-related payments, employee share ownership payments), which would you recommend for Sara and why?

Essential reading

Antoni, C. H., et al. (2017) Reward management: linking employee motivation and organisational performance. *Journal of Personnel Psychology, 16*: 57–60.

Kuvass, B., Buch, R. and Dysvik, A. (April 2018) Individual variable pay for performance, incentive effects, and employee motivation. *Academy of Management Annual Meeting Proceedings, 1*: 12393.

Long, R. D., et al. (Winter 2012) Effects of and preference for pay for performance: an analogue analysis. *Journal of Applied Behaviour Analysis, 45*(4): 821–6.

Ogbonnaya, C., Daniels, K. and Nielsen, K. (January 2017) Does contingent pay encourage positive employee attitudes and intensify work? *Human Resource Management Journal, 27*(1): 94–112.

Pendleton, A. and Robinson, A. (November 2017) The productivity effects of multiple pay incentives. *Economic and Industrial Democracy, 38*(4): 588–608.

Note: This case was contributed by Lori Rilkoff.

*Basil Café is a fictitious name.

Further reading

Dorling, D. (2019) *Inequality and the 1%*. London: Verso.

Gerhart, B. (2018) Compensation. In J. Storey, P. M. Wright and D. Ulrich (eds) *The Routledge Companion to Strategic Human Resource Management*, (pp. 224–44). London: Routledge.

Jones, S. E. and Perkins, S. J. (2020) *Reward Management: Alternatives, Consequences and Contexts* (4th edn). London: CIPD.

Joshi, H., Bryson, A., Wilkinson, D. and Ward, K. (2021) The gender gap in wages over the life course: evidence from a British cohort born in 1958. *Gender, Work & Organization, 28*: 397–415. Available at: https://onlinelibrary.wiley.com/doi/epdf/10.1111/gwao.12580.

Landivar, L. C. (2015) The gender gap in employment hours: do work-hour regulations matter? *Work, Employment and Society*, 1–21. DOI: 10.1177/0950017014568139

Nyberg, A. J., Maltarich, M. A., Abdulsalam, D. D., Essman, S. M. and Cragun, O. (2018) Collective pay for performance: a cross-disciplinary review and meta-analysis. *Journal of Management, 44*(6): 2433–72.

PART 4

MANAGING THE EMPLOYMENT RELATIONSHIP

CHAPTER 9

Labour Relations and Collective Bargaining

CHAPTER 10

Employee Relations and Conflict Management

CHAPTER 9

LABOUR RELATIONS AND COLLECTIVE BARGAINING

outline

- Introduction
- The nature of labour relations
- The legal context of labour relations
- HRM and labour relations strategies
- Trade unions
- Collective bargaining
- Critiquing labour relations
- Summary
- Further reading

Source: Guy Smallman/Getty Images

objectives

After studying this chapter, you should be able to:

1. Define and describe contemporary trends in labour relations
2. Describe the core legal principles relating to union–management relations
3. Explain and critically evaluate different types of union–management strategy.
4. Explain the meaning of union density, union structure and collective bargaining

Introduction

During the global pandemic, British Gas imposed a 'fire and rehire' scheme in an attempt to reduce labour costs and improve the productivity of the engineers (Ambrose, 2021). British Airways unilaterally imposed on its cabin crew staff a 20 per cent basic pay cut and change in working patterns, and in addition the company laid off 12,000 workers, up to 30 per cent of its workforce, after coronavirus grounded almost all passenger flights (Topham, 2020). Severely impacted by the coronavirus-induced collapse of international travel, the decision by US plane maker, Boeing, manufacturer of the 787 Dreamliner, to move production entirely from its union-organised plant north of Seattle, in Washington State, to the non-union state of South Carolina will cause over 1,000 workers to lose their jobs (Johnson, 2020). The central significance of these actions by high-profile companies is to remind us that the employment relationship has a political dimension which reflects a distribution of power that underpins management-union relations. As explained in Chapter 1, there can be an individual employment relationship or a collective employment relationship, with the former determined unilaterally by the employer, and the latter bilaterally or jointly by the employer and a trade union(s) (Kelly, 2005). Labour relations is concerned with the theory and practice associated with the bilateral employment relationship. In particular it is concerned with the process of determining the terms and conditions of employment through negotiations between management and the trade union(s) representing the workers. It is important to note that the terms of the collective agreement negotiated are incorporated into the individual contracts of employment of *all* workers (i.e. union *and* non-union workers) in the bargaining group (Farnham, 2015).

PART 4

We begin the chapter by defining labour relations and the scope of this interdisciplinary field of study. Next, we examine a number of strategic decisions that management must take with regard to trade unions. After providing an overview of the legal context, the chapter will examine some important developments in labour relations in recent years. Finally, the chapter will turn to the issue of social partnership and an assessment of unions' influence and response to the post-2020 recession, Covid-19 and other developments impacting the workplace.

Reflective question

It is important to examine your own values and life experiences, and therefore your own perspective on trade unions. Do you think that unions have a role to play in the new knowledge-based economy or are they 'dinosaurs' from a past era?

The nature of labour relations

As a field of study, the academic community has used different terms to describe the collective employment relationship, including 'industrial relations', 'labour relations' and 'union–management relations' (see Burchill, 2014; Farnham, 2015; Gunderson et al., 2005; Kelly, 2005). Industrial relations is the traditional term used to refer to the theory and practice of management and trade union relations, together with collective bargaining between the two parties. It is argued that the term 'industrial relations' and its traditional subject boundaries have now become outdated (Wood, 2000). In this book, we use the contemporary term 'labour relations' because it is less synonymous with heavy manufacturing and mining, which has been in decline for at least four decades in many parts of Europe.

In post-industrial economies, therefore, the term labour relations is a better descriptor of the collective employment relationship in both private and public sector organisations.

Since the rise of neoliberalism, labour relations in Britain has been so radically transformed by economic, political and social factors that the 2021 workplace would be 'incomprehensible' to the average worker in work in 1980 (Brown et al., 2009, p. 1). Successive workplace surveys have demonstrated with clarity the transformation 'in the shadow' of the post-financial global crisis (van Wanrooy et al., 2013a). Running parallel with (and not unrelated to) these changes has, of course, been the increasing reliance of financialisation for the accumulation of profits (Davis and Kim, 2015) and, of course, the ascendancy of the HRM paradigm (Godard, 2005; Guest, 1995). The radical transformation of labour relations has not been limited to the UK. In the US and the European Union (EU), the traditional pattern of labour relations has also undergone profound modifications in the intervening period (Boltanski and Chiapello, 2018). European trade unions have been weakened both numerically and politically. The response to intensified global competition has not, however, been the same in every EU member state. Thus, in some respects, the pattern of European labour relations systems has always sharply diversified, 'a contradictory mix of market liberalization and social regulation', representing a complex interaction between 'Europeanization' and 'Anglicization' forms of employment relations (Hyman, 2010).

In light of these profound contextual and institutional changes, it has become widely accepted that labour relations must be reconceptualised and extend its focus of inquiry and analysis beyond traditional issues to a broader concern with all the contextual forces, the structural bases of conflict and cooperation between employer and workers, and the institutional processes that shape the employment relationship (Blyton and Turnbull, 2004; Colling and Terry, 2010; Gunderson et al., 2005). Burchill (2014, p. 1) points to the 'economic forces' in shaping the behaviour of the principal labour relations actors. It is acknowledged that the primary object of inquiry that defines the field of labour relations is not management, trade unions or strikes, but the analysis of the social relationship that generates these phenomena, that is, the employment relationship (Klerck, 2019). In labour relations literature it is possible to discern a growing tendency to focus on and define the distinctive characteristics of the employment relationship in terms of:

- indeterminacy, which derives from the fact that the labour contract involves an exchange for pay for a potential level of performance;
- power, which is unequally distributed between the two parties;
- its dynamic nature, which emphasises the uncertainty, resistance and conflict associated with managing labour. (Colling and Terry, 2010, pp. 7–8)

Thus, labour relations examines explicitly facets of the employment relationship few mainstream HRM scholars address: the power of capital and the resistance of labour to management strategic decisions. Specifically, the field engages with the political dimension of the employment relationship. Organisational politics and power shape the ways in which HRM professionals and management manage work and people (Clegg and Dunkerley, 1980; Edwards and Kuruvilla, 2005). Further, labour relations encompass dynamic ways in which employers may respond to unionisation and how labour may contest management practices and collective conflict, spheres of people management neglected to a large degree in unitarist studies of HRM studies.

In the context of finance capitalism, at organisational level, financialisation manifests itself in maximising shareholder value (MSV) and the outsourcing production activities to low-wage economies –

the process of 'Nikefication' (Davis and Kim, 2015, p. 210). The orientation toward 'Nikefication' has influenced organisational design and work and inevitably refashioned both the individual and collective employment relationship (Davis, 2016; Martin and Quick, 2020). The trend towards outsourcing, offshoring and greater emphasis on MSV have had pervasive consequences for economic inequality, power and labour relations. As Peck (1996, p. 240) observes, 'the contours of labour control are [continuously] reworked and remade' under industrial capitalism, change, uncertainty and conflict. Arguably, finance capitalism is inherently more unstable at workplace level, in part because finance activities are disconnected from the internal value generating activities (Thompson, 2013). This observation suggests that employment relations can never be in 'equilibrium'. In particular, management-driven work entails the two principles of control and consent, and these facets are 'necessarily in contradiction ... An IR system can never be in equilibrium because it rests on the need to manage actively these contradictory pressures', argues Edwards (2003b, p. 339). Therefore, the purpose of labour relations is the control, reworking, and regulation of the employment relationship (Edwards, 1995). Likewise, Hyman (1975, p. 31) argues the 'control over work relations' is a central feature of labour relations. It is in this context that we define labour relations as:

> The relations between organised employees (represented by a union) and management, the processes that regulate the employment contract, the *context* within which a union and an employer interact.

PART 4

Let us briefly expand on the components of this definition. The *'relations'* between the workers and management are both economic and social: they are an economic relation because employers buy workers' potential physical and mental abilities, and they are a social relation because, when workers enter into a contract, they agree to comply with the employer's standards and rules. These relationships between workers and management may be played out in different arenas – at the workplace level, at industry level and at the national level – where union, employer and government representatives participate in a social dialogue on economic and employment-related issues.

The word *'processes'* refers to collective bargaining, by which unions represent their members' interests through formal negotiations with management representatives. Through collective bargaining, a hierarchy of rules and regulations affecting employment and workplace behaviour is generated, and this is the process that may provide the focal point for studying the *mediating* effects of key variables in the HRM–performance causal chain, often referred to as the 'HR black box' (see Chapter 2).

The third key feature of the definition, *'context'*, refers to the economic, legal and political conditions and constraints within which management and union relations take place. Our definition of labour relations recognises the fluidity of contexts and the processes of control over the employment relationship. This dynamic mix means that, in a unionised environment, managing the interactions between union and management representatives can be a significant area of HRM activity.

The rest of this chapter examines the legal context of labour relations, the strategic choices of employers for dealing with trade unions, the influence of trade unions on the collective employment relationship and the process of collective bargaining that determines the terms and conditions of the employment contract.

Ethical Insight

Is a union-avoidance strategy unethical?

Source: Spencer Davis on Unsplash

For decades, trade union membership has been in decline across most advanced economies. In 1985, 30% of workers in OECD countries were members of a trade union, however, by 2019 this had fallen to 16% (OECD, 2020a). The decrease has been attributed to a range of factors, including the changing composition of the labour force, new patterns of industrial relations and the effects of globalisation (Dundon, 2003), as well as employers 'turning their back on unions – preferring to "go" or "remain" non-union' (Bryson and Blanchflower, 2008). However, there is evidence of a modest reversal of this trend. In the UK, for example, trade union membership reached a low of 6.23 million (or 23.5% of the workforce) in 2016 (Stone, 2020). However, in May 2020, the Department for Business, Energy and Industrial Strategy (BEIS) reported that the number of workers who are a member of a trade union rose by 91,000 in 2019. This is due, at least in part, to large numbers of women joining, predominantly from the heavily unionised fields of education and health and social care (Stone, 2020). In addition to growth amongst traditional trade unions, there have also been grassroots efforts to organise new unions for workers in atypical or precarious forms of employment, such as the gig economy.

Some employers have – to varying degrees – opposed the unionisation of their workforce. In the United States, for example, a 'union avoidance' industry has developed, 'dedicated to defeating union organizing campaigns and keeping their clients – including many multinational corporations (MNCs) – union free' (Logan, 2020, p. 76). Having 'perfected' their techniques, the industry, which predominantly comprises law firms, has begun to extend their activities globally (Logan, 2020). Commentators have raised concerns that union avoidance firms are using international labour standards 'offensively', arguing that 'employers have a right – and even an obligation – to oppose unionization' (Logan, 2020, p. 76). The rationale underpinning this position is that International Labour Organization (ILO) jurisprudence states that employees should have access to 'information, opinions and ideas' that allow them to make an informed choice in relation to membership (Logan, 2020, p. 79), for example, by presenting evidence that unions may lead to increased unemployment by raising the price of labour and reducing the capacity of organisations to compete. However, organisations (with or without the support of union avoidance firms) may attempt to prevent union access to the workplace so that they can present the case in favour of unionisation. Anti-union behaviour and control strategies may go further, straying into what has been termed 'fear stuff' (where employer behaviour includes blatant intimidation of workers, with the objective of instilling fear of management reprisals) or 'harm stuff' (where the employer seeks to effectively marginalise collective employee voice, often through non-union communication channels) (Dundon, 2003; Roy, 1980).

Stop! What is your view: are union avoidance strategies unethical?

Essential reading

Logan, J. (2020) The US union avoidance industry goes global. *New Labor Forum*, *29*(1): 76–81.

Note: This feature was contributed by Laura Steele.

The legal context of labour relations

Labour law is an aspect of labour relations that interacts with the institutions, processes and behaviour of the key actors in the system. As a body of statutes and cases, labour law regulates union organisation and governance, the main concerns being relations between different unions, union recognition by employers, the process of collective bargaining, and manifestations of collective conflict, such as strikes, arising from the managerial function. Whereas individual labour law governs the relations between individual employees and their employer, collective labour law governs the collective aspects of the employment relationship. Labour relations processes and outcomes are also influenced through *third-party intervention* (as, for example, in Britain, by the Advisory, Conciliation and Arbitration Service – ACAS).

When trade unions organised in eighteenth-century Britain, they faced illegality under both criminal and civil law. The Combination Acts of 1799 and 1800 were only part of a battery of more than 40 statutes that criminalised trade union activities. Fast forward to the twentieth century, the Conservative governments of the 1980s and 1990s significantly remodelled the legal framework for labour relations that had been established between 1870 and 1906 and developed by the Labour governments of the 1970s (McIlroy, 1988).

The New Labour government's Employment Relations Act 1999 provides a more supportive statutory framework for union organisation and governance and collective bargaining, including provision for statutory union recognition, changed balloting procedures and increased protection for union members when participating in official industrial action (see Emir, 2014). Employers' anti-union activities remain a feature of HRM in Britain. Gall (2006), for example, using an array of primary and secondary sources, provides evidence and analysis of employers' attempts to resist campaigns for union recognition and to undermine newly granted recognition agreements. A critical review of trade union rights is also offered by Smith and Morton (2006, p. 414). The authors contend that, to strengthen workers' power, legislation is needed to establish 'a statutory right of trade partnership agreements' and that unions should have access to, and assembly at, the workplace.

The Conservative government's Trade Union Act 2016 aims to reform various aspects of the law on trade union activities and industrial action. Key features of the Act include the following: a new 'opt-in' process for union political funds; a new minimum voter turnout – at least 50 per cent of eligible members must have voted in favour of strike action – a requirement made in no other part of British democracy; additional minimum thresholds for workers in 'important public services', for example health services, education, fire services and transport services; and a new definition of, and restrictions on, picketing at or near a place of work in contemplation or furtherance of a trade dispute for the purpose of obtaining or communicating information. Labour relations scholars and a United Nations (UN) body have expressed concerns about the Act, suggesting that the 'draconian' provisions amount to 'the most sustained attack on trade union and workers' rights since the Combination laws of the early 19th century' (Stuart, 2015, p. 30). The International Labour Organization, a UN agency dealing with employment and union issues, expressed concern that the Trade Union Act 2016 contravenes international labour law (Perraudin, 2016).

A direct consequence in Britain of ever-complex legal rules regulating strike action was the injunction preventing the airline cabin crew's union Unite calling a strike against British Airways in 2010. The landmark decision by Mr Justice McCombe granted the injunction against the strike, overturning an 81 per cent vote by BA's cabin crew in favour of industrial action. The judge ruled that Unite had not complied with a particularly esoteric point of the 1992 Trade Union and Labour Relations (Consolidation) Act that orders unions to notify not just the result of any secret ballot to all eligible voters, but also the exact breakdown of votes, including spoiled ballot papers, of which there were 11 (Milmo and Pidd,

2010). Reacting to the verdict, the joint general secretaries of Unite, Tony Woodley and Derek Simpson (quoted by Milmo and Pidd, 2010, p. 1), said:

> This judgement is an absolute disgrace and will rank as a landmark attack on free trade unionism and the right to take industrial action. Its implication is that it is now all but impossible to take legally protected strike action against an employer who wishes to seek an injunction on even the most trivial grounds.

The traditional attitude of the English courts is that there is no 'right to strike': Parliament has granted unions immunities not rights (as set out in the case *Express Newspapers v McShane* [1979]). The judge in this case, Lord Denning, held that trade unions had no right 'to break the law or do wrong by inducing people to break contracts ... only immunity if they did'. Pre-Brexit, that view was open to question once English law incorporated the European Convention on Human Rights through the Human Rights Act 1998. Article 11 of the Convention recognises a right to freedom of association, which has been interpreted as incorporating a right to strike. In *British Airways Plc v Unite Union* [2010], Judge McCombe seemed to resurrect Lord Denning's view.

Source: iStock.com/Pattanaphong-Khuankaew

Although the traditional attitude of the English courts is that there is no 'right to strike', there is a consensus that some form of a right to strike must be respected if that is really the democratic will of union members.

However, at the Court of Appeal it was held that Unite had complied with the Trade Union and Labour Relations (Consolidation) Act 1992. The Lord Chief Justice described the ballot as having been 'impeccably conducted'. The Court of Appeal did not clarify the argument of whether the right to strike is recognised in Britain as a fundamental human right: 'The judgments of the majority do, however, seem to assume that some form of a right to strike must be respected if that is really the democratic will of union members' (Eady and Motraghi, 2010, p. 1). Despite promoting 'social partnerships' and, most recently, 'employee representation' on company boards, the effects of the legal strategies pursued by governments has thus considerably restricted lawful industrial action (Dickens and Hall, 2010).

Before 31 December 2020, EU law and regulations have also influenced labour relations in Britain. In 2007, for example, the landmark judgements of the European Court of Justice in the Viking and Laval cases adopted the legal concept of proportionality. The general principle of proportionality is complex but briefly it entails a three-part test: first, is the measure suitable to achieve a legitimate objective, second, is the measure necessary to achieve that objective or are less restrictive means available, and third, whether the measure has an excessive effect on the applicant's interests. The application of proportionality in labour relations meant that, irrespective of national law, work stoppages that interfered with freedom of movement were lawful only if they satisfied a 'proportionality' test. That is, they are both appropriate and necessary (Hyman, 2010). The ramifications of the UK withdrawal from the European Union for labour law will take years to emerge and will not become clear until we know what elements of EU law/regulations are passed into UK law (Hillage, 2016).

Reflective question

Reflecting on this brief overview of labour relations law, what is your view – should trade unions have more or fewer rights?

HRM in Practice

Unions and green groups call for a sustainable Covid-19 recovery

The UK must prioritise a green economic recovery while driving a new 'industrial revolution' to help the unemployed. This is the vision of trade unionists as urgent calls are made for increased levels of government investment as part of the UK's Covid-19 recovery, urging the government to learn lessons from the first post-war Labour government. As outlined in the Trades Union Congress (TUC) report 'Just transition to a greener, fairer economy', investment in environmental sustainability policies and practices as part of an economic recovery strategy would cut carbon dioxide emissions and create jobs. In Scotland, the Scottish Trades Union Congress (STUC) has proposed a new Future Jobs Fund to support a green construction and retrofit housing programme, to make existing homes more environmentally friendly, while creating 'good quality' jobs (Williams, 2020). Similarly, a Scottish Government advisory group on economic recovery has made 25 recommendations to 'build a robust, resilient wellbeing economy' and invest in a 'green economic recovery' by seeking to end insecure and low-pay jobs and invest in renewable energy (Beaton, 2020). Green advocacy groups have also called for a sustainable Covid-19 recovery and advocated for a more joined-up approach to rebuilding low-carbon economies, such as the European Green Deal, with collaboration between governments, companies, unions and the youth movement. Jennifer Morgan, Executive Director of Greenpeace International, suggests (Whiting, 2020a):

> Government funds need to be invested in people for long-term jobs. We have an opportunity to shift coal miners who have been working in those types of jobs into other ones over time. It can't be either/or. We need to be thinking about these things together.

However, critics argue that governments advocating for green policies will face a backlash from citizens. Charles Grant, director of the Centre for European Reform thinktank, points to the *gilets jaunes* protests in France, which emerged in response to rises in fuel taxes intended to reduce carbon emissions (Harvey and Rankin, 2020). He said:

> The green agenda will meet more and more opposition as voters start to realise it will make them poorer and affect their lifestyles, and they will worry about Europe becoming less competitive than, say, India and China, which won't be going carbon-neutral.

Similarly, left wing campaigners have also criticised the European Green Deal taking issue with the 'just transition' mechanism, arguing that there is insufficient support for communities negatively affected by the shift away from fossil fuels (Varoufakis and Adler, 2020). This highlights the inherent tensions linked to the sustainable use of natural resources and the economy. Critical scholars suggest that a more inclusive, participatory and worker-led just transition is needed to build a society that lives within its ecological limits while reversing social and economic inequality.

Stop! What is your understanding of the age-old 'jobs versus environment narrative'? How can trade unions help with the transition towards a more equitable low-carbon future?

Essential reading

Harvey, F. and Rankin, J. (2020) What is the European Green Deal and will it really cost €1tn? *The Guardian*, 9 March; Whiting, K. (2020) How the world can 'reset' itself after COVID-19-according to these experts. *World Economic Forum*, 3 June; Williams, M. (2020) Coronavirus - what now: unions' grand green plan for Scottish jobs and economy. *The Herald*, 24 May; Varoufakis, Y. and Adler, D. (2020) The EU's green deal is a colossal exercise in greenwashing. *The Guardian*, 7 February. You can read more about the work of the Trades Union Congress at www.tuc.org.uk/ABetterRecovery.

Note: This feature was contributed by Andrew Bratton.

HRM and labour relations strategies

The HRM function plays a predominant role in constructing collective relations in the workplace, with HRM professionals and senior managers shaping the options and largely determining the outcomes (Hyman, 1997a). Unilateral regulation is that part of the employment relationship managed by managers alone, and it is the preferred method of managing labour around the globe (Farnham, 2015). Numerous studies have emphasised the differences in managerial behaviour and competences of managers between neoliberal market economies (NMEs) and coordinated market economies (CMEs) towards managing the collective employment relationship, in response to falling profits, public policy and employment law (Boltanski and Chiapello, 2018; van Wanrooy et al., 2013). There is no straightforward relationship between fall in profitability or increase in unemployment and different approaches to managing people and trade unions.

A labour relations strategy refers to the plans and policies chosen by HRM professionals and senior management to deal with trade unions (Gospel and Littler, 1983). The idea of choice among alternative labour relations strategies is closely linked to the concept of 'HR strategy'. The choice of a strategy towards unions is substantially influenced and constrained by a number of complex factors, including historical legacies, managerial ideology, path dependency, union power, existing bargaining structures and global competition (Hyman, 1999; Jacoby, 2005; Purcell and Sisson, 1983; Thompson and Ponak, 2005). The 'varieties of capitalism' approach (Hall and Soskice, 2001) highlighted the differences in managerial styles between neoliberal market economies – e.g. the US and Britain – and coordinated market economies – e.g. Finland and Iceland – national culture and national institutions that substantially constrain – as well as explain – the choice of a labour relations strategy.

Managerial ideology can influence choice of strategy. Unitarist and pluralist ideologies, for example, are bundles of values and assumptions pertaining to the interests of capital and labour (Budd and Bhave, 2008, p. 93). It is possible to discern, Purcell and Sisson, (1983) argue, a typology of management approaches to people and union management based on the degree to which pluralism and unitarism are emphasised. Although it is simplifying a complex phenomenon, the various strategic alternatives can, for analytical purposes, be classified into a typology of four labour relations strategies mirroring the dominance of pluralism and unitarism ideology (Thompson and Ponak, 2005): union acceptance, union resistance, union replacement and union avoidance.

The *union-acceptance* strategy is defined here as a decision by top managers to accept the legitimacy of the union role and, in turn, of collective bargaining as a process for regulating the employment relationship to support their corporate strategy. A pluralist orientation to HRM, the *union-acceptance* strategy is considered a 'sophisticated human relations' model based on a combination of individualism and collectivism (Purcell and Sisson, 1983). Union-acceptance organisations are characterised as 'partnerships' combining individual and collective processes for the management of people (Guest and Conway, 1999). Survey evidence indicates that, even in the inimical environment of the 1980s, a number of important Japanese companies chose a union-acceptance strategy, albeit in a modified form, to achieve their employment objectives (Bassett, 1987; Bratton, 1992; Wickens, 1987). This suggests that high-flexible and high-commitment HR practices and workplace unionism are not necessarily mutually exclusive and, as Bratton (1992) cited, there are a number of cases in which union representatives facilitated and contributed to the achievement of high-performance practices – teams, total quality control, just-in-time production. In 2011, however, UK survey data indicated that, overall, the number of organisations opting for a bilateral arrangement had significantly declined. In the private sector, for example, the proportion of workplaces adopting a union-acceptance/recognition strategy was only 16 per cent, compared with 44 per cent in the public sector (Kersley et al., 2006; van Wanrooy et al., 2013).

Management's choice of a union-acceptance strategy will be influenced by their assessment of whether bilateral arrangements will benefit or damage the organisation. The extant literature on the direct relationship between unions and organisational performance, however, shows inconsistent results and emphasises the difficulty of generalising across different industries, countries, years and workplace HR and labour relations practices (Verma, 2005). Pohler and Luchak (2015) argue that determining whether unions are a benefit or a detriment to an organisation will depend on whether a cooperative or competitive union–management relationship exists between the parties. Their research found that where management's intentions towards cooperation were clear and where they espouse a 'high employee-focused' strategy, the union was more likely to reciprocate with cooperative behaviours that create the potential for win–win outcomes. In contrast, the presence of a 'low employee-focused' strategy tends to send a mixed signal to the union about whether or not its interests are aligned with those of management. In this situation, the union is more likely to respond by seeking to regulate work effort and to resist the potential threat to itself and its membership, with negative implications for organisational performance.

The existing literature reports that non-union strategy is the most common form of employment relationship globally (Farnham, 2015, p. 381), and three strategies can create a non-union environment.

First, the *union-resistance* strategy describes a benign form of unitarist orientation to HRM. Although the HRM function and senior management may accept the legitimacy of their existing unions, the strategy is to contain the spread and influence of unionisation to other sections of the company's workforce, for example, a company might tolerate the unionisation of manual workers, but robustly discourage the unionisation of knowledge workers. A firm might do this by communicating to its white-collar workforce that improvements in pay and conditions are due to management initiative, not union pressure. Google, for example, has long resisted efforts to organise its engineers and other white-collar employees. The US high-tech industry has reputationally been anti-union. In 2019, an unusual event happened; after years of campaigning, more than 225 Google engineers formed a union; the Alphabet Workers Union after Google's parent company Alphabet. It follows increasing demands by workers at Google for policy changes on pay and the handling of sexual harassment. Union activism at one of the world's largest companies presented 'a rare beachhead for labour organisers in staunchly anti-union Silicon Valley' (Conger, 2021). Critical scholars on financialisation point out that MSV companies may aim deliberately to load the firm with debt as part of a union-resistance strategy (Martin and Quick, 2020). The study by Heery and Simms (2010, p. 9) gives two graphic illustrations of outright anti-union action by employers:

> Example 1: There are surveillance cameras at the only entrance of the building. Staff were afraid to even stop and speak to us at the gate. Management had previously sacked the last employee who spoke about getting a union.
>
> Example 2: When we first started the [union] campaign factory-gating, the factory manager, who is Asian, called all the Asian workers together on the shopfloor and told them that he would sack anyone who joined the union. That week, he phoned them all at home and told them again that they would be sacked.

Second, the *union-replacement* strategy describes a more belligerent unitarist approach to HRM. This strategy means that the firm's senior management have decided to achieve their strategic goals without any influence from trade unions. De-recognition refers to a decision by management to withdraw from collective bargaining in favour of unilateral arrangements for managing employment relations. The decision by Boeing, the US plane maker, to shift production entirely from its union-organised plant in Washington State, to the non-union state of South Carolina is an example of a *union-replacement* strategy. The decision would improve operational efficiency, claimed Boeing, as the non-union plant in South Carolina offers lower labour costs. Further, the decision to move across the country to the non-union state of South Carolina was 'a culmination of a years-old board-led strategy to reduce reliance on Washington State, where Boeing has had stormy relations with unions' (Johnson, 2020, p. B3). Numerous studies provide convincing evidence of an increase in de-recognition or substitution strategies (see, for example, Gall and McKay, 1994; Heery and Simms, 2010; Smith and Morton, 1993). The union-replacement scenario describes a case in which a union is no longer formally recognised by the company. Management may install a non-union employee representation arrangement as 'a deliberate attempt to pre-empt the return of a union voice' (Butler, 2009, p. 207).

Survey findings show union-replacement strategy was evident in UK workplaces with 6 per cent of all workplaces de-recognising unions between 1990 and 1998 (Millward et al., 2000). Bacon and Storey's (2000) analysis reveals a 'disjuncture between unions and "new" corporate thinking'. One manager (quoted in Bacon and Storey, 2000, p. 412) expressed the new management thinking towards unions like this:

> Collectivism via trade unions is something we want to remove ... We are not anti-union; it is just that they are incompatible with our current direction. I think we can win by edict in the current climate and drive through changes against any opposition and hope that in the end people will see there is no choice.

One interesting aspect of Bacon and Storey's study is the evidence suggesting that British management did not take full advantage of its power. Two reasons are given for this. First, the 'heavy threats' to the unions contributed to higher levels of mistrust of management. This observation can be linked to the importance of the psychological contract. With this in mind, Bacon and Storey's (2000, p. 423) note that managers were 'reluctant to sacrifice employee trust' is important. The second reason managers did not use their power to de-recognise the unions was because the very threat of such action alone 'allowed managers to introduce many of the changes they had wanted to drive through' in the workplace (Bacon and Storey, 2000, pp. 413–14). Overall, then, although most managers have an enduring preference for non-union relations, pragmatic considerations in these cases deterred the adoption of a union-replacement strategy.

The third strategy, *union avoidance*, is defined here as a decision to maintain the status quo of a non-union workforce by either closing or threatening to relocate the business or by barring union members from employment, often referred to as 'blacklisting'. The traditional unitarist company Wal-Mart prioritises individualised HR practices and the individual management of its staff but it is also known to fiercely oppose unionisation. In 2004, 190 Canadian workers in Jonquière, Quebec voted to unionise with the United Food and Commercial Workers Union. The Jonquière establishment was the first successful unionisation of an entire Wal-Mart store in North America. Shortly thereafter, Wal-Mart closed the store. After years of litigation, the Supreme Court of Canada ruled that the closure was an unlawful effect to avoid union recognition. The Supreme Court of Canada upheld the original arbitrator's decision, which read: 'It was in fact reasonable to find that a reasonable employer would not close an establishment that "was performing very well" and whose "objectives were being met" to such an extent that bonuses were being promised.' (Marin, 2014).

Refusing to employ known union members is an alternative union avoidance tactic. In 2016, for example, major UK construction companies, including Robert McAlpine and Balfour Beatty, to avoid going to trial, agreed compensation and issued an 'unreserved and sincere' apology in the high court to hundreds of building workers for putting them on an illegal blacklist and denying them work for two decades (Boffey, 2016b, p. 10). In his penetrating account of the collapse of Carillion, one of Britain's largest construction companies, Wylie (2020, p. 140–2) details evidence that the company's HR management was responsible for 'blacklisting people'. In 2016, over a decade after the supposed end of Carillion blacklisting, the company was prepared to pay out more than £10 million for its 'blacklisting crimes'. Legal strategies to avoid unions include HR practices that give employees a 'voice' (see Chapter 10) and/or better employment conditions to negate the need for unions. The iconic retailer Marks & Spencer exemplifies what can be described as a 'soft' union-avoidance strategy. The company's individualised approach to HRM offers favourable working conditions to deter the need for staff to unionise. However, from an employee's perspective M&S's strategy has limits. In 2020, in response to a 'material shift in trade' due to the coronavirus, the retailer cut 7,000 jobs across its stores (Onita, 2020),

In Britain, between 1998 and 2004, a period that was relatively favourable to trade unions, there was no single dominant labour relations strategy – 'support, suppression and substitution' were all evident (Heery and Simms, 2010). The significance of this debate for labour relations strategies is this: the HRM model is not restricted to a 'union-exclusion' environment. Guest (1995) analyses the strategic options in terms of labour relations that are available to management, the 'new realism' option appearing to illustrate the case of HRM and labour relations operating in tandem. Pre-Brexit, it was argued that British labour relations have been 'Europeanized' (Hyman, 2010), and managers were beginning to take a more proactive approach towards union involvement in workplace decision-making. However, Hyman (2015, p. 269) argues that globalised financial capitalism 'is one of the grave diggers of social democracy'. He suggests that the precipitous decline of union organisation over the past 30 years is 'in part ideological in causation' (p. 273). As an important constituent of social democracy, the travails of trade unions will fluctuate as HRM labour strategies change depending on the ideological and economic climate. In addition, different labour strategies can be applied to different firms within the same industrial sector and to different groups of workers within the same organisation. More broadly, the economic climate in Western economies, such as Britain in the context of Brexit and the recession at the time of writing, will compel firms, as illustrated by retailer Marks & Spencer, to make strategic choices about their business operations and labour relations strategies and policies in response to the economic and public health crises.

Global HRM

Do police unions lead to more violence?

Source: Alex Young on Unsplash

Growing controversy surrounds the influence of labour unions on police behaviour in the United States. As protests over the killing of George Floyd spread across the nation, protesters, community organisers and elected officials increasingly called for defunding the police as a way to end police violence. Critics argue that unions are one of the biggest barriers to organisational reform and insulate officers from discipline for misconduct (Greenhouse, 2020). However, collective bargaining tends to increase wages and has a positive effect on training levels, which could improve law enforcement behaviour.

Since the 1960s, when police unions first became like traditional unions and won the right to bargain collectively, they have had a controversial history. Studies suggest that their political and bargaining power has enabled them to shield police from both public and departmental accountability by multiple layers of contractual and legislative protection. Walker's (2008) research highlights that virtually all of the published research on the impact of police unions regards them as having a negative effect, particularly on accountability, innovation and police-community relations. A recent study found that extending collective-bargaining rights to Florida sheriffs' deputies resulted in a substantial increase in violent incidents of misconduct (Dharmapala et al., 2019). Police contracts have also made it harder to hold officers accountable for improper use of force or other misconduct. For example, a study of police-union contracts in 82 cities found that most required departments to erase disciplinary records, in some cases after six months (Levinson, 2017).

The string of police killings captured on mobile phones increased public unease with police unions. After the killing of George Floyd, many protesters, and even some unions, including the Writers Guild of America, East (WGAE), have called on the AFL-CIO, the nation's main labour federation, to expel the International Union of Police Associations, which represents a hundred thousand law-enforcement officers. Hamilton Nolan, elected WGEA council member who voted to approve the resolution said: 'The motivation for the current campaign to take police unions out of the labour movement is to *empower* working people by ensuring that the AFL-CIO is not forced to represent a slice of the workforce that is structurally opposed to its broader mission of freedom and equality for the sort of people most likely to be harassed by the police' (Nolan, 2020). The question now is whether police unions will be receptive to the message that they should not think of only protecting their members, but they should also think of the original purpose of labour unions: protecting all workers – in other words, protecting the public.

Stop! How should police union leaders respond to the criticism that they enable and conceal abuses of power? What are some practical steps that police unions could take to improve accountability and police-community relations?

Essential reading

Dharmapala, D., McAdams, R. H. and Rappaport, J. (2019) Collective bargaining rights and police misconduct: evidence from Florida. *University of Chicago Coase-Sandor Institute for Law & Economics Research Paper* (831); Greenhouse, S. (2020) How police unions enable and conceal abuses of power. *The New Yorker*, 18 June; Hager, E. and Li, W. (2020) White US police union bosses protect officers accused of racism. *The Guardian*, 10 June; Levinson, R. (2017) Across the US, police contracts shield officers from scrutiny and discipline. *Reuters*, 13 January; Nolan, H. (2020) It's time to kick police unions out of the labor movement. They aren't allies. *The Guardian*, 13 June.

Note: This feature was contributed by Andrew Bratton.

Trade unions

Most students using this textbook will be probably be surprised to learn that, four decades ago, trade unions in Britain were considered to be powerful social institutions that merited close study. Indeed, an eminent labour relations scholar referred to trade unions as 'one of the most powerful forces shaping our society' (Clegg, 1976, p. 1). This section examines recent developments in trade union membership in the belief that a knowledge of these changes is important for a better understanding of the employment relationship, HRM and income inequality. But first, we pose the question: Why do workers join trade unions?

Understanding why employees join trade unions

Workers join unions for a wide variety of reasons (Schnabel, 2003). First, they may be motivated to join a union for *economic* reasons. In a classic study, Sidney and Beatrice Webb (1911) suggested that workers' pursuit of improved pay and conditions expressed a basic motive to tilt the balance of power towards labour and reduce domination by their employers. Contemporary surveys of UK workplaces have found that workers' motive for joining a union was for economic reasons (Waddington and Whitston, 1997). Second, workers may also join a union because of perceived and actual extreme income equality (Checchi et al., 2010). Equity theory posits that workers will engage in social action to the extent that they perceive the situation to be equitable (Bratton, 2021).

Third, in addition to economic and equity rationales, workers join unions because they want to gain a *voice* in decision-making in their workplace. North America and UK survey findings suggest that workers' perceptions of the imbalance of power between 'them' (the management) and 'us' (the workers) necessitate some form of collective voice or representation in the form of a union (see Chapter 10). Fourth, in a democratic society, workers may make a decision to unionise in order to lobby politicians for political action on work-related or societal improvements. The participation of unions in civil society can also help to bring about the demise of authoritarian regimes. The democratisation of Poland, for example, was led by the trade union Solidarity (Frost and Taris, 2005, p. 40).

Reflective question

What factors make unions relevant today? What factors make them irrelevant? And what do employees want from unions?

Source: T.H. Chia on Unsplash

It's the duty of every employer to ensure the health, safety and welfare of all workers. Making sure an employer adheres to the Health & safety at Work Act 1974 is just one of the issues that unions campaign for.

Trade unions in action

In a non-unionised workplace, managers have flexibility in designing work, selecting, promoting and training staff, and determining rewards and other HR policies and practices, but much of this can change when workers join a union. After recognising the union, representatives from union and management negotiate a collective agreement that spells out the details of the employment relationship that will be jointly determined. This can typically include establishing some control over core HR policies and practices, including rewards, recruitment and selection, employee learning and development and health, safety and well-being:

- First and foremost, unions seek to counter downward pressures on wages caused by fluctuations in the labour market, and to control *rewards* and attempt to maximise the pay side of the wage–effort contract.
- Perhaps most controversially, the whole practice of *individual performance appraisal* (IPA) poses challenges to the unions. The central tenet of traditional unionism has been the collectivist culture, namely the insistence on pay according to the same definite standard and its application in the workplace. Such collectivist goals have resulted in unions strongly resisting workforce atomisation and performance appraisal based on individual performance.
- In the area of *recruitment and selection*, unions, in some industries at least (for example, construction, film, theatre and health care), may have some control over external recruiting.
- Unions also take an active interest in work-related *learning* and *employee development*, trying to ensure that learning opportunities are distributed equitably and that employers adhere to the principle of maintained earnings during training.
- Union goals can extend to issues of sexual harassment (see Chapter 10). In 2018, for example, more than 20,000 Google workers staged a walkout to protest how the company handled sexual harassment. Grievances beyond pay were instrumental in forming a new union by more than 250 Google engineers (Conger, 2021).
- Occupational *health hazards*, the *effects of Covid-19* and environmental pollution disproportionately affect those in the lower social class strata, the working class. Unions have a long history of campaigning and negotiating for the removal of toxic substances and for healthier and safer workplaces.

Union membership

In the European Union, substantial cross-country variation in unionisation levels remain, but around one in four workers are a member of a trade union. However, union membership and density rates have declined in most EU countries (Vandaele, 2019). However, nowhere in the OECD has union membership fallen more than in the US, where in 2019 fewer than 10 per cent of the labour force are union members (Rubin, 2020). A feature of the data is that European unionisation reflect shared political-legal characteristics that shape each country's labour relations system and therefore the countries can be grouped together (Gumbrell-McCormick and Hyman, 2013). Table 9.1 shows such country groupings, with the averages in trade union density and collective bargaining coverage in 2017–18.

Table 9.1 Average trade union membership, union density and collective bargaining coverage in selective European countries, 2018

Country	Union membership (in millions)	Union density (%)	Collective bargaining coverage (%)	Productivity levels[1]
Denmark	1.7	67	79	81
Finland	1.3	62	87	67
Iceland	0.2	90	92	69
Norway	1.3	51	73	93
Sweden	3.0	66	90	73
Germany	6.4	17	58	72
Netherlands	1.1	17	84	74
France	2.6	11	98	74
Italy	6.0	34	80	59
Spain	2.3	17	87	56
Ireland	0.5	24	32	104
UK	6.4	23	29	63

Source: Vandaele (2019), Table 1, p. 21.

Note: (1) Labour productivity levels, 2018, expressed as US dollar to allow international comparisons, OECD Stats.

PART 4

The Nordic countries all share the highest rates of union density and bargaining coverage. In contrast, neoliberal market economies (NMEs), such as Ireland and the UK, are characterised by voluntarist labour relations systems, and share low rates of union density and bargaining coverage.

Decline in union membership 'is not ubiquitous', however (Vandaele, 2019, p. 6). Indeed, in some of the selected European countries listed here, a rise in union membership over the last decade has been recorded, for example in Spain (+0.2%), France (+2.5%), Norway (+9.6%), Italy (+10.7%) and Iceland (+10.9%).

While data on union membership corresponds to the number of employees belonging to a union, trade union density expresses its proportion. As Vandaele (2019) points out, this ratio is likely overestimated, as the denominator does not include all workers 'relevant' for unions, such as the self-employed and workers in the gig economy. Table 9.1 shows union density ranges from a low 11 per cent in France to 90 per cent in Iceland. It also shows labour productivity levels presented as GDP per capita and in a common currency from 56 in Spain to 104 in Ireland. Trade union data matters. Union density is a general indicator for comparing the bargaining power of workers across industries or occupations (Sullivan, 2009; Vandaele, 2019; Visser, 2006).

Despite the country differences in union membership and density, there are similarities in unionisation across countries in terms of their gender and whether they are employed in the private or public sectors. Union membership among women has marginally increased in most countries, which is related to the proliferation of employment in personal, public sector occupations (Vandaele, 2019; Visser 2019;). Whereas, union members are predominantly concentrated in the public sector, in contrast, the private services sector is characterised by low unionisation rates.

Vandaele's (2019) analysis corroborates that union membership levels have been in decline in Europe since the 1990s, however, the downward trend is especially pronounced in Britain as shown in

Source: Getty Images/Jose Luiz Pelaez Inc.

Union membership among women has marginally increased in most EU countries, which is related to the proliferation of employment in personal, public sector occupations.

Table 9.2. In 1979, when the late Margaret Thatcher was first elected Prime Minister of Britain, union membership stood at over 12 million. Since then, membership has fallen by over 6 million, or 49.9 per cent. In 2019, union membership in Britain stood at 6.44 million, which amounts to 23.5 per cent of the workforce (Roper, 2020).

Table 9.3 describes the pattern of union membership across private and public sectors of the British economy from 1996 to 2018. The trajectory of union presence in private sector workplaces shows a downward trend, from 36 per cent in 1996 to 32 per cent in 2018, and the demographic phenomenon of just 4.4 per cent of 16 to 24-year-olds being union members (Gall, 2020). The majority of union presence is in private manufacturing, rather than private services. The trade union presence in public sector establishments over the two decades remained relatively stable, falling from 90 per cent in 1996 to 88 per cent in 2018. Similar to economies in the EU, union membership is predominantly concentrated in the public sector, including local government, education and health, a feature which mirrors a rising proportion of women within unions. In both private manufacturing and services, the decline was 'more substantial in small workplaces' and among traditionally 'male-dominated' workplaces (Millward et al., 2000, p. 86). Unsurprisingly, workers on zero-hours contracts and part-time workers are less likely to be unionised than workers with an open-ended, permanent contract (OECD, 2019).

Table 9.2 Average union membership in the UK, 1971–2019

5-year annual average	Members (000s)	% of employed
1971–75	11,548 (+1.5)	50.0
1976–80	12,916 (+1.5)	55.9
1981–85	11,350 (−3.5)	49.1
1986–90	10,299 (−1.7)	44.6
1991–95	8,740 (−4.0)	37.8
1996–2000	7,910 (−9.5)	34.2
2003–05	7,772 (−1.7)	33.6
2006–11	7,436 (−4.3)	28.0
2011–15	6,463 (−13.1)	25.0
2015–19	6, 440 (−0.4)	23.5

Source: Data from UK Department for Business, Energy & Industrial Strategy, (May 2020) and the EIRO website.

Table 9.3 UK average union density from 1996 to 2018, by broad sector

	Percentages						
	1996	**2000**	**2004**	**2008**	**2012**	**2016**	**2018**
All establishments	31	30	29	28	26	24	23
Sector of ownership							
Private sector[1]	36	42	39	38	35	33	32
Public sector	90	93	92	92	91	88	88

Note: (1) This table only refers to the 'private' sector – both manufacturing and services. Figures are rounded.
Source: Statista (2020).

Interpreting union decline

Although the general pattern clearly indicates that union membership and union density across Europe, and in Britain particularly, have fallen continually since 1979, there is a debate over the precise scale of the trend and the cause of union decline. Relevant here is the well-known statistical mantra, 'correlation is not causation' (Green, 2012). This means that just because two things correlate does not necessarily mean that one causes the other. Therefore, just because the emergence of HRM coincided with the decline of UK union membership does not mean HRM *caused* the decline of organised labour. An early influential study by Bain and Price (1983) explained the decline in unionisation by: (1) fluctuations in the labour market at macro-level; (2) public policy; (3) the restructuring of work; (4) the outsourcing of manufacturing to low-wage economies; and (5) employer policy. Vandaele's (2019) explanation adds normative attitudes towards unionism at individual and societal level and the 'greying' of trade unions. These studies provide plausible explanations, but it is difficult to disentangle the relative importance of each of the determinants in interpreting aggregate union decline across Europe.

Within the macro-economic framework, a plausible explanation of union decline is the effect of globalisation and financialisation. Financialisation in the economy, particularly the doctrine of MSV, has had dysfunctional outcomes for workers and trade unions. Financial practices such as using profits to buy back company shares, high corporate debt, non-production activities, for example, the leasing of motor vehicles, undermine union wage-bargaining because labour's structural power – the ability to withdraw their labour – stems from production wealth creation (Davis and Kim, 2015; Thompson, 2013). The outsourcing of productive activities, as part of restructuring for maximising shareholder value, changes a host of management strategies and governance structures (Cushen and Thompson, 2012; Davis and Kim, 2015; Froud et al., 2000) The MSV logic intensifies the process of organisational 'disaggregation', leading to stratified and atomised workforces. The process thereby makes it difficult for unions to engage in effective wage bargaining because their direct employer might only have a small profit margin, and collective unity among dispersed sub-contractors is more difficult (Martin and Quick, 2020, p. 28). In parallel to the creation of free trade zones and the process of financialisation, public policy towards trade unions in Britain was overtly hostile and changes to labour relations helped to further reduce union density and the associated undercutting of wages (Freeman and Pelletier, 1990). Related is the change to trade union law prohibiting compulsory unionism – the 'closed shop' – among workers (Wright, 1996). This type of analysis is, however, fraught with problems: it is difficult to disentangle cause and effect when dealing with trade union law (Disney, 1990).

Organisational restructuring impacts unionisation levels. Strong union access to and presence in the workplace are essential for unionisation (Toubøl and Jensen, 2014). The degree of access is associated with organisational size, and it is no coincidence that union members are more likely to be employed in large organisations. Social custom and organisational culture eases union recruitment efforts based on reputational effects – not conforming to the custom may lead to a reputation loss (Visser, 2002). Employers' labour relations and HR policies and practices will significantly influence workers' access to union representation. As noted, the strategic de-recognition of trade unions has been associated with the growing adoption of the 'Americanized' HRM model (Brown et al., 1997). Hyman (2015) argues that part of the neoliberal agenda is an 'ideological revolution' against unions. Similar arguments are made by Toubøl and Jensen (2014) and Boltanski and Chiapello (2018) that the ideological and political attitudes of workers influence their likelihood to join a union.

Levels of unionisation are strongly influenced by employers' corporate strategy to outsource productive activities and HR practices such as, for example, the shift to precarious employment contracts. Strong workplace access to unions helps union recruitment, so, unsurprisingly, union membership tends to be low among workers on part-time or precarious contracts (Vandaele, 2019). The challenges of organising precarious workers by existing unions (in Britain, for example, the GMB, UNISON and Unite) has focused attention on the organising efforts of new 'grassroots' unions, such as the Cleaners and Allied Independent Workers' Union (CAIWU – established 2016). Gall (2020), for example, argues that the contrast between the 'long-standing' and 'new' unions raises a number of issues: that the long-standing unions are too diverse (e.g. Unite) or too specific (e.g. RMT) in their memberships to have prioritised organising precarious workers; that precarious workers are too resource intensive for existing unions to devote time and resources organising these workers; and that long-standing unions are 'too bureaucratic' to organise precarious workers. Furthermore, the 'Americanised' HRM model is associated with individualised reward based on individual performance (see Chapter 8), as opposed to the collective determination of reward. Strong employer support for centralised collective bargaining over pay and conditions is also associated with higher levels of unionisation and institutionalised workplace collaboration (Rasmussen & Høgedahl, 2020).

Finally, over the past ten years in most European countries, fewer young people (below the age 30) have joined a union. This has contributed to the 'greying' of trade unions. The generation gap in unionisation is important for trade union renaissance or 'revitalisation' (Hyman, 2007) because, as others argue, it is more likely for a worker to join a union when they are young and entering the workplace than later on. Put differently, 'the window of opportunity for unions to organise workers becomes decidedly smaller, the older they get' (Budd, 2010, and cited by Vandaele, 2019, p. 24).

Trade union structure

The word 'structure' in relation to trade unions denotes the 'external shape' of trade unions (Hyman, 1975) or job territories – the areas of the labour market from which trade unions aim to recruit. We should note that the word '*trade*' unions is an anachronism and it would be better to adopt the North American term 'labour' unions. However, we justify the use of the term 'trade unions', in part, in recognition of the terminology used in UK employment law (Burchill, 2014). There are many variants of trade union structure within countries, traditionally expressed as ideal types: craft (e.g. tinsmiths), industrial (e.g. mining) general (e.g. stevedores) and white-collar (e.g. technicians) unions. The wave of union mergers has reduced the number of unions from 237 in 1999 to 142 in 2019, which has resulted in the formation of 'super-unions' (Ebbinghaus and Waddington, 2000). The union Unite, for example, with a membership of over 1.23 million is the largest union in Britain. Unite was created in 2007 through the merger of Amicus and the Transport and General Workers Union, with Amicus itself being created in 2002 through the merger of the Manufacturing Science and Finance Union and the Amalgamated Engineering and Electrical Union (Clark, 2019). The expectation was that the new enlarged union would give working people the largest resources in industrial disputes. In explaining merger activity, formal union links to the British Labour Party, what is called a 'political logic', are also influential (Waddington and Whitston, 1994).

The three TUC-affiliated 'super-unions' – Unite, UNISON, GMB – with a combined membership of over 3 million members accounted for almost 50 per cent of the entire union membership. Mergers have created 'chaotic' union structures that can seem bewildering and incomprehensible (Hyman, 1997b). The major structural characteristic of British trade unions in 2020 was the predominance of 'conglomerate' unions, that is, large individual unions whose members were distributed over a wide range of different industries, a trend evident among European trade unions (see, for example, Ebbinghaus and Waddington, 2000).

Collective bargaining

The previous sections have examined the principal 'actors' in labour relations: management and the unions. We will now focus our attention on a central activity – collective bargaining – that regulates the employment relationship for over 40 million employees in the EU, plus Britain. The extent of collective bargaining coverage is an alternative indicator for measuring the influence of trade unions and their effectiveness in labour markets (Hayter and Visser, 2018). We define collective bargaining here as:

> An institutional system of formal negotiation in which the making, interpretation and administration of rules, as well as the application of statutory controls affecting the employment relationship, are decided within union–management negotiating committees.

PART 4

Several important points arise from this definition. First, formal collective bargaining, often referred to as wage-bargaining, is a process through which representatives of the union and management *jointly* determine some of the rules and regulations appertaining to the employment contract. Second, there are two types of rules: *substantive* and *procedural*. Substantive rules establish terms and conditions of employment (e.g. pay), whereas procedural rules regulate the way in which substantive rules are made and interpreted, and indicate how workplace conflicts (see Chapter 10) are to be resolved. Third, the parties negotiating the collective agreement also *enforce* the agreement. Collective agreements are, with a few exceptions, not regarded as contracts of legal enforcement between the parties (see Davies and Freedland, 1994). Fourth, informal social relations help to shape and lubricate the formal collective employment relationship. The influential Donovan Commission reported that Britain had both a 'formal' and 'informal' system of labour relations, and the latter was created 'by the actual behaviour of managers, shop stewards and workers' (Donovan, 1968, p. 12). Recent research (see, for instance, Findlay et al., 2009; Sennett, 2012) has shed further light on the role and importance of informal social relations and the complexity of the interdependencies, levels of trust and reciprocal obligations that define and lubricate the formal negotiating process itself. Although informal bonds and workplace friendships do not eliminate conflict, they help to create civility in the organisation.

Collective bargaining structure

The structure of collective bargaining is the framework within which negotiations take place and defines the scope of the employers and employees covered by the collective agreement. In Britain, for much of the post-1945 period, there was no single uniform structure of collective bargaining, the major structural characteristic of the system being diversity. Collective bargaining was conducted at several levels – workplace, corporate or industry-wide. In practice, survey evidence showed that collective bargaining structures were closely linked with business structures and 'profit centres'. Industry-wide collective agreements covering core pay, hours and holidays items were, however, unlike in Nordic economies, never dominant in Britain (Hutton, 2015a, p. 184), In the early 1980s, around 70 per cent of workers had their pay determined by union–management bargaining. But from

1980–84 onwards, collective bargaining coverage started to decline, and this has continued into the twenty-first century. In 2020, the pay and employment conditions of the majority of employees in the UK are not collectively negotiated.

The demise of pay bargaining is a significant feature of the 'transformation' in UK employment relations (Millward et al., 2000, p. 234). Surveys show that the proportion of UK employees covered by collective bargaining in 2018 was only 29 per cent (Table 9.1). However, collective bargaining coverage is not even across the economy. The proportion of public sector employees covered by collective bargaining is 64 per cent, compared with only 16 per cent in the private sector. Therefore, coverage in the sector has diminished to 'a patchy and ... shrinking minority of workers' (Brown and Nash, 2008, p. 102). As Brown (2010, p. 258) observes, the demise in collective bargaining coverage has meant that, for the vast majority of private sector workers, 'the only cushion against the vagaries of an open labour market has been provided by the state' through the statutory national minimum wage. The latest findings on the scope of collective bargaining in the private sector are strongly reminiscent of those published in earlier WERS studies (see, for instance, van Wanrooy et al., 2013).

The steep decline in collective bargaining coverage is largely confined to Britain. Across the EU, the proportion of employees covered by collective bargaining in the 27 EU states plus Norway varies from over 90 per cent to 15 per cent. Countries with a high coverage, associated with multi-employer bargaining, in general show stability, except for Greece (-43%), which witnessed a drastic decline in coverage due to legislative changes. In the periods 2000–09 and 2010–16, bargaining coverage has only declined slightly in most EU member states with medium to low coverage marked by either less-dominant systems of multi-employer bargaining or single-employer bargaining. An exception to this pattern is Ireland (-10 per cent), featuring a decrease of ten percentage points (Vandaele, 2019, p. 16). As Table 9.1 shows, the countries at the top of the table either have high levels of union membership and density, as in Iceland (92 per cent), Sweden (90 per cent), Finland (87 per cent) and Denmark (79 per cent), or have legal structures which ensure that collective agreements have a wide coverage (ETUI, 2020). In the countries at the bottom of the table, for instance Ireland and Britain, company level bargaining dominates.

Collective bargaining is the *raison d'être* of trade unionism, but the latest data underscores how little involved unions are in influencing the employment contract in twenty-first-century Britain. Similar arguments about the decline of union membership have been put forward to explain the sustained collapse in collective bargaining. Brown (2010), for example, cites the destabilising forces of globalisation. However, globalisation does not fully explain why collective bargaining remains relatively stable in EU member states. Others point to the shift in power towards management. As Hyman (1975, p. 26) explains, 'In every workplace there exists an invisible frontier of control ... a frontier which is defined and redefined in a continuous process of pressure and counter-pressure, conflict and accommodation, overt and tacit struggle'. The absence of support from the state has been a significant contributing factor to the diminishing significance of collective bargaining as a means of regulating the employment relationship (Sullivan, 2010).

The collective agreement: an overview

The outcome of wage-bargaining is a collective agreement that provides for the terms and conditions of employment of those employees covered by the agreement, also specifying the procedures, for instance the handling of grievances and disciplinary action (see Chapter 10), that will govern the relationship between the signatories. In Britain, the terms of the collective agreement are binding in law on the parties if they are incorporated into the individual contract of employment (see Emir, 2014, for a legal discussion on incorporation). For management, the formal negotiation of a collective agreement is an instrument for rewriting the 'rules' governing the workplace. For trade unions, the process of negotiating a collective agreement offers an opportunity for union representatives to become 'embedded' in workplace governance (Findlay et al., 2009). A key determinant of the contents of the agreement is the balance of power between the parties (Brown, 2010).

Digital Spotlight

Bargaining disruptive technological change: a case of mutual gains?

Technological advancements have long impacted on labour relations. On 1 December 1913, for example, Henry Ford introduced the first moving assembly line for the mass production of an automobile. Ford's innovation had the effect of drastically reducing the average time it took to build a car (Manokha, 2017). However, it also had repercussions for labour relations within the company: workers struggled to keep pace and employee turnover increased dramatically. It has been reported that, in order to raise the headcount by 100, Ford had to hire 963 staff to account for the number that rapidly resigned (Manokha, 2017). Over a century later, as technology has advanced at a seemingly exponential rate, so too have concerns regarding its impact on labour relations. An area of particular attention has been wearable technologies. Wearables can take a number of forms, including smart watches, smart glasses, hearables (wireless in-ear devices that can be used for communication, medical monitoring or fitness tracking) and exoskeletons/exosuits that support the body. It has been suggested that these products can enhance workers' physical and perceptual abilities, giving them 'superhuman strength, endurance, vision, hearing, and awareness' (Schatsky and Kumar, 2018). In addition, many employers put forward the argument that wearables can help protect the health and safety of workers (Nicastro, 2018). It is this rationale that has been demonstrated to be most convincing for employees, alongside the use of incentives such as money, gift cards or time off (Jacobs et al., 2019).

The next step after a device that sits *on* the skin, is one that is inserted *under* it. Such a suggestion no longer rests firmly in the realm of science fiction. In July 2017, it was reported that employees at a Wisconsin-based technology company could choose to have a radio-frequency identification (RFID) microchip embedded between their thumb and index finger (Astor, 2017). The device would allow them to swipe into the office or pay for food in the cafeteria with a wave of their hand. The initiative was not mandatory, but more than 50 of the company's 80 employees volunteered (Astor, 2017). There has been widespread criticism of such developments. In addition to fears about data security, Alessandro Acquisti of Carnegie Mellon University notes that technology designed for one purpose may later be used for another (Astor, 2017). A microchip implanted to allow an employee effortless access to and egress from their workplace could subsequently be used to track the length of their lunch or bathroom breaks, without their knowledge or consent. The TUC expressed concerns that employees could be coerced into being microchipped, adding that, 'microchipping would give bosses even more power and control over their workers', while the Confederation of British Industry (CBI), lamented that firms 'should be concentrating on rather more immediate priorities and focusing on engaging their employees' (Kollewe, 2018). Moreover, the surge in homeworking during the coronavirus pandemic has seen a growing demand for surveillance software (Jones, 2020).

Stop! Should trade unions seek to negotiate clauses that protect their members against RFID chips being implanted by employers and other surveillance technology? Why/why not?

Essential reading

Jacobs, J. V., Hettinger, L. J., Huang, Y-H., Jeffries, S., Lesch, M. F., Simmons, L. A., Verma, S. K. and Willets, J. L. (2019) Employee acceptance of wearable technology in the workplace. *Applied Ergonomics*, *78*: 148–56.

Note: This feature was contributed by Laura Steele.

PART 4

Critiquing labour relations

The dominant narrative of HRM offers few meaningful insights into the political dimension of the employment relationship, the distribution of power between capital and labour and employer strategies designed to create a non-union workplace. Earlier chapters have emphasised that central to strategic HRM is the connectedness of all HR practices in alignment with the organisation's strategic goals. In this context, strategic labour relations, designed to secure the 'new pay' strategy of individualised performance-based pay, is a core component in any inclusive HR strategy. Further, a critical interpretation of an HR strategy that undermines workplace trade unionism and influence can be viewed as playing a crucial role in constituting an atomised 'neoliberal self' (Boltanski and Chiapello, 2018).

Critical labour relations scholars view trade unions as a countervailing power against management-driven work and systems of pay. Moreover, in any democratic society, the freedom for workers to bargain collectively is a core human right (Adams, 2006). In Canada, for example, the Charter of Rights protects the right to collective bargaining in the workplace. In a landmark judgement in Canada in 2007, Chief Justice Beverley McLachlin and Mr Justice Louis LeBel (quoted by Makin, 2007, p. A4) wrote:

> The right to bargain collectively with an employer enhances the human dignity, liberty and autonomy of workers by giving them the opportunity to influence the establishment of workplace rules and thereby gain some control over a major aspect of their lives, namely their work.

Collective bargaining therefore is a form of workplace democracy (Adams, 2006). The precipitous decline in union density and wage-bargaining coverage provides the backcloth for a critical analysis of union density and influence over management decisions and public policy considered detrimental to the interests of labour. In terms of public policy, post-2008 wage austerity has been a feature of labour markets in Germany, France, the UK and the US (Flassbeck and Lapavitsas, 2015; Piketty, 2014; Stiglitz, 2015). Alongside wage austerity, there has also been 'stratospheric levels' of income inequality, with top UK executives now earning 117 times more than the average full-time worker (Thomas, 2020).

Building on the disconnected capitalism thesis (DCT), there is a growing body of critical work that interrogates the dynamics and connections between financialisation in the economy and longer-term trends such as income inequality and the decreasing power and influence of trade unions in wage-bargaining. The financial practice of growing corporate debt in order to invest in share buybacks or to speculate on the financial markets is, arguably, a strategy designed to justify the company's inability to increase pay or invest in human capital. As Martin and Quick (2020, p. 14) observe, debt loading 'weakens workers' position when bargaining for better wages and conditions, or indeed, make it hard to bargain at all'. Increasing corporate debt can also undermine the viability of the whole company with subsequent job losses (Wylie, 2020). Critical orthodox explanations of growing income inequality emphasise changes in the labour market and downward pressures on wages as part of the financialisation phenomenon. It is argued that the doctrine of MSV is a central cause of income inequality and pay gulf between corporate elites and workers. The massive gap between CEO earnings and the pay of an average worker is the cornerstone of social inequality. Part of the inequality narrative, at least in the US and Britain, is the emasculation of trade unions and the collapse of wage-bargaining over the last four decades. Kumhof et al. (2012) pinpointed the rise of inequality to the decline of collective bargaining and its effect on real wages. This, Hutton (2015a, p. 180) observes, 'is what hap-

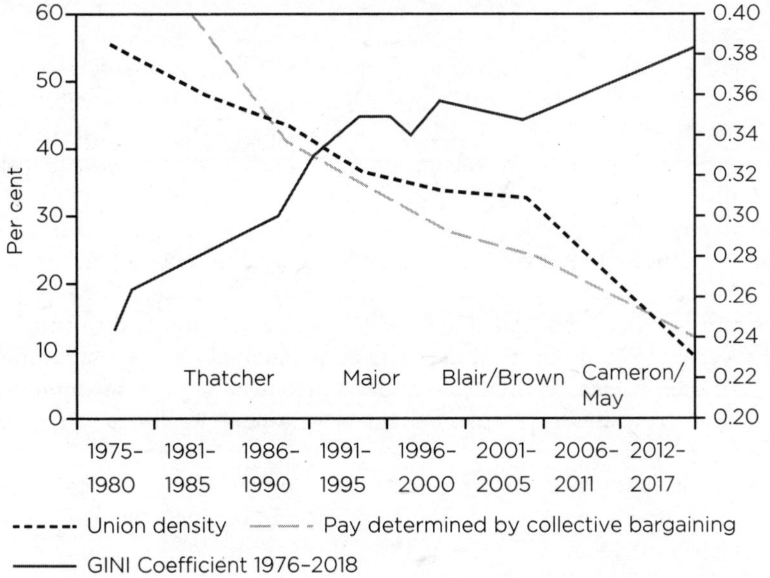

Figure 9.1 UK trade union density, private sector collective bargaining and rising income inequality

Sources: Millward et al. (2000); Kersley et al. (2006); van Wanrooy et al. (2013); TUC Research Bulletin (July 2011); The Equality Trust (2015).

PART 4

pened: the fall in union density ... was associated with an accumulative decline in real wages 7 per cent below what they would otherwise have been'. But, the decisive decline of organised labour has meant that effectively there has been no substantial countervailing challenge to MSV from trade unions (Wylie, 2020).

The available data shows a correlation between reduced levels of union density and income inequality (Ewing and Hendy, 2013). Figure 9.1 shows, between 1979 and 2018, a correlation between falling levels of union density and pay bargaining and a widening gap between the incomes of rich and poor in the UK (Wilkinson and Pickett, 2010). Since 1979, income inequality, as shown by the Gini coefficient, has increased significantly, levelling in the 1990s and, after a slight fall, reaching a new peak of 0.38 in 2017. As Wilkinson and Pickett, 2010, p. 239) observe, 'Few other developed countries have shown quite such dramatic increases over this period.'

The cumulative decline in collective bargaining coverage and real wages partly explains why the UK, along with the US, is one of the lowest ranked economies for equality. The concept of distributive justice – the outcomes and allocations emerging from organisational processes – is useful to help us understand the possible reaction to extreme income inequality (Bratton, 2020). Faced with the triple crises of the global pandemic, the climate emergency and Britain's deep recession, critical perspectives on the role of HRM and labour relations have to analyse the destructive contradiction between unsustainable short-term 'quarterly focused' business strategies that destroy the ecosystem and those which partner with trade union and environmental movements in the quest to achieve a *just* low-carbon, eco-friendly economy (see, Klein, 2015).

Summary

This chapter has examined the political dimension of the employment relationship and the distribution of power between unions and employers. It has highlighted the transformation in labour relations in Britain and its response to the country's economic and socio-political context. The analysis shows the interface between models of HRM and labour relations in a framework that emphasises, on the one hand, pluralist, trade union recognition and collectivised HR policies and practices and, on the other, employment relations, denoting unitarism and individualised HR practices.

The analysis shows that there is a remarkable decline in trade union membership, union density and collective bargaining in the post-industrial context. To a great extent this can be attributed to the influence of pro-market neoliberal ideology, the financialisation of the economy and the doctrine of maximising shareholder value, the long-term contraction of the manufacturing sector brought about and pursued by British capital interests, and the deregulation of the economy and labour markets to give greater flexibility and freedom to managers to respond to changes in the organisation's external context.

The decline in unionisation and collective bargaining coverage has coincided with a commensurate rise in non-unionism. A non-union workplace and individualised HR practices is the norm in British workplaces. The argument here is that this shift in power towards employers makes it more likely that managers will be tempted to take the short-term 'low road' HRM to profitability that, amongst other things, can potentially violate the psychological contract.

Review questions

1. What might be management's motives for choosing (a) a 'union acceptance' or (b) a 'union replacement' strategy? What are the potential benefits and disadvantages of each strategy?
2. How is collective bargaining in Britain different to that found in EU economies? To what extent does the financialisation of the economy undermine wage-bargaining?
3. Can union agency, together with coalitional support from green environmental groups, be a countervailing power in both the labour market and society? Has the decline in union density and collective bargaining contributed to income inequality and low productivity?

Search & Watch

Go to the video hub at **www.bloomsbury.pub/bratton-hrm** and watch the interview with **Ray Fletcher OBE, Director of Personnel and Development, Unite the Union.** Ray has worked in personnel in the automobile and building materials industries before moving to the not-for-profit sector, where he became Executive Director of HR and External Affairs at Remploy. Ray was awarded an OBE in 2004 for his work there. He currently works at the trade union, Unite, where he has been for ten years. He is a Fellow of the CIPD and has 40 years' experience in HRM. Watch him talking about trade unions in the contemporary workplace, their contribution to workplace learning and possibilities for union-green coalitions, and then think about the following questions: (1) According to Ray, in the context of change and restructuring, does the role of HR change? (2) What does Unite do to promote learning at work? (3) Can a balance be found between green policies and the interests of union members?

Legal Focus

The statutory definition and the purpose of a trade union is found in section 1(a) of the Trade Union and Labour Relations (Consolidation) Act 1992, which defines a trade union as an organisation which 'consists wholly or mainly of workers of one or more descriptions and whose principal purposes include the regulation of relations between workers of that description ... and employers'. The definition describes a union as consisting of workers. As such, professional bodies such as The Law Society are not trade unions. To fulfil its primary purpose of regulating the employment relationship, a union has to be recognised by the employer. The Employment Relations Act 1999 provides two ways by which this can occur: (a) where the employer recognises the union voluntarily; or (b) where the union has invoked the statutory recognition procedure and thus the employer has to recognise the union for collective bargaining purposes.

Virtually all forms of workplace disputes will constitute a breach of contract by the employee. A strike is a situation where the employee is withdrawing their labour and refusing to work. Hence, it constitutes a breach of the work-wage bargain. In 2008, in *Demir and Baykara v Turkey*, the European Court of Human Rights protected the right of freedom of association (the right to join a trade union), also a right to collective bargaining. In 2009, in *Enerji Yapi-Yol v Turkey*, the Court went further and held workers had a right to strike. The recognition of a right to strike in English law was rejected by the Court of Appeal in *Metrobus Ltd v Unite* [2009]. The Trade Union & Labour Relations Act 2016 imposed new requirements on minimum levels of participation in a ballot for strike action.

Task Search online for government information in your jurisdiction on legislation affecting workers ability to take part in lawful industrial action. (1) Does the law achieve the right balance between the competing interests? (2) Should workers have the legal right to join a trade union, and if necessary, withdraw their labour?

Reference

See Deborah Lockton and Tom Brown's *Employment Law* (2020), pp. 415–18 on the legal status of trade unions; pp. 420–6 on union recognition and pp. 462–8, for a discussion on the English courts' reluctance to recognise the right to strike.

PART 4

HRM web links

Visit **www.bloomsbury.pub/bratton-hrm** for a list of the key legislative provisions related to labour relations in Britain. To what extent, if at all, have the changes to trade union and labour relations legislation listed given more power to employers?

Chapter case: Rajah Apparel Co.

The setting

In the early twentieth century, the rapid expansion of industry and the growth of the working class in India led to an increase of skilled and literate workers who set the stage for unions to flourish in the workplace. The country's first trade union was formed in 1918, followed by the creation of the regulatory India Trades Union Act in 1926. As per the latest data released for 2011–12, union density across the total workforce stood at 10.7%. Among non-agricultural workers, union density was 17.5%, increasingly marginally compared to the 1993–94 levels. Overall, trade union density in India is relatively low compared to other emerging economies such as South Africa and Brazil, which indicates the limited scope unions have to bargain for improvements in working conditions (Hayter and Lee, 2018).

Men overwhelmingly represent the majority of trade union membership in the country. Union density among female workers is half that of male workers. The active participation of women in the trade union movement has historically been low, with social, historical, biological and religious constraints creating barriers to the higher paying opportunities that unionised workplaces can offer. Although the trade unions were successful in helping to establish the Maternity Benefit Act in 1961, Indian women are still under-represented at all levels of union leadership and decision-making, and their issues have not taken centre stage in union struggles.

One striking exception to trade union membership for women is in the garment industry, a major source of exports for India. More than 80% of the 3 million people who work in the industry are women, and women can make up as many as 70% of total union members. However, despite the presence of unions in the industry, the work is still characterised by long hours, low wages and minimal regulation. The Boohoo clothes factory scandal in Leicester, where workers were paid as little as £3.50 an hour and were not wearing protective masks to stop the spread of Covid-19, highlights that the garment industry in both India and the UK appears to be prone to a 'cost-minimisation' HR strategy (Davies and Kelly, 2020).

The problem

Twenty-year-old Asha recently arrived in Baddi, an industrial town in northern India, to find work in the garment industry. She had followed her cousin Devi, who had fled their rural village several months earlier after failing to find local work that would pay enough to help support her family. Although both women knew the wages in Baddi's garment industry were low, a job in a factory would still pay more than they could earn performing the traditional agricultural or domestic work available to women in their village. Asha's father was severely ill, and her mother was depending on Asha to provide additional money for his medication. The women also wanted to continue their education, a goal that would be highly unlikely if they remained at home.

Devi, who had had some experience as a seamstress, quickly found work in the tailoring section at one of the newer Baddi factories called Rajah. She told Asha that the factory management preferred to hire young women, saying that women were more efficient and disciplined than men. Devi managed to get Asha an interview with the supervisor of the factory she worked for. At the interview, the supervisor talked to Asha about job responsibilities and salary, and then ended the meeting by saying that she should not get involved in any kind of unionism. 'It's unproductive,' he said. 'You must pay attention only to your work.' Asha nodded and was happy to learn that she was hired for the job, although the money she would earn would still not be enough to pay for all of her father's medical bills.

On her first day on the job, Asha noticed that although there were a few men on the factory floor, the vast majority of her co-workers were women. The work was routine and the hours were long, but Asha was appreciative of the opportunity the factory management had given her. Within her first few weeks, she was able to send home money to help support her parents and buy her father's medicine.

Shortly after Asha had completed her first year at the factory, her father's condition worsened and he required more medication, putting a further strain on the family's finances. Kapil, who had been hired at the same time as Asha, approached her when they began their shift. He told her that he had contacted a trade union leader to start the process of unionising the workers and asked for her support. 'The union can help improve our working conditions and get us an increment in pay.' Kapil stressed that he needed the women in the factory to get involved as there were far more of them than men. 'We will never become unionised unless the women come forward,' he said. 'It's for their benefit too.' He asked Asha to meet him the next day to work out a strategy to get the other women to support the idea.

When Asha told Devi what Kapil had said, Devi warned Asha about talking to Kapil any further about unions. 'We cannot take this risk as it is the best work option we have. The men are always trying to bring in the union because it is easier for them to find work elsewhere if the factory lets us go. The other women will not cooperate with the men in trying to unionise our workplace'. Later that day, Asha read a notice that management had posted on the factory floor bulletin board warning that other factories in Baddi had been shut down because of unions protesting against work conditions. It also mentioned that management was reviewing possible pay increments, but only if the factory remained non-unionised. Asha spent that night worrying about how she was going to continue to support her family and wondered if helping Kapil bring in the union was the right thing to do.

The assignment

Working either alone or in a study group, prepare a PowerPoint presentation with notes drawing on this chapter and other recommended material addressing the following:

1. How does India's patriarchal society play a role in Asha's situation and for Indian women in general?
2. What type of industrial relations strategy is Rajah's management applying? What national features of India's society and economy might be contributing to their choice of strategy?
3. If you were Asha, would you help Kapil bring in the union? Why or why not?

Essential reading

Chakravarty, D. (2007) 'Docile oriental women' and organised labour: a case study of the Indian garment manufacturing industry. *Indian Journal of Gender Studies*, *14*: 439–60.

Davies, R. and Kelly, A. (2020) More than £1bn wiped off Boohoo value as it investigates Leicester factory. *The Guardian*, 6 July. https://www.theguardian.com/business/2020/jul/06/boohoo-leicester-factory-conditions-covid-19.

Hayter, S. and Lee, C. H. (eds) (2018) *Industrial Relations in Emerging Economies: The Quest for Inclusive Development*. Cheltenham, UK: Edward Elgar Publishing.

O'Connor, S. (2018) Dark factories: labour exploitation in Britain's garment industry. *The Financial Times*, 17 May. https://www.ft.com/content/e427327e-5892-11e8-b8b2-d6ceb45fa9d0.

Note: This case was contributed by Lori Rilkoff and updated by Andrew Bratton.

Further reading

Budd, J. W. and Bhave, D. (2008) Values, ideologies, and frames of reference in industrial relations. In P. Blyton, E. Heery, N. Bacon and J. Fiorito (eds) *The Sage Handbook of Industrial Relations* (pp. 92–112). London: Sage,

Findlay, P., McKinlay, A., Marks, A. and Thompson, P. (2009) Collective bargaining and new work regimes: 'too important to be left to bosses'. *Industrial Relations Journal*, *40*(3), 235–51.

Heery, E. and Simms, M. (2010) Employer responses to union organising: patterns and effects. *Human Resource Management Journal*, *20*(1): 3–22.

Martin, A. and Quick, A. (2020) *Unions Renewed*. Cambridge, UK: Polity.

Pohler, D. and Luchak, A. (2015) Are unions good or bad for organisations? The moderating role of management's response. *British Journal of Industrial Relations*, *53*(3): 423–59. DOI: 10.1111/bjir.12042 53

Vachon, T. E., Wallace, M. and Hyde, A. (2016) Union decline in a neoliberal age: globalization, financialization, European integration, and union density in 18 affluent democracies. *Socius: Sociological Research for a Dynamic World*, *2*: 1–22. DOI: 10.1177/2378023116656847

Vandaele, K. (2019) *Bleak Prospects: Mapping Trade Union Membership in Europe since 2000*. Brussels: European Trade Union Institute. Available from: https://www.researchgate.net/publication/332511266_Bleak_prospects_mapping_trade_union_membership_in_Europe_since_2000.

PART 4

CHAPTER 10

EMPLOYEE RELATIONS AND CONFLICT MANAGEMENT

outline

- Introduction
- The nature of employee relations
- Understanding conflict and conflict management
- Employee grievance
- Employee discipline
- Employee voice
- Employee communication
- Critiquing employee relations
- Summary
- Further reading

Source: Antenna on Unsplash

objectives

After studying this chapter, you should be able to:

1. Define employee relations and its relationship to HRM
2. Describe the meaning of conflict and how it is manifested in the workplace
3. Explain the concepts of workplace communication, employee involvement, participation and voice and outline why managers might want to increase their use of employee voice, taking into account the notion of strategic 'high-commitment' management
4. Explain the meaning of grievance and discipline processes and how these are used to manage dissatisfaction and conflict in the workplace

Introduction

As previously explained, the employment relationship can be created in three ways: unilaterally, bilaterally and trilaterally. Whereas conventionally the field of 'labour relations' is conceived in narrow terms as addressing the bilateral or collective dimension of the employment relationship, the field of 'employee relations' has traditionally focused on the unilateral or individual aspect of employer and employee relationships. The HRM literature proposes that employee relations offer a more inclusive conception of employee-employer relations (Guest and Bryson, 2009). Here, 'employee relations' is concerned with the theory and HR practices associated with the management and regulation of the individual dimension of the employment relationship and the handling of worker dissatisfaction, tension or overt conflict when either the worker or employer perceives the explicit or implicit contract has been violated. The employment relationship is based on managerial prerogative, the ideological assumption that employers or managers, as agents of capital, have 'the right to manage' (Farnham, 2015, p. xvi) and therefore reflects managerial power.

We begin this chapter by explaining the nature of employee relations and then proceed to explore the meaning of conflict and how it is expressed in the workplace. We then go on to explain the concept and importance of communication and the various forms of worker voice before examining some well-known approaches to managing conflict with a focus on the processes governing individual employee grievance and management discipline.

The nature of employee relations

Exactly what constitutes employee relations (ER) is not explicable. As we noted in Chapter 9, some authors use the terms 'industrial relations' and 'employee relations' interchangeably, while other scholars argue that there are identifiable differences in the subject matter that justify the use of each term. Blyton and Turnbull (1998, pp. 7–9) adopted the term 'employee relations' partly because 'industrial relations' was too closely associated with trade unions, collective bargaining and industrial action, though they acknowledge that 'the management of employees, both individual and collective, remain a central feature of organisational life (2004, p. 3). Marchington and Wilkinson (1996, p. 223) justify the use of the term 'employee relations' principally because it is increasingly used by practitioners to describe workplace employment relations, both collective and individual, and it epitomises the shift in focus to management issues, though they acknowledge that they use the terms interchangeably. Other scholars define ER to include both non-union and union dimensions of the employment relationship. Leat (2007, p. 7), for example, uses the term ER to:

> Encompass both individual and collective dimensions, union and non-union relationships, the changing nature of work and the employment relationship, and the wider contexts within which the employment relationship occurs. I do not take a managerial perspective or standpoint.

From a managerial perspective, the CIPD justify the use of the term 'employee relations' because the term 'industrial relations' is no longer widely used by employers and does not describe today's employment relationships, except in specific sectors and, even there, in modified form. Thus, the CIPD offers an inclusive conception of employee relations:

> Encompasses individual as well as collective workplace relationships. It reflects the increasing individualisation of the employment relationship following the rise of individual

> workplace rights and the decline in trade union reach and influence. In line with this focus, there's an increasing emphasis on helping line managers to establish trust-based relationships with employees. (CIPD, 2020d)

The CIPD's definition reflects the historic decline in workplace unionism and how areas traditionally of concern to labour relations scholars have been 'colonized by HRM' (Ackers and Wilkinson, 2005, p. 448). The HRM literature presents a number of different definitions and perspectives but share in common that the new ER paradigm views employee relations as a wider concept than the traditional term industrial relations.

Here the term employee relations is used to encompass both individual and collective dimensions of the employment relationship, but the focus in this chapter is given to the individual employee relations processes, skills and competencies as opposed to the collective relationship. As such we examine the management of the employment relationship, taking into account the implications of the notion of the psychological contract, without trade unions. The focus is on an assortment of HR policies and practices that shape and influence employer or manager-employee relationships with the objective of improving individual and organisational performance. This means dealing with employees on an individual basis; communicating with employees; providing employees with a voice or input into decision-making; handling workplace conflict and individual grievances; and dealing with poor performance or unacceptable behaviour through a disciplinary procedure. These core activities are shown in Figure 10.1.

The focus here on the individual employment relationship should not be interpreted to mean that 'union voice' is unimportant in the workplace – far from it. Edwards and Sengupta's (2010) evidence highlighting the 'social relations of performance' as a contested arena indicates that both employee voice and union voice are important for the achievement of both worker influence and sustainable organisational performance.

The four dimensions of employee relations can be operationalised both informally or formally and without or with a union voice (Edwards and Sengupta, 2010). The concepts of *formal* and *informal* employee relations relate to the nature of relationships and the processes in the workplace. A formal *communication* process mirrors the literal structure of the organisation with its organisational chart and hierarchical reporting relationships. Informal communication, on the other hand, often called the grapevine, is the unstructured and informal communication network based around social relationships rather than organisational charts. A formal *employee voice* scheme can include managers, individual employees and/or their union representatives participating in decision-making in committee or governing body, such as a works council. On the other hand, informal employee voice may simply involve line managers engaging with staff and listening to their work-related suggestions. Further, if an employee's

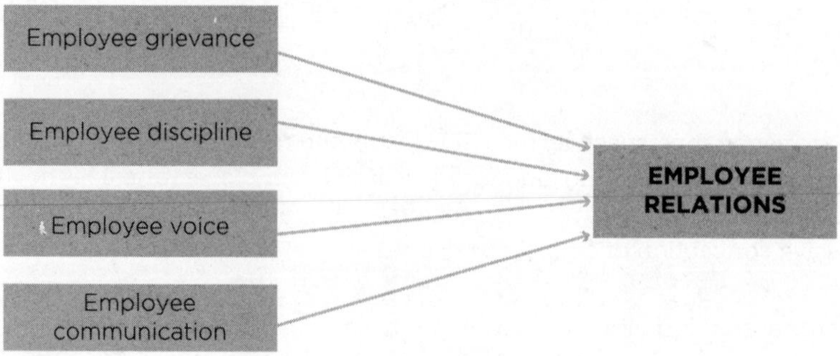

Figure 10.1 Four important dimensions of employee relations

conduct or performance does not meet organisational standards or targets, a line manager can seek to improve the employee's behaviour through informal ongoing conversation (see Chapter 6). However, if the employee's poor conduct or performance continues, a formal *disciplinary* procedure can be activated. The formal disciplinary procedure should – at the very least – comply with the statutory dismissal and disciplinary procedures and might, providing the employer recognises trade unions, include a union representative in the proceedings. In a unionised environment, if the disciplinary process is deemed to be unlawful, unfair or biased, it could lead to a union *grievance* or third-party intervention (e.g. employment tribunal or court) Thus, there can be a significant interaction between individual and collective forms of employee voice, grievance-handling and disciplinary processes.

Reflective question

Looking at the four key dimensions of employee relations, how can HR practices in each area impact positively and negatively on the employment relationship? Try to think about your own work experience of 'good' and 'poor' employee relations.

Digital Spotlight

The surveillance of workers in a 'digital cage'

Source: Agence Olloweb on Unsplash

Recent technological advancements have facilitated the development of an array of new tools that employers can utilise to surveil their staff. Digital platforms, such as those offered by Teramind and InterGuard, can be installed overtly or covertly on devices and, in effect, act as an 'all-seeing eye'. They can capture the most granular level of detail: every keystroke made, email exchanged, website visited, app opened, file edited and much more. Key word triggers can be established that result in an automatic alert being sent to an administrator when they are identified within text. In addition, some systems can automatically compile reports, which may be used in disciplinary or dismissal cases. Most – though not all – platform providers, however, draw a line at accessing workers webcams.

During the coronavirus pandemic, demand for surveillance software reportedly surged as many people were forced to work from home and employers sought to monitor their activity (Jones, 2020). However, employee surveillance has serious legal and ethical implications. In regard to the former, legislation varies significantly between countries. For example, in the EU the General Data Protection Regulations have implications in relation to the collection and processing of employee data, for example, that obtained through the monitoring of digital devices. From an ethical perspective, it risks infringing on a number of fundamental rights, notably the right to privacy. Justifications offered for its use typically include the prevention and detection of accidents and injuries, workplace harassment and violence, theft (of both property and, increasingly, identity), and/or a desire to enhance productivity. Surveillance and monitoring companies often put forward arguments based on notions of paternalism and benevolence. Brad Miller of InterGuard, for example, states, 'If you are a parent and you have a teenage son or daughter coming home late and not doing their homework you might wonder what they are doing. It's the same as employees' (Solon, 2017). However, the TUC (2018) argues that invasive forms of monitoring can breed 'fear and distrust'. Indeed, Jathas Sadowski, a research fellow at Monash University, states that, 'these are technologies of discipline and domination ... they are ways of exerting power over employees'. Sadowski continues that while many businesses install the software covertly, 'others are very upfront about it, because that's part of the disciplinary power, knowing that screenshots are being taken, that you are being watched and tracked and recorded' (Wood, 2020).

The use of surveillance and monitoring technology risks placing workers in a 'digital cage', echoing German sociologist Max Weber's (1930) concept of an 'iron cage'. According to Weber, the increased rationalisation inherent in social life, especially within Western capitalist societies, creates an iron cage that can limit freedom and agency. However, those born into the cage rarely question their confinement. The digital cage may be equally powerful. Sanjeev Patni of employee surveillance platform Crossover argues that reluctant employees are soon persuaded of the 'benefits' of monitoring: 'The response is "OK, I'm being monitored, but if the company is paying for my time how does it matter if it's recording what I'm doing? It's only for my betterment"' (Solon, 2017).

Stop! What role can HR professionals play in terms of ensuring that employers strike the correct balance between protecting business assets and respecting the privacy of employees?

Essential reading

Sayre, G. M. and Dahling, J. J. (2016) Surveillance 2.0: How personality qualifies reactions to social media monitoring policies. *Differences*, *90*: 254–59.

Note: This feature was contributed by Laura Steele.

Understanding conflict and conflict management

Employee relations is fundamental to managing people as it 'brings the formal agreement, the employment contract, to life' (Aylott, 2018, p. 1). Perhaps the most animated feature of the contract is overt conflict. As we discussed in the preceeding chapter, negotiating and third-party intervention is viewed as a means of reconciling divergent interests, whereas in non-unionised workplaces with shallower forms of employee voice dissatisfaction, tension and conflict is managed using alternative HR processes. The employment relationship has been conceptualised as having several dimensions – economic, legal, psychological – and each facet has the potential for conflict, if either party perceives the formal contract or unspoken informal understanding has been breached. This is why we include in our coverage of employee relations an introduction to behaviours that challenge people management – resistance and conflict. Sennett's (2012) 'social triangle' concept – authority, mutual respect and cooperation – remind us that people are different from other 'resources' because their cooperation and commitment always have to be won and sustained by managers. Importantly, employees have the capacity to resist management's decisions and actions and to engage in work stoppages, sabotage, non-cooperation or simply being absent. Therefore, a critical analysis takes as axiomatic that employee relations are inevitably characterised by structured power, cooperation and conflict. How far, and in what ways, do employees contest or resist the power of management? What happens when the employer or the employee is deemed to have breached the employment relationship? In this section we examine different types of conflict in organisations, before explaining some well-known approaches to conflict resolution.

Types of conflict

Worker resistance, dissent, misbehaviour and, sometimes, overt conflict are significant elements of everyday organisational life (Farnham, 2015). There are numerous definitions of conflict (Tjosvold et al., 2014). Conflict has traditionally been defined in terms of opposing interests involving scarce resources, goal divergence and frustration (Pondy, 1967). It can refer to all expressions of dissatisfaction resulting from a breach of the formal employment contract, especially those pertaining to the effort–reward bargain (Scott and Marshall, 2009). Members of organisations without opposing interests or dissonance not only can, but often do, have conflicts (Tjosvold et al., 2014, p. 547). There are many expressions of employee dissatisfaction and discord at work. Typically, these have been divided into two broad categories – formal and informal:

- *Formal conflict* describes organised expressions of discontent that are articulated typically through a union-employer grievance process. Formal conflict is more associated with labour relations.
- *Informal conflict* is not based on any recognisable coordinated organisation and results from an actual or perceived breach of the employment contract or it is taken in defence of one's dignity. (Karlsson, 2012)

Conflict may further be classified as 'organised' and 'unorganised', with the involvement of trade unions or individual employees, respectively (Hyman, 1989).

- *Organised conflict* occurs when a group of workers engage in planned action, for example, a trade union authorised strike or an unofficial stoppage of work, sometimes referred to as 'wildcat' strike in the US, without union authorisation, or a boycott of working overtime or the occupation of the employer's premises to change the source of the dissatisfaction. Where a union's bargaining power is weak, because of high unemployment or restrictive employment laws, for instance, organised conflict is less likely (Farnham, 2015). Thus, organised conflict is closely related to theories of labour relations and negotiating power.
- *Unorganised conflict* occurs when an individual employee responds to dissatisfaction by, for instance, exiting the organisation, being absent or sabotaging a computer.

There is no single theoretical framework for analysing employee conflict and resistance. However, drawing on the concepts examined so far, a two-dimensional model of employee discord is presented in Figure 10.2.

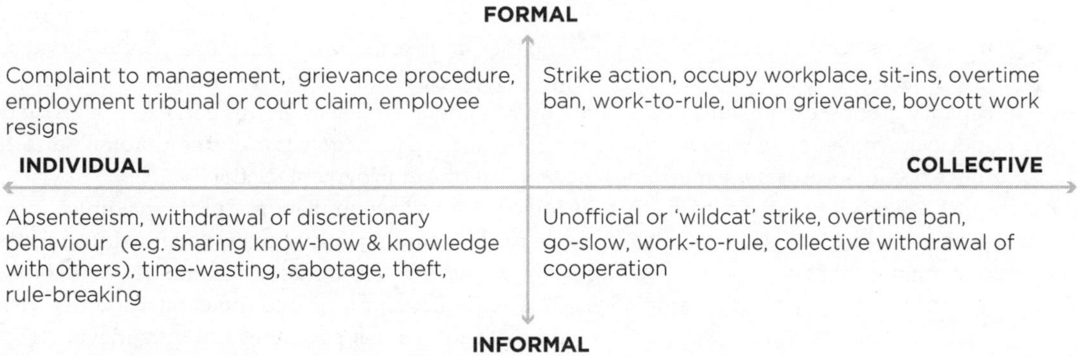

Figure 10.2 Manifestations of organisational conflict

Source: Farnham (2015).

Figure 10.2 shows both formal and informal types of resistance and individual/group and collective forms of resistance. Formal individual/group types of resistance range from absenteeism (employee avoiding the conflict), to formal complaints to line managers, to leaving the organisation. Formal types of collective resistance include work stoppages or strikes or the union pursuing the grievance through a process up to an employment tribunal. A key feature of UK labour relations over the last four decades is the decline in the number of strikes. In 1974, for example, 14.8 million working days were lost due to strikes compared to only 273,000 working days in 2018, the sixth-lowest annual total since records began in 1891 (Clegg, 2019). The effect of trade union law restricting the ability of unions to strike has meant that the UK has now fallen below the average strike rate of other OECD countries in every year since 1992.

One effect of the decline in official strikes is the contribution to a perception of workplace 'harmony'. However, informal individual/group types of resistance covering a wide variety of behaviours, including withholding effort, sabotaging machinery, theft and non-cooperation, still occurs, albeit mainly unrecorded. Informal 'misbehaviour' in organisations is not limited to subordinate workers alone. Corporate executives also 'misbehave' through corporate fraud and tax avoidance (Farnham, 2015, p. 412). Informal types of collective resistance include occupying the workplace, 'wildcat' strikes, banning overtime and working to contract, all of which negatively affect organisational performance. As explained in Chapter 9, employers also have recourse to a variety of actions aimed at expressing dissatisfaction with the collective workforce (e.g. imposing a lockout or relocating the business) or individuals (e.g. instigating disciplinary action).

Reflective question

Thinking about your own experience at work or at university working in small groups, or reports in newspapers, what factors are most likely to cause dissatisfaction and discord? Is conflict inevitable at work? How is conflict between individuals or groups typically resolved?

Causes of conflict

At this point in your HRM studies, it will be no surprise to you that there are different perspectives on what causes workplace conflict. Fox's (1966) classic contribution distinguished four different perspectives, which, by now, you should be familiar with. These are unitarist, pluralist, radical and interactionist. The *unitarist perspective* views organisations as harmonious, cooperative entities and assumes a commonality of interests between managers and non-managers. It explains observable conflict in psychological terms – a personality clash – or as something that 'trouble-makers' cause (Ackroyd and Thompson, 1999). The *pluralist perspective* considers the organisation as a microcosm of society, as a collection of many separate groups, each of which have their own legitimate interests. In this context, workplace conflict is inevitable, indeed endemic. All parties recognise the need for negotiation and compromise and the occurrence of conflict provides a mechanism to 'regulate' the employment relation.

The *radical perspective* holds that the logic of capital accumulation – profit maximisation – necessitates that employers relentlessly minimise costs, including labour costs, and maximise control of the operating or service process. It views the workplace as an arena of conflict between managers (as agents of capital) and other employees. Thus, conflict is intrinsic to the capitalist employment relationship. The fourth perspective, *interactionist*, believes that conflict is not only inevitable, but it can also release positive energy and improve group or organisational performance. Indeed, it is suggested that some managers deliberately 'engineer' conflict to encourage reflexivity, self-criticism and change (Xenikou and Furnham, 2013).

Given these contrasting perspectives on conflict, there has been much debate concerning whether or not conflict is detrimental or beneficial. It seems intuitively plausible that conflict within organisations is always harmful (De Dreu, 2008). But, counter intuitively, different types of conflict can be a catalyst for beneficial change. Organisational behaviour (OB) scholars propose that different types of conflict have different effects and not all conflict is uniformly bad or good for the organisation (De Dreu, 2012). Tjosvold (2008), for example, has argued that conflict can lead to improvements by employees sharing their experience and knowledge to generate creative ideas. Such views gave rise to functional and dysfunctional conflict:

- *Functional conflict* supports the goals of the organisation, and has the effect of improving its performance, and is a constructive form of workplace conflict. For example, disagreement among team members over how to efficiently complete a task can be considered functional conflict.
- *Dysfunctional conflict* has the effect of hindering organisational performance. Acts of aggression or abuse in a department or team that distract from the task in hand are dysfunctional conflict.

Both types of conflict can relate to the content and goals of the work in hand – called *task conflict* – or about how the work gets completed – called *process conflict* – or relate to disputes about interpersonal relationships – referred to as *relationship or dyadic conflict* (Jehn, 1997). Much of the literature examines intragroup conflict (conflict within the group) as opposed to intergroup conflict (between groups). Collinson (1994) argues that, despite the decline of organised conflict in workplaces, non-organised conflict continues in diffuse and pervasive forms. He contends that knowledge and information are key aspects of power and, despite its seemingly uneven distribution, other forms of knowledge (that is, technical and production-based knowledge) are available to workers. These alternative resources can be mobilised by workers and this accounts for the very uneven and variegated results of power struggles in organisations. Of course, management in this framework tries to use the opposite strategies of extracting and restricting information, respectively, and this results in a complex spiral of control resistance, greater efforts at control and so on, or rather a series of strategies and counter strategies.

PART 4

The key point we make here is that, although high levels of unemployment and low opportunities of changing jobs at a time of economic turbulence may reduce workplace discord and overt conflict, an absence of conflict must not be confused with job satisfaction or organisational commitment. Moreover, power is often revealed in overt forms of conflict (such as strikes), both subtle and covert forms of human agency (action) can be identified, which suggests 'everyone has power' (Giddens, 1984). In the context of employee relations, the workplace is a highly complex configuration of ongoing micro-political power conflicts at individual, group and organisational levels, in which strategising human agency inside and outwith the organisation interact with each other and create temporary balances of power that shape how formal employment relations and processes actually work in practice (Morgan and Kristensen, 2006). We next examine management practices which critical workplace theorists argue can, at best, only mitigate, and not prevent, the occurrence of conflict.

Conflict management

Conflict management is the process of limiting the negative aspects of discord while resolving dissatisfaction, tension and disagreement within or between social groups or individuals. The literature provides alternative methods of handling workplace conflict. Four common approaches are discussed below.

Negotiation

In unionised workplaces organised conflict can be managed through negotiations or collective bargaining (see Chapter 9). Negotiation is a process that occurs between two or more parties, with each party having its own goals and needs, but with each seeking to establish common ground in order to reach an agreement to resolve a conflict or settle a matter of mutual concern. Walton and McKersie (1991) distinguished between 'distributive' and 'integrative' negotiating strategies. *Distributive bargaining* aims to divide up a fixed amount of valued resources – cutting up a 'pie' is a commonly used metaphor – thereby creating a 'win–lose' solution. It therefore operates under zero-sum conditions. Sometimes called mutual gains bargaining, *integrative bargaining* aims to create a 'win–win' situation. A collective agreement that increased both productivity (lowering costs) and pay would be an example of integrated bargaining because the size of the 'pie' would be increased.

Third-party intervention

In organisations with or without a trade union presence, a common way to manage conflict is to make use of third-party intervention, which can involve the third party adopting the role of a mediator or arbitrator. The UK Advisory, Conciliation and Arbitration Service (ACAS) defines *mediation* as a process that involves a neutral third party bringing the two sides together with the aim of reaching a mutual agreement. Mediation can be especially effective when used in the initial phase of any disagreement, before conflict escalates in the organisation. *Arbitration* is a process whereby an employer and trade union in dispute agree to hand over to an independent third party the responsibility for deciding how their differences should be settled. The arbitrator is asked to make a decision on a dispute. The two sides present evidence to an arbitrator, who then makes a decision that they have agreed in advance to abide by. Thus, the process is a confidential alternative to a tribunal or court of law.

Grievance procedure

A *grievance* is generally defined as a claim by an employee that they are adversely affected by the misbehaviour of a manager or the misinterpretation or misapplication of company *policy* or collectively bargained agreement. To address an employee's grievance, employers typically implement a *grievance procedure* (ACAS). SMEs typically have less sophisticated procedures for handling expressions of conflict. A formal grievance procedure has increasingly come to be regarded as a legitimate management tool to manage conflict and to receive redress for alleged unfair or unreasonable treatment at work. We examine the procedure in more detail below.

Source: iStock.com/Joa_Souza

After the strike, occupation of the workplace is probably the most well-known form of organised conflict. Unorganised and informal forms of conflict are often managed through employee relations tools, such as grievance and disciplinary procedures, consultation, effective communications.

Disciplinary procedure

Generally, employee conduct meriting discipline stems from violation of the employer's rules, unacceptable behaviour or unacceptable performance. An employer uses a disciplinary procedure to express dissatisfaction with an employee and to address an employee's behaviour or performance. Importantly, the employer is not obligated to exercise progressive discipline (see below).

Employee grievance

A grievance is an overt form of conflict which involves an employee complaining about the behaviour of a manager or another co-worker which is perceived to be unfair or damaging to them. Figure 10.2 depicts an array of means through which workers can express their dissatisfaction by initiating a grievance procedure. Indeed, a grievance procedure is an important aspect of fairness and dignity at work. The formal grievance procedure, which may or may not involve a union representative, plays an important role in introducing democracy into the workplace (Craig and Solomon, 1996, p. 334) and is also a form of *direct* employee voice (Marchington, 2008, p. 237). From management's perspective, the formal grievance procedure allows an employee to express dissatisfaction that, if not resolved, can result in unsatisfactory (mis)behaviour (Ackroyd and Thompson, 1999) and performance.

The non-union models of grievance-handling vary widely from one workplace to another and may have fewer than or as many procedural steps as are found in union models; in all instances, the grievance-handling process mirrors the management hierarchy. At a minimum, prescriptive HR advisers recommend that a grievance workplace policy should:

- investigate the complaint;
- take appropriate action to resolve the complaint to the mutual satisfaction of the complainant and the management;
- resolve the grievance in a timely manner (see Gennard and Judge, 2005, p. 300).

Employee complaints that require formal grievance management cover a myriad of workplace issues, including undignified or demeaning treatment by front-line managers or other co-workers, workplace bullying and harassment.

Sexual harassment as an employee relations issue

Analysis has shown that the negative consequences of sexual harassment and a misogynistic workplace extend beyond individual targets to include co-workers, work groups and whole organisations (Bowling and Hershcovis, 2017; Miner-Rubino and Cortina, 2004). As Keith (2000, p. 287) points out, sexual harassment 'poisons the atmosphere in the workplace'. It is an important issue for management, centring as it does on issues of social justice and efficiency. Sexual harassment in the workplace is unlawful, and the courts have increasingly viewed its prevention as the employer's responsibility. The legal concept of 'detriment' is important here. Sexual harassment is a 'detriment' per se; it can lead to an employment-related detriment to the female employee and, as such, has serious implications for management. In 1986, the European Parliament passed a resolution on violence against women, commissioning a report on the dignity of women at work, which led to the adoption of the EU code of practice (Figure 10.3).

The allegations of sexual impropriety against US President Bill Clinton in 1998, the case of former International Monetary Fund chief Dominique Strauss-Kahn in 2011 and the case of Hollywood producer Harvey Weinstein in 2020, found guilty of sex crimes, highlight some of the difficulties seen in cases of sexual harassment in the workplace. The first issue is credibility because there is seldom a witness to support

Source: iStock.com/Andrii Yalanskyi

The EU code of practice defines sexual harassment as 'unwanted conduct of a sexual nature' affecting 'the dignity of women and men at work'. It defines harassment as largely subjective, in that it is for the individual to decide whether the conduct is acceptable or offensive.

The code says that member states should take action in the public sector and that employers should be encouraged to:

- issue a policy statement
- communicate it effectively to all employees
- designate someone to provide advice to employees subjected to harassment
- adopt a formal complaints procedure
- treat sexual harassment as a disciplinary offence.

Figure 10.3 The European code on sexual harassment

whether the conduct being complained about actually happened. There are, for example, no witnesses to the alleged conduct of Mr Clinton and the White House employee Monica Lewinsky or to the sexual encounter between Mr Strauss-Kahn and the hotel maid, Nafissatou Diallo, a 32-year-old immigrant from Guinea, or the dozens of women who brought allegations of sexual assault against Mr Weinstein. Credibility and circumstantial evidence are under scrutiny here. Who has more credibility? Is there indirect evidence that might support or dismiss the allegations? The Clinton case raises another issue that often applies to workplace investigations: the question of containment. In the presidential investigation, the public prosecutor apparently had no interest in limiting the scope of the investigation, but for many HR professionals, containment, in addition to what is legitimate and necessary in terms of conducting the investigation into a complaint of sexual harassment, is also an issue. The aim will be to contain the allegation and limit knowledge about the complaint to those who need to know.

For many women, Weinstein's conviction was a watershed moment for the #MeToo movement and 'a crucial test in the effort to hold powerful men accountable for sexual harassment in the workplace' (Ransom, 2020). However, despite workplace sexual harassment being 'the most intimate manifestation of employment discrimination faced by women' (Keith, 2000, p. 277), legal protection against it is complex, sensitive and stressful. There is concern expressed by some authors about how women are treated in law, contending that women are disadvantaged because of a patriarchal or sexist jurisprudence. Debono (2001), for example, found that there are sexist elements to the jurisprudence related to workplace sexual harassment decisions in the UK, the USA and New Zealand. Although the legislation is progressive, it is argued that 'sexist attitudes still remain with those who have the power to use the legislation to compensate the victims' (Debono, 2001, p. 338).

The intervention of co-workers witnessing sexual harassment is another response to the problem. McDonald et al.'s (2016) study of sexual harassment in Australian workplaces reveals that despite the hidden nature of sexual harassment, the intervention of bystanders who are not direct targets can potentially be an effective response to the persistent and damaging problem of workplace sexual harassment. The use of social networking presents additional risks to employees and employers alike. For example, the posting of inappropriate material can be discriminatory, derogatory and may constitute cyber-bullying. The cases of *Otomewo v Carphone Warehouse Ltd*, ET/2330554/2011 and *Taggart v TeleTech UK Ltd*, NIIT/704/11 illustrate that employers can be held vicariously liable for the actions of employees on social networking

HRM in Practice

Online activism: how should HR respond?

With traditional union membership in decline, employees are finding new ways to voice their opposition to corporate decisions, as shown by the global Google protests when thousands of Google workers in London, Tokyo and New York staged a series of walkouts targeting claims of sexual harassment, gender inequality and systemic racism (Wakabayashi et al., 2018). So why is employee activism on the rise? According to Richard Saundry, professor of HRM and employment relations at the University of Plymouth, we have seen 'significantly reduced union density and membership' in both the UK and the US and little has emerged to fill the gap (Faragher, 2019):

> 'It's not necessarily a wave of unrest - but it does point to more diverse forms of employee opposition, compared with traditional forms of industrial action,' he says. 'There's a general feeling that employees are becoming more politically motivated and will call out inequality; they're pushing for better quality jobs ... Workers at grassroots levels at companies like Deliveroo are using new methods to join together, such as social media; technology is helping them to get organised.'

This suggests that union membership is in decline, yet grassroots and digital activism is on the rise. Critics argue that social media is central to this trend. Phillipa Foster Back, director of the Institute of Business Ethics, points out that new technology enables employees to communicate their dissent, not just externally, but internally using communication platforms such as Yammer and Slack, which means an increasing number of workers are connected with each other in the same team, workplace or even country (Faragher, 2019). She explains that something may begin as an internal online petition, but if workers are not listened to, they may feel the need to shout louder. For example, workers at grassroots levels at companies like Uber Eats and Deliveroo are using social media and personal communication platforms such as WhatsApp to help them get organised, and traditional unions have invested in new social media initiatives to broaden their appeal and stimulate membership. Research suggest that social media also has the potential to improve the historic under-representation of women and youth workers in the union movement. For instance, research from Australia suggests that the use of social media can improve gender inclusion and is 'having a significant positive impact on women's involvement in unions' (Thornthwaite et al., 2018, p. 413). However, a study on the way in which three British unions use social media to engage younger workers reveals that while social media has the potential to engage new, young audience members, in reality unions are heading further into 'the echo chamber' (Hodder and Houghton, 2020, p. 56), with only those already active becoming increasingly active and the potential reach ultimately diminished.

Stop! Studies to date have concentrated on Twitter - are different messages being posted on different social media platforms? What impact do private messenger apps such as WhatsApp have on union activity and organisation?

Essential reading

Wakabayashi, D., Griffith, E., Tsang., A. and Conger, K. (2018) Google walkout: employees stage protest over handling of sexual harassment. *The New York Times*, 1 November; Hodder, A. and Houghton, D. J. (2020) Unions, social media and young workers - evidence from the UK. *New Technology, Work and Employment*, *35*(1): 40–59; Thornthwaite, L., Balnave, N. and Barnes, A. (2018) Unions and social media: prospects for gender inclusion. *Gender, Work & Organisation*, *25*(4), 401–17.

Note: This feature was contributed by Andrew Bratton.

PART 4

sites if they occur 'in the course of employment'. Studies tend to emphasise that exposure to workplace bullying impacts negatively on the quality of employee relations and is, moreover, associated with impaired employee well-being and individual performance (Bowling and Hershcovis, 2017).

Employee discipline

The modern workplace is pervaded by rules established by management to regulate the behaviour of workers. Indeed, it is argued that obedience underscores the relationship between employer and employee: 'There is certainly nothing more essential to the contractual relation between master and servant than the duty of obedience' (Cairns, 1974, quoted in Wedderburn, 1986, p. 187). *Rules* set standards of conduct and performance in the workplace, whereas *procedures* help to ensure that the standards are adhered to and also provide a fair method of dealing with alleged failures to observe them. A breach of management rules by an employee or group of employees can be interpreted as an expression of conflict. In such circumstances, employers have recourse to disciplinary procedures when individual employees are deemed to have breached one or more of the explicit and implied rules that govern the employment relationship. Disciplinary procedures are designed for promoting orderly employee relations as well as fairness and consistency in the treatment of individuals (Klass, 2009).

Disciplinary action ranges from the subtle persuasions of mentoring to dismissal, but managers have to ensure that their actions are dealt with fairly and consistently (CIPD, 2019c). As you hopefully should know by now, the employment relationship involves a legal relationship, and for those employers and managers who share a less-than-sophisticated management style known as 'my way or the highway', there is a framework of legal rights regulating the process dealing with alleged inappropriate or unacceptable behaviour.

Disciplinary concepts

Discipline can be defined as the process that maintains compliance with employment rules in order to produce a controlled and effective performance. The purpose of discipline in the workplace is threefold:

- *Improvement* – the disciplinary process is seen as one of counselling the disobedient employee back to acceptable behaviour.
- *Punishment* – the disciplinary process is seen as being about imposing penalties.
- *Deterrent* – the process is seen as educational to deter others.

Corrective discipline refers to management action that follows the infraction of a rule. In Canada, the 'hot-stove rule' metaphor is used to guide correct discipline. This states that disciplinary action (for example, warnings or suspension from work) should have the same characteristics as the penalty an individual receives from touching a hot stove. These characteristics are that discipline should be, with warning, immediate, consistent and impersonal.

Most organisations apply a policy of *progressive discipline*, which means that the employer notifies employees of unacceptable conduct and provides them with an adequate opportunity to correct it. A policy of progressive discipline typically includes seven steps:

1. *Verbal caution:* An employee will receive a verbal caution when they engage in unacceptable behaviour.
2. *Verbal warning:* An employee will receive a verbal warning when they continue to misbehave while a verbal caution is in effect. A verbal warning is documented.
3. *Written warning:* A written warning will be issued when an employee continues to engage in behaviour that warrants such a warning, or they engage in unacceptable behaviour while a verbal warning is in effect. A written warning is kept in an employee's personnel file.
4. *Suspension:* An employee will be suspended without pay when they engage in conduct that warrants it, or the employee continues to engage in unacceptable behaviour while a written warning is in effect. An employee's suspension is kept in an employee's personnel file.

5. *Decision-making leave:* Following a suspension, an employee will usually be given limited time to reflect on whether they wish to continue working for the employer.
6. *Termination:* The employer will terminate an employee when they engage in conduct that justifies this action or do not correct the behaviour that resulted in prior discipline.
7. *Appeals process:* Employees will be permitted to refute information the employer has used as the basis for disciplinary action.

Research has found that managers have different handling styles when dealing with disciplinary situations. The less serious disciplinary cases tend to attract a prescriptive autocratic style, whereas in more serious cases managers tend to adopt less prescriptive approaches and involve the employee to a greater extent, which, in theory, is more likely to bring about the desired change in employee behaviour (Rollinson et al., 1996). It is important to note that an effective disciplinary process incorporates the requirements of *natural justice*, which means that employees should be informed in advance of any disciplinary hearing of the alleged misconduct, be given the right to challenge the alleged evidence, have the right to representation and to have witnesses, and be given the right to appeal against any decisions taken by management (Emir, 2014).

Global HRM

International assignments can be tough for LGBTQ+ staff

One of the clearer case studies on the intersection of human resources management and social justice is how organisations have handled the rise of LGBTQ+ rights. For many years, employers have been working to improve their internal practices on LGBTQ+ issues, investing in culture, benefits and marketing to welcome LGBTQ+ workers and customers (Shortall, 2019). Working overseas is a chance for employees to experience a new culture and develop communication skills and confidence which might help them progress their career. However, short-term assignments to countries where homosexuality is illegal may leave LGBTQ+ workers at risk of arrest and harassment. In those places where same-sex relationships and parental rights of LGBTQ+ parents are not recognised, it can create difficult challenges for accompanying partners and children. As Stonewall, the LGBTQ+ rights charity, reports: 'Sexual acts between people of the same sex are criminalised in more than 70 countries and only a small minority of states recognise same-sex partnerships [or the gender identity of trans people]' (Jacobs, 2018). Additionally, in more than half the world, LGBTQ+ people may have no protection from discrimination by workplace law.

In 2019, the University of Birmingham faced criticism after issuing guidance on its website suggesting its LGBTQ+ employees should hide their sexuality when travelling to its new campus in Dubai, United Arab Emirates. According to the guide, created by members of the Rainbow Network, a group of LGBTQ+ employees and PhD students at the university, queer and transgendered workers are urged to not wear clothes or accessories which could be considered a 'form of LGBTQ+ advocacy'. Employees were also told they should not disclose their sexuality or gender identity publicly on social media. While their intentions were to safeguard LGBTQ+ workers from violence and harassment, critics argue that the guidance undermines the university's commitment to equality and diversity. Jo Grady, general secretary of the University and College Union, said:

> Before entering into these kinds of partnerships, universities need to set out clearly how they will protect their staff and ensure all their campuses are safe for all staff and students. Not to clumsily ask staff to keep their head down and stay out of trouble ... This advice highlights a disregard for LGBT+ staff and is a dereliction of the university's duty to stand up for human rights and academic freedom. (Busby, E., 2019)

As the university increases its global activity and presence, this issue highlights the challenge of how to translate a commitment to equality and diversity in countries that have significant legal, social and cultural differences to the United Kingdom. LGBTQ+ rights are extremely suppressed in the United Arab Emirates, where any sexual relations outside of a heterosexual marriage is considered a crime. Punishment can range from a prison sentence, fines, flogging, deportation or execution. Adultery and fornication are also crimes punishable by death.

Stop! How can an employer best support LGBTQ+ employees in the workplace? Can you identify ways to support LGBTQ+ employees abroad?

Essential reading

Busby, E. (2019) University criticised for suggesting staff hide their sexuality when travelling to Dubai campus. *The Independent*, 3 December; Shortall, J. (2019) Why many businesses are becoming more vocal in support of LGBTQ rights. *Harvard Business Review*, 7 March.

Note: This feature was contributed by Andrew Bratton.

Employee voice

In considering worker dissatisfaction, discord and conflict management, so far, we have been focusing on grievance and disciplinary procedures initiated by an employee or union and by the employer respectively. However, for a select segment of enlightened management, a key dimension of employee relations, employee voice (EV), aspires to engage and win commitment from workers (Storey et al., 2018). Employee voice mechanisms can be a means of articulating workers' dissatisfaction and can help reduce discord. As union membership and influence has decreased, interest in the various aspects of employee voice has increased across sectors (e.g. Johnstone and Ackers, 2015; Marchington, 2008; Storey et al., 2018). The concept of 'employee voice' can perhaps best be seen as the holy grail of employee relations (Emmott, 2015, p. vii). Beardwell (1998, p. 32) defined employee voice as the 'expression of employee perspectives within [their] organisation'. It might be conceived from within the unitarist traditions as a process for fostering a harmonious 'high-commitment' relationship built on trust, fairness and respect (Emmott, 2015). Alternatively, within the pluralist tradition, employee voice is interpreted as a mechanism for representing workers' collective interests, primarily financial interests, and for ensuring those interests are taken into account in organisational decision-making (Ackers, 2007). For Marchington (2008), employee voice appears to be a vogue term used to describe HR practices designed to permit workers some 'say' in workplace decision-making.

Processes that provide for employee voice include *direct* employee involvement and participation (EIP) in decision-making, whether via upward quality control techniques or *indirect* participative arrangements such as a works council (Wilkinson et al., 2014). Previous variants to describe these activities include industrial democracy, employee participation and employee involvement (Marchington, 2008, p. 231). The terms 'employee participation' and 'employee involvement' have different meanings, however. In essence, *employee participation* involves workers exerting a countervailing and upward pressure on management control, which need not imply unity of purpose between managers and non-managers. *Employee involvement* is, in contrast, perceived to be a softer form of participation, implying a commonality of interest between workers and management, and stressing that involvement should be directed at the workforce as a whole rather than being restricted to trade union channels. As Guest (1986, p. 687) states: 'involvement is considered to be more flexible and better geared to the goal of securing commitment and shared interest'.

The concept of '*employee engagement*' has attracted much attention from academics and practitioners (Storey et al., 2018). However, it is a contested phenomenon (Farnham, 2015, p. 226) and the global interest has produced multiple definitions. MacLeod and Clarke (2009, p. 9) define employee engagement as:

> A workplace approach designed to ensure that employees are committed to their organization's goals and values, motivated to contribute to organizational success, and able at the same time to enhance their own sense of well-being.

The definition suggests that to be engaged workers must have a cognitive understanding of the organisation's goals and values, they must have an emotional or effective attachment to these goals and values and, third, they must have the motivation to exert discretionary effort beyond the requirements of the formal contract. Bridger (2015) identifies three dimensions to employee engagement:

- *intellectual* engagement – employee thinking about the job and how to do it better;
- *affective* engagement – employee feeling positively about doing a good job;
- *social* engagement – employees actively taking opportunities to discuss work-related improvement.

Storey and his colleagues make a salient point that most definitions of worker engagement define the construct in terms of its outcomes (e.g. increasing employee commitment) more than the construct itself (2018, p. 300). Employee engagement can be seen as a management tool 'to leverage the employment relationship to the benefit of the organisation' (Guest, 2015, p. 61). It can also be seen as a psychological state characterised by vigour, dedication and absorption: the antithesis of Marx's notion of alienation (Bratton, 2021, p. 59).

HR practices can strengthen employee engagement, but it is also acknowledged that the 'enablers' or antecedents of attitudinal and behavioural engagement include leadership, engaging line managers, integrity, trust and voice (Guest, 2015, pp. 47–8). In this context, variants of employee voice aim to encourage cooperative and productive modes of employment interaction. According to Dundon et al. (2004), employee voice can be viewed as:

- a form of contribution to decision-making;
- an articulation of individual dissatisfaction (or satisfaction);
- a demonstration of collective organisation.

The search for causal links between strategic HRM and organisational performance has elevated the importance of understanding the relationship between employee voice and performance. Employee voice practices can be seen as a management-designed means to transform the climate of employee relations by long-term changes in workers' attitudes and commitment that shape 'organisational citizenship' (Guest, 2008). However, Boxall and Purcell (2016) remind us that managers' choices are not solely about the economic 'bottom line'. The beliefs and values of managers, employees and society at large – the notion of social legitimacy – provide a crucial non-economic dimension.

Definitions of employee voice do not always reflect the range of possibilities available – from having some say over how work is designed and executed to exerting a significant influence over strategic decisions. Strauss (1998) maintains that meaningful employee participation in decision-making demands that workers are able to exert influence over their working environment. He observes that employee voice 'is meaningless if the message is ignored' Strauss (2006, p. 803). He adds, 'it is actual influence, not a *feeling of influence* that is important' (Strauss, 2006, p. 778, emphasis added). Token employee voice practices, which are aimed at engendering a 'feeling' of influence or 'belonging' among employees, but which have no effect on decision-making, do not provide 'intersubjective ethical legitimacy' (Fryer, 2019, p. 111).

The plurality of ways in which EV works gives rise to differing *form*, *level*, *scope* and *influence* in the workplace. Figure 10.4 provides a framework within which different forms of EV can be examined and shows the relationship between three constituent elements:

- The forms of voice – range from direct to indirect.
- The level of voice – the setting within the hierarchy in which decisions are made.
- The scope of voice – the types of issues dealt with, ranging from office seating to organisational strategy.
- The influence of voice – the extent to which workers are able to effect management decision-making.

Figure 10.4 shows a continuum of EV from a situation in which employees have no autonomy (for example, a downward communication), to problem-solving and team-based arrangements to enable a voice on operational decisions, to works councils with greater scope and potentially high degrees of influence on strategic decision-making. Current forms of employee voice fall along this continuum,

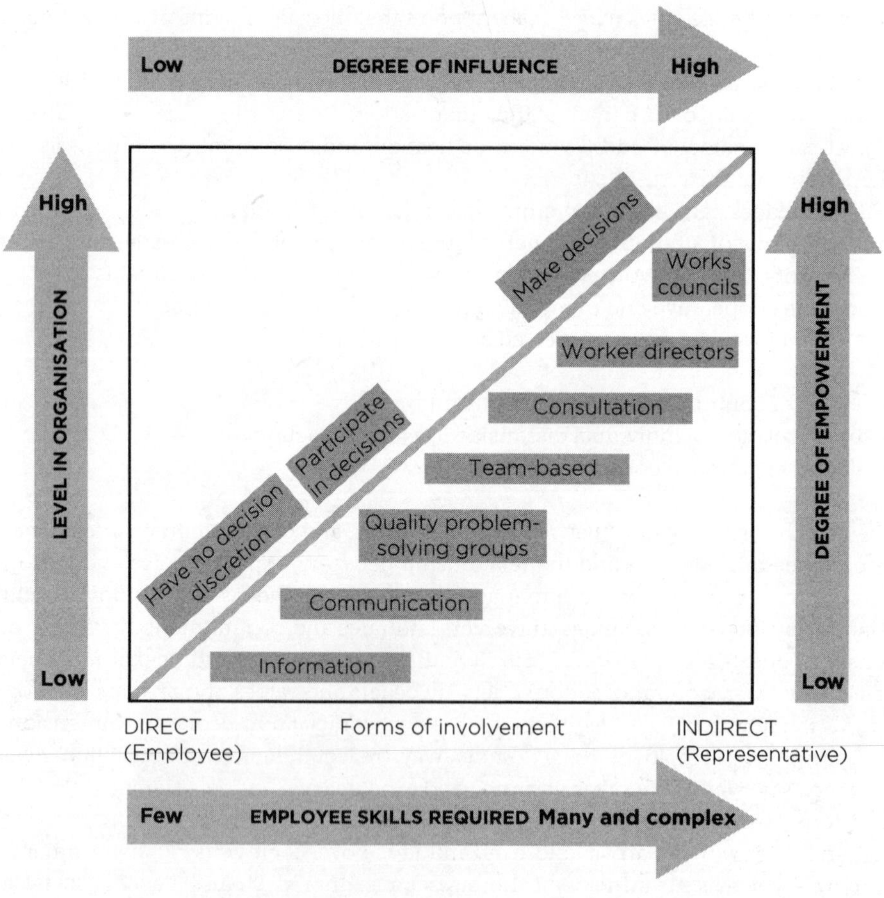

Figure 10.4 Framework for analysing employee voice

which is called an 'escalator' of participation by Marchington and Wilkinson (2000, p. 343). The choice of employee voice mechanism within organisations is shaped by a number of factors such as the size of an organisation, the context of national regulation and whether unionised or not. In SMEs, the form of employee voice (and the HR function) is likely to be less formalised, which means that managers may tend towards informal team briefings and limited information sharing. Conversely, large organisations with dedicated HR professionals, may have more structured employee voice mechanisms.

Reflective question

What might be management's motives for introducing mechanisms for employee voice? Is employee voice plausible in SMEs? Why/why not?

Forms of employee voice

The form of employee voice might range from *direct* forms, in which individual employees, albeit often in a very limited way, are given input or 'say' in decision-making processes that affect their everyday work routines. Examples of direct EV include task-based, quality-problem-solving participation, and high-performance work systems (HPWS). *Indirect* forms of employee voice typically involve employee representatives participating in the decision-making process through a formal meeting arrangement. Examples of indirect voice include Joint Consultative Councils, works councils and 'worker directors', all forms that are associated with the broader notion of 'industrial democracy' (Bullock, 1977). More recently, as a consequence of the precipitous decline in trade union density and collective bargaining coverage, research has increasingly focused on non-union models of employee representation (Butler, 2009; Kim et al., 2010; Marchington, 2008).

Research on EV arrangements in multinational corporations (MNCs) reveals a complex picture. Studies have found that UK-owned MNCs are more likely to have a hybrid arrangement of union and non-union employee representation, consistent with a shift away from union-based employee representation. US-based MNCs have a preference for direct forms of employee voice. Nordic-based and Japanese-based MNCs are, however, no more likely to have employee representative structures than their US counterparts. In the main Anglophone countries, there is a trajectory towards non-union employee representation (Marginson et al., 2010). Indirect EV through the process of collective bargaining was examined in Chapter 9. Before examining forms of EV in detail, however, let us address the question, 'Why the enthusiasm for direct forms of EV?'

Reflective question

The different forms of EV need to be understood as part of an HR strategy. Before reading on, review Figure 2.5 and its accompanying text. What is the connection between business strategy, HR strategy and EV? Thinking about the post-pandemic 2020 debate on new ways of working and business survival, which forms of EV would generate ideas and 'buy-in' among employees? Why?

A general theory of employee voice

The literature puts forward three main reasons why senior management might support direct forms of EV – *ethical, economic* and *behavioural* (Verma, 1995). The ethical reason has roots in the argument that, in a democratic society, workers should have a say in how their workplaces are run when the outcomes of any decisions impact on their lives. EV therefore presents a socially acceptable management style. EV reflects well on the company's image or 'brand' and their desire to project 'a socially responsible stance on such issues' (Marchington and Wilding, 1983, p. 32).

The economic reason for EV is championed by the 'model of excellence' school in North America, and is derived from the utilitarian principle that EV improves the quality of decision-making and performance. There is evidence that EV potentially improves productivity and energises workers (Verma and Taras, 2001), increases employees' job satisfaction (Sisodia at al., 2014, p. 69), heightens trust in management (Mabey et al., 1998a) and, during organisational restructuring, can help to reduce anxiety, stress and resentment (Marchington and Kynighou, 2012). Therefore, research appears to support the theory that giving workers a voice on a range of workplace decisions yields benefits to both the organisation and the workforce (Heller et al., 1998).

The behavioural justification for employee voice derives from the perennial managerial problems associated with perceived dysfunctional behaviour. In particular, resistance to change, absenteeism and conflict (Beer et al., 1984). EV is seen as a solution to these dysfunctional human behaviours. According to Beer et al. (1984, p. 53), by introducing EV schemes:

> Employers hope that participative mechanisms will create a greater coincidence of interests between employers and employees, thereby increasing trust, reducing the potential for conflict, and increasing the potential for an effective mutual influence process.

Source: ide alien on Unsplash

Research shows that EV potentially improves the quality of a decision and its chances of successful implementation in the workplace.

Extending the behavioural explanation for EV, it is important to recall the discussion on managing the employment relationship. Managers have to continually address two interlinked problems – those of control and commitment – with regard to managing the employment relationship. Fox (1985) argues that, faced with the management problem of securing employee compliance, identification and commitment, management has adopted a range of employment strategies including employee voice. The current enthusiasm for improved EV needs to be viewed within the context of changing business and corresponding HR strategies in which its purpose is to secure employee support, engagement and commitment to new technologies and work designs in order to improve performance (Marchington, 2008). Support for management investing in new technologies, such as robots, is much more likely if workers are given the opportunity or a 'voice' to influence when and how technology is used in the workplace (Partington, 2019). The engagement–performance link is based on a number of assumptions, the first being that giving workers more autonomy over work tasks will strengthen emotional and intellectual connection workers have with their job, co-workers or organisation, which will in turn result in enhanced individual and organisational performance. The engagement–commitment cycle is depicted in Figure 10.5.

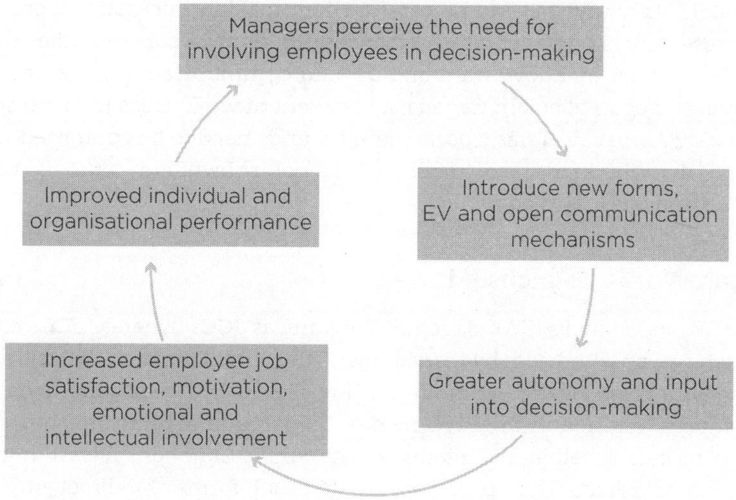

Figure 10.5 The engagement–commitment cycle

Performance process is a communication style that attempts to build a strong internal culture encouraging initiative, learning, creativity and greater employee identification with the organisation.

Indirect employee voice

Joint consultation is a key type of employee voice (Cregan and Brown, 2010). In its simplest form, joint consultation may take the form of an informal exchange of views between a group of workers and their manager on an incoming piece of technology or a reorganisation of the office. When, however, the size of the organisation makes it difficult for workers to access management, a more formal and indirect employee voice network needs to be established. The committee usually includes representatives of management and workers. The intent is to provide a meeting forum that acts as a channel for employee voice on matters affecting the workplace.

Joint consultation is different from collective bargaining examined in the last chapter. The difference rests on the idea that both conflict and a common interest are inherent elements of the employment relationship that need to be handled in different ways. Joint consultation is viewed as a means of promoting action when there are no obvious conflicts of interest, whereas collective bargaining is a means of reconciling divergent interests, although, as emphasised throughout our discussion on managing people, every aspect of the employment relationship has the potential for conflict. The balance between joint consultation and collective bargaining will depend upon the power of trade unions (Daniel and Millward, 1983).

Joint consultative committees

Here we define Joint Consultative Committees (JCCs) as workplace-based committees of managers and other employees that tend towards shallower forms of consultation, rather than more consequential negotiating, about workplace change. In some organisations they are known as Works Councils and union representatives often sit on JCCs but, equally, many function without union involvement. Survey evidence of UK workplaces with 100 to 249 employees found that there has been a statistically significant increase in JCCs, from 9 per cent in 2004 to 18 per cent in 2011 (Van Wanrooy et al., 2013, p.

61). Although we always have to be careful when making international comparisons – because, for example, researchers often define HR practices differently – survey studies show that, across Western Europe EV practices and downward and upward communication increased by an average of 52 per cent (Mayrhofer et al., 2000). In Canada, 43 per cent of workplaces reported some form of EV in decision-making (Verma and Taras, 2001). These findings need to be contrasted with more critical studies suggesting that EV in decision-making has not shown any sign of substantive improvement (Thompson and McHugh, 2009).

European Works Councils

European Works Councils (EWCs) are not the same as JCCs: whereas JCCs are voluntary committees, and as such can be withdrawn by management, the term 'European Works Council' is used to describe only mandatory consultative committees. Pre-Brexit, UK managers, trade unions and academics became more interested in the EWC model (Gilman and Marginson, 2002). However, post-Brexit, it remains to be seen whether this interest will continue. Although, at least in the UK, the EWC model is still in its infancy, Frege (2002, p. 221) argues that such forms of indirect employee voice are 'the most prominent, widespread and powerful form of industrial democracy in contemporary capitalist societies'. Frege (2002, p. 223) defines works councils as:

> Institutionalised bodies of collective worker participation at the workplace level, with specific informatory, consultative and codetermination rights in personnel, social and economic affairs.

Works councils are legally independent of trade unions, and their members are elected in a ballot of *all* employees rather than just union members. The key functions of EWCs are:

- establishing two-way communication between employees and management, and union and management;
- maintaining peaceful and cooperative employment relations (as EWCs are not allowed to initiate a stoppage of work);
- providing training for representatives.

EWCs have differing degrees of power (Mayrhofer et al., 2000): in Germany, for example, employee representatives can resort to the courts to prevent or delay managerial decisions in areas such as changing working practices and dismissals. The range of issues discussed and the degree of legislative support for EWCs would, note Mayrhofer et al. (2000, p. 226), 'shock US managers brought up on the theories of "manager's right to manage"'. In another study, it was found that Germany's employee voice rights provided a 'crucial source of countervailing power in negotiations over work reorganisation' (Doellgast, 2010, p. 395). Frege (2002, p. 241) observes, 'we know much about the ontology of works councils (what is a works council, what does it do) but much less about the determinants, outcomes and underlying causal relations'. In terms of outcomes, Addison et al. (2000) using data from Germany and Britain, contend that mandatory indirect participation in decision-making is associated with higher productivity in workplaces with more than 100 workers and in economies with centralised pay bargaining (for example, Germany).

Employee communication

The research focus on the engagement–commitment cycle, on 'followership' and the antecedents of leadership behaviours (Bratton and Francis, 2020) as it applies to the HRM–performance debate, underscore the importance of interpersonal dialogic *communication* in the workplace. Witherspoon (1997, p. x), a specialist in leadership and communication, argues that 'leadership is to a great extent a communication process'. In our three-dimensional model of management (see Figure 1.2), communication is part of the process of influence by which managers 'personalise' and implement HR policies and practices, which is an element of the HR 'black box'. (See Chapter 1 for an extended discussion on the so-called HR 'black box'.)

A simple definition of employee communication focuses on information disclosure:

> Employee communications means the provision and exchange of information and instructions which enable an organisation to function efficiently and employees to be properly informed about developments. It covers the information to be provided, the channels along which it passes, and the way it is communicated. (ACAS, 2014, p. 3)

Meaning is a core concept in communication, and communication researchers define their discipline in complex behavioural and contextual terms. Byers (1997), for example, incorporates three ideas associated with communication – behaviour, meaning and context – and defines communication in the workplace as (p. 4):

> Both behaviours and symbols, generated either intentionally or unintentionally, occurring between and among people who assign meaning to them, within an organizational setting.

Communication is symbolic, which means that the words managers and workers speak or the gestures they make have no inherent meaning. Symbolic meanings conveyed both verbally and non-verbally only 'gain their significance from an agreed-upon meaning' (Martin and Nakayama, 2000, p. 61).

Downward communication patterns from managers to non-managers need to be explored within the wider context of organisational culture. Information exchange and the transmission of meaning are the essence of organisational life. Information about the organisation – its products and services, its external environment and its people – is a prerequisite for effective employee involvement in decision-making. A strong advocate of high-involvement work systems, Pfeffer (1998, p. 93), not surprisingly, argues that 'the sharing of information on such things as financial performance, strategy, and operational measures conveys to the organization's people that they are trusted'. However, the communication process is complicated by organisational characteristics such as hierarchy and power relations, and by the fact that managers and non-managers all have idiosyncrasies, abilities and biases.

Communication strategies will be determined by the way work is designed; for example, the more the organisation relies on knowledge workers and innovation to competitively survive, the more important the mode of communications become. All managers engage in *downward* communication in one form or another, but communication scholars emphasise that, to be effective, employee communication must be a two-way or dialogic process to give employees the opportunity to participate on a regular basis. Researchers, academics and practitioners have also stressed some key issues related to communications in the workplace (Figure 10.6).

Communicating is the fundamental process of organising

Understanding communication provides insights into management strategies

Senior management should be committed to open communication

Communication skills are the basis for effective leadership

Management should take the initiative in devising and maintaining the communication system

Messages should occur in a form that can be readily understood

Information should be perceived to be relevant to employees

Efficacy - desired effect or effectiveness of written versus face-to-face channels of communication

Messages should be consistent with actions

Male and female managers communicate differently in the workplace

Cross-cultural communication is an increasing feature of a diverse work organisation

Training in communication skills increases the effectiveness of the system

Communication systems should be monitored and evaluated

Figure 10.6 Key issues related to communication in the workplace

Communication methods

Organisation communication is a process by which information is exchanged between a sender and a receiver. This can be done three ways:

- verbal;
- non-verbal;
- written.

Verbal communication ranges from a casual conversation between two employees to a formal speech by the managing director. In face-to-face meetings, the meaning of the information being conveyed by the sender can be expressed through gesture or facial expressions, which are referred to as *non-verbal* communication. *Written* communication ranges from a casual email note to a co-worker to an annual company report to shareholders. Social media platforms, including Facebook, Twitter, blogs, LinkedIn, WhatsApp, TikTok, podcasts, YouTube and Zoom, are an increasingly popular form of communication within and across organisations and are revolutionising business communications. The content of any message consists of what is being communicated, and the way in which content is communicated – through the various channels – describes the sender's communication style. In turn, different communication styles, will also, importantly, affect the perception of a message or set of messages.

People communicate differently depending on their class, gender and national culture (Coates and Pichler, 2011; Rees, 1998; Tan, 1998). In Britain, language is particularly associated with social class. Research suggests that there is sometimes implicit prejudice against certain accents or regional dialects (Plimmer, 2015b, p. S1). An accent is a speech pattern, and everyone has one, 'but it can be a huge barrier at work, affecting productivity, engagement and morale' (Judy Ravin, president and cofounder of Accents International and quoted by Plimmer, 2015b, p. S1).

Viewing communication as a linear process is a contextually impoverished model of employee communication that neglects cross-cultural norms. Thinking globally, how do new forms of communications technology impact on managing people?

Language, gender and power intersect. The interplay of language and power comes through clearly in how Western people use masculine words to signify greater force, significance or value. For instance, the positive word 'seminal', meaning ground-breaking, is derived from the word 'semen' or 'male seed'. The positive adjective 'virtuous', meaning morally worthy, is derived from the Latin word *vir*, meaning man. In contrast, the disparaging adjective 'hysterical' comes from the Greek word *hustera*, meaning uterus or womb (Bratton 2021, p. 278). Therefore, it is argued that in the process of gender redefinition, communication is an ideological act.

Ethnographic research shows that most workplaces are predominantly masculine domains with masculine norms of behaviour, which of course includes ways of communicating (see, for example, Coates and Pichler, 2011). Language scholars posit that language and gender intersect, and this contributes to different interpretations of meaning in workplace communications. Effective communicators, both female and male, typically draw on a diverse discursive repertoire of social and linguistic practices, ranging from normative 'feminine' to normatively 'masculine' ways of talking (Holmes, 2006). Studies suggest, for example, that male managers tend to be loud, direct, dominant and aggressive. Women, on the other hand, tend to be more open and self-revealing when they speak, and are better at decoding non-verbal communication (Aries, 1996). Cross-cultural literature focus on culture, because it shapes our perception of reality, and thereby influences communication processes: 'All communities in all places at all times manifest their own view of reality in what they do: The entire culture reflects the contemporary model of reality' (Burke, 1985, quoted in Martin and Nakayama, 2000, p. 62).

The traditional approach to communication, in particular simply viewing communication as a linear process, is a contextually impoverished model of employee communication that needs to be improved upon by sensitivity to cross-cultural norms and mores, as well as to the organisational context that gives rise to the shared meanings through which interpersonal communication occurs.

Ethical Insight

Can we accord ethical legitimacy to 'pseudo-employee voice'?

Over the last four decades, the concept of employee voice has received significant attention from both academics and practitioners. Wilkinson et al. (2018) suggest that within the HRM literature employee voice is viewed as a fundamental democratic right. Therefore, failure to afford workers legitimate voice represents a threat to their dignity. In contrast, OB perspectives tend to emphasise the role of employee voice in identifying organisational improvements that, if implemented, may enhance performance (Wilkinson et al., 2018). This approach, however, risks employee voice being viewed as an 'optional extra' that can be discarded when it becomes inconvenient (Barry and Wilkinson, 2016).

While most of the literature on employee voice highlights the positive impact it may have at the individual, group and organisational levels, there are a small number of studies that urge caution. De Vries and Jehn (2012, p. 221), for example, address the issue of 'pseudo voice', which occurs when 'the manager encourages employees to share their views about work-related issues without the intention to really consider their input'. Employers may, for example, conduct an employee satisfaction survey but fail to disclose or act upon the results. Torka et al. (2008, p. 151) quote an operator from a textile factory who describes their experience of pseudo voice: 'It's always been the same here that it's already been agreed upon before they even ask your opinion. So, actually, it's virtually all arranged and then you can come along and say what you think.' Pseudo voice is, in other words, autocracy covered with a veneer of democracy (Sagie and Aycan, 2003).

De Vries and Jehn (2012, p. 222) importantly note that, 'it all boils down to whether or not employees *perceive* pseudo voice; they may perceive pseudo voice when it is absent by objective criteria, and vice versa'. The impression of pseudo voice (whether or not this reflects reality) may cause employees to become angry, cynical and disengaged. They may cease to offer their thoughts and opinions in the belief that there is little, if anything, to be gained. This is known as 'employee silence' (Van Dyne et al., 2003). In such a situation, the organisation fails to benefit from their insights and ideas. Worse, de Vries and Jehn (2012) argue that pseudo voice may lead to increased intragroup conflict. The authors cite a number of reasons for this, including a poor organisational atmosphere stemming from feelings of deceit, unfairness and outrage. Employees may start to engage in counterproductive work behaviour, such as sabotage and interpersonal aggression, because they feel that management lacks legitimacy (de Vries and Jehn, 2012). In addition, workers who perceive pseudo voice and, as a result, withhold their opinions, have no input into decision-making outcomes. Instead, de Vries and Jehn (2012) argue, they may attempt to regain a sense of control by acting in an aggressive manner towards management or, more commonly, their co-workers.

Stop! What actions can managers take to ensure that employee voice mechanisms are not only legitimate but are perceived to be so?

Essential reading

de Vries, G. and Jehn, K. A. (2012) When employees stop talking and start fighting: the detrimental effects of pseudo voice in organizations. *Journal of Business Ethics*, *105*: 221–30.

Note: This feature was contributed by Laura Steele.

Critiquing employee relations

Employee relations are socially embedded and express societal and government values. For example, an overwhelming majority of the people living in Britain believe the practice of firing workers only to rehire them on worse employment terms should be outlawed (Savage, 2021). The pandemic has not only highlighted the various ways in which it has increased inequality but also exposed 'low-road' HR practices that have created abysmal working conditions for many workers. In 2019, the UK government promised that it would bring forward new employment legislation to improve people's rights at work. The government was accused of negating on its promise to enhance workers' rights, after ministers failed to include an employment bill in the 2021 Queen's Speech (TUC, 2021). In addition, employee relations practices reflect the philosophy of organisational leaders on what sort of relationships are wanted between management and workers.. Within critical theory employee relations practices are conceived as being designed and largely driven by an employer's agenda and help to 'naturalize' and legitimise capitalist exploitative relations (Klerck, 2019, p. 311). The forms of employee voice arrangements initiated by management contain contradictions and paradoxes. Stohl and Cheney (2001), for example, analyse four main forms of employee voice paradox: structure, agency, identity and power. The authors posit that paradox is inherent in mainstream EV processes and that these paradoxes set limits that constrain the effectiveness of EV networks. Organisational *structures* tend to eliminate workers voice from the most influential network: the executive. Strauss (1998) posits that direct employee voice mechanisms provide opportunities to make changes only at the margins of managerial decision-making. It is senior management that make the 'really important decisions', for example investment in sustainable energy. Put another way, 'Learn, innovate and voice your opinions as I have planned!'

The notion of *agency* relates to an individual's sense of being and a feeling that they can or do make a difference (Giddens, 1984). One paradox of agency references the tensions and contradictions present in high-commitment, high-performance workplaces, in which teams may rely on the active subordination of team members to the will of the team. Thus, 'Do things our way but in a way that is still distinctively your own!' The paradox of *identity* addresses issues of boundaries, space and the divide between the in-group and the out-group (Stohl and Cheney, 2001; Wang et al., 2018). The paradox is linked to the notion of employee commitment. At one level, EV implies commitment to the processes of learning and dialogue. At another level, however, 'commitment is expected to equal agreement' (Stohl and Cheney, 2001, p. 380). In a so-called 'learning organisation', the paradox of identity may be expressed as 'Be a self-directed learner to meet organisational priorities'. The fourth paradox is that of *power*, which centres on issues of access to resources, opportunities for independent voice and the shaping of employee behaviour. Stohl and Cheney (2001, p. 388) provide persuasive evidence of EV regimes 'getting workers to make decisions that management would have made themselves'. In other words, 'Be an independent thinker, just as I have commanded you!'

That tension and contradictions are found within the existing EV literature should be no surprise. These mirror the inherent contradiction contained within the capitalist employment relationship, that is, the need of management to be able to manage workers as an objectified commodity, but at the same time to call upon the cooperation of employees (Clayton, 2000). It is a mistake to assume that employee voice can serve as an effective alternative to other more robust forms of union-based worker voice such as collective bargaining (Heery, 2000) or 'bottom-up' employee-owned enterprises (Erdal, 2011). The HRM literature has tended to give much attention to employer-sponsored employee voice arrangements across the Anglophone economies, and their capacity to bridge the 'representation gap' – workers who desire union representation but who currently do not have access to a union (Freeman et al., 2007, p. 4 and cited by Heery, 2009, p. 325). For Heery (2009, p. 331) indirect EV in the form of works councils 'must fit with and not undermine trade union-based participation'. More broadly, the variables used to evaluate the EV contribution, such as high levels of worker commitment and engagement and low levels of dissatisfaction and conflict, implicitly assume a stable and permanent workforce (Wilkinson et al., 2013). However, in the wake of Covid-19, the worst recession statistically on record, and when it was recorded that one million Britons were on zero-hour contracts, the enlightened employer-sponsored employee voice formulas may be less plausible or effective in the new business environment. The challenge for managers, workers, trade unions and governments is whether the Covid-19-driven crisis of capitalism will generate a new debate over union-based employee voice systems.

Summary

This chapter has conceptualised employee relations as an assortment of rules, regulations and HR policies and practices by which employees are managed both as individuals and as a collective group. Employee relations systems are driven by management's concern with how to gain employee's commitment to the organisation's goals and operational objectives. In this context we examined workplace conflict and different processes for managing or mismanaging conflict.

The chapter examined four dimensions of employee relations: grievances and discipline procedures, employee voice and communications. Formal non-union grievance procedures are designed to allow workers to articulate dissatisfaction about an issue directly to management. For managers, a grievance process can be seen as a useful tool to identify and resolve conflict and inappropriate behaviour, such as bullying or harassment. Discipline procedures vary between national legal systems, but to avoid litigation and to avoid violations of the psychological contract, managers should design and apply discipline practices with due regard to the requirements of *natural justice*.

Employee voice (EV) potentially provides an opportunity for workers to take an active role in management decision-making. EV may be direct or indirect and may range from a shallow form, such as a manager sharing information with workers, to their complete participation in major investment or reorganisation decisions. In this chapter, we also examined communication, which we argued is the fundamental process of managing people in the workplace. It includes written, verbal and non-verbal communication, which flows downwards, upwards and horizontally in organisations. Critical scholars are unanimously supportive of the conceptualisation of communication as being constructed and reconstructed through class, gender and national culture.

Review questions

1. Explain the difference between organised and unorganised conflict. Is conflict always perceived as dysfunctional in organisations?
2. What is meant by employee voice and employee engagement? Can the growth of EV be explained by employer 'needs', or are there other reasons driving this HR practice?
3. Explain the difference between grievance and discipline in the organisation. What is the purpose of grievance and discipline processes? Why is an effective response to incidents of sexual harassment in the workplace important for the employer?

Search & Watch

Go to the video hub at www.bloomsbury.pub/bratton-hrm and view the interview with **Keith Hanlon-Smith, Employee Relations Director, Norland Managed Services**. Keith has been with Norland since 2006, and has previously worked as HR Manager at Sony DADC and Quantum Business Media, as well as having been Employee Relations Manager at Earls Court Olympia Ltd. He is a member of the HR Professionals Network. In the interview, Keith talks about employee relations, the employment relationship and how Norland's HR practices fit with its business strategy. After watching the interview, think about the following questions: (1) How is HR embedded in the business at Norland Managed Services? (2) What is Keith's view on changes in employee relations? (3) How does Keith think that 'agendas' affect priorities?

Legal Focus

The right to be treated fairly and equitably is fundamental to employee relations. Indeed 'Employment rights are human rights' (Barber, 2007, p. vii) that form an integral part of a workplace where employees can expect respect, and dignity *in* and *at* work. As we have explained elsewhere, individual employment rights, embodied in Australian, Canadian, EU and UK legislation, for example, regulate the behaviour of employers and employees. The UK Equality Act 2010 for instance, addresses the issue of harassment at work. The EA 2010 gives protection against unwanted conduct harassment, sexual harassment and non-submission harassment. In Canada, the Canadian Human Rights Act 1977 provides the similar protection for workers employed by the federal government, First Nations governments and federally regulated private companies, with provincial and territorial human rights laws covering most other workplaces.

Task Search online for information in your jurisdiction about employment protection and compare and contrast it with another country, such as Australia or Canada. (1) How does the legislation define harassment in the workplace? (2) How does the legislation protect employees against 'victimisation'? (3) What are the differences, if any, between these two countries' approaches to harassment in the workplace?

Reference
See Deborah Lockton and Tom Brown's *Employment Law* (2020), pp. 193–6, for a discussion on the Equality Act 2010, section 26, covering the three forms of sexual harassment and case law related to harassment in the workplace.

PART 4

Chapter case: Rising tensions at Solas Resort and Spa*

The setting

According to the OCED (2020c), job retention schemes were one of the main policy tools used by governments around the world to mitigate the economic and social consequences of Covid-19. By May 2020, the organisation reported that such initiatives were supporting approximately 50 million workers across the OECD. The specific details varied between countries. The overarching aim, however, was the same: to prevent a rapid surge in unemployment. It was believed that this would, in turn, reduce the risk of financial hardship and a steep drop in aggregate demand (the total amount of demand for all finished goods and services in an economy). In Australia, the scheme was named the 'JobKeeper Payment' (ATO, 2020). It enabled employers, sole traders and other eligible entities to apply to receive AUS $1,500 per employee per fortnight. The government set aside AUS $130bn to cover the first six months of the scheme (Hurst and Karp, 2020). The JobKeeper Payment was due to end on 28 September 2020; however, it was subsequently extended for a further six months and eligibility criteria relaxed after it became apparent that the country's economic recovery was going to be slower and more painful than initially predicted (Cridland and Moloney, 2020).

The problem

Solas Resort and Spa in the Gold Coast, Queensland, is a large hotel set within a sprawling estate. Solas employs over 180 people, including managers, administrators, front desk staff, events planners, chefs, waiters and waitresses, and housekeepers. The impact of the pandemic on the hotel was swift and devastating. Within days, the occupancy rate had dropped to almost zero. The Central Reservations Office at Solas was usually staffed by the Reservations Manager, Kirra Jones, and nine Reservations Agents. At the end of March 2020, the General Manager, Tim Hawthorne, announced that six of the Reservations Agents were to be put on the JobKeeper scheme. While there were almost no new bookings, for several months Kirra and the remaining agents dealt with an avalanche of enquiries from customers seeking information and refunds. Their days were long and frequently stressful.

One morning Kirra was approached by Olivia Lin, a hardworking agent who had been with the company for just over five years. 'Kirra,' Olivia said, 'I am really struggling with the fact that we are in the office working long, intense shifts only to go home, log on to social media, and see that our co-workers on the job retention scheme are spending their days reading, baking and enjoying the sunshine. It feels very unfair'. Kirra reassured her that, now that the situation was beginning to ease, their colleagues would be returning soon to share the workload. Privately, however, Kirra feared that this was only the beginning of the problems.

Unfortunately, Kirra's concerns proved correct. The six agents who had been placed on the scheme returned in early September 2020. Within days, tensions began to emerge. Kirra asked Olivia to come into her office and enquired how things were going. Olivia responded, 'I thought things would improve now that they are back in the office, but in some ways its actually worse. I feel like they are not pulling their weight. It's like they have forgotten how to do their jobs. Plus, those of us who worked throughout are exhausted, while they are well rested and actually accrued holidays while they were off. I just feel very angry, and it is hard not to let that impact my relationship with them'. As Olivia shifted her chair to get up and leave, Kirra thought, 'I am going to have to deal with this before the situation deteriorates further and we are dealing with outright conflict, but where do I even start?'

The assignment

You are the assistant HR manager at Solas Resort and Spa. You are asked to attend a meeting with the HR manager, Sara Sato, and Kirra Jones. At the meeting, Kirra relays recent events to you and expresses her concern that, unless something is done, the situation is likely to get worse. Sara laments that the Central Reservations Office is unlikely to be the only area of the business affected by such tensions. She asks you: (1) to conduct brief research into the issue of employee conflict, with a specific focus on the impact of the pandemic and (2) to outline in a written report some potential solutions for addressing the problem.

Essential reading

Bartsch, S., Weber, E., Büttgen, M. and Huber, A. (2020) Leadership matters in crisis-induced digital transformation: how to lead service employees effectively during the COVID-19 pandemic. *Journal of Service Management, 32*(1): 71–85. Avalable at: https://doi.org/10.1108/JOSM-05-2020-0160.

CIPD (2020) *Dealing with Conflict at Work: A Guide for People Managers*. CIPD, 21 January. Available at: https://www.cipd.co.uk/knowledge/fundamentals/relations/disputes/workplace-conflict-people-manager-guide.

Note: This case was contributed by Laura Steele.

*The name of the hotel is fictitious, but the case is based on actual data and reports.

Further reading

Bratton, J. and Francis, H. (2020) Followers, communication and leadership. In J. Bratton (ed.) *Organizational Leadership* (pp. 289–315). London: Sage.

Jammers, E. and Williams, J. (2021) Care for the self, overcompensation and bodily crafting: the work-life balance of disabled people. *Gender, Work and Organization, 28:* 119–37.

McDonald, P. Charlesworth, S. and Graham, T. (2016) Action or inaction: bystander intervention in workplace sexual harassment. *The International Journal of Human Resource Management, 27*(5): 548–66. DOI: 10.1080/09585192.2015.1023331

Medina-Garrido, J. A., Biedma-Ferrer, J. and Ramos-Rodríguez, A. R. (2021) Moderating effects of gender and family responsibilities on the relations between work-family policies and job performance. *International Journal of Human Resource Management, 32*(5): 1006–37.

Roy, A. L. and Perrin, C. (2021) Managing conflicts in the nonprofit sector through organizational culture change. *Journal of Organizational Change Management, 34*(1): 60–83. Available at: https://doi.org/10.1108/JOCM-11-2016-0254.

Smith, A. and McBride, J. (2021) 'Working to live, not living to work': low-paid multiple employment and work-life articulation. *Work, Employment and Society, 35*(2): 256–76.

Storey, J., Ulrich, D., Welbourne, T. and Wright, P. (2018) Employee engagement. In J. Storey, P. Wright and D. Ulrich (eds) *The Routledge Companion to Strategic Human Resource Management* (pp. 299–316). London: Routledge.

Valitova, A. and Besson, D. (2021) Interpersonal communications at core of conflicts' escalation in organization: the interplay of interpersonal communication escalation, people's habitus and psycho-sociological processes are more important than contextual factors. *Journal of Organizational Change Management, 34*(1): 3–27. Available at: https://doi.org/10.1108/JOCM-04-2017-0131.

PART 5

CONTEMPORARY ISSUES

CHAPTER 11

HRM, Health and Well-Being

CHAPTER 12

Sustainable HRM and Environmental Sustainability

CHAPTER 13

International HRM in a Globalised Capitalism

CHAPTER 14

Back to the Future: Reimagining HRM in a Post-Pandemic Capitalism

CHAPTER 11

HRM, HEALTH AND WELL-BEING

outline

- Introduction
- Sustainable health and safety and human resource management
- The importance of health, safety and wellness
- Workplace health and safety issues
- Workplace wellness
- Critiquing workplace health, safety and well-being
- Summary
- Further reading

Source: Deniz Altindas on Unsplash

objectives

After studying this chapter, you should be able to:

1. Explain the benefits of a health, safety and wellness strategy
2. Describe some common hazards in the contemporary workplace
3. Describe the components of a workplace wellness programme
4. Critique management strategies for health, safety and well-being in the workplace

Introduction

On 4 August 2020, a large blast tore through the Lebanese capital, Beirut, killing at least 200 people, including multiple port workers and a team of firefighters, and injuring 5,000 more (BBC, 2020). Videos of the event showed smoke billowing from the city's busy port, followed by a fiery explosion. The aftermath was described as being 'like a war zone' (Regencia et al., 2020). The incident was soon traced to a hangar, where almost three thousand tonnes of ammonium nitrate, an agricultural fertiliser and explosive, was being stored without appropriate safety measures. The chemical, which has been linked to several other deadly industrial accidents, had arrived into the country in September 2013 on board a cargo ship bound for Mozambique. The vessel was forced to dock in Beirut due to technical problems but concerned officials prevented it from departing. Abandoned by its owners, the dangerous cargo was eventually unloaded into the hangar where it remained for almost seven years. The initial investigation suggested that a spark from a welder's torch ultimately triggered the explosion. The tragedy in Beirut represents an extreme example of a common problem: the environments in which we work can be unhealthy, unsafe and, at times, even deadly. The mismanagement of occupational health and safety (OHS) issues can have devastating repercussions for individuals, organisations, communities and even countries.

This chapter will begin by considering the importance of health, safety and well-being in the management of work and people, before discussing some common health and safety concerns in the modern workplace. Next, we will evaluate the importance of health, safety and well-being, before concluding with a critique of these concepts.

Reflective question

Who are the stakeholders in health and safety? What are the responsibilities of employers to ensure that work is conducted in a safe and healthy environment? What role should governments play in terms of regulating workplace health and safety?

Sustainable health and safety and HRM

The World Health Organization (WHO) (2020) defines health as 'a state of complete physical, mental and social well-being and not merely the absence of disease or infirmity'. The organisation adds that the 'enjoyment of the highest attainable standard of health is one of the fundamental rights of every human being without distinction of race, religion, political belief, economic or social condition'. Accordingly, managers and, in workplaces where they are organised, trade union representatives, are immersed in one of society's greatest challenges – the design and maintenance of sustainable work systems that both support the organisation's objectives and provide an environment that is safe and healthy for its workers.

Traditionally, OHS encapsulated distinct yet intrinsically related concepts concerned with the identification and control of work-induced ill health and accidents. Whereas accidents, such as the one described in the introduction, are visible or measurable, not without cause and largely preventable, work-induced ill health is largely invisible and can develop over a long period of time. OHS evolved from a separate function predominantly staffed by engineers and industrial hygienists to become a core aspect of the overall management of many organisations (Hart, 2010); a shift in part attributable to the move towards HRM. OHS encompasses both 'prevention' (of hazards) and 'promotion' (of health) (Iavicoli et al., 2018).

Although workplace health and safety have long been legitimate areas for regulation, as evidenced by health and safety legislation, in recent decades greater emphasis has been placed on workers' well-being (Black and Frost, 2011; van Wanrooy et al., 2013). There is, however, a lack of consensus in relation to the definition of 'well-being' and it has been conceptualised in a multitude of different ways (Kowalski and Loretto, 2017). For example, a distinction is usually drawn within the literature between hedonic and eudemonic well-being. The hedonic approach focuses on the type of affective feelings, both positive and negative, that the worker experiences in relation to their work. In contrast, the eudemonic approach centres on feelings that are considered to demonstrate good mental health, such as whether the worker derives a sense of purpose from their job (Bryson et al., 2014). An overview of the different approaches to measuring well-being is provided in Table 11.1.

Table 11.1 Differing approaches to well-being at work

Hedonic well-being		Eudemonic well-being
Affective feelings engendered by the job	**Satisfaction with the job**	**Psychological functioning associated with the job**
Sub-components include:	Sub-components include:	Sub-components include:
Anxiety	Satisfaction with work tasks	Sense of meaning or purpose
Boredom	Satisfaction with pay	Sense of vitality
Enthusiasm	Satisfaction with job security	Sense of achieving your potential
Contentment	Satisfaction with job training	Sense of personal development

Source: Bryson et al. (2014).

Reflective question

Can you think of jobs where the individual might experience a high level of eudemonic well-being, but lower levels of hedonic well-being, and vice versa?

In recent decades we have witnessed the development of a substantial body of literature on sustainable business strategies, as well as growing interest in 'triple', or even 'quadruple', bottom line performance (see chapters 2 and 12). Combined with clear evidence of the link between inequality and poor health and well-being (Pickett and Wilkinson, 2015), this has served to expand the scope and coverage of 'green' or 'sustainable' health and safety management to the point where they are no longer marginal but now mainstream concepts. The UN Sustainable Development Goals (SDGs) adopted in 2015, for example, make specific reference to 'Good Health and Well-being', as well as 'Decent Work'. The UN has called upon businesses of all sizes to contribute towards achieving the SDGs by acting responsibly and seeking ways to solve societal challenges through innovation and collaboration.

Over the last two decades many new issues have come to the fore that have an impact on OHS (Iavicoli et al., 2018). These include changes to the nature of work, including the rise in remote working and development of the platform economy, economic turmoil, demographic shifts, the development and introduction of new technologies, and increased globalisation. In addition, the workforce in most countries is becoming more diverse, with increasing numbers of women, older people and migrants participating (Iavicoli et al., 2018). These changes present both opportunities and challenges for organisational stakeholders, including worker representatives, managers, employers, government bodies and professional associations. For example, ageing is often associated with a general decline in health, as well as increased risk of injury and the development of chronic conditions, such as arthritis (Vanajan et al., 2019). As people work into old age, either by choice or necessity, employers will need to play a role in terms of supporting longer, healthier working lives. This may include introducing more flexible working arrangements and making physical adjustments to workspaces, as well as addressing negative stereotypes directed towards older workers.

The employer has a legal duty to maintain a healthy and safe workplace. On the question of the importance of OHS, although economic cost and HR considerations will always be predominant for the organisation, the costs of ill health and work-related accidents are not only borne by the victims, the families and their employers; they are also clearly borne by the taxpayer and public sector services. The health-care sector, for example, bears the costs of workplace ill health and accidents. Reliable estimates of the total cost of occupational ill health and accidents are incomplete, which is perhaps symptomatic of the low priority given to this area of work. The UK Health and Safety Executive (HSE) has estimated the cost of workplace injuries and ill health to be £15 billion (HSE, 2020a), however, the true figure may be much higher.

Although there has been a deluge of research on HRM problems and issues, workplace health and safety remains under-researched by workplace scholars, partly because it has entered the HRM discourse in only a marginal way. Rising costs associated with work-induced injuries and ill health, issues relating to the psychological contract, new laws and growing concerns about protecting the environment are important reasons why workplace health, safety and wellness should be part of any introduction to the field of HRM. But there is another important reason why HRM scholars and practitioners need to pay more attention to health and wellness: if strategic HRM means anything, it must encompass the development and promotion of a set of health and wellness policies to protect the organisation's most valued asset – its people.

Ethical Insight
Employee genetic testing

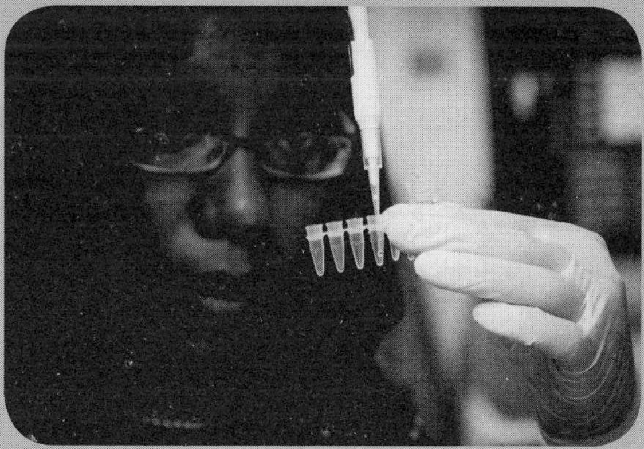

Source: National Cancer Institute on Unsplash

Many companies offer health and wellness-related benefits, such as gym memberships, in order to attract and retain talent. Some, however, are taking it a step further and, quite literally, digging into their employees' DNA. Genetic disease risk screening is becoming an increasingly popular 'perk', particularly in the United States where businesses including Apple are offering free tests to employees within their headquarters (Farr, 2019). From their perspective, it is hoped that the intervention will encourage staff to take preventative health measures based on the results. In turn, this may enhance productivity and, eventually, reduce business health-care costs. It is also possible to use genetic testing to identify those at increased risk of specific occupational hazards or illnesses. For employees, test results may offer valuable insight into their chances of developing certain inherited diseases. However, significant concerns have been raised in relation to both the efficacy and ethics of employee genetic testing.

Regarding the first issue, the accuracy of many tests is still in doubt and evidence suggests that there are only a few instances where genes appear to have a strong influence over susceptibility to certain common illnesses (US National Library of Medicine, 2020a). Environmental factors may have an equally powerful impact on an individual's health and well-being. Second, the results of the testing, particularly if they reveal negative information, can have emotional, social and financial consequences for the subject. They may feel anxious, depressed or even angry about what has been revealed, particularly if they do not receive appropriate support afterwards. There are also fears that if the results of the tests become known to employers, the individual could become the victim of 'genetic discrimination' (Riley Chapman et al., 2019). Genetic discrimination occurs when people are treated differently by their employers because they possess a gene mutation that causes or increases the risk of an inherited disorder (US National Library of Medicine, 2020b). In many countries there are laws in place to prevent workplace genetic discrimination, however, it may be subtle and difficult to prove.

Most genetic screening companies stress that they adhere to the highest standards of data protection and will not reveal results to employers without the individual's consent. However, in 2017, legislation was proposed in the US that could have made the situation significantly more complex and ethically ambiguous. Most Americans under the age of 65 receive their health insurance from work-based plans. The 'Preserving Employee Wellness Programs Act' allowed employers to request genetic data from workers (and potentially their family members) in order to access company health insurance (Thompson, 2017). While it would not be mandatory, those who refused could see their health-care costs increase by up to 50%. The legislation was not passed but, nonetheless, fears remain that if the results of DNA tests become tied to recruitment and promotion, for instance, employees may find themselves with little choice but to hand over their genetic code.

Stop! Do you think it is ethical to compel employees to disclose their genetic information to their employer? Provide a rationale for your answer.

Essential reading

Riley Chapman, C., Mehta, K. S., Parent, B. and Caplan, R. L. (2019) Genetic discrimination: emerging ethical challenges in the context of advancing technology. *Journal of Law and the Biosciences, 7*(1): 1-23.

Note: This feature was contributed by Laura Steele.

The importance of health, safety and wellness

There are strong economic, legal, psychological and ethical reasons why managers should take health and safety seriously, and these will be discussed in turn below.

Economic considerations

An important consideration, and one that is sometimes overlooked, is that OHS can contribute to the economic viability of an organisation. A safe and healthy work environment, built on sustainable principles, can reduce operating costs and improve organisational effectiveness (Dyck, 2002; Mearns and Hope, 2005). The European Agency for Safety and Health at Work (2014) has set out the 'business case' for OHS. In particular, they highlight how small and medium-sized Enterprises (SMEs), which account for 67 per cent of employment within the European economy, are the site of 82 per cent of occupational injuries. Managers within SMEs may, however, be reluctant to invest in OHS interventions due to actual or perceived costs, as well as difficulties in assessing and monitoring the risks associated with certain activities (Bianchini et al., 2017).

In considering the economics of an unhealthy and unsafe workplace, it is necessary to distinguish between costs falling upon the organisation and costs falling upon government-funded bodies such as hospitals. It is not difficult for an organisation to calculate the economic costs of a work-related accident. In addition to direct costs related to lost production due to accidents and illness, there are also indirect costs. These include the overtime payments necessary to make up for lost production, the cost of retraining a replacement employee and the legal cost associated with court hearings in contested cases. The indirect costs of workplace accidents and illnesses also fall on society through the extra need for health-care provision. The economic costs of work-related accidents, and the techniques for assessing them, require further research (Byram et al., 2016; Georgiou et al., 2009).

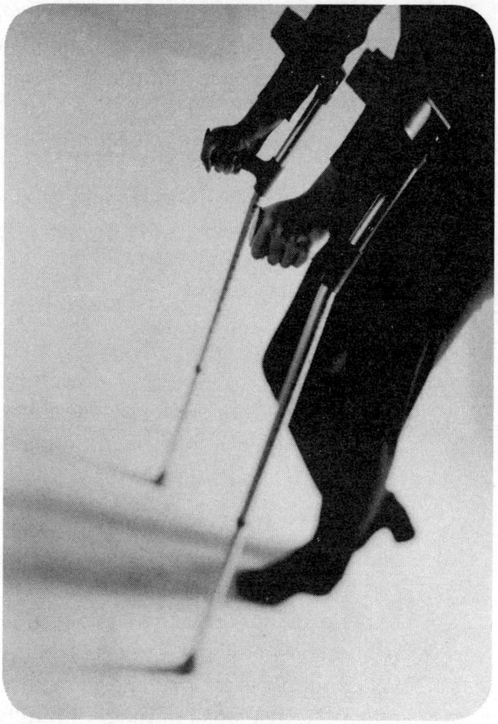

Source: Stockbyte/PunchStock/Getty Images

Work-related accidents have economic costs. There are direct costs related to lost production and indirect costs including the cost of retraining a replacement employee, and the legal cost associated with court hearings.

Legal considerations

With respect to workplace health and safety, the legal rights of workers can be categorised into two broad classes: *individual* and *collective*. The first source of *individual* rights evolves from common law. Every employer has a vicarious common law duty to provide a safe working environment for their workers. But the primary source of individual rights arises from statute law. In Great Britain, an example is the Health and Safety at Work etc. Act 1974. Within the European Union (EU), individual rights stemming from directives under Article 189 of the Treaty of Rome are a second important source of legislated protection standards promoting safe working environments. Questions have been raised as to what, if any, impact the UK's exit from the EU may have on the legislative landscape. In the short term at least, the government's approach appears to reflect a desire to maintain the status quo. The Health and Safety at Work etc. Act 1974 will remain the primary source of health and safety legislation. In addition, steps have been taken to convert key EU health and safety regulations into domestic law. However, as the government seeks to negotiate trade deals with other countries, concerns have been expressed that a need to compete internationally could drive deregulation. In the event this did occur, however, the economic and ethical arguments for OHS may forestall a steep decline in standards.

The main source of *collective* health and safety rights arises from the negotiated collective agreements between unions and management. In many countries, including Australia, New Zealand, the UK and the USA, workers have the legal right to refuse to perform unsafe or unhealthy work. Such provisions became particularly pertinent during the coronavirus pandemic. Some workers, including many teachers, expressed concerns about returning to workplaces where it is difficult to maintain social distancing or where hygiene standards may be insufficient to prevent the spread of the virus. In the EU and the USA, failure to provide a safe working environment may result in the employer being prosecuted for *corporate manslaughter*. Following the death of over 50 hospital and care home workers in the UK from Covid-19 in 2020, it was suggested that employers could be sued for corporate manslaughter for failure to supply adequate Personal Protective Equipment (PPE) or otherwise ensure safe working conditions (Dodd and Campbell, 2020).

Psychological considerations

Apart from economic and legal considerations, a healthy and safe work environment helps to facilitate worker commitment and improve industrial relations. In Beer et al.'s (1984) model of HRM, it is recognised that, going beyond the legal requirement of 'due diligence', a healthy organisation can have a highly positive effect on the psychological contract by strengthening employees' commitment, motivation and loyalty (p. 153):

> There is some evidence to indicate that work system design may have effects on physical health, mental health, and longevity of life itself.

A survey of UK workplaces found a strong relationship between worker reports of a 'healthier workplace' and greater experience of HR practices. Healthier workplaces are also associated with a more positive state of the psychological contract and lower reported levels of stress (Guest, 2004). In regard to performance, Bryson and colleagues (2014, p.62) note that there is strong evidence of a positive correlation between employee well-being and performance at the individual level, however, the evidence is less robust at the workplace or firm level. They attribute this to several factors, including 'spillover effects' from a small number of highly disaffected employees and greater opportunities for other factors to intervene.

Ethical considerations

The ethical dimension of occupational health, safety and well-being is understudied and requires further investigation (Artvinli, 2016). It is, however, generally accepted that employers have a moral duty to safeguard their workers against hazards. The ethical aspect is usually most apparent in the 'grey areas' of occupational health, safety, and well-being that do not fall within the scope of legislation. Doherty and Tyson (2000) argue that managers are not innocent bystanders with regard to worker health and well-being: their actions – such as the choice of production processes and substances, work speed-up – can have adverse effects on employees' work–life balance, as well as their physical and mental well-being.

Artvinli (2016) draws attention to the concept of informed consent. In the work context, for a worker to be able to give informed consent they should be *competent* to assess the risk, *understand* the risk, be *fully informed* about the risks and *voluntarily* accept the risks. If any of these conditions are not met, for example, if an employer fails to fully apprise the worker of the risks involved or coerces them into engaging in an unsafe activity, then informed consent has not been given. Informed consent, or lack thereof, is a particular issue when it comes to industrial chemicals. According to a UN report (United Nations General Assembly, 2018a), a worker dies of toxic exposure every 30 seconds, with cancer the largest contributor to these deaths. For example, in 2008 a 23-year-old Samsung Electronics employee in South Korea, Hwang Yumi, died of leukaemia after being exposed to noxious chemicals at work (United Nations General Assembly, 2018b). The report paints a grim picture of the factory at which Hwang worked, with workers complaining of chronic stress stemming from long shifts and high production targets.

Ethics is distinct from, but closely related to, the concepts of corporate social responsibility, sustainability and global governance. Rather than addressing underlying issues, there is evidence of some multinational companies relocating hazardous work to countries with more lax health and safety regulations, effectively outsourcing the problem. Providing a safe and healthy work environment for employees is clearly a major challenge for managers. In addition to a pervasive portfolio of OHS legislation, economic and ethical considerations also shape organisational policy. As a result, the HR practitioner has a critical role to play in terms of advising line managers in relation to their obligations.

Reflective question

Do you think how businesses treat their employees has an impact on whether or not consumers choose to purchase goods or services from them? Would learning that a company had mistreated its workers make you less likely to engage with them? Why/why not?

Global HRM

Supporting the mental health of Black employees

Most Black Americans, regardless of education, socioeconomic status or job title, experience one or more forms of racism every day and continue to face both explicit racism and subtle forms of racism in the workplace (Roberts and Mayo, 2019). On 25 May 2020, George Floyd, a 46-year-old Black man, was arrested in Minneapolis, Minnesota when he allegedly bought cigarettes with a counterfeit $20 bill. Police officers held him down, choking him for nearly nine minutes until he was unconscious and died. After his death, protests against police violence towards Black people quickly spread across the United States and internationally. Neal-Barnett (2020) explains that for Black people, watching the death of George Floyd on video was a painful and traumatising experience:

> First, it's important to understand that when Black Americans watched the video of George Floyd being killed by a white police officer, we saw ourselves. In those eight minutes and 46 seconds, we were horrified, enraged, and anguished as a man who could have been our spouse, our brother, our son, our nephew, our cousin, or us was killed. Collectively, Black Americans were traumatized.

Trauma is the experience of severe psychological distress following any terrible or life-threatening incident. With the placement of the police officer's knee on George Floyd's neck, racism shifted from a chronic stressor to a trauma trigger. For Black Americans, witnessing the events before and after the killing of George Floyd is a form of racism know as racial trauma. Neal-Barnett (2020) explains that racism takes three forms, each of which is a chronic stressor: (1) *systemic racism* is experienced when ideologies, institutions and policies operate to produce racial and ethnic inequality; (2) *interpersonal racism* involves two or more people and can be manifested through bigotry, bias, prejudice and microaggressions; and (3) *internalised racism* is the acceptance of negative stereotypes and societal beliefs about one's racial group.

To address the needs of a racially traumatised workforce organisational leaders must take concrete action (Neal-Barnett, 2020). First, it is important to understand that racism impacts Black workers emotionally, mentally and physically. This may require the creation of a safe place within the organisation and bringing in a skilled expert in racial trauma to help Black workers process what they are experiencing and feeling. Second, action should be taken to demonstrate support at the organisational level to show that the organisation stands with Black workers. For example, many organisations may issue an internal

PART 5

statement of support acknowledging Black employees' current state of emotions and to recognise their anger, grief and trauma. Third, organisational leaders should ensure that Black workers are part of the organisation's daily decision-making body, senior management or board of directors. Fourth, it is important to develop a plan and include target dates in that plan. Finally, most importantly, organisational leaders must listen to what Black workers are saying and convert ideas and recommendations into action.

Stop! Are you confident you recognise the organisational and individual behaviours that maintain racist practices in the workplace? How can HR professionals help people tackle racism and racial discrimination at work?

Essential reading

Neal-Barnett, A. (2020) How organisations can support the mental health of Black employees. *Harvard Business Review*, 11 June; Roberts, L. and Mayo, A. (2019) Toward a racially just workplace: diversity efforts are failing Black employees. Here's a better approach. *Harvard Business Review*, 20 November; Tharps, L. (2014) The case for Black with a capital B. *The New York Times*, 18 November.

Note: This feature was contributed by Andrew Bratton.

Workplace health and safety issues

This section examines several health issues of special concern to today's managers, specifically mental health, stress and burnout, workplace violence, workplace bullying, alcohol and drug abuse, and sick building syndrome (SBS).

Mental health at work

The coronavirus pandemic is likely to increase the number of people in Britain experiencing a mental health problem in the next two years (Sinclair et al., 2020). Prior to the Covid-19 crisis, mental health at work had become an area of increasing scholarly interest. Research suggests that one in four people will experience a mental health problem of some kind each year, with depression and/or anxiety the most common disorders (Mind, 2020). The number of people with common mental health problems increased by 20 per cent between 1993 and 2014 (Mind, 2020). While anyone can be affected by mental ill health, evidence suggests that certain groups, such as people who identify as lesbian, gay, bisexual and transgender (LGBTQ+), and Black, Asian and minority ethnic (BAME), as well as women aged 16 to 24, are at greater risk. This has been attributed to several factors, including experiencing social inequality and disadvantage, discrimination and social exclusion, and traumatic events such as assault (Mind, 2020).

According to the UK's Health and Safety Executive (HSE) (2019a), in 2018–19, work-related stress, depression or anxiety accounted for 44 per cent of work-related illness and 54 per cent of working days lost. In turn, the WHO (2019) estimates that these issues cost the global economy approximately US$1 trillion annually in lost productivity. Work can have a positive influence on mental well-being, for example, by bolstering self-esteem and facilitating the development of mutually supportive relationships. Indeed, unemployment is a recognised risk factor in terms of mental health problems, while returning to work, or getting a job, is protective (WHO, 2019). However, there is growing awareness of the negative impact work may have on mental health. Risks to mental well-being include excessive workloads, unclear tasks or organisational objectives, poor communication and management practices, low levels of support for employees, limited participation in decision-making or low control over one's work, inflexible working hours, and inadequate health and safety policies (WHO, 2019). As noted below, violence and bullying are other common sources of work-related stress and may result in both mental and physical ill health. In addition, some jobs by their very nature carry a higher personal risk than others, for example, first responders such as the firefighters mentioned in the introduction, which can place additional strain on the individual.

Despite the prevalence of many mental health conditions, a significant stigma remains, discouraging workers from disclosing them for fear of the repercussions. Such concerns are not unfounded: a study conducted by Mind (2014) reported that 22 per cent of workers who disclosed a mental health problem to their employers had either been sacked or forced out of their jobs. In addition to the strong ethical case for addressing the stigma around mental illness, there is also a robust economic argument. The financial cost to employers, the government and the economy as a whole is high. In relation to employers, this is estimated at between £33 billion and £42 billion. Half of this figure is attributable to 'presenteeism', where individuals are less productive as the result of struggling with poor mental health, with the remaining costs including sickness absence and staff turnover. The impact on the economy, estimated at between £74 billion and £99 billion, comes from lost output (Stevenson and Farmer, 2017).

In 2017, the UK government commissioned Lord Denis Stevenson and Paul Farmer, the Chief Executive of mental health charity Mind, to independently review the role employers can play in supporting individuals with mental health conditions in the workplace. In their report, *Thriving at Work* (2017), Stevenson and Farmer developed a set of 'Core Standards' that they recommend workplaces of all sizes can and should put into place. These include that employers should:

1. Produce, implement and communicate a mental health at work plan.
2. Develop mental health awareness among employees.
3. Encourage open conversations about mental health and the support available when employees are struggling.
4. Provide employees with good working conditions.
5. Promote effective people management.
6. Routinely monitor employee mental health and well-being.

Source: Arif Riyanto on Unsplash

A significant stigma remains discouraging employees from disclosing mental health conditions for fear of the repercussions. A study conducted found that 22 per cent of employees who disclosed a mental health problem to their employers had either been dismissed or forced out of their jobs.

Disrupting the traditional narrative, St-Hilaire and colleagues (2019) ask the question, what if subordinates took care of managers' mental health at work? The authors note that managers' mental health is an increasing subject of concern. However, workplace interventions (and research studies) predominantly focus on employees, rather than managers. The limited evidence available suggests that subordinates have an impact on managers' stress levels (Glowinkowski and Cooper, 1986). St-Hilaire and colleagues (2019) found that subordinates can reduce managers' exposure to stress through various practices including assisting with tasks (support practices), promoting a positive climate (affiliation practices), taking the initiative (contributing practices), and being open and transparent (ethical practices). However, could charging employees with supporting managers' mental health – beyond the standard of professional behaviour expected of all workers – simply place another burden upon them rather than, perhaps, addressing systemic problems within the organisation?

The coronavirus pandemic rapidly changed the employment conditions of tens of millions of people around the world. Some lost their jobs, while others worked throughout (often while carrying concerns about contracting the virus). A large number worked from home, often for the first time, with many finding themselves also juggling childcare and home-schooling responsibilities. In addition, in many countries, including the UK, a significant proportion of the population was placed on job retention schemes. Such uncertainty and change can put a strain on mental health. In August 2020, 33 leading organisations, including Barclays, Santander and Unilever, signed an open letter published in *The Times* (Gosden, 2020) committing to prioritising the mental health of their employees as they returned to the workplace. The letter cited research from Mind, which found that 35 per cent of employees described their mental health as either 'poor' or 'very poor', and that the prospect of returning to work was causing them anxiety. The results of this survey are in line with findings from the CIPD (Wells, 2020), who found that 43 per cent of employees said their general mental health had worsened since the coronavirus outbreak, increasing to 52 per cent for those with an existing mental health condition. The CIPD (Wells, 2020) have outlined a number of ways employers can support those returning to work, including preparing a detailed communication plan covering practical issues, such as hygiene and maintaining social distancing to allay concerns; providing manager training on mental health conditions, including signs and symptoms; and introducing an Employee Assistance Programme (EAP), if one is not currently in place.

Workplace stress and burnout

As noted above, workplace stress and burnout may be contributing factors in relation to both mental and physical ill health. The word 'stress' is now part of the regular vocabulary of managers and other employees. Stress is an unavoidable part of working life (Gallo, 2011; Nelson and Simmons, 2011). Certain forms of stress can have a positive impact, for example, by enhancing productivity, performance and innovation (Ren and Zhang, 2015). However, if stress is repeated or prolonged, individuals experience physical and psychological discomfort. There is widespread recognition that tension and stress have increased in UK workplaces, and this is supported by evidence of work intensification. So, what is driving workplace stress? According to the Health and Safety Executive (2020b), workload, in particular tight deadlines, too much work, and excessive pressure or responsibility, was the primary cause of pressure. This was followed, in order, by lack of support, violence, threats or bullying, changes at work, role uncertainty and lack of control (HSE, 2020b). In addition, the ubiquity of the Internet and 'smart' devices such as phones and tablets have helped to create a 24/7, on-demand lifestyle, that results in the intrusion of work into private life (Bittman et al., 2009). This was compounded by the coronavirus pandemic, which saw unprecedented numbers of people working from home. Figure 11.1 illustrates some common symptoms of stress.

Job-related stress and burnout is a serious human resource issue that affects performance and retention (McCormack and Cotter, 2013). Research shows that employees affected by burnout approach their day-to-day work interactions with cynicism, exhaustion and inefficiency (Maslach et al., 2001).

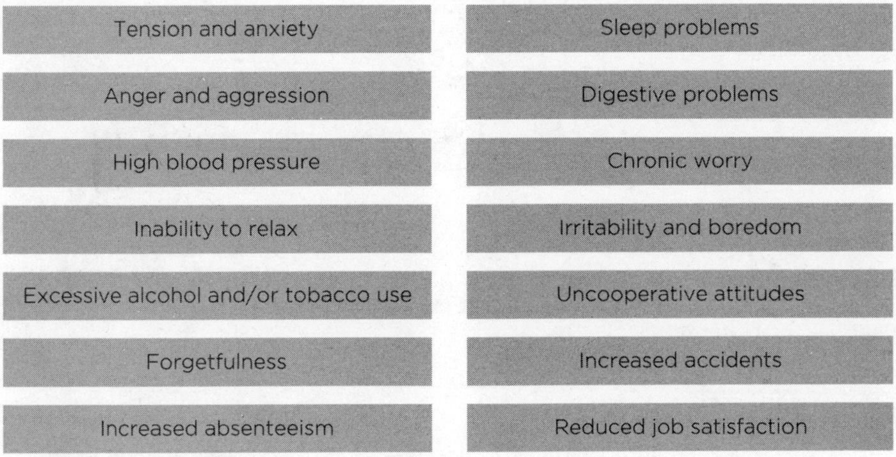

Figure 11.1 Typical symptoms of workplace stress

However, they may not realise they are afflicted (McCormack and Cotter, 2013). Much of the research into job-related stress has tended to focus on 'executive burnout' and individuals at the upper echelons of the organisational hierarchy. However, stress can affect employees at every level, in any organisation. Using data from the UK Labour Force Survey, the HSE (2020b) found that those in the professional occupations category reported significantly higher rates of stress than their counterparts in the likes of sales and customer service, administrative and secretarial roles, and managers, directors and senior officials. There was also evidence of a gender divide: women were found to have notably higher rates of work-related stress, depression or anxiety compared to men. This was particularly acute amongst those aged 25–54. The research suggests that smaller workplaces (less than 50 employees) had lower rates of work-related stress, depression or anxiety while large workplaces (over 250 staff) had significantly higher rates.

The nature of work has changed significantly over the last two decades, with more people finding themselves in 'atypical' or precarious forms of employment (Apouey and Stabile, 2020). This has been driven by a range of factors, including advances in technology and the rise of the gig and platform economies. Research suggests that non-standard working hours and job insecurity can be a source of work-related stress. Zeytinoglu et al. (2015), for example, examined the relationship between home care workers' health and non-standard hours and insecurity. Their findings show that casual, part-time work and job insecurity are strongly correlated with symptoms of stress. More recently, Mousteri et al. (2020) found that underemployment, defined as part-time workers preferring to work more hours, resulted in a level of distress comparable to that of losing a job. It is important to note, however, that there are a small number of studies that contradict these findings and suggest that, for example, self-employment in the gig economy can increase some measures of mental health and well-being (Apouey and Stabile, 2020).

Stress from an individual's personal life can frequently spill over into their professional life, and vice versa. For example, an employee may be dealing with illness within their family or the breakdown of a relationship that is placing them under significant pressure. Alternatively, bullying or harassment in the workplace may cause them to be anxious or short-tempered at home. Researchers have explored the antecedents of workplace stress. In particular, studies have examined work-related factors, including role ambiguity and job design, as well as individual factors, such as debt worries and workplace bullying (Hadikin and O'Driscoll, 2000). Findings appear to suggest 'dual-role syndrome' as an explanation of work-related stress. According to a Canadian study, stress is triggered by employees trying to balance family and work (Ross and MacDonald, 1997). However, research conducted by Zheng et al. (2016) in Australia on work–life balance (WLB) found that individual employees with positive attitudes and life-coping strategies were more capable of achieving overall well-being.

Source: iStock.com/NoSystem images

Stress caused by the 'dual-role' syndrome

Work-related stress is a multifaceted workplace phenomenon caused by multiple social and environmental factors. While once the prevailing view may have been that occupational stress is a personal problem, now it is widely recognised that it represents a major health problem and that management within organisations have a responsibility to eliminate or reduce the causes of work-related stress. As a result, the findings of the studies outlined above have implications for employers, HR managers, trade unionists and policy makers.

Reflective question

Think about a time when you felt under considerable stress. What were the causes of that stress? Could any of the work-related stressors have been eliminated or reduced? If not, explain why.

Workplace violence

For many employees, particularly those at the front end of service delivery, violence is a critical safety issue. The HSE describes workplace violence as 'Any incident in which a person is abused, threatened, or assaulted in circumstances relating to their work' (HSE, 2020c). Workplace violence can be physical, psychological and/or sexual in nature, and may take the form of a one-off incident or a systematic pattern of behaviour. It can be perpetrated by subordinates, peers, superiors or third parties such as clients, customers or suppliers. According to the HSE (2019b), in the 2018–19 period, there were 739,000 incidents of violence at work affecting 344,000 people in the UK. Of these, 54 per cent caused an injury, such as bruising or a black eye, cuts or scratches. In the US, in 2018 there were 453 fatalities resulting from workplace violence (NSC, 2020). Certain industries, including health care, service provision and education are more prone to violence than others. In the US, taxi drivers, for example, are 20 times more likely to be murdered while on the job than any other worker (NSC, 2020).

In recent years, movements such as #MeToo and the Everyday Sexism Project have brought accounts of sexual harassment and abuse to the fore, including acts perpetrated within the workplace. According to McDonald and Charlesworth (2016), men are overwhelmingly responsible for harassment against women in the workplace. However, anyone can be the victim, or the perpetrator. Research conducted by the TUC (2016) found that over half of all women have experienced some form of sexual harassment at work, rising to nearly two-thirds (63 per cent) amongst those aged 18–24. However, four out of five did not report it to their employer. Some respondents stated that they feared that they would be viewed as 'humourless' or 'unable to take a joke' if they challenged or reported the behaviour. Workplace sexual harassment is often dismissed as 'just a bit of banter' (TUC 2016). The TUC (2019b) also surveyed more than 1,000 lesbian, gay, bisexual and transgender (LGBTQ+) people and found that 68 per cent had been sexually harassed at work. Almost one in eight (12 per cent) of LGBTQ+ women surveyed had been seriously sexually assaulted or raped at work.

There are four major forms of workplace violence (Ceplenski, 2013):

- Type 1: Criminal Intent – The perpetrator has no legitimate relationship to the business or its employees, and is usually committing a criminal act, such as robbery or shoplifting, in conjunction with the violence. Retail and service industry employees are those most exposed to this form of workplace violence.
- Type 2: Customer/Client – The perpetrator has a legitimate relationship with the organisation, for example, a customer, client, patient, student or any other group to which the organisation provides goods or services. This form of violence is particularly common in the health and social care field.
- Type 3: Worker-on-Worker – Violence between co-workers is also referred to as lateral or horizontal violence. It includes bullying and harassment, and frequently manifests as verbal and emotional abuse. However, it can also be physical in nature, sometimes even resulting in homicide.
- Type 4: Personal Relationship – Here, the perpetrator has a relationship with the employee outside of work, for example, their partner or spouse, and targets them in or around their workplace. Other employees may find themselves subject to the violence either by accident or deliberate intention. There is growing awareness of the fact that domestic violence may spill out of the home and into the workplace.

Research suggests that many incidents of workplace violence go unrecorded. However, the consequences of workplace violence go beyond immediate physical injury or death. The trauma caused by the violence has negative results for both the individual employee's well-being (that is, in terms of impaired mental and physical health) and the organisation (that is, decreased commitment, retention and performance) (Montgomery and Kelloway, 2002).

Workplace bullying

Workplace bullying is a troublesome and ubiquitous reality of institutional life, which may be considered an extreme form of 'dysfunctional organisational behaviour' (Soylu and Sheehy-Skeffington, 2015). As a result of the increased involvement of line managers in HRM, understanding this complex phenomenon has become especially important. Over the last 30 years a substantial body of literature on workplace bullying has developed, however, an agreed-upon definition remains elusive (Rai and Agarwal, 2018). Three key features distinguish bullying from other negative workplace phenomena such as workplace aggression, deviance and harassment, specifically: persistency (the escalating nature of the phenomenon), power disparities and hostility (Einarsen et al., 2003; Rai and Agarwal, 2018). Workplace bullying can therefore be defined as:

> The systematic mistreatment of a subordinate, a colleague, or a superior, which if continued and long-lasting, may cause severe social, psychological and psychosomatic problems in the target. (Einarsen et al., 2011, p. 4)

Workplace bullying can range from subtle and covert, to explicit and identifiable (Stouten et al., 2010). Einarsen et al. (2009) consider bullying behaviours to fall into three categories: work-related (such as withholding information, setting unreasonable deadlines or creating an unmanageable workload); person-related (humiliation in connection with work, repeated reminders of mistakes, persistent criticism); and physical intimidation (insults, threats). Einarsen (2000) argues that the prevalence of workplace bullying varies markedly between countries due to the influence of national culture. Supporting this, Ciby and Raya (2015) found that the lowest prevalence of victims was observed in Denmark (1 per cent), while the highest levels were found in Turkey and Pakistan (over 52 per cent). The authors attribute this to cultural dimensions such as power distance and masculine-feminine values, as identified by Hofstede (1980). However, they note that differences in terms of defining and measuring workplace bullying makes comparison between countries and continents challenging.

In terms of the impact on the victim, research has demonstrated that workplace bullying can be detrimental to both mental and physical health. In regard to the former, it may lead to depression; anxiety; post-traumatic stress disorder; poor self-esteem; emotional damage, such as a sense of humiliation, doubt and stress; violation of the psychological contract; and vicious cycles of counterproductive work behaviour (Field, 1996; Fox and Stallworth, 2010; Hoel et al., 2004; O'Moore et al., 1998; Parzefall and Salin, 2010). At the organisational level, the negative effects of bullying include costs associated with higher turnover rates, absenteeism, reduced productivity, diminished organisational performance, legal expenses, reputational damage, and decreased loyalty and commitment (Branch et al., 2009; Fox and Stallworth, 2010; Glambek et al., 2014; Hoel et al., 2011). Despite the severe consequences for both the individual and the wider organisation, a report by the CIPD (2020g) found that a quarter of employees surveyed felt their company turned a 'blind eye' to workplace bullying and harassment. Although 15 per cent of respondents had experienced bullying in the previous three years, over half chose not to report it. The primary reason cited was fear of the repercussions, with some expressing a concern that they would be blamed for the situation. Fox and Cowan (2015) contend that because HR professionals have the prime responsibility for dealing with the victim and perpetrator of bullying, they should have a voice in assessing and dealing with cases of bullying. However, they also report that HR professionals experience difficulties in effectively responding to employee complaints of bullying due to a number of factors, including conflicts among multiple HR roles in the organisation, a paucity of specific organisational policies and guidelines for dealing with bullying, and ambiguous definitions and criteria for behaviour to be considered bullying.

Recent research into workplace bullying supports the notion that it is an elusive, complex social phenomenon, which, according to some, has its origins outside the organisation (Soylu and Sheehy-Skeffington, 2015). An important variation to the concept of workplace bullying and possibly a societal – gender or/and religious – dimension, is that bullying is deployed 'strategically', to achieve goals beyond those of the perpetrators themselves. Thus, according to Soylu and Sheehy-Skeffington's (2015) study, bullying is used either as a calculated means of getting rid of unwanted employees, or as a subtle, but no less pernicious, way of achieving the dominance of one sociocultural worldview over another and, in turn, a mechanism through which inequality is maintained and reproduced (2015, p. 24). In addition, research has identified a link between economic conditions and bullying, with studies predicting that the threat of job loss is likely to cause an increase in workplace bullying, as is the decline of trade unions and of collective representation (Hirch, 2010). This is particularly pertinent in the context of the coronavirus pandemic, which plunged many countries around the world into a deep recession (Partington, 2020a). This led to a vast number of redundancies, with many of those who survived the initial phase fearful for their long-term prospects. This can produce an opportune environment for workplace bullying to take hold.

In August 2020, the Commonwealth of Puerto Rico, a US territory, became the first jurisdiction within the country to adopt a specific law against workplace bullying. The controversial legislation faced significant opposition, largely from the private sector (Santos and Colón-Acevedo, 2020), and raised questions as to whether other areas within the US will follow suit. To date, only a small number of countries have introduced OHS legislation that specifically deals with workplace bullying. Instead, it tends to fall within the remit of laws related to workplace harassment or violence, as is the case in the US and UK (Pinkos Cobb, 2017). However, this can result in legislative voids where workers are unable to make a claim because their particular circumstances mean that there are no relevant options available to them. As a result, campaigners in many countries have been advocating the development and introduction of specific legislation on workplace bullying. Their case was advanced in 2019, when the International Labour Organization (ILO) ratified the first international treaty to address violence and harassment in the workplace, called the Violence and Harassment Convention 2019. The treaty aims to provide a clear framework for action to shape a future of work based on dignity and respect. Due to the lack of agreed-upon definition, the ILO took a broad approach describing violence and harassment as 'a range of unacceptable behaviours and practices'. This potentially covers an array of behaviours, including bullying.

It is recommended that organisations develop and implement a policy on workplace bullying. These documents may be standalone, incorporated into a wider harassment policy, or included in an even broader dignity at work policy that examines situations where dignity and respect have allegedly been violated (Rayner and Lewis, 2011). Ferris et al. (2018), conducted an extensive review of best practice regarding the development and implementation of workplace bullying policies. They argue that, when developing a policy, a small group representing a broad range of stakeholders should be involved, for example, representatives from senior management, HR, OHS, unions (where they are operating), workers and possibly external consultants. Ferris et al. (2018) continue that the purpose of the policy should be clearly stated, and the document should reference core organisational values. Workplace bullying should be described using definitions contained in any relevant legislation or guidance within the jurisdiction, and illustrative examples of bullying behaviour included. According to the authors, resolution options should be set out. Depending on the level of the bullying, for the victim these may include an apology, coaching, mentoring or financial compensation. In turn, depending on the severity of the bullying, the perpetrator may be subject to disciplinary action up to and including dismissal. It is important that the policy is written in clear language and widely accessible. Finally, it should be kept under regular review. New legislation or novel cases may prompt organisational learning and, as a result, it may be necessary to update policies, procedures and training programmes to reflect this.

Workplace bullying is a significant issue for worker well-being and for achieving dignity *at* work. In conclusion, Aryanne Oade writes, 'Being subject to workplace bullying is among the most horrible workplace experiences you might have' (2009, p. 159). Although it is under analysed, research shows that workplace bullying can have a detrimental effect upon individual and organisational performance and, consequently, necessitates a response from management and worker representatives, including an effective preventative policy and process.

PART 5

Reflective question

What challenges might managers and HR professionals encounter when attempting to tackle bullying in the workplace? How might these be overcome?

Alcohol and drug abuse

Levels of alcohol consumption vary significantly across the world. For example, alcohol consumption is very low in North Africa and the Middle East and higher in Europe. Since the early 1980s, the amount of alcohol that people in the UK consume increased steadily, before peaking in 2008 and declining slightly thereafter (Public Health England, 2019). Drinking habits are shaped by a variety of factors, including age, gender, education level, relationship status and household composition (for example, whether or not someone lives alone). In the UK, men are more likely to drink alcohol than women (61.9 per cent compared to 52.4 per cent), and the highest consumption is found amongst those aged 45 to 64 (ONS, 2018a). In contrast, the lowest consumption is amongst those aged 16 to 24. However, when they did drink, this group was more likely to 'binge' on alcohol. Binge drinking is defined as males who consume more than eight units of alcohol and females who consume more than six units of alcohol on their heaviest drinking day (ONS, 2018a). Alcohol misuse contributes – wholly or partially – to approximately 200 health conditions, including depression, certain cancers, heart disease and stroke (Public Health England, 2019). According to the ONS (2018a), people working in managerial and professional occupations, such as architects, doctors, lawyers and teachers, were the most likely to say that they had consumed alcohol in the previous week.

Obtaining an accurate picture of drug use is difficult because, unlike alcohol, substances such as cannabis, cocaine and MDMA/Ecstasy are illegal in many countries. The 2018–19 Crime Survey for England, for example, reported that 9.4 per cent of adults aged 16 to 59 had taken a drug in the last year and 34.2 per cent of adults aged 16 to 59 had taken drugs at some point during their lifetime (Home Office, 2019). However, the authors note that the report may not provide a true measure of problematic drug use, as many such users may be unable or unwilling to participate in the research. While many people associate drug misuse with illegal substances, there is growing awareness of the problem of prescription drug abuse. Misuse of prescription medications encompasses taking medication in a manner or dose other than prescribed, taking someone else's medication or taking a medication to feel a sense of euphoria (to 'get high'). The most commonly misused prescription drugs are opioids used to treat pain, central nervous system depressants used to treat anxiety and sleep disorders, and stimulants, most often prescribed to treat attention-deficit hyperactivity disorder (ADHD) (NIDA, 2020). Prescription drug misuse has increased significantly in the last 15 years in many countries. In the US, for example, commentators have spoken of an 'opioid crisis' that has seen deaths involving prescription medications increase fivefold between 1999 and 2016 (NIDA, 2020).

Employers must strike a balance between respecting the employee's private life and protecting the health, safety and well-being of the employee, their co-workers and anyone else with whom they interact. According to research conducted by the CIPD (2020h), just over a third of employers had disciplined someone in the previous two years for alcohol misuse and just over a quarter for drug misuse. Around a fifth had dismissed someone in the same period where alcohol and/or drug misuse was a significant reason. Alcohol and drug misuse can pose a particular risk when the individual is involved in safety-critical work, such as the use of heavy machinery, electrical devices, or driving and operating heavy lifting equipment HSE (2020d). According to the HSE (2020d), warning signs of alcohol or drug misuse may include unexplained or frequent absences, a change in behaviour, unexplained dips in productivity, more accidents or near-misses, and performance or conduct issues. However, these may also be symptoms of other issues, such as stress or bullying.

The HSE recommends that all organisations develop a policy on alcohol and drug misuse. This can either be a standalone document or form part of the organisation's broader health and safety policy. In either case it should be bolstered by training for line managers on the appropriate way to address concerns regarding alcohol and/or drug misuse by employees. The HSE stresses that, if an employee reports a problem, the first step should be to offer help and support, rather than seek to dismiss them.

However, a survey by the CIPD (2020h) found that just 27 per cent of organisations provided information for employees on how to disclose a problem with alcohol or drugs. Some organisations have introduced alcohol and drug screening as part of their policy. However, this is an issue that must be given careful consideration. There may be a case for screening in certain occupations where alcohol and drug misuse can have devastating consequences for the employee, their co-workers, members of the public and the environment, for example, airline pilots, train drivers or sea captains (HSE, 2020c). However, in the UK employees must consent to being screened, though they may potentially face disciplinary action if they refuse. In addition, screening can be costly, erode trust and may fail to address the problems caused by (or, indeed, leading to) alcohol and drug misuse.

The culture or social climate within the workplace can be a significant factor in terms of setting norms in relation to drinking and drug use. In predominantly female occupations, for example, research indicates that both male and female employees are less likely to have substance abuse problems, compared to employees of both genders in male-dominated occupations (Messick Svare et al., 2004). In contrast, in male-dominated occupations, such as construction, mining and drilling, employees may build solidarity through a culture of heavy drinking (French et al., 2011; Tynan et al., 2017). Employers must, therefore, be mindful of the culture within their organisation and how the decisions they take may shape it for good or ill.

Sick building syndrome

Research suggests that in North America and Europe, the average person spends approximately 90 per cent of their time indoors, which includes their place of work (EPA, 1996). Interest in the physical aspects of the work building, as a factor affecting employee performance, goes back to at least the 1930s with the Hawthorne experiments in the USA. More recently, the construction of 'closed' office buildings with air-conditioning systems has focused research attention on the impact such environments have on employees, particularly knowledge workers.

In 1983, sick building syndrome (SBS) was recognised by the World Health Organization as occurring where a cluster of work-related symptoms of unknown cause were significantly more prevalent among the occupants of certain buildings in comparison with others. Researchers have identified numerous symptoms of SBS, including respiratory symptoms (e.g. cough, breathing difficulties, wheezing), mucosal irritation (e.g. dry throat, eye irritation), neurotoxic symptoms (e.g. dizziness, headaches, nausea) and dermal complaints (e.g. skin rashes) (Gül, 2011). For SBS to be diagnosed, at least 20 per cent of the occupants of a building must experience symptoms that persist for more than two weeks (Jansz, 2011). It is difficult to obtain a clear picture of the prevalence of SBS, however, one study by the HSE calculated that the staff of 30–50 per cent of newly 'remodelled' buildings in Britain suffered a high incidence of SBS-related illnesses. In Canada, it has been estimated that there are 1,800 'sick' buildings affecting 250,000 office workers. As a result, from a worker well-being perspective, SBS can be considered a significant problem (Redman et al., 2010).

Physical and environmental factors, such as poor air quality, inadequate ventilation, unsuitable lighting and airborne pollutants have been identified as contributing to SBS. In addition, other researchers have highlighted the complex interplay between individual, psychosocial and environmental factors. Bain and Baldry (1995) and Bain et al. (1999), for example, propose that, in a context of high energy costs, SBS is related to cost reductions and the intensification of knowledge work. They conclude that, 'Changes in the balance of power in the office environment have undoubtedly made it easier for management to gain employee acceptance of much more demanding practices and patterns of work' (Bain and Baldry, 1995, p. 30). SBS is negatively associated with job satisfaction and is associated with 'increased management-employment conflict' (Redman et al., 2010, p. 23). SBS is also a 'stressor' and positively associated with emotional exhaustion that can increase labour costs via lower performance and absenteeism. It may in turn undermine the empowerment approach associated with high-commitment work models as managers resort to disciplinary measures to reduce absenteeism. The coronavirus pandemic has renewed interest in SBS, as a result of both physical and psychological concerns that poor air quality, a lack of ventilation and insufficient surface cleaning may facilitate the spread of the virus (Allen, 2020; Wedekind, 2020).

HRM in Practice
Employee perceptions of work-related stress

The incidence of work-related stress appeared to increase rapidly at the end of the twentieth century, bringing into the spotlight the importance of the health and well-being of employees at work. A research drive followed, attempting to understand the consequences for individuals (for example, psychological and physical ill health), for teams (such as conflict between team members) and for organisations (for example, short- and long-term absence). Significant effort was also invested in understanding the work-related causes of stress and the effectiveness of different interventions for preventing, managing and treating it. As a result, plentiful amounts of information and resources are now available for organisations to better manage this aspect of their employees' experience, and the advice given to HR and organisations is fairly consistent. Most advocate a series of linked interventions to manage stress, prioritising an employee risk assessment of specific work characteristics identified as potentially stressful. Employees are typically asked to rate features of their jobs, such as the amount of control and discretion allowed in their role, usually via questionnaires.

Many of these approaches can describe themselves as evidence-based, in that they directly link to recent research. Examples are the HSE's Management Standards for Work-related Stress and the toolkits and training courses specifically available for HR practitioners. But, for all this, are these approaches missing something? There are those who think so, as Kevin Daniels, who has researched and written about work-related stress for over a decade describes (2011, p. 33):

> The dominant approach to policy and practice in the areas of work stress and well-being has focused on jobs and job redesign but has evolved to ignore how workers interpret their work and how they act to shape their work.

Research reveals a much more active role for individual employees in shaping how they think, feel and behave at work. It portrays a more complex and dynamic interaction between individuals, for example their personality, coping styles, expectations and motivations, and their work. Individuals make decisions about their choice of jobs and therefore about their exposure to potential stressors; once in the job, they differently interpret its remit, and their coping abilities can influence how they respond to potentially stressful situations. These differences of interpretation can be the result of their personality, abilities and previous experience, and also of the group, organisation or national culture they work in.

Before the Covid-19 pandemic, stress, burnout and anxiety were already significant issues in the workplace. Data from the Labour Force Survey in the UK showed that incidences of work-related stress, depression and anxiety have increased steadily since 2014–15 and mental health was the most common type of work-related ill health, accounting for 44 per cent of all work illness (Palmer, 2019). This brings into question approaches to work-related stress that assume relatively universal relationships between stable, 'bad' work characteristics and related emotional and physical distress, as seen in popular measurements of stress at work. More flexible and employee-centred research methods might therefore be needed to generate meaningful insight into employees' experience at work.

Stop! What do you think of the idea of standardised measures of stress at work? What are the advantages of this approach, but what might its limitations be, in light of the discussion above?

Essential reading

Daniels, K. (2006) Rethinking job characteristics in work stress research. *Human Relations*, *59*(3): 267–90.

Daniels, K. (2011) Stress and well-being are still issues and something still needs to be done: or why agency and interpretation are important for policy and practice. In G. P. Hodgkinson and J. K. Ford (eds) *International Review of Industrial and Organizational Psychology*, (Vol 25, pp. 1–46). Chichester: John Wiley & Sons.

Palmer, S. (2019) 12 million working days lost to work-related mental health conditions last year. *People Management*, 20 November.

Note: This feature was contributed by Chiara Amati and updated by Andrew Bratton.

Workplace wellness

Workplace wellness programmes are intended to increase productivity, enhance well-being and reduce spending on medical care (Jones et al., 2019). The latter is particularly important in countries where health care often forms part of the wider employment package, such as the US, and therefore represents a significant expense for organisations. Interest in workplace wellness initiatives has been amplified by evidence of an epidemic of 'lifestyle diseases' stemming from inactivity, poor nutrition, tobacco use and excessive alcohol consumption that are considered to be increasing absenteeism and reducing productivity (Mattke et al., 2013). The workplace wellness industry in the US, for example, more than tripled in size to US$8 billion between 2010 and 2019 (Jones et al., 2019). Programmes often take the form of screening activities, designed to identify health risks, and interventions to promote healthier lifestyles (Mattke et al., 2013).

Source: Getty Images/Assembly

Workplace wellness models typically focus on behavioural change at the individual level, for example, supporting the employee to quit smoking, take more exercise or improve their diet. However, workplace wellness can refer to any voluntary health-improving programme and activity instigated by the employer to effect changes in non-occupational health behaviours. Apple, Google and Facebook, for example, offer female employees financial support to freeze their eggs if they wish to have children at a later date and Netflix and Goldman Sachs will help to pay for gender reassignment procedures, such as hormone therapy (Nguyen, 2018). Common initiatives that fall under the wellness promotion strategy that have been instigated in organisations with 500 or more employees, include part or all of the following:

- a smoke-free workplace;
- employer-sponsored sports;
- discounted gym facilities;

- health examinations offered to employees;
- 'health fairs' hosted on the premises;
- wellness newsletters;
- smoking cessation incentives;
- weight loss incentives;
- blood pressure and cholesterol testing;
- energy-based therapy seminars;
- EAPs.

An EAP provides confidential professional assistance to employees and their families to help resolve problems affecting their personal lives and, in some cases, their job performance. Typically, an EAP covers services such as alcohol and drug abuse, legal, financial, crisis and marriage counselling. These various workplace wellness initiatives tend to operate independently and focus on the goals of the individual employee. Research on the effectiveness of wellness programmes is limited. A recent study involving over 30,000 employees found that worksites with a wellness programme had higher numbers of workers who reported engaging in exercise and actively managing their weight, however, there was no significant difference in other measures, such as clinical markers of health, absenteeism and job performance, when compared to worksites without such programmes (Song and Baicker, 2019).

Reflective question

If you were asked to design a workplace wellness programme, what elements would you include and why?

Digital Spotlight

OHS and well-being in Industry 4.0

We are now considered to be living through the Fourth Industrial Revolution or in the age of Industry 4.0 (Marr, 2018). Industry 4.0 is characterised by the development and rapid diffusion of technologies such as artificial intelligence, big data, cloud computing, remote sensing and robotics. The First Industrial Revolution was associated with appalling working conditions for men, women and children, with illness, injury and even death commonplace within many factories (Badri et al., 2018). The absence of effective OHS combined with ambivalence on the part of employers for the safety of their workers, had devastating consequences. In response to public and trade union pressure, governments in industrialised countries were impelled to introduce regulation. Workplace conditions were slowly transformed in many, if not all, countries (Badri et al., 2018). As this chapter highlights, the focus for many organisations is now not only on preventing illness or injury, but also enhancing wellness. The dawn of Industry 4.0, however, presents new challenges and opportunities. Badri et al. (2018, p. 403) argue that if the technologies underpinning the Fourth Industrial Revolution are developed without due consideration of their effect, 'the net impact on OHS will be negative'.

The potential impact of Industry 4.0 on workers may be both psychological and physical. Regarding the former, the rapid proliferation of new technologies may stimulate both excitement and fear amongst employees. Some may be concerned that they will be replaced by robots. Such anxieties are not unfounded. McKinsey (2017) reported that around 50% of jobs globally could theoretically be automated. Those in low paid work with limited qualifications are most likely to be impacted. While automation may enhance productivity and create new job opportunities, if this societal shift is not managed correctly it may serve to deepen inequalities. Indeed, a recent report revealed that the use of robots in poorer regions led to the loss of almost twice as many jobs as in wealthier ones (Oxford Economics, 2019). Compounding the problem, there is evidence that workers are not being consulted about the integration of new technologies. While many staff were positive about the potential benefits, they felt they lacked a 'voice' in terms of when and how they were introduced (Partington, 2019). Finally, people will increasingly find themselves working alongside, or perhaps even for, artificial intelligences. This may have an impact in terms of an individual's perception of their dignity *in* and *at* work (Bolton, 2007). Reflecting on the physical dimension, robots may help to create safer, healthier workplaces. They can relieve human workers of some dull, dirty, dangerous or degrading tasks. However, they are often large and have fast-moving automated arms, which in turn presents a danger. Weighing both the positive and negative aspects of Industry 4.0, it seems that managers have a challenge ahead in terms of ensuring humans and machines can coexist in an emotionally and physically safe manner.

Stop! How could HR professionals support managers and employees to ensure that new technologies are integrated in a safe and healthy manner?

Essential reading

Badri, A., Boudreau-Trudel, B. and Souissi, A. (2018) Occupational health and safety in the Industry 4.0 era: a cause for major concern? *Safety Science*, *109*: 403–11.

Note: This feature was contributed by Laura Steele.

Critiquing workplace health, safety and well-being

As has been highlighted throughout this chapter, occupational health, safety and well-being is replete with paradox. Many organisations, for example, cite a strong commitment to these concepts on their website and social media channels, as well as in recruitment materials and communications to staff. However, employees may sense a gap between the espoused values of the organisation ('we care for our workers', 'we encourage a healthy work–life balance') and their lived experience of long hours, heavy workloads and increasing expectations. This can breed cynicism and contempt. In addition, most employers since the Industrial Revolution have opposed OHS and environmental regulation, citing global competition and the need to level the playing fields. Indeed, the economic cost of OHS and wellness is a double-edged sword for the organisation. On the one hand, OHS measures that protect employee well-being from physical or chemical hazards can conflict with management's objective of containing production costs. On the other, as we have explained, effective health and wellness interventions can improve the performance of employees and the organisation by reducing the cost associated with accidents, disabilities, absenteeism and illness. Arguably, HRM (at least the rhetoric) has raised the ethical stakes over OHS. Yet, despite this claim, the driving force for the majority of employers to provide a safe and healthy working environment has all too often been framed through a 'business case' lens, for example the reduction in sick leave and time lost from accidents.

Paradox stems from multiple consequences of a single management action that seems to conflict with those of another. The work-related symptoms of stress presented in Figure 11.1 can be illuminated using a single health and wellness case.

Technology in the form of devices such as mobile phones, tablets and laptops, combined with the ubiquity of email and development of platforms such as Slack and Teams, has enabled us to be connected to the organisation 24 hours a day, 7 days a week. This has undoubtedly brought many benefits, for example, by allowing a vast number of people to work from home during the coronavirus pandemic.

However, we must also be aware of the dark side of such developments. Two decades ago, Drohan (2000, p. B15) described early iterations of these technologies as 'electronic versions of a ball and chain, keeping us in work mode around the clock'. The intended effect of these technologies is improved productivity, but the unanticipated consequence of high-tech communications has yielded a major problem of stress and burnout caused by the inability of individuals to maintain a boundary between work and home.

OHS and wellness form an important part of the HRM context, but it is not simply a technical issue of, for example, supplying hard hats and goggles (or, in the context of the coronavirus pandemic, appropriate PPE). Above all, OHS underscores the fact that employment relations involve an economic and power relationship. In terms of economics, 'pure market' ideology panders to the shareholder and 'profitability over safety' is favoured (Glasbeek, 1991, p. 196). Regarding power, it is argued (Sass, 1982, p. 52; quoted in Giles and Iain, 1989) that:

> In all technical questions pertaining to workplace health and safety there is the social element. That is ... the power relations in production: who tells whom to do what and how fast.

Wellness management also contains a social element. It is arguably about organisations attempting to appropriate the employee's whole body as a matter of surveillance and control (Haunschild, 2003), and wellness management represents a process of discipline since activities such as medical screening and lifestyle counselling are connected to selection and promotion (Townley, 1994). As noted above, companies such as Facebook and Google offer 'social egg freezing' to female employees so that they have the option to have children later in life. Some commentators have lauded this decision, stating that it frees women to pursue their career ambitions unfettered by concerns about fertility. Others have lamented that it fails to address the deep structural issues in business and society that still force many women to choose between a fulfilling career and family life. As a result, 'we end up with huge corporations offering female employees the possibility of reproduction at a later date in return for the "best" years of their lives' (Moore, 2017). Rather than a 'perk', Moore (2017) suggests that it is a 'bribe' and, given that only 27 per cent of women become pregnant when using their own thawed eggs (RCOG, 2018), it may be one that is never actually paid.

To manage the employment relationship effectively, it also needs to be recognised that the employer's perspective on OHS and wellness issues can affect an individual's beliefs, levels of trust and psychological contract (Guest, 2008). Talk of a reciprocal commitment and a psychological contract has a hollow ring for many manual workers: more pressing may be malodorous processes and dangerous work systems. Critical, too, is the ability of global companies to relocate to other parts of the world to avoid stringent health and safety laws and regulations. Global trading agreements, such as the NAFTA and TTIP, put growth and protectionist polemics ahead of concern for the environment and community health (Klein, 2015, p. 84). Following numerous catastrophic events, such as the Bhopal disaster in 1984 when over 500,000 people were exposed to methyl isocyanate (MIC) gas at the Union Carbide pesticide plant in Madhya Pradesh, India, the explosion on the Deepwater Horizon in the Gulf of Mexico in 2010, the Fukushima Daiichi nuclear disaster in 2011 and the 2020 blast in the Port of Beirut, there is growing public awareness of the links between work systems, OHS and environmental protection. An identifiable current concern is how the UK's withdrawal from the EU will affect health and safety standards and protection as the country seeks to negotiate trade deals with other nations with weaker legislation. An appreciation of OHS provides a better understanding of managing the employment relationship. Indeed, the discussion on paradox goes back to basics in reminding us of some of the complexities and tensions inherent in the employment relationship. The key point is that OHS and wellness policies and practices must, as with other aspects of the HR strategy, be properly integrated in the sense that they are both complementary to, and compatible with, corporate strategy.

Summary

This chapter has argued that OHS and well-being should be an important aspect of managing the employment relationship. It began by discussing sustainable health, safety and human resource management, highlighting in particular the growing interest in the concept of well-being and the plethora of new issues that have come to the fore over the last two decades that have an impact on OHS. Next, we established the importance of health, safety and well-being from economic, legal, psychological and ethical perspectives. Following this, we examined some contemporary health issues, including mental health, stress and burnout, workplace violence, workplace bullying, drug and alcohol abuse, and sick building syndrome, as well as the key elements of a workplace wellness programme.

Critical analysis of OHS and wellness management draws attention to the fact that employment relations involve an economic and power relationship. Shareholder interests and return on investment may come before workers' health and safety. Wellness management is arguably a distraction because it manages the consequences rather than causes of ill health. In addition, we examined how the economic cost of workplace health and wellness is a double-edged sword for the organisation. On the one hand, it protects employees' well-being from physical or chemical hazards, but it can also be at odds with management's objective of containing costs. However, effective health and wellness interventions can improve the performance of employees and the organisation by reducing the cost associated with accidents, disabilities, absenteeism and illness.

Review questions

1. 'Spending money on a health and wellness programmes is a luxury most small organisations cannot afford.' Build an argument to support this statement, and an argument to negate it.
2. What is workplace bullying and why is it important for managers to understand its antecedents and its effects of on targets? What can an organisation do to alleviate workplace bullying?
3. What role can line managers play in the development of a sustainable and healthy workplace?

PART 5

Search & Watch

Go to the video hub at **www.bloomsbury.pub/bratton-hrm** and view three short films:

- The explosion in Beirut in August 2020.
  1. What caused the explosion?
  2. Could this type of industrial accident happen in your jurisdiction, if not, why not?
- Oxley, T. (2018) Workplace mental health – all you need to know (for now). *TEDxNorwich*, 16 July.
  1. What is the key learning point for managers from this video?
- Johns Hopkins University (2015). Extraordinary workplace wellness programmes. *Johns Hopkins University*, 18 July.
  1. What role should managers play in creating workplaces that are 'extraordinary' in terms of wellness?
  2. Should OHS and wellness be the responsibility of companies or government? Why?

Legal Focus

In most English-speaking jurisdictions OHS law can be categorised into two broad categories: individual and collective. The first source of individual rights evolves from common law. Every employer has a vicarious common law duty to provide a safe working environment for their employees. However, the primary source of individual rights arises from legislation. In Britain, for example, the Health and Safety at Work Act (HASAWA) 1974, Section 2(1) lays down the general duty on employers to ensure, so far as reasonably possible, the health, safety and welfare of all of their employees. The main source of collective OHS rights arises from the negotiations between unions and management. In Britain, breach of the common law can lead to criminal prosecution for breach of the HASAWA, and therefore the two areas are interlinked (Lockton and Brown, 2020). In Canada, the US and New Zealand, workers have legal rights to refuse to perform unsafe or unhealthy work (Pye et al., 2001). In the EU, the US and Britain, failure to provide a safe working environment may result in the organisation being prosecuted for corporate manslaughter.

Task Search online for information in your jurisdiction for provision for OHS protection and compare and contrast it with another country, such as Australia or Canada. (1) What general duty is placed on employers to ensure the health and wellness of their employees? (2) What are the differences, if any, between these two countries' approaches to OHS?

Reference

See Deborah Lockton and Tom Brown's *Employment Law* (2020), pp. 114–24, for a discussion on the HASAWA 1974, covering health and safety at work, working time regulations and corporate manslaughter.

Chapter case: Lagan Meadows Care Home* – caring for the carers

The setting

In June 2020, it was reported that aged care homes in Northern Ireland (NI) had suffered 130 times the number of Covid-19 deaths per head amongst their residents compared to the general population. This equates to around 45% of all coronavirus deaths within the country (Blevins, 2020). These grim statistics led to allegations that care homes had become 'ground zero' for the pandemic in NI. Care workers have historically been underpaid and undervalued within society. Further, the pandemic arrived at a time when health and social care systems in NI were already under strain, as evidenced by high rates of mental illness, burnout and low morale among care workers (McMurray, 2020).

The impact of the coronavirus crisis on care workers has been both physical and psychological. There were numerous reports that staff could not get access to appropriate Personal Protective Equipment (PPE). Many care workers contracted Covid-19 themselves, resulting in an absence rate of around 10% (Booth, 2020). In the early stages of the pandemic, because most care workers were not paid sick leave, some employees went in to work ill thereby compounding the problem (UNISON, 2020). This, in turn, placed additional pressure on those who were in work and had to cover for colleagues who were sick or self-isolating. In terms of the psychological impact, emerging research on the impact of Covid-19 suggests that health and social care workers are at increased risk of adverse mental health outcomes (Kwong and Marshall, 2020), including Post Traumatic Stress Disorder (PTSD). Individuals with PTSD often relive the traumatic incident through flashbacks and nightmares. It is not difficult to see how care workers could be at risk of experiencing the disorder, with some having had to deal with the deaths of multiple residents in a single day.

The problem

Lagan Meadows is a large for-profit care home based in Belfast, NI. It employs two managers, four administrators, eight cooks, eight nurses and thirty-six care workers. All employees work shifts to maintain 24/7 care for residents. Like many care homes in NI, Lagan Meadows pays care workers National Minimum Wage, even though their role is both physically and emotionally demanding. Despite the best efforts of management, at the beginning of the pandemic PPE was difficult to source and it was some weeks before staff had access to all the resources they required. While the facility fared better than many of its counterparts, an outbreak of Covid-19 in April 2020 resulted in over twenty residents contracting the illness, with eight subsequently dying. In addition, ten staff members caught the disease, though all have since recovered and returned to work. While the threat presented by Covid-19 appears to be under control, an informal staff survey, conducted by an HR consultancy firm, revealed that a high proportion of employees are feeling anxious, exhausted and deeply upset at the loss of those under their care. Several respondents expressed that the thought of a second wave of cases within Lagan Meadows is keeping them awake at night. Martha Bugler, one of the managers responsible for HR issues, called a meeting to discuss the staff survey. After opening the meeting, the most senior care assistant, Nora McGrath, who had contracted the virus herself, stated: 'We love our residents that much we just want to see them come out the other side. You don't really think about yourself. You just go in and get on with it. We love them like our own' (Blevins, 2020). 'But who is there to care for us?' Richard Tennant, an administrator with responsibility for finance, retorted, 'We do value our staff Nora, but in the current economic climate, Lagan Meadows will not survive if costs continue to rise or unless revenue substantially increases.'

The assignment

You have recently been appointed as the assistant HR manager at Lagan Meadows. At the interview, the panel were particularly impressed by the knowledge of health, safety and wellness you displayed. Martha Bugler has asked you to prepare a short report outlining ways in which the organisation could address the challenges posed by Covid-19. In your answer, address the following:

1. What role should the HR function play in supporting the mental and physical well-being of care workers in the wake of the pandemic?
2. Offer three recommendations for HR interventions to support the physical and/or mental health of care workers. Provide a rationale for the options you have selected.
3. What barriers may be encountered in terms of implementing the recommendations made in your report?

Essential reading

Greenwood, K. and Krol, N. (2020) 8 ways managers can support employees' mental health. *Harvard Business Review*, 7 August.

Also, visit www.cipd.co.uk/news-views/coronavirus for advice, guidance and resources on dealing with the effects of the pandemic for employers and HR professionals.

Note: This case was contributed by Laura Steele.

*The name of the care home is fictitious, but the case is based on actual NI data and reports.

Further reading

Byram, M., Ünğan, M. C. and Ardıç, K. (2016) The relationships between OHS prevention costs, safety performance, employee satisfaction and accident costs. *International Journal of Occupational Safety and Ergonomics*, *23*(2): 285–96.

Fox, S. and Cowan, R. L. (2015) Revision of the workplace bullying checklist: the importance of human resource management's role in defining and addressing workplace bullying. *Human Resource Management Journal*, *25*(1): 116–30.

Gallo, A. (2011) Turning stress into an asset. *Harvard Business Review*, 28 June [online]. Available at: <https://hbr.org/2011/06/turning-stress-into-an-asset>.

Gregory, K. (2021) 'My life is more valuable than this': understanding risk among on-demand food couriers in Edinburgh. *Work, Employment and Society, 35*(2): 316–31.

Hennekam, S., Follmer, K. and Beatty, J. (2021) Exploring mental illness in the workplace: the role of HR professionals and processes. *International Journal of Human Resource Management, 32*(15): 3135–56.

Iavicoli, S., Valenti, A., Gagliardi, D. and Rantanen, J. (2018) Ethics and occupational health in the contemporary world of work. *International Journal of Environmental Research and Public Health*, *15*(8): 1713–30.

Kowalski, T. H. and Loretto, W. (2017) Well-being and HRM in the changing workplace. *International Journal of Human Resource Management*, *28*(16): 2229–55.

Note: This chapter was written by Laura Steele and John Bratton.

CHAPTER 12

SUSTAINABLE HRM AND ENVIRONMENTAL SUSTAINABILITY

outline

- Introduction
- The nature of environmental sustainability
- Workers' pro-environmental behaviours
- Environmental management systems
- Motivators for embedding sustainability strategies
- Environmental leadership and culture
- Creating a low-carbon workplace through sustainable HRM
- Employee voice in environmental sustainability
- Critiquing corporate-oriented sustainability
- Summary
- Further reading

Source: Ricardo Gomez Angel on Unsplash

objectives

After studying this chapter, you should be able to:

1. Explain the nature of environmental sustainability
2. Explain the role of organisational leadership in influencing environmental sustainability
3. Critically analyse sustainable HRM strategies
4. Explain the meaning of 'employee voice' and how it contributes to environmental sustainability in the workplace

Introduction

During the Covid-19 pandemic, health-care professionals from more than 200 organisations representing over 40 million workers, sent an open letter to G20 leaders calling on them to ensure an environmentally sustainable economic recovery from the coronavirus crisis that takes into account climate change and air pollution (Harvey, 2020). The emerging consensus is that when taxpayers' money is used to rescue business due to the Covid-19 crisis, employers must create low-carbon jobs and not bail out polluting, carbon-intensive industries. There is a growing consensus too that organisations are both part of the problem, as well as part of the solution to the climate crisis. Organisations need to orient themselves beyond a focus on the financial performance imperative but shift towards a multi-stakeholder model including sustainable pro-environmental performance (Stahl et al., 2020).

It is within this context that HRM scholars advocate a proactive role for HRM in creating more environmentally sustainable workplaces. Environmental sustainability incorporates ecological or environmental considerations (e.g. carbon emissions) with organisational needs (e.g. profitability) in such a way as to promote benefits for the environment (Norton et al., 2015). Here, environmental sustainability reflects multiple stakeholder calls for action to reduce workplace emissions, and to add low-carbon jobs and duties to existing HR processes (Renwick et al., 2016, p. 114). As discussed in Chapter 2, greater attention to environmental sustainability can be examined as part of a wider consideration of corporate social responsibility (CSR) and it should come as no surprise that efforts to tackle climate change and recovery from the Covid-19 pandemic have become major concerns for humanity (Figueres and Zycher, 2020).

This chapter begins by introducing the concept of environmental sustainability and discusses its importance to contemporary management. Drawing on the author's own research, it then identifies the main drivers of sustainable workplace practices and behaviours before going on to explain the role of HRM in creating a low-carbon workplace (LCW). The chapter critically examines how effective practices are at encouraging workers' pro-environmental behaviour.

Reflective question

What do you understand by the term 'sustainability' as it relates to work organisations?

The nature of environmental sustainability

The sustainability discourse evolved in the 1970s and 1980s with publications on the ecological limits of economic growth (e.g. Meadows et al., 1972). The issue of sustainability was initially debated at the 1972 United Nations Conference on the Human Environment in Stockholm (Sumner, 2005, p. 79). A significant development came with the formation of the UN's World Commission on Environment and Development (WCED; also known as the Bruntland Commission), which subsequently provided the now classical definition of *sustainable development*: 'development that meets the needs of the present without compromising the ability of future generations to meet their own needs' (1987, p. 43).

Conceptually, the meaning of sustainability, as cited in the Bruntland Commission, 'can be understood as an overarching worldview recognizing the interconnectedness of ecological, social, and economic factors in human activity' (Docherty et al., 2009, p. 6). The Commission's report also introduced 'the concept of justice (within and between generations, global justice and justice through participation and democratic arrangements) as a central issue in relation to efforts to enhance sustainability' (Lund, 2004, p. 43).

Sustainability science is an interdisciplinary field that seeks to enhance sustainability by integrating knowledge from a range of disciplines including natural sciences, engineering, social sciences and the humanities (Kates et al., 2001). The challenge for sustainability science is to ensure that knowledge production is a communal effort that links academic research with industry and government, and benefits individuals and society (Wiek et al., 2011). Sustainability science is embedded within broader social processes of understanding, and thus contributes to organisational decision-making processes through the creation of knowledge (particularly analyses of risks and consequences) derived from emergent interdisciplinary enquiry (Kasemir et al., 2003). Although it is recognised that there is a multiplicity of viewpoints, sustainability is, for an increasing number of organisational and environmental writers, the ultimate goal: that is, 'living within the regenerative capacity of the biosphere' (Wackernagel et al., 2002, p. 9,266). Importantly, in terms of managing work and people, scholars of sustainability science advocate participatory and collaborative approaches to the co-generation of knowledge and environmental decision-making (Blackstock et al., 2007).

Environmental management is an attempt to control the human impact on and interaction with the natural environment in order to preserve natural resources. At the organisational level, *corporate environmental performance* refers to 'organisational performance in managing natural resources and the natural environment in the process of conducting business' (Ones and Dilchert, 2012, p. 450). Corporate environmental performance includes both environmental outcomes and the pro-environmental initiatives that organisations implement. The former represent the ecological impact or 'footprint' of organisational activities; the latter focus on what organisations do for environmental sustainability. In the workplace, this includes encouraging energy efficiency, waste reduction and recycling, water conservation, and workers' use of alternative low-carbon forms of transportation (e.g. a bus, train or bicycle). At the individual level, workplace pro-environmental behaviour (WPEB) can be defined as 'a systematic set of actions from a collective network of organizational actors spread across a company, team, and/or value chain' (Kennedy et al., 2015, p. 370). For workers, this entails changes to their existing job duties, additional requirements of their position and, in some cases, the creation of entirely new occupational opportunities, such as 'environmental manager' (Ones and Dilchert, 2012).

Source: Max Bender on Unsplash

Environmental management is an attempt to control the human impact on and interaction with the natural environment in order to preserve natural resources.

Although sustainability has been debated for decades, it is an emerging concept in the business world, and the existing literature provides numerous and varied interpretations of it. In contemporary management parlance, sustainability has been used to refer to values and ethics, as well as goals such as corporate social responsibility (CSR). In 1997, expert John Elkington, for example, coined the term 'triple bottom line' or 'P3' (People, Planet and Profit) which emphasises that, in sustainable workplaces, human and social resources along with ecological and economic resources should be able to grow and develop. Bratton and Gold (2017, p. 48) extend the concept further to the pursuit of *quadruple bottom line* performance which includes culture as a fourth pillar of sustainability to encourage leaders to recognise and build on distinctive cultural characteristics, including the shared values, of the communities where organisations are embedded.

From a work systems perspective, sustainability has been described as an ongoing process of efficiency and improved environmental and social performance (Docherty et al., 2009). For Norton and his colleagues (2015), organisational efficiency and improvements to the planet are combined in the concept of *environmental sustainability*. In the organisational context, this means that environmental sustainability incorporates business needs (e.g. profitability) with environmental consideration (e.g. lower carbon emissions) in such a way as to be ecologically beneficial to the planet. Therefore, WPEBs are necessary but not sufficient for environmental (corporate) sustainability. Popular corporate strategy authors have been optimistic, arguing that although the concept is understood to mean different things to different people, it has nevertheless made a positive social and environmental impact. For example, management strategy expert Michael Porter, championing the concept of creating competitive advantage and shared value, has argued that the ongoing efforts of certain corporations are helping to transform sustainability from a 'cliché term' to an innovative and enduring business strategy (Porter and Kramer, 2011).

Informed by a social justice perspective (i.e. justice in terms of the distribution of wealth, opportunities and privileges within a society) a number of critical social scientists (e.g. Holden et al., 2017) and advocacy associations (notably Friends of the Earth Scotland) are attempting to re-orient the term 'sustainability' around concepts of equity, social justice, participatory democracy and ecological limits. This more inclusive view of sustainability is captured by Agyeman and colleagues who argue that:

> Sustainability ... cannot be simply a 'green', or 'environmental' concern, important though 'environmental' aspects of sustainability are. A truly sustainable society is one where wider questions of social needs and welfare, and economic opportunity are integrally related to environmental limits imposed by supporting ecosystems. (2002, p. 78)

PART 5

There is a requirement to define environmental sustainability that recognises the need to ensure a better quality of life for all, in the present and into the future, in a just and equitable manner, while living within environmental limits (Agyeman et al., 2016; Schlosberg, 2013); that is, an economy that meets emission targets and is environmentally sustainable and socially just. This more inclusive definition focuses on four core areas: (1) quality of life; (2) present and future generations; (3) equity and justice in resource allocation; and (4) living within environmental limits. While mainstream corporate notions of sustainability have little to say about contemporary human conditions, this definition includes both intra-generational and intergenerational equity (equality within and between different generation groups). This more egalitarian perspective of sustainability draws the connection between environmentalism, equity and fairness. Emerging definitions of sustainability are shifting towards 'just sustainability' (the nexus between social justice and environmentalism), a broader approach that prioritises social justice but does not downplay the limits of supporting ecosystems. The 'environmental justice' definition has more explicit emphasis on the social conditions of citizens and workers both locally and internationally, and also acknowledges that multiple stakeholder decision-making needs to address environmental and social inequality (see e.g. Agyeman et al., 2013).

More recently, as a reaction to the criticism of corporate sustainability business models to effectively address the 'grand challenges' of our time, interest is growing among academics and practitioners alike in alternative 'outside-in' models that seek to resolve sustainability challenges (Aust, et al. 2020). The *Common Good HRM* approach marks a fundamental shift in understanding organisations and assumes that it is the responsibility of business to 'make an effective contribution to resolving the sustainability challenges we are collectively facing' (Dyllick and Muff, 2016, p. 156). This assumption is built on the understanding that despite the prevalence of organisational sustainability initiatives, quadruple bottom line frameworks and environmental management practices, they have had, whether studied individually or collectively, limited positive societal or environmental impacts (Aust et al., 2020). Boxall et al.'s (2008) third characteristic of analytical HRM examines 'for whom and how well' with assessing the outcomes of HRM. The 'Common Good' HRM approach extends the scope of analysis to include human rights and environmental protection.

The burgeoning literature demonstrates that sustainability is no longer a fringe issue. Corporate titans, for example retailer Wal-mart (2018), Google (2018) and BP (2017) have embraced elements of sustainability. In the twentieth century, occupational health and safety was always an issue for trade unions, but in the twenty-first century, institutions such as the International Labour Organization, the European Trade Union Confederation and the British Trades Union Congress (TUC, 2020a) in the UK have also embraced the wider concept of sustainability. Sustainability is particularly relevant to 'mission-driven organizations, such as governments, charities, and universities, because they are not evaluated in traditional financial terms, and have missions that go beyond the bottom line' (Boudreau and Ramstad, 2005, p. 130). This trend towards sustainability, no doubt influenced by the environmental movement of the 1980s and the CSR movement of the 1990s, has influenced organisational leaders to become increasingly aware of the need to build positive relations with stakeholders, both internal and external to the organisation (Stahl et al., 2020), and more government and investors' pressure on organisations to serve the common good (Crifo et al., 2019).

In summary, the concept of sustainability has evolved since its first usage over 30 years ago. There is a general consensus in the literature that the concept of sustainability is linked to nature, and the notion of resource conservation. Contemporary interpretations of the term have been influenced primarily by three different stakeholder groups: ecologists, business strategy scholars and the United Nations (Dyllick and Hockerts, 2002). Following the perspective throughout this textbook, sustainability is examined here through a prism that recognises that the employment relationship is, by necessity, cooperative but also entails unavoidable structural conflict between the managers and workers (Van Buren, 2020).

HRM in Practice
Carney issues climate change warning to companies

Organisations introduce sustainability strategies for both internal and external reasons. The internal reasons include the personal pro-environmental values of leaders, environmental champions, among the managers, the need to reduce operational costs and pressure from investors. The external drivers of change, on the other hand, are associated with legislative and regulatory compliance and pressure from consumers. Customer boycotts can be effective. If an organisation adopts an environmentally sustainable business model because of customer boycotts, its action is driven by self-interest, especially if the customer happens to be a pension fund looking for 'green' investment. Greater transparency on the organisation's carbon emissions may act to drive change. Mark Carney, former governor of the Bank of England and United Nations Special Envoy for Climate Action and Finance, has argued that the financial sector has begun to curb investments in fossil fuels – but far too slowly:

> 'The concern is whether we will spend another decade doing worthy things but not enough ... and we will blow through the 1.5C mark very quickly' ... He re-iterated his warning that unless firms woke up to what he called the climate crisis, many of their assets would become worthless. 'If we were to burn all those oil and gas [reserves], there's no way we would meet carbon budget ... A question for every company, every financial institution, every asset manager, pension fund or insurer: what's our plan?', he said. (Harrabin, 2019)

The Royal Bank of Canada (RBC) is one financial institution that has acted; the RBC will not provide direct financing for exploration or development projects in the Arctic National Wildlife Refuge in north-eastern Alaska. In a joint statement, the RBC and the Yukon's Vuntut Gwitchin First Nation said, 'We are committed to finding ways to balance the transition to a low-carbon economy.' ... 'It is promising to see a leading Canadian chartered bank developing environmentally conscious policies and we are hopeful that other Canadian financial institutions will follow their lead,' said Ken Smith, the grand chief of the tribal council (Blaze Baum and Bradshaw, 2020, p. B3).

There are multiple external and internal drivers that cause organisations to develop environmentally conscious business models. The STEPLE framework - **S**ocial, **T**echnological, **E**conomic, **P**olitical, **L**egal and **E**cological - provides a wide-ranging audit of the organisation's external context with the purpose of using the information to guide strategic decisions around issues such as environmental sustainability (see Bratton, 2020).

Stop! Mark Carney warned that the 'age of irresponsibility' was coming to an end. What is the most effective way to make multinational corporations act responsibly towards the natural environment: is it through legislation, market forces or consumer boycotts? In the light of the Paris accord and the actions of financial institutions, such as the RBC, what role do organisational leaders have in promoting workplace pro-environmental behaviours? And, in a Covid-19-defined economy, what is the role, if any, of the HR professional?

Essential reading

Harrabin, R. (2019) Bank of England chief Mark Carney issues climate change warning. BBC News, 30 December; Lozano, R. (2015) A holistic perspective on corporate sustainability drivers. *Corporate Social Responsibility and Environmental Management*, *22*(1), 32–44; Blaze Baum, K. and Bradshaw, J. (2020) RBC refuses to finance Arctic drilling and puts restrictions on coal under new investment guidelines. *The Globe and Mail*, Toronto, 3 October.

Note: This feature was contributed by John Bratton and Andrew Bratton.

PART 5

Workers' pro-environmental behaviours

The extant literature on sustainable workplaces raises the possibility that work organisations, through appropriate policies, processes and practices, can make strategic choices that can enhance natural resource efficiency and reduce the amount of greenhouse gases emitted into the atmosphere (Cox et al., 2012). It is in the workplace, therefore, where HR policies and practices have their effects on the issue of work itself and, by extension, on worker behaviour, labour productivity and environmental sustainability (Bratton and Bratton, 2015). It is to the workplace that one must look to examine how managers' and workers' behaviours and own goals combine to create more environmentally sustainable workplaces. The workplace is a site where social relationships shape interests, motives and the actions of managers and workers, and where cooperation and resistance around management objectives takes place in a 'contested terrain' (Edwards, 1979). Workplace sustainability is therefore more than a technical challenge – it goes to the very heart of managing people.

Ultimately, the solution to reducing carbon emissions in the workplace lies with the social sciences that are tasked with changing employee behaviour. In this regard, Boiral et al. (2015) provide some insight into the nature and scope of employees' pro-environmental behaviours, and Renwick et al. (2016) examine the role of 'sustainable' or Green HRM (GHRM), which we will go on to consider in the next section.

Source: Getty Images/ Kasipat Phonlamai/ EyeEm

Workplace pro-environmental behaviours include all types of voluntary or prescribed activity undertaken by employees that aim to protect the natural environment or improve organisational practices that decarbonise the workplace.

The role of employees' pro-environmental behaviours has been highlighted in many environmental studies (e.g. Davis et al., 2020; Yuriev et al., 2018). Pro-environmental behaviour is a multifaceted concept used to describe a broad range of actions intended to benefit the natural environment. Ones and Dilchert (2012, p. 452) define *employees' pro-environmental behaviours* as 'scalable actions and behaviours that employees engage in that are linked with and contribute to or detract from environmental sustainability'. This definition focuses on environmental behaviours inside organisations at the individual level, and excludes those behaviours rooted in employees' own lifestyles. Notwithstanding the value of the definition, Ones and Dilchert focus only on measurable behaviour at the employee level and exclude actions taken by employees to support organisational practices or informal initiatives. The attraction of conceptualising pro-environmental behaviours in such a way is its adoption as part of a performance appraisal system (see Chapter 6).

A more inclusive definition of WPEB includes 'all types of voluntary or prescribed activity undertaken by individuals at work that aim to protect the natural environment or improve organizational practices in this area' (Boiral et al., 2015, p. 21). This definition highlights the diverse nature of informal and formal employee-level behaviour and organisational initiatives, and the voluntary or prescribed nature of the pro-environmental behaviours of employees and managers alike. Employee pro-environmental behaviours mostly comprise task performance or organisational citizenship (commitment and engagement) behaviours. Empirical research in this area has demonstrated that effective environmental sustainability change depends, to a large extent, on various behaviours intended to reduce pollution, internalise environmental management practices, and contribute to eco-innovations (Saeed et al., 2019).

Environmental management systems

Within the emergent sustainable workplace literature, it has been argued that in order to work towards the goal of environmental sustainability, organisational managers must develop an environmental management system (EMS). An EMS is the most widely recognised tool for managing the impacts of an organisation's activities on the environment. It refers to the management of an organisation's environmental impact in a comprehensive, systematic, planned and documented manner. It incorporates people, procedures and working practices into a formal structure, involves all members of an organisation as appropriate, promotes continual improvement including periodically evaluating environmental performance, and actively engages senior management in support of the EMS (see, for example, Zutshi and Sohal, 2004). EMS enables organisations to achieve more environmentally sustainable processes, practices and outcomes (see, for example, Jabbour et al., 2010). Thus, the focus is on improving environmental performance and maintaining compliance with environmental regulations. As EMS and risk management are analogous activities, EMS supports an organisation's overall approach to environmental risk management.

Reflective question

Based on your own experience of work or of being a customer of an organisation, how important to you is the issue of 'green' products and low-carbon practices?

Ethical Insight

A just transition to a low-carbon economy: a question of ethics, economics or politics?

It is now largely – though by no means universally – accepted that a transition to a low-carbon economy is essential. Carbon emissions resulting from human activity are a primary driver of climate change. In turn, the current and potential impacts of climate change include, amongst other concerns, extreme weather, environmental degradation, and compromised water and food supplies. Barry and colleagues (2013) state that the normative analysis of climate change – and the justifications put forward for addressing it – fall into three distinct but related categories: moral/ethical, economic/technological and political/policy/legal.

In regard to the moral/ethical perspective, this encompasses both the causes and effects of climate change and includes debates regarding injustice and inequality in the distribution of harms (and benefits); intergenerational and global justice considerations; and the categorisation of harms caused by climate change as forms of human rights violations (Barry et al., 2013). The ethical case for decarbonisation (and, indeed, sustainability more broadly) is compelling. However, Sovacool et al. (2019) argue that we must nonetheless be cautious as the transition to low-carbon economies 'can in fact create new injustices and vulnerabilities'. In particular, the authors highlight how those on low incomes often have to bear the cost of subsidies for government sustainability initiatives but, due to lack of finances, may not be able to reap the benefits (for example, even when discounted, solar panels can be prohibitively expensive).

It has been suggested that the moral/ethical perspective on climate change has, at times, been 'side-lined' or 'marginalised' in favour of the economic/technical approach (Mabon et al., 2015). The latter tends to focus on, for example, the unsustainability of the capitalist economic system; the possibility of 'greening' capitalism; and the role of markets in climate change mitigation (Barry et al., 2013). Elements of this approach may be viewed as being more 'palatable' to the business community. Indeed, Deloitte (2020), for example, cites findings from the New Climate Economy that low-carbon growth can deliver US$26tn in economic benefits globally by 2030. In addition, a visible commitment to sustainability and decarbonisation can attract investors, strengthen brand and reputation, increase customer appeal, and facilitate access to tax allowances and other fiscal incentives (Deliotte, 2020). However, the danger in relying strictly on the economic arguments is that there may be times when there is a strong 'business case' for engaging in destructive behaviours, such as the illicit dumping of toxic waste.

Finally, the political/policy/legal perspective addresses, amongst other issues, the shifting role of political actors and structures in defining and addressing climate change and the regulatory systems required for this (Barry et al., 2013). According to the authors, this encompasses the 'ideological battle for hearts and minds around climate change', including those who are sceptical about or deny its existence.

Stop! What is your view: does it matter if arguments for decarbonisation and/or sustainability are underpinned by an economic, ethical or political rationale?

Essential reading

Barry, J., Mol, A. P. J. and Zito, A. R. (2013) Climate change ethics, rights, and policies: an introduction. *Environmental Politics*, *22*(3): 361–76.

Note: This feature was contributed by Laura Steele.

PART 5

Motivators for embedding sustainability strategies

Managers attempting to create sustainable workplaces are often less effective than they might be because they do not understand the 'drivers' of change (Saifulina and Carballo-Penela, 2017). Here, drawing on data from the author's own research, we give a brief overview of the internal and external drivers towards sustainable LCWs. In order to create an LCW, change agents need to know and reflect upon a number of cause-effect mediating variables, including employees' attitudes (for example, commitment to the workplace), employees' behaviours (for example, conforming to a 'green' policy), external regulatory bodies and the management of organisational risk. Change agents also need to understand that their own leadership behaviour and the organisation's culture directly and indirectly affect managers' and other employees' behaviours and the overall success of a low-carbon strategy (Chen et al., 2020).

Despite the research on organisations' sustainability strategies, it remains unclear why some organisations adopt sustainability initiatives beyond regulatory compliance (Engert et al., 2016). The drivers of sustainability initiatives can be grouped into internal and external drivers. Internal drivers include, personal or ethical values of managers; employee environmental champions; desire to reduce operational costs; employee engagement; organisational culture; investor pressure; and, since the 1990s, corporate social responsibility (Gabzdylova et al., 2009; Lozano, 2015; Walker et al., 2008). External drivers of change, on the other hand, are associated with legislative and regulatory compliance. For example, the Climate Change Act (Scotland) 2009 was often noted as a key driver for sustainability initiatives. A manager explained it this way:

> That is by far the biggest driver ... Within the policy it is substantial enough, it looks at waste, it looks at producing sustainable development plans that go to the government for review, it looks at annual self-assessment to make sure we are matching the requirements from the good corporate citizenship level. (Bratton, 2016, p. 111)

Other external drivers of change include increased energy costs, gaining competitive advantage, access to government funds, customer demands for sustainable products and services, as well as pressures from suppliers, environmental groups, trade unions and public opinion that impinge on the organisation (see, for example, Haigh and Jones, 2006). Guerci et al.'s (2016) study of HR managers and supply chain managers operating in Italy examined how low-carbon practices can be implemented in response to stakeholder pressures. The authors found that 'green' HR practices mediated the relationship between pressures on environmental issues from external stakeholders (customers and regulatory stakeholders) and environmental performance.

Change management 'trigger-response' theories, proposing that the stimulus of external change prompts management action, have been critiqued on the grounds of 'environmental determinism' (Duncan, 1972), and for considering that the external 'context' and 'organisation' are discrete spheres, which tends to downplay the importance of strategic choice (Child, 1972). Changes in these various internal and external drivers might cause managers to consider the need for sustainability initiatives, but every organisation has its own peculiar history and context. The context and character of the sector in which the organisation is located shapes some of these drivers of change. The top six internal and external drivers encountered in Bratton's (2016) study of six large public and private sector workplaces in Scotland is shown in Table 12.1.

With regard to internal factors, reducing organisational risk exposure was considered to be 'very important' in four out of the six cases. Risk has been defined as, 'an uncertain (generally adverse) consequence of an event or activity with respect to something that humans value' (International Risk Gov-

Table 12.1 Rank order of environmental managers' perceptions of drivers of sustainability initiatives

Internal	External
1. Reducing organisational risk	1. Regulatory compliance
2. New product / service opportunities	2. Reducing the impact on local environment
3. Promoting social responsibility	3. Providing assurance to stakeholders and regulators
4. Ethical reasons	4. Customer demand
5. Reducing costs / efficiency savings	5. Maintaining rapport with government agencies and non-governmental organisations
6. Health and safety	6. Maintaining a 'license to operate'
7. Brand reputation / green marketing	7. Improve stakeholder engagement

ernance Council, 2005, p. 4). Correspondingly, risk governance is concerned with the identification, assessment, management and communication of risks in a board context (IRGC, 2005). Concern with reputational risk was highlighted in the author's research in six case studies. Several interviewees reported that, because their organisation is well known and in the public eye, they are under considerable pressure and scrutiny from different stakeholders to address environmental issues. For example, commenting on the potential reputational risk associated with poor recycling performance on trains, one interviewee observed:

> It is very visual that we don't do it. All it takes is a couple of concerned people on the train to say, 'you are not recycling, I'll Tweet that or Facebook that'. (Bratton, 2016, p. 105)

PART 5

Evidence can be found in abundance that the reduction of operating costs is a key driver of change. In Bratton's (2016) study, the majority of respondents indicated that reducing costs was either a 'very important' or 'important' driver. In all six cases, sustainability initiatives involving electricity use were seen as an effective strategy to reduce overall energy costs. In the public sector cases, energy reduction programmes were seen as a strategy to reduce costs and maintain service levels. Unsurprisingly, in the transport industry, a significant motivator behind the implementation of low-carbon technology was the desire to reduce fuel costs. For example, transport companies recognised that pollution reflects hidden costs and that, by implementing eco-driving training and driver assistance technology, management could improve fuel efficiency and decrease the overall cost of fuel. One driver interviewed explained:

> The services are now recognizing reducing energy costs is one of the measures that they can take to reduce their overall costs. There is a lot of talk in the council about revenue generation and ideas for that, but gradually people are coming around to the idea that resource efficiency and reducing consumption can also come from the bottom-up to support that. (Bratton, 2016, p. 108)

In the public sector cases, government budget cuts and increased energy prices provided the financial context to certain sustainability initiatives. This was most evident where so-called 'agile' working and office rationalisation programmes were introduced, first, as a cost-saving measure and second, as a carbon reduction initiative.

The evidence suggests that, in the context of UK and Scottish government budget cuts, sustainability activities have been seen as a strategy to control and reduce operating costs and maintain service levels. These findings are consistent with research by Cox et al. (2012) and Zibarras and Ballinger (2011) that reports initiatives to reduce energy as one of most common sustainability initiatives.

Table 12.1 shows that the promotion of social responsibility and ethical considerations ranked third and fourth, respectively, of the internal drivers. In three cases, health and safety was a 'very important' consideration. The mantra of CSR is based on the belief that organisations are expected to provide 'green' measures that reduce carbon emissions or waste (Docherty et al., 2009). Again, in Bratton's (2016) research of Scottish private and public sector organisations, a number of interviewees expressed a 'moral' imperative for their sustainability initiatives, articulating a belief that encouraging low-carbon behaviour is the 'right' thing to do. For example, in both the public and private sector, ethical considerations motivated senior managers to increase engagement in sustainability at a workplace level. The notion of ethical environmental behaviour was expressed in such terms: 'To start with (economics) was not a driver it was mostly it is the right thing to do' (Bratton, 2016, p. 106).

With regard to external factors, research found that regulatory compliance seems to underpin the different sustainability initiatives, and is the context for other observed drivers (Bratton, 2016). The study found that, in four out of six case studies, environmental managers considered that meeting regulatory compliance requirements was 'very important'. In all of the cases, sustainability initiatives involving waste and recycling were driven by Waste (Scotland) Regulations 2012. In terms of energy initiatives, at one company in the study government legislation drove investment in sustainability initiatives through a combination of higher costs associated with increased taxes and reputational risk. Environmental legislation underpinned many of the sustainability initiatives, and provided the context for other observed drivers.

The Climate Change (Scotland) Act 2009 is the centrepiece of the Scottish Government's climate change policy framework. The Act includes an emissions target, set for the year 2050, for a reduction of at least 80 per cent from the baseline year, 1990. The Act requires public sector bodies to engage in climate change mitigation and adaptation activities, integrate greenhouse gases into decision-making, and act in ways that it considers most sustainable. For example, the Act requires public bodies to set annual greenhouse gas emissions targets and demonstrate compliance with duties through transparent and open reporting.

In Bratton's (2016) study, interviewees from both public and private sector organisations noted the importance of the Act and highlighted their responsibility to reduce greenhouse gas emissions and to help with decarbonising the economy. For example, a Programme Manager at one public sector organisation described the role of government legislation in shaping organisational activities like this: 'We are a public body so we are required to carry out a number of duties laid down in the Climate Change legislation of 2009 that the Scottish Government passed and we have obligation to work toward the low-carbon Scotland' (Bratton, 2016, p. 111). The Climate Change Act (Scotland) 2009 was often noted as a key driver for sustainability initiatives. Other common external drivers were reducing the overall impact on the local environment and providing assurance to stakeholders and regulators, which were ranked second and third, respectively.

Reflective question

Think of an organisation where you have worked or volunteer group of which you were a member. Do you feel top leadership valued sustainability?

Global HRM

US and UK unions call for climate jobs and just transition

Reducing carbon emissions impacts differently on employers and trade unions, and while unions globally are beginning to support environmental issues, in some instances forming links with environmental groups - a blue-green alliance - unions and their members are affected in different ways (see, for example, Goods, 2017). For example, curbing the use of fossil fuels, nuclear energy and air travel will have a negative effect on employment and union membership in those sectors. Increasing the supply of renewable energy with onshore and offshore wind, wave power or tidal power will create new employment opportunities. There is little hope, writes Canadian environmental activist, Naomi Klein, of bringing the fossil fuel companies onside to renewable energy - the profits they stand to lose are too great. However, that is not the case for workers whose jobs are tied to fossil extraction and combustion. She writes (2015, pp. 126–7):

> What is known is this: trade unions can be counted on to fiercely protect jobs, however dirty, if these are the only jobs on offer. On the other hand, when workers in dirty sectors are offered good jobs in clean sectors (like the former autoworkers at the Silfab factory in Toronto, Canada), and are enlisted as active participants in a green transition, then progress can happen at lightning speed.

Given the will, there is an opportunity to create decent, fairly paid, low-carbon jobs. In the US, this path is advocated by the BlueGreen Alliance, a coalition of America's major labour unions and environmental organisations. They believe that the creation of good jobs goes 'hand-in-hand' with the protection of the environment (BlueGreen Alliance). For example, one of the many initiatives that they support is energy-efficient housing products. As governments look to reduce carbon emissions and people become more aware of energy cost savings, the markets for these products are predicted to grow from $300 billion globally in 2014 to $620 billion in 2023 (Navigant Research quoted in BlueGreen Alliance Foundation, 2016).

There is a debate on whether the market will create climate jobs on a large scale or whether this can only be done by government involvement and thoughtful policy and planning. The body representing British trade unions, the TUC, in its document *One Million Climate Jobs*, estimated that one million workers could be employed for a decade for less than the government gave to the banks in one year (TUC, 2010). The climate case for rethinking government intervention, long-term planning and alternative business models is particularly strong when it comes to energy and transport. Since economy and ecology have the same root, perhaps it is not so remarkable that unions around the world are beginning to cooperate and form alliances with the environmental movement.

Stop! What do you think of Klein's argument? To what extent can it be argued that the contradictory position of capital and labour renders any cooperation between work organisations, unions and environmental groups to curb carbon emission a problematic endeavour?

Essential reading

Cha, M. and Brecher, J. (2019) Reject the 'jobs versus environment' narrative - we can do both. *The Guardian*, 10 September; Goods, C. (2017) Climate change and employment relations. *Journal of Industrial Relations*, *59*(5): 670–9. You can read about the BlueGreen Alliance at www.bluegreenalliance.org.

Note: This feature was contributed by John Bratton and Andrew Bratton.

PART 5

Environmental leadership and culture

A growing body of research has highlighted the importance of leadership (Robertson and Barling, 2015) and organisational culture (Norton et al., 2015) to drive both organisational and employee-level pro-environmental performance. The focus in this chapter is on how leaders affect their organisation's environmental performance through influencing the behaviour of individual employees and by changing organisational practices and culture.

Environmental leadership

Although employees' pro-environmental behaviours are critical to the effectiveness of environmental sustainability initiatives, there is insufficient understanding of the role of leadership to support these behaviours (Afsar et al., 2018). Within the strategic management context, the goal of environmental leadership is to motivate followers to achieve high levels of environmental performance (see e.g. Ren et al., 2020). Egri and Herman (2000, p. 572) define environmental leadership as 'the ability to influence individuals and mobilise organisations to realise a vision of long-term ecological sustainability'. This definition is based on the notion that, guided by eco-centric values and assumptions, environmental leaders seek to change economic and social systems that they perceive as currently and potentially threatening to the health of the biophysical environment. Robertson and Barling's (2015, p. 166) framework for pro-environmental leadership highlights the importance of leaders, inspired by their own personal values, attitudes and perceptions, striving 'to influence others at all levels of the organisation in an effort to benefit the natural environment'.

Pro-environmental leaders typically demonstrate transformational patterns of behaviour including charisma, two-way communication, collaboration and orientation towards changing work systems that reduce the environmental impact of an organisation. For example, Portugal and Yukl (1994, p. 274) report transformational leadership behaviours such as 'articulating an appealing vision with environmental issues, changing perceptions about environmental issues, and taking symbolic actions to demonstrate personal commitment to environmental issues'. Importantly, leaders' supportive behaviours have been shown to be a crucial component of environmental leadership (Robertson and Barling, 2015). Environmental leadership can be defined as:

> A process to create a shared vision of environmental sustainability and motivate others to create sustainable organizations in an equitable manner whilst living within the limits of ecosystems'. (Bratton, 2020, p. 367)

This definition emphasises the importance of vision to help align individuals and motivate followers, that the coordinated pro-environmental initiatives must be sustainable and viable for the organisation and, at the same time, marries pro-environmental leadership with notions of social justice and ecological limits.

A *sustainability leader* can extend beyond senior managers (Ferdig, 2007). Robertson and Barling (2015, p. 169) found that pro-environmental leaders are more likely to: (1) possess personal values that go beyond self-interest; (2) have favourable attitudes towards the natural environment; (3) perceive social pressure to support environmental and sustainability initiatives; and (4) view environmental issues as commercial opportunities for their organisation. Other studies have identified different types of behaviours enacted by sustainability leaders, including line-management supportive behaviours (Ramus, 2001). These behaviours include encouraging innovation among employees, competence-building, communicating ideas on sustainability, dissemination of information, rewards and recognition, and management of goals and responsibilities by disseminating environmental targets and responsibilities. Kotter (2012) points to the importance of leadership behaviours that encourage employee involvement and participation in organisational change. Participation at all levels of management is essential to the introduction of environmental sustainability change (Davis and Coan, 2015). However, internal workplace stakeholders – specifically front-line managers – are seen to be critical to the overall success of an organisation's sustainability strategy (Bratton and Bratton, 2015).

Source: Jonathan Kemper on Unsplash

The goal of environmental leadership is to motivate followers to achieve high levels of environmental awareness and performance.

Reframing organisational culture

What role does culture play in developing employees' pro-environmental behaviours? Findings across several studies consistently show that, when implementing strategic change, managers need to consider organisational culture and climate (e.g. Chen et al., 2020; Roscoe et al., 2019). Norton et al. (2015) define a pro-environmental organisational culture as

> a pattern of shared basic assumptions learned by a group as it adapts to the challenges posed by human activity's impact on the natural environment in a way that permits day-to-day functioning, which has worked well enough to be considered valid and, therefore, to be taught to new members as the correct way to perceive, think, and feel in relation to environmental sustainability. (Norton et al., 2015: 329–30)

PART 5

At the individual level, a pro-environmental climate – defined as employees' shared perceptions of pro-environmental policies and practices that management tangibly supports – acts as a go-between between the perception of management's pro-environmental behaviour and the pro-environmental behaviour of employees. Research suggests leaders and organisational culture and climate influence employees' and their organisations' environmental performance. There is debate regarding whether organisations need to have an underlying 'moral commitment to sustainability' (Davis and Coan, 2015, p. 247), which suggests that there is a need for the principles, assumptions and values that underpin the organisation's norms and rules to be changed if sustainability is to be achieved (see e.g. Hayes, 2014). This introduces the concept of 'cultural congruence'; that is, for an organisation to become environmentally sustainable, its underlying values and assumptions must be aligned with sustainability interventions in such a way that employees' attitudes and behaviours support the organisation's overall low-carbon strategic objectives (see, for example, Russell and McIntosh, 2011). A sustainable workplace is therefore associated with specific pro-environmental attitudes, values and behaviours. Taken together, the available research findings identify two key antecedents or enablers of pro-environmental behaviours and initiatives, which are leadership and a pro-environmental culture and climate.

In this context, organisational behaviour theorists have tried to identify effective ways to change manifestations of organisational culture: visible artefacts, including language and shared behaviour; work values, which are invisible, but can be espoused; and various sets of HRM practices that reinforce culture. Research shows that the three main strategies of planned culture change are:

- leadership processes that create the motivation to change behaviour, with a particular emphasis on their symbolic content; for example, replacing office plastic cups with ceramic;
- reframing social networks of symbols and meanings through artefacts, language, rituals and ceremonies; for example, a 'best employee' award for an initiative that helps to decarbonise the organisation;
- initiating new HRM practices to change work conduct; for example, training new and existing employees about the need and benefits of reducing carbon emissions in the workplace.

Harris and Crane (2002) identify an undeveloped conception of organisational culture in the sustainable HRM literature, with non-functionalist views of culture largely being ignored. The comparative case study research by Fineman (1996, 1997) has been referred to as 'something of an antidote to the non-empirical and largely uncritical literature on green organizational culture' (Harris and Crane, 2002, p. 217). It suggests that even in the 'most progressive firms', environmental values and beliefs tend to be absorbed into existing cultural assumptions and beliefs rather than eliciting any kind of cultural transformation. Newton and Harte (1997) expose the over-reliance on simplistic formulae for green change, the overselling of voluntary change as a solution to environmental issues, and the lack of a critical perspective into how and why culture change might occur. A simplistic formula, for example, would be to believe that the organisation can impact climate change just by replacing single-use plastic cups, that individual efforts rather than enforceable carbon-reducing legislation is a solution to high-carbon workplaces, and neglecting the role of values in nudging human behaviour towards more pro-environment action.

The extant literature on organisational culture and business strategy highlights how important it is that the prevailing business strategy and organisational culture are consistent with each other (internal fit) and with the wider operation of the organisation (external fit) (e.g. Chow and Liu, 2009). For example, a company may be targeting sales of a new craft beer to the 19- to 24-year-old age group but its processing system uses traditional methods, which is energy inefficient and pollutes a nearby river. Extending the best-fit debate, theory and empirical research suggest that a green HR strategy should coincide with the organisation's business strategy and create an appropriate culture in which to enhance environmental performance. Broadly, the HRM approach to building a low-carbon workplace is to develop and support the workplace's environmental sustainability initiatives.

Creating a low-carbon workplace through sustainable HRM

A critical issue in the theory of strategic HRM is that HR practices should be integrated with the organisation's goals (Boxall and Purcell, 2016). Too much of the public discourse on the 'green economy' continues to disregard human behaviour in the workplace that affects environmental performance. In this section, we consider the main ways in which HR practices can develop managers' and workers' pro-environmental behaviours. While 'specific contingency' factors must always be considered (Boxall and Purcell, 2016, p. 78), serial research suggests that green HR practices improve environmental sustainability (see, for example, Chaudhary, 2020). The established use of HR processes in occupational health and safety, minimum waste production as part of a 'lean' manufacturing system and cultural management make HRM well positioned to coordinate the goals of a sustainable workplace (Oliveira and Pinheiro, 2009). Indeed, as already noted, the influential CIPD considers sustainable HRM central to promoting pro-environmental behaviours that will act to de-carbonise the workplace (Houghton, 2019).

An early contribution to the debate on the links between HRM and environmental management was made by Wehrmeyer's (1996) edited book, *Greening People: Human Resources and Environmental Management*. In it, HRM is associated with a distinctive HR philosophy, strategy and set of determinate HR practices (see Chapter 2) to create a *high-performance work system* (HPWS). Building on the HPWS concept, Bratton and Bratton define a low-carbon work system as:

> A planned approach to organization design, culture, and HR practices to deliver low-carbon outcomes in the workplace as well as to align the organization and its processes to achieve innovation and sustainable high-quality results for the organization, workforce, and customers. (2015, p. 277)

A *low-carbon work system* (LCWS) requires new roles and low-carbon behavioural activities for leaders, managers and other employees. Low-carbon behaviours occur at three levels: individual, social and material (Cox et al., 2012):

- Individual-level influences act on individual motivations (e.g. personal rewards).
- Social-level influences act on employees when operating in teams or groups (e.g. social norms, shared understandings and communities of practice).
- Material level influences act on organisational structure and processes (e.g. products, technology and environment).

The research by Cox et al., (2012) suggests that behavioural interventions tend to be most successful when they consider these three dimensions holistically, and do not simply focus on trying to change individual employee attitudes or just install new technology. In other words, when establishing a LCWS, the goal should be to take an integrated approach that raises awareness and improves understanding with individual employees and groups, builds social meaning and norms around pro-environmental, 'low-carbon' or 'sustainable' working practices, and supports employees with the technology they need, backed up with consistent policies.

HRM scholars have tried to identify effective ways to change manifestations of an environmentally sustainable organisational culture through modified HR practices. The emergent literature on sustainable HRM emphasises that a set of integrated HR practices covering recruitment, selection, performance management, rewards, training and development, and employment relations can promote pro-environmental behaviours at work and build a more environmentally sustainable organisational culture.

Existing sustainable HRM studies highlight the opportunity for improved environmental performance when the goals, policies and procedures of EMSs are more closely aligned or 'embedded' (Purcell and Kinnie, 2008) with HR practices and wider activities of the organisation (see, for example, Chen, 2011; Jørgensen, 2000). However, this convergence between HR practices and organisational culture is considered secondary in classic studies of organisational sustainability (see, for example, Shrivastava, 1995). A central question that arises from the literature is whether effective environmental sustainability initiatives can develop from top-down management-driven exercises, or whether they are more likely to be successful if they are part of a more grass-roots, employee-led initiative for environmental sustainability in the workplace. To date, much of the sustainable HRM research has focused on core HR practices.

Recruitment and selection

Environmental sustainability has become an important dimension shaping the recruitment and selection process. Research suggests that attracting top candidates is easier for organisations known for their superior environmental stewardship (Chaudhary, 2018; Gully et al., 2013; Pham and Paillé, 2019; Rupp et al., 2013). An Italian study found, for example, that 'green recruiting practices' could have a distinct and direct effect on attracting applicants (Guerci et al., 2016). One obvious way to build a sustainable workplace is through self-selection of prospective employees. For example, German companies such as chemical and pharmaceutical company Bayer and engineering company Siemens, use their environmental reputation to attract competent employees who are committed to the environment (Jabbour and Santos, 2008). The published research suggests that, given a choice, people are attracted to green employers that are keenly attuned to climate change issues and have a strong ecological approach (Philips, 2007). Environmentally sensitive job previews combined with accurate portrayal of the organisation's culture can attract talented people with values that match and promote sustainability (Jabbour, 2011).

Another way to embed ecological values in the workplace is by selecting people with green-related skills and values. The selection process may be designed to ensure that 'employees committed to the environmental issue have a potential to be hired more than those who do not show an ability to lead the environmental management in a company' (Jabbour and Santos, 2008, p. 53). Studies also suggest that it may be expedient to start hiring managers who have a proven track record of environmental performance and value environmental protection (see e.g. Ramus, 2002). Personality- and competency-based tests provide the tools that enable managers to find talented individuals who seem to fit the new culture. Selection tests based on attitudinal and behavioural profiling can also be used to screen applicants for green values.

Pro-environmental learning and development

Consensus is growing among academics that the issues of sustainability, learning and development are closely interrelated. From a socio-technical systems approach, creating individual and collective learning opportunities is an important part of designing a sustainable work system (Zink, 2014). Training is a primary intervention for developing pro-environmental behaviours (see e.g. Bratton, 2018; Joshi and Dhar, 2020) and 'green' training is positively associated with career growth (Xie et al., 2020). Much of company training appears to be related to improving employees' health and safety, energy saving and waste management. For example, the US company 3M has encouraged employees to find creative ways to reduce pollution through their Pollution Prevention Pays (3Ps) programme, which has saved the company close to $300 million (Renwick et al., 2008, p. 7). Learning and development is a necessary component of advanced environmental management systems. The literature suggests that a major factor in a successful EMS is a comprehensive training programme that provides all employees, at all levels of the organisation, with the tools and understanding necessary to conduct themselves in an environmentally aware manner, foster innovation, make environmentally responsible decisions and contribute to continued environmental improvements (Daily and Huang, 2001).

Research suggests that the level of employee environmental awareness is one of the most important predictors of the level of adoption and success of an organisation's environmental initiatives. Perron et al. (2006, p. 553) report, for example, that the intent of clause 4.4.2 of ISO 14001 is to 'ensure that employees at all levels of the organization understand the goals of the EMS and the ways their job activities impact the environment and the achievement of EMS goals' (ISO, 2015). This understanding allows employees to participate in environmental management efforts and could lead to improved environmental performance of an organisation. Zilahy's (2003) study of the factors restricting the implementation of energy efficiency improvement indicates that perhaps the most salient restrictive factor was the level of employee environmental awareness. Research findings support the importance of employees being well versed in environmental issues, environmental processes and the overall functioning of environmental management systems to ensure that an organisation's environmental targets and objectives were achieved (see e.g. Pham, 2020).

Performance management and sustainability

Performance management, examined in Chapter 6, was conceptualised not as a single event, but as an ongoing holistic process. It has become fashionable in emergent studies in environmental management (Garavan and McGuire, 2010) to argue that, in those organisations with proactive environmental sustainability programmes, performance management systems (PMSs) can improve the effectiveness of environmental management over time (Milliman and Clair, 1996). In ongoing performance conversations leaders can promote pro-environmental employees' behaviour and actions towards enhanced environmental performance outcomes. Jabbour et al. (2010) report that Brazilian manufacturing companies are establishing environmental objectives for their employees, whose performance is evaluated as one of the criteria of the performance appraisal. For example, the business services Xerox Corporation has a reward system that recognises employees who meet certain levels of innovation in terms of how they deal with waste reduction, reuse and recycling (Milliman and Clair, 1996). Without performance appraisal, pro-environmental behaviours may come to a standstill. Chinander (2001) highlights how many environmental management programmes fail to emphasise the importance of feedback on environmental issues. The performance appraisal (PA) plays a crucial role in determining appropriate rewards and for employee training and development. Indeed, the current HRM wisdom emphasises that it is through the process of continual observation, monitoring and serial performance conversations that workers are made aware of the link between their environmental performance outcomes, rewards and development (Govindarajulu and Daily, 2004).

Rewarding pro-environmental behaviours

The organisation's reward system provides a good indication of the seriousness of its commitment to environmental sustainability management (Berrone and Gomez-Mejia, 2009). The rewards can be monetary or non-monetary, and could be tied to individual, group or organisational actions (see Chapter 7). Monetary rewards may be one of the strongest motivators for encouraging employees to participate in environmental improvement activity. For example, aligning compensation practices with environmental strategy has been implemented in North American companies such as Huntsman Corporation (chemicals), Browning-Ferris Industries (waste management) and Coors Brewing Company (Milliman and Clair, 1996), where financial rewards are tied to employees' environmental performance. In this regard, managers will need to determine whether environmental responsibilities and initiatives should be incorporated into managers' and employees' performance appraisals. Denton (1999) observes that, even in some of the best-known companies for encouraging environmental initiatives, financial rewards are rarely tied to environmental performance.

Studies suggest that many workplaces are encouraging environmental activities using non-monetary rewards such as employee recognition schemes, time off from work, gift certificates and paid vacations (Govindarajulu and Daily, 2004). For example, Dow Chemical Company, a leading American multinational corporation, motivates its employees by awarding plaques to employees who develop innovative waste reduction ideas (Denton, 1999). Some employees may be more motivated by formal or informal recognition rather than financial incentives. Empirical findings from six environmentally proactive European firms have shown that two of the most important factors for engaging employees and encouraging creative ideas are management support and company environmental awards (Ramus, 2002). This suggests that front-line managers should seek environmental ideas from all employees, and seek opportunities to provide feedback to encourage employees' engagement in environmental sustainability. Whether rewards are monetary or non-monetary in nature, the reward system has to be supported by an effective communication plan (Parker and Wright, 2001), rewards must be tied to the achievement of environmental objectives (Starik and Rands, 1995), and they must be consistent with other aspects of the rewards system (May and Flannery, 1995).

Digital Spotlight
Key metrics for sustainability

The concept of sustainability has, to a greater or lesser extent, become embedded in all functions of management, including HRM (see, for example, Ehnert et al., 2016). Assessing and reporting on environmental performance is now a core activity within many organisations and there is evidence it may yield significant business benefits, such as cost reductions and increases in efficiency (Zutshi and Sohal, 2004). In addition, current and potential employees, customers and investors are increasingly demanding that businesses behave in an environmentally sustainable manner or risk losing their 'social licence to operate' (Hurst et al., 2020). In order to facilitate assessment and reporting, organisations may introduce an Environmental Management System (EMS). The system can be of their own bespoke design or, alternatively, they may opt to follow guidelines developed by a third party. Perhaps the best know EMS certification scheme is ISO 140001, which requires organisations to determine the criteria by which they will evaluate their environmental performance. Typical metrics include the use of natural resources (water, electricity, gas, paper, etc.); discharges to air, land and water; incidents and potential incidents; and proactive measures (for example, risk reduction activities). Increasingly, organisations are also choosing to incorporate reference to the UN Sustainable Development Goals (SDGs) into their reports on sustainability. (Indeed, Target 12.6 within the SDGs specifically encourages companies to adopt sustainable practices and integrate sustainability information into their reporting). The SDGs are more broadly scoped than many previous initiatives, which predominantly focused on the environment and, therefore, required businesses to expand their definition of sustainability. For example, they are relevant in the context of occupational health and safety (SDG 3: Good Health and Well-being); learning and development (SDG 4: Quality Education); and job and work design (SDG 8: Decent Work and Economic Growth), to highlight just a few of the relevant 'Global Goals'.

It is clear that, just as the concept of sustainability has expanded, so too has the amount of data that businesses must collect, analyse and report upon. Much of this information is likely already held by the organisation, for example, in relation to energy use, water use, vehicle fuel use and/or mileage figures, or the gender and ethnicity of their employees. However, it is likely located across multiple departments and/or geographical locations and in various different formats. This presents a significant challenge. Advances in technology, including the centralisation of systems, are helping to present a solution. In addition, a number of platforms, such as Intelex and the SDG Action Manager have been specifically developed to capture and report on environmental and other sustainability goals.

Stop! Read about the SDG Action Manager at https://www.unglobalcompact.org/take-action/sdg-action-manager. What role can HR professionals play in terms of helping to achieve the UN Sustainable Development Goals by the deadline of 2030 and how might technology be able to facilitate this?

Essential reading

Ehnert, I., Parsa, S., Roper, I., Wagner, M. and Muller-Camen, M. (2016) Reporting on sustainability and HRM: a comparative study of sustainability reporting practices by the world's largest companies. *International Journal of Human Resource Management*, *27*(1): 88–108.

Note: This feature was contributed by Laura Steele.

Employee voice in environmental sustainability

Employee voice can operate informally and formally and with or without a trade union voice, as explained in Chapter 10. An example of informal employee voice would be a line manager listening to suggestions from an individual or team members (see Marchington, 2008). An example of formal employee voice would be a scheme involving managers, individual workers and/or their union representatives participating in a decision-making group. In this section we extend the discussion by critically examining how worker and trade union voice can support the creation of a sustainable workplace and improve environmental management (Antonioli and Mazzanti, 2017; Farnhill, 2018; Hampton, 2015; Markey and McIvor, 2019; Markey et al., 2019). Recent sustainable HRM studies (e.g. Montabon et al., 2016) have tended to focus on non-union processes, and most only go so far as to suggest that managers should use various employee representation arrangements to encourage employee 'voice' (Del Brio et al., 2007). As Perron et al. (2006, p. 556) opine, 'the many small actions and decisions that all members of an organisation can make in their everyday work can cumulate to large improvements in the environmental impacts of the organisation'. The research suggests that when workers are 'engaged' through employee participation processes they will better understand how they can contribute towards environmental sustainability. This highlights further that without the ingenuity and expertise of workers, environmental management initiatives may be limited and superficial.

Lund's classification (Table 12.2) shows different levels of employee participation from the perspective of workplace democracy. The distinction between 'employee involvement' and 'participation' may be conceptualised in terms of six categories: (1) information; (2) practical involvement; (3) consultation; (4) negotiation; (5) codetermination; and (6) self-management (Lund, 2004, p. 53). These categories only relate with the question of 'how' employees participate, and therefore must also be combined with categories describing the subject of participation. These subject categories can be described in terms of increasing levels of participation in managerial decisions such as: (1) welfare decisions; (2) shop-floor operational decisions; (3) tactical business decisions; and (4) strategic business decisions (Walters and Frick, 2000).

PART 5

Although trade union membership and influence has significantly declined over the last four decades (see Chapter 9), unions in the developed economies have responded to climate change issues. For example, in Britain in 2019, the TUC published its report, 'A just transition to a greener, fairer economy',

Table 12.2 Different concepts of involvement and participation

Elements within management	Employee involvement	Employee participation
Decision-making process	Management initiated and controlled	Dialectics between top-down and bottom-up managerial tasks allocated to workers
Level of competence	Limited to assignments and functions	Involves high-level decisions
Forms of consultation	Individual only	Collective and individual representation
Strategy for innovation/ change	Management through goals and visions	Dialogue and cooperation
Views on the employees' role in workplace changes	Employees as important production factors	Employees as political actors

Source: Adapted from Lund (2004).

which aimed to place workers at the centre of achieving a successful transition to a sustainable, low-carbon economy. The TUC (2020a, pp. 3–6) focuses on the role of worker voice in helping to build a greener, fairer economy:

> The voices of workers who are at the forefront of dealing with the challenge of climate change must be at the centre of achieving a successful transition ... Workers also have transition-related knowledge. A company or organisation moving from fossil-based to a cleaner energy system, or whole sector transitioning towards cleaner technologies, will have to adapt to specific processes and workers are most likely to understand how to do this effectively. It makes business sense to give workers a stronger voice and higher visibility in such circumstances.

The TUC's just transition statement sets out a number of ambitious industrial relations policies designed to give workers a central voice in the move to a low-carbon economy. Although trade unions globally are beginning to support environmental issues, for example, the campaign for One Million Climate Jobs and the proposals for a Green New Deal in the US and Europe, the labour movement is divided. The union that organises many workers in the US construction and energy industries, LIUNA, argues the case against the Green New Deal like this:

> While rhetorically mimicking one of the most successful government initiatives in our country's history, there is a significant difference between the real New Deal and the 'Green New Deal'. The real New Deal put green in working people's pockets, won massive public support and lifted our nation out of despair. The latter threatens to destroy workers' livelihoods, increase divisions and inequality, and undermine the very goals it seeks to reach. (LIUNA, 2019)

If pro-environment change is desired, the notion of 'dialogic communication', a mode of communication driven by an *exchange* of views (Bratton and Francis, 2020, p. 307), underscores the value of workers' engagement and agency in shaping individual and organisational behaviours. For example, employee voice mechanisms such as 'green teams' (Daily et al., 2007) and 'eco-champions' (Brosse, 2010) are major elements of the sustainable HRM strategy because they provide followers with an opportunity to use their intimate knowledge of work and discretion at work to generate creative eco-friendly initiatives rather than rely solely on leaders.

In the UK, the climate of employment relations has changed radically over the last three decades (Farnham, 2015, p. 231). In the post-Covid-19 recession, a key question remains: 'Who gains what from being involved?' Leaders and managers have the power to drive (or not) employee participation. It is plausible therefore to assume that leaders and managers expect to see some advantage from investing in time-consuming voice mechanisms, and HR practices which critics might see as 'an expensive waste of time' (Wilkinson et al., 2010, p. 5).

Reflective question

Does the primacy of the profit motive prevent organisations adopting a strategy that is environmentally sustainable?

Critiquing corporate-oriented sustainability

Mainstream environmental studies tend not to engage sufficiently with conflicts inherent in the employment relationship (Lund, 2004, pp. 48–9); they also tend to largely neglect the role of the state in combating climate change (Betsill and Rabe, 2009). Critical authors three decades ago argued that the term *sustainability* had become a purposeful distraction, 'deliberately vague [...] so that endless streams of academics and diplomats could spend many comfortable hours trying to define it without success' (O'Riordan, 1988, p. 37). Later, others added to this critique, arguing that the sustainability debate had become too 'technocratic, mere rhetoric, in-egalitarian, and for being a *smokescreen for perpetuation of the status quo, vacuous, politically correct sloganeering*' (Buttel, 1998, p. 262, emphasis added).

But most environmental studies mirror mainstream management by neglecting the close relationship of the state to corporate interests (Kelly, 1998). The role of the state in the environmental management discourse should not be downplayed or disregarded. The state, through macro-economic policy, trade agreements, labour market reforms, environmental legislation or investment in renewable technology, plays a central role in the economy. For example, governments project an image of neutrality on the issue of fracking, a drilling process used in the extraction of gas from shale rock, and downplay environmental damage while citing the benefits of job creation. Those opposed to fracking accuse governments and fracking companies of providing misinformation and 'keeping secret the impacts of shale gas extraction' (BBC, 2014). Heyes and Nolan observe that:

> The state is viewed as a benign force composed of multiple sites of authority none of which is dominant. It acts to create institutions and networks that facilitate information sharing, innovative behaviours, coordination and joint problem solving by social actors ... Yet pluralism lacks a clear theory of the state, certainly lacks a theory of the capitalist state and therefore fails to problematize the nature of the state's relationship to capital and labour. (2010, p. 121)

It has been argued that mainstream management approaches to environmental sustainability fail to engage with the dynamics of capitalism and the nature of the capitalist state. A critical analysis requires that researchers recognise the importance of macro social structures (e.g. population changes), social movements (e.g. Greenpeace), international trade agreements and environmental legislation in supporting or undermining environmental sustainability.

At the workplace level, a critical analysis gives consideration to bottom-up, stakeholder input 'which would, by necessity, involve dialogical communication' (Sumner, 2005, p. 91). This, it is argued, is best developed if deliberative democracy principles are employed and there is recognition by stakeholders of 'their interdependencies and power differences and the development of a shared will to move beyond the immediate self-interest of the affected parties' (Benn et al., 2009, p. 1,572). Such stakeholder-centred approaches accept the inevitability of change in the nature of environmental risks or human perceptions of environmental risks and assume that organisations have reflexive capacity to respond to the process of 'mutual learning' between a range of stakeholders (Carlsson and Berkes, 2005). A stakeholder-centred approach would also give greater prominence to effective followers (Uhl-Bien et al., 2014). Potentially, voice would make every member of the organisation an effective follower for pro-environmental creativity and innovation (Stahl et al., 2020). Organisational leaders, senior managers and other employees are central to facilitating change and supporting better environmental outcomes. For example, employees and their union representatives could be involved in strategic decision-making with potential for 'social partnership' (Johnstone and Ackers, 2015) for better environmental outcomes in the workplace.

Summary

The goal of this chapter is to establish the role of human resource management in enabling and improving environmental sustainability in the workplace. Given that questions of organisational leadership, culture and managerial behaviour are increasingly seen to fall within HRM theory and research, this chapter brings together distinct streams of literature to focus on environmental sustainability and human resource management in the workplace.

We explained that an EMS is the most widely recognised tool for managing the impacts of an organisation's environmental impact in a comprehensive, systematic, planned and documented manner. With regards to the motivators of change, all the evidence points to a variety of internal and external drivers including organisational values, regulation, demand from customers, society and competition, for implementing sustainability initiatives. The review of environmental leadership and organisational culture literature highlights the need to examine the role of leaders' influence in creating sustainable, low-carbon workplaces.

The review of sustainable HRM literature focuses attention on how selective HR practices can drive change through formal and informal levers. In this regard, the emerging sustainable HRM literature focuses on a cluster of HR practices including selection, appraisal, rewards and training that can influence employees' attitudes and behaviours.

Finally, the chapter focused attention on the limitations of sustainable HRM studies, including the importance of context and the nature of the employment relationship, insufficient recognition of alternative voices, particularly those of employees and unions, and the 'fatally flawed' assumption that line managers enact sustainable HR policies and practices.

Review questions

1. What is your understanding of a sustainable workplace?
2. What are the internal and external drivers of change towards more environmentally sustainable workplace practices?
3. What role can HRM play in creating a low-carbon workplace? What are the challenges?

Search & Watch

Go to the video hub at www.bloomsbury.pub/bratton-hrm and watch the interview with **Markus Hiemann, Sustainability Manager for NHS National Services Scotland**. NHS National Services Scotland (NSS) provides national strategic support services and expert advice to NHS Scotland, including procurement, legal services and public health intelligence. Markus is responsible for the Health Board's sustainability strategy and delivery of Good Corporate Citizenship programmes across the workforce, procurement, community engagement and climate change adaptation. Click on Markus's photo in your *ebook* to watch him speaking about ways to encourage sustainability and how it relates to HR practice, and then think about the following questions: (1) How has the idea of sustainability evolved over time? (2) Should sustainability be driven from the top down or from the bottom up? (3) How can sustainability goals be combined with performance management?

Legal Focus

The primary purpose of a trade union is to protect and promote its members and the way it achieves this is by collective bargaining. Mainstream environmental studies tend to largely neglect the role of trade unions in creating low-carbon workplaces and combating climate change. Reducing carbon emissions and creating low-carbon jobs could be part of a trade union's collective bargaining agenda. However, pro-environmental clauses in collective agreements are rare, and are as likely to be driven by management as by unions (Markey and McIvor, 2019).

As previously mentioned (see Legal Focus in Chapter 9), in the case of *Demir and Baykara v Turkey*, the European Court of Human Rights protected the right for unions to engage in collective bargaining, in 2008. The Trade Union & Labour Relations (Consolidation) Act (TULR(C)A) 1992 defined a collective agreement as 'any agreement made by or on behalf of one or more trade unions and one or more employer or employer's association and relating to one or more of the matters specified'. The specified matters include terms and conditions of employment. The parties to these agreements are the union and the employer, not the employees. Unlike jurisdictions such as Canada, collective agreements in the UK have been presumed not to be legally enforceable between the collective parties. Employment terms (e.g. pay and hours of work) need to become part of the individual's contract to be enforceable against the employer. This is normally done by what is referred to as 'express' or 'implied' incorporation.

Task Search online for government information in your jurisdiction on legislation about collective bargaining. Answer the following questions: (1) What matters are specified that are within the remit of collective negotiations? (2) How do the provisions compare to Canada or Australia? (3) Should pro-environmental clauses be part of a formal collective agreement? Explain your reasoning.

Reference

See Deborah Lockton and Tom Brown's *Employment Law* (2020), pp. 57–66 on collective bargaining and implied and express incorporation of the terms of a collective agreement.

Chapter case: RailCo

The setting

RailCo is a train operating company in Scotland owned by Transport Group plc, a large transport company, registered in the UK. The Transport Group operates bus, coach, rail and tram services in the United States, Canada, Denmark, UK and Ireland. The company reports that it employs approximately 124,000 people globally with revenues of over £6.5 billion per annum. The majority of Scotland's 340 passenger stations are operated by RailCo and are under Network Rail ownership. The core occupations are characterised by large gender imbalances with 80% of the workforce being male. It operates with a two-tier payroll system, reducing the overall wage costs by hiring new employees at a wage less than incumbent employees, which potentially impacts on employment relations. RailCo has a high level of union membership, especially train drivers, with over 90% unionisation. Train drivers, engineers, conductors and ticket collectors, hospitality and other stations employees are members of three transport unions ASLEF, RMT, TSSA and the general union Unite. The case provides an example of how unions and employers can constructively contribute to creating sustainable practices and behaviours through cooperation on workplace learning for driver environmental training and accreditation.

Source: Chris Yang on Unsplash

RailCo's sustainability strategy demonstrates the relevance and value of trade union involvement when organisations introduce sustainable low-carbon practices. For example, the introduction of eco-driving techniques and new technology that helps train drivers operate their trains in a more energy-efficient manner.

The problem

Rewards and recognition are often seen as key features of an organisation's strategic drive to achieving a low-carbon workplace. In terms of environmental management, pay-for-environmental performance (PEP) aims to guide employees' actions towards desired environmental performance outcomes. Mainstream sustainable HRM scholars suggest that without an effective rewards management strategy, employee environmental improvement effort may falter. However, integrating rewards management with sustainability objectives presents many challenges, particularly in the implementation process when new eco-technology and performance-related financial participation is first introduced. The formal link between employee environmental performance and pay is established in the performance appraisal system (PAS). At least in theory, financial participation has the potential to encourage train drivers to operate their trains in a more energy-efficient manner. In practice, however, managers and workers expressed concern that there were unresolved union-management negotiations on eco-driving technology and performance-related financial participation. At a meeting held to discuss some of the issues, one RailCo manager said:

> There is certainly scope for consensus ... if we had business benefits through cooperation, through a consensual approach, then maybe there is an opportunity for gainshare there.

Commenting on the perceived lack of management consultation and support for PEP, a union representative expressed concern:

> Where management have made a mess is they didn't engage with the unions ... And right away there is a bit of animosity between the staff and management towards the whole ozone, eco-driving ... There are guys that are not interested so the most beneficial way to encourage them is to give them a bonus.

Rachelle Wong, the HR Director, who was chairing the meeting, summarised the main concerns of the managers and trade union representatives and added that their experiences mirror published evidence drawing attention to the need for employee participation when implementing performance-related pay in a highly unionised workplace. She promised to consider the views of the union representative and organise a joint consultative committee (JCC) meeting to consider how PEP could be implemented. Rachelle Wong prides herself on her use of evidence-based HR management to design policies.

The assignment

Working as a group or on your own, prepare a report for Rachelle Wong drawing on the material from this chapter and address the following:

1. How can rewards management help this organisation meet its sustainability objectives?
2. What role, if any, should unions play in implementing pay-for-environmental performance (PEP)?
3. What are the challenges associated with integrating rewards management with sustainability objectives?

Essential reading

Berrone, P. and Gomez-Mejia, L. R. (2009) Environmental performance and executive compensation: an integrated agency-institutional perspective. *Academy of Management Journal*, *52*(1): 103–26.

Markey, R. and McIvor, J. (2019). Environmental bargaining in Australia. *Journal of Industrial Relations*, *61*(1): 79–104.

Note: This case was contributed by Andrew Bratton.

Further reading

Aust, I., Matthews, B. and Muller-Camen, M. (2020) Common good HRM: a paradigm shift in Sustainable HRM? *Human Resource Management Review*, *30*(3): 100705.

Farnhill, T. (2018) Union renewal and workplace greening – three case studies. *British Journal of Industrial Relations*, *56*(4): 716–43.

Houghton, E. (2019) *Sustainable HR: A 'Green' Fad, or a Realistic Model for Change?* London: CIPD.

Stahl, G. K., Brewster, C. J., Collings, D. G. and Hajro, A. (2020) Enhancing the role of human resource management in corporate sustainability and social responsibility: a multi-stakeholder, multidimensional approach to HRM. *Human Resource Management Review*, *30*(3): 100708.

Note: This chapter was written by Andrew Bratton.

CHAPTER 13

INTERNATIONAL HRM IN A GLOBALISED CAPITALISM

outline

- Introduction
- Globalisation and typologies of global business strategy
- The nature of international HRM
- A model of SIHRM
- HR strategy in MNCs
- The convergence/ divergence debate
- Critiquing international HRM
- Summary
- Further reading

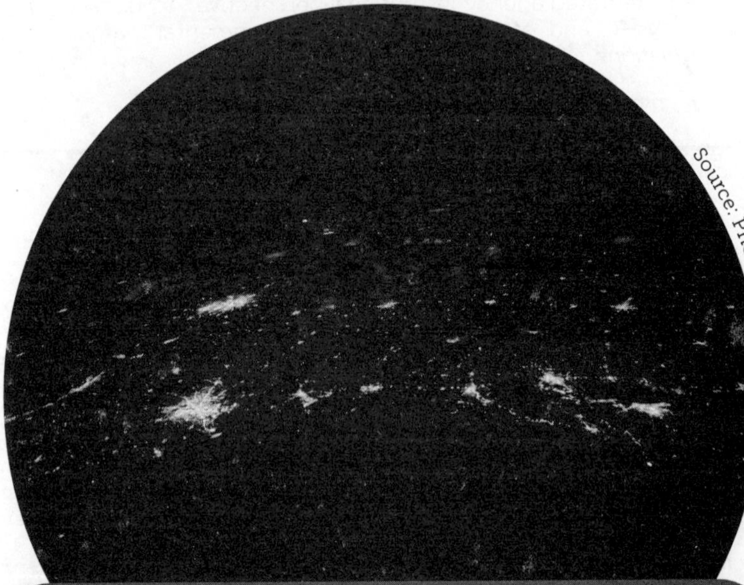

Source: Photo by NASA on Unsplash

objectives

After studying this chapter, you should be able to:

1. Explain how developments in global capitalism affect corporate strategies and patterns of employment relations
2. Describe the difference between strategic international human resource management (SIHRM) and international human resource management (IHRM)
3. Explain how SIHRM is linked to different global business strategies
4. To critically evaluate the key approaches to global staffing and managing labour in MNCs
5. To critically analyse the debate on global convergence or divergence in HRM policies and practices

Introduction

The international management literature emphasises that successful global business strategies depend on the 'quality of the people' who are in charge of its implementation in overseas operations (Lasserre, 2012, p. 335). The challenge of securing talented workers to manage in a global context is therefore of crucial importance for multinational corporations (MNCs). The various orientations MNCs can have towards staffing and managing people in organisations that straddle national borders constitute the field of *international* human resource management (IHRM). The literature has focused on the issue of standardisation versus localisation in the global development and diffusion of HR policies and practices. International HRM can be distinguished from domestic HRM by the fact that core HR activities have to be culturally sensitive and effective in a cross-cultural, multinational context (Scullion and Linehan, 2005). As such, Collings et al. (2019, p. 378) posit that IHRM 'has acquired an important niche in the field of HRM and become a key issue for practitioners in MNCs'.

The focus of this chapter is IHRM. We begin with an overview of three alternative theories relating to the impact of global processes on domestic patterns of employment relations. This is followed by an examination of the various orientations MNCs can have towards the management of labour in their overseas subsidiaries including staffing, learning and development, and reward management. It concludes by exploring a pivotal argument in IHRM on whether global capitalism is causing a convergence or a divergence in employment management.

Globalisation and typologies of global business strategy

The social networking platform Facebook, with over 2.6 billion monthly active users globally as of the first quarter of 2020, exemplifies the globalisation of capitalism and the converging lifestyles worldwide (Statista, 2020). Europeans managing foreign operations and the analysis of globalised capitalism are not new, both go back to the eighteenth and nineteenth century respectively. The relationship between the slave trade, slavery and economic development remains a contested field of British and European history (Devine, 2015). But the plantation economies needed a constant supply of competent middle-class administrators and overseers to manage slave labour and operations. A racist ideology shaped the ways in which European companies managed their overseas workforce. Expatriates (people living and working outside their native country) were typically employed in key managerial (roles. Locals were perceived as 'lazy' and generally inferior and only capable of manual labour or lower-level administrative jobs while parent country nationals (PCNs) staffed management positions in foreign operations (Moore and Lewis, 1999).

Marx (1894) was among the early classical social theorists to recognise the global character of industrial capitalism (Bratton and Denham, 2019; Edgell and Granter, 2020, p. 284). The need to supply European factories with raw materials and constantly expand markets for their products, compelled early capitalists and their agents to settle, establish connections and trade across the globe. Industrial capitalism was the impulse to the globalisation of production and exchange. The Marxist economist Rosa Luxemburg extended Marx's analysis of mature capitalism. Whereas Marx identified the transformation of rural peasants into an urban-based proletariat class, as well as the appropriation of human (e.g. slaves) and material (e.g. cotton) resources from colonised countries, Luxemburg posits that Marx treats these processes as 'incidental' – the travails by which the capitalist mode of production emerges from a feudal society. Her critique was that these processes are indispensable for capital accumulation:

> Since capitalist production can develop fully *only* with complete access to all territories and climes, it can no more confine itself to the natural resources and productive forces of

> the temperate zone than it can manage with white labour alone. Capital needs other races to exploit territories where the white man cannot work. (Luxemburg, 1913/2003, pp. 342–3, emphasis added)

The essence of Luxemburg's polemic is that mature capitalism needs to constantly expand across the globe for 'untrammelled accumulation', (i.e. maximise profit) and this impulse is the economic reason for colonial wars between the super-powers (Bratton and Denham, 2019, pp. 288–91). As we discuss below, a key critique of much IHRM theorising is that it neglects the impact of power. Luxemburg's prescient analysis that 'political power is nothing but a vehicle for the economic process' (1913/2003, p. 343) can contribute to our understanding of the behaviour and management of MNCs.

Over the last 50 years, the character of globalisation has changed with finance capital rather than products dominating international exchanges between European and US corporations and emerging economies. Contemporary mainstream analysis of globalisation has focused on the expansion of global markets, global supply chains, global boundaryless organisations and, especially in the last 20 years, foreign direct investment (FDI) by MNCs in emerging economies such as Brazil, Russia, India, China and South Africa (BRICS). Even before the pandemic, the UN (2019) reported some softening in economic momentum in the BRICS economies. The BRICS nations have become a major source of cross-border acquisitions and, interestingly, while the diverging long-term economic trajectory of the BRICS countries weakens the analytical value of viewing these economies as a coherent economic grouping, the operations of their business and financial institutions represent a different way of doing business to the traditional *modus operandi* of Western MNCs (Petrone, 2019). Studying globalisation from a critical perspective allows for a more in-depth understanding of the multiple dimensions involved that extend beyond economic considerations.

Critical scholars are divided on whether contemporary globalisation is merely a continuation of past developments (e.g. Hirst and Thompson, 1996) or is fundamentally different (Beck, 2000; Castells, 2001). Castells' (2001) theory of the 'network society' illustrates the interrelated character of the driving forces behind globalisation. It is the information revolution that provides the 'indispensable, material basis for the creation of the new global economy' (Castells, 2001, p. 77). Moreover, global interconnectedness, made possible by information and communications technology (ICT), is historically unprecedented and as such the nature of contemporary globalisation is both 'quantitatively and qualitatively' distinctive. Therefore, twenty-first-century globalisation is characterised by extensive networks, intensive flows within networks and instantaneous global human interactions, all of which affect all areas of economic, cultural and political life, and affect everyone in the world to a greater or lesser extent (for a fuller discussion of globalisation, including its links to precarious employment, see Edgell and Granter, 2020).

Global business strategies

The domain of IHRM connects to issues of significance in the field of global business and the internationalisation process (Boxall et al., 2008; Morris et al., 2009). Global business strategies are connected to the generic business-level strategies of cost-leadership and differentiation that were examined in Chapter 2. A global business strategy means effectively and efficiently matching an MNC's internal strengths (relative to competitors) with the opportunities and challenges found in geographically dispersed markets that cross international borders. Such matching is said to be a pre-condition to creating value and satisfying stakeholder goals, both domestically and internationally (Verbeke, 2013).

Bartlett and Ghoshal's (1989) conceptualisation of global business strategies has been highly influential in influencing IHRM research. Their framework therefore is a useful starting point for understanding the various orientations global corporations can have towards overseas operations. Bartlett and Ghoshal's central premise is that MNCs face tension from two types of business pressure. MNCs face, on the one hand, demands for global cost reductions and integration, and, on the other hand, demands for differentiation and local responsiveness.

MNCs strive for global efficiency by rationalising their product lines, standardising their parts design and integrating their global manufacturing and control systems. The pressures for integration can be high in technologically intensive enterprises or where the product is universal and requires minimal modification to local needs. This typically occurs with goods such as petroleum, steel and chemicals, and is also typical for consumer electronics, for instance mobile phones and personal computers. Demands for integration are also high in industries in which there is excess capacity or in which consumers face low switching costs. For example, the demand for integration has been globally intense in the steel industry, in which differentiation is difficult and price is the main competitive variable (Hill et al., 2016).

Countering global strategies and organisational efficiency imperatives are local realities and customer needs. MNCs have to satisfy consumer tastes and preferences in diverse locations, so competitive advantage may be derived from producing a product or service that is more sensitive to national cultures and local tastes in the host countries where the corporation operates. Culture differentiates one locale from another, and the duality of culture – its pervasiveness yet its uniqueness – impacts on global business strategy (Mintzberg et al., 2008). Pressures to be locally responsive arise from consumer tastes and preferences, differences in the host country's infrastructure and the regulations of the national business environment imposed by the host government. For example, when the Swedish home furnishing company IKEA entered the US market in the 1990s, it offered cut-price standardised products, which had sold well across Europe, based on huge economies of scale. However, IKEA soon found that it had to be responsive to North American tastes and physiques: IKEA's glasses were too small for North American consumers, who tend to add ice to their drinks, and Swedish beds were too narrow for American body sizes (Hill et al., 2016).

A second set of demands for local responsiveness arises from differences in the host country's infrastructure. For example, some EU member states use 240-volt consumer electric systems, whereas in North America 110-volt systems tend to be standard. Thus, differences in the national infrastructure require MNCs to customise domestic electrical appliances. This diversity in infrastructure has been identified as a barrier to European competitiveness and was behind the Single Europe Act of 1986. The Act aimed to stimulate pan-European trade by harmonising technical standards governing the production and distribution of goods (Hendry, 1994).

Source: Kelly Sikkema on Unsplash

Differences in the national infrastructure can be a barrier for MNCs. This diversity in infrastructure has been identified as a barrier to European competitiveness and was behind the Single Europe Act of 1986.

PART 5

A third set of demands for local responsiveness emanates from nationally based regulatory regimes constructed and maintained by host governments. The regulation of employment relations, consumer products (for example, automobile exhaust emissions), ecological controls and local testing (for example, clinical trials of pharmaceutical products according to domestic standards) may dictate that MNCs be responsive to local conditions. Global corporations can be enticed to relocate by national governments deregulating safety, environmental or employment standards.

The major chemical accident that occurred in Bhopal, India, for example, illustrates the dangers implicit in reducing standards to attract Western investment. A chemical plant owned by the US multinational company Union Carbide engaged in chemical production under conditions that would have been illegal in the US. On 3 December 1984, the plant experienced a major leak. Within hours, 3,000 people were dead, 15,000 more dying in the aftermath. A further 200,000 were seriously injured, and half a million still carry special health cards. Eventually, the MNC paid out just $470 million in compensation (Saul, 2005). More recently, the Indian government gave tax exemptions and deregulated the telecommunications industry in order to increase foreign investment in call centres (Maitra and Sangha, 2005).

Through a wide variety of national or regional policy mechanisms, host governments can effectively shape national business systems and therefore the ability of MNCs to optimise profits (Cooke, 2006). Prahalad and Doz (1987, p. 251) therefore suggest that, 'MNCs can approach strategy as a process of "negotiation" with host governments'; they call this process 'negotiated strategies'. The national business context in the host country, as well as the relative economic dominance and power of the parties, is significant in explaining not only the spatial location of MNCs' subsidiaries but also the HR strategy in the subsidiaries (Cooke, 2006; Edwards et al., 2013; Ferner and Quintanilla, 1998). MNCs are crucial agents in the transformation of national employment management systems (Marginson and Meardi, 2010). They are widely held to have differing preferences over arrangements for managing the employment relationship: union representation, non-union representation or none at all, direct or indirect forms of employee voice (Cooke, 2006; Marginson et al., 2010). The point we wish to make here is, therefore, that the cost efficiency–responsiveness strategic mix may well depend on the MNC's calculation to exploit cross-national differences, including the model of capitalism that prevails in the host country and that country's political will and ability to safeguard the health and safety of its people and protect the planet.

Source: Daniel Berehulak/Getty Images

The chemical accident in Bhopal, India, killed thousands of people illustrating the dangers implicit in reducing health and safety standards to attract MNCs.

The integration–responsiveness grid

Local realities are the classic barrier to universal theories of global efficiency. Two pressures – cost efficiencies and rationalisation, and differentiation and local responsiveness – form the two dimensions of what Bartlett and Ghoshal (1989) call the integration–responsiveness grid. The authors offer a typology – global, multidomestic and transnational – as solutions to the dual pressure for cost efficiency and responsiveness.

Global strategy

Global corporations that pursue a global strategy focus on increasing profit margins through cost efficiencies arising from economies of scale and economies of location. These MNCs are pursuing a low-cost leadership strategy. The operations of the MNCs will be concentrated in a few favourable host economies and will tend not to customise their goods to local situations. A global strategy is typically associated with high demands for integration and low demands for local responsiveness. Texas Instruments, a company that once dominated the market in pocket calculators and digital watches by focusing persistently on cost reductions and price at the expense of understanding consumers' needs, is an example of an MNC that, until 1982, followed a global strategy (Hill et al., 2016).

Multidomestic strategy

MNCs pursuing a multidomestic strategy design their operations to maximise local responsiveness. These companies tend to customise both their product offering and marketing strategy to different local customer tastes and preferences. A multidomestic MNC such as ITT developed a 'strategic posture and organisational ability that enables it to be very sensitive and responsive to differences in national environments' (Bartlett and Ghoshal, 1989, p. 14). A multidomestic strategy is typically associated with low demands for integration and high demands for local responsiveness.

Transnational strategy

MNCs following a transnational strategy strive for competitive advantage worldwide by rationalising and integrating resources to achieve superior cost efficiencies from economies of scale and economies of location, by being sensitive and capable of responding to local needs, and by sharing knowledge throughout their global operations. In a transnational corporation (TNC), knowledge and distinctive competencies flow to and from each of the company's operations as part of a larger process of 'global learning' that encompasses 'every member of the company' (Bartlett and Ghoshal, 1989, p. 59).

PART 5

In essence, a TNC simultaneously achieves low-cost leadership and a competitive advantage in terms of differentiation. The effect is 'a complex configuration of assets and capabilities that are distributed, yet specialized [and] the company integrates the dispersed resources through strong interdependencies ... Such interdependencies may be reciprocal rather than sequential' (Bartlett and Ghoshal, 1989, p. 60). Therefore, a world-scale production plant in Brazil may depend on world-scale component plants in Australia, China and Germany; major sales subsidiaries worldwide may in turn depend on Brazil for their finished products. The TNC's resources and capabilities are represented as an integrated network, a term emphasising the significant flows of components, products, resources, information and people. Unilever is an example of an MNC that has pursued a transnational strategy, with 17 different and largely decentralised detergent plants in Europe alone. The integration–responsiveness grid is a simple and impressive model for explaining the strategic choices shaping the strategies and organisational networks of MNCs. Bartlett and Ghoshal's typology has been supported by case study research (see Harzing, 2000; Morris et al., 2009) and, importantly, it has also been influential in the IHRM field.

Reflective question

How has Britain's exit from the European Union and Covid-19 impacted global and local business trends?

Global HRM
Can quotas achieve gender equality?

Source: Keren Levand on Unsplash

It has long been recognised that there is a 'glass ceiling' preventing women from achieving top positions in management. Norway is seen as a global leader in gender equality and in many regards is seen as an international leader in the field of quotes on company boards. In 2006, the Norwegian government introduced a quota law that required both public limited companies (PLCs) and state-owned companies to have 40% female board representation by 2008. Failure to meet the target resulted in fines or company closures. In Europe, Austria, Belgium, France, Germany, Iceland, Italy, the Netherlands, Portugal and Spain introduced quota regulations after Norway (see Mensi-Klarbach and Seierstad, 2020). The primary objective of this reform in Norway was to increase the representation of women in top leadership positions in the corporate sector and decrease the gender gap in earnings within the sector. After the law came into effect in 2008, international researchers, politicians and business leaders visited Norway, keen to observe the effect of gender quotas. Research suggests that gender gap in earnings within boards fell substantially and the selection process for board members is reported to be fairer and more transparent. For example, research suggests a greater perceived equality within the PLC board setting, with respect to recruitment, gendered ideas of suitability, increased formalisation and professionalisation. As one female director explained:

> The election committees work completely different now. When I got my first directorship in the early 2000s, you sort of got a phone call, you accepted, and you were in. Now, the nomination committee meets all the directors, interviews them, conducts board evaluations, meets potential candidates, reviews the 'board mix' and evaluates the competencies needed, really engaging and understanding the complementarity of skills among the directors so that the board is ready for the challenges the specific companies are facing. (Seierstad et al., 2020, p. 17)

The use of board evaluations in the search process was seen to create greater transparency and challenge gendered organising practices. However, concerning female labour outcomes more generally, there is no evidence that the reform benefited the larger set of women employed in the companies subject to the quota. Ten years later, the number of female directors has increased but any trickle-down effects to the wider female workforce are hard to see. Of the 213 public limited companies in 2017, just 15 were run by a woman – 7% of the total. Bertrand et al.'s (2019, p. 191) research on the effect of board quotas on female labour market outcomes in Norway suggests that seven years after the board quota policy fully came into effect 'it had very little discernible impact on women in business beyond its direct effect on the women who made it into boardrooms'. Even in Norway, a country ranked second of 144 countries in the World Economic Forum's Gender Gap Index in 2020, there is still much progress to be made in improving gender equality in organisations.

Stop! Quotas in the business world can be controversial. Advocates suggest that they can put an end to the 'old boys' networks and ensure that qualified women are no longer denied access to leadership positions because of their gender. What do you think about quotas to help rectify women's under-representation in leadership positions?

Essential reading

Mensi-Klarbach, H. and Seierstad, C. (2020) Gender quotas on corporate boards: similarities and differences in quota scenarios. *European Management Review*; Seierstad, C., Healy, G., Sønju Le Bruyn Goldeng, E. and Fjellvær, H. (2020) A 'quota silo' or positive equality reach? The equality impact of gender quotas on corporate boards in Norway. *Human Resource Management Journal, 31*(1): 165–86.

Note: This feature was contributed by Andrew Bratton.

The nature of international HRM

In an earlier chapter, we explained that the doctrine of maximising shareholder value (MSV) has had a pervasive influence on corporate structure and strategy. Corporations that pursue tactics of MSV are more likely to reduce investment and employment in their country of origin and outsource production activities in low-wage economies, a phenomenon called 'Nikefication' in honour of the company that pioneered this strategy (Davis and Kim, 2015, p. 210). As Nikefication has spread widely across the Anglo-Saxon variant of capitalism, academics and practitioners alike have increasingly begun to explore the complexities of organising work and managing people with heterogeneous beliefs and values, cognitive and emotional orientations. Thus, MNCs face significant challenges, *inter alia*, external factors relating to the host-country sociocultural contexts and internal factors relating to the alignment of HR strategy to the organisation's corporate strategy, and the nature of the headquarters–subsidiary relationship (Brewster et al., 2016; Budhwar, 2012; Edwards and Kuruvilla, 2005). A full understanding of these multifaceted issues involves three streams of analysis: organisation embeddedness, comparative HRM and IHRM (Brewster et al., 2016).

The notion of organisational embeddedness draws heavily from sociological, anthropological and organisational behaviour concepts and approaches to understand the embeddedness of economic activity in wider social structures, inter-organisational relations and organisation-environment relations (Dacin et al., 1999). Comparative HRM is a complex domain that identifies and analyses the roles of institutions, culture and other societal conditions in understanding differences and similarities in HRM across countries. Both culture and institutional heterogeneity mean that analysis in the meaning and practice of HRM in different countries has to avoid 'false universalism'. There are obvious differences between the role of HRM and labour relations strategies in the US, Europe, BRICS and Japan. And, within Europe, different regional patterns can be distinguished, underpinning the notion of 'varieties of capitalism' (Brewster and Mayrhofer, 2019).

In this section, we focus on IHRM rather than comparative HRM and, in so doing, seek to understand the explicit connection between global competition and HR strategy in MNCs and their subsidiaries. We begin by identifying three alternative theories relating to the impact of global processes on domestic patterns of employment relations. We will then explain the concepts of IHRM and strategic IHRM (SIHRM) and critically examine the links between global strategic management and SIHRM and IHRM. Finally, we will look at a model of strategic IHRM first developed by Schuler et al. (1993).

MNCs and employment relations

The developments in global capitalism have generated much debate on how MNCs balance the pressures to develop globally integrated employment relations and HR policies and practices on the one hand, while trying to adapt to local cultural and institutional pressures on the other: the global versus local question. The existing literature identifies three alternative paradigms for examining this question: economic, institutionalist and integrated (Bamber et al., 2004).

The *economic* approach follows the classical neoliberal premise that global business activity has become so interconnected, and that competitive imperatives are so dominant, that they offer little scope for domestic differences in patterns of employment relations. This influential economic approach predicts that international markets operate in accordance with universal principles and will result in a 'convergence' of national employment relations. Economic imperatives will, for example, create 'efficiencies' by driving wages down and eroding employment standards.

The *institutionalist* approach to the impact of globalisation contends that global forces are more fluid in their dynamics and more contradictory in their outcome. Moreover, nationally-based regulatory institutions form an independent dynamic that structures, controls and legitimates business activities and outcomes. Global trends are mediated by national or local institutional regimes and changed into 'divergent' power struggles over particular national employment practices (Hyman, 1999). By highlighting national differences in how societies shape economic and social outcomes, the institutionalist approach emphasises the variability of market economies and highlights why 'varieties of capitalism' are likely to persist in the future (see, for example, Hall and Soskice, 2009). Furthermore, nationally embedded institutions, for example universities, can confer a comparative competitive advantage, especially in the sphere of innovation.

Bamber et al. (2004) put forward an *integrated* approach to globalisation and national patterns of employment relations and HR practices. They suggest that both global economic trends and nationally based institutions are important in structuring national patterns of employment practices. However, because different kinds of market economy are integrated into the global economy in different ways, global economic pressures are likely to be divergent. The integrated approach thus focuses on the effects of global economic developments on the 'interests of different groups of employers, workers and policy-makers within different institutional settings' (Bamber et al., 2004, p. 1,483).

IHRM and SIHRM

Before we consider models of SIHRM that have been developed to explain how the HRM function is configured in MNCs, it is important to distinguish between IHRM and SIHRM. There are competing definitions of IHRM, although most scholarship in the field has focused on issues associated with the cross-national transfer of expatriates (that is, global staffing and managing individual managers in international job assignments). Taylor et al. (1996, p. 960) define IHRM as:

> The set of distinct activities, functions and processes that are directed at attracting, developing and maintaining a MNC's human resources. It is thus the aggregate of the various HRM systems used to manage people in the MNC, both at home and overseas.

Scullion (2001, p. 288) defines IHRM as:

> The HRM issues and problems arising from the internationalization of business, and the HRM strategies, policies and practices which firms pursue in response to the internationalization process.

More recent definitions have extended the field to cover the need to adapt to local contexts, the global coordination of overseas subsidiaries, global knowledge management and global leadership (Scullion and Linehan, 2005). For Lazarova (2006) it is important to distinguish domestic HRM from international HRM by reference to the additional layers of complexity when operating in dissimilar cultural and institutional contexts combined with the requirement to manage three diverse employee groups: domestic, host and third-country nationals. IHRM is further distinguished from domestic HRM as HR professionals have to be deal with the consequences of political resistance to centralised-corporate HR policy in overseas subsidiaries (Ahlvik and Björkman, 2015).

The IHRM literature tends to celebrate a Western hegemonic culture, one that emphasises the subordination of domestic culture and domestic employment practices to corporate culture and corporate HRM practices (Boxall, 1995). As such, many contemporary studies of IHRM tend to be seen as a managerial strategic instrument unashamedly connected to the neoliberalism agenda (Farazmand, 2002). It is the principal discourse of neoliberalism that provides insights into related debates around labour market rigidities, flexibility, outsourcing, privatisation, European integration, shifting macro-economic policy paradigms and international HR practices. IHRM is thus the sum of the various labour relations and HR policies and practices used to manage the workforce in MNCs operating in multiple countries.

As we showed in Chapter 2, strategic HRM is the process of explicitly linking the HRM function with the strategic management goals of the organisation. Thus, SIHRM is the process of explicitly linking IHRM with the strategy of the MNC. In defining SIHRM, we draw on the work of Scullion and Linehan (2005) and Stahl and Björkman (2006). Schuler et al. (1993, p. 720) define SIHRM as:

> The HRM issues, functions and policies and practices that result from the strategic activities of multinational enterprises and that impact the international concerns and goals of those enterprises.

PART 5

Emphasising that the study of IHRM is a relatively new area of research, Stahl and Björkman (2006, p. 1) define the sub-field simply as: 'all issues related to the management of people in an international context'. Here we define SIHRM as:

> An array of HR practices and issues related to the management of people that arise from the global competitive activities of MNCs and that explicitly link international HR practices and processes with the worldwide strategic goals of those companies.

SIHRM builds on strategic HRM that aims to connect HRM explicitly with strategic management processes. In so doing, SIHRM recognises the need to address the tension between the global and the local. This tension is related to balancing global competitiveness (rationalisation and integration) and local responsiveness (flexibility) strategies pursued by MNCs while simultaneously leveraging global learning within and across the MNC. As such, SIHRM links 'IHRM explicitly with the strategy and with the MNC' (Scullion and Linehan, 2005, p. 23). This highly dynamic and complex context is the arena of SIHRM.

A model of SIHRM

We have focused so far on some global business strategies and the meaning of IHRM and SIHRM. A key theme in the IHRM literature interrogates the extent the HR function in the multinational transfers

HR and labour relations (LR) policies and practices to cross-border subsidiaries. Adding to the complexity is evidence to suggest that British, German, Swedish, US, Japanese and Chinese multinationals, for example, behave in significantly different ways, specifically in respect of the cross-border HR/LR issues. While a thorough examination of the differing theoretical perspectives on transfer of HR/LR policies is beyond the scope of this chapter, we introduce an integrative theoretical framework that, among other things, provides insight into understanding the reasons why MNCs behave differently in regard to HR/LM and the myriad variables impacting SIHRM. Figure 13.1 draws primarily from Schuler et al. (1993) but is also informed by the work of Bartlett and Ghoshal (1989), Ferner (1997), Edwards and Ferner (2002), Perlmutter (1969) and Taylor et al. (1996).

Schuler et al.'s original integrative framework consisted of four core components:

1. Exogenous factors
2. Endogenous factors
3. SIHRM
4. The pressures and goals of the MNC

To this, we have added a fifth component – the corporate SIHRM orientation. The lines and arrows in Figure 13.1 denote the reciprocal relationships between exogenous factors, SIHRM and the pressures and goals of the MNC.

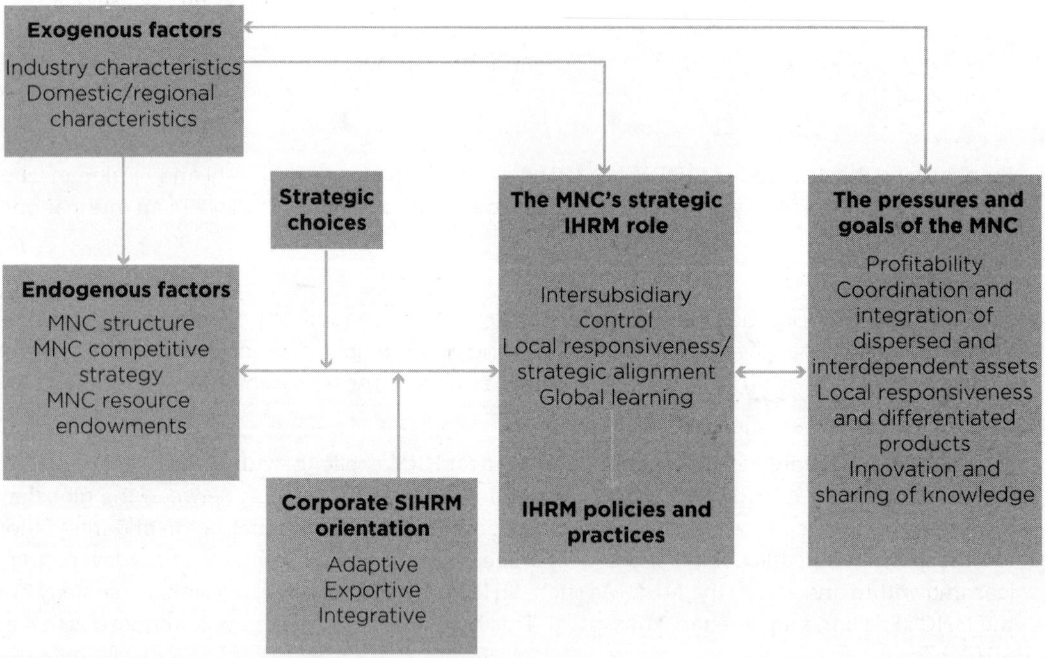

Figure 13.1 An integrated framework of SIHRM

Source: Based on the theories of Schuler et al. (1993); Scullion and Linehan (2005); Perlmutter (1969); Taylor et al. (1996) and Bartlett and Ghoshal (1989).

(1) Exogenous factors

Exogenous factors relate to issues external to the MNC. A theoretical framework for the analysis of SIHRM decisions is provided by Edwards and Ferner (2002). This framework presents a classification of three major exogenous influences on the nature and design of SIHRM practices transferred to cross-border subsidiaries. The influences comprise country-of-origin, dominance and host country effects.

Country-of-origin effects

The country-of-origin effects (Ferner, 1997) emphasise that a multinational's country of origin foists a distinctive national effect on management behaviour and HR/LR practices within an MNC. The premise is that multinationals are embedded in a national specific culture and institutional architecture which together make up national business systems. These national specific characteristics are likely to influence MNCs' international HR/LR policies and practices. For example, US multinationals are distinctive in terms of formalised approaches to HR policy and antipathy towards trade union involvement in negotiating the employment contract (e.g. Ferner et al., 2013; Gunnigle et al., 2005). Therefore, if a US MNC perceives such an HR strategy to be a source of competitive advantage, it will, unless compelled otherwise, have a preference to replicate it in its overseas subsidiaries.

Dominance effects

The dominance effects draw attention to the hegemonic position of the US economy and the ability of US multinationals to impose standardised management practices on their overseas subsidiaries (Edwards and Ferner, 2002).

Host country effects

PART 5

The host country effects refer to the host institutional architecture, legal and cultural values and mores which can impose limits on MNCs' attempts to diffuse HR/LR practices to subsidiaries (e.g. Gunnigle et al., 2002). However, MNCs can threaten to relocate out of the host country to leverage preferred HR/LR policies and practices on subsidiaries (Ferner et al., 2001). The European Union is a powerful regulator of business. However, Europe's second-highest court overturned an EU ruling that the iPhone maker Apple should pay a £11.7 billion (€13 billion) tax bill to the Irish government highlighting the host country effect. The Republic of Ireland, to protect its low tax regime and jobs, supported Apple's case (Boffey, 2020). De Cieri and Dowling (1999) argue that exogenous factors exert a direct influence on endogenous factors, SIHRM and the pressures and goals of the MNC.

(2) Endogenous factors

Endogenous factors relate to internal organisational issues, such as work design, intra-organisational networks, control systems and 'global integration' effects on MNCs. *Global integration* refers to the generation of inter-unit supply chains across national borders (see Edwards et al., 2013). This endogenous factor influences the transfer of HR/LR as evidence suggests that high levels of global integration can lead to centralisation of decision-making on HR/LR issues (Marginson et al., 1995).

(3) SIHRM

SIHRM relates to issues of coordination and control, local responsiveness and worldwide learning. It is concerned with 'Developing a fit between exogenous and endogenous factors and balancing the competing demands of global versus local requirements as well as the needs of coordination, control and autonomy' (Schuler et al., 1993, p. 451).

(4) Pressures and goals

Pressures and goals of the MNC relate to profitability, the dual demands for cost reductions and local responsiveness, and the global transfer of innovation. The framework suggests that there are reciprocal relationships between exogenous factors, SIHRM and the pressures and goals of the MNC (Scullion and Linehan, 2005). SIHRM is expected to buttress the MNC's global goals.

(5) SIHRM orientation

The corporate *SIHRM orientation* refers to the four approaches – polycentric/adaptive; ethnocentric/exportive; geocentric/integrative; and regiocentric – taken by the MNC's top management in designing its total IHRM system (see below).

Among the many HR issues facing MNCs is global staffing (Stahl and Björkman, 2006). For example, a Swedish-based multinational has a vacancy for a new marketing director for its Canadian subsidiary. It has to make a decision whether to select from its talented marketing team available in the company's parent country, Sweden (i.e. a parent country national – PCN), or to recruit a Canadian marketing director (i.e. a host country national – HCN). Alternatively, the Swedish company could recruit from one of its other overseas subsidiaries, for example, Britain (i.e. a third-country national – TCN). Perlmutter (1969) and Taylor et al. (1996) identified three orientations to the staffing of MNCs: ethnocentric/exportive; polycentric/adaptive; and geocentric/integrative. Perlmutter developed a fourth orientation, the regiocentric approach (Heenan and Perlmutter, 1979). Table 13.1 shows the linkages between Perlmutter's and Taylor's typologies and Bartlett and Ghoshal's global business strategies. (for a more detailed discussion of the different orientations to staffing, see Dowling et al., 2017 and Collings and Scullion, 2006). The four SIHRM orientations are discussed below:

Table 13.1 MNCs IHRM orientation and global business strategies

Bartlett and Ghoshal's (1989) business strategies	Perlmutter's (1969) SIHRM typologies	Taylor's et al. (1996) SIHRM typologies
Global	Ethnocentric	Exportive
Multidomestic	Polycentric	Adaptive
Transnational	Geocentric	Integrative
	Regiocentric	

Ethnocentric orientation

An ethnocentric SIHRM orientation develops and implements HR systems for subsidiaries based upon headquarters' policies and practices with little consideration for national difference. The ethnocentric orientation is similar to Taylor et al.'s (1996) exportive approach. Top managers at corporate head office fill key positions in foreign operations from the parent company (i.e. a PCN) and give zero or restricted autonomy to the cross-border subsidiaries. This approach gives better control and coordination of the company's activities. The ethnocentric or exportive orientation is consistent with Bartlett and Ghoshal's (1989) conceptualisation of a global business strategy, which is characterised by standardisation and cost efficiency.

Polycentric orientation

A polycentric organisation is primarily host-country oriented. Foreign subsidiaries are permitted to develop their own HR systems thereby reflecting local cultural and institutional conditions with minimal interference from the parent company. The polycentric orientation is similar to Taylor et al.'s (1996) adaptive approach. Local managers fill key positions in foreign operations either internally or from the local labour market (i.e. an HCN). Cross-border subsidiaries are given virtually unrestricted autonomy and are controlled through sophisticated financial monitoring. The polycentric or adaptive orientation is consistent with Bartlett and Ghoshal's (1989) conceptualisation of a multidomestic business strategy, which is characterised by a need for local responsiveness and differentiation of product or service.

Geocentric orientation

A geocentric SIHRM orientation focuses on transferring the 'best' HR policies and practices regardless of where they originate within the MNC, to construct a global HRM system. In terms of staffing, key positions at headquarters or at any subsidiary are filled with the 'best person for the job' regardless of nationality (i.e. potentially a TCN). The geocentric orientation is similar to Taylor et al.'s (1996) integrative approach. The geocentric or integrative orientation is consistent with Bartlett and Ghoshal's (1989) conceptualisation of a transnational business strategy which is characterised by agility and flexibility enabling the MNC's sub-units to respond to emerging opportunities in the business contexts. The central theoretical argument of the geocentric/integrative model is, therefore, that SIHRM should be explicitly related to the MNC's global business strategy and that its changing forms must be understood in relation to the strategic evolution of the MNC (Scullion and Linehan, 2005; Taylor et al., 1996).

Regiocentric orientation

A regiocentric organisation is primarily regional oriented. Cross-border subsidiaries within the region, for example, Europe, Canada and the US or Asia-Pacific, may have a high degree of autonomy. Corporate communications and HR policies and practices are generally mediated through the regional headquarters. Vacancies for key management positions are generally filled from a pool on the basis of 'best in the region'. The increasing significance of regional trading blocs such as the EU and NAFTA and the difficulties associated with implementing global strategies in MNCs as a result of geo-politics, for example, trade disputes between China, the US and Britain, has made a regiocentric strategy more attractive in recent years (Collings et al., 2019).

Global companies share with their domestic counterparts the intractable problem of managing the employment relationship to reduce the indeterminacy that results from the unspecified nature of the employment contract. If we adopt Townley's (1994) perspective on IHRM, the role of knowledge to render people in the workplace 'governable' is made problematic by the intertwining of highly complex local, regional, national and global cultures (Crane, 1994). It is the *complexity* of operating in different socio-culturally diverse environments and employing different national categories of workers, rather than the HR practices as such, which differentiates national and international HRM (Dowling et al., 2017).

HRM in Practice
'We are expendable ...'

In May 2020, three workers at a Cranswick food processing facility in Wombwell, England, which supplies UK supermarkets, were confirmed to have died after testing positive for coronavirus. Speaking on condition of anonymity, the family of a worker at the UK-based company, which has about £1.5 annual revenue, revealed (Levit, 2020):

> If you don't feel well and know if you don't go to work you're only going to get the statutory sick pay [£95.85 a week] and are not going to be able to pay bills, what are you going to do? I am scared he could bring it home to us and our kids. They [plant workers] have not been happy, but they're all scared to say anything because of losing their jobs. It's a shit way to go for £9 an hour [worker is paid £9.40 an hour].

This was the latest episode to add to the growing concern over the employment conditions faced by the large number of workers in the UK, particularly in agriculture. The Gangmasters Licensing Authority itself was set up in the aftermath of the death of Chinese shellfish collectors in Morecombe Bay in 2004 with the aim to protect vulnerable and exploited workers. There is, however, evidence that parts of the agriculture sector are still ignoring or undermining minimum labour standards; in August 2015, for example, a group of Lithuanian workers were found being severely abused and exploited while working as chicken catchers, rounding up hens on the UK's largest poultry farms.

Moreover, agriculture has always been characterised by a seasonal use of migrant and temporary labour as the agricultural cycle makes it uneconomical to retain a permanent labour force: the use of labour contractors makes achieving numerical flexibility easier for the grower. Rogaly (2008) looked at the increasing use of migrant workers in this sector and concluded that the shift of power away from producers to a small number of powerful retailers had pressured growers to intensify production to compensate for the smaller margins dictated by the supermarkets. This was done through a combination of innovations in growing techniques, manipulation of piecework regimes and innovations in labour control.

Migrants have a strong monetary incentive, and the cutting of piecework rates ensures a higher daily output before the minimum wage equivalent is reached. Growers have preferred non-UK nationals because of their 'work ethic', but these workers form a vulnerable group in the labour market due to factors such as immigration status, a general lack of information and language barriers. Rogaly argues that this vulnerability is used to ensure a compliant labour force. The agencies can exercise power over the workers through being the source of information about jobs, offering transport to the work location and providing credit and, importantly, accommodation. Such workers are more amenable to working irregular hours and may be easier to dispose of when harvesting is over: 'they can easily be turned on and they can easily be turned off', said one grower.

Stop! Should we be prepared to pay more for our food if it guarantees better working conditions for food production workers?

Essential reading

Levitt, T. (2020) A terrible way to go for £9 an hour: fear at meat plant after three coronavirus deaths, *The Guardian*, 20 May; Lawrence, F. (2015) Lithuanian migrants trafficked to UK egg farms sue 'worst gangmaster ever'. *The Guardian*, 10 August.

Note: This feature was contributed by Chris Baldry and updated by Andrew Bratton.

HR strategy in MNCs

The international HRM literature has traditionally focused on MNCs as a 'head-office' driven entity (Ferner, 1997), but societal analysis has tended to discount universalistic HR strategies (Maurice and Sorge, 2000; Trompenaars and Hampden-Turner, 2012). One important aspect of IHRM relates to the 'best practice' versus 'best fit' debate. The former argues for the universal application of certain HR practices, while the latter recognises the importance of context and societal embeddedness in HRM. It is argued that MNCs in general engage in the straightforward transfer of their own, 'nationally idiosyncratic' HR policies and practices across borders (Sayim, 2010). As an independent variable, however, sociocultural embeddedness can have an important influence on the development of IHRM policies and practices and their subsequent effect on global performance (Paauwe and Boselie, 2008, p. 167). Expatriate managers, for example, are required to fit in and be 'legitimated' by the host country nationals (HCNs) but local legitimacy is also dependent on compliance with local norms and mores (Brewster and Bennett, 2010).

In shaping international HR policies and practices, an MNC will need to consider a number of objectives. First, each area of HR activity, like structure and systems, should be consistent with its business strategy, and hence contribute to the MNC's international performance. Second, the array of HR practices needs to recruit, retain, motivate and facilitate the transfer of talented workers internationally. Third, the MNC will want to ensure that the HR practices are equitable and comply with the host country's cultural values (Zhang and Albrecht, 2010) and employment law. Fourth, the IHRM literature emphasises the added dimension of cultural diversity. MNCs by definition have multicultural workforces made up of workers with a variety of ethnic, racial, religious and cultural values and mores. Indeed, it has been suggested that the central *modus operandi* of the MNC is the creation and effective management of multicultural work teams that represent diversity in competencies, levels of experience, and cultural and language backgrounds. As a whole, the above considerations inevitably raise the potential for countless complexities (Dowling et al., 2017; Varma et al., 2011).

Reflective question

Thinking of cultural diversity, when an MNC adopts a global business strategy, what new challenges does it present for managing Fombrun et al.'s (1984) four dimensions of recruitment and selection, rewards, training and development, and performance appraisal? For further information on cultural diversity, go to http://www.ethnoconnect.com and www.shrm.org/diversity.

International staffing

MNCs do not simply transmit capital: they invariably transmit management 'know-how'. As such, international staffing is seen as a crucial aspect of the management of people in the MNC. First, talented managers are key to controlling and coordinating MNCs' spatially dispersed global operations (Collings and Scullion, 2007; Pucik et al., 2016). Second, expatriate managers, while playing a critical role in the transfer of both explicit knowledge and the tacit knowledge of the MNC's practices to the overseas affiliates (Gamble, 2003), face the challenges of local cultures. Third, in a post-Covid-19 world, restrictions on international travel and health concerns, in addition to terrorism and security concerns, pose significant global staffing problems for MNCs (Collings and Isichei, 2018).

Much of the IHRM literature on staffing has focused on three alternative categories of global staffing: selecting a parent country national (PCN), recruiting a host country national (HCN) or hiring a third-country national (TCN). In theory, drawing from these three pools of potential workers seems logical in global staffing as they mirror the wider dilemma of central versus de-central or local, in that the choice is whether to transfer the dominant norms of the MNC's national culture or make use of those of the local or another culture. In practice, however, expatriate selection appears to be more a matter of 'good luck than good management' (Anderson, 2005, p. 580). In addition, staff at the MNC's head office may have little idea what culturally derived expectations are needed to 'fit' the local context (Gamble, 2003). Moreover, informal ad hoc selection practices may be frequent, and decisions of intercultural reach may frequently be affected by illogical or irrational elements such as ethnocentrism, ignorance and stereotyping (Torbiörn, 2005).

Further, local culture and norms where the MNC's corporate office is located can exhibit discriminatory staffing practices. Almeida et al.'s (2015) research examines the influence of similarity effect in recruitment decision-making involving immigrant information technology (IT) professionals in Australia. In particular, the authors investigated how the level of exposure to diversity, the decision maker's origin and the diversity of clientele can moderate the assessment of the candidate's fit to the organisation. The discriminatory effect can also extend to gender. Research shows that, despite women's increased presence in Western organisational hierarchies, the number of female expatriates remains only a fraction of those in senior management positions, and 'only in rare circumstances' are female managers offered global assignments (Linehan, 2005, p. 197). The low number of women chosen for global assignments provides evidence that staffing decisions in MNCs may often be irrational, and sometimes discriminatory (e.g. Caligiuri and Tung, 1999). In all capitalist countries, it is argued, men control economic and political power – management is consequently androcentric.

Reflective question

The term 'glass border' describes the irrational assumptions held by parent country senior management about the suitability of female managers for overseas appointments. To what extent is gender still relevant as a criterion for selecting female expatriates? If gender is still relevant, what can be done to promote equal opportunity for female managers to undertake international assignments?

International reward

Reward management needs to support overall business strategy in order to attract, retain and motivate needed workers (see Chapter 8). Managing international rewards requires that managers responsible for implementing HR policies and practices are familiar with a range of other issues, including the

HCNs, the host country's employment law, national labour relations, the availability of particular allowances or benefits, and currency fluctuations in particular host countries. Even within the 'scant' international reward literature, much of the focus has been on reward for expatriates and far less on other categories of workers, such as host country and third-country nationals (Mahajan, 2011). Although the issue of generous renumeration packages for globally mobile corporate elites has become part of the public discourse on what constitutes 'responsible capitalism', most of the reward literature deals with technical rather than strategic or ethical issues of rewards, that is, with how to design effective remuneration packages for expatriates (Bonache and Fernández, 2005). Part of that technical discussion includes deciding which currency it is beneficial to pay rewards in so that, in terms of tax efficiency, the outcome motivates the expatriate.

Bonache and Fernández (2005) present a theory-based approach to expatriate rewards based on the costs and benefits. They suggest that when salary and non-salary costs (for example, training) are taken into account, and in certain circumstances (for example, the need to exploit company-specific knowledge), expatriates can be a cost-effective solution. Other studies provide evidence that effective performance management requires expatriates to know whether and how their performance in their overseas assignment is linked to pay and the next step in their career (Tahvanainen and Suutari, 2005). In developing a global reward policy, an MNC will need to include the HCN's perspective. According to Mahajan, a 'cultural alignment' pay system will be more acceptable to HCNs than ethnocentric reward policies 'as it increases perceived status similarity and reduces intergroup conflict between expatriates and HCNs [and] will facilitate adjustment of expatriates and favourably impact overall effectiveness of [MNCs]' (2011, p. 131). While there is evidence of 'strong "pull" factors' for the transfer of contemporary reward practices to HCNs (Sayim, 2010), the need to elicit HCNs' voluntary cooperation and knowledge-sharing with expatriates makes international reward management inevitably complex.

Source: iStock.com/michaeljung

MNCs are embedded in a national culture and institutional structures and these national specific characteristics are likely to influence MNCs international HR practices. Despite women's increased presence in Western management, only in rare circumstances are female managers offered global assignments.

International learning and development

The HRM literature emphasises learning intervention as a strategic instrument to transfer the distinctive management practices from the parent headquarters to the subsidiaries and to nurture a 'strong' culture, or what Bartlett and Ghoshal (1989, p. 175) call the 'global glue' that counterbalances the centrifugal forces of decentralised operations and processes. Evidence suggests that MNCs pursuing a global strategy will place greater emphasis on learning interventions that provide expatriate managers with the competencies needed to function effectively in the host country. A particular focus in this area has been the predeparture training of expatriates to be 'interculturally competent', that is, to communicate both verbally and non-verbally with HCNs – and 'cognitive competence', which avoids the use of crude stereotypes to judge people (see, for example, Caligiuri et al., 2005; Mabey et al., 1998b). MNCs pursuing a multidomestic strategy tend to transfer almost all their HR practices to the host country subsidiaries. MNCs pursuing a transnational strategy clearly require the most complex learning and development strategy because managers will be recruited from a worldwide pool of workers, regardless of nationality. Irrespective of global business strategy and training and performance linkages, learning and development interventions in MNCs typically include cross-cultural training and competencies associated with global leadership. Table 13.2 summarises these interventions and their respective goals. (See Chapter 7 for a more detailed discussion on learning and development.)

Table 13.2 Examples of learning and development interventions in MNCs

Learning and development initiatives	Goals
Cross-cultural orientation (predeparture)	Comfortably live and work in host country
Cross-cultural training (in-country)	Increase cross-cultural adjustment
Diversity training	Increase ability to understand and appreciate multiple cultural perspectives
Language training	Fluency in another language
Traditional education in international management	Increase international business acumen and knowledge
Individualised coaching or mentoring on cultural experiences	Build cultural awareness; work on cultural 'blind spots'; develop competencies for becoming an effective global leader
Immersion cultural experiences	Build extensive understanding of the local culture and increase ability to understand and appreciate multiple cultural perspectives
Cross-border global teams with debriefing	Learn skills to be a better leader (or team member) with multiple cultures involved in the team
Global meetings with debriefing or coaching	Learn skills to conduct a better meeting when multiple cultures are involved in the meeting
International assignment rotations with debriefing or coaching	Develop a deep appreciation for the challenges of working in another culture; increase global leadership competence

Source: Caligiuri et al. (2005).

International performance appraisal

As we discussed in Chapter 6, performance appraisal (PA) has become a key feature of managing the employment relationship. Here, we will consider questions of 'why' and 'how' related to international performance appraisal. Sparrow et al. (2004) argue that five interrelated organisational 'drivers' – core business cost efficiencies, information exchange, building a global presence, global learning and localised decision-making – are together creating an obvious logic of being as effective as possible across the organisation's whole global operations, as well as creating a need for the cross-national transfer of HR practices that are perceived in the parent company as superior to local management practices. Performance appraisal is the favoured way to ensure that strategic employee competencies, employee behaviour and motivation are performed effectively in the host country.

How far does PA in an international context resemble the Anglo-American model and practice? PA is a political activity. It is about making judgements on a subordinate's work effort and reward. Expatriate PA in a global context is affected by volatility in the international environment (for example, fluctuating currency exchange rates), which is outside the expatriate's scope of control, and by cultural and political factors inside the host country (for example, acts of terrorism). PA in a host country requires more than technical and interpersonal skills, the process demands sensitivity to different cultural and socio-political experiences. For example, Chou (2005) found that Anglo-Saxon-style PA was undermined in China because of the collectivist, relationship-oriented or 'Communist neo-traditionalism' socio-political culture. Many managers 'manipulated appraisal results' and refrained from rating subordinates' performance as 'unsatisfactory' because of the importance placed on a 'reciprocal relationship and organisational harmony' (Chou, 2005, p. 54). The study illustrates that the cross-national transfer of Anglo-Saxon HR practices require some degree of cultural sensitivity, as well as consultation with HCNs about local suitability (Mabey et al., 1998b).

Repatriation

Much of the early IHRM literature focuses on expatriates returning to the parent company – repatriation. The foremost reason for a premature return or an ineffective international assignment is a failure of the expatriate and their family to adapt to the new setting (Fischlmayr and Kollinger, 2010). In the context of strategic IHRM discussed in this chapter, managing expatriates or 'flex-patriates' (Mayerhofer et al., 2004) returning to the parent company may be the least of the challenges facing a global manager in a post-9/11 and Covid-19 world. Nonetheless, for many MNCs, the failure to repatriate managers successfully has caused many expatriates to resign from the company owing to what has been termed re-entry shock. Repatriation failures can also impact negatively on the ability of MNCs to attract management talent for their global operations.

The complexity of the repatriation problem varies from individual to individual. Linehan and Mayrhofer (2005) point out that a violation of the psychological contract may lead to a negative psychological reaction to repatriation. Anecdotal and empirical evidence of re-entry shock indicates that loss of autonomy, loss of status and loss of career opportunities, together with problems of family members readjusting to the parent culture, are often relevant (e.g. Brewster and Scullion, 1997; Dowling et al., 2017; Suutari and Brewster, 2003;). Nga Thi Thuy Ho et al.'s (2016) study found three pull–push factors associated with home and host countries that have a significant impact on expatriates' self-initiated intention to re-expatriate: dissatisfaction with career and life in their home country, culture shock and quality-of-life outcomes from re-expatriation. Even before the attacks on the World Trade Center in New York in 2001, civil war in North Africa in 2011 and acts of terrorism in the Middle East, MNCs had begun to experience difficulty attracting managers to accept overseas assignments. The coronavirus pandemic will be an additional contributing factor in this reluctance to accept international assignments.

Digital Spotlight

How technology drives the globalisation of work and employment

In August 2020, the government of Bermuda launched a one-year 'Work from Bermuda' residential certificate in order to attract 'digital nomads' and others wishing to work remotely from the sub-tropical island (York, 2020). For the government, the scheme represents a partial solution to declining birth rates and a 30% drop in retail sales due to the coronavirus pandemic (York, 2020). In turn, the lure for potential expats includes sun-soaked beaches and the promise of a better work-life balance. More broadly, the initiative serves to illustrate how technological advancements have played an instrumental role in the globalisation of work and employment.

The capacity of technology to facilitate the global labour market is not a new phenomenon. Previously, it tended to take the form of companies located in high-income nations outsourcing certain services to businesses based in countries with lower capital and labour costs (known as the 'offshoring country'). For example, as the result of advances in telecommunication, since the 1990s India, Bangladesh and the Philippines have each developed sizeable business process outsourcing industries providing, amongst other services, call centres for companies based in the UK, US and Australia. (However, these jobs which one wave of technological innovation facilitated, are now being threatened by AI-powered chatbots (Reed et al., 2020). More recently, there has been a focus on digital labour platforms, such as Amazon Mechanical Turk and Upwork, that create a direct connection between the customer and the worker. These include web-based platforms, where work is outsourced through an open call to a geographically dispersed group ('crowdwork'), and location-based applications (apps), which allocate tasks to individuals in a specific geographical area (Berg et al., 2018).

The benefits for businesses of using digital labour platforms are easy to identify: workers are available 'just-in-time', they are often paid less than a traditional employee, and are rarely entitled to employment benefits (De Stefano, 2016). In turn, an individual may seek out work via a digital labour platform for a variety of reasons, such as a lack of other opportunities in the place they live, to supplement their wages from another job, to allow them to work from home (or abroad), or because health conditions prevent them from engaging in full-time employment (Berg et al., 2018). However, there are concerns that such platforms may lead to the offshoring of work performed by traditionally self-employed individuals, such as graphic or web designers, in higher-income countries (Schwellnus et al., 2019). In addition, it has been suggested that the more the platform economy encroaches on activities also carried out by workers in standard employment contracts, the more this will put a downward pressure on wages in the sectors affected (Hancké, 2018).

Stop! Do you think online labour platforms are a positive development? What steps could companies take when utilising online labour platforms to try to ensure that they do not exploit workers?

Essential reading

Schwellnus, C., Geva, A., Pak, M. and Veiel, R. (2019) Gig economy platforms: boon or bane? Economics Department Working Papers, No. 1550. *OECD*, 15 May.

Note: This feature was contributed by Laura Steele.

The convergence/divergence debate

Throughout this text, we have drawn attention to the contentious nature of the employment relationship and the HR/LR policies and practices that seek to manage it. A common theme in the comparative and IHRM literature has been 'convergence' and 'divergence' in HR practices, resulting from globalisation. Historically, orthodox economists have held the belief that unfettered flows of capital and trade would allow rich and emerging economies eventually to converge to similar levels of per capita income, as capital investment would migrate from developed economies, where it would be abundant and returns limited, to emerging economies, where capital would be scarce and returns higher. This convergence process should also, according to prevailing management wisdom, result in a convergence of national business environments, including HR practices, towards homogeneity. The power of capital from the parent country, and the weakness and 'receptiveness' of the subordinate host country, both underscore notions of how globalisation creates uniformity in national business patterns (Rowley and Bae, 2002).

The major challenge to a universal vision of order, equilibrium and convergence arises from local rationalities, local realities, local ideologies and local culture (Clegg et al., 1999). An example of divergence theory applied to IHRM is the freedom of lesbian, gay, bisexual and transgender (LGBT) expatriates to disclose their identity when on international assignments. Although LGBTQ+ employees are becoming increasingly acknowledged in diversity management practices, they are under-researched in IHRM. In Paisley and Yayar's (2016) study the concept of convergent and divergent intersectionality is introduced to explain how the multiple identities of LGBT+ expatriates are redefined during an international work assignment.

Evidence of continued diversity in local or national patterns of economic activity and employment relations has contributed to the notion of 'varieties of capitalism' (see Hall and Soskice, 2001; Hancké, 2009). Within the 'varieties of capitalism' literature, academics have highlighted the importance of national culture, national economic and political conditions, institutions and historical legacies that substantially shape, if not determine, employment relations. Societal analysis searches for an understanding of what is contextually unique and why. Thus, it has been persuasively argued that, with the existence of distinct national contexts and cross-cultural differences, the 'universalist' assumption that Anglo-American or European HR 'best practices' are directly transferable is wrong (Brewster and Mayrhofer, 2019; Elenkov, 1998), and that understanding strikingly resilient differences between and within HRM in various cultural and institutional contexts and what the antecedents of those differences are provide a more nuanced understanding of divergent employment relations and HR practices (cf. Clark and Pugh, 2000; Jacoby, 2005; Paik et al., 1996).

To examine whether globalisation brings into being a convergence of HR/LR, we have drawn on Rowley and Bae's (2002) model, Figure 13.2. The two dimensions in the model are the unit of analysis – *country* versus *organisation* – and the foci – *practices* versus *people*. Changes in HR/LR practices within MNCs are mediated by environmental changes and notions of universal 'best practices'. However, the framework draws attention to 'gaps' between universalism versus national culture, and HR/LR practices newly adopted versus the organisational culture or the 'shared mindset' of people in the organisation. For example, the change from a regulated to a more market-driven form of capitalism in China, India and Singapore with greater flexibility and unemployment would provide a cultural shock for the nationals of these countries.

Different national institutional systems (e.g. laws, core values) can explain 'divergence' between the parent and host local establishments. Brewster (2001) makes a strong case that the likelihood of a generic HRM model is impossible because the idiosyncratic national institutional settings are so variable in HCNs.

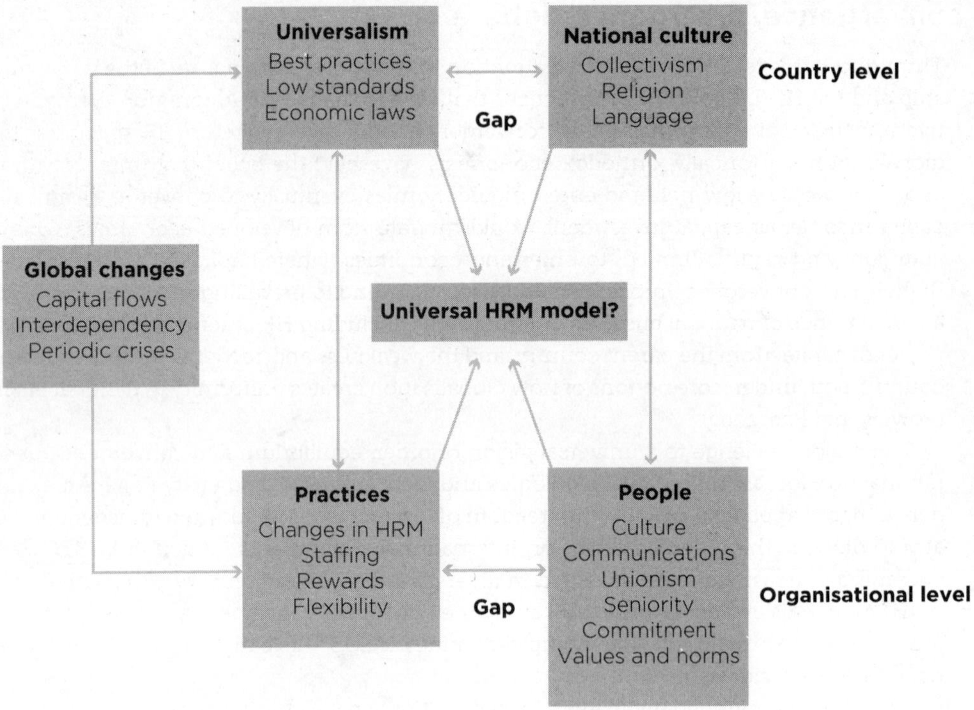

Figure 13.2 Globalisation and HRM models

Source: Adapted from Rowley and Bae (2002).

Similarly, Rowley and Bae (2002) point out the gap between changes in IHRM practices and what they call the 'shared mindset' of managers and workers. Successful transfer, it is argued, depends upon two processes:

- The '*implementation*' of the IHRM practices, whereby workers in the recipient subsidiary change their behaviours in respect of the transferred practice.
- The '*internalisation*' of the IHRM practices, whereby workers fully accept and approve the practices.

The gaps reflect a failure to inculcate IHRM practices with embedded core 'values'. Therefore, 'even if there are 'best practices', they would not bring positive effects until people fully accepted and approved them', assert Rowley and Bae (2002, p. 544). The gaps problematise any grand narrative on the conversion to either US, European or Asian models of HRM and their efficacy. Brewster captured the inconclusiveness of the convergence/divergence debate when he concluded (2007, p. 212):

> Those looking to defend one position, or another can easily find evidence to support their case. Thus, there do seem to be trends ... that are widespread, even if they do not seem to be diminishing the differences between the countries in the way they manage their HRM.

Understanding the disjuncture between universal theory and idiosyncratic national institutions and cultures becomes a key competency of the global manager. Although the debate remains equivocal, we can be more confident in affirming that the study of IHRM and comparative HRM is no longer a marginal area of interest.

Ethical Insight
Decarbonising the Global North at the expense of the Global South?

'In June 2019, the UK became the first major economy to set a legally binding commitment to reach net zero emissions by 2050' (PwC, 2019b). The pledge builds upon existing efforts that have seen the country achieve the highest average decarbonisation rate of any G20 country in the twenty-first century (PwC, 2020). As of June 2020, a further 19 countries and regions around the world had followed suit and formally adopted net zero targets (Levin and Davis, 2020). While there is undoubtedly progress to acknowledge and (cautiously) celebrate, some argue that the decarbonisation of Western economies is resulting in higher levels of pollution in the emerging economies.

Roser (2016) argues that Europeans, for example, 'bear a particularly large responsibility for climate change mitigation – due to both our historical emission record and our economic capacity to address it'. However, even if Europeans (rightly) live up to their responsibilities and completely decarbonise by 2030, we would still fall far short of the reductions needed to prevent a global rise in temperature. Therefore, he suggests, our ethical responsibility is to focus on policies that best advance deep, global decarbonisation, rather than only near-term, local decarbonisation (Roser, 2016). Fischer (2014) states that 'decarbonization must be accompanied by a massive scaling up of redistribution from the global North to South if the agenda is to be founded on a social justice approach'. In order for decarbonisation to occur in the South, large-scale capital infrastructure would need to be put in place. However, this is both costly and import intensive. In addition, there is a long-standing tendency in the global economy to siphon resources from the South to the North (Fischer, 2014). In large part this has been driven by powerful corporations based in the North, who possess high levels of control over flows of value and wealth (Fisher, 2014).

A further concern is that as demand for low-carbon technologies, such as electric vehicles and solar panels, increases this will result in the further exploitation of nations in the Global South (Sovacool et al., 2020). Many of these innovations rely upon minerals and metals that are extracted in countries including the Democratic Republic of Congo and Ghana. The mining of such materials presents serious risks to both public health and the environment. There are also significant concerns regarding the use of child labour. As a result, 'at present, the transition to low carbon-technology for cleaner production in the Global North is taking place at the expense of environmental and social harm in the Global South. In global perspective, contemporary decarbonization is neither sustainable nor renewable' (Payne, 2020).

Stop! Is the decarbonisation of economies in the Global North coming at the expense of those in the Global South?

Essential reading

Sovacool, B. K., Hook, A., Martiskainen, M., Brock, A. and Turnheim, B. (2020) The decarbonisation divide: contextualising landscapes of low-carbon exploitation and toxicity in Africa. *Global Environmental Change, 60*: 1–19.

Note: This feature was contributed by Laura Steele.

PART 5

Critiquing international HRM

The proliferation of IHRM literature springs directly from the globalisation of markets, the pursuit of MSV, in particular the development of complex just-in-time supply chains (Davie and Kim, 2015; Morris et al., 2009), the dominance of neoliberal capitalism (Harvey, 2007) and the exponential growth in international students attending Western universities and undertaking research-based degrees. Critical perspectives view globalisation not just in terms of capital flows and global interconnectivity, but rather as a driver of the gig economy and precarious employment (Edgell and Granter, 2020). Critics argue that MSV-oriented conglomerates and the process of 'Nikefication' has created the new international division of labour, causing the transfer from old industrialised regions of high-wage manufacturing jobs to low-wage developing economies. Even before the Covid-19 pandemic, mainstream economists, for example, Larry Summers, former economic adviser to US President Barack Obama, deliberated about the negative impact of a 'race to the bottom' in national regulations and the dominance effect of MNCs to depress labour standards. The orthodox economic theory of 'efficient markets' has been thoroughly discredited along with the supposedly unmitigated virtues of self-regulation (see, for example Aldred, 2020). It is observable that organisational designs that rely on global just-in-time supply chains are susceptible to disruption with serious consequences for the business operation. For example, the coronavirus crisis disrupted Samsung's supply chain, causing the company to fly electronic components for its latest Galaxy smartphone from China to its factories in Vietnam (Reed and Jung-A, 2020). The severe disruption of global supply chains has triggered a paradigmatic shift in economic thinking (Hutton, 2020a), which is likely to impact on MNC behaviour in both the short and long term.

The pandemic and post-Brexit conditions in Europe may lead some corporations to consider repatriating production rather than more offshoring to guarantee domestic labour and components, while others may outsource more to take advantage of Britain's low-wage, less-regulated economy. Indeed, the interesting analysis by Rubery and Johnson (2019) and Thompson (2013) of HRM in the aftermath of the 2008 GFC is relevant to analysing IHRM in an era of the global pandemic crisis (GPC) and economic depression. In assessing how MNCs will respond to the triple crises – Covid-19, economic depression and climate change – what is clear is that the effects will place heavy demands on the HR function as the crises undermine a central assumption that MNCs have total control over their own destinies and can thereby enter into long-term policies of high-commitment IHRM. Further, how MNCs change their IHRM policies and practices in response to capitalism's triple crises may undermine the principles on which global business models have been built, thereby adding further layers of complexity in IHRM.

Bartlett and Ghoshal's (1989) integration–responsiveness typology is helpful for examining the link between global business strategies and IHRM, and for identifying a comprehensive range of factors that influence SIHRM in MNCs. However, a key critique of the model is that it depicts an 'ideal type' of global strategy that MNCs strive for, but not necessarily enact. Moreover, models are just that: they are a conceptual construct and have been disparaged because the alleged direction of the causal relationships within them is ambiguous. For example, the argument that exogenous factors exert a direct effect on endogenous factors may privilege external factors as the actor when MNCs have actually become global giants that wield titanic political power. Corporations in fact determine the 'rules of the game', and governments enforce the rules laid down by MNCs (Hertz, 2002). As the environmental and political activist George Monbiot (2017) argues, MNCs follow the doctrine of neoliberalism that is not only an expression of power – it is a source of power. For Monbiot, MNCs champion a certain kind of freedom: freedom from environmental constraints, freedom from collective bargaining with trade unions, and freedom from the demands of social justice. Therefore, arguably the MNC is the dominant actor.

Critical analysis serves as an antidote to the mainstream assumption found in much of the IHRM literature that the MNC is an integrated and harmonious entity in which management and other employees all share a common purpose – the unitarist perspective. Interrogating IHRM through a labour relations lens would, it is argued, provide a better understanding of the management challenge in MNCs (Collings, 2008). Specifically, such a pluralist orientation would compel IHRM scholars to engage with a myriad of issues typically neglected in the IHRM literature, including trade union avoidance, collective bargaining and the role of other actors, such as the state in host countries. Further, researching the dynamics of collective bargaining in MNCs offers latitude lacking in many unitarist studies to examine how the balance of power between the actors affects management in MNCs (for more discussion of these issues, see Collings, 2008).

The rhetoric of IHRM suggests that the phenomenon of internationalisation of HR practices has immense potential to foster a global approach to managing human capital in emerging economies following the paradigmatic Anglo-American model (Farazmand, 2002; Sparrow et al., 2004). However, the reality of managing people in a global environment can fall well below rhetorical 'good' practices. Alleged erratic payment of wages, intimidation and debt bondage (Pattisson, 2016), and reports of Brazilian meat-processing workers presented with a stark choice: risk potentially being infected with Covid-19, or risk losing their jobs (TUC, 2020c), offer an alarming insight into what can be called a 'dark' side of global HR management.

Orthodox IHRM studies typically conceptualise organisational culture as being continuously constructed and reconstructed through human interactions between specific social contexts (Frenkel, 2008). From this perspective, critical scholars view MNC's corporate culture as a powerful strategic tool not just to facilitate integration and cooperation, but rather to exert control over the host country's workforce (Kramar and Syed, 2012; Said, 1993). An important measure of an MNC's orientation towards the management of their cross-border subsidiaries transpires through staffing decisions. Critical analysis of global staffing decisions brings to the fore a gender dimension often lacking in many mainstream IHRM studies. The phrase 'think manager, think male', was coined by Schein et al. (1996) to describe the effect of sex-role stereotypes on what it takes to be an effective manager (see Bratton, 2021, pp. 156–60). Many studies point to stereotypical perceptions of women's managerial abilities to undertake overseas assignments, which, along with general discrimination against women, act as major social barriers to women expanding their career horizons through access to global management positions. Countering one myth, studies by Taylor and Napier (1996) found that there were no significant differences between male and female expatriates in their business performance, even in male-dominated cultures such as South Korea and Japan (cf. Adler, 1994; Caligiuri and Tung, 1999; Linehan, 2005; Taylor and Napier, 1996).

Summary

In this chapter, we explained how global corporations typically face tension from two types of business pressure. On the one hand, pressures for global cost reductions and rationalisation and, on the other hand, demands for differentiation and local responsiveness. We also discussed how IHRM is closely tied to international business strategies and briefly explained three fashionable business strategies – global, multidomestic and transnational – as solutions to the dual pressure for cost efficiencies and responsiveness.

An integrative model explored how IHRM should be explicitly linked to the global business strategy of the MNC and how its changing forms must be understood in relation to the strategic evolution of the MNC. We discussed how the cross-national transfer of Anglo-Saxon HR practices will require some degree of cultural sensitivity, as well as consultation with HCNs about local suitability.

We discussed how variations in national regulatory systems, the labour markets, cultural and polyethnic contexts are likely to constrain or shape any tendency towards 'convergence' or a 'universal' model of 'better' HR practice. The sheer variation of capitalist economies and cultures makes claims for convergence both simplistic and problematic. Finally, we can note that it has been easier to formulate questions than answers, and we have taken the easier rather than the more difficult route. Yet there is value in asking questions. Questions can stimulate reflection and increase our understanding of IHRM. Our object here has been to do both.

Review questions

1. Explain how MNCs address the tension between the dual imperatives of global integration and local responsiveness.
2. Discuss how differences in national institutional systems might influence a corporation's decision to locate its profit-making operations.
3. Explain how global business strategies are linked to approaches to global staffing. What are the advantages and disadvantages of using parent country nationals in cross-border management positions? Does gender and sexuality influence global staffing decisions?

Search & Watch

Go to the video hub at www.bloomsbury.pub/bratton-hrm and watch the interview with **Lesley White, Human Resources Director UK and Ireland, Huawei Technologies** (www.huawei.com). Huawei is a multinational networking and telecommunications company that provides information and communications technology (ICT) solutions and products to its customers. Huawei is headquartered in Shenzhen in China. Lesley White is an HR professional with more than 20 years' experience, having started as an HR Assistant. She specialised for nine years in European Compensation and Benefits, designing reward strategies and associated policies to attract, retain and motivate employees. Her current role covers all areas of HRM, with a key focus on strategy planning and implementation. Click on Lesley's picture to watch her talking about the challenges of working in a UK-based HR department for a company headquartered in China, cultural differences in working and management styles, and the place of HR in Huawei's business strategy, and then think about the following questions: (1) What are the key features of working in HR in a global organisation, according to Lesley? (2) In Lesley's view, how do Chinese managers respond to directives compared with Europeans, and why? (3) In 2020, the British government cancelled the 5G contract with Huawei, how do you see this decision affecting British-Chinese relations?

Legal Focus

The outsourcing of business activities has long existed but with the rise of economic globalisation it has become more common and bigger in scale in those economies that have embraced the neoliberal ('free market') ideology, countries like the US and UK. Outsourcing entails the contracting out of an organisational activity to an external party within or outwith a country. Outsourcing may involve the transfer of tangible assets (e.g. machinery) and/or employees from one business entity to a new party that is to perform the outsourced activity. Outsourcing has clear ramifications for individual employees and communities. UK labour law and European Union Acquired Rights Directive aim to ensure that, on the transfer of an organisational activity or undertaking, the acquired rights of the employees (contractual and statutory) are maintained. In the UK, important rights for employees are contained in the Transfer of Undertakings (Protection of Employment) Regulation (TUPE) 2006. The Regulations 2006 protect the rights of employees on a relevant transfer of business activity (e.g. contracting out a service). A relevant transfer is a transfer of an economic entity which retains its identity or a service provision change, impacting a group of employees whose main purpose is carrying out those activities outsourced or transferred from one contractor to another. Dismissal due to the transfer is normally automatically unfair, unless the reason for dismissal is an economic or organisational reason entailing changes in the workforce.

Task Search online for government information in your jurisdiction on the transfer of undertakings. Answer the following: (1) What is meant by a 'relevant transfer' of undertakings? (2) What rights do relevant employees have if a transfer falls within the TUPE Regulation 2006?

Reference

See Deborah Lockton and Tom Brown's *Employment Law* (2020), pp. 137–49, for a discussion on the Transfer of Undertakings (Protection of Employment) Regulation 2006, covering statutory provisions and case law related to the effect of a relevant transfer on the employment contract.

PART 5

Chapter case: IKAN

The setting

IKAN, established in 1972 in Finland by Onni Lehtinen, has experienced considerable growth since Finland joined the EU in the 1990s, to become one of the largest manufacturers of home furnishings. The parent company is located in Tampere and employs 1,750 employees made up of skilled and semi-skilled workers. Two hundred and thirty employees work in design and development and other highly skilled areas. All the employees belong to one trade union. The company has a profit-sharing scheme and an excellent pension scheme.

Since 1972, IKAN has sold a basic range of typically 'Scandinavian' home furnishings in six stores, only one of which – in Helsinki – is inside Finland. The company remains primarily production-oriented, its Finnish management and design group deciding what it is going to manufacture in the most cost-effective way and then how it will sell it to the European homeowner, often with very little market research outside Finland. The company has emphasised its Finnish roots in its European advertising, including the adoption of the colours blue and white, from the Finnish national flag, for its retail outlets and advertising material.

The foundation of IKAN's success has been to offer consumers good value for money, distinctive branding and a good network of suppliers. A supplier for IKAN gains long-term contracts and leased equipment from the company. In return, IKAN demands an exclusive contract and low prices. IKAN's expatriate managers seconded to the subsidiary standardise products and integrate production to gain maximum savings on the final products at a low cost. IKAN sells its avant-garde furniture to customers as self-assembly kits. In this way, the company reaps economies of scale from the large production runs. IKAN operates over 275 stores in 38 countries/territories. In 2019, only 5% of its sales were generated in Finland, the balance coming from Germany (15%), the US (13%), France (8%), the UK (7%) and China (6%). IKAN's online store accounts for 10% of total sales. This strategy allows IKAN to match its competitors on quality but undercut them by up to 30% on price, while maintaining an after-tax return on sales of around 7%.

The problem

In 2018, IKAN decided to establish a factory in Toronto and two retail stores in Canada, followed by six in the US. The Canadian subsidiary was built on a green-field site on the west side of Toronto and employed 320 employees by the end of 2020. Informed that trade union density in Canada was well below that of Finland, expatriate managers were told that unionisation was a 'non-issue' and that the company's profit-sharing scheme, similar to the Finnish scheme, would ensure employee loyalty and commitment. The operation side of the business was meeting output targets. Preliminary reports, however, indicated that the new North American retail stores were not meeting sales and profit targets as planned. Finnish home furnishings, which sold well in Western Europe, clashed with Canadian and US tastes and sometimes physiques. In addition, the new Canadian factory was experiencing quality control problems and some challenges in managing the workforce.

Sofia Koski, the operations director, called a meeting of the Canadian management team. Aada Alvesson, an experienced Finnish marketing manager, gave the first presentation to the assembled IKAN managers. He explained that sales had not reached expected targets because the standard furniture did not meet North American tastes and preferences. He said, for example, 'Our Finnish kitchen cupboards are too narrow to take large dinner plates needed for pizza. And our beds are too narrow for American preferences.'

Emma Hokkanen, the finance manager at the Canadian subsidiary, explained that some of the Canadian managers resented the degree of control exerted over how they managed their units. In addition, she had heard through various supervisors that some employees had been overheard talking about 'bringing in a union' to achieve higher wages. Eric Lynch, one of three Canadian-born and Canadian-educated managers present at the meeting, interjected at this point and said, 'The union isn't the problem; it's poor communications. Many staff can't understand the expatriate managers! I've heard that shop-floor supervisors leave their encounters with Finnish managers feeling frustrated by their inability to understand and relate to them.' Hokkanen also said they needed to recruit a senior HR manager to deal with the issues raised. 'The fact that Ontario, like the other provinces in Canada, has its own labour relations statutes makes dealing with Canadian unions more difficult and frustrating, especially if we open a factory in Vancouver,' she added. 'We should bring in an experienced HR professional from head office; someone with experience of dealing with labour unions', said Koski. 'I'm unsure, but I'll investigate', replied Hokkanen.

The assignment

Given the pressures facing IKAN in the marketplace, prepare a written report to Sofia Koski:

1. Explain how IKAN can be both competitive and locally responsive and detailing why IKAN's SIHRM orientation should be linked to its international business strategy and what this would mean for the role of the HR department at IKAN's Canadian subsidiary.
2. Explain the advantages and disadvantages of recruiting an HR manager from Finland, a parent country national.

Essential reading

Farndale, E., Brewster, C., Ligthart, P. and Poutsma, E. (2017) The effects of market economy type and foreign MNE subsidiaries on the convergence and divergence of HRM. *Journal of International Business Studies*, *48*(9): 1065–86.

Collings, D. G. and Isichei, M. (2018) The shifting boundaries of global staffing: integrating global talent management, alternative forms of international assignments and non-employees into the discussion. *International Journal of Human Resource Management, 29*(1): 165–87.

Note: This feature was written by John Bratton and updated by Andrew Bratton.

Further reading

Dowling, P., Festing, M. and Engle, A. (2017) *International Human Resource Management*. London: Thomson.

Edwards, T., Marginson, P. and Ferner, A. (2013) Multinational companies in cross-national context: integration, differentiation, and the interactions between MNCs and nation states: Introduction to a Special Issue of the ILR Review. *ILR Review*, *66*(3): 547–87.

Galang, M.C. and Osman, I. (2016) HR managers in five countries: what do they do and why does it matter?, *International Journal of Human Resource Management*, *27*(13): 1341–72. DOI: http://dx.doi.org/10.1080/09585192.2015.1072099.

Hancké, B. (ed.) (2009) *Debating Varieties of Capitalism: A Reader*. Oxford: Oxford University Press.

Paisley, V. and Yayar, M. (2016) Lesbian, gay, bisexual and transgender (LGBT) expatriates: an intersectionality perspective. *The International Journal of Human Resource Management*, *27*(7): 766–80. DOI:10.1080/09585192.2015.1111249

CHAPTER 14

BACK TO THE FUTURE

REIMAGINING HRM IN A POST-PANDEMIC CAPITALISM

outline

- Introduction
- Past and present
- Post-pandemic capitalism
- Reimagining HRM
- A final word
- Further reading

Source: Peter Parks/Getty Images

objectives

After studying this chapter, you should be able to:

1. Describe some common themes and the different ways in which the preceding chapters relate to one another
2. Appreciate some possible contextual changes in which HRM operates
3. Understand some possible scenarios for the future of HRM

Introduction

As dramatised in director Robert Zemeckis's 1985 science fiction film, *Back to the Future*, the present and the future depend on the route taken in the past. In post-pandemic capitalism, where HRM is going in the future depends upon its past and how academics, HRM professionals and policy makers have intellectually travelled from the past to the present. The Covid-19 pandemic has laid bare multiple workplace injustices, not least the total lack of employment protection afforded to many workers (Jones, 2020). From the precarious lives of workers engaged in non-standard employment and gig work, to the greater death toll among low-paid essential public-facing workers in homecare, transport and public services, the consequences of a 'low-road' HRM model devoid of employment rights and security could hardly be starker. Emergency national lockdowns hit workplaces dominated by women and young people, as restaurants, hotels, childcare and high-street retail businesses closed their doors, thus, entrenching inequality and amplifying precarity among these demographics.

The preceding chapters have drawn from mainstream and critical work-related scholarship to provide readers with a knowledgeable and critical introduction of the key issues surrounding both the theory and practice of HRM. In so doing, we have frequently highlighted the disjuncture between the positive rhetoric and reality of HRM. Without that disjuncture the contemporary workplace would look a very different place. Thus, the critical interrogation of HR practices and pedagogical features contained in the preceding chapters provide the basis for reimagining HRM in a post-pandemic world.

The purpose of this chapter is to examine developments in political economy that influence, if not determine, the long-term business and HR strategies of companies and organisations. This sets the scene for exploring the future of work and employment relations against the background development in post-pandemic capitalism and corporate governance.

Past and present

The long-term effects of the pandemic on our workplaces and cities are just beginning to be revealed. The metropolises are where pre-Covid-19 life and work patterns have been most disrupted. Does it mean high-density urban apartments are unliveable, and that everyone is migrating to the suburbs and beyond? What does this mean for public transport, travel times and the future of high-street retailing? Will working at home be a permanent feature making high-rise offices a relic of the past (Moore, 2020)? What does it mean for the traditional workplace and HR practices? Will there be a faster shift towards 'surveillance capitalism' (Zuboff, 2015; 2019) as traditional human supervision is replaced by computer surveillance? Graeber (2018) observes, 'humans are social beings that begin to atrophy – even to physical decay – if they are denied regular contact with other human beings' (pp. 101–2). If people are isolated working at home separated from their co-workers, what does that mean for worker well-being? At the time of writing, November 2021, it is too early to tell. However, it is likely that pre-Covid-19 trends, such as working at home, perhaps outside large cities, and virtual meetings, are likely to get intensified rather than redirected (Berridge, 2020). Prior to the coronavirus crisis, for example, 68 per cent of British workers never worked from home. Survey evidence shows that people enjoyed the experience and once the crisis is over, 57 per cent expressed a preference to be able to continue working from home (Smith, 2020).

Anglo-American elites have been indifferent to the growth of social inequality. But the pandemic has highlighted the need for stronger employment rights and income security for workers, especially those in non-standard forms of employment. The important lesson from Asia is that more equal societies have the social capital and mutual support to allow social distancing, self-isolation, quarantining and lockdowns to work, even for the poorest. Western societies can achieve the same goals using different tools, of which furlough arrangements, income support and sick pay are central (Hutton, 2020b). Wage subsidy schemes introduced by many governments attempt to address the income support challenges of workers furloughed due to national lockdowns. Although the programmes are temporary, the concerns about income-related stability and insecurity are not. After the previous recession in 2008–9, work-sharing programmes were introduced in a number of EU countries which had significant effects in preserving employment and disposable income (Messenger and Ghosheh, 2013).

Over the time it has taken us to write this new edition, global capitalism has been shaken by the coronavirus pandemic, while Brexit has caused convulsions within British capitalism. The Covid-19 virus has upended the belief in the conviction that a short-term approach to employment is the best model to manage employment relations. There is a cacophony of voices calling for significant changes in employment and labour market regulations that in principle should affect employer behaviour and HR practices post-pandemic. Rethinking HRM is explored later in this chapter, but two main areas are highlighted here: employment protection and pay systems. With respect to employment protection, there needs to be an upgrading of employment rights. Already, governments in some jurisdictions have decided to apply traditional employment models to many gig workers and independent contractors, for example, reclassifying many as employees (Mahboubi, 2020). With respect to pay systems, workers in non-standard employment need more than temporary government income relief. In both the UK and the US, a general stagnation or decline in real pay for many workers has been matched by the decline of pay bargaining. Wages on, in some cases below, the legal minima have been the experience for many gig workers. A whole set of regulations designed to increase both workplace trade unionism and pay bargaining needs to be implemented in order to address stagnating real wages and pay inequality. Whichever the direction governments and companies take in relation to economic interventions and employment relations, those actions will be overshadowed by the climate crisis and the economic crisis as Britain adjusts to its exit from the European Union. That the triple crises – Covid-19, global warming, Brexit – should entail changes in the way work and people are managed is not merely advisable, it is absolutely necessary.

In Part 2 of the book, we conceptualised HRM as a strategic approach, one that seeks to leverage people's capabilities and commitment with the goal of enhancing performance and dignity *in* and *at* work. These HRM goals, we pointed out, are accomplished by a set of integrated employment policies and practices within an organisational and societal context. Further, we discussed some specific contextual factors affecting corporate strategy and examined the meaning of strategic HRM and its relation to corporate strategy. In the aftermath of Covid-19 the whole notion of what constitutes an 'effective' long-term HR strategy is coming under intense scrutiny. Pre-pandemic the focus of most SHRM research is on the interests of shareholders and the maximisation of shareholder value (MSV) model. Put in more colloquial language, the focus has been on the 'bottom line' with little attention given to the well-being of the workforce reflected in physical and mental ill-health, insecurity and inequitable rewards.

In Part 3 we described and critiqued a range of research and core professional HR practices covering job design, workforce planning, recruitment and selection, performance appraisal, learning and development, and rewards. Part 4 was devoted to managing employment relations with a focus on labour relations and the role of collective bargaining and employee relations with an examination of conflict management. Finally, in Part 5, we examined some contemporary HRM issues: health, safety and worker well-being, sustainable HRM and international HRM. Globalisation has created the new international division of labour, causing the transfer from European and North American industrialised regions of high-wage manufacturing jobs to low-wage developing economies, notably China. The coronavirus crisis, however, has upended the belief in the supremacy of global just-in-time supply chains which are susceptible to disruption (Hutton, 2020a). What should be self-evident is that HRM – in whatever form – is shaped by its context – *external* in the form of deep structural economic forces and cultural-political dynamics as well as *internal* gravitational forces, pulling in many contradictory directions that generate cooperation and conflict. If large workplaces are conceived in such a way HRM is difficult to execute and, like capitalism, is full of tension and contradiction.

Macroeconomic stability could be considered a precondition for a developmental-high-commitment HR strategy. The effects of the Covid-19-induced economic crisis directly put into question the presumptions underpinning strategic HRM. During the crisis, there was a belated recognition of the importance of people doing work often labelled as 'low skill', but which the emergency showed to be essential for society to function. These workers, relentlessly squeezed to do more and exploited on low pay, the majority of whom are women, are too often marginalised in academic HRM research and discourse. The pandemic exposed the unsustainability of traditional HRM models and, in 'building anew', at the heart of HRM ought to be fair reward, basic rights, security and dignities to *all* workers. How companies and organisations might respond to eruptions in the economic environment, and what are the long-term implications of Covid-19 for restructuring and the way people are managed, are topics we explore in the rest of the chapter.

Post-pandemic capitalism

> The capitalist class ... create their own contradictions, throw up opposing classes, provoke class struggles, set in train economic, political, and cultural changes. History, far from being at an end, has hardly begun! (Leslie Sklair, cited in Bratton and Denham, 2009, p. 293)

Studying capitalism is important for understanding how companies and organisations respond to changes in the political economy in a post-pandemic world. In particular, analysis provides insight into the connection between corporate strategy and models of HR strategy (Rubery and Johnson, 2019). This section will consider three key questions. First, how is the 2020–21 public health crisis (PHC) different from the 2008 global financial crisis (GFC)? Second, what options are there to economic dislocation and mass unemployment? Third, what are the longer-term implications of the 2020–21 PHC for managing employment relations?

Since the millennium, global capitalism has faced two major economic crises: the 2008 GFC and the 2020–21 pandemic. Much has been written about the 2008 financial crisis, so we only here have to provide a brief summary of the cause and effect. Not since the Great Depression of 1929 had Western capitalism experienced such an economic shock to the financial system. In 2008, GFC occurred despite the efforts of the US Federal Reserve and Department of the Treasury and the Bank of England. In the US, Lehman Brothers went bankrupt and blue-chip financial institutions Merrill Lynch, AIG, the world's biggest insurance company, Freddie Mac and Fannie Mae, had to be rescued. The Bank of England had to rescue the Royal Bank of Scotland, HBOS, the UK's biggest mortgage provider, Bradford & Bingley and Alliance & Leicester. The global financial system came closer to total collapse than at any time since 1929 (Mathiason, 2008). Free-market capitalism is intrinsically unstable, but the depth and scope of the crisis was associated with the process of 'financialisation' or the creation of massive fictitious financial wealth, that began in the 1980s and with the hegemony of neoliberal ideology (Bresser-Pereira, 2010). Financialisation is a distorted financial system disconnected from real wealth or from the production of goods and services.

Neoliberalism was the ideological impulse behind the deregulation in the US and UK financial system. Among professional economists, John Maynard Keynes's disparaging vision of financial markets as a 'casino' was replaced by 'efficient market' theory (Krugman, 2009). In the US, the Financial Services Modernization Act of 1999 (Gramm-Leach-Bliley Act) allowed banks to use deposits to invest in high-risk hedge fund trading with derivatives, and the Commodity Futures Modernization Act of 2000 overruled any state regulations and exempted derivatives from regulatory oversight (Amadeo, 2020). Similarly, in Britain, the Financial Services Act of 1986, passed by Margaret Thatcher's Conservative government, began to deregulate the city of London and its banks (Fishman, 1993). The phrase 'Big Bang' was used to describe the speed of deregulation of financial markets. The crisis led to the Great Recession, causing US housing prices to plunge, and unemployment to soar. Two years after the recession ended, unemployment was still above 9 per cent (Amadeo, 2020). In Britain, a decade later, compounded by 'austerity economics', the 'scarring' effects were particularly acute among millennials entering the job market. A survey found that average pay for workers in their thirties was still 7 per cent below its pre-crisis peak in 2018 (Inman, 2019). Critical scholarship contends that the 2008 GFC was, in essence, a traditional endogenous crisis of laissez-faire capitalism stemming from over production, in this case in the form of complex high-risk financial products, and of the hegemony of neoliberalism, which relied upon self-regulation of the banks and financial institutions. Pre-2008 most of the financial instruments of the 1990s and 2000s bore a resemblance to a Ponzi scheme.

The 2020–21 economic crisis, in contrast, was, arguably, triggered by exogenous factors – the Covid-19 pandemic. The deadly virus caused every component of aggregate demand – consumption, capital spending, exports – to massively fall. In 1957, the H2N2 pandemic (a.k.a. 'Asian Flu') claimed an estimated 1.1 million lives worldwide and triggered a 10 per cent fall in gross domestic product (GDP). The global economy recovered rapidly from the virus; by the third quarter of 1958 growth had spiked to 10 per cent– a 20 percentage-point swing (Rubin, 2020, p. x). Perhaps it was the 1957 pandemic that emboldened some economic pundits to predict V-shaped or L-shaped downturns (either a sharp downturn followed by rapid recovery or decline followed by stagnation); it is evident that the Covid-19 crisis is neither V- nor L-shaped, but more likely I-shaped: a vertical line representing an unprecedented collapse of economic activity followed by severe contraction of the real economy (Roubini, 2020). The Covid-19 crisis has laid bare weaknesses in the global and national economy and exposed existing tensions and inequalities which proceeding chapters have highlighted. The Covid-19 crisis has also disproportionately affected certain sectors of the economy – including hospitality, high-street retail and the airline and aircraft production industry – with negative repercussions for women, Black, Asian and minority ethnic (BAME), and young workers. While widespread furloughing curbed the rise in unemployment in the early phase of the pandemic, BAME and young workers were disproportionately affected. Over 20 per cent of BAME workers, and around 20 per cent of young people who were furloughed during the 2020–21 national lockdowns lost their jobs (Resolution Foundation, 2020).

However, the pandemic effect has been uneven on different sectors of the economy. Other services, usually defined as the FAIRE sector (finance, artificial intelligence, insurance, real estate), have seen demand and profits increase. The percentage of FAIRE-oriented jobs has rapidly increased since the latter half of the twentieth century (Graeber, 2018) and, therefore, the crisis has accelerated an existing trend – the rise of the digital classes and decline of the traditional manual labouring classes. This trend is one factor explaining the rise of right-wing popularism and support for Trump in the US (cf. Rubin, 2020). The 2008–9 and 2020–21 crises, however, do share something in common: global interconnectedness. The way the financial and Covid-19 crises spread signifies the scope and depth of a global interconnectedness which enabled the fast transmission of negative convulsions across economies through multiple channels.

In the case of Europe, studying changes in capitalism and the links to corporate strategy and models of HR strategy is further complicated by Brexit. Britain formally left the European Union on 1 January 2020. There then followed a further 12 months of intense negotiations on the future post-Brexit relationship. Numerous self-imposed deadlines were set and passed, without agreement, until final agreement on Christmas Eve, 24 December, 2020. The 1,200-page agreement covers everything from trade and fishing rights to transportation and nuclear power. For the first time in over four decades, UK and EU exporters will face border controls and cope with regulations governing a myriad of issues, including work visas and 'rules of origin', which dictate whether import taxes, called tariffs, must be paid based on where a product's parts or ingredients come from and where it has come from in international trade (Stojanovic, 2020). The treaty also sets up more than 20 councils, committees and working groups to monitor its implementation and handle disputes. 'Brexit is far from over', said Anand Menon, director of the think-tank UK in a Changing Europe (cited by Dellanna, 2020). It is predicted that the UK will be consumed by Brexit for the foreseeable future as it enters 'this liminal swamp of permanent negotiations' (Ash, 2021, p. O2). While the treaty was viewed as a political victory for Prime Minister Johnson, economically it will mean goods traded with the EU will be slower and more expensive, and for trading services, which accounts for 80 per cent of the UK economy, it will become far more expensive.

The developing consensus is that 1 January 2021 marked a decisive rupture. Britain went one way, the EU another. There is a chorus of opinion representing two broad perspectives, that Brexit will, on the one hand, represent a new beginning, with 'Britannia unchained' negotiating new free trade deals or, on the other, the Brexit apocalypse will leave 'Global Britain' isolated and people impoverished. These polar opposite views are likely to be confounded by the simple geographic and economic realities of Europe and global capitalism. Britain remains a significant part of the European economy and vice-versa. What this means in practice is that despite the formal disengagement, Britain's new relationship to the EU will constantly mutate. For HRM scholars and practitioners alike, a key question is: what is the future of the post-Brexit, labour market?

Forecasting whether labour markets will simply go back to 'normal' or fundamentally change, will depend on whether the disruptions have been cyclical or structural (Levine, 2013). Distinguishing cyclical from structural unemployment is important because their relative contribution to the increase in the unemployment rate has different implications for which macroeconomic policies are most appropriate to lower an unemployment rate. The term cyclical unemployment is used by economists to describe how employment tends to fluctuate with the business cycle. During a recession, at the bottom of the cycle, demand for workers is weak and employers shed workers. As the economy picks up, generally workers are typically rehired and at the top of the cycle, demand for workers is strong and employment is high. The Covid-19 virus inflicted havoc with employment in 2020–21 both in terms of unemployment and the effects. Unemployment increased as employers cut staff in the face of three waves of infections leading to tighter restrictions which particularly impacted the hospitality sector. Official data shows the largest annual fall in employment in Britain for a decade, as the unemployment rate increased to 4.9 per cent in the three months to October 2020 (Strauss, 2020). The extent to which jobs will return to pre-pandemic levels, albeit with a time lag, will depend on structural change in the labour markets. Post-pandemic, AI and robotics could change manufacturing or data processing operations in that employers may need fewer workers in those sectors. Equally, structural change could arise from changing work habits as an increasing number of people work at home or eat out less, or as organisations switch away from global to local or regional just-in-time supply chains. Arguably, with diminished workers' rights and union influence, free movement of labour has helped entrench Britain's reputation as a low-wage, low-investment, low-productivity economy (Elliott, 2020).

Post-pandemic and post-Brexit labour markets may significantly change because of the disruptions to supply chains. In the pre-Covid-19 era, mainstream economic wisdom celebrated the advantages of economic specialisation and the international division of labour, which saw the unrelenting offshoring of factory jobs to low-wage economies. Coordinated market economies (CMEs) are likely to reassess globalisation. There will be some reshoring and shortening of supply chains (Goodhart, 2020). Today, the economic benefits of globalisation, which relies upon long venerable just-in-time supply chains, no longer seem quite so advantageous as they did only yesterday. As Rubin (2020, p. 295) observes:

> The advantages of economic specialization and the international division of labour ... may sound great in theory, but when the factory on the other side of the world – the one you're relying on to supply vitally needed medical equipment – has been closed or some government official decides where the goods are made at that factory can be shipped, local sourcing all of a sudden sounds like a very good idea.

Just-in-time production was identified as a 'high-dependency', high-risk business model in the early 1990s (cf. Bratton, 1992). As quarantined factories in Asia sever or disrupt just-in-time supply chains Covid-19 may well usher in the polar opposite of globalisation: a return to local sourcing. A sustained pivot away from offshoring towards onshore sourcing will have significant consequences for HRM. As Rubin (2020) optimistically predicts, onshore sourcing will boost local labour markets and wages: 'Local sourcing means local production by local workers paid at local wage rates' (p. 295). This will mean that many workers will not be quite as 'expendable'. In post-Brexit Britain, car manufacturers faced with high export tariffs and rules of origin are reported to be considering doing things differently: investing in new plant and machinery and onshore sourcing (Carroll, 2020). Others are considering building onshore capacity for life-sciences products to guarantee the supply of the Covid-19 vaccine (Chakrabortty, 2021). In Britain, Brexit and the pandemic has reportedly created recruitment problems, particularly in the hospitality sector (CIPD, 2021). It is too early to know the extent of these changes, but, in the short and medium term, it would be surprising if labour shortages and the pivot to new ways of working did not incentivise employers to review wages and job quality (Partington, 2021b). The pandemic and containment measures have resulted in unprecedented job losses (OECD, 2020a). But the experience of workers under the effect of the pandemic is complex and multidimensional. The pandemic has had a greater effect on young people and women workers. Whereas non-medical professionals, managers and white-collar workers were able to work at home, public-facing medical workers, care workers, supermarket tellers and shelf stackers, bus, taxi and lorry drivers, Deliveroo riders on their bikes, refuse collectors and food processors faced the greatest risk. Millions of 'essential' public-facing workers are low-paid and unable to qualify for sickness benefits. Covid-19 mortality among male and female BAME workers has been higher compared to those of white ethnic background. According to the Office for National Statistics this is due to socioeconomic factors not genetics (White and Avoubkhani, 2020). BAME workers are in those low-pay, insecure and high-exposure jobs. In other words, it has largely to do with class, not ethnicity or race. Mitigating the effects of structural changes in labour markets will need organisational and government measures. Rebuilding labour markets after the coronavirus pandemic requires investing in a sustainable green transition from fossil fuels to a low-carbon economy (Barbier, 2020). Government priorities include support for green innovation and infrastructure, and pricing carbon and pollution. The Organisation for Economic Cooperation and Development (OECD) examining the future of labour markets, recommends, among other measures, investment in learning and development programmes, and targeting those most at risk of being affected by new technologies, including low-skilled workers (OECD, 2020a). Together, the pandemic, Brexit and a newly functioning global trading network will challenge every aspect of how companies and organisations operate including the role and responsibilities of the HRM function.

Reimagining HRM

We who dream together, achieve together. Benjamin Zephaniah[1]

What will the pandemic-induced recession and Brexit mean for HRM? Reflecting on the post-2008 crisis, the discernible differences in the way Western economies and employers reacted to the crisis provide a clue to how employers will react to the unprecedented fall in aggregate demand. The varieties of capitalism theses (Hall and Soskice, 2001) emphasised the differences in employers' reactions between coordinated market economies (CMEs), for example, France, Germany and the Netherlands, and liberal market economies (LMEs), for instance, the US and UK. Organisations in CME countries interfaced with government institutional arrangements and were more able to achieve competitive advantage by adopting a long-term human investment in firm specific skills, and thus favouring high-ended manufacturing. In contrast, organisations in LME countries tended to take a more short-term approach, dictated by short-term pressures associated with shareholder capitalism (see Rubery and Johnson, 2019). Consequently, despite pronouncements that capitalism must reform on the 'put your house in order' concept the changes were insufficient to achieve global economic stability or reverse growing inequality (Bini Smaghi, 2010). In Britain, a distinctive approach to competing can be identified: a flexi-workforce consisting of a shrinking core of secure, relatively well-paid occupations for sought-after 'talent' and an ever-growing number of jobs on short-term non-standard contracts. Thus, economic precarity is rampant in post-Brexit Britain.

Although there is much evidence that different models of HRM are concentrated in different countries and different workplaces, ultimately, much of the diversity in HRM can be understood in terms of how investors and their agents – CEOs and senior managers – governments and national institutions respond to the crises, as well as the macro-political and economic forces that shape their agendas. The convulsions of Brexit and the 2020–21 pandemic are events that remind us that private and public sector organisations and HR practices are deeply embedded in the wider sociocultural and environmental context in which they operate. Throughout this book, we have emphasised that a deep understanding of contemporary HRM is not possible without appreciating the nature of the capitalist employment relationship. We also underlined the interrelatedness of economics and HRM issues and argued that an HRM perspective on the changing organisation of work and employment which neglects change in macroeconomic variables lacks credibility. As stated in Chapter 1, critical approaches to both globalisation and HRM start by asking, *'Cui bono?'* 'Who benefits?'

In January 2018, Carillion, the UK's largest public works contractor, outsourcer of enormous government building contracts, went into administration. Contracts were frozen, more than 20,000 workers lost their jobs and the collapse left major building projects unfinished. The Carillion case study illustrates corporate malfeasance at the heart of contemporary British capitalism. In his eye-opening book *Bandit Capitalism* (2020), author Bob Wylie argues trenchantly that corporate dishonesty, incompetence and self-enrichment caused the collapse of Carillion. Further, Wylie lays bare the failures of British capitalism, in particular the absence of regulations, the imperative of the maximisation of shareholder value and the grotesque income inequality that transpired with it; and the shortcomings of the company's HRM. The company collapsed with only £29 million in the bank and debts and liabilities of over £6.9 billion. Carillion's collapse left 30,000 SMEs owed £2 billion. Under the Pensions Act 2004, company directors have legal obligations to ensure appropriate assets and funding are available

1 Martin Luther King's 'Dream' speech reimagined by Benjamin Zephaniah (28 August 2020). Available at: https://www.bbc.co.uk/sounds/play/p08px03s.

to meet their liabilities in providing for worker pensions. At the time of Carillion's collapse the deficit in the pension fund was a massive £2.6 billion. By the statutes of the 2004 Act Carillion's directors were accused of gross negligence and that they 'abrogated their responsibilities and failed their employees' (Wylie, 2020, p. 3).

Why did Carillion collapse? The co-chair of a House of Commons inquiry into the collapse of the company, Frank Field MP, summed up the behaviour of its directors as: 'It's greed on stilts, pure and simple' (cited by Wylie, 2020, p. 64). Between 2009 and 2015 Carillion distributed £554 million in dividends to its shareholders, while its income for the same period was just £594 million and bank debts grew from £242 million to £1.3 billion. While Carillion's debts increased by almost 300 per cent over the period, assets grew by 14 per cent. In the 2016 accounts, Carillion's chairman, Philip Green, stated: 'Given ... our customer-focused culture and integrated business model, we have a good platform from which to develop the business in 2017' (Wylie, 2020, p. 22). As part of the top 1 per cent in the UK, Carillion's directors lived in a parallel country to most of us. The directors paid themselves enormous salaries and bonuses. Over that period, Richard Adam, the company's former financial director, who left the company in December 2016, to 'spend more time with his family', received a 'golden goodbye' touching £2 million and three months later, at the earliest opportunity cashed in a first tranche of Carillion shares, making £534,000. In 2016, his last year at Carillion, Richard Howson, the former chief executive, received earnings of £1.5 million and over that period took £7.2m in salary and pensions.

In addition to self-enrichment, corporate incompetence caused Carillion's collapse. Illustrative examples include the Royal Liverpool Hospital which in 2017 had forecasted losses of £83 million and the Midlands Metropolitan Hospital with projected losses of £48 million. Major delays and serious structural defects in the building were discovered at the Royal Liverpool. The construction of the Aberdeen bypass road project suffered losses of £91 million. The bid price was too low, inadequately resourced and riven with problems management had not factored into the bid, such as avoiding oil company pipelines, peat deposits and water courses. Carillion had no experience of managing public-sector prisons. Unsurprisingly, therefore, the £200 million contract on prisons in England and Wales was losing £15 million a year. According to Wylie (2020, p. 20) the company resembled a sophisticated, corporate Ponzi scheme where the business could only continue by maintaining cash flow, whether or not the contracts would produce future profits and using the new income to service historic debt. The Ponzi scheme was made possible by deploying 'aggressive accounting', all legal, of course, but which made Carillion's business model unsustainable. Richard Adam, as Finance Director between 2007 and 2016, masterminded Carillion's aggressive accounting policies, which included inflating 'goodwill' intangibles in the balance sheet, taking out short-term loans to be paid back after accounts were published to make net debt look better, and counting profits from joint ventures as though they were Carillion's alone. In addition, insufficient payments were allotted to the worker pension fund. The pension deficit when Adam left the company was £990m. The chair of the Carillion pension fund trustees, Richard Ellison, told a Commons select committee that he believed that Adam viewed pension schemes as 'a waste of money'. Adam has strenuously denied making the statement. In 2017 consultants reported on Carillion's accounting practices which 'enhanced reported financial performance above underlying operating performance' (cited by Wylie, 2020, p. 77). That is accounting-speak for the accounts completely misrepresenting the way the business was presented to the marketplace.

Carillion was managed by oligarchs that rewarded the top elite above their abilities and competence. The reward system is a classic case of maximising shareholder value (MSV) and Carillion's directors were spectacularly rewarded for failure. As we noted in an early chapter, 'strategic' HRM offered, rhetorically at least, the possibility of senior HR professionals joining the top management decision-making team. However, the Carillion case study with regard to the influence of HR representation at board level is less than magnanimous. HR played a role of protecting executive bonuses despite calamitous deterioration of Carillion's finances. Carillion's reward policy was established at the AGM in 2014 and, due to time limits, it had to be renewed at the AGM in 2017. In 2016 Carillion's Remuneration Committee (RemCo), chaired by Alison Horner, Tesco's HR director, was tasked to evaluate the existing reward policy and make recommendations for change. The continued payment of substantial bonuses to directors is, Wylie elaborates, a quintessential example of 'largesse at the top of Carillion' and Horner's culpability for it (Wylie, 2020, p. 65). Indeed, RemCo's recommendation to investors was to support an increase in potential bonus payments to directors from 100 per cent of base salary to 150 per cent of base salary. The chair of RemCo suggested that this increase was intended 'to continue to provide competitive remuneration packages in order to attract and retain Executive Directors of the calibre required' (cited by Wylie, 2020, p. 65). In July 2017, when Carillion's senior managers had presided over a crisis write-down in profits, in hundreds of millions, the Remuneration Committee recommended increases in salary for the executive team as well as generous 'retention bonuses' to motivate them to stay with Carillion. As Wylie contends, rather than challenging the culture of self-entitlement, greed and 'largesse at the top', board members, including the company's top HR representatives, provided explanations to investors as to why salaries and the bonus bonanza were totally justified. Bob Wylie's book exposed any notion that the egregious behaviour of Carillion's directors was a result of 'one or two bad apples', but rather it was about the whole barrel or system.

The collapse of Carillion is more than the demise of a company; it is about the development of British corporate capitalism over the last four decades, it is about government deregulation of business and, notwithstanding the positive aspects of the developmental variant of HRM, the story illustrates, for practical purposes, how the economic and cultural-political context drives corporate behaviour and differences in approaches to employment relations. If Carillion is cited as an exemplar of the state Anglo-American HRM is in, then the answer to the question obviously has to go beyond Carillion. The deeper structural economic forces that drive corporate changes are different from the cultural and political factors that determine, or at least shape, corporate behaviour. The rise of neoliberalism had significance for how Carillion was managed. Important changes in the economic environment include the deregulation of the banks, the rise of financial capitalism and the shift from stakeholder to shareholder capitalism. These variables are interconnected, and the outcome is to recalibrate an existing form of capitalism to a more laissez-faire, free-market model, with corporation behemoths more able to take a short-term approach, reinforced by legal arrangements that favour shareholder capitalism. The hegemony of shareholder capitalism in corporate America and Britain can be explained by the development of the doctrine of maximisation of shareholder value (see Chapter 8). As Wylie (2020, p. 164) observes, Carillion directors' obsession with dividends and the 'largesse at the top' 'cannot be understood without first examining MSV'. Moreover, Carillion's directors could pursue MSV because the cultural-political institutions, notably governments and trade unions, offered no substantial countervailing force to challenge the power of the corporate class.

A reimagined HRM – reformed practices and research priorities – has six core elements, none of which are 'silver bullets' to improving performance or the well-being of workers and stopping the degradation of the natural habitat and the planet, but each contribute to a realignment which has enormous implications for managing work and people, from changes in management sensibilities to changes in the direction of how work and jobs are designed to reforms of human rights and the creation of a more equal society. It would be arrogant to suggest I can offer grand employment-related solutions to the acute problems that HRM has caused in Britain. So, my purpose here, though, is not to detail HRM and employment policies, but simply to provide a broad policy framework that will help change attitudes towards the management of work and people. The idea for reimagining HRM draws from the academic work of Henderson (2020), Wylie's critique of Carillion and the Fair Work Framework developed by academics at the Centre for Employment Research, University of Strathclyde, Glasgow, after consulting with a wide range of organisations including unions. The context of the Fair

Work Framework is the worldview of the Scottish Government that the Scottish economy needs to be more efficient and productive in order to generate more employment and the public tax revenues to fund its social programme (Gall, 2016). The stated vision of the Fair Work Framework (FWF) is that:

> By 2025, people in Scotland will have a world-leading working life where fair work drives success, wellbeing and prosperity for individuals, businesses, organisations and society. (FWF, 2016, p. 5)

Fair work is defined as that which offers effective voice, opportunity, security, fulfilment and respect; that balances the rights and responsibilities of employers and workers and that can generate benefits for individuals, organisations and society. *Effective voice* is defined as a safe workplace where dialogue and challenge are dealt with constructively and where workers' views are sought out, listened to and can make a difference. In unionised workplaces, collective bargaining can provide the context for effective voice. *Opportunity* allows people equal access to work and to progress in employment and is a crucial dimension of fair work. Fair opportunity can be supported in a variety of different ways: through robust recruitment and selection procedures; paid internship arrangements equally open to all; and training and development to support access to work for all. *Security* at work can be achieved by building stability into contractual arrangements and by having collective bargaining arrangements for pay and conditions of employment. *Fulfilling* work involves workers having some control over their work and using and developing their skills. Fulfilment can be supported through work and job design that focuses on skills use, autonomy and empowerment. Finally, *respect* involves recognising others as dignified human beings and recognising their standing and personal worth. At its most basic, respect involves ensuring the health, safety and well-being of others. Respect can be supported through HR policies and practices on dignity *in* and *at* work; through health, safety and well-being policies and practices and established procedural arrangements negotiated with unions. The FWF emphasise the importance of benchmarking policy, practice, behaviours and outcomes against the set goals.

The intellectual roots of the FWF are found in Douglas McGregor's *The Human Side of Enterprise* (1960), and in two UK studies *Reports on Trade Unions and Employers' Association* (Donovan, 1968) and the *Report of the Committee of Inquiry on Industrial Democracy* (Bullock, 1977). The Reports were very much a product of the times, in that both advocated a culture of workplace collectivism rather than atomisation, and more recent literature on high-performance systems (HPWS). The FWF, as conceived, is a pluralistic, multi-stakeholder approach to work and employment. That is, fair work is delivered by employers and workers and, where present, union representatives, and interests extend beyond maximising shareholder value (MSV). Its weakness, as Gall (2016) points out, is the absence of statutory underpinning to achieve its aspirations. Although it promotes 'progressive' job design principles and some elements of social justice and social equality, 'it does not seek to redistribute wealth or use the state to act to change market outcomes by way of public ownership, regulation and intervention' (Gall, 2016, pp. 1–2). The authors of the FWF acknowledge that it is only the first step of a long journey toward fairer work. The FWF is described as a 'voluntary commitment by companies to adopt fair and progressive HR practices'. To the degree that there is an evidence-based case that the five dimensions of fair work improve individual and organisational performance, there is a case for addressing inequality, industrial democracy and climate change through government regulation and intervention in the economy. Therefore, the argument here is that the FWF is necessary but insufficient to reimagine HRM.

A reimagined HRM model has an additional six key elements, which, potentially, combined with the five dimensions of the FWF have significant synergies. First, the 'shareholder' capitalist model needs to be challenged and replaced. After four decades of neoliberalism and the recognition that the maximisation of shareholder value model is deleterious to the living standards of the many, a new model is needed that restores the social contract between capital and labour. The element of a reimagined HRM means that the scope of HRM research needs to go beyond workplace level analysis. To investigate the well-being of workers, researchers have to engage in intersectional thinking and analysis. This approach suggests that HRM cannot be understood without explaining the cultural-political dynamics by which strategic considerations and HR practices first come into being.

Second, a reimagined HRM has to reinforce effective voice and workers' power. Trade unions are a source of effective voice and worker empowerment. Employment legislation is needed to establish a statutory right for trade unions to have access to, and assembly at, the workplace. Across OECD economies, workers are defaulted to being non-union in employment relationships. Harcourt et al. (2019) argue that a union default would likely strengthen the extent and effectiveness of workplace union representation. Changing the social-political culture is a crucial route to improving employment and trade union rights practice so that employment and trade union law is understood to be just as powerful as that on the freedom of information etc. (Ewart, 2020). Trade union representation in the workplace, the rebuilding of collective bargaining structures across sectors, and the involvement of trade unions in pay bargaining and organisational decision-making will, as is evidenced in coordinated market economies (CMEs), help reduce short-termism associated with the MSV model of capitalism and improve investment in human skills and low-carbon technology.

Third, a reimagined HRM needs to address the huge gap between the top and bottom levels of firms. Reward systems are central to strategic HRM. As documented in previous chapters, pay for most workers is increasingly based on output or results. Top managerial pay, however, is increasingly based on share value, which, as the collapse of Carillion demonstrates, sometimes incentivises risk taking (Richbell and Wood, 2019). In the 2000s, in both the US and the UK, a disproportionate rise in pay for top executives has been matched by the rise in the doctrine of maximising shareholder value (MSV). The huge gulf in 'tournament-like' pay is a cornerstone of economic and social inequality. In Britain, the ratio between the typical FTSE 100 chief executive pay and that of an average full time worker was 48:1 in 1998, and by 2020 it had risen to 120:1 (High Pay Centre, 2021). This means that the average FTSE 100 CEO's earnings for 2021 has surpassed the average annual wage for a full-time worker in the UK at around 5:30 pm on 6 January. In Canada, the ratio between the highest-paid CEOs and the average worker was 202:1 in 2019. The British TUC argues that pay ratios between the CEO and the average worker's pay should aim to be no more than 20:1, and to avoid 'largesse at the top' a maximum of 10 per cent of CEO remuneration should be paid in incentives. Related, the Carillion collapse is testimony to the lack of accountability and objectivity in the pay system covering top executives in British companies and organisations. Adding share options on to CEO accounts in the form of Long-Term Incentive Plans (LTIPs), for example, was prohibited in the Republic of Ireland in the aftermath of the Irish banking crisis (Wylie, 2020). During the pandemic Western governments introduced wage subsidies to companies, yet CEOs still received their annual bonuses. The Canadian Centre for Policy Alternatives has recommended that the federal government should follow the Netherlands and Spain and explicitly prohibit bonuses and dividends being paid to chief executives if their companies receive wage subsidies (Marowits, 2021, p. B3). A reimagined HRM will provide a policy, underpinned by employment law legally guaranteeing worker or union representation on the Remuneration Committee for companies and organisations with more than 250 workers. A reformed organisational governance structure will restrict the primacy of shareholders, act as a brake on the more egregious demands for CEO rewards and be a source of information for the entire workforce. Democracy in large organisations would be enhanced if executive pay proposals were put to a binding vote for the entire company and organisation workforce (Sikka et al., 2018).

Fourth, a reimagined HRM has to bolster the security at work dimension through a new approach to reward management for those at the bottom end of the pay scale. Earlier chapters have traced the change from negotiated rates for a job to an emphasis on payment for performance. Since the early 1980s, in the UK and the US, there has been a decline or stagnation in real pay for workers at the bottom end of the pay scale. In step with these changes has been an ongoing and cumulatively dramatic contraction of unionisation and collective bargaining, particularly in the private sector. Mainstream analysis of the strategic reward paradigm has focused little on the relationship between pay options and power. A fundamental workplace right which we all should enjoy equally, is the right to an adequate standard of living and the right to the highest attainable standard of physical and mental health (Ewart, 2020). The Covid-19 virus that thrived on inequality revealed the fragility of civilisations built on social injustices, short-term policies and a dangerous disregard for the environment (Anonymous, 2021). Covid-19 demonstrates the interconnectivity of society: that a supermarket checkout worker is connected not only to a shopper but also to the shopper's family, their co-workers and friends. Moreover, the coronavirus exposed how social inequality and income insecurity is entwined with public health. Britain's low level of statutory sick pay (SSP) is one reason why its test-and-trace system is dysfunctional because many low-pay and temporary workers who do receive the payment cannot afford to take time off when they are required to self-isolate (see TUC, 2020f). The CIPD and TUC have called for eligibility of SSP to be widened by removing the lower earnings limit and the rate to be raised closer to the equivalent of someone earning the national living wage (Owen, 2020). Therefore, to fulfil the security goal, a reimagined HRM will address issues of low wages, sick pay and precariousness which are endemic in Britain.

The pandemic has graphically exposed social inequalities and injustices across our society. Low-paid workers, the so-called 'precariat' and public-facing workers, many classified as 'essential', have experienced economic hardship, ill-health and higher mortality rates. As the British economy adjusts to the convulsions of the pandemic and Brexit, early indications are the Conservative government is favouring a deregulated approach to securing competitive advantage through low wages and fewer employment rights – the so-called 'race to the bottom' (Miliband, 2021). Under plans drawn up by the Conservative government, the post-Brexit UK labour markets will be reformed by weakening worker protections enshrined in EU law. The package of deregulatory measures is reported to include renouncing the EU Working Time Directive which stipulates a maximum 48-hour working week and guarantees the statutory right to rest breaks at work, which is vital for key workers, such as those in front-line health care, airlines and haulage, and not including overtime pay when calculating some holiday pay entitlements. A change in the calculation of holiday pay could be 'a significant monetary loss' for a low-paid worker often forced into overtime to increase their earnings (Foster et al., 2021). The move will potentially mark a clear divergence from EU labour market standards, but the UK will only face retaliation from Brussels under the terms of its new post-Brexit trade treaty if the EU can demonstrate the changes had a material impact on competition. Labour market deregulation will benefit a small number of employers at immense cost to workers. Though deregulation does not have a simple predictable effect on employer behaviour (Rubery and Johnson, 2019), regulations designed to reduce wage costs as a comparative competitive strategy accelerate the trend of precarity. Reimagining HRM will take a long-term approach, underpinned by statutory rights, and prohibit precarious, zero-hours contracts, the practice of 'fire and rehire' and enforce the payment of the National Minimum Wage. The challenges of organising precarious workers in the largely non-union private service economy, where bilateral agreements are not established, means there is a strong case for giving legal protections by reintroducing former wage councils to enforce the payment of the National Minimum Wage and to regulate hours of paid work (Gall, 2020).

Fifth, a reimagined HRM has to tackle the insecurity of workers' pensions. When Carillion collapsed, employees lost 10 per cent of their pension entitlement and the Pension Protection Fund, and taxpayers were left with a £2.6 billion liability. Carillion directors arguably privatised profits and socialised the company pensions. The Carillion Inquiry exposed the ineffectiveness of the Pension Regulator. An amendment to the Pension Act has been proposed that will help avoid the pension debacle at Carillion. If a company has a deficit on employee pensions it cannot pay into directors' pensions until a recovery plan has been agreed (Wylie, 2020, p. 252). The FWF, reform of corporate governance and rewards management offer potentially promising pathways forward to reimagining HRM but tackling insecurity and inequality can only be addressed through political action and by strengthening employment protection laws so, as a discipline, the scope of analytical HRM needs to give consideration to issues which are often neglected in mainstream HRM literature, including the role of the state in shaping employment relations, trade unions and collective bargaining, and employee and trade union participation in organisational decision-making.

Sixth, promoting and scaffolding pro-environment organisational behaviours form a key plank in a reimagined HRM. Environmentalists have long argued that climate stabilisation and decarbonising the workplace must be the cornerstone of political and organisational leaders' agency. Indeed, with regard to governments, climate change is a priority for newly elected President Biden and his administration, beginning with cancelling support for the Canada-US Keystone XL oil pipeline, the US re-joining the Paris Accord and actively supporting the climate world summit scheduled for 2021 in Glasgow, Scotland (Lynch and Deegan, 2021). Companies and organisations are both part of the problem, as well as part of the solution to the climate crisis (cf. Robertson and Barling, 2015). Organisations need to pivot toward a multi-stakeholder model including sustainable pro-environmental performance (Stahl et al., 2020). It is within this context that a reimagined HRM should play a pro-active role in creating more environmentally sustainable workplaces. The concept of environmental sustainability integrates environmental considerations (e.g. carbon emissions) with organisational needs (e.g. profitability) and worker needs (e.g. health and well-being) in such a way as to promote benefits for the environment. The CIPD considers sustainable HRM central to promoting pro-environmental behaviours that will act to de-carbonise the workplace (Houghton, 2019).

Mainstream political discourse tends to view the state as a benign force (Heyes and Nolan, 2010). This is reflected in academic HRM which tends to give too little credence to the capitalist state and fails to problematise the nature of the state's relationship to corporate business and the environment. Yet too much focus on economic freedom leads to the destruction of the social and natural world. One important lesson to learn from the pandemic is, do not count on the efficiency of the markets (Rubin, 2020). Real problems of public health, social inequality and global warming require more robust solutions than markets are likely to provide. Active government intervention is required. As Henderson (2020, p. 29) observes, 'we will only be able to tackle problems like climate change and inequality with state help – and this will require rebuilding our institutions and bringing markets and governments back in balance.' A reimagined HRM is part of a reformed business model and political culture.

A reimaged HRM will need to consider the effects of financialised modes of profit-making on work and employment relations, as well as HRM theories and practices. In previous chapters, while we have drawn attention to the financialisation of the economy, as others have pointed out, workplace scholars need to better understand how financialised mechanisms operate in non-financial organisations and how these dynamics are translated into outcomes for workers and the consequences for HRM modelling (Cushen and Thompson, 2016). In this chapter we have offered a critique of the economic and social dynamics that drive management and an outline of work, employment and HRM reforms that are necessary to address current failures. It is understood that a greater effect will be achieved by the sum of the public policies and HR practices rather than just focusing on individual actions. Perhaps the most important lesson of this book is just how difficult it is to separate HRM from the wider political-cultural and economic context, and it may be that such an exercise is theoretically unwarranted because it does not make sense to suggest that HRM operates without regard to corporate strategy or outside a context. Under capitalism, cyclical and structural change and conflict means that employment relations can never be in symmetry. Managing the competing forces of neoliberal economics and social justice is a central challenge facing social democratic politicians. And as a microcosm of this social-economic dynamic, managing change and the contradictions and tensions within employment relations is a central challenge facing HRM. As John Storey (2007, p. 17), pronounced, the position of HRM in contemporary organisations is 'no panacea; no set of employment policies ever will be'.

Transforming HRM and employment relations proposed in these pages will not be easy or rapid. Neither will the changes really challenge structures of power and social injustice in society. But the reforms outlined are significant, at least for me, because they start to address the inequalities at the heart of HRM. At the time of writing, not surprisingly, the eyes of the world have been captivated by the shocking physical violence of the US presidential transition and President Joe Biden's agenda to tackle multiple crises – Covid-19, unemployment, climate change, racism – in which the country finds itself (Morrow, 2021). In considering the task of transforming HRM, the words of US President Abraham Lincoln, delivered 160 years ago, are pertinent: 'Capital is only the fruit of labour, and could never have existed if labour had not first existed. Labour is the superior of capital, and deserves much the higher consideration' (Lincoln, 1861, cited by Graeber, 2018, p. 230). Although Lincoln's address to Congress seems extreme to a contemporary ear, the words are a reflection of the 'common sense' view of the time – the labour theory of value. That labour created all wealth was embraced by the Scottish philosopher Adam Smith (1776), the founder of economic science, and later developed in Marx's *Capital* (1867). Hopefully, a reimagined HRM will give workers the higher consideration they deserve and create the conditions for unfamiliar rights in contemporary society – the right to fairer work, the right to secure high-paid work, the right of workers and unions to have an effective voice and participate in decision-making, and the right to expect organisations to protect nature and the planet.

A final word

I would like to end this book with a few thoughts about reflective learning and leadership. There is perhaps a tradition in Britain of anti-intellectualism and that may affect our insouciance towards our study of work and management. Reflectivity may help to avoid indifference. Reflection, or to use an ancient Irish word, 'Machnamh' which encompasses reflection, contemplation, meditation and thought (Higgins, 2021), is like using a mirror to help us to look back on our actions and thought processes. Reflective learning occurs where we have experiences and then step back from them to evaluate the learning we have experienced. There are several ways of carrying out reflection. One approach is to look at the additional reading listed at the end of each chapter in this book. Other sources of information, particularly material that tends to differ from the approach in this book, provide mirrors for us and allow us to look at topics from another perspective. Further, other people – friends, relatives and co-workers – provide mirrors for us, allowing us to understand work and people management from another perspective. Talk to other people about the topics covered in *HRM: A Critical Approach*. Your own experience of the workplace is also excellent material for reflection and can provide insight into HRM. To help you start the reflection process, go back to the beginning of each chapter and consider whether you have personally achieved the major learning objectives.

In previous editions, we have avoided proposing concrete policy recommendations, instead we have focused on the critique of both theory and practice of HRM. The main point of this chapter is to start us thinking and arguing about better ways of managing work and people that bring dignity and security to paid work and to mitigate the gross inequalities that exist in workplaces. In *Reimagining Capitalism*, which inspired the title for this chapter, Rebecca Henderson reminds us that it's easy to fall into the trap of thinking only charismatic leaders can change the world. Effective leaders learn to ride the wave of change they find surrounding them. Nelson Mandela, for example, did not singlehandedly end apartheid in South Africa. He rode the wave of change in which tens of thousands of people engaged in direct action and thousands died. Greta Thunberg was a fifteen-year-old school student when she began protesting outside the Swedish Parliament that governments were not doing enough to deal with the climate crisis. In September 2019 an estimated 1.6 million students from 125 countries came out of school to join a global climate strike. You can make a difference to how companies and organisations manage work, people and the planet's finite resources. The metaphor of the single pebble moving down a mountain that causes an avalanche and picks up mass and momentum, is used by writers to illustrate the importance of social change starting by a single individual. Your actions can make a difference and cause transformative change. The message is don't wait for others, take action now. Reduce your carbon footprint, drive less, try to buy from firms that treat their employees with dignity and are committed to confronting the realities of climate change. You do not have to be in a formal leadership position to drive change. You can help to reduce carbon emissions by avoiding waste, changing lightbulbs, building local supply chains. Spread the word through social media platforms: your actions will help encourage others to adopt pro-environmental behaviour. A seemingly trivial change when implemented across the organisation is analogous to a pebble that starts an avalanche. As Henderson opines, 'You don't need to transform the structure of the modern corporation single-handedly to make a difference. If you can make even a small part of a single firm a better place to work, you will change lives' (2020, p. 264). Finally, I hope our journey with you has proved worthwhile, and that you remain positive yet sceptical rather than negative and cynical, after all if Marty McFly had been the latter he would never have got back to the future.

John Bratton
Edinburgh
November 2021

Further reading

Eaton, A. and Heckscher, C. (2021) COVID's impacts on the field of labour and employment relations. *Journal of Management Studies*, *58*(1): 275–9.

Fair Work Convention (2016) *Fair Work Framework*. London. Available at: https://www.fairworkconvention.scot/.

Gall, G. (2016) *The Fair Work Framework: A Critique*. Glasgow: The Jimmy Reid Foundation.

Goodhart, D. (2020) *Head Hand Heart: The Struggle for Dignity and Status in the 21st-century*. London: Allen Lane.

Hadjisolomou, A. (2021) Profit over people? Evaluating morality on the front line during the covid-19 crisis: a front-line service manager's confession and regrets. *Work, Employment and Society*, *35*(2): 396–405.

Henderson, R. (2020) *Reimagining Capitalism*. London: Penguin.

Mazzucato, M. (2021) *Mission Economy: A Moonshot Guide to Changing Capitalism*. London: Allen Lane.

Rubin, J. (2020) *The Expendables*. London: Scribe.

Wylie, B. (2020) *Bandit Capitalism*. Edinburgh: Birlinn.

GLOSSARY

Diversity: Refers to the total composition of the employee workforce and the amount of equality of opportunity and employment without any bias because of employees' gender, race, ethnicity or sexual orientation.

Equal opportunities: Aims to achieve equality of opportunity regardless of gender, race, ethnicity, sexual orientation, disability, age or any other social categorisation.

Financialisation: A term used to describe the role and pre-eminence of financial markets, financial institutions, financial actors and financial logics over real production activities, product markets, labour and daily life.

HR analytics: Data collected by HR systems that enables professionals to gain insights into their workforce and HR policies and practices.

Leadership development: A process of learning for leaders and managers through recognised opportunities.

Learning & development: A process that facilitates the acquisition of knowledge, skills and attitudes that enables and results in learning at and through work.

Learning organisation: Refers to collective or organisational-wide learning that results from individual, communities of practice or group learning.

Learning: A relatively permanent change of behaviour or human capabilities resulting from processing new knowledge, practice or experience.

Performance appraisal: Aims to provide adequate feedback to each worker on their performance, modify or change work behaviour, and provide data to judge future assignments, training or reward.

Performance management: An integrated series of reciprocal interactions and conversations about setting goals and performance appraisal, as well as learning, development and reward decisions.

Precarity: A life lived without predictability, and thus without security.

SWOT analysis: A study undertaken by an organisation to identify its internal strengths and weaknesses, as well as its external opportunities and threats.

Tacit knowledge: The ability to deal with different situations, known and unknown, often responding spontaneously to surprise through improvisation and without thought.

Workplace learning: A metaphor for capturing formal, nonformal, self-directed, collective and even tacit informal learning activities in the workplace.

REFERENCES

Acikgoz, Y. and Bergman, S. M. (2016) Social media and employee recruitment: chasing the run away bandwagon. In R. Landers and G. Schmidt (eds) *Social Media in Employee Selection and Recruitment* (pp. 175–95). Cham: Springer.

Acker, J. (2016) Inequality regimes: gender, class, and race in organizations. *Gender & Society*, *20*(4): 441–64.

Ackers, P. (2007) Collective bargaining as industrial democracy: Hugh Clegg and the political foundations of British industrial relations pluralism. *British Journal of Industrial Relations*, *45*(1): 77–101.

Ackers, P. and Wilkinson, A. (2005) British industrial relations paradigm: a critical outline history and prognosis. *Journal of Industrial Relations*, *47*(4): 443–56.

Ackroyd, S. and Thompson, P. (1999) *Organizational Misbehaviour*. Thousand Oaks, CA: Sage.

Adams, J. S. (1965) Inequality in social exchange. In L. Berkowitz (ed.) *Advances in Experimental Social Psychology* (pp. 267–99). New York: Academic Press.

Adams, J. S. and Freedman, S. (1976) Equity theory revisited: comments and annotated bibliography. *Advances in Experimental Social Psychology*, *9*: 43–90. Academic Press.

Adams, R. J. (2006) *Labour Left Out*. Ottawa: Canadian Centre for Policy Alternatives.

Addison, J., Siebert, W., Wagner, J. and Wei, X. (2000) Worker participation and firm performance. *British Journal of Industrial Relations*, *38*(1): 7–48.

Adler, N. J. (1994) Competitive frontiers: women managing across borders. In N. J. Adler and D. N. Izraeli (eds) *Competitive Frontiers: Women Managers in a Global Economy* (pp. 22–40). Oxford: Blackwell.

Advisory, Conciliation and Arbitration Service (ACAS) (2020) Zero-hours contracts. ACAS. Available at: https://www.acas.org.uk/zero-hours-contracts. Accessed 7 October 2020.

Afsar, B., Shahjehan, A. and Shah, I. (2018) Leadership and employee pro-environmental behaviours. In *Research Handbook on Employee Pro-Environmental Behaviour* (pp. 185–209). Cheltenham, UK: Edward Elgar.

Agarwal, P. (2018) Here is how bias can affect recruitment in your organization. *Forbes*, 19 October online. Available at: https://www.forbes.com/sites/pragyaagarwaleurope/2018/10/19/how-can-bias-during-interviews-affect-recruitment-in-your-organization/#5b7219ef1951. Accessed 12 August 2020.

Agashae, Z. and Bratton, J. (2001) Leader–follower dynamics: developing a learning organization. *Journal of Workplace Learning*, *13*(3): 89–102.

Aguinis, H. (2009) *Performance Management* (2nd edn). Upper Saddle River, NJ: Pearson Prentice-Hall.

Aguinis, H., Joo, H. and Gottfredson, R. K. (2013) What monetary rewards can and cannot do: how to show employees the money. *Business Horizons*, *56*(2): 241–9.

Agyeman, J., Bullard, R. D. and Evans, B. (2002) Exploring the nexus: bringing together sustainability, environmental justice and equity. *Space and Polity*, *6*(1): 77–90.

Agyeman, J., Schlosberg, D., Craven, L. and Matthews, C. (2016) Trends and directions in environmental justice: from inequity to everyday life, community, and just sustainabilities. *Annual Review of Environment and Resources*, *41*, 321–40.

Ahlvik, C. and Björkman, I. (2015) Towards explaining subsidiary implementation, integration, and internalization of MNC headquarters HRM practices. *International Business Review*, *24*(3): 497–505.

Ahmad, S. and Schroeder, R. G. (2003) The impact of human resource management practices on operational performance: recognizing country and industry differences. *Journal of Operations Management*, *21*(1): 19–43.

Ahmad, R. and Scott, N. (2019) Technology innovations towards reducing hospitality human resource costs in Langkawi, Malaysia, *Tourism Review*, *74*(3): 547–62.

Ahmed, S., Tahir, H. and Warsi, S. W. (2015) E-Recruitment transforming the dimensions of online job seeking: a case of Pakistan. *International Journal of Human Resource Studies*, *5*(1): 96.

Akerjordet, K. and Severinsson, E. (2009) Emotional intelligence, Part 1: the development of scales and psychometric testing. *Nursing and Health Sciences*, *11*: 58–63.

Al-Sharif, R., Searle, R. and Nienaber, A. M. (2019) The impact of stereotype threat on organisational justice and trust: recruitment and selection of Muslims in the UK banking sector. Enlighten.

Alagaraja, M. and Wang, G. (2012) Development of a national HRD strategy model. *Human Resource Development Review*, *11*(4): 407–29.

Albizu, E. and Olazaran, M. (2006) BPR implementation in Europe: the adaptation of a management concept. *New Technology, Work and Employment*, *21*(1): 43–58.

Aldred, J. (2020) This pandemic has exposed the uselessness of orthodox economics. *The Guardian*, 5 July. Available at: https://www.theguardian.com/commentisfree/2020/jul/05/pandemic-orthodox-economics-covid-19. Accessed 21 July 2020.

Alis, D., Karsten, L. and Leopold, J. (2006) From gods to goddesses. *Time and Society*, *15*(1): 81–104.

Allas, T., Canal, M. and Hunt, V. (2020) COVID-19 in the United Kingdom: Assessing jobs at risk and the impact on people and places. McKinsey & Company, 11 May. Available at: https://www.mckinsey.com/industries/public-sector/our-insights/covid-19-in-the-united-kingdom-assessing-jobs-at-risk-and-the-impact-on-people-and-places. Accessed 16 June 2020.

Allen, D., Biggane, J. E., Pittis, M., Otondo, R. and Van Scotter, J. (2013) Reactions to recruitment web sites: visual and verbal attention, attraction, and intentions to pursue employment. *Journal of Business Psychology*, *28*(3): 263–85.

Almeida, S., Fernando, M., Hannif, Z. and Dharmage, S. C. (2015) Fitting the mould: the role of employer perceptions in immigrant recruitment decision-making. *International Journal of Human Resource Management*, *26*(22): 2811–32.

Alvesson, M. (2018) Critical perspectives on strategic HRM. In J. Storey, P. Wright and D. Ulrich (eds) *The Routledge Companion to Strategic Human Resource Management* (pp. 52–67). London: Routledge.

Alvesson, M. and Sveningsson, S. (2016) *Changing Organizational Culture: Cultural Change Work in Progress*. London: Routledge.

Alvesson, M., Bridgman, T. and Willmott, H. (eds) (2009) *The Oxford Handbook of Critical Management Studies*. Oxford: Oxford University Press.

Amadeo, K. (2020) 2008 Financial crisis causes, costs, and whether it could happen again, The Balance. Available at: https://www.thebalance.com/2008-financial-crisis-3305679. Accessed 9 December 2020.

Amadxarif, Z., Angeli, M., Haldane, A. G. and Zemaityte, G. (2020) Understanding pay gaps, Bank of England Staff Working Paper No. 877. *Bank of England*, July. Available at: https://www.bankofengland.co.uk/-/media/boe/files/working-paper/2020/understanding-pay-gaps.pdf. Accessed 15 October 2020.

Ambrose, J. (2021) Thousands of British Gas customers threaten to switch over 'fire and rehire' policy. *The Guardian*, 1 April. Available at: https://www.theguardian.com/business/2021/apr/01/thousands-british-gas-customers-switch-fire-rehire-plan. Accessed 9 May 2021.

Anand, N. and Daft, R. L. (2007). What is the right organization design? *Organizational Dynamics*, 36 (4):329–44.

Anderson, B. A. (2005) Expatriate selection: good management or good luck? *International Journal of Human Resource Management*, *16*(4): 567–83.

Anderson, C., Keltner, D. and John, O. P. (2003) Emotional convergence between people over time. *Journal of Personality and Social Psychology*, *84*: 1054–68.

Anderson, N., Lievens, F., Van Dam, K. and Ryan, A. M. (2004) Future perspectives on employee selection: key directions for future research and practice. *Applied Psychology*, *53*(4): 487–501.

Anderson, V. (2007) *The Value of Learning: A New Model of Value and Evaluation*. London: Chartered Institute of Personnel and Development.

Andolšek, D. M. and Štebe, J. (2005) Devolution or (de)centralization of HRM function in European organizations. *International Journal of Human Resource Management*, *16*(3): 311–29.

Angrave, D., Charlwood, A., Kirkpatrick, I., Lawrence, M. and Stuart, M. (2016) HR and analytics: why HR is set to fail the big data challenge. *Human Resource Management Journal*, *26*(1): 1–11. Available at: https://doi.org/10.1111/1748-8583.12090. Accessed 7 May 2021.

Anonymous (2021) Editorial: Health as a foundation for society, *The Lancet*, 2 January, 397 (10268): 1. Available at: https://www.thelancet.com/journals/lancet/article/PIIS0140-6736(20)32751-3/fulltext. Accessed 14 January 2021.

Anseel, F. and Lievens, F. (2009) The mediating role of feedback acceptance in the relationship between feedback and attitudinal and performance outcomes. *International Journal of Selection and Assessment*, *17*(4): 362–75.

Antai, I. (2011) A theory of the competing supply chain: alternatives for development. *International Business Review*, *4*: 74–85.

Antonacopoulou, E. (2010) Making the business school more 'critical': reflexive critique based on phronesis as a foundation for impact. *British Journal of Management*, *21*: S6–S25.

Antonacopoulou, E. P. (1999) Training does not imply learning: the individual perspective. *International Journal of Training and Development*, *3*(1): 14–23.

Antoni, C. H., et al. (2017) Reward management: linking employee motivation and organisational performance. *Journal of Personnel Psychology*, *16*: 57–60.

Antonioli, D. and Mazzanti, M. (2017) Towards a green economy through innovations: the role of trade union involvement. *Ecological Economics*, *131*: 286–99.

Apedoe-Dzidza, D. Y., Haligah, R. D. and Mensah, D. K. D. (2008) Human resource planning in organisations. *Journal of Business & Retail Management Research*, *2*(2): 64–72.

Apouey, B. and Stabile, M. (2020) The effects of Uber diffusion on mental heath in the UK. INSEAD Working Paper No. 2020/12/EPS.

Appelbaum, E., Bailey, T., Berg, P. and Kalleberg, A. (2000) *Manufacturing Advantage: Why High-Performance Systems Pay Off*. Ithaca, NY: ILR Press.

Aries, E. (1996) *Men and Women in Interaction: Reconsidering the Differences*. New York: Oxford University Press.

Armstrong, M. (2012) *Armstrong's Handbook of Management and Leadership: Developing Effective People Skills for Better Leadership and Management*. Kogan Page Publishers.

Armstrong, M. and Brown, D. (2019) Strategic Human Resource Management: back to the future. Available at: www.employment-studies.co.uk/system/files/resources/files/517_Strategic-Human-Resource-Management-Back-to-the-future-IES-CIPD-2019.pdf. Accessed 7 August 2020.

Armstrong, M. and Murlis, H. (2007) *Reward Management* (5th edn). London: Kogan Page.

Armstrong, M. and Taylor, S. (2014) *Armstrong's Handbook of Human Resource Management Practice* (13th edn). London: Kogan Page.

Armstrong, S. J., Cools, E. and Sadler-Smith, E. (2012) Role of cognitive styles in business and management: reviewing 40 years of research. *International Journal of Management Reviews*, *14*: 238–62.

Arnett, D. and Wittman, M. (2014) Improving marketing success: the role of tacit knowledge exchange between sales and marketing. *Journal of Business Research*, *67*: 324–31.

Arnold, J. (2017) How to calculate the total cost of your workforce, *HR Magazine*, 23 May.

Arthur, J. (1994) Effects of human resources systems on manufacturing performance and turnover. *Academy of Management Journal*, *37*: 670–87.

Arvey, R. D. and Campion, J. E. (1982) The employment interview: a summary and review of recent research. *Personnel Psychology*, *35*: 281–322.

Ash, T. G. (2021) Far from a done deal, Brexit will consume the UK and the EU for years to come. *The Globe and Mail*, 16 January, p. O2.

Ashcroft, K. and Allen, B. (2003) The radical foundation of organizational communication. *Communication Theory*, *13*, pp. 5–38.

Ashford, S. J., Blatt, R. and VandeWalle, D. (2003) Reflections on the looking glass: a review of research on feedback-seeking behavior in organizations. *Journal of Management*, *29*(6): 773–99.

Ashikali, T. and Groeneveld, S. (2015) Diversity management in public organizations and its effect on employees' affective commitment: the role of transformational leadership and the inclusiveness of the organizational culture. *Review of Public Personnel Administration*, *35*(2): 146–68.

Ashley, L., Duberley, J., Sommerlad, H. and Scholarios, D. (2015) *A Qualitative Evaluation of Non-educational Barriers to the Elite Professions*. London: Social Mobility and Child Poverty Commission.

Astor, M. (2017) Microchip implants for employees? One company says yes. *The New York Times*, 25 July. Available at: https://www.nytimes.com/2017/07/25/technology/microchips-wisconsin-company-employees.html. Accessed 4 October 2020.

Atkinson, J. S. and Meager, N. (1985) Introduction and summary of main findings. In *Changing Work Patterns* (pp. 2–11). London: National Economic Development Office.

Aust, I., Matthews, B. and Müller-Camen, M. (2020) Common Good HRM: a paradigm shift in Sustainable HRM? *Human Resource Management Review*, *30*(3): 100705.

Australian Tax Office (ATO) (2020) JobKeeper Payment. Australian Tax Office. Available at: https://www.ato.gov.au/general/jobkeeper-payment. Accessed 12 August 2020.

Aylott, E. (2018) *Employee Relations: A Practical Introduction*. London: Kogan Page

Azasu, S. (2009) Reward and performance of Swedish real estate firms. *Compensation & Benefits Review*, *41*(4): 19–28.

Bacon, N. and Hoque, K. (2005) HRM in the SME sector: valuable employees and coercive networks. *International Journal of Human Resource Management*, *16*(11): 1976–99. DOI: 10.1080/09585190500314706

Bacon, N. and Storey, J. (2000) New employee relations strategies in Britain: towards individualism or partnership? *British Journal of Industrial Relations*, *38*(3): 407–27.

Badri, A., Boudreau-Trudel, B. and. and Souissi, A. (2018) Occupational health and safety in the Industry 4.0 era: a cause for major concern? *Safety Science*, *109*: 403–11.

Bagilhole, B. (2009) *Understanding Equal Opportunities and Diversity: The Social Differentiations and Intersections of Inequality*. London: Policy Press.

Bailey, C., Mankin, D., Kelliher, C. and Garavan, T. (2018) *Strategic Human Resource Management*. Oxford: Oxford University Press.

Bain, G. S. and Price, R. (1983) Union growth: determinants, and density. In G. S. Bain (ed.) *Industrial Relations in Britain* (pp. 3–33). Oxford: Blackwell.

Bain, P. and Baldry, C. (1995) Sickness and control in the office – the sick building syndrome. *New Technology, Work and Employment*, *10*(1): 19–31.

Bain, P., Taylor, P. and Baldry, C. (1999) Sick building syndrome and the industrial relations of occupational health. *International Journal of Employment Studies*, *7*(1): 125–48.

Baird, L. and Meshoulam, I. (1988) Managing two fits of strategic human resource management. *Academy of Management Review*, *13*(1): 116–28.

Bajorek, Z. (2020) The squeezed middle. Institute for Employment Studies. February 2020. Available at: https://www.employment-studies.co.uk/system/files/resources/files/The%20Squeezed%20Middle%20IES%20Report.pdf. Accessed 23 June 2020.

Bakan, J. (2004) *The Corporation: The Pathological Pursuit of Power and Profit*. New York: Free Press.

Baker, D. T. and Kelan, E.K. (2019) HRM practices to diversity management: individualization, precariousness and precarity. In D. Collings, G. Wood and L. Szamosi (eds) *Human Resource Management: A Critical Approach* (2nd edn) (pp. 117–34). London: Routledge.

Baker, M., Halberstam, Y., Kroft, K., Mas, A. and Messacar, D. (2020) Can transparency laws fix the gender wage gap? *Harvard Business Review*, 26 February.

Bal, P. M. and Dorenbosch, L. (2015) Age-related differences in the relations between individualized HRM and organisational performance: a large-scale employer survey. *Human Resource Management Journal*, *25*(1): 41–61.

Balabanova, E., Ehrnrooth, M., Koveshnikov, A. and Efendiev, A. (2019) Employee exit and constructive voice as behavioral responses to psychological contract breach in Finland and Russia: a within-and between-culture examination. *International Journal of Human Resource Management*, 1–32.

Baldamus, W. (1961) *Efficiency and Effort: An Analysis of Industrial Administration*. London: Tavistock.

Balaguer, E., Cheese, P. and Marchetti, C. (2006) *The high-performance workforce study*. New York: Accenture Consulting.

Baldwin, T. T. and Ford, J. K. (1988) Transfer of training: a review and directions for future research. *Personnel Psychology*, *41*: 63–105.

Ballantyne, I. and Povah, N. (2004) *Assessment and Development Centres*. Gower: Aldershot.

Bamber, G., Ryan, S. and Wailes, N. (2004) Globalization, employment relations and human indicators in ten developed market economies: international data sets. *International Journal of Human Resource Management*, *15*(8): 1481–516.

Bamberger, P. and Meshoulam, I. (2000) *Human Resource Management Strategy*. Thousand Oaks, CA: Sage.

Bamberger, P. and Phillips, B. (1991) Organizational environment and business strategy: parallel versus conflicting influences on human resource strategy in the pharmaceutical industry. *Human Resource Management*, *30*, 153–82.

Bondarouk, T., Parry, E. and Furtmueller, E. (2017) Electronic HRM: four decades of research on adoption and consequences. *International Journal of Human Resource Management*, *28*(1): 98–131.

Bandura, A. (1977) *Social Learning Theory*. Englewood Cliffs, NJ: Prentice Hall.

Bandura, A. (1986) *Social Foundations of Thought and Action*. Englewood Cliffs, NJ: Prentice Hall.

Bandura, A. and Locke, E. A. (2003) Negative self-efficacy and goal effects revisited. *Journal of Applied Psychology, 88*(1): 87.

Bangerter, A., Roulin, N. and König, C. J. (2012) Personnel selection as a signaling game. *Journal of Applied Psychology, 97*(4): 719–38.

Banks, K. and Harvey, R. (2020) Is your company actually fighting racism, or just talking about it. *Harvard Business Review*, 11 June. Available at: https://hbr.org/2020/06/is-your-company-actually-fighting-racism-or-just-talking-about-it. Accessed 19 June 2020.

Baran, P. A. and Sweezy, P. A. (1968) *Monopoly Capital*. London: Penguin.

Barber, A. E. and Bretz, R. (2000) Compensation, attraction and retention. In S. Rynes and B. Gerhart (eds) *Compensation in Organizations: Current Research and Practice* (pp. 32–60). San Francisco, CA: Jossey-Bass.

Barber, B. (2007) Foreword. In S. Bolton (ed.) *Dimensions of Dignity at Work* (pp. viii–x). Amsterdam: Elsevier.

Barbier, E. B. (2020) Greening the post-pandemic recovery in the G20. *Environmental Resource Economic 76*|: 685–703. Available at: https://doi.org/10.1007/s10640-020-00437.

Barclay, J. (1999) Employee selection: a question of structure. *Personnel Review, 28*(1/2): 134–51.

Barclay, J. (2001) Improving selection interviews with structure: organisations' use of 'behavioural' interviews. *Personnel Review, 30*(1): 81–101.

Barclays (2020) Diversity and Inclusion Report 2020. London: Barclays PLC. Available at: https://home.barclays/content/dam/home-barclays/documents/investor-relations/reports-and-events/annual-reports/2020/Barclays-PLC-Diversity-and-Inclusion-Report-2020.pdf. Accessed 7 May 2021.

Barlow, G. (1989) Deficiencies and the perpetuation of power: latent functions in management appraisal. *Journal of Management Studies, 26*(5): 499–517.

Barnett, N. (2018) The Political Environment. In L. Hamilton and P. Webster (eds) *The International Business Environment* (4th edn) (pp. 289–321). Oxford: Oxford University Press.

Barney, J. B. (1991) Firm resources and sustained competitive advantage. *Journal of Management, 17*(1): 99–120.

Barney, J. B. (1995) Looking inside for competitive advantage. *Academy of Management Executive, 9*(4): 49–61.

Baron, A. (2009) *Performance Management: A Discussion Paper*. London: Chartered Institute of Personnel and Development.

Baron, A., Clake, R., Turner, P. and Pass, S. (2010) *Workforce Planning: Right People, Right Time, Right Skills*. London: CIPD.

Barry, J., Mol, A. P. J. and Zito, A. R. (2013) Climate change ethics, rights, and policies: an introduction. *Environmental Politics, 22*(3): 361–76.

Barry, M. and Wilkinson, A. (2016) Pro-social or pro management: a critique of the conception of employee voice as a pro-social behaviour within Organisational Behaviour. *British Journal of Industrial Relations, 54*(2): 261–84.

Bartholomew, D. J. (1971) The statistical approach to manpower planning. *Statistician, 20*: 3–26.

Bartlett, C. A. and Ghoshal, S. (1989) *Managing across Borders: The Transnational Solution*. Boston, MA: Harvard Business School Press.

Bartoletti, I. (2020) *An Artificial Revolution: On Power, Politics and AI*. Indigo Press.

Bassett, P. (1987) *Strike Free: New Industrial Relations in Britain*. London: Papermac.

Bartsch, S., Weber, E., Büttgen, M. and Huber, A. (2020) Leadership matters in crisis-induced digital transformation: how to lead service employees effectively during the COVID-19 pandemic. *Journal of Service Management, 32*(1): 71–85. Available at: https://doi.org/10.1108/JOSM-05-2020-0160.

Battisti, M., Fraccaroli, F., Fasol, R. and Depolo, M. (2007) Psychological contract and quality of organizational life: an empirical study on workers at a rest home. *Industrial Relations, 62*: 664–88.

Baum, M., Schafer, M. and Kabst, R. (2016) Modeling the impact of advertisement-image congruity on applicant attraction. *Human Resource Management, 55*(1): 7–24.

Baum, T., Mooney, S. K. K., Robinson, R. N. S. and Solnet, D. (2020) COVID-19's impact on the hospitality workforce – new crisis or amplification of the norm? *International Journal of Contemporary Hospitality Management, 32*(9): 2813–29. Available at: https://doi.org/10.1108/IJCHM-04-2020-0314.

BBC (2014) Anti-fracking protesters cause disruption in UK cities. *BBC News*, 18 August 2014. Retrieved from https://www.bbc.co.uk/news/uk-wales-south-west-wales-28832520 in November 2019.

BBC (2019) Olivia Bland's Web Applications UK interview 'humiliating'. *BBC News*, 31 January. Available at: https://www.bbc.co.uk/news/uk-england-manchester-47071423. Accessed 7 October 2020.

BBC (2020a) Beirut explosion: What we know so far. *BBC News*, 11 August. Available at: https://www.bbc.co.uk/news/world-middle-east-53668493. Accessed 2 September 2020.

BBC (2020b) Coronavirus: Campaign to encourage workers back to offices. *BBC News*, 28 August. Available at: https://www.bbc.co.uk/news/uk-53942542. Accessed 6 October 2020.

Beardwell, I. (1998) Voices on. *People Management, 4*(11): 32–6.

Beardwell, J. (2001) An introduction to human resource management: Strategy, style or outcome. In I. Beardwell and L. Holden (eds) *Human Resource Management: A Contemporary Approach*, (3rd edn). Harlow: Prentice Hall.

Beaton, A. (2020) Youth job guarantee, fiscal flexibility and investment in green busines key to economic recovery, expert panel says Holyrood, June 2020. Available at: https://www.holyrood.com/news/view,youth-job-guarantee-fiscal-flexibility-and-investment-in-green-business-key_15666.htm Accessed 22 June 2020.

Beattie, J. (2020) Poll: Care homes families demand Public Inquiry after 'scandalous' situation. *Belfast Live* online. Available at: https://www.belfastlive.co.uk/news/poll-care-homes-call-public-18338735. Accessed 9 August 2020.

Beatty, C. A. and Barker-Scott, B. (2004) *Building Smart Teams: A Roadmap to High Performance.* London: Sage.

Beck, U. (2000) *What is Globalisation?* Cambridge: Polity Press.

Beck, U., Lash, S. and Wynne, B. (1992) *Risk Society: Towards a New Modernity* London: Sage.

Beckett, D. and Hager, P. (2002) *Life, Work and Learning: Practice in Postmodernity*. London: Routledge.

Beckett, D. and Hager, P. (2013) *Life, Work and Learning*. London: Routledge.

Beer, M., Boselie, P. and Brewster, C. (2015) Back to the future: implications for the field of HRM of the multistakeholder perspective proposed 30 years ago. *Human Resource Management, 54*(3): 427– 38.

Beer, M., Spector, B., Lawrence, P. R., Quin Mills, D. and Walton, R. E. (1984) *Managing Human Assets*. New York: Free Press.

Beer, M., Spector, B., Lawrence, P. R., Quinn Mills, D. and Walton, R. E. (1984) *Managing Human Assets*. New York: The Free Press.

Beevers, K. and Rea, A. (2016) *Learning and Development Practice in the Workplace* (3rd edn). London: CIPD.

Begum, H. (2020) So the ethnicity pay gap is over? If only things were that simple. *The Guardian*, 15 October. Available at: https://www.theguardian.com/commentisfree/2020/oct/15/ethnicity-pay-gap-disparities-minority-workers-unemployed-precarious-work. Accessed 15 October 2020.

Behnam, M. and Rasche, A. (2009) Are strategist from Mars and ethicists from Venus?' – strategizing as ethical reflection. *Journal of Business Ethics, 84*: 79–88.

Beioley, K., Parker, G., Strauss, D., Hancock, A. and Venkataramakrishnan, S. (2021) UK companies look to make Covid-19 vaccinations mandatory. *The Financial Times*, 16 February. Available at: https://www.ft.com/content/965dfaf0-f070-4dae-93a6-28bedbdb75da. Accessed 1 March 2021.

Bell, D. (1973) *The Coming of the Post-Industrial Society*. New York: Basic Books

Bell, D. N. F. and Blanchflower, D. G. (2013) Underemployment in the UK revisited. *National Institute Economic Review, 224*(1): F8–22.

Belt, V. and Giles, L. (2009) *High Performance Working: A Synthesis of Key Literature*. Evidence Report No. 4. Wath-upon-Dearne: UK Commission for Employment and Skills.

Benda, J. (1928/2006) *The Treason of the Intellectuals* (translated by R. Aldington). London: W. W. Norton.

Bendal, S. E., Bottomley, C. R. and Cleverly, P. M. (1998) Building a new proposition for staff at NatWest UK. In P. Sparrow and M. Marchington (eds) *Human Resource Management: The New Agenda* (pp. 90–105). London: Financial Times/Pitman.

Bendle, R. and Hofmann, R. (2017) Queer perspectives fuelling diversity management discourse. In R. Bendle, I. Bleijenbergh, E. Henttonen and A. Mills (eds) *The Oxford Handbook of Diversity in Organizations* (pp. 195–217). Oxford: Oxford University Press.

Bendle, R., Bleijenbergh, I., Henttonen, E. and Mills A. (eds) (2017) *The Oxford Handbook of Diversity in Organizations*. Oxford: Oxford University Press.

Benn, S., Dunphy, D. and Martin, A. (2009) Governance of environmental risk: new approaches to managing stakeholder involvement. *Journal of Environmental Management, 90*(4): 1567–75.

Bennett, C. (2020) As statues of slave traders are torn down, their heirs sit untouched in the Lords. *The Observer*, 14 June, p. 39.

Benschop, Y. and Doorewaard, H. (1998) Covered by equality: the gender subtext of organizations. *Organization Studies, 19*(5): 787–805.

Benschop, Y., Holgersson, C., Van Den Brink, M. and Wahl, A. (2017) Future challenges for practices of diversity management in organizations. In R. Bendl, I. Bleijenbergh, E. Henttonen and A. Mills (eds) *Oxford Handbook of Diversity Management* (pp. 553–74). Oxford: Oxford University Press.

Berg, J., Furrer, M., Harmon, E., Rani, U. and Silberman, M. S. (2018) *Digital Labour Platforms and the Future of Work: Towards Decent Work in the Online World*. Geneva: International Labour Organization. Available at: https://www.ilo.org/wcmsp5/groups/public/---dgreports/---dcomm/---publ/documents/publication/wcms_645337.pdf. Accessed 3 October 2020.

Berkhout, E., Galasso, N., Lawson, M., Rivero Morales, P. A., Taneja, A. and Vázquez Pimentel, D.A. (2021) *The Inequality Virus: Bringing Together a World Torn Apart by Coronavirus Through a Fair, Just and Sustainable Economy*. Oxford, UK: Oxfam International. Available at: https://oxfamilibrary.openrepository.com/bitstream/handle/10546/621149/bp-the-inequality-virus-250121-en.pdf. Accessed 26 January 2021.

Bernardin, H. J. and Villanova, P. (2005) Research streams in rater self-efficacy. *Group & Organization Management, 30*(1): 61–88.

Berridge, J. (2020) Are Canada's biggest cities headed for decline? *The Globe and Mail*, 3 October, p. 01.

Bertrand, M., Black, S. E., Jensen, S. and Lleras-Muney, A. (2019) Breaking the glass ceiling? The effect of board quotas on female labour market outcomes in Norway. *The Review of Economic Studies, 86*(1): 191–239.

Bertua, C., Anderson, N. and Salgado, J. (2005) The predictive validity of cognitive ability tests: a UK meta-analysis. *Journal of Occupational and Organizational Psychology, 78*: 387–409.

Betcherman, G., McMullen, K., Leckie, N. and Caron, C. (1994) *The Canadian Workplace in Transition*. Queen's University, Kingston, Ontario: IRC Press.

Betsill, M. M. and Rabe, B. G. (2009) Climate change and multilevel governance: the evolving state and local roles. In D. Mazmanian (ed.) *Toward Sustainable Communities: Transition and Transformations in Environmental Policy* (pp. 201–25). MIT Press.

Bevan, G. and Hood, C. (2006) What's measured is what matters: targets and gaming in the English public health care system. *Public administration, 84*(3): 517–38.

Beynon, H. (1984) *Working for Ford*. Harmondsworth: Penguin.

Bhuiyan, F., Chowdhury, M. M. and Ferdous, F. (2014) Historical evolution of human resource information system (HRIS): An interface between HR and computer technology. *Human Resources Management Research, 4*(4): 75–80.

Bianchini, A., Donini, F., Pellegrini, M. and Saccani, C. (2017) An innovative methodology for measuring the effective implementation of an Occupational Health and Safety Management System in the European Union. *Safety Science*, *92*: 26–33.

Bibby, J. (2020) Will COVID-19 be a watershed moment for health inequalities? The Health Foundation. Available at: https://www.health.org.uk/publications/long-reads/will-covid-19-be-a-watershed-moment-for-health-inequalities. Accessed 14 July 2020.

Bierema, L. and Callahan, J. (2014) Transforming HRD: a framework for critical HRD practice. *Advances in Developing Human Resources*, *16*(4): 429–44.

Billett, S. (2006) Constituting the workplace curriculum. *Journal of Curriculum Studies*, *38*(1): 31–48.

Bini Smaghi, L. (2010) What has the financial crisis taught us? The global dimension and international policy cooperation, Brussels: European Central Bank. Available at: https://www.ecb.europa.eu/press/key/date/2010/html/sp100907.en.html. Accessed 11 December 2020.

Biswas, S. (2019) AI in Human Capital Management (HCM): the what, why and how. *HR Technologist*, 30 April. Available at: https://www.hrtechnologist.com/articles/digital-transformation/ai-in-human-capital-management-hcm-the-what-why-and-how.Accessed 16 May 2021.

Bittman, M., Brown, J. and Wajcman, J. (2009) The mobile phone, perpetual contact and time pressure. *Work, Employment and Society*, *23*(4): 673–91.

Bjarnason, E. and Hauser, C. (2018) Iceland makes companies prove they're not paying women less. *The New York Times*, 3 January. Available at: https://www.nytimes.com/2018/01/03/world/europe/iceland equal pay.html. Accessed 6 July 2020.

Black, C. and Frost, D. (2011) *Health at Work – An Independent Review of Sickness Absence*. Great Britain, Department for Work and Pensions. Available at: https://assets.publishing.service.gov.uk/government/uploads/system/uploads/attachment_data/file/181060/health at work.pdf. Accessed 20 September 2020.

Blackstock, K. L., Kelly, G. J. and Horsey, B. L. (2007) Developing and applying a framework to evaluate participatory research for sustainability. *Ecological Economics*, *60*(4): 726–42.

Blakeley, G. (2019) *Stolen: How to Save the World from Financialisation*. London: Repeater.

Blau, P. (1964) *Exchange and Power in Social Life*. New York: John Wiley & Sons.

Blaze Baum, K. and Bradshaw, J. (2020) RBC refuses to finance Arctic drilling and puts restrictions on coal under new investment guidelines. *The Globe and Mail*, Toronto, 3 October.

Blevins, D. (2020) Coronavirus: Inside the Northern Ireland care home where staff believe they are beating Covid-19. *Sky News* online. Available at: https://news.sky.com/story/coronavirus-inside-the-northern-ireland-care-home-where-staff-believe-they-are-beating-covid-19-11989176. Accessed 9 August 2020.

Bloom, M. and Milkovich, G. T. (1998) Relationships among risk, incentive pay, and organizational performance. *Academy of Management Journal*, *41*(3): 283–97.

Bloom, N., Conway, N., Mole, K., Moslein, K., Neely, A. and Frost, C. (2004) *Solving the Skills Gap*. Summary Report from the AIM/CIHE Management Research Forum. London: Advanced Institute of Management Research.

BlueGreen Alliance (no date) *About us*. Available at: https://www.bluegreenalliance.org. Accessed December 2016.

BlueGreen Alliance Foundation (2016) *Energy Efficient Housing Products for Multifamily Buildings*. Available at: http://www.bgafoundation.org/news/energy-efficient-housing-products-for-multifamily-buildings. Accessed September 2021.

Blyton, P. and Turnbull, P. (2004) *The Dynamic of Employee Relations* (3rd edn). Basingstoke: Palgrave Macmillan.

Boak, G. and Crabbe, S. (2019) Evaluating the impact of coaching skills training on individual and corporate behaviour. *European Journal of Training and Development*, *43*(1–2): 153–65.

Boffey, D. (2012) Revealed: class divide at the heart of unpaid internships. *The Observer*, 2 December, p. 16.

Boffey, D. (2016) Top headhunters admit: UK bosses' pay 'absurdly high'. *The Observer*, 6 March, p. 1.

Boffey, D. (2016b) Bosses 'tried to destroy evidence of blacklist', say building workers. *The Observer*, 15 May, p. 10.

Boffey, D. (2020) Apple does not need to pay €13bn Irish tax bill, EU court rules. *The Guardian*, 15 July. Available at: https://www.theguardian.com/technology/2020/jul/15/apple-does-not-need-to-pay-13bn-irish-tax-bill-court-rules. Accessed 25 July 2020.

Bogen, M. (2019) All the ways hiring algorithms can introduce bias. *Harvard Business Review*, 6 May online. Available at: https://hbr.org/2019/05/all-the-ways-hiring-algorithms-can-introduce-bias#:~:text=Unfortunately%2C%20most%20hiring%20algorithms%20will,equity%2C%20rather%20than%20erode%20it. Accessed 12 August 2020.

Boiral, O., Paillé, P. and Raineri, N. (2015) The nature of employees' pro-environmental behaviors. In J. L. Robertson and J. Barling (eds) *The Psychology of Green Organizations* (pp. 12–33). New York: Oxford University Press.

Boltanski, L. and Chiapello, E. (2018) *The New Spirit of Capitalism*. London: Verso

Bolton, S. C. (2005) *Emotion Management in the Workplace*. Basingstoke: Palgrave Macmillan.

Bolton, S. C. (2009) Getting to the heart of the emotional labour process: a reply to Brook. *Work, Employment and Society* *23*(3): 549–60.

Bolton, S. C. (ed.) (2007) *Dimensions of Dignity at Work*. Amsterdam: Elsevier.

Bolton, S. C. and Houlihan, M. (eds) (2007) *Searching for the Human in Human Resource Management: Theory, Practice and Contexts*. Basingstoke: Palgrave Macmillan.

Bonache, J. and Fernández, Z. V. (2005) International compensation: costs and benefits of international assignments. In H. Scullion and M. Linehan (eds) *International Human Resource Management* (pp. 114–30). Basingstoke: Palgrave Macmillan.

Bondarouk, T., Parry, E. and Furtmueller, E. (2017) Electronic HRM: four decades of research on adoption and consequences. *International Journal of Human Resource Management*, *28*(1): 98–131.

Booth, R. (2020) Ministers urged to raise pay for care home staff during Covid-19 crisis. *The Guardian* online. Available at: https://www.theguardian.com/world/2020/

apr/14/ministers-urged-to-raise-pay-for-care-home-staff-during-covid-19-crisis. Accessed 9 August 2020.

Borman, W. C., White, L. A. and Dorsey, D. W. (1995) Effects of ratee task performance and interpersonal factors on supervisor and peer performance ratings. *Journal of Applied Psychology*, *80*(1): 168.

Boselie, P., Dietz, G. and Boon, C. (2005) Commonalities and contradictions in HRM and performance research. *Human Resource Management Journal*, *15*(3): 67–94.

Boudreau, J. W. and Ramstad, P. M. (2005) Talentship, talent segmentation, and sustainability: a new HR decision science paradigm for a new strategy definition. *Human Resource Management*, *44*(2): 129–36.

Bou-Llusar, J. C., Beltrán-Martín, I., Roca-Puig, V. and Escrig-Tena, A. B. (2016) Single- and multiple-informant research designs to examine the human resource management–performance relationship. *British Journal of Management*, *27*(3): 646–68.

Bowling, N.A. and Hershcovis, M.S. (2017) (eds) *Research and Theory on Workplace Aggression*, New York: Cambridge University Press.

Boxall, P. F. (1992) Strategic human resource management: beginnings of a new theoretical sophistication? *Human Resource Management Journal*, *2*(3): 60–79.

Boxall, P. (2008) The goals of HRM. In P. Boxall, J. Purcell and P. Wright (eds) *The Oxford Handbook of Human Resource Management* (pp. 48–67). Oxford: Oxford University Press.

Boxall, P. (2018) The development of strategic HRM: reflections on a 30-year journey. *Labour & Industry: A Journal of the Social and Economic Relations of Work*, *28*(1): 21–30.

Boxall, P. and Macky, K. (2009) Research and theory on high-performance work systems: progressing the high-involvement stream. *Human Resource Management Journal*, *19*(1): 3–23.

Boxall, P. and Purcell, J. (2016) *Strategy and Human Resource Management* (4th edn). London: Palgrave Macmillan.

Boxall, P., Purcell, J. and Wright, P. (2008) Human resource management: scope, analysis and significance. In Boxall, J. Purcell, and P. Wright (eds) *The Oxford Handbook of Human Resource Management* (pp. 1–16). Oxford: Oxford University Press.

Boxall, P., Hutchison, A. and Wassenaar, B. (2015) How do high-involvement work processes influence employee outcomes? An examination of the mediating roles of skill utilisation and intrinsic motivation. *International Journal of Human Ressource Management*, *26*(13): 1737–52.

Boyatzis, R. (1982) *The Competent Manager: A Model for Effective Performance*. New York: John Wiley & Sons.

Boyatzis, R. E., Smith, M. L. and Blaize, N. (2006) Developing sustainable leaders through coaching and compassion. *Academy of Management Learning and Education*, *5*(1): 8–24.

Boyne, G. A. and Walker, R. M. (2010) Strategic management and public service performance: the way ahead. *Public Administration Review*, *70*(1): 185–92.

Bradbury, H. (eds) (2015) *Handbook of Action Research*. London: Sage.

Bradley, A., Beevers-Cowling, F., Norton, C., Hill, C., Pelopida, B. and Quigley, M. (2020) Falling at the first hurdle: undergraduate students' readiness to navigate the graduate recruitment process, *Studies in Higher Education*. DOI: 10.1080/03075079.2019.1709164

Bratton, A. (2018) The role of talent development in environmentally sustainable hospitality: a case study of a scottish national health service conference centre. *Worldwide Hospitality and Tourism Themes*, *10*(1): 69–85.

Bratton, A. (2020) Leading pro-environmental change. In J. Bratton (ed.) *Organizational Leadership* (pp. 359–83). London: Sage.

Bratton, A. and Bratton, J. (2015) Human resource management approaches. In J. Robertson and J. Barling (eds) *The Psychology of Green Organizations* (pp. 275–95). New York: Oxford University Press.

Bratton, A. and Francis, H. (2020) Followers, communication and leadership. In J. Bratton (ed.) *Organizational Leadership* (pp. 289–315). London: Sage.

Bratton, J. (1992) *Japanization at Work: Managerial Studies for the 1990s*. Basingstoke: Palgrave Macmillan.

Bratton, J. (1999) Gaps in the workplace learning paradigm: labour flexibility and job design. Paper presented at the 1st International Conference on Researching Work and Learning, University of Leeds, UK.

Bratton, J. (2001) Why workers are reluctant learners: the case of the Canadian pulp and paper industry. *Journal of Workplace Learning*, *13*(7/8): 333–43.

Bratton, J. (2015) *Work and Organizational Behaviour*, London: Palgrave.

Bratton, J. (2021) *Work and Organizational Behaviour* (4th edn). London: Macmillan.

Bratton, J. (ed.) (2020) *Organizational Leadership*. London: SAGE Publications Limited.

Bratton, J. and Denham, D. (2009) *Capitalism and Classical Sociological Theory* (1st edn). Toronto, Ontario: University of Toronto Press.

Bratton, J. and Denham, D. (2014) *Capitalism and Classical Sociological Theory* (2nd edn). Toronto, Ontario: University of Toronto Press.

Bratton, J. and Denham, D. (2019) *Capitalism and Classical Sociological Theory* (3rd edn). Toronto, Ontario: University of Toronto Press.

Bratton, J. and Francis, H. (2020) Followers, Communication and Leadership. In J. Bratton (ed.) *Organizational Leadership* (pp. 289–315). London: Sage.

Bratton, J. and Gold, J. (2015) Towards critical human resource management education (CHRME): a sociological imagination approach. *Work, Employment and Society*, *29*(3): 496–507.

Bratton, J. and Gold, J. (2017) *Human Resource Management: Theory and Practice*. London: Palgrave.

Bratton, J. and Sawchuk, P. (2001) Editorial. *Journal of Workplace Learning*. *13*(7/8): 269–73.

Bratton, J., Helms Mills, J., Pyrch, T. and Sawchuk, P. (2004) *Workplace Learning: A Critical Introduction*. Toronto: Garamond.

Braverman, H. (1974) *Labor and Monopoly Capital*. New York: Monthly Review Press.

Breaugh, J., Labrador, J., Frye, K., Lee, D., Lammers, V. and Cox, J. (2014) The value of biodata for selecting employees: comparable results for job incumbent and job applicant samples? *Journal of Organizational Psychology*, *14*(1): 41–51.

Bresser-Pereira, L. C. (2010) The global financial crisis and a new capitalism? *Journal of Post Keynesian Economics, 32*(4): 499–534.

Brewster, C. (2001) HRM: 'the comparative dimension'. In J. Storey (ed.) *Human Resource Management: A Critical Text* (pp. 255–71). London: Thompson Learning.

Brewster, C. and Bennett, C. V. (2010) Perceptions of business cultures in eastern Europe and their implications for international HRM. *International Journal of Human Resource Management, 21*(14): 2568–88.

Brewster, C. and Mayrhofer, W. (2019) Comparative HRM: The debates and Evidence. In D. G. Collings, G. T. Wood and L. T. Szamosi (eds) *Human Resource Management: A Critical Approach* (pp. 358–77). London: Routledge.

Brewster, C. and Scullion H. (1997) A review and an agenda for expatriate HRM. *Human Resource Management Journal, 7*(3): 32–41.

Brewster, C., Mayrhofer, W. and Smale, A. (2016) Crossing the streams: HRM in multinational enterprises and comparative HRM. *Human Resource Management Review, 26*(4): 285-297.

Brey, P. and Soraker, J. H. (2009) *Philosophy of Computing and Information Technology*. Amsterdam: Elsevier.

Bridger, E. (2015) *Employee Engagement*. London: Kogan Page.

Broadbridge, A., Maxwell, G. A. and Ogden, S. M. (2009) Selling retailing to Generation Y graduates: recruitment challenges and opportunities. *International Review of Retail, Distribution and Consumer Research, 19*(4): 405–20.

Brockbank, W. and Ulrich, D. (2018) HR Competencies that make a difference. In J. Storey, P. M. Wright and D. Ulrich (eds) *The Routledge Companion to Strategic Human Resource Management* (pp. 167–81). London: Routledge.

Brosse, M. (2010) Trends affecting the workforce. *Employment Relations Today, 36*, 79–84.

Brown, B., Hanson, M., Liverman, D. and Merideth, R. (1987) Global sustainability: towards a definition. *Environmental Management, 11*(6): 713–19.

Brown, D. (2010) *Performance Management: Can the Practice Ever Deliver the Policy*. Brighton: Institute of Employment Studies.

Brown, D. (2014) The future of reward management: from total reward strategies to smart rewards. *Compensation & Benefits Review, 46*(3): 147–51.

Brown, J. N. (2011) *The Complete Guide to Recruitment: A Step-by-step Approach to Selecting, Assessing and Hiring the Right People* (1st edn). London: Kogan Page Publishers.

Brown, J. S. and Duguid, P. (1991) Organizational learning and communities-of-practice: toward a unified view of working, learning and innovation. *Organization Science, 2*(1): 40–7.

Brown, M. and Lim, V. S. (2013) Understanding performance management and appraisal: supervisory and employee perspectives. In A. Wilkinson, N. bacon, T. Redman and S. Snell (eds) *The Sage Handbook of Human Resource Management* (pp. 191–209). London: Sage.

Brown, M., Hyatt, D. and Benson, J. (2010) Consequences of the performance appraisal experience. *Personnel Review, 39*(3): 375–96.

Brown, R. (1988) The employment relationship in sociological theory. In D. Gallie (ed.) *Employment in Britain* (pp. 33–66). Oxford: Blackwell.

Brown, V. R. and Vaughn, E. D. (2011) The writing on the (Facebook) wall: the use of social networking sites in hiring decisions. *Journal of Business and Psychology, 26*(2): 219–25.

Brown, W. (1989) Managing remuneration. In K. Sisson (ed.) *Personnel Management in Britain* (pp. 249–70). Oxford: Blackwell.

Brown, W. and Nash, D. (2008) What has happening to collective bargaining under New Labour? Interpreting WERS 2004. *Industrial Relations Journal, 39*(2): 91–103.

Brown, W., Bryson, J. and Whitfield, K. (2009) *The Evolution of the Modern Workplace*. Cambridge: Cambridge University Press.

Brown, W., Deakin, S. and Ryan, P. (1997) The effects of British industrial relations legislation. *National Institute Economic Review, 161*: 69–83.

Brumbach, G. B. (1988) Some ideas, issues and predictions about performance management. *Public Personnel Management*, Winter: 387–402.

Brunow, S. B. U. (2014) Effects of cultural diversity on individual establishments. *International Journal of Manpower, 35*(1/2): 166–86.

Bryan, M. and Bryson, A. (2016) Has performance pay increased wage inequality in Britain? *Labour Economics, 41*, 149–61

Bryman, A. (2015) *Social Science Methods*. Oxford: Oxford University Press.

Brynjolfsson, E. and McAfee, A. (2014) *The Second Machine Age: Work, Progress and Prosperity in a Time of Brilliant Technologies*. New York: WW Norton & Co.

Bryson, A. (2004) Management responsiveness to union and nonunion worker voice in Britain. *Industrial Relations, 43*(1): 213–41.

Bryson, A. and Blanchflower, D. (2008) In brief... The end of trade unionism as we know it? *London School of Economics CentrePiece*, Autumn. Available at: http://cep.lse.ac.uk/pubs/download/cp268.pdf. Accessed 11 October 2020.

Bryson, A., Forth, J. and Stokes, L. (2014) Does worker wellbeing affect workplace performance? London: Department for Business, Innovation and Skills. Available at: https://assets.publishing.service.gov.uk/government/uploads/system/uploads/attachment_data/file/366637/bis-14-1120-does-worker-wellbeing-affect-workplace-performance-final.pdf. Accessed 2 September 2020.

Buckingham, M. (2016) Reinventing Performance Management, Global leadership Network. Available at: https://globalleadership.org/articles/leading-others/reinventing-performance-management-marcus-buckingham-ashley-goodall/. Accessed 20 June 2020.

Buckingham, M. and Goodall, A. (2015) Reinventing performance management. *Harvard Business Review, 93*(4): 40–50. Available at: https://hbr.org/2015/04/reinventing-performance-management. Accessed 26 June 2020.

Buckley, R. and Caple, J. (2007) *The Theory and Practice of Training* (5th edn). London: Kogan Page.

Budd, J. W. (2020) The psychologisation of employment relations, alternative models of the employment relationship, and the OB turn. *Human Resource*

Management Journal, 30: 73–83. Available at: https://doi.org/10.1111/1748-8583.12274

Budd, J. W. and Bhave, D. (2008) Values, ideologies, and frames of reference in industrial relations. In P. Blyton, E. Heery, N. Bacon and J. Fiorito (eds) *The Sage Handbook of Industrial Relations* (pp. 92–112). London: Sage.

Budd, J. W. and Bhave, D. P. (2013) The employment relationship: Key elements, alternative frames of reference, and implications for HRM. *The SAGE Handbook of Human Resource Management, 41*. London: Sage.

Budhwar, P. (2012) Management of human resources in foreign firms operating in India: the role of HR in country-specific headquarters. *International Journal of Human Resource Management, 23*(12): 2514–31.

Bullock, Lord (1977) *Report of the Committee of Inquiry on Industrial Democracy*. Cmnd 6706. London: HMSO.

Bunglawala, Z (2019) Please, don't call me BAME or BME. Civil Service Blog, 8 July. Available at: https://civilservice.blog.gov.uk/2019/07/08/please-dont-call-me-bame-or-bme/. Accessed 20 June 2020.

Burawoy, M. (1979) *Manufacturing Consent: Changes in the Labour Process Under Monopoly Capitalism*. Chicago, IL: Chicago University Press.

Burchill, F. (2014) *Labour Relations* (4th edn). Basingstoke: Palgrave Macmillan.

Burgoyne, J., Hirsh, W. and Williams, S. (2004) *The Development of Leadership and Management Capability and its Contribution to Performance: The Evidence, the Prospects and the Research Need*. Report No. 560. London: Department for Education and Skills.

Busby, E. (2019) University criticised for suggesting staff hide their sexuality when travelling to Dubai campus. *The Independent*, 3 December. Available at: https://www.independent.co.uk/news/education/education-news/university-birmingham-dubai-campus-lgbt-sexuality-guidance-academics-students-a9231541.html. Accessed 2 July 2020.

Busby, M. (2019) Record number of UK workers paid below minimum wage – report. *The Guardian*, 26 April. Available at: https://www.theguardian.com/society/2019/apr/26/record-number-of-uk-workers-paid-below-minimum-wage-report. Accessed 13 July 2020.

Business in the Community (2020) The Business Case for Diversity. *Business in the Community* online. Available at: https://www.bitc.org.uk/fact-sheet/the-business-case-for-diversity. Accessed 12 October 2020.

Business Leader (2020) Junk rating for Rolls-Royce signals importance of state support. *The Observer*, 31 May, p. 51.

Butler, P. (2009) Non-union employee representation: exploring the riddle of management strategy. *Industrial Relations Journal, 40*(3): 198–214.

Butler, P. (2020) UK's poorest 'skip meals and go hungry' during coronavirus crisis. *The Guardian*, 13 August, Available at: https://www.theguardian.com/uk-news/2020/aug/12/coronavirus-lockdown-hits-nutritional-health-of-uks-poorest. Accessed 22 October, 2020.

Butler, S. (2020a) Coronavirus lockdown to hit low-paid, young and women hardest, warns IFS. *The Guardian*, 6 April. Available at: https://www.theguardian.com/business/2020/apr/06/coronavirus-lockdown-to-hit-low-paid-young-and-women-hardest-warns-ifs. Retrieved 11 June 2020.

Butler, S. (2020b) Covid and Brexit could see UK manufacturers bringing it all back home. *The Guardian*, 23 November. Available at: https://www.theguardian.com/business/2020/nov/23/covid-and-brexit-could-see-uk-manufacturers-bringing-it-all-back-home. Accessed 4 March 2021.

Byers, P. Y. (ed.) (1997) *Organizational Communication: Theory and Behavior*. Boston: Allyn & Bacon.

Byram, M., Üngan, M. C. and Ardıç, K. (2016) The relationships between OHS prevention costs, safety performance, employee satisfaction and accident costs. *International Journal of Occupational Safety and Ergonomics, 23*(2): 285–96.

Caffarella, R. (1993) Self-directed learning. *New Directions for Adult and Continuing Education, 57*: 25–35.

Calás, M. B. and Smircich, L. (1999) From 'the woman's' point of view: feminist approaches to organizational studies. In S. R. Clegg and C. Hardy (eds) *Studying Organization: Theory and Method* (pp. 212–51). London: Sage.

Caligiuri, P. M. and Tung, R. (1999) Comparing the success of male and female expatriates from a US based company. *International Journal of Human Resource Management, 10*(5): 763–82.

Caligiuri, P. M., Lazarova, M. and Tarique, I. (2005) Training, learning and development in multinational organizations. In H. Scullion and M. Linehan (eds) *International Human Resource Management* (pp. 71–90). Basingstoke: Palgrave Macmillan.

Callaghan, G. and Thompson, P. (2001) Edwards revisited: technical control and worker agency in call centres. *Economic and Industrial Democracy, 22*: 13–37.

Callesen, J. (2020) Here's what the first coronavirus 'swab robot' can teach us about fast innovation. World Economic Forum, 24 June. Available at: https://www.weforum.org/agenda/2020/06/first-swab-robot-can-teach-about-fast-innovation-covid-19/. Accessed 1 July 2020.

Callinicos, A. (2006) *Universities in a Neoliberal World*. London: Bookmarks.

Cameron, C. (2020) Coronavirus in Scotland: Wages drop at record rate. *The Times*, 8 July. Available at: https://www.thetimes.co.uk/article/coronavirus-in-scotland-wages-drop-at-record-rate-z0d6v959h Accessed 9 July 2020.

Caminiti, S. (2020) Royal Dutch Shell reskills workers in artificial intelligence as part of huge energy transition. *CNBC*, 3 April online. Available at: https://www.cnbc.com/2020/04/03/royal-dutch-shell-reskills-workers-in-ai-part-of-energy-transition.html. Accessed 12 August 2020.

Campbell, D. (2010) The binge working culture is taking its toll. *The Observer*, 16 May, p. 37.

Campbell, D. (2020a) One in three surgeons don't have enough protective kit. *The Observer*, 12 April, p. 17.

Campbell, D. (2020b) Racism contributed to disproportionate UK BAME coronavirus deaths, inquiry finds. *The Guardian*, 14 June. Available at: https://www.theguardian.com/education/2019/sep/18/25-of-teachers-in-england-work-more-than-60-hours-a-week-study. Accessed 16 June 2020.

Carabantes, M. (2020) Black-box artificial intelligence: an epistemological and critical analysis. *AI and Society, 35*: 309–17.

Carless, S. A. (2006) Applicant reactions to multiple selection procedures for the police force. *Applied Psychology, 55*(2): 145–67.

Carlsson, L. and Berkes, F. (2005) Co-management: concepts and methodological implications. *Journal of Environmental Management, 75*(1): 65–76.

Carr, H. (2019) History according to EH Carr, *New Stateman*, 8 May. Available at: https://www.newstatesman.com/culture/books/2019/05/eh-carr-what-is-history-truth-subjectivity-facts/. Accessed 10 October 2020.

Carroll, B. (2015) Leadership learning and development. In B. Carroll, J. Ford and S. Taylor (eds) *Leadership: Contemporary Critical Perspectives* (pp. 89–108). London: Sage.

Carroll, L. (2020) UK carmakers face higher tariffs as EU rejects component plea. *The Guardian*, 30 September. Available at: https://www.theguardian.com/politics/2020/sep/30/uk-carmakers-face-higher-tariffs-as-eu-rejects-component-plea-brexit. Accessed 11 January 2021.

Carter, M. Z., Armenakis, A. A., Feild, H. S. and Mossholder, K. W. (2013) Transformational leadership, relationship quality, and employee performance during continuous incremental organizational change. *Journal of Organizational Behavior, 34*(7): 942–58.

Caruth, D. and Handlogten, G. (2001) *Managing Compensation: A Handbook for the Perplexed*. Westport, CT: Quorum.

Cascio, W. F. (2006) Decency means more than 'always low prices': a comparison of Costco to Wal-Mart's Sam's club. *Academy of Management Perspectives, 20*(3): 26–37.

Cascio, W. F. (2015) Strategic HRM: too important for an insular approach. *Human Resource Management, 54*(3): 423–6.

Case, A. and Deaton, A. (2020) *Deaths of Despair and the Future of Capitalism*. Princeton, NJ: Princeton University Press.

Castellanos, S. (2020) Shell Aims to Enroll Thousands in Online Artificial Intelligence Training. *Wall Street Journal*, 13 February online. Available at: https://www.wsj.com/articles/shell-enrolls-thousands-in-online-artificial-intelligence-training-11581622566. Accessed 12 August 2020.

Castells, M. (2001) *The Internet Galaxy. Reflections on the Internet, Business and Society*. Oxford: Oxford University Press

Cawley, B. D., Keeping, L. M. and Levy, P. E. (1998) Participation in the performance appraisal process and employee reactions: a meta-analytic review of field investigations. *Journal of Applied Psychology, 83*(4): 615–33.

Celik, H., Abma, T., Klinge, I. and Widder, G. (2012) Process evaluation of a diversity training program: the method strategy. *Evaluation and Programme Planning, 35*: 54–65.

Ceplenski, C. (2013) 4 types of workplace violence. *HR Daily Advisor*, 27 December online. Available at: https://hrdailyadvisor.blr.com/2013/12/27/4-types-of-workplace-violence. Accessed 20 September 2020.

Cha, M. and Brecher, J. (2019) Reject the 'jobs versus environment' narrative—we can do both. *The Guardian*, 10 September. Available at: https://www.theguardian.com/commentisfree/2019/sep/10/jobs-environment-unions-green-new-deal. Accessed 29 June 2020.

Chakrabortty, A. (2021) Britain could be mass-producing its Covid shot. Shame we junked our industrial base. *The Guardian*, 6 January. Available at: https://www.theguardian.com/commentisfree/2021/jan/06/britain-covid-shot-industrial-base-uk-manufacturing-national-security. Accessed 12 January 2021.

Chakravarty, D. (2007) 'Docile oriental women' and organised labour: a case study of the Indian garment manufacturing industry. *Indian Journal of Gender Studies, 14*: 439–60.

Champy, J. (1996) *Reengineering Management: The Mandate for New Leadership*. New York: HarperCollins.

Chance, P. (2009) *Learning and Behavior* (6th edn). Belmont, CA: Wadsworth.

Chand, M. (2010) The impact of HRM practices on service quality, customer satisfaction and performance in the Indian hotel industry. *International Journal of Human Resource Management, 21*(4): 551–66.

Chapman, D. S. and Zweig, D. I. (2005) Developing a nomological network for interview structure: antecedents and consequences of the structured selection interview. *Personnel Psychology, 58*: 673–702.

Chapman, D. S., Uggerslev, K. L., Carroll, S. A., Piasentin, K. A. and Jones, D. A. (2005) Applicant attraction to organizations and job choice: a meta-analytic review of the correlates of recruiting outcomes. *Journal of Applied Psychology, 90*(5): 928–37.

Chartered Institute of Personnel and Development (2008) Smart Working: How smart is UK PLC? Findings from organizational practice. London, CIPD

Chartered Institute of Personnel and Development (2009) *Performance Management in Action*. London: CIPD.

Chartered Institute of Personnel and Development (2010a) *The Talent Perspective. What Does it Feel Like to Be Talent-Managed?* London: CIPD.

Chartered Institute of Personnel and Development (2010b) *Next Generation HR*. London: CIPD.

Chartered Institute of Personnel and Development (2010c) *Opening Up Talent for Business Success*. London: CIPD.

Chartered Institute of Personnel and Development (2010d) *Resourcing and Talent Planning*. London: CIPD.

Chartered Institute of Personnel and Development (2011) *Sustainable Organisation Performance*. London: CIPD.

Chartered Institute of Personnel and Development (2015a) *The Role of Line Managers*. London: CIPD.

Chartered Institute of Personnel and Development (2015b) *Over-qualification and Skills Mismatch in the Graduate Labour Market*. London: CIPD.

Chartered Institute of Personnel and Development (2015c) *Human Capital Reporting: Investing for Sustainable Growth*. London: CIPD

Chartered Institute of Personnel and Development (2015d) *Resourcing and Talent Planning*. London: CIPD. Available at: https://www.cipd.co.uk/Images/resourcing-talent-planning_2015_tcm18-11303.pdf. Accessed 3 June 2020.

Chartered Institute of Personnel and Development (2016) *Could Do Better? Assessing what Works in Performance Management*. London: CIPD.

Chartered Institute of Personnel and Development (2018) *PESTLE analysis: Factsheet*. Available at: https://www.

cipd.ie/news-resources/practical-guidance/factsheets/pestle-analysis. Accessed 28 October 2019.

Chartered Institute of Personnel and Development (2019a) *Brexit Impact on Workforce Trends.* London: CIPD. Available at: https://www.cipd.co.uk/news-views/brexit-hub/workforce-trends.

Chartered Institute of Personnel and Development (2019b) *Corporate Responsibility: An Introduction – Factsheet.* London: CIPD. Available at: https://Www.Cipd.Co.Uk/Knowledge/Strategy/Corporate-Responsibility/Factsheet. Accessed 14 June 2020.

Chartered Institute of Personnel and Development (2019c) *Discipline and Grievance at Work: Factsheet*. Available at: https://www.cipd.co.uk/knowledge/fundamentals/emp-law/discipline/factsheet. Accessed 3 August 2020.

Chartered Institute of Personnel and Development (2019d) *Diversity Management that Works: An Evidence-based View.* London: CIPD. Available at: https://www.cipd.co.uk/knowledge/fundamentals/relations/diversity/management-recommendations.

Chartered Institute of Personnel and Development (2019e) *Ethics at Work: An Employer's Guide*. London: CIPD.

Chartered Institute of Personnel and Development (2019f) *Executive Pay in the FTSE 100 – 2019 review*. London: CIPD. Available at: https://www.cipd.co.uk/knowledge/strategy/reward/executive-pay-ftse-100-2019. Accessed 13 July 2020.

Chartered Institute of Personnel and Development (2019g) *Line Managers' Role in Supporting the People Profession: Factsheet*. Available at: https://www.cipd.co.uk/knowledge/fundamentals/people/hr/line-managers-factsheet. Accessed 10 April 2020.

Chartered Institute of Personnel and Development (2019h) *Performance management: An Introduction. Factsheet.* Available at: https://www.cipd.co.uk/knowledge/fundamentals/people/performance/factsheet. Accessed 26 June, 2020.

Chartered Institute of Personnel and Development (2019h) *Selection Methods: Factsheet*. London: CIPD. Available at: https://www.cipd.co.uk/knowledge/fundamentals/people/recruitment/selection-factsheet. Accessed 9 June 2020.

Chartered Institute of Personnel and Development (2020a) *Business Partnering: Factsheet*. September. Available at: https://www.cipd.co.uk/knowledge/fundamentals/people/hr/business-partnering-factsheet. Accessed 10 May 2021.

Chartered Institute of Personnel and Development (2020b) *Dealing with Conflict at Work: A Guide for People Managers*. CIPD, 21 January. Available at: https://www.cipd.co.uk/knowledge/fundamentals/relations/disputes/workplace-conflict-people-manager-guide. Accessed 20 September 2020

Chartered Institute of Personnel and Development (2020c) *Diversity and Inclusion in the Workplace*. London: CIPD. Available at: https://www.cipd.co.uk/knowledge/fundamentals/relations/diversity/factsheet#gref. Accessed 7 May 2021.

Chartered Institute of Personnel and Development (2020d) *Employee Relations: An Introduction. Factsheet.* Available at: https://www.cipd.co.uk/knowledge/fundamentals/relations/employees/factsheet Accessed 29 July 2020.

Chartered Institute of Personnel and Development (2020e) *Labour Market Outlook*. London: CIPD. Available at: https://www.cipd.co.uk/Images/labour-market-outlook-spring-2020_tcm18-76992.pdf. Accessed 3 June 2020.

Chartered Institute of Personnel and Development (2020f) *Learning and Development Strategy and policy: Factsheet.* August. London: CIPD. Available at: https://www.cipd.co.uk/knowledge/strategy/development/factsheet#gref. Accessed 10 May 2021.

Chartered Institute of Personnel and Development (2020g) *Managing Conflict in the Modern Workplace*. CIPD online. Available at: https://www.cipd.co.uk/Images/managing-conflict-in-the-workplace-1_tcm18-70655.pdf. Accessed 20 September 2020.

Chartered Institute of Personnel and Development (2020h) *Managing Drug and Alcohol Misuse at Work*. CIPD online. Available at: https://www.cipd.co.uk/knowledge/culture/well-being/drug-alcohol-misuse-work-report. Accessed 20 September 2020.

Chartered Institute of Personnel and Development (2020i) *Recruitment: An Introduction: Factsheet*. London: CIPD. Available at: https://www.cipd.co.uk/knowledge/fundamentals/people/recruitment/factsheet. Accessed 4 June 2020.

Chartered Institute of Personnel and Development (2020j) *Succession Planning: Factsheet*. London: CIPD. Available at: https://www.cipd.co.uk/knowledge/strategy/resourcing/succession-planning-factsheet. Accessed 16 May 2020.

Chartered Institute of Personnel and Development (2021) *Labour Market Outlook, Spring 2021*. London: CIPD. Available at: https://www.cipd.co.uk/Images/labour-market-outlook-spring-2021_tcm18-95263.pdf. Accessed 18 May 2021.

Chartered Institute of Personnel and Development/Simplyhealth (2012) *Absence Management Survey*. London: CIPD/Simplyhealth.

Chartered Management Institute (2014) *Management 2020. The Commission on the Future of Management and Leadership*. London: CMI.

Chaudhary, R. (2018) Can green human resource management attract young talent? An empirical analysis. *Evidence-based HRM, 6*(3): 305–19.

Chaudhary, R. (2020) Green human resource management and employee green behavior: an empirical analysis. *Corporate Social Responsibility and Environmental Management, 27*(2): 630–41.

Cheatham, B., Javanmardian, K. and Samandari, H. (2019) *Confronting the Risks of Artificial Intelligence*. McKinsey Quarterly, April.

Checchi, D., Visser, J. and van de Werfhorst, H. (2010) Inequality and union membership: the influence of relative earnings and inequality attitudes. *British Journal of Industrial Relations, 48*(1): 84–108.

Chen, L., Mislove, A. and Wilson, C. (2015) Peeking beneath the hood of uber. Paper presented at the Proceedings of the 2015 Internet Measurement Conference: 495–508. Available at: https://doi.org/10.1145/2815675.2815681.

Chen, T., Wu, P. and Leung, K. (2011) Individual performance appraisal and appraisee reactions to workgroups. *Personnel Review, 40*(1): 87–105.

Chen, Y. (2011) Green organizational identity: sources and consequence, *Management Decision*, *49*(3): 384–404.

Chen, Y. S., Lin, S. H., Lin, C. Y., Hung, S. T., Chang, C. W. and Huang, C. W. (2020) Improving green product development performance from green vision and organizational culture perspectives. *Corporate Social Responsibility and Environmental Management*, *27*(1): 222–31.

Chiaburu, D. and Tekleab, A. (2005) Individual and contextual influences on multiple dimensions of training effectiveness. *Journal of European Industrial Training*, *29*(8): 604–26.

Child, J. (1972) Organizational structure, environment and performance: the role of strategic choice. *Sociology*, *6*(1):1–22. DOI:10.1177/003803857200600101

Child, J. (2015) *Organization: Contemporary Principles and Practice* (2nd edn). Chichester: John Wiley & Sons.

Chinander, K. R. (2001) Aligning accountability and awareness for environmental performance in operations. *Production and Operations Management*, *10*(3): 276–91.

Choi, S. and Rainey, H. G. (2014) Organizational fairness and diversity management in public organizations: does fairness matter in managing diversity. *Review of Public Personnel Administration*, *34*(4): 307–31.

Chomsky, N. (1999) *Profit over People*. New York: Seven Stories Press.

Chou, B. K. (2005) Implementing the reform of performance appraisal in China's civil service. *China Information*, *19*(1): 39–65.

Chou, T. (2013) Where are the numbers? *Medium*. 11 October. Available at: www.medium.com/@triketora/where-are-the-numbers-cb997a57252. Accessed 5 July 2020.

Chouhan, V. S. and Srivastava, S. (2014) Understanding competencies and competency modelling – a literature survey. *IOSR Journal of Business and Management*, *6*(1): 14–23.

Chow, I. H. S. and Liu, S.S. (2009) The effects of aligning organizational culture and business strategy with HR systems on firm performance in Chinese enterprises. *International Journal of Human Resource Management*, *20*: 2292–310.

Christophers, B. (2020) *Rentier Capitalism: Who Owns the Economy, and Who Pays for It?* London: Verso.

Chuai, X., Preece, D. and Iles, P. (2008) Is talent management just 'old wine in new bottles'? *Management Research News*, *31*(12): 901–11.

Chui, C., Manyika, J. and Miremadi, M. (2016) Where machines could replace humans – and where they can't (yet). *McKinsey Quarterly*, 8 July online. Available at: https://www.mckinsey.com/business-functions/mckinsey-digital/our-insights/where-machines-could-replace-humans-and-where-they-cant-yet#. Accessed 30 September 2020.

Chun, J., Brocker, J. and De Cremer, D. (2018) People don't want to be compared with others in performance reviews. They want to be compared with themselves. Harvard Business Review. 22 March. Available at: https://hbr.org/2018/03/people-dont-want-to-be-compared-with-others-in-performance-reviews-they-want-to-be-compared-with-themselves Accessed 7 July 2020.

Churchill, F. (2020) Learning is key to addressing racism, Amaechi tells Festival of Work. *People Management*, 11 June. Available at: https://www.peoplemanagement.co.uk/news/articles/learning-is-key-to-addressing-racism-issues-amaechi-tells-festival-of-work. Accessed 20 June 2020.

Ciby, M. and Raya, R. P. (2015) Workplace bullying: a review of defining features, measurement methods and prevalence across continents. *IIM Kozhikode Society & Management Review*, *4*(1): 38–47.

Clark, D. (2019) *Trade Union Density in the United Kingdom (UK) 1995 to 2018*. London: Statista. Available at: https://www.statista.com/statistics/287232/trade-union-density-united-kingdom-uk-y-on-y/. Accessed 20 August 2020.

Clark, D. (2020) Post-coronavirus unemployment rate forecast in the UK 2020–2021. 10 September. Statista. Available at: https://www.statista.com/statistics/1107870/uk-unemployment-forecast/. Accessed 10 October 2020.

Clark, I. (2009) Owners and managers: disconnecting managerial capitalism? Understanding the private-equity business model. *Work, Employment and Society* 23(4): 775–86.

Clark, T. and Pugh, D. (2000) Similarities and differences in European conceptions of human resource management. *International Studies of Management and Organizations*, *29*(4): 84–100.

Claxton, J. and Gold, J. (2013) Leadership and Management Development. In J. Gold, R. Holden, P. Iles, J. Stewart, and J. Beardwell (eds) *Human Resource Development* (2nd edn) (pp. 259–85). *Human Resource Development: Theory and Practice*. London: Palgrave.

Clayton, T. (1998) Problematizing partnerships: the prospects for a cooperative bargaining agenda. In P. Sparrow and M. Marchington (eds) *Human Resource Management: The New Agenda* (pp. 180–92). London: Financial Times Management.

Clayton, T. (2000) Employee participation and involvement. In D. Winstanley and J. Woodall (eds) *Ethical Issues in Contemporary Human Resource Management* (pp. 208–23). Basingstoke: Palgrave Macmillan.

Clegg, H. (1976) *Trade Unionism Under Collective Bargaining*. Oxford: Blackwell.

Clegg, R. (2019) Labour Disputes, annual estimates, UK. National Statistics: London. Available at: https://www.ons.gov.uk/employmentandlabourmarket/peopleinwork/workplacedisputesandworkingconditions/articles/labourdisputes/2018. Accessed 24 August 2020.

Clegg, S. and Dunkerley, D. (1980) *Organization, Class and Control*. London: Routledge & Kegan Paul.

Clegg, S., Hardy, C. and Nord, W. (eds) (1999) *Managing Organizations: Current Issues*. Thousand Oaks, CA: Sage.

Clegg, S. R. (2016) Foreword. In A. Prasad, P. Prasad, A.J. Mills and J. Helm Mills (eds) *The Routledge Companion to Critical Management* (pp. xxiii–xxiv). London: Routledge.

Clegg, S. R., Kornberger, M. and Pitsis, T. S. (2016) *Managing & Organizations: An Introduction to Theory and Practice* (4th edn). SAGE Publications.

Clifford, B. (2016) 'Clock-watching and box-ticking': British local authority planners, professionalism and performance targets. *Planning Practice & Research*, *31*(4): 383–401.

Coates, D. (1975) *The Labour Party and the Struggle for Socialism*. CUP Archive.

Coates, D. (2018) Changing labour markets and the future of work. In J. Storey, P. M. Wright, and D. O. Ulrich (eds) *The Routledge Companion to Strategic Human Resource Management* (pp. 106–122). London: Routledge.

Coates, J. and Pichler, P. (eds) (2011) *Language and Gender: A Reader* (2nd edn). Chichester: Wiley-Blackwell.

Cockburn, C. (1991) *In the Way of Women: Men's Resistance to Sex Equality in Organizations* (No. 18). Ithaca, NY: Cornell University Press.

Coens, T. and Jenkins, M. (2002) *Abolishing Performance Appraisals*. San Francisco, CA: Berrett-Koehler.

Colling, T. and Terry, M. (eds) (2010) Work, the employment relationship and the field of industrial relations. In T. Colling and M. Terry (eds) *Industrial Relations: Theory and Practice* (3rd edn) (pp. 3–25). Chichester: John Wiley & Sons.

Collings, C. J. and Kehoe, R. R. (2018) Recruitment and selection. In J. Storey, P. Wright and D. Ulrich (eds) *The Routledge Companion to Strategic Human Resource Management,* (pp. 209–23). London: Routledge.

Collings, D. G. (2008) Multinational corporations and industrial relations research: a road less travelled. *International Journal of Management Reviews, 10*(2): 173–93.

Collings, D. G. and Isichei, M. (2018) The shifting boundaries of global staffing: Integrating global talent management, alternative forms of international assignments and non-employees into the discussion. *International Journal of Human Resource Management, 29*(1): 165–87.

Collings, D.G. and Scullion, H. (2006) Approaches to international staffing. In H. Scullion and D. G. Collings (eds) *Global Staffing*. London: Routledge.

Collings, D. G. and Scullion, H. (2007) Global staffing and multinational enterprise. In J. Storey (ed.) *Human Resource Management: A Critical Text* (3rd edn) (pp. 215–31). London: Thomson Learning.

Collings, D. G., Scullian, H. and Curran, D. (2019) 'International human resource management. In D. G. Collings, G. T. Wood and L. T. Szamosi (eds) *Human Resource Management: A Critical Approach* (pp. 378–95). London: Routledge.

Collington, R. (2020) The myth of the 'efficient' private sector has been busted by Covid. *The Guardian*, 24 October. Available at: https://www.theguardian.com/commentisfree/2020/oct/24/efficient-private-sector-covid-pandemic-uk. Accessed 24 October 2020.

Collins, H. M. (2001) Tacit knowledge, trust, and the Q of sapphire. *Social Studies of Science, 31*(1): 71–85.

Collins, J. M. and Muchinsky, P. M. (1993) An assessment of the construct validity of three job evaluation methods: a field experiment. *Academy of Management Journal, 36*: 895–904.

Collins, P. H. and Bilge, S. (2020) *Intersectionality*. London: John Wiley & Sons.

Collinson, D. (1994) Strategies of resistance: power, knowledge and subjectivity in the workplace. In J. Jermier, D. Knights and W. Nord (eds) *Strategies of Resistance: Power, Knowledge and Subjectivity in the Workplace* (pp. 25–68). London: Routledge.

Colquitt, J. A., Conlon, D. E., Wesson, M. J., Porter, C. O. and Ng, K. Y. (2001) Justice at the millennium: a meta-analytic review of 25 years of organizational justice research. *Journal of Applied Psychology, 86*(3): 425–45.

Colthart, I., Cameron, N., McKinstry, B. and Blaney, D. (2008) What do doctors really think about the relevance and impact of GP appraisal 3 years on? A survey of Scottish GPs. *British Journal of General Practice, 58*: 82–7.

Colville, I. D., Waterman, R. H. and Weick, K. E. (1999) Organizing and the search for excellence: making sense of the times in theory and practice. *Organization, 6*(1): 129–48.

Conger, K. (2021) Google union marks landmark moment. *The Globe and Mail*, 5 January, p. B4.

Connell, J., Nankervis, A. and Burgess, J. (2015) The challenges of an ageing workforce: an introduction to the workforce management issues. *Labour and Industry, 25*(4): 257–64.

Connelly, C. E. and Turel, O. (2016) Effects of team emotional authenticity on virtual team performance. *Frontiers in Psychology, 7*: 1336.

Contractor, F. J., Kumar, V., Kundu, S. K. and Pedersen, T. (2010) Reconceptualizing the firm in a world of outsourcing and offshoring: the organizational and geographical relocation of high-value company functions. *Journal of Management Studies, 47*(8): 1417–33.

Cook, M. (1994) *Personnel Selection and Productivity*. Chichester: John Wiley & Sons.

Cooke, W. N. (2006) Industrial relations in MNCs. In M. J. Morley, P. Gunnigle and D. G. Collings (eds) *Global Industrial Relations*. London: Routledge.

Coombs, J. E. and Bierly, P. E. (2006) Measuring technological capability and performance. *R&D Management, 36*(4): 421–38.

Corby, S., Palmer, S. and Lindop, E. (eds) (2009) *Rethinking Reward.* Basingstoke: Palgrave Macmillan.

Corritore, M., Goldberg, A. and Srivastava, S. B. (2020) Duality in Diversity: How Intrapersonal and Interpersonal Cultural Heterogeneity Relate to Firm Performance. *Administrative Science Quarterly, 65*(2): 359–394. Available at: https://doi.org/10.1177/0001839219844175.

Corstjens, J., Lievens, F. and Krumm, S. (2017) Situational Judgement Tests for Selection. In H. W. Goldstein, E. D. Pulakos, J. Passmore and C. Semedo (eds) *The Wiley Blackwell Handbook of the Psychology of Recruitment, Selection and Employee Retention.* Available at: https://doi.org/10.1002/9781118972472.

Cotton, C. (2020) Foreword. In S. E. Jones and S. J. Perkins, *Reward Management: Alternatives, Consequences and Contexts* (4th edn) (p. xvi). London: CIPD.

Cousins, S. (2020) Migrant workers can't afford a lockdown. *Foreign Policy*, 8 April.

Cowling, A. and Walters, M. (1990) Manpower planning – where are we today? *Personnel Review, 19*(3): 3–8.

Cox, A., Higgins, T., Gloster, R. and Foley, B. (2012) The impact of workplace initiatives on low carbon behaviours: case study report. Available at: www.scotland.gov.uk/Publications/2012/03/2237 Accessed 13 August 2016.

Craig, A. W. J. and Solomon, N. (1996) *The System of Industrial Relations in Canada* (5th edn). Scarborough, Ontario: Prentice-Hall.

Crane, A., Matten, D. and Moon, J. (2008) The emergence of corporate citizenship: Historical development and alternative perspectives. In *Handbook of Research on*

Global Corporate Citizenship (pp. 25–49). Cheltenham: Edward Elgar.

Crane, A., Matten, D., Glozer, S. and Spence, L. (2019) *Business Ethics* (5th edn). Oxford: Oxford University Press.

Crane, D. (ed.) (1994) *The Sociology of Culture*. Cambridge, MA: Blackwell.

Cregan, C. and Brown, M. (2010) The influence of union membership status on workers' willingness to participate in joint consultation. *Human Relations*, *63*(3): 331–48.

Cridland, M. and Moloney, M. (2020) Covid-19: (Australia) JobKeeper 2.0 – Expanded Eligibility. *The National Law Review*, X (225). Available at: https://www.natlawreview.com/article/covid-19-australia-jobkeeper-20-expanded-eligibility. Accessed 12 August 2020.

Crifo, P., Durand, R. and Gond, J. P. (2019) Encouraging investors to enable corporate sustainability transitions: The case of responsible investment in France. *Organization & Environment*, *32*(2): 125–44.

Croft, J. and Venkataramakrishnan, S. (2021) Uber loses landmark UK battle as Supreme Court rules drivers are workers. *Financial Times*, 19 February. Available at: https://www.ft.com/content/9ef3a1c5-328c-460d-9261-33ea991cae62. Accessed 22 February 2021.

Crossan, M. M. and Apaydin, M. (2010) A multi-dimensional framework of organizational innovation: a systematic review of the literature. *Journal of Management Studies*, *47*(6): 1154–91.

Crossan, M., Lane, H. and White, R. (1999) An organizational learning framework: from intuition to institution. *Academy of Management Review*, *24*: 522–37.

Cullinane, N. and Dundon, T. (2006) The Psychological contract: a critical review. *International Journal of Management Reviews*, *8*(2): 113–29.

Currie, G., Knights, D. and Starkey, K. (2010) Introduction: a post-crisis critical reflection on business schools. *British Journal of Management*, *21*: S1–S5.

Curson, J. (2006) Crystal-ball gazing: planning the medical workforce. *British Journal of Hospital Medicine*, *67*(8): 1141–7.

Curson, J. A., Dell, M. E., Wilson, R. A., Bosworth, D. L. and Baldauf, B. (2010) Who does workforce planning well?: workforce review team rapid review summary. *International Journal of Health Care Quality Assurance*, *23*(1): 110–19.

Cushen J and Thompson P (2012) Doing the right thing? HRM and the angry knowledge worker. *New Technology, Work and Employment* 27(2): 79–92.

Cushen, J. and Thompson, P. (2016) Financialization and value: why labour and the labour process still matter. *Work, Employment and Society*, *30*(2): 352–65. Available at: https://doi.org/10.1177/0950017015617676.

Czerny, A. (2004) Not so quick and easy. *People Management*, February *26*: 14–15.

D'Netto, B., Shen, J., Chelliah, J. and Monga, M. (2014) Human resource diversity management practices in the Australian manufacturing sector. *International Journal of Human Resource Management*, *25*(9): 1243–66.

Da Costa, P. N. (2017) Here's Why Millions of Americans Feel Left Behind. Business Insider, 28 September. Available at: https://www.businessinsider.in/heres-why-millions-of-americans-feel-left-behind-by-the-economic-recovery/articleshow/60874110.cms?mobile=no.

Dacin, M. T., Ventresca, M. J. and Beal, B. D. (1999) The Embeddedness of Organizations: Dialogue & Directions, *Journal of Management*, *25*(3): 317–56.

Daft, R. (2015) *Organizational Theory and Design* (12th edn). Boston, MA: Cengage Learning.

Daily, B. F. and Huang S. (2001) Achieving sustainability through attention to human resource factors in environmental management. *International Journal of Operations and Production Management*, *21*: 1539–52.

Daily, B. F., Bishop, J. and Steiner R. (2007) The mediating role of EMS teamwork as it pertains to HR factors and perceived environmental performance. *Journal of Applied Business Research*, *23*, 95–109.

Danford, A., Richardson, M., Stewart, P., Tailby, S. and Upchurch, M. (2008) Partnership, high performance work systems and quality of working life. *New Technology, Work and Employment*, *23*(3): 151–66.

Daniel, W. W. and Millward, N. (1983) *Workplace Industrial Relations in Britain*. London: Heinemann.

Daniels, C. (2004) 50 best companies for minorities. *Fortune*, *149*(13): 136–42.

Daniels, K. (2006) Rethinking job characteristics in work stress research. *Human Relations*, *59*(3): 267–90.

Daniels, K. (2011) Stress and well-being are still issues and something still needs to be done: or why agency and interpretation are important for policy and practice. In G. P. Hodgkinson and J. K. Ford (eds) *International Review of Industrial and Organizational Psychology*, (Vol 25, pp. 1-46). Chichester: John Wiley & Sons.

Daniels, K., Gedikli, C., Watson, D., Semkina, A. and Vaughn, O. (2017) Job design, employment practices and well-being: a systematic review of intervention studies, *Ergonomics*, *60*(9): 1177–96. DOI: 10.1080/00140139.2017.1303085

Darlington, R. (ed.) (2009) *What's the Point of Industrial Relations? In Defence of Critical Social Science*. Manchester: British Universities Industrial Relations Association.

Das, S. C. and Ahmed, I. Z. (2014) The perception of employer branding to enhance recruitment and selection processes. *European Journal of Business and Management*, *6*(6): 138–44.

Datta, D., Guthrie, J., Basuil, D. and Pandey, A. (2010) Causes and effects of employee downsizing: a review and synthesis. *Journal of Management*, *36*(1): 281–348.

Datta, N., Giupponi, G. and Machin, S. (2019) Zero-hours contracts and labour market policy. *Economic Policy*, 34(99): 369-427.

Davey, R., Fearon, C. and McLaughlin, H. (2013) Organizational grief: an emotional perspective on understanding employee reactions to job redundancy. *Development and Learning in Organizations: An International Journal*, *27*(2): 5–8.

Davie, G. (1986) *The Crisis of the Democratic Intellect*. Edinburgh: Polygon.

Davies, P. and Freedland, M. (1994) *Labour Law: Text and Materials*. London: Weidenfeld & Nicolson.

Davies, R. (2015) It's all to play for as employers turn to recruitment apps. *The Observer*, 29 November, p. 44.

Davies, R. and Kelly, A. (2020) More than £1bn wiped off Boohoo value as it investigates Leicester factory. *The Guardian*, 6 July. Available at: https://www.theguardian.

com/business/2020/jul/06/boohoo-leicester-factory-conditions-covid-19. Accessed 9 July 2020.

Davis, A., Kimball, W. and Gould, E. (2015) *The Class of 2015*. Economic Policy Institute Briefing Paper No. 401. Washington, DC: EPI.

Davis, G. F. (2016) *The Vanishing American Corporation*. Oakland, CA: Berrett-Koehler Publishers.

Davis, G. F. and Kim, S. (2015) Financialization of the Economy. *Annual Review of Sociology, 41*, pp. 203–21.

Davis, M. C. and Coan, P. (2015) Organizational change. In J. L. Robertson and J. Barling (eds) *The Psychology of Green Organizations* (pp. 244–74). New York: Oxford University Press.

Davis, M. C., Unsworth, K. L., Russell, S. V. and Galvan, J. J. (2020) Can green behaviors really be increased for all employees? Trade-offs for 'deep greens' in a goal-oriented green human resource management intervention. *Business Strategy and the Environment, 29*(2): 335–46.

Davis-Blake, A. and Broschak, J. P. (2009) Outsourcing and the changing nature of work. *Annual Review of Sociology, 35*, 321–40.

De Cieri, H. and Dowling, P. (1999) Strategic human resource management in multinational enterprises: theoretical and empirical developments. In P. Wright, L. Dyer, J. Boudreau and G. Milkovich (eds) *Research in Personnel and Human Resource Management* (pp. 305–27). Stanford, CT: JA Press.

De Dreu, C. K. W. (2008) The virtue and vice of workplace conflict: food for (pessimistic) thought. *Journal of Organizational Behaviour, 29*(1): 5–18.

De Dreu, C. K. W. (2012) Conflict at work: basic principles and applied issues. In S. Zedeck (ed.) *APA Handbook of Industrial and Organizational Psychology* (pp. 461–93). Washington, DC: APA Press.

De Gieter, S. and Hofmans, J. (2015) How reward satisfaction affects employees' turnover intentions and performance: an individual differences approach. *Human Resource Management Journal, 25*(2): 200–16.

De Leede, J. and Kraijenbrink, J. (2014) The mediating role of trust and social cohesion in the effects of new ways of working: a Dutch case study. In T. Bondarouk and M. R. Olvias-Lujan (eds) *Human Resource Management Social Innovation and Technology*. Advanced Series in Management No. 14 (pp. 2–20). Bingley: Emerald Publishing Group.

De Stefano, V. (2015) The rise of the just-in-time workforce: on-demand work, crowdwork, and labor protection in the gig-economy. *Comparative Labor Law & Policy Journal, 37*: 471–85.

De Stefano, V. (2016) *The Rise of the 'Just-In-Time Workforce': On-Demand Work, Crowdwork and Labour Protection in the 'Gig Economy'*. Geneva: International Labour Organisation. Available at: https://www.ilo.org/wcmsp5/groups/public/---ed_protect/---protrav/---travail/documents/publication/wcms_443267.pdf. Accessed 5 October 2020.

de Vries, G. and Jehn, K. A. (2012) When employees stop talking and start fighting: the detrimental effects of pseudo voice in organizations. *Journal of Business Ethics, 105*: 221–30.

Debono, J. (2001) Sexual harassment in employment: an examination of decisions looking for evidence of a sexist jurisprudence. *New Zealand Journal of Industrial Relations, 26*(3): 329–40.

Deci, E. L. and Ryan, R. M. (2000) The 'what' and 'why' of goal pursuits: human needs and the self-determination of behavior. *Psychological Inquiry, 11*(4): 227–68.

Dehghan, S. K. (2020) Qatar eases exit rules but concerns linger over abuse of domestic workers. *The Guardian*, 23 January.

Del Brio, J. A., Fernandez, E. and Junquera, B. (2007) Management and employee involvement in achieving an environmental action-based competitive advantage: An empirical study. *International Journal of Human Resource Management, 18*(4): 491–522.

Delbridge, R. and Keenoy, T. (2010) Beyond managerialism? *International Journal of Human Resource Management, 21*(6): 799–817.

Delery, J. E. and Doty, H. D. (1996) Modes of theorizing in strategic human resource management: tests of universalistic, contingency, and configurational performance. *Academy of Management Journal, 39*(4): 802–835.

Delery, J. and Gupta, N. (2016) Human resource management practices and organizational effectiveness: internal fit matters. *Journal of Organizational Effectiveness: People and Performance, 3*(2): 139–63.

Delery, J. E. and Roumpi, D. (2017) Strategic human resource management, human capital and competitive advantage: is the field going in circles? *Human Resource Management Journal, 27*(1): 1–21.

Dellanna, A. (2020) Trade deal signed but 'Brexit is far from over,' expert tells *Euronews*. *Euronews*, 30 December. Available at: https://www.euronews.com/2020/12/30/trade-deal-signed-but-brexit-is-far-from-over-expert-tells-euronews. Accessed 7 January 2021.

Deloitte (2018) *Power Up: UK skills Boosting Transferable Skills to Achieve Inclusive Growth and Mobility*. London: Deloitte.

Deloitte (2020) Extracting value from decarbonisation. *Deliotte* online. Available at: https://www2.deloitte.com/content/dam/Deloitte/au/Documents/risk/deloitte-au-risk-decarbonisation-extracting-value-from-decarbonisation-05032020.pdf. Accessed 13 October 2020.

Deloitte Consulting and Deloitte & Touche (2000) The Future of B2B: A New Genesis. Available at: http://www.netmarketmakers.com.

DeNisi, A. S. and Kluger, A. N. (2000) Feedback effectiveness: can 360-degree appraisals be improved? *Academy of Management Perspectives, 14*(1), 129–139.

Den Hartog, D. N. and Verburg, R. M. (2004) High performance work systems, organizational culture and firm effectiveness. *Human Resource Management Journal, 14*(1): 55–78.

Denham, D. and Bratton, J. (2020) Culture and Leadership. In J. Bratton (ed.) *Organizational Leadership* (pp. 79–100). London: Sage.

Denti, L. and Hemlin, S. (2012) Leadership and innovation in organizations: a systematic review of factors that mediate or moderate the relationship. *International Journal of Innovation Management, 16*(3): 1–20.

Denton, D. K. (1999) Employee involvement, pollution control, and pieces to the puzzle. *Environmental Management and Health, 10*: 105–11.

Department of Business, Energy and Industrial Strategy (2020) *Trade Union Membership, UK 1995–2019*. London: National Statistics. Available at: https://assets.publishing.service.gov.uk/government/uploads/system/uploads/attachment_data/file/887740/Trade-union-membership-2019-statistical-bulletin.pdf. Accessed 17 August 2020.

Derlien, H. U. and Peters, B. G. (2008) *The State at Work* Vol. 1: Public sector Employment in ten western Countries. Cheltenham: Edward Elgar Publishing.

Devanna, M., Fombrun, C. and Tichy, N. (1984) A framework for strategic human resource management. In C. Fombrun, N. Tichy and M. Devanna (eds) *Strategic Human Resource Management* (pp. 3–18). New York: John Wiley & Sons,

Devine, T. M. (2015) *Recovering Scotland's Slavery Past*. Edinburgh: Edinburgh University Press.

Devlin, H. (2018) Unconscious bias: what is it and can it be eliminated? *The Guardian*, 2 December, online. Available at: https://www.theguardian.com/uk-news/2018/dec/02/unconscious-bias-what-is-it-and-can-it-be-eliminated. Accessed 12 October 2020.

Dharmapala, D., McAdams, R. H. and Rappaport, J. (2019) Collective bargaining rights and police misconduct: evidence from Florida. *University of Chicago Coase-Sandor Institute for Law & Economics Research Paper* (831).

Dickens, L. and Hall, M. (2010) The changing legal framework of employment relations. In T. Colling and M. Terry (eds) *Industrial Relations: Theory and Practice* (3rd edn) (pp. 298–322). Chichester: John Wiley & Sons.

Dickinson, J. (2006) Employees' preferences for the bases of pay differentials. *Employee Relations*, *28*(2):164–83. Available at: https://doi.org/10.1108/01425450610639383.

Diekma, A. B. and Eagly, A. H. (2000) Stereotypes as dynamic constructs: women and men of the past, present, and future. *Personality and Social Psychology Bulletin*, *26*: 1171–88.

Dijk, H., Engen, M. and Paauwe, J. (2012) Reframing the business case: a values and virtues perspective. *Journal of Business Ethics*, *111*: 73–84.

Disney, R. (1990) Explanations of the decline in trade union density in Britain: an appraisal. *British Journal of Industrial Relations*, *28*(2): 165–77.

Dobbins, T., Plows, A. and Lloyd-Williams, H. (2014) *Work, Employment and Society*, *28*(4): 515–32.

Docherty, P., Kira, M. and Shani, A. B. (2009) *Creating Sustainable Work Systems* (2nd edn). London: Routledge.

Dodd, V. and Campbell, D. (2020) UK health watchdog may investigate coronavirus deaths. *The Guardian*, 8 May, online. Available at: https://www.theguardian.com/world/2020/may/08/uk-health-watchdog-may-investigate-coronavirus-deaths. Accessed 2 September 2020.

Doellgast, V. (2010) Collective voice under decentralized bargaining: a comparative study of work reorganization in US and German call centres. *British Journal of Industrial Relations*, *48*(2): 375–99.

Doeringer, P. and Piore, M. J. (1971) *Internal labor markets and manpower adjustment*. New York: D. C. Heath.

Doherty, M. (2009) When the working day is through: the end of work as identity? *Work, Employment and Society*, *23*(1): 84–101.

Doherty, N. and Tyson, S. (2000) HRM and employee well-being: raising the ethical stakes. In D. Winstanley and J. Woodall (eds) *Ethical Issues in Contemporary Human Resource Management* (pp. 102–15). Basingstoke: Palgrave.

Donkin, R. (2010) *The Future of Work*. Basingstoke: Palgrave Macmillan.

Donovan, L. (1968) Report of the Royal Commission on Trade Unions and Employers Associations. Cmnd 3623. London: HMSO.

Doolittle, R. and Wang, C. (2021) Power Gap. *The Globe and Mail*, 23 January, pp. E1–10.

Doran, T., Fullwood, C., Reeves, D., Gravelle, H. and Roland, M. (2008) Exclusion of patients from pay-for-performance targets by English physicians. *New England Journal of Medicine*, *359*(3): 274–84.

Doward, J. and Munro, M. (2017) It's not what you know ... poorer graduates struggle for job as unpaid internships. *The Observer*, 16 April, p. 5.

Dowling, P., Festing, M. and Eagle, S. (2017) *International Human Resource Management* (7th edn). Melbourne: Cengage Learning.

Downey, M. (1999) *Effective Coaching*. London: Orion Business.

Downey, S. N., van der Werff, L., Thomas, K. M. and Plaut, V. C. (2015) The role of diversity practices and inclusion in promoting trust and employee engagement. *Journal of Applied Social Psychology*, *45*(1): 35–44.

Drohan, M. (2000) Technology comes with a price: stress and depression. *Globe and Mail*, 11 October, p. B15.

Drucker, P. (1961) *The Practice of Management*. London: Mercury Books.

Drucker, P. F. (1999) *Management: Tasks, Responsibilities*, Practices. Oxford: Butterworth-Heinemann.

Du Gay, P. (2000) *In Praise of Bureaucracy: Weber – Organization – Ethics*. London: Sage.

Duggan, K. 92015) Why the annual performance review is going extinct. Fast Company, 21 October. Available at: https://www.fastcompany.com/3052135/why-the-annual-performance-review-is-going-extinct Accessed 26 June 2020.

Dulewicz, V. and Higgs, M. (2000) Emotional intelligence: a review and evaluation. *Journal of Managerial Psychology*, *15*(4): 341–72.

Duncan, R. B. (1972) Characteristics of organizational environments and perceived environmental uncertainty. *Administrative Science Quarterly*, *17*(3): 313–27.

Dundon, T. (2003) Employer opposition and union avoidance in the UK. *Industrial Relations Journal*, *33*(3): 234–45.

Dundon, T. and Rafferty, A. (2018) The (potential) demise of HRM? *Human Resource Management Journal*, *28*(3): 377–91.

Dundon, T., Wilkinson, A., Marchington, M. and Ackers, P. (2004) The meaning and purpose of employee voice. *International Journal of Human Resource Management*, *15*(6): 1149–70.

Dunkley, E. (2020) HSBC hires strategy chief amid push into Asia. *The Sunday Times*, 31 May, p. B1.

Duxbury, L. and Higgins, C. (2002) Telework: a primer for the millennium introduction. In C. L. Cooper and R. J. Burke (eds) *The New World of Work: Challenges and Opportunities* (pp. 157–200). Oxford: Blackwell.

Dweck, C. S. (1999) *Self-theories: Their role in Motivation, Personality, and Development*. Philadelphia, PA: Psychology Press.

Dwelly, T. and Bennion, Y. (2003) *Time To Go Home: Embracing the Home-working Revolution*. London: Work Foundation.

Dyck, D. E. (2002) *Disability Management: Theory, Strategy and Industrial Practice* (2nd edn). Markham, Ontario: Butterworths.

Dyer, L. and Holder, G. (1988) A strategic perspective of human resource management. In L. Dyer (ed.) *Human Resource Management: Evolving Roles and Responsibilities*. Washington: BNA.

Dyllick, T. and Hockerts, K. (2002) Beyond the business case for corporate sustainability. *Business Strategy and the Environment, 11*(2): 130–41.

Eady, J. and Motraghi, N. (2010) United action. *New Law Journal*, 160 (7423).

Eagly, A. (1987) *Sex differences in social behavior: a social-role interpretation*. Hillsdale, NJ: Lawrence Erlbaum.

Ebbinghaus, B. and Waddington, J. (2000) United Kingdom/ Great Britain. In B. Ebbinghaus and J. Visser (eds) *The Societies of Europe: Trade Unions in Western Europe Since 1945* (pp. 705–56). Basingstoke: Palgrave Macmillan.

Edgell, S. and Granter, E. (2020) *The Sociology of Work: Continuity and Change in Paid and Unpaid Work* (3rd edn). London: Sage.

Edwards, G., Elliott, C., Iszatt-White, M. and Schedlitzki, D. (2013) Critical and alternative approaches to leadership learning and development. *Management Learning, 44*(1): 3–10.

Edwards, M. R. and Edwards, K. (2019) *Predictive HR Analytics: Mastering the HR Metric* (2nd edn). London: Kogan Page.

Edwards, P. and Sengupta, S. (2010) Industrial relations and economic performance. In T. Colling and M. Terry (eds) *Industrial Relations: Theory and Practice* (3rd edn) (pp. 378–97). Chichester: John Wiley & Sons.

Edwards, P., Belanger, J. and Wright, M. (2002) The social relations of productivity. *Relations Industrielles/Industrial Relations, 57*(2): 309–28.

Edwards, P. K. (1995) From industrial relations to the employment relationship: the development of research in Britain. *Relations Industrielles/Industrial Relations, 50*(1): 39–65.

Edwards, P. K. (2003a) The employment relationship. In P. Edwards (ed.) *Industrial Relations: Theory and Practice in Britain* (pp. 1–36). Oxford: Blackwell.

Edwards, P. K. (2003b) The future of industrial relations. In P. Ackers and A. Wilkinson (eds) *Understanding Work and Employment: Industrial Relations in Transition*, (pp. 337–58). Oxford: Oxford University Press..

Edwards, R. (1979) *Contested Terrain: The Transformation of the Workplace in the Twentieth Century*. London: Heinemann.

Edwards, T. and Ferner, A. (2002) The renewed 'American Challenge': a review of employment practice in US multinationals. *Industrial Relations Journal, 33*(2): 94–111.

Edwards, T. and Kuruvilla, S. (2005) International HRM: national business systems, organizational politics and the international division of labour in MNCs. *International Journal of Human Resource Management, 16*(1): 1–21.

Egan, J. (2004) Putting job evaluation to work: tips from the front line. *IRS Employment Review, 792*: 8–15.

Egan, M. (2016) 5,300 Wells Fargo employees fired over 2 million phony accounts. *CNN Business*, 9 September online. Available at: https://money.cnn.com/2016/09/08/investing/wells-fargo-created-phony-accounts-bank-fees/index.html Accessed 11 October 2020.

Egan, M. (2020) US government fines Wells Fargo $3 billion for its 'staggering' fake-accounts scandal. *CNN Business*, 24 February online. Available at: https://edition.cnn.com/2020/02/21/business/wells-fargo-settlement-doj-sec/index.html#:~:text=Weather-,US%20government%20fines%20Wells%20Fargo%20%243%20billion,'staggering'%20fake%2Daccounts%20scandal&text=New%20York%20(CNN%20Business)%20Wells,troubled%20bank%20over%20many%20years. Accessed 7 October 2020.

Egri, C. P. and Herman, S. (2000) Leadership in the North American environmental sector: values, leadership styles, and contexts of environmental leaders and their organizations. *Academy of Management Journal, 34*(4): 571–604.

Ehnert, I., Parsa, S., Roper, I., Wagner, M. and Muller-Camen, M. (2016) Reporting on sustainability and HRM: a comparative study of sustainability reporting practices by the world's largest companies. *International Journal of Human Resource Management, 27*(1): 88–108.

Eichinger, R. W. and Lombardo, M. M. (2003) Knowledge Summary Series: 360-Degree Assessment. *Human Resource Planning, 26*(4).

Ehrke, F., Berthold, A. and Steffens, M. C. (2014) How diversity training can change attitudes: increasing perceived complexity of superordinate groups to improve intergroup relations. *Journal of Experimental Social Psychology, 53*: 193–206.

Einarsen, S. (2000) Harassment and bullying at work: a review of the Scandinavian approach. *Aggression and Violent Behavior, 5*(4): 379–401.

Einarsen, S., Hoel, H., Zapf, D. and Cooper, C. L. (2003) The concept of bullying at work: the European tradition. In S. Einarsen, H. Hoel, D. Zapf and C. L. Cooper (eds) *Bullying and Emotional Abuse in the Workplace: International Perspectives in Research and Practice* (pp. 3–30). New York, NY: Taylor and Francis.

Einarsen, S., Hoel, H. and Notelaers, G. (2009) Measuring exposure to bullying and harassment at work: validity, factor structure and psychometric properties of the Negative Acts Questionnaire-Revised. *Work and Stress*, 23(1): 24–44.

Einarsen, S., Hoel, H., Zapf, D. and Cooper, C. L. (2011) The concept of bullying and harassment at work: the European tradition. In S. Einarsen, H. Hoel, D. Zapf and C. L. Cooper (eds) *Bullying and Harassment in the Workplace* (2nd edn) (pp. 3–41). Boca Raton, FL: Taylor & Francis.

Elena-Iuliana, I. and Maria, C. (2016) Organizational performance: a concept that seeks to find itself. *Annals of 'Constantin Brancusi' University of Targu-Jiu. Economy Series*, (4): 179–83. Available at: https://pdfs.semanticscholar.org/2a4a/ffed8b1f9b05f52535ff37d8288264aefaff.pdf. Accessed 22 June 2020.

Elenkov, D. (1998) Can American management concepts work in Russia?: a cross-cultural comparative study. *California Management Review, 40*(4): 133–56.

Elger, T. and Smith, C. (eds) (2010) *Global Japanization?: The Transnational Transformation of the Labour Process*. London: Routledge.

Ellinger, A. D. (2015) Coaching and mentoring. In R. F. Poell, T. S. Rocco and G. L. Roth (eds) *The Routledge Companion to Human Resource Development* (pp. 258–71). London: Routledge.

Elliott, L. (2016) A zero-hours contract is not 'flexibility' but exploitation – and it's rising. *The Guardian*, 9 March online. Available at: https://www.theguardian.com/business/2016/mar/09/zero-hour-contract-is-not-flexiblity-but-exploitation-and-its-rising. Accessed 7 October 2020.

Elliot, L. (2020) The left must stop mourning Brexit – and start seeing its huge potential, *The Guardian*, 31 December. Available at: https://www.theguardian.com/commentisfree/2020/dec/31/the-left-brexit-economic-uk. Accessed 11 January 2021.

Elliott, L. and Treanor, J. (2015) Bank of England's disarray in the face of financial crisis revealed. *The Guardian*, 7 January, p. 27.

Elorza, U., Aritzeta, A. and Ayestarán, S. (2011) Exploring the black box in Spanish firms: the effect of the actual and perceived system on employees' commitment and organizational performance. *International Journal of Human Resource Management, 22*(7): 1401–22.

Emir, A. (2014) *Selwyn's Law of Employment* (18th edn). Oxford: Oxford University Press.

Emmott, M. (2015) Foreword. In S. Johnstone and P. Ackers, *Finding a Voice at Work?* (pp. vii–xii). Oxford: Oxford University Press.

Engert, S., Rauter, R. and Baumgartner, R. J. (2016) Exploring the integration of corporate sustainability into strategic management: a literature review. *Journal of Cleaner Production, 112*: 2833–50.

Environmental Protection Agency (1996) *Indoor Air Pollution: An Introduction for Health Professionals*. Washington, DC: Environmental Protection Agency. Available at: https://www.epa.gov/sites/production/files/2015-01/documents/indoor_air_pollution.pdf. Accessed 20 September 2020.

Epitropaki, O., Martin, R. and Thomas, G. (2018) Relational Leadership. In J. Antonakis and D. Day (eds) *The Nature of Leadership* (3rd edn) (pp. 109–37). Los Angeles, CA: Sage.

Epstein, G. (2015) *Financialization: There's Something Happening Here. Political Economy Research Institute*. Amherst, MA: University of Massachusetts. Available at: https://www.peri.umass.edu/publication/item/684-financialization-there-s-something-happening-here.

Eraut, M. (2000) Non-formal learning and tacit knowledge in professional work. *British Journal of Educational Psychology, 70*: 113–36.

Erdal, D. (2011) *Beyond the Corporation: Humanity at Work*. New York: Random House.

Eswaran, V. (2019) The business case for diversity in the workplace is now overwhelming. *World Economic Forum*, 29 April.

ETUI (2020) Worker Participation. Brussels: European Trade Union Institute. Available at: https://www.worker-participation.eu/National-Industrial-Relations/Across-Europe. Accessed 21 August 2020.

Etzioni, A. (1988) *The Moral Dimension*. New York: Free Press.

EU (2020) Commission moves to ensure supply of personal protective equipment in the EU, European Union: Brussels. Available at: https://trade.ec.europa.eu/doclib/press/index.cfm?id=2122 Accessed 16 May 2020.

Eubanks, B. (2019) *Artificial Intelligence for HR*. London: Kogan Page.

European Commission (2008) *Restructuring in Europe*. Brussels: European Commission.

Evans, R. (2015) Blacklisted: the secret war between big business and union activists – a book review. *The Guardian*, 9 July. Available at: https://www.theguardian.com/uk-news/undercover-with-paul-lewis-and-rob-evans/2015/jul/09/blacklisted-the-secret-war-between-big-business-and-union-activists-a-book-review. Accessed 15 July 2016.

Evans, S., Vladimirova, D., Holgado, M., Van Fossen, K., Yang, M., Silva, E. A. and Barlow, C. Y. (2017) Business model innovation for sustainability: towards a unified perspective for Creation of sustainable business models. *Business Strategy and the Environment, 26*(5): 597–608.

Everett, C. (2020) What will shape the managers of the future? *Personnel Today*, 16 July. Available at: https://www.personneltoday.com/hr/what-will-shape-the-managers-of-the-future/. Accessed 23 June 2020.

Ewart, C. (2020) *Update on Human Rights Protection in Scotland: Recommendations to Review and Revitalise Collective Action*. Glasgow: Jimmy Reid Foundation.

Ewing, K. D. E. and Hendy, J. (2013) *Reconstruction after the Crisis: A Manifesto for Collective Bargaining*. Liverpool: Institute of Employment Rights.

EY (2020) Beyond Covid-19: What will be the 'new' normal? Available at: https://assets.ey.com/content/dam/ey-sites/ey-com/fi_fi/pdf/beyond-covid-19-what-will-define-the-new-normal.pdf. Accessed 20 May 2020.

Fairclough, N. (2013) *Critical Discourse Analysis* (2nd edn). London: Routledge.

Fairholm, G. W. (1996) Spiritual leadership: fulfilling whole-self needs at work. *Leadership and Organizational Development, 17*(5): 11–17.

The Fair Work Convention (2016) *Putting Fair Work at the Heart of Scotland's Workplaces and Economy*. Glasgow: Fair Work Convention. Available at: https://www.fairworkconvention.scot/.

Fang, M. and Gerhart, B. (2012) Does pay for performance diminish intrinsic interest? *International Journal of Human Resource Management, 23*(6): 1176–96.

Faragher, J. (2019) How employees are using activism to make their voices heard. *Personnel Today*, 16 July. Available at: https://www.personneltoday.com/hr/how-employees-are-using-social-activism-to-make-their-voices-heard/. Accessed 23 June 2020.

Farazmand, A. (2002) Privatization and globalization: a critical analysis with implications for public management education and training. *International Review of Administrative Sciences, 68*: 355–71.

Farina, E., Green, C. and McVicar, D. (2019) Zero hours contracts and their growth. *British Journal of Industrial Relations, 58*(3): 507–31.

Farndale, E., Brewster, C., Ligthart, P. and Poutsma, E. (2017) The effects of market economy type and foreign MNE subsidiaries on the convergence and divergence of HRM. *Journal of International Business Studies, 48*(9): 1065–86.

Farnham, D. (2015) *The Changing Faces of Employment Relations*. London: Palgrave.

Farnhill, T. (2018) Union renewal and workplace greening – three case studies. *British Journal of Industrial Relations, 56*(4): 716–43.

Farr, C. (2019) Apple is offering free genetic tests to all its Silicon Valley employees. *CNBC* online. Available at: https://www.cnbc.com/2019/12/13/apple-teams-with-color-to-offer-free-dna-tests-to-employees.html#:~:text=Apple%20employees%20in%20Silicon%20Valley,pilot%20partnership%20with%20Color%20Genomics.&text=The%20idea%20is%20to%20move,health%20risks%20down%20the%20line. Accessed 7 August 2020.

Farr, J. L., Fairchild, J. and Cassidy, S. E. (2008) Technology and performance appraisal. In M. D. Coovert and L. Foster Thompson (eds) *The Psychology of Workplace Technology* (pp. 77–98). New York: Routledge.

Farrell, A. and Hart, M. (1998) What does sustainability really mean? The search for useful indicators. *Environment, 40*(9): 4–31.

Farrell, D. (2005) Offshoring: value creation through economic change. *Journal of Management Studies, 42*(3): 675–83.

Felstead, A. and Henseke, G. (2017) Assessing the growth of remote working and its consequences for effort, well-being and work-life balance. *New Technology, Work and Employment, 32*(3): 195–212.

Felstead, A., Jewson, N., Phizacklea, A. and Walters, S. (2002) Opportunities to work at home in the context of work–life balance. *Human Resource Management Journal, 12*(1): 54–76.

Fenwick, T. (2001) *Sociocultural Perspectives on Learning through Work*, Number 92, San Francisco, CA: Jossey-Bass.

Ferguson, D. (2019) Record levels of stress 'put teachers at breaking point'. *The Guardian*, 10 November.

Ferlie, E. and Ongaro, E. (2015) *Strategic Management in Public Service Organizations*. London: Routledge.

Fernandez Campbell, A. (2019) CEOs made 287 times more money last year than their workers did. Vox. Available at: https://www.vox.com/policy-and-politics/2019/6/26/18744304/ceo-pay-ratio-disclosure-2018#:~:text=The%20average%20chief%20executive%20of,the%20AFL%2DCIO%20labor%20federation. Accessed 13 July 2020.

Ferner, A. (1997) Country of origin effects and HRM in multinational companies. *Human Resources Management Journal, 7*: 19–37.

Ferner, A. and Quintanilla, J. (1998) Multinationals, national business systems and HRM: the enduring influence of national identity or a process of 'Anglo-Saxonization'. *International Journal of Human Resource Management, 9*(4): 710–31.

Ferner, A., Quintanilla, J. and Varul, M. Z. (2001) Country-of-origin effects, host-country effects, and the management of HR in multinationals: German companies in Britain and Spain. *Journal of World Business, 36*(2): 107–27.

Ferner, A., Bélanger, J., Tregaskis, O., Morley, M. and Quintanilla, J. (2013) US multinationals and the control of subsidiary employment policies. *ILR Review, 66*(3): 645–69.

Ferrant, G., Pesando, L. M. and Nowacka, K. (2014) *Unpaid Care Work: the missing link in the analysis of gender gaps in labour outcomes*. Boulogne Billancourt: OECD Development Center.

Ferris, P., Deakin, R. and Mathieson, S. (2018) Workplace bullying policies: A review of best practices and research on effectiveness. In P. D'Cruz, E. Noronha, C. Caponecchia, J. Escartín, D. Salin, and M. Tuckey (eds) *Dignity and Inclusion at Work. Handbooks of Workplace Bullying, Emotional Abuse and Harassment*, vol 3. Springer, Singapore.

Field, L. (2004) Rethinking 'Organizational learning'. In G. Foley (ed.) *Dimensions of Adult Learning: Adult Education and Training in a Global Era* (pp. 201–18). Crows Nest, New South Wales, AU: Allen & Unwin.

Field, T. (1996) *Bully in Sight: How to Predict, Resist, Challenge and Combat Workplace Bullying*. Wantage: Wessex Press.

Fieschi, C. (2019) *Populocracy*. Newcastle upon Tyne: Agenda Publishing.

Figueres, C. and Zycher, B. (2020) Can we tackle both climate change and Covid-19 recovery? *The Financial Times*, 7 May.

Findlay, P. and Thompson, P. (2017) Contemporary work: its meanings and demands. *Journal of Industrial Relations, 59*(2): 122–38.

Findlay, P., McKinlay, A., Marks, A. and Thompson, P. (2009) Collective bargaining and new work regimes: 'too important to be left to bosses'. *Industrial Relations Journal, 40*(3): 235–51.

Fine, B. (1998) *Labour Market Theory: A Constructive Reassessment*. London: Routledge.

Fine, C., Sojo, V. and Lawford-Smith, H. (2020) Why does workplace gender diversity matter? Justice, organizational benefits, and policy. *Social Issues and Policy Review, 14*(1): 36–72.

Fineman, S. (1996) Emotional subtexts in corporate greening. *Organizational Studies, 17*(3): 479–500.

Fineman, S. (1997) Constructing the green manager. *British Journal of Management, 8*(1): 31–38.

Finkelstein, L. M. (2015) Older workers, stereotypes, and discrimination in the context of the employment relationship. In P. M. Bal., D. T. A. M. Kooij and D. M. Rousseau (eds) *Aging Workers and the Employee-Employer Relationship* (pp. 13–32). Heidelberg: Springer.

Fiscal Commission, (2013) *First Report – Macroeconomic Framework*. Edinburgh: Scottish Government.

Fischer, A. M. (2014) Redistribution as social justice for decarbonising the global economy. *The Economic and Labour Relations Review, 25*(4): 574–86.

Fischlmayr, I. and Kollinger, I. (2010) Work-life balance – a neglected issue among Austrian female expatriates. *International Journal of Human Resource Management, 21*(4): 455–87.

Fishman, C. (2007) *The Wal-Mart Effect: How an Out-of-town Superstore Became a Superpower*. London: Penguin.

Fishman, J. (1993) *The Transformation of Threadneedle Street: The Deregulation and Reregulation of Britain's Financial Services*. Durham, NC: Carolina Academic Press.

Flanders, A. (1964) *The Fawley Productivity Agreements*. London: Faber.

Flassbeck, H. and Lapavitsas, C. (2015) *Against the Troika: Crisis and Austerity in the Eurozone*. London: Veso.

Follett, M. P. (1927) *Dynamic Administration* (reprint 1942). New York: Harper & Brothers Publishers.

Fombrun, C. J. (1984) The external context of human resource management. In C. Fombrun, N. M. Tichy and M. A. Devanna (eds) *Strategic Human Resource Management* (pp. 3–18). New York: John Wiley & Sons.

Fombrun, C. J., Tichy, N. M. and Devanna, M. A. (eds) (1984) *Strategic Human Resource Management*. New York: John Wiley & Sons.

Ford, H. (1926) *Today and Tomorrow*. New York: Doubleday, Page and Co.

Forde, C., Stuart, M., Gardiner, J., Greenwood, I., MacKenzie, R. and Perett, R. (2008) *Socially Responsible Restructuring in an Era of Mass Layoffs*. CERIC Working Paper No. 5. Leeds: Leeds University.

Fortson, D. (2020) Big brands decide that Black lives matter – except in the boardroom. *The Sunday Times*, 7 June, p. 5.

Foster, P., Pickard, J., Strauss, D. and Brunsden, J. (2021) UK workers' rights at risk in plans to rip up EU labour market rules. *Financial Times*, 14 January. Available at: https://www.ft.com/content/55588f86-a4f8-4cf3-aecb-38723b787569. Accessed 15 January 2021.

Foucault M. (1998) *History of Sexuality*. London: Penguin Books.

Fox, A. (1966) *Industrial Sociology and Industrial Relations*. London: HMSO.

Fox, A. (1974) *Beyond Contract: Work, Power and Trust Relations*. London: Faber & Faber.

Fox, A. (1985) *Man Mismanagement* (2nd edn). London: Hutchinson.

Fox, S. and Cowan, R. L. (2015) Revision of the workplace bullying checklist: the importance of human resource management's role in defining and addressing workplace bullying. *Human Resource Management Journal*, *25*(1): 116–30.

Fox, S. and Stallworth, L. E. (2010) The battered apple: An application of stressor-emotion-control/support theory to teachers' experience of violence and bullying. *Human Relations*, *63*(7):927-54. Available at: https://journals.sagepub.com/doi/10.1177/0018726709349518. Accessed 29 May 2021.

Francis, H. and Keegan, A. (2006) The changing face of HRM: in search of balance. *Human Resource Management Journal*, *16*(3): 231–49.

Francis, R. (2013) *Report of the Mid Staffordshire NHS Foundation Trust Public Inquiry*. London: HMSO.

Frege, C. M. (2002) A critical assessment of the theoretical and empirical research on works councils. *British Journal of Industrial Relations*, *40*(2): 221–48.

French, J., Jr. and Raven, B. (1960) The bases for social power. In D. Cartwright and A. Zander (eds) *Group Dynamics* (pp. 607–2). New York: Harper & Row.

French, M. T., Maclean, J. C., Sindelar, J. L. and Fang, H. (2011) The morning after: alcohol misuse and employment problems. *Applied Economics*, *43*(21): 2705–20.

Frenkel, M. (2008) The multicultural corporation as a third space: rethinking international management discourse on knowledge transfer through Homi Bhabba. *Academy of Management Review*, *33*(4): 924–42.

Frese, M., Brodbeck, F., Heinbokel, T., Mooser, C., Schleiffenbaum, E. and Thiemann, P. (1991) Errors in training computer skills: On the positive function of errors. *Human-Computer Interaction*, *6*(1):77–93.

Friedan, B. (1963). *The Feminine Mystique*. WW Norton & Company.

Friedberg, B. A. (2020) Are We in a Baby Boomer Retirement Crisis? Available at: https://www.investopedia.com/articles/personal-finance/032216/are-we-baby-boomer-retirement-crisis.asp. Accessed 22 May, 2020

Friedman, A. (1977) *Industry and Labour: Class Struggle at Work and Monopoly Capitalism*. London: Macmillan.

Friedman, G. (2014) Workers without employers: shadow corporations and the rise of the gig economy. *Review of Keynesian Economics*, *2*(2): 171–88.

Fröbel, P. and Marchington, M. (2005) Teamworking structures and worker perceptions: a cross-national study in pharmaceuticals. *International Journal of Human Resource Management*, *16*(2): 256–76.

Frost, A. and Taris, D. (2005) Understanding the unionization decision. In M. Gunderson, A. Ponak and D. Taras (eds) *Union-Management Relations in Canada* (5th edn) (pp. 23–57). Toronto: Pearson.

Froud, J., Haslam, C. S., Johal, S. and Williams, K. (2000) Restructuring for shareholder value and its implications for labour. *Cambridge Journal of Economics*, *24*(6): 771–97.

Fry, H. (2018) *Hello World: How to be Human in the Age of the Machine*. New York: Norton & Company.

Fryer, M. (2019) HRM: an ethical issue. In D. Collings, G. Wood and L. Szamosi (eds) *Human Resource Management: A Critical Approach* (2nd edn) (pp. 98-116). London: Routledge.

Furnham, A. (2008) HR professionals' beliefs about, and knowledge of, assessment techniques and psychometric tests. *International Journal of Selection and Assessment*, *16*(3): 300–5.

Fyfe, J. (1986) Putting people back into the manpower planning equation. *Personnel Management*, October: 64–9.

Gabris, G. T. and Ihrke, D. M. (2001) Does performance appraisal contribute to heightened levels of employee burnout? The results of one study. *Public Personnel Management*, *30*(2): 157–72.

Gabzdylova, B., Raffensperger, J. F. and Castka, P. (2009) Sustainability in the New Zealand wine industry: drivers, stakeholders and practices. *Journal of Cleaner Production*, *17*(11): 992–8.

Gager, S., Bowley, R., Cruz, E. and Batty, R. (2015) Global recruiting trends. LinkedIn.

Galin, A. and Benoliel, B. (1990) Does the way you dress affect your performance rating. *Personnel*, *67*(8): 49–52.

Gall, G. (2016) *The Fair Work Framework: a critique*. Glasgow: The Jimmy Reid Foundation.

Gall, G. (2020) Emerging forms of worker collectivism among the precariat: When will capital's 'gig' be up? *Capital & Class*, February, pp. 1–8. Available at: https://doi.org/10.1177/0309816820906344.

Gall, G. and McKay, S. (1994) Trade union derecognition in Britain, 1988–1994. *British Journal of Industrial Relations*, *32*(3): 433–48.

Gallacher, G. and Hossain, I. (2020) Remote work and employment dynamics under COVID-19: evidence from Canada. *Canadian Public Policy*, *46*(S1): S44–S54.

Gallagher, P. (2000) *Human Resource Planning*. Ohio University: Scitech Educational.

Gallie, D., Felstead, A., Green, F. and Inanc, H. (2013) Fear at work in Britain: first findings from the Skills and Employment Survey 2012. Available at: https://www.cardiff.ac.uk/__data/assets/pdf_file/0003/118641/4.-Fear-at-Work-Minireport.pdf. Accessed 28 May 2021.

Gallo, A. (2011) Turning stress into an asset. *Harvard Business Review*, 28 June online. Available at: https://hbr.org/2011/06/turning-stress-into-an-asset. Accessed 20 September 2020.

Gamble, J. (2003) Transferring human resource practices from the United Kingdom to China: the limits and potential for convergence. *International Journal of Human Resource Management*, *14*(3): 369–87.

Garavan, T. (2007) A strategic perspective on human resource development. *Advances in Developing Human Resources*, *9*(1): 11–30.

Garavan, T. and McGuire, D. (2010) Human resource development and society: human resource development's role in embedding corporate social responsibility, sustainability, and ethics in organizations. *Advances in Developing Human Resources*, *12*(5): 487–507.

Garavan, T. N. (1997) The learning organization: a review and an evaluation. *Learning Organization*, *4*(1): 18–29.

Garengo, P., Biazzo, S. and Bititci, U. (2005) Performance measurement systems in SMEs: a review for a research agenda. *International Journal of Management Reviews*, *7*(1): 25–47.

Garvey, R., Stokes, P. and Megginson, D. (2009) *Coaching and Mentoring: Theory and Practice*. London: Sage.

Garvey, R., Megginson, D. and Stokes, P. (2014) *Coaching and Mentoring* (2nd edn). London: Sage.

Geary, J. F. and Dobbins, A. (2001) Teamworking: a new dynamic in pursuit of management control. *Human Resource Management Journal*, *11*(1): 3–23.

Gegenfurtner, A., Veermans, K., Festner, D. and Gruber, H. (2009) Motivation to transfer training: an integrative literature review. *Human Resource Development Review*, *8*(3): 403–423.

Gennard, J. and Kelly, J. (1997) The unimportance of labels: the diffusion of the personnel/HRM function. *Industrial Relations Journal*, *28*(1): 27–42.

Gentle, S. (2019) UK employees suffer 'appraisal apathy' as productivity sees sharpest fall in five years. *Onrec*, 21 October online. Available at: https://www.onrec.com/news/statistics/uk-employees-suffer-%E2%80%98appraisal-apathy%E2%80%99-as-productivity-sees-sharpest-fall-in-five. Accessed 2 October 2020.

Georgiou, S., Thomson, M., Richardson-Owen, A. and Edwards, H. (2009) The costs of workplace injuries and work-related ill health in the UK. *Ege Academic Review*, *9*(3): 1035–46. Available at: eab.ege.edu.tr/pdf/9_3/C9-53-M13 pdf. Accessed 2010.

Gerhart, B. (2007) Horizontal and vertical fit in human resource systems. In C. Ostroff and T. Judge (eds) *Perspectives on Organizational Fit*, SIOP Organizational Frontiers Series (pp.317–48). New York: Lawrence Erlbaum Associates, Taylor & Francis Group.

Gerhart, B. (2008) Modelling HRM and performance linkages. In P. Boxall, J. Purcell and P. Wright (eds) *The Oxford Handbook of Human Resource Management* (pp. 552–80). Oxford: Oxford University Press.

Gerhart, B. (2018) Compensation. In J. Storey, P. M. Wright and D. Ulrich (eds) *The Routledge Companion to Strategic Human Resource Management* (pp. 224–44). London: Routledge.

Gershgorn, D. (2018) Companies are on the hook if their hiring algorithms are biased. *Quartz*, 22 October online. Available at: https://qz.com/1427621/companies-are-on-the-hook-if-their-hiring-algorithms-are-biased. Accessed 12 August 2020.

Gheyoh Ndzi, E. (2019) Zero-hours contracts have a devastating impact on career progression – Labour is right to ban them. *The Conversation*, 24 September online. Available at: https://theconversation.com/zero-hours-contracts-have-a-devastating-impact-on-career-progression-labour-is-right-to-ban-them-123066. Accessed 7 October 2020.

Gibb, S. (2003) Line manager involvement in learning and development: small beer or big deal? *Employee Relations*, *25*(3): 281–93.

Giddens, A. (1984) *The Constitution of Society*. Berkeley, CA: University of California Press.

Gilbert, C., De Winne, S. and Sels, L. (2011a) The influence of line managers and HR departments on employees' affective commitment. *International Journal of Human Resource Management*, *22*(8): 1618–37.

Gilbert, C., De Winne, S. and Sels, L. (2011b) Antecedents of front-line managers' perceptions of HR role stressor. *Personnel Review*, *40*(5): 549–69.

Giles, A. and Iain, H. (1989) The collective agreement. In J. Anderson, M. Gunderson, and A. Ponak (eds) *Union Relations in Canada* (2nd edn). Don Mills, Ontario: Addison-Wesley.

Giles, C. (2020) BoE warns UK set to enter worst recession for 300 years. *Financial Times*, 7 May. Available at: https://www.ft.com/content/734e604b-93d9-43a6-a6ec-19e8b22dad3c. Accessed 14 June 2020.

Giles, W. F., Findley, H. M. and Feild, H. S. (1997) Procedural fairness in performance appraisal: Beyond the review session. *Journal of Business and Psychology*, *11*(4): 493–506.

Gillborn, D. (2015) Intersectionality, critical race theory, and the primacy of racism: race, class, gender, and disability in education. *Qualitative Inquiry*, *21*(3): 277–87. Available at: https://doi.org/10.1177/1077800414557827.

Gillinsky, A., Newton, S. K. and Vega, R. F. (2016) Sustainability in the global wine industry: concepts and cases. *Agriculture and Agricultural Science Procedia*, *8*: 37–49.

Gilman, M. and Marginson, P. (2002) Negotiating European Works Councils: contours of constrained choice. *Industrial Relations Journal*, *33*(1): 36–51.

Ginsberg, B. (2011) *The Fall of the Faculty*. Oxford: Oxford University Press.

Glaister, A. (2014) HR outsourcing: the impact on HR role, competency development and relationships. *Human Resource Management Journal*, *24*(2): 211–22.

Glasbeek, H. (1991) The worker as a victim. In D. Poff and W. Waluchow (eds) *Business Ethics in Canada* (2nd edn) (pp. 199–204). Scarborough, Ontario: Prentice Hall.

Glowinkowski, S. P. and Cooper, C. L. (1986) Managers and professionals in business/industrial settings: the research evidence. *Journal of Organizational Behavior Management, 8*(2): 177–193.

Godard, J. (1991) The progressive HRM paradigm: a theoretical and empirical re-examination. *Relations Industrielles/Industrial Relations, 46*(2): 378–99.

Godard, J. (2004) A critical assessment of the high-performance paradigm. *British Journal of Industrial Relations, 42*(2): 349–78.

Godard, J. (2005) *Industrial Relations: The Economy and Society* (3rd edn). Concord, Ontario: Captus Press.

Godard, J. (2014) The psychologization of employment relations? *Human Resource Management Journal, 24*: 1-18. Available at: https://doi.org/10.1111/1748-8583.12030.

Godfrey, M. M., Andersson-Gare, B., Nelson, E. C., Nilsson, M. and Ahlstrom, G. (2014) Coaching interprofessional health care improvement teams: the coachee, the coach and the leader perspectives. *Journal of Nursing Management, 22*(4): 452–64.

Gold, J. (2014) Revans reversed: focusing on the positive for a change. *Action Learning: Research and Practice,11*(3): 264–77.

Gold, J. and Bratton, J. (2014) Towards critical human resource development education (CHRDE): using the sociological imagination to make the HRD profession more critical in the post-crisis era. *Human Resource Development International, 17*(4): 400–15. DOI: 10.1080/13678868.2014.928135

Gold, J. and Thorpe, R. (2008) 'Training, it's a load of crap!': the story of the hairdresser and his 'suit'. *Human Resource Development International, 11*(4): 385–99.

Gold, J. and Yeo, R. (2013) Experiential learning and learning cycles – towards an integrative perspective. In C. Valentin and J. Walton (eds) *Human Resource Development: Practices and Orthodoxies* (pp. 33–57). Basingstoke: Palgrave Macmillan.

Gold, J., Thorpe, R. and Mumford, A. (2010) How leaders and managers learn. *The Gower Handbook of Leadership and Management Development.* (pp. 261–278). Aldershot: Gower.

Gold, J., Holden, R., Iles, P., Stewart, J. and Beardwell, J. (eds) (2013) *Human Resource Development: Theory and Practice* (2nd edn). Basingstoke: Palgrave Macmillan.

Gold, J., Nichol, L. and Harrison, P. (2020) 'L&D must be a participant not a bystander in machine learning', *People Management*, 10 September. Available at: https://www.peoplemanagement.co.uk/voices/comment/ld-must-be-participants-not-bystanders-in-machine-learning. Accessed 10 September 2020.

Goleman, D. (2006) *Emotional Intelligence* (10th anniversary edition). London: Bantam.

Gomez-Mejia, L. R., Berrone, P. and Franco-Santos, M. (2010) *Compensation and Organizational Performance: Theory, Research, and Practice*. London: Routledge.

Gong, Y., Wang, M., Huang, J. C. and Cheung, S. Y. (2014) Toward a goal orientation-based feedback-seeking typology implications for employee performance outcomes. *Journal of Management, 20*(10): 1–27.

Gonsalves, L. (2020) From face time to flex time: the role of physical space in worker temporal flexibility. *Administrative Science Quarterly*. Available at: https://doi.org/10.1177/0001839220907891.

Gonzales, P. M., Blanton, H. and Williams, K. J. (2002) The effects of stereotype threat and double-minority status on the test performance of Latino women. *Personality and Social Psychology Bulletin, 28*(5): 659–70.

Goodfellow, I., Bengio, Y. and Courville, A. (2016) *Deep Learning*. Cambridge, MA: MIT Press.

Goodhart, D. (2020) *Head Hand Heart: The Struggle for Dignity and Status in the 21st-century*. London: Allen Lane.

Goods, C. (2017) Climate change and employment relations. *Journal of Industrial Relations, 59*(5): 670-79.

Goodstein, E. S. (1999) *Economics of the Environment*. Englewood Cliffs, NJ: Prentice Hall.

Gopal, P. (2019) Call racism by its name. That's how to rein it in. *The Guardian*, 9 October, p. J5.

Gopinath, M., Nair, A. and Thangaraj, V. (2018) Espoused and enacted values in an organization: workforce implications. *Management and Labour Studies, 43*(4): 277–93.

Gordon, M. (2020) Covid-19 and the campaign against climate change and a just transition. *Scottish Left Review, 118*, 14.

Gordon, T. J. and Todorova, M. (2019) *Future Studies and Counterfactual Analysis: Seeds of the Future*. London: Palgrave Macmillan.

Gore, E. (2020) COVID-19 and racial capitalism in the UK: why race and class matter for understanding the coronavirus pandemic. Sheffield Political Economy Research Institute. 1 May. Available at: http://speri.dept.shef.ac.uk/2020/05/01/covid-19-and-racial-capitalism-in-the-uk-why-race-and-class-matter-for-understanding-the-coronavirus-pandemic/. Accessed 22 June 2020.

Gorz, A. (ed.) (1976) *The Division of Labour: The Labour Process and Class-Struggle in Modern Capitalism* (Vol. 2). Brighton: Harvester Press.

Gorz, A. (1982) *Farewell to the Working Class*. London: Pluto.

Gosden, E. (2020) Mental health 'is a priority'. *The Times*, 25 August online. Available at: https://www.thetimes.co.uk/edition/business/mental-health-is-a-priority-lfd27dr3b. Accessed 2 September 2020.

Gospel, H. (2013) Human Resource Management: a historical perspective. In A. Wilkinson, N. Bacon, T. Redman and S. Snell (eds) *The Sage Handbook of Human Resource Management* (pp. 12–30). London: Sage.

Gospel, H. F. and Littler, C. R. (eds) (1983) *Managerial Strategies and Industrial Relations*. London: Heinemann.

Gould, A. (2010) Working at McDonalds: some redeeming features of McJobs. *Work, Employment and Society, 24*(4): 780–802.

Gourlay, S. (2006) Towards conceptual clarity for 'tacit knowledge': a review of empirical studies. *Knowledge Management Research and Practice, 4*(1):60–9.

Govindarajulu, N. and Daily, B. F. (2004) Motivating employees for environmental improvement. *Industrial Management and Data Systems, 104*: 364–72.

Graeber, D. (2014) Savage capitalism is back – and it will not tame itself. *The Guardian*, 30 May. Available at: https://www.theguardian.com/commentisfree/2014/may/30/savage-capitalism-back-radical-challenge Accessed 30 August 2016.

Graeber, D. (2018) *Bullshit Jobs: A Theory*. New York: Simon & Schuster.

Grant, K., Maxwell, G. and Ogden, S. (2014) Skills utilisation in Scotland: exploring the views of managers and employees. *Employee Relations*, *36*(5): 458–79.

Grant, R. M. (2016) *Contemporary Strategy Analysis: Text and Cases Edition*. Chichester: John Wiley & Sons.

Green, F., Felstead, A., Gallie, D. and Henseke, G. (2018) Work intensity in Britain: First findings from the Skills and Employment Survey 2017

Green, N. (2012) Correlation is not causation, *The Guardian*, 6 January. Available at: https://www.theguardian.com/science/blog/2012/jan/06/correlation-causation#:~:text=%22Correlation%20is%20not%20causation%22%20means,that%20one%20causes%20the%20other.&text=Correlations%20between%20two%20things%20can,wheel%20is%20called%20a%20confounder. Accessed 26 November 2020.

Greene, A. and Kirton, G. (2011) Diversity management meets downsizing: the case of a government department. *Employee Relations*, *33*: 22–39.

Greenhouse, S. (2020) How police unions enable and conceal abuses of power. *The New Yorker*, 18 June. Available at: https://www.theguardian.com/commentisfree/2020/jun/13/police-unions-afl-cio-labor-movement. Accessed 29 June 2020.

Greenwood, R. G. (1981) Management by Objectives: As Developed by Peter Drucker, Assisted by Harold Smiddy. *Academy of Management Review*, *6*(2): 225–30.

Grey, C. (2005) *Studying Organizations*. London: Sage.

Griffiths, S. and Calver, T. (2020) Mothers driven back to sink, cooker and homeschooling. *Sunday Times*, 24 May, p. 7.

Grimshaw, D. and Rubery, J. (2003) Economics and industrial relations: an unsatisfactory marriage of stereotypes? In P. Ackers and A. Wilkinson (eds) *Understanding Work and Employment: Industrial Relations in Transition* (pp. 44–69). Oxford: Oxford University Press.

Grimshaw, D. and Rubery, J. (2008) Economics and HRM. In P. Boxall, J. Purcell and P. Wright, (eds) *The Oxford Handbook of Human Resource Management*. Oxford: Oxford University Press.

Grint, K. (2011) A History of leadership. In A. Bryman, D. Collinson, K. Grint, B. Jackson, and M. Uhl-Bien, (eds) *The Sage Handbook of Leadership* (pp. 3–14). London: Sage.

Grint, K. and Willcocks, L. (1995) Business process re-engineering in theory and practice: business paradise regained? *New Technology, Work and Employment*, *10*(2): 99–108.

Grossman, R. and Salas, E. (2011) The transfer of training: what really matters. *International Journal of Training and Development*, *15*(2): 103–20.

Grote, R. (1996) *The Complete Guide to Performance Appraisal*. New York: American Management Association.

Grugulis, I. (2019) Human resource development. In D. Collings, G. T. Wood and L. T. Szamosi (eds) *Human Resource Management: A Critical Approach* (2nd edn) (pp. 295–310). London: Routledge.

Guardian, The (2011) News of the World phone-hacking whistleblower found dead. Available at: www.theguardian.com/media/2011/jul/18/news-of-the-world-sean-hoare Accessed 14 September 2016.

Guardian, The (2015) Sports Direct: a mega-success, but also big British capitalism at its grubbiest. *The Guardian*, *9* September, p. 34.

Guba, E. G. and Lincoln, Y. S. (1989) *Fourth Generation Evaluation*. London: Sage.

Guerci, M. and Carollo, L. (2016) A paradox view on green human resource management: insights from the Italian context. *International Journal of Human Resource Management*, *27*(2): 212–38.

Guerci, M., Longoni, A. and Luzzini, D. (2016) Translating stakeholder pressures into environmental performance – the mediating role of green HRM practices. *International Journal of Human Resource Management*, *27*(2): 262–89. DOI:10.1080/09585192.2015.1065431

Guest, D. (1987) Human resource management and industrial relations. *Journal of Management Studies*, *24*(5): 503–21.

Guest, D. (1990) Human resource management and the American dream. *Journal of Management Studies*, *27*(4): 377–97.

Guest, D. (2008) HRM and the worker: towards a new psychological contract? In P. Boxall, J. Purcell and P. Wright (eds) *The Oxford Handbook of Human Resource Management* (pp. 128–46). Oxford: Oxford University Press.

Guest, D. (2015) Voice and employee engagement. In S. Johnstone and P. Ackers (eds) *Finding a Voice at Work?* (pp. 44–66). Oxford: Oxford University Press.

Guest, D. and Bryson, A. (2009) From industrial relations to human resource management: the changing role of the personnel function, in W. Brown, A. Bryson, J. Forth and K. Whitfield (eds) *The Evolution of the Modern Workplace* (pp. 120–50). Cambridge: Cambridge University Press.

Guest, D. and Conway, N. (1999) Peering into the black hole: the downside of the new employment relations in the UK. *British Journal of Industrial Relations*, *37*(3): 367–89.

Guest, D. and Conway, N. (2002) Communicating the psychological contract: an employer perspective. *Human Resource Management Journal*, *12*(2): 22–38.

Guest, D. and Conway, N. (2011) The impact of HR practices, HR effectiveness and a 'strong HR system' on organisational outcomes: a stakeholder perspective. *International Journal of Human Resource Management*, *22*(8): 1686–02.

Guest, D. and King, Z. (2004) Power, innovation and problem solving: the personnel managers' three steps to heaven? *Journal of Management Studies*, *41*(3): 401–23.

Guest, D., Iskasson, K. and De Witte, H. (eds) (2010) *Employment Contracts, Psychological Contracts, and Employee Well-Being*, Oxford: Oxford University Press.

Guest, D. E. (1986) Worker participation and personnel policy in the UK: some case studies. *International Labour Review*, *125*(6): 406–27.

Guest, D. E. (1995) Human resource management, trade unions and industrial relations. In J. Storey (ed.) *Human Resource Management: A Critical Text* (pp. 110–41). London: Routledge.

Guest, D. E. (1997) Human resource management and performance: a review and research agenda. *International Journal of Human Resource Management*, *8*(3): 263–76.

Guest D. E. (2017) Human resource management and employee wellbeing: towards a new analytical framework. *Human Resource Management Journal, 22*(1): 22–38.

Guest, D. E., Michie, J., Conway, N. and Sheehan, M. (2003) Human resource management and corporate performance in the UK. *British Journal of Industrial Relations, 41*(2): 291–314.

Gül, H. (2011) Sick building syndrome from the perspective of occupational and public health. In S. A. Abdul-Wahab (ed) *Sick Building Syndrome in Public Buildings and Workplaces* (pp. 89–104). Heidelberg: Springer.

Gulati, R. (2018) Structure that's not stifling. *Harvard Business Review, 96*(3): 68–79.

Gully, S. M., Phillips, J. M., Castellano, W. G., Han, K. and Kim, A. (2013) A mediated moderation model of recruiting socially and environmentally responsible job applicants. *Personnel Psychology, 66*: 935–73.

Gumbrell-McCormick R. and Hyman R. (2013) *Trade Unions in Western Europe: Hard Times, Hard Choices*. Oxford: Oxford University Press.

Gunderson, M., Ponak, A. and Taras, D. (eds) (2005) *Union–Management Relations in Canada* (5th edn). Toronto, Ontario: Pearson.

Gunnigle, P., Murphy, K. R., Cleveland, J. N., Heraty, N. and Morley, M. (2002) Localization in human resource management: Comparing American and European multinational corporations. *Advances in Comparative International Management, 14*: 259–84.

Gunnigle, P., Collings, D. G. and Morley, M. (2005) Exploring the dynamics of industrial relations in US multinationals: evidence from the Republic of Ireland. *Industrial Relations Journal, 36*(3): 241–56.

Gunnigle, P., Turner, T., Lavell, J. and McDonnell, A. (2014) Pay and performance management in MNCs in Ireland. In B. Harney and K. Monks (eds) *Strategic HRM: Research and Practice in Ireland* (pp. 95–116). Dublin: Orpen Press.

Guthrie, J. P. (2008) Remuneration: pay effects on work. In P. Boxall, J. Purcell and P. Wright (eds) *The Oxford Handbook of Human Resource Management* (pp. 344 63). Oxford: Oxford University Press.

Guthrie, J. P., Flood, P., Liu, W. and MacCurtain, S. (2009) High performance work systems in Ireland: human resource and organizational outcomes. *International Journal of Human Resource Management, 20*(1): 112–25.

Habraken, M. and Bondarouk, T. (2017) Smart industry research in the field of HRM: resetting job design as an example of upcoming challenges. In T. Bondarouk, H. Ruel and E. Parry (eds) *Electronic HRM in the Smart Era* (pp. 221–59). Bingley: Emerald Publishing.

Hackman, J. R. and Oldham, G. R. (1980) *Work Redesign*. New York: Addison-Wesley.

Haddock-Millar, J., Sanyal, C. and Müller-Camen, M. (2016) Green human resource management: a comparative qualitative case study of a United States multinational corporation. *International Journal of Human Resource Management, 27*(2): 192–211.

Hadikin, R. and O'Driscoll, M. (2000) *The Bullying Culture: Causes, Effect, Harm Reduction*. Melbourne: Books for Midwives.

Hager, E. and Li, W. (2020) White US police union bosses protect officers accused of racism. *The Guardian*, 10 June.

Haigh, M. and Jones, M. T. (2006) The drivers of corporate social responsibility: a critical review. In *GBER 2006: Proceedings of the 2006 Global Business and Economics Research Conference* (pp. 1–8).

Haigh, M. and Jones, M. T. (2006) The drivers of corporate social responsibility: a critical review. *Business Review, 5*(2): 245–51.

Ha-Joon Chang (2013) There's a new jobs crisis – we need to focus on the quality of life at work. *The Guardian*, 22 December. Available at: https://www.theguardian.com/commentisfree/2013/dec/22/jobs-crisis-quality-of-life-at-work. Accessed 27 April 2021.

Hales, C. P. (1986) What do managers do? A critical review of the evidence. *Journal of Management Studies, 23*(1): 88–115.

Hall, D. T. (1984) Human resource Development and organizational effectiveness. In C. Fombrun, N. M. Tichy and M. A. Devanna (eds) *Strategic Human Resource Management* (pp. 159–81). New York: John Wiley & Sons.

Hall, P. and Soskice, D. (2001) *Varieties of Capitalism*. Oxford: Oxford University Press.

Hall, P. A. and Soskice, D. (2009) An introduction to varieties of capitalism. In B. Hancke (ed.) *Debating Varieties of Capitalism: A Reader* (pp. 21–74). Oxford: Oxford University Press.

Hall, R. and Bowles, K. (2016) Re-engineering higher education: the subsumption of academic labour and the exploitation of anxiety. *Workplace: A Journal of Academic Labor, 28*: 30–47.

Hallock, K. F., Jin, X. and Barrington, L. (2014) Estimating pay gaps for workers with disabilities: Implications from broadening definitions and datasets. *Rehabilitation Research, Policy and Education: Journal of the National Council on Rehabilitation Education, 28*(4): 264–90.

Halman, F. and Fletcher, C. (2000) The impact of development centre participation and the role of individual differences in changing self-assessments. *Journal of Occupational and Organizational Psychology, 73*: 423–42.

Hamel, G. (2000) *Leading the Revolution*. Boston, Mass: Harvard Business School Press.

Hammer, M. (1997) *Beyond Reengineering*. New York: HarperCollins.

Hammer, M. and Champy, J. (1993) *Reengineering the Corporation*. London: Nicholas Brealey.

Hampton, P. (2015) *Workers and trade unions for climate solidarity: Tackling climate change in a neoliberal world*. London: Routledge.

Hanappi-Egger, E. and Ortlieb, R. (2017) The intersectionalies of age, ethncity, and classs in organizations. In R. Bendl, I. Bleijenbergh, E. Henttonen and A. J. Mills (eds) (2017) *The Oxford Handbook of Diversity in Organizations* (pp. 454–68). Oxford: Oxford University Press.

Hancké, B. (2009) (ed.) *Debating Varieties of Capitalism: A Reader*. Oxford: Oxford University Press.

Hancké, B. (2018) Wages in the gig economy and beyond. London School of Economics, 25 October online. Available at: https://blogs.lse.ac.uk/netuf/2018/10/25/wages-in-the-gig-economy-and-beyond. Accessed 3 October 2020.

Harcourt, M., Gall, G., Kumar, R.V. Croucher, R. (2019) A union default: a policy to raise union membership, promote the freedom to associate, protect the freedom not to associate and progress union representation, *Industrial Law Journal*, *48*(1): 66–97. Available at: https://doi.org/10.1093/indlaw/dwy005.

Hardy, C. and Clegg, S. R. (1999) Some dare call it power. In S. R. Clegg and C. Hardy (eds) *Studying Organization: Theory and Method* (pp. 368–87). London: Sage.

Harland, C., Knight, L., Lamming, R. and Walker, H. (2005) Outsourcing: assessing the risks and benefits for organisations, sectors and nations. *International Journal of Operations and Production Management*, *25*(9): 831–50.

Harrabin, R. (2019) Bank of England chief Mark Carney issues climate change warning. *BBC News*, 30 December. Available at: https://www.bbc.co.uk/news/business-50868717 Accessed 15 June 2020.

Harrabin, R. (2020) Bank of England chief Mark Carney issues climate change warning. *BBC News*, 20 December.

Harris, L. C. and Crane, A. (2002) The greening of organisational culture: management views on the depth, degree and diffusion of change. *Journal of Organizational Change Management*, *15*(3): 214–34.

Harrison, P., Nichol, L. and Gold, J. (2020) Redefining HRD Roles and Practice in the Machine Learning Revolution. In M. Loon, J, Stewart and S. Nachmias (eds) *The Future of HRD, Volume I Innovation and Technology* (pp. 143–66). Palgrave Macmillan, London.

Harrison, R. (2009) *Learning and Development* (5th edn). London, CIPD.

Hart, S. M. (2010) Self-regulation, corporate social responsibility, and the business case: do they work in achieving workplace equality and safety? *Journal of Business Ethics*, *92*(4): 585–600.

Harvey, D. (2005) *A Brief History of Neoliberalism*. Oxford: Oxford University Press.

Harvey, D. (2007) *A Brief History of Neo-Liberalism*. Oxford: Oxford University Press.

Harvey, F. (2020) World health leaders urge green recovery from coronavirus crisis. *The Guardian. Guardian News and Media*, 26 May.

Harvey, F. and Rankin, J. (2020) What is the European Green Deal and will it really cost €1tn? *The Guardian*, 9 March. Available at: https://www.theguardian.com/world/2020/mar/09/what-is-the-european-green-deal-and-will-it-really-cost-1tn Accessed 22 June 2020.

Harvey, G. and Turnbull, P. (2010) On the go: walking the high road at a low cost airline. *International Journal of Human Resource Management*, *21*(2): 230–41.

Harvey, G. and Turnbull, P. (2020) Ricardo flies Ryanair: Strategic human resource management and competitive advantage in a Single European Aviation Market. *Human Resource Management Journal*, *30*(4): 553–65.

Harvey, G., Rhodes, C., Vachhani, S. J. and Williams, K. (2017) Neo-villeiny and the service sector: the case of hyper flexible and precarious work in fitness centres. *Work, Employment and Society*, *31*(1): 19–35.

Harzing, A. W. (2000) An empirical analysis and extension of the Bartlett and Ghoshal typology of multinational companies. *Journal of International Business Studies*, *31*(1): 101–20.

Hastings, R. and Meyer, E. (2020) *No Rules Rules: Netflix and the Culture of Reinvention*. London: Penguin.

Haunschild, A. (2003) Humanization through discipline? Foucault and the goodness of employee programmes. *Journal of Critical Postmodern Organization Science*, *2*(3): 46–59.

Hayes, J. (2014) *The Theory and Practice of Change Management*. London: Palgrave Macmillan.

Hayter, S. and Lee, C. H. (eds) (2018) *Industrial Relations in Emerging Economies: The Quest for Inclusive Development*. Cheltenham: Edward Elgar Publishing.

Hayter S. and Visser J. (eds) (2018) Collective agreements: extending labour protection. Geneva, International Labour Office.

Health and Safety Executive (2019a) Work-related stress, anxiety or depression statistics in Great Britain, 2019. *HSE* online. Available at: https://www.hse.gov.uk/statistics/causdis/stress.pdf. Accessed 2 September 2020.

Health and Safety Executive (2019b) Violence at work, 2018/19. *HSE* online. Available at: https://www.hse.gov.uk/statistics/causinj/violence/index.htm. Accessed 20 September 2020.

Health and Safety Executive (2020a) Costs to Great Britain of workplace injuries and new cases of work-related ill health – 2017/18. *HSE* online. Available at: https://www.hse.gov.uk/statistics/cost.htm#:~:text=The%20total%20costs%20of%20workplace%20self%2Dreported%20injuries%20and%20ill,costs%20(%C2%A35.2%20billion). Accessed 2 September 2020.

Health and Safety Executive (2020b) Work-related stress, anxiety or depression statistics in Great Britain, 2020. *Health and Safety Executive*, 4 November. Available at: https://www.hse.gov.uk/statistics/causdis/stress.pdf Accessed 29 May 2021.

Health and Safety Executive (2020c) Work related violence – Frequently asked questions. *HSE* online. Available at: https://www.hse.gov.uk/violence/toolkit/faqs.htm. Accessed 20 September 2020.

Health and Safety Executive (2020d) Managing drug and alcohol misuse at work. *HSE* online. Available at: https://www.hse.gov.uk/alcoholdrugs. Accessed 20 September 2020.

Healy, C. and Niven, K. (2016) When tough performance goals lead to cheating. *Harvard Business Review*, 8 September online. Available at: https://hbr.org/2016/09/when-tough-performance-goals-lead-to-cheating. Accessed 11 October 2020.

Healy, G., Tatli, A., Ipek, G., Öztürk, M., Seierstad, C. and Wright, T. (2019) In the steps of Joan Acker: A journey in researching inequality regimes and intersectional inequalities. *Gender, Work & Organization*, *26*(12): 1749–62. Available at: https://doi.org/10.1111/gwao.12252.

Hearn, J. and Louvrier, J. (2017) Theories of Difference, Diversity, and Intersectionality: What Do They Bring to Diversity Management? In R. Bendle, I. Bleijenbergh, E. Henttonen and A. Mills (eds) *The Oxford Handbook of Diversity in Organizations* (pp. 62–82). Oxford: Oxford University Press.

Heath, A. (2019) *New CSI Report on Ethnic Minority Job Discrimination*. Oxford: Centre for Social Investigation, Nuffield College. Available at: https://www.nuffield.ox.ac.uk/news-events/news/new-csi-report-on-ethnic-minority-job-discrimination/ Accessed 10 June 2020.

Heenan, D. A. and Perlmutter, H. V. (1979) *Multinational Organization Development*. Addison-Wesley.

Heery, E. (2000) The new pay: risk and representation at work. In D. Winstanley and J. Woodall (eds) *Ethical Issues in Contemporary Human Resource Management* (pp. 172–88). Basingstoke: Palgrave Macmillan.

Heery, E. (2009) The representation gap and the future of worker representation. *Industrial Relations Journal, 40*(4): 324–36.

Heery, E. and Simms, M. (2010) Employer responses to union organizing: patterns and effects. *Human Resource Management Journal, 20*(1): 3–22.

Heffernan, M. and Dundon, T. (2012) Researching Employee Reactions to High Performance Work Systems in the Service Sector: The Role of Organisational Justice Theory. 16th ILERA (IIRA) World Congress.

Heffernan, M., Harney, B., Cafferkey, K. and Dundon, T. (2016) Exploring the HRM-performance relationship: the role of creativity climate and strategy. *Employee Relations*.

Heffernan, M., Harney, B., Cafferkey, K. and Dundon, T. (2009, August) Exploring the relationship between HRM, creativity climate and organisational performance: evidence from Ireland. In *Academy of Management Conference* (pp. 1–35).

Heller, F., Pusic, E., Strauss, G. and Wilpert, B. (1998) *Organizational Participation: Myth and Reality*. Oxford: Oxford University Press.

Henley, J. (2016) White and Wealthy Voters Gave Victory to Donald Trump, Exit Polls Show. *The Guardian*, 9 November.

Hendry, C. (1994) The single European market and the HRM response. In P. Kirkbride (ed.) *Human Resource Management in Europe* (pp. 93–113). London: Routledge.

Hendry, C. and Pettigrew, A. (1990) Human resource management: an agenda for the 1990s. *International Journal of Human Resource Management, 1*(1): 17–43.

Henderson, R. (2020) *Reimagining Capitalism: How Business Can Save the World.* London: Penguin.

Henkens, K., Remery, C. and Schippers, J. (2005) Recruiting personnel in a tight labour market: an analysis of employers' behaviour. *International Journal of Manpower, 26*(5): 421–33.

Henry, A. E. (2018) *Understanding Strategic Management* (3rd edn). Oxford: Oxford University Press.

Hern, A. (2018) 'Alarming' lack of diversity in UK tech sector, report reveals. *The Guardian*, 14 November, p. 35.

Herod, A., Rainnie, A. and McGrath-Champ, S. (2007) Working space: why incorporating the geographical is central to theorizing work and employment practices. *Work, Employment and Society, 21*(2): 247–64.

Herriot, P. (1987) The selection interview. In P. Warr (ed.) *Psychology at Work*. London: Penguin.

Hertz, N. (2002) *The Silent Takeover: Global Capitalism and the Death of Democracy*. London: Arrow.

Herzberg, F (1968) One more time: how do you motivate employees? *Harvard Business Review*, January–February: 109–20.

Hesketh, A. (2014) *Managing the Value of Your Talent*. London: Chartered Institute of Personnel and Development.

Heyes, J. and Nolan, P. (2010) State, capital and labour relations in crisis. In T. Colling and M. Terry (eds) *Industrial Relations: Theory and Practice* (pp. 106–24). Chichester: John Wiley & Sons.

Higgins, M. D. (2021) Empire shaped Ireland's past. A century after partition, it still shapes our present. *The Guardian*, 11 February. Available at: https://www.theguardian.com/commentisfree/2021/feb/11/empire-ireland-century-partition-present-britain-history. Accessed 18 March 2021.

High Pay Centre (2021) 'High pay day' 2021. London. Available at: https://highpaycentre.org/high-pay-day-2021-ceos-earnings-for-2021-will-surpass-the-median-uk-full-time-salary-today/. Accessed 6 January 2021.

Hill, C. W., Schilling, M. A. and Jones, G. R. (2016) *Strategic Management: An Integrated Approach: Theory & Cases* (12th edn). Boston, MA: Cengage Learning.

Hillage, J. (2016) What does Brexit mean for employment? June. Available at: www.employment-studies.co.uk/news/what-does-brexit-mean-employment. Accessed 1 August 2016.

Hinsliff, G. (2017) Why the working class lose out on the career ladder. *The Guardian*, 26 January. Available at: https://www.theguardian.com/commentisfree/2017/jan/26/working-class-career-ladder-gap-earnings. Accessed 7 May 2021.

Hirch, A. (2010) Bullying in the workplace on the rise. *The Guardian*, 4 January. Available at: https://www.theguardian.com/money/2010/jan/04/bullying-workplace-recession. Accessed 20 September 2020.

Hirsh, W. and Tamkin, P. (2005) *Planning Training for your Business*. Report No. 422. Brighton: Institute of Employment Studies.

Hirst, P. and Thompson, P. (1996) *Globalisation in Question*, Second edition. Cambridge: Polity Press.

Ho, K. (2019) Half of Singaporeans would be less likely to hire a candidate with a tattoo. YouGov, 29 May. Available at: https://sg.yougov.com/en-sg/news/2019/05/29/half-singaporeans-would-be-less-likely-hire-candid/. Accessed 29 June 2020.

Hochschild, A. R. (1983) *The Managed Heart: Commercialization of Human Feeling*. Berkeley, CA: University of California Press.

Hochschild, A. R. (2012) *The Managed Heart: Commercialization of Human Feeling* (3rd edn). Berkeley, CA: University of California Press.

Hodder, A. and Houghton, D. J. (2020) Unions, social media and young workers – evidence from the UK. *New Technology, Work and Employment, 35*(1): 40–59.

Hodgkinson, G. P. and Clarke, I. (2007) Exploring the cognitive significance of organizational strategizing: a dual-process framework and research agenda. *Human Relations, 60*: 243–55.

Hoel, H., Sheehan, M. J., Cooper, C. L. and Einarsen, S. (2011) Organisational effects of workplace bullying. In Einarsen, S., Hoel, H., Zapf, D. and Cooper, C. (eds) *Bullying and Harassment in the Workplace: Developments in Theory, Research, and Practice* (2nd edn) (pp. 129–48). London: Taylor & Francis.

Hofmans, J., De Gieter, S. and Pepermans, R. (2013) Individual differences in the relationship between satisfaction with job rewards and job satisfaction. *Journal of Vocational Behavior, 82*(1): 1–9.

Hofstede, G. (1980) *Culture's Consequences: International Differences in Work Related Values*. Newbury Park, CA: SAGE Publications.

Holbeche, L. (2018) *The Agile Organization: How to Build an Engaged, Innovative and Resilient Business* (2nd edn). London: Kogan Page Publishers.

Holden, E., Linnerud, K., Banister, D., Schwanitz, V. J. and Wierling, A. (2017) *The Imperatives of Sustainable Development: Needs, Justice, Limits*. Routledge.

Holmes, J. (2006) *Gender Talk at Work*. Oxford: Blackwell.

Holtz, B. C., Ployhart, R. E. and Dominguez, A. (2005) Testing the rules of justice: The effects of frame-of-reference and pre-test validity information on personality test responses and test perceptions. *International Journal of Selection and Assessment, 13*(1): 75–86.

Holzer, M., Ballard, A., Kim, M., Peng, S. and Deat, F. (2019) Obstacles and opportunities for sustaining performance management systems. *International Journal of Public Administration, 42*(2): 132–43.

Holton, E. F., Bates, R. A., Bookter, A. I. and Yamkovenko, V. B. (2007) Convergent and divergent validity of the learning transfer system inventory. *Human Resource Development Quarterly, 18*(3): 385–419.

Home Office (2019) Drug Misuse: Findings from the 2018/19 Crime Survey for England and Wales, Statistical Bulletin: 21/19. *Home Office*, 19 September online] Available at: https://assets.publishing.service.gov.uk/government/uploads/system/uploads/attachment_data/file/832533/drug-misuse-2019-hosb2119.pdf. Accessed 20 September 2020.

Honeyball, S. (2010) *Honeyball and Bower's Textbook on Employment Law* (11th edn). Oxford: Oxford University Press.

Hoogvelt, A. (2001) *Globalization and the Postcolonial World* (2nd edn). Basingstoke: Palgrave Macmillan.

Houghton, E. (2019) *Sustainable HR: A 'Green' Fad, or a Realistic Model for Change?* London: CIPD. Available at: https://www.cipd.co.uk/news-views/changing-work-views/future-work/thought-pieces/sustainable-hr. Accessed 14 June 2020.

Howe, C. L., Auflick, P. and Freiberger, G. (2011) Upward evaluation at the Arizona Health Sciences Library. *Journal of the Medical Library Association, 99*(1): 91–4.

Howlett, E. (2020a) Number of over-50s on zero-hours contracts surges, official figures show. *People Management*, 13 March online. Available at: https://www.peoplemanagement.co.uk/news/articles/number-over-50s-zero-hours-contracts-surges-official-figures. Accessed 7 October 2020.

Howlett, E. (2020b) Work is detrimental to employee wellbeing, CIPD survey finds. *People Management*, 4 June. Available at: https://www.peoplemanagement.co.uk/news/articles/work-detrimental-to-employee-wellbeing-CIPD. Accessed 19 June 2020.

Hughes, E. and Dundon, T. (2018) Wage councils could address endemic pay inequality in the UK. *The Conversation, 5*. Available at: https://theconversation.com/wage-councils-could-address-endemic-pay-inequality-in-the-uk-economy-102682.

Hughes, J. (2008) *The High Performance Work Paradigm: A Review and Evaluation*. Learning as Work Research Paper No. 16. Cardiff: Cardiff School of Social Sciences, Cardiff University.

Hughes, P. and Grant, M. (2007) *Learning and Development Outlook: Are We Learning Enough?* Toronto: Conference Board of Canada.

Hurst, B., Johnston, K. A. and Lane, A. B. (2020) Engaging for a social licence to operate (SLO). *Public Relations Review, 46*(4): 1–9.

Hurst, D. and Karp, P. (2020) Australia to subsidise wages of up to 6m workers in $130bn coronavirus plan. *The Guardian*, 30 March online. Available at: https://www.theguardian.com/world/2020/mar/30/australia-to-subsidise-wages-of-up-to-6m-workers-in-130bn-coronavirus-plan. Accessed 12 August 2020.

Huselid, M. A. (1995) The impact of HRM practices on turnover, productivity, and corporate financial performance. *Academy of Management Journal, 38*(3): 635–72.

Hutchinson, S. and Purcell, J. (2003) *Bringing Policies to Life*. London: Chartered Institute of Personnel and Development.

Hutton, W. (2014) It's easy to moan about bonuses, but just how do we fix banks? *The Observer*, 27 April, p. 42.

Hutton, W. (2015a) *How Good We Can Be*. London: Abacus.

Hutton, W. (2015b) Quarterly capitalism is short-term, myopic, greedy and dysfunctional. *The Observer*, 26 July, p. 32.

Hutton, W. (2020a) The looming economic disaster will only be worse if those leading us stick to dogma. *The Observer*, 17 May, p. 44.

Hutton, W. (2020b) Western societies have failed the deadly Covid test. They must learn lessons from Asia. *The Guardian*, 1 November. Available at: https://www.theguardian.com/commentisfree/2020/nov/01/western-societies-have-failed-the-deadly-covid-test-they-must-learn-lessons-from-asia. Accessed 18 November 2020.

Hutton, W. and Adonis, A. (2018) *Saving Britain: How We Must Change to Prosper in Europe*. London: Abacus.

Huws, U. (1997) *Teleworking: Guidelines for Good Practice*. Report No. 329. Brighton: Institute for Employment Studies.

Hyman, R. (1975) *Industrial Relations: A Marxist Introduction*. Basingstoke: Macmillan.

Hyman, R. (1987) Trade unions and the law: papering over the cracks? *Capital and Class, 31*: 43–63.

Hyman, R. (1989) *The Political Economy of Industrial Relations*. Basingstoke: Palgrave Macmillan.

Hyman, R. (1997a) The future of employee representation. *British Journal of Industrial Relations, 35*(3): 309–36.

Hyman, R. (1997b) Editorial. *European Journal of Industrial Relations, 3*(1): 5–6.

Hyman, R. (1999) National industrial relations systems and transnational challenges: an essay review. *European Journal of Industrial Relations, 5*(1): 89–110.

Hyman, R. (2007) How can trade unions act strategically? *Transfer, 13*(2): 193–210.

Hyman, R. (2010) British industrial relations: the European dimension. In T. Colling and M. Terry (eds) *Industrial Relations: Theory and Practice* (3rd edn) (pp. 54–79). Chichester: John Wiley & Sons.

Hyman, R. (2015) Making voice effective: imagining trade union responses to an era of post-industrial democracy. In S. Johnstone and P. Ackers, *Finding a Voice at Work?* (pp. 265–77). Oxford: Oxford University Press

Hynie, M., Jensen, K., Johnny, M., Wedlock, J. and Phipps, D. (2011) Student internships bridge research to real world problems. *Education and Training, 53*(1): 45–56.

Iavicoli, S., Valenti, A., Gagliardi, D. and Rantanen, J. (2018) Ethics and Occupational Health in the Contemporary World of Work. *International Journal of Environmental Research and Public Health*, *15*(8): 1713–30.

Ichniowski, C., Kochan, T., Levine, D., Olson, C. and Strauss, G. (1996) What works at work: overview and assessment. *Industrial Relations, 35*(3): 299–333.

Ichniowski, C., Shaw, K. and Prennushi, G. (1997) The effects of human resource management on productivity: a case study of steel finishing lines. *American Economic Review, 87*(3): 291–313.

Iddekinge, C. H. van., Lanivich, S. E., Roth, P. L. and Junco, E. (2013) Social media for selection? Validity and adverse impact potential of a Facebook-based assessment. *Journal of Management*. DOI:10.1177/0149206313515524

Iles, P. (2001) Employee resourcing. In J. Storey (ed.) *Human Resource Management: A Critical Text* (2nd edn) (pp. 133–64). London: Thomson Learning.

Iles, P. and Preece, D. (2010) Talent management and career development. In Gold, J., Thorpe, R. and Mumford, A. (eds) *Gower Handbook of Leadership and Management Development* (pp. 243–60). Aldershot: Gower Press.

Iles, P. and Salaman, G. (1995) Recruitment, selection and assessment. In Storey, J. (ed.) *Human Resource Management* (pp. 203–33). London: Routledge.

Ilgen, D. R., Fisher, C. D. and Taylor, M. S. (1979) Consequences of individual feedback on behavior in organizations. *Journal of Applied Psychology*, *64*(4): 349–71.

Inesi, M. E. and Cable, D. M. (2014) When accomplishments come back to haunt you: the negative effect of competence signals on women's performance evaluations. *Personnel Psychology*, *68*(3): 615–57.

Inman, P. (2019) Millennials' pay still stunted by the 2008 financial crash, *The Observer*, 3 February. Available at: https://www.theguardian.com/money/2019/feb/03/millennials-pay-still-stunted-by-financial-crash-resolution-foundation. Accessed 9 December 2020.

Inman, P. (2020) Number of people in poverty in working families hits record high. *The Guardian*, 7 February. Available at: https://www.theguardian.com/business/2020/feb/07/uk-live-poverty-charity-joseph-rowntree-foundation Accessed 14 June 2020.

Institute of Business Ethics (IBE) (2020) Performance. *Institute of Business Ethics* online. Available at: https://www.ibe.org.uk/knowledge-hub/pay/performance.html. Accessed 7 October 2020.

International Risk Governance Council (2005) *Risk Governance: Towards an Integrative Approach*. White paper. Geneva: IRGC.

International Risk Governance Council (IRGC) (2005) Risk governance: Towards an integrative approach. White paper.

Iqbal, N. (2020) 'They just got away with paying men more...' Major milestone looms in Asda equal pay fight', *The Observer*, 12 July, p. 14.

Jabbour, C. J. C. (2011) How green are HRM practices, organizational culture, learning and teamwork? A Brazilian study. *Industrial and Commercial Training*, *43*(2): 98–105.

Jabbour, C. J. C. and Santos, F. C. A. (2008) The central role of human resource management in the search for sustainable organizations. *International Journal of Human Resource Management*, *19*: 2133–54.

Jabbour, C. J. C., Santos, F. C. A. and Nagano, S. M. (2010) Contributions of HRM throughout the stages of environmental management: methodological triangulation applied to companies in Brazil. *International Journal of Human Resource Management*, *21*(7): 1049–89.

Jack, G., Greenwood, M. and Schapper, J. (2012) Frontiers, intersections, and engagement of ethics and HRM. *Journal of Business Ethics*, 111: 1–12.

Jacobs, E. (2019) Why radical transparency about salaries can pay off. *The Financial Times*, 6 May online. Available at: https://www.ft.com/content/11403170-6cc9-11e9-a9a5-351eeaef6d84. Accessed 15 October 2020.

Jacobs, J. V., Hettinger, L. J., Huang, Y-H., Jeffries, S., Lesch, M. F., Simmons, L. A., Verma, S. K. and Willets, J. L. (2019) Employee acceptance of wearable technology in the workplace. *Applied Ergonomics*, *78*: 148–56.

Jacobs, K. (2016) CIFF's fresh approach to performance management. *HR Magazine*, 17 March.

Jacobs, M. (2018) LGBT employees face hurdles at home and abroad. *The Financial Times*, 7 May. Available at: https://www.ft.com/content/957504b2-4de8-11e8-97e4-13afc22d86d4. Accessed 2 July 2020.

Jacoby, S. M. (2005) *The Embedded Corporation: Corporate Governance and Employment Relations in Japan and the United States*. Princeton, NJ: Princeton University Press.

Jaeger, J. (2020) Three former Wells Fargo execs settle with OCC for fake account scandal roles. *Compliance Week*, 22 September online. Available at: https://www.complianceweek.com/regulatory-enforcement/former-wells-fargo-execs-settle-with-occ-for-fake-account-scandal-roles/29500.article. Accessed 7 October 2020.

Jaffee, D. (2001) *Organization Theory: Tension and Change*. Boston: McGraw-Hill.

Jain, N. and Bhatt, P. (2014) Employment preferences of job applicants: unfolding employer branding determinants. *Journal of Management Development*, *34*(6): 634–52.

Jang, B. (2011) Air Canada to launch cut-rate carrier. *Globe and Mail*, 12 April, pp. B1, B4.

Jansz, J. (2011) Introduction to Sick Building Syndrome. In S. A. Abdul-Wahab (ed.) *Sick Building Syndrome in Public Buildings and Workplaces* (pp. 1–24). Heidelberg: Springer.

Järvensivu, P., Toivanen, T., Vadén, T., Lähde, V., Majava, A. and Eronen, J. T. (2019) Governance of economic transition, Unpublished Paper, Helsinki: Allto University.

Jarvis, H. and Pratt, A. C. (2006) Bringing it all back home: The extensification and 'overflowing'of work: The case of San Francisco's new media households. *Geoforum*, *37*(3): 331–9.

Jarvis, P. (ed.) (1991) *Twentieth Century Thinkers in Adult Education*. London: Routledge.

Jayanetti, C. (2019) Wealthiest 10% cash in as average family income falls. *The Guardian*, 27 July. Available online at: https://www.theguardian.com/money/2019/jul/27/hmrc-data-shows-unearned-income-britain-wealthiest-doubles-in-five-years. Accessed 21 October 2020.

Jehn, K. A. (1997) A qualitative analysis of conflict types and dimensions in organizational groups. *Administrative Science Quarterly*, pp. 530–57.

Jenkins, S. (2021) Covid has made inequality even worse. The only answer: squeeze the super-rich. *The Guardian*,

26 January. Available at: https://www.theguardian.com/news/commentisfree/2021/jan/26/covid-inequality-worse-squeeze-super-rich. Accessed 26 January 2021.

Jewson, N. and Mason, D. (1986) The theory and practice of equal opportunities policies: liberal and radical approaches. *Sociological Review*, *34*(2): 307–34.

John, O. P., Naumann, L. P. and Soto, C. J. (2008) Paradigm shift to the integrative big five trait taxonomy. *Handbook of Personality: Theory and research*, *3*(2): 114–58.

Johnson, C. (2015) Autumn statement: Apprenticeships levy to raise £3bn. www.bbc.co.uk/news/business-34923235 Accessed 14 September 2016.

Johnson, E. M. (2020) Boeing to move all Dreamliner production next year. *The Globe and Mail*, 2 October, p. B3.

Johnson, P., Joyce, R. and Platt, L. (2021) The IFS Review of Inequalities: a New Year's message. Institute for Fiscal Studies, January 5. Available at: https://www.ifs.org.uk/publications/15241. Accessed 11 January 2021.

Johnson, P., Wood, G. T., Dibben, P., Cullen, J., Meira, J., Bonnin, D., Miranda, L., Crockett, G. and Linhares, C. (2019) Reconfiguration and regulation of supply chains and HRM in times of economic crisis. In D. G. Collings, G. T. Wood and L. T. Szamosi (eds) *Human Resource Management: A Critical Approach* (2nd edn) (pp. 156–70). London: Routledge.

Johnston, D. (2015) Are zero hours contracts in danger of becoming a golem for business? *Reuters Events*, 21 May online. Available at: https://www.reutersevents.com/sustainability/stakeholder-engagement/are-zero-hours-contracts-danger-becoming-golem-business#:~:text=Employees%20on%20zero%2Dhours%20contracts,to%20the%20organisation's%20ethical%20principles.&text=If%20an%20organisation%20does%20not,interest%20in%20doing%20business%20ethically. Accessed 11 October 2020.

Johnstone, S. and Ackers, P. (2015) *Finding a Voice at Work?* Oxford: Oxford University Press.

Jolly, J. (2020) Homeworking boom could tumble London's skyscrapers. *The Observer*, 28 June, pp. 54–5.

Jones, A., Visser, F., Coats, D., Bevan, S. and McVerry, A. (2007) *Transforming Work*. London: Work Foundation.

Jones, D. C., Kalmi, P. and Kauhanen, A. (2010) How does employee involvement stack up? The effects of human resource management policies on performance in a retail firm. *Industrial Relations: A Journal of Economy and Society*, *49*(1):1–21.

Jones, D., Molitor, D. and Reif, J. (2019) What do workplace wellness programs do? Evidence from the Illinois workplace wellness study. *The Quarterly Journal of Economics*, *134*(4): 1747–91.

Jones, O. (2016) Our private school elite's dominance is not just unfair – it damages us all. *The Guardian*, 25 February, p. 33.

Jones, O. (2020) The right-wing press is trying to bully workers back to the office. *The Guardian*, 28 August. Available at: https://www.theguardian.com/commentisfree/2020/aug/28/rightwing-press-bully-workers-back-to-the-office-britain. Accessed 16 October 2020.

Jones, O. (2021) The combination of Covid and class has been devasting for Britain's poorest. *The Guardian*, 26 January. Available at: https://www.theguardian.com/commentisfree/2021/jan/26/combination-covid-class-devastating-britain-poorest. Accessed 26 January 2021.

Jordan, A. and Audia, P. (2012) Self-enhancement and learning from performance feedback. *Academy of Management Review*, *37*(2): 211–31.

Jørgensen, H. H., Owen, L. and Neus, A. (2008) *Making change work*. Available at: www-07.ibm.com/au/pdf/making_change_work.pdf. Accessed 4 July 2015.

Joshi, G. and Dhar, R. L. (2020) Green training in enhancing green creativity via green dynamic capabilities in the Indian handicraft sector: the moderating effect of resource commitment. *Journal of Cleaner Production*. Available at: https://doi.org/10.1016/j.jclepro.2020.121948. Accessed 29 May 2021.

Judd, C. M. and Park, B. (1993) Definition and assessment of accuracy in social stereotypes. *Psychological Review*, *100*(1): 109–28.

Judge, T. A. and Cable, D. M. (1997) Applicant personality, organizational culture and organization attraction. *Personnel Psychology*, *50*: 359–94.

Kalev, A. (2020) Research: U.S. Unemployment Rising Faster for Women and People of Color. *Harvard Business Review*, 20 April online. Available at: https://hbr.org/2020/04/research-u-s-unemployment-rising-faster-for-women-and-people-of-color. Accessed 12 October 2020.

Kantor, J. and Streitfeld, D. (2015) Inside Amazon: wrestling big ideas in a bruising workplace. *New York Times*, 15 August.

Kaplan, R. S. and Norton, D. P. (1992) The Balanced Scorecard: measures that drive performance. *Harvard Business Review* (January–February): 71–79.

Kapoor, C. (2011) Defining diversity: the evolution of diversity. *Worldwide Hospitality and Tourism Themes*, *3*(4): 284–93.

Karasek, R. A. and Theorell, T. (1990) *Healthy Work: Stress, Productivity, and the Reconstruction of Working Life*. New York: Basic Books.

Karlsson, J. C. (2012) *Organizational Misbehaviour in the Workplace*. London: Palgrave Macmillan.

Kasemir, B., Jäger, J., Jaeger, C. C. and Gardner, M. T. (eds) (2003) *Public Participation in Sustainability Science: A Handbook*. Cambridge University Press.

Katz, H. C., Kochan, T. A., Keefe, J. H., Lazear, E. and Eads, G. C. (1987) Industrial relations and productivity in the US automobile industry. *Brookings Papers on Economic Activity*, *1987*(3): 685–727.

Katzenbach, J. R. and Smith, D. K. (2015) *The Wisdom of Teams: Creating the High-performance Organization*. Harvard Business Review Press.

Kaufman, B. (2008) The development of HRM in historical and international perspective. In P. Boxall, J. Purcell and P. Wright (eds) *The Oxford Handbook of Human Resource Management* (pp. 19–47). Oxford: Oxford University Press.

Kaufman, B. (2010) SHRM theory in the post-Huselid era: why its fundamentally misspecified. *Industrial Relations*, *49*(2): 286–313.

Kaufman, B. E. (2012) Strategic human resource management research in the United States: a failing grade after 30 years? *Academy of Management Perspectives, 26*(2): 12–36.

Kaufman, B. E. (2015) Evolution of strategic HRM as seen through two founding books: a 30th anniversary perspective on development of the field. *Human Resource Management, 54*(3): 389–407.

Kaufman, B. E. and Miller, B. I. (2011) The firm's choice of HRM practices: economics meets strategic human resource management. *Industrial and Labor Rlations Review, 64*(3): 526–57.

Kaye, L. (1999) Strategic human resources management in Australia: the human cost. *International Journal of Manpower, 20*(8): 577–87.

Keegan, A. and Francis, H. (2010) Practitioner talk: the changing textscape of HRM and emergence of HR business partnership. *International Journal of Human Resource Management, 21*(6): 873–98.

Keenoy, T. (1990) Human resource management: rhetoric, reality and contradiction. *International Journal of Human Resource Management,* 3(1): 363–84.

Keep, E. (1989) Corporate training strategies: the vital component. In G. Salaman (ed.) *Human Resource Strategies*, London: Sage.

Kehoe, R. R. and Han, J. H. (2020) An expanded conceptualization of line managers' involvement in human resource management. *Journal of Applied Psychology, 105*(2): 111.

Kehoe, R. R. and Wright, P. M. (2013) The impact of high performance HR practices on employees' attitudes and behaviour. *Journal of Management, 39*: 366–91.

Keith, M. (2000) Sexual harassment case law under the Employment Contracts Act 1991. *New Zealand Journal of Industrial Relations, 25*(3): 277–89.

Kelliher, C. and Anderson, D. (2008) For better or for worse? An analysis of how flexible working practices influence employees' perceptions of job quality. *International Journal of Human Resource Management, 19*(3): 421–33.

Kellner, A., Cafferkey, K. and Townsend, K. (2019) Ability, Motivation and Opportunity: a Formula for employee performance? In K. Townsend, A. M. McDermott, K. Cafferkey and T. Dundon (eds) *Elgar Introduction to Theories of Human Resources and Employment Relations* (pp. 311–23). London: Edward Elgar Publishing.

Kelly, J. (1998) *Rethinking Industrial Relations: Mobilisation, Collectivism and Long Waves*. London: Routledge.

Kelly, J. E. (1985) Management's redesign of work: labour process, labour markets and product markets. In D. Knights, H. Willmott and D. Collinson (eds) *Job Design: Critical Perspectives on the Labour Process* (pp. 30–51). Aldershot: Gower.

Kelly, J. E. (2005) Industrial relations approaches to the employment relationship. In J. A.-M. Coyle-Shapiro, L. Shore, S. Taylor and L. Tetrick (eds) *The Employment Relationship: Examining Psychological and Contextual Perspectives* (pp. 48–64). Oxford: Oxford University Press.

Kennedy, S., Whiteman, G. and Williams, A. (2015) Workplace pro-environmental behavior as a collective driver for continuous improvement. In J. L. Robertson and J. Barling (eds) *The Psychology of Green Organizations* (pp. 351–77). New York: Oxford University Press.

Kerr, C. (1963/2001) *The Uses of the University*. Cambridge, MA: Harvard University Press.

Kersley, B., Alpin, C., Forth, J., Bryson, A., Bewley, H., Dix, G. and Oxenbridge, S. (2005) *Inside the Workplace: First Findings from the 2004 Workplace Employment Relations Survey (WERS 2004)*. London: DTI/ESRC/ACAS/PSI.

Kessler, I. (1994) Performance pay. In K. Sisson (ed.) *Personnel Management* (2nd edn). Oxford: Blackwell.

Kessler, I. (1995) Reward systems. In J. Storey (ed.) *Human Resource Management: A Critical Text* (pp. 254–79). London: Routledge.

Kessler, I. (2007) Reward choices: strategy and equity. In J. Storey (ed.) *Human Resource Management: A Critical Text* (3rd edn) (pp. 159–76) London: Thomson Learning.

Kessler, I. and Purcell, J. (1992) Performance related pay: objectives and application. *Human Resource Management Journal, 2*(3): 16–33.

Kessler, S. (2018) *Gigged: The Gig Economy, The End of the Job and the Future of Work*. London: Penguin.

Kim, H. and Gong, Y. (2009) The roles of tacit knowledge and OCB in the relationship between group-based pay and firm performance. *Human Resource Management Journal, 19*(2): 120–39.

Kim, J., MacDuffie, J. P. and Pil, F. (2010) Employee voice and organizational performance: team versus representative influence. *Human Relations, 63*(3): 371–94.

Kim, J., Egan, T. and Tolson, H. (2015) Examining the Dimensions of the Learning Organization Questionnaire: a review and critique of research utilizing the DLOQ. *Human Resource Development Review, 14*(1): 91–112.

Kirkpatrick, D. L. (1998) *Evaluating Training Programs* (2nd edn). San Francisco, CA: Berrett-Koehler.

Kispal-Vitai, Z. and Wood, G. T. (2019) HR planning: Institutions, strategy, tools and techniques', in David G. Collings, G. T. Wood and L. T. Szamosi (eds) *Human Resource Management: A Critical Approach* (2nd edn) (pp. 238–61). London: Routledge.

Klass, B. S. (2009) Discipline and grievances. In A. Wilkinson, N. Bacon, T. Redman and S. Snell (eds) *The Sage Handbook of Human Resource Management* (pp. 322–39). London: Sage.

Klein, N. (2015) *This Changes Everything*. London: Penguin.

Klerck, G. (2019) Industrial relationships and human resource management. In D. Collings, G. Wood and L. Szamosi (eds) *Human Resource Management: A Critical Approach* (2nd edn) (pp. 311–34). London: Routledge.

Klikauer, T. (2013) What is managerialism? *Critical Sociology. 41* (7–8): 1103–19. DOI:10.1177/0896920513501351

Kluger, A. N. and DeNisi, A. S. (1996) The effects of feedback interventions on performance: a historical review, a metaanalysis, and a preliminary feedback intervention theory. *Psychological Bulletin, 119*: 254–84.

Kluger, A. N. and Nir, D. (2009) The feedforward interview. *Human Resource Management Review, 20*: 235–46.

Knights, A. and Poppleton, A. (2008) *Developing Coaching Capability in Organisations*. London: Chartered Institute of Personnel and Development.

Knights, D. and Willmott, H. (eds) (1986) *Gender and the Labour Process*. Aldershot: Gower.

Knowles, M. (1998) *The Adult Learner* (5th edn). Houston, TX: Gulf Publishing.

Kolb, D. A. (1984) *Experiential Learning*. Englewood Cliffs, NJ: Prentice Hall.

Kollewe, J. (2018) Alarm over talks to implant UK employees with microchips. *The Guardian*, 11 November online. Available at: <https://www.theguardian.com/technology/2018/nov/11/alarm-over-talks-to-implant-uk-employees-with-microchips. Accessed 4 October 2020.

Kotter, J. (2012) How the most innovative companies capitalise on today's rapid-fire strategic challenges – and still make their numbers. *Harvard Business Review, 90*(11): 43–58.

Kowalski, T. H. and Loretto, W. (2017) Well-being and HRM in the changing workplace. *International Journal of Human Resource Management, 28*(16): 2229–55.

KPMG (2013) People are the real numbers: HR analytics has come of age. KPMG International. Avaliable at: https://assets.kpmg/content/dam/kpmg/pdf/2014/01/workforce-analytics-download.pdf. Accessed 28 September 2020.

Krahé, B. (1992) *Personality and Social Psychology: Towards a synthesis*. London: Sage.

Kramar, R. and Syed, J. (2012) *Human Resource Management in a Global Context*. Basingstoke: Palgrave Macmillan.

Kramer, A. and Kramer, K.Z. (2020) The potential impact of the COVID-19 pandemic on occupational status, work from home, and occupational mobility. *Journal of Vocational Behavior, 119*: 1034422.

Krashinsky Robertson, S. (2020) Why Netflix's uncomfortable office culture works. *The Globe and Mail*, Canada, p. B2;

Krippner G.R. (2005) The financialization of the American economy. *Socio-Economic Review, 3*: 173–208.

Krugman, P. (2009) How Did Economists Get It So Wrong? *New York Times*, 2 September. Available at: https://www.nytimes.com/2009/09/06/magazine/06Economic-t.html. Accessed 10 December 2020.

Krugman, P. (2012) *End This Depression Now!* (2nd edn). New York: W. W. Norton.

Krugman, P. (2020) *Arguing with Zombies: Economics, Politics, and the Fight for a Better Future,* New York: Norton & Company.

Kuhl, J. S. (2014) Investing in Millennials for the future of your organization. *Leader to Leader, 71*: 25–30.

Kuhn, K. M. (2009) Compensation as a signal of organizational culture: the effects of advertising individual or collective incentives. *International Journal of Human Resource Management, 20*(7): 1634–48.

Kultalahti, S. and Viitala, R. (2015) Generation Y – challenging clients for HRM? *Journal of Managerial Psychology, 30*(1): 101–14.

Kumhof, M., Lebarz, C., Rancière, R., Richter, D. A. and Throckmorton, N. (2012) *Income Inequality and Current Account Imbalances*. IMF Working Paper 12/08. Washington, DC: International Monetary Fund.

Kuvass, B., Buch, R. and Dysvik, A. (April 2018) Individual variable pay for performance, incentive effects, and employee motivation. *Academy of Management Annual Meeting Proceedings, 1*: 12393.

Kwong, E. and Marshall, L. (2020) Emerging evidence of COVID-19's unequal mental health impacts on health and social care staff. *The Health Foundation*, 31 July. Available at: https://www.health.org.uk/news-and-comment/blogs/emerging-evidence-of-covid-19s-unequal-mental-health-impacts-on-health-and. Accessed 29 May 2021.

La Prade, A., Mertens, J., Moore, T. and Wright, A. (2019) The enterprise guide to closing the skills gap: Strategies for building and maintaining a skilled workforce. *IBM* online. Available at: https://www.ibm.com/thought-leadership/institute-business-value/report/closing-skills-gap#. Accessed 4 October 2020.

Laborers' International Union of North America (LIUNA) (2019) LIUNA on the Green New Deal. Press release. 7 February. Available at: https://www.liuna.org/news/story/liuna-on-the-green-new-deal. Accessed 6 October 2020.

Langer, M., König, C. J. and Krause, K. (2017) Examining digital interviews for personnel selection: Applicant reactions and interviewer ratings. *International Journal of Selection and Assessment, 25*(4): 371–82.

Latham, G., Sulsky, L. M. and MacDonald, H. (2008) Performance management. In P. Boxall, J. Purcell and P. Wright (eds) *The Oxford Handbook of Human Resource Management* (pp. 364–81). Oxford: Oxford University Press.

Latham, G. P. (1984) The Appraisal System as a Strategic Control. In C. Fombrun, N. M. Tichy and M. A. Devanna (eds) *Strategic Human Resource Management*, (pp. 87–100). New York: John Wiley & Sons.

Latham, G. P. and Locke, E. A. (1979) Goal setting – A motivational technique that works. *Organizational Dynamics, 8*(2): 68–80.

Latham, G. P. and Wexley, K. N. (1994) *Increasing Productivity through Performance Appraisal*. Reading, MA: Addison-Wesley.

Latham, G. P., Saari, L. M., Pursell, E. D. and Campion, M. A. (1980) The situational interview. *Journal of Applied Psychology, 65*: 422–7.

Latimer, J. and Skeggs, B. (2011) The politics of imagination: keeping open and critical. *Sociological Review,* 59(3): 393–410.

Laud, R. L. (1984) Performance appraisal practices in the Future 1300. In C. Fombrun, N. M. Tichy and M. A. Devanna (eds) *Strategic Human Resource Management*, (pp. 101–26). New York: John Wiley & Sons.

Lave, J. and Wenger, E. (1991) *Situated Learning. Legitimate Peripheral Participation*. Cambridge: Cambridge University Press.

Lawler, E. (2000) *Rewarding Excellence*. San Francisco, CA: Jossey-Bass.

Lawler, E. E. (1971) *Pay and Organizational Effectiveness*. New York: McGraw-Hill.

Lawler, E. E. (2011) Creating a New Employment Deal: Total Rewards and the New Workforce, *Organizational Dynamics*, 40(4): 302–9. Available at: https://ceo.usc.edu/wp-content/uploads/2011/07/2011-09-G11-09-Creating_New_Employment_Deal.pdf Accessed 13 July 2020.

Lawler, E. E. (2014) HR should own organizational effectiveness. *Forbes.* Available at: https://www.forbes.com/sites/edwardlawler/2014/02/11/hr-should-own-organizational-effectiveness/#497a9b181e46. Accessed 23 October 2020.

Lawler, E. E. (2017) *Reinventing Talent Management: Principles and Practices for the New World of Work*. Oakland: Berrett-Koehler Publishers.

Lawler, E. E., Benson, G. S. and McDermott, M. (2012) What makes performance appraisals effective? *Compensation & Benefits Review, 44*(4): 191–200.

Lawler III, E. E. (1973) *Motivation in Work Organizations*. Monterey, CA: Brooks/Cole.

Lawrence, F. (2015) Lithuanian migrants trafficked to UK egg farms sue 'worst gangmaster every'. *The Guardian*, 10 August. Available at: https://www.theguardian.com/world/2015/aug/10/lithuanian-migrants-chicken-catchers-trafficked-uk-egg-farms-sue-worst-gangmaster-ever. Accessed 15 June 2020.

Lawrence, T. B. and Phillips, N. (2019) *Constructing Organizational Life: How Social-Symbolic Work Shapes Selves, Organizations, and Institutions*. Oxford University Press.

Lazarova, M. (2006) 'International human resource management in global perspective. In M. J. Morley, N. Heraty and D. G. Collings (eds) *International Human Resource Management and International Assignments*. London: Palgrave MacMillan.

Lazear, E. P. (2000) The power of incentives. *American Economic Review*, pp. 410–14.

Leat, M. (2007) *Exploring Employee Relations* (2nd edn). Oxford: Butterworth-Heinemann.

Lee, M. Y. and Edmondson, A. C. (2017) Self-managing organizations: exploring the limits of less-hierarchical organizing. *Research in Organizational Behavior, 37*: 35–58.

Lefkowitz, J. (2000) The role of interpersonal affective regard in supervisory performance ratings: a literature review and proposed causal model. *Journal of occupational and Organizational Psychology, 73*(1): 67–85.

Legge, K. (1978) *Power, Innovation, and Problem-solving in Personnel Management*. London: McGraw-Hill.

Legge, K. (1986) Women in personnel management. In A. Spencer and D. Podmore (eds) *A Man's World* (pp. 33–60). London: Tavistock.

Legge, K. (1995) *Human Resource Management: Rhetorics and Realities*. Basingstoke: Macmillan.

Legge, K. (1998) The morality of HRM. In C. Mabey, D. Skinner and Clark, T. (eds) *Experiencing Human Resource Management* (pp. 14–32). London: Sage.

Legge, K. (2005) *Human Resource Management: Rhetorics and Realities* (anniversary edn). Basingstoke: Palgrave Macmillan.

Legge, K. (2007) Networked organizations and the negation of HRM? In J. Storey (ed.) *Human Resource Management: A Critical Text* (3rd edn) (pp. 39–56). London: Thomson Learning.

Leonard, N. H., Beauvais, L. L. and Scholl, R. W. (1999) Work motivation: the incorporation of self-concept-based processes. *Human Relations, 52*(8): 969–98.

Leonard-Barton, D. (1992) Core capabilities and core rigidities: a paradox in managing new product development. *Strategic Management Journal*, Summer Special Issue, *13*: 111–25.

Leslie, J. and McCurdy, C. (2020) *The economic effects of coronavirus in the UK*. London: Resolution Foundation. Available at: https://www.resolutionfoundation.org/publications/the-economic-effects-of-coronavirus-in-the-uk/. Accessed 13 July 2020.

Leslie, L. M. (2019) Diversity initiative effectiveness: a typological theory of unintended consequences. *Academy of Management Review 44*(3): 538–63.

Levashina, J. and Campion, M. A. (2006) A model of faking likelihood in the employment interview. *International Journal of Selection and Assessment, 14*: 299–316.

Levin, K. and Davis, C. (2020) What does 'Net-Zero Emissions' mean? 6 common questions, answered. *World Resources Institute* online. Available at: https://www.wri.org/blog/2019/09/what-does-net-zero-emissions-mean-6-common-questions-answered#:~:text=Twenty%20countries%20and%20regions%20adopted,Switzerland%20and%20the%20United%20Kingdom. Accessed 13 October 2020.

Levine, L. (2013) *The Increase in Unemployment Since 2007: Is It Cyclical or Structural?* Washington, Congressional Research Service.

Levinson, R. (2017) Across the US, police contracts shield officers from scrutiny and discipline. *Reuters*, 13 January. Available at: https://www.reuters.com/investigates/special-report/usa-police-unions/. Accessed 29 June 2020.

Levitt, T. (2020) A terrible way to go for £9 an hour: fear at meat plant after three coronavirus deaths. *The Guardian*, 20 May. Available at: https://www.theguardian.com/environment/2020/may/20/its-a-terrible-way-to-go-for-9-an-hour-fear-at-meat-plant-after-three-deaths-coronavirus. Accessed 15 June 2020.

Lewin, D. (2008) HRM in the 21st century. In C. Wankel (ed.) *Handbook of 21st Century Management*. London: Sage.

Lian, H., Brown, D. J., Ferris, D. L., Liang, L. H., Keeping, L. M. and Morrison, R. (2014) Abusive supervision and retaliation: a self-control framework. *Academy of Management Journal, 57*(1): 116–39.

Lievens, F. and Harris, M. M. (2003) Research on Internet recruiting and testing: current status and future directions. In C. L. Cooper and I. T. Robertson (eds) *International Review of Industrial and Organizational Psychology, 16*: 131–65.

Lievens, F., Peeters, H. and Schollaert, E. (2008) Situational judgment tests: a review of recent research. *Personnel Review, 37*(4): 426–41.

Liff, S. (1997) Two routes to managing diversity: individual differences or social group characteristics. *Employee Relations, 19*(1): 11–26.

Lin, C. A., Atkin, D. J., Cappotto, C., Davis, C., Dean, J., Eisenbaum, J., House, `k., Lange, R., Merceron, A., Metzer, J., Mitchum, A., Nicholls, H. and Vidican, S. (2015) Ethnicity, digital divides and uses of the Internet for health information. *Computers in Human Behavior, 51*: 216–23.

Lin, M. H. and Chen, H. G. (2017) A study of the effects of digital learning on learning motivation and learning outcome. *Eurasia Journal of Mathematics, Science and Technology Education, 13*(7): 3553–64.

Linehan, M. (2005) Women in international management. In H. Scullion and M. Linehan (eds) *International Human Resource Management* (pp. 181–201). Basingstoke: Palgrave Macmillan.

Linehan, M. and Mayrhofer, W. (2005) International careers and repatriation. In H. Scullion and M. Linehan (eds) *International Human Resource Management* (pp. 131–55). Basingstoke: Palgrave Macmillan.

Little, P. (2020) College sector is certain to play a vital and central role in scotland's post-Covid-19 economic recovery. *BusinessHQ, 14*: 116.

Littler, C. R. (1982) *The Development of the Labour Process in Capitalist Societies*. London: Heinemann.

Littler, C. R. and Salaman, G. (1984) *Class at Work: The Design, Allocation and Control of Jobs*. London: Batsford.

Livingstone, D. W. (1999) Exploring the icebergs of adult learning: Findings of the first Canadian survey of informal learning practices. *Canadian Journal for the Study of Adult Education, 13*(2): 49–72.

Lo Piano, S. (2020) Ethical principles in machine learning and artificial intelligence: cases from the field and possible ways forward. *Humanities and Social Sciences Communications, 7*(9): 1–7.

Locke, E. A. (1968) Towards a theory of task motivation and incentives. *Organizational Behavior and Human Performance, 3*: 152–89.

Logan, J. (2020) The US union avoidance industry goes global. *New Labor Forum, 29*(1): 76–81.

London, M. and Mone, E. M. (2018) Strategic performance appraisal. In J. Storey, P. M. Wright and D. Ulrich (eds) *The Routledge Companion to Strategic Human Resource Management* (pp. 245–61). London: Routledge.

Long, R. D., Wilder, D.A., Betz, A. and Dutta, A. (2012) Effects of and preference for pay for performance: an analogue analysis. *Journal of Applied Behaviour Analysis, 45*(4): 821–6.

Long, R. J. and Singh, P. (2017) *Strategic Compensation in Canada* (6th edn). Toronto: Nelson.

Lopez-Cabrales, A. and Valle-Cabrera, R. (2020) Sustainable HRM strategies and employment relationships as drivers of the triple bottom line. *Human Resource Management Review, 30*(3): 100689.

Lorange, P. and Murphy, D. (1984) Bringing human resources into strategic planning: systems design considerations. In C. Fombrun, N. M. Tichy and M. A. Devanna (eds) *Strategic Human Resources Management* (pp. 275–96). New York: John Wiley & Sons.

Lorenz, C. (2012) If you're so smart, why are you under surveillance? Universities, neoliberalism, and new public management. *Critical Inquiry, 38*(3): 599–629.

Lovelace, J. B., Neely, B. H., Allen, J. B. and Hunter, S. T. (2019) Charismatic, ideological, & pragmatic (CIP) model of leadership: a critical review and agenda for future research. *The Leadership Quarterly, 30*(1): 96–110.

Loya, M. A. and Cuevas, M. (2010) Teaching racism: using experiential learning to challenge the status quo. *Journal of Teaching in Social Work, 30*(3): 288–99.

Lozano, R. (2015) A holistic perspective on corporate sustainability drivers. *Corporate Social Responsibility and Environmental Management, 22*(1): 32–44.

LTHT (2019) *Improving workforce planning and intelligence.* Leeds. Leeds Teaching Hospitals NHS Trust. Available at: https://improvement.nhs.uk/documents/4332/Improving_workforce_planning_and_intelligence.pdf. Accessed 15 May 2020.

Lub, X. D., Bal, P. M., Blomme, R. J. and Schalk, R. (2016) One job, one deal ... or not: do generations respond differently to psychological contract fulfillment? *International Journal of Human Resource Management, 27*(6): 653–80.

Lund, H, L. (2004) Strategies for sustainable business and the handling of workers' interests: integrated management systems and worker participation. *Economic and Industrial Democracy, 25(*1): 41–74.

Luxemburg, R. (1913/2003) *The Accumulation of Capital.* London: Routledge.

Lynch, D., Hughes, J. and Arnold, M (2016) JPMorgan to pay $264m penalty for hiring 'princelings'. *Financial Times*, 17 November.

Lynch, K. and Deegan, P. (2021) Team America. *The Globe and Mail*, 16 January, p. O8. Toronto, Canada.

Mabey, C., Skinner, D. and Clark, D. (eds) (1998a) *Experiencing Human Resource Management*. London: Sage.

Mabey, C., Salaman, G. and Storey, J. (eds) (1998b) *Human Resource Management: A Strategic Introduction*. Oxford: Blackwell.

Mabon, L., Shackley, S., Vercelli, S. Anderlucci, J. and Boot, K. (2015) Framework for Low-Carbon Energy through the Case of Carbon Dioxide Capture and Storage. *Environment and Planning C: Politics and Space*, 33(2): 256–71.

Macintosh, R. and MacLean, D. (2015) *Strategic Management*. London: Palgrave Macmillan.

Macionis, J. and Gerber, L. M. (2011) *Sociology* (7th Canadian edn). Toronto, Ontario: Pearson.

Macky, K. and Boxall, P. (2007) The relationship between 'high-performance work practices' and employee attitudes: an investigation of additive and interaction effects. *International Journal of Human Resource Management, 18*(4): 537–67.

MacLeod, D. and Clarke, N. (2009) *Engaging for Success: Enhancing Performance through Employee Engagement*. London: Department for Business, Innovation and Skills.

Macwhirter, I. (2020) In 2008, Labour bailed out the banks – in 2020, the Tories have bailed out the workers, *The Herald*, 21 March, Avaliable at: https://www.heraldscotland.com/news/18325009.iain-macwhirter-2008-labour-bailed-banks---2020-tories-bailed-workers/. Accessed 27 April 2021.

Maes, J. D. and Weldy, T. G. (2018) Building effective virtual teams: expanding OD research and practice. *Organisation Development Journal, 36*(3): 83–90.

Mahajan, A. (2011) Host country national's reactions to expatriate pay policies: making a case for a cultural alignment model. *International Journal of Human Resource Management, 22*(1): 121–37.

Mahboubi, P. (2020) Canada's gig workers need more than temporary government relief, *The Globe and Mail*, October 16, p. B4.

Mahmood, M. (2015) Strategy, structure, and HRM policy orientation: Employee recruitment and selection practices in multinational subsidiaries. *Asia Pacific Journal of Human Resources, 53*(3): 331–50.

Mahoney, J. and Fine, S. (2020) Will vaccine be mandatory for certain workers? *The Globe and Mail,* 18 December, p. A4.

Main, P., Curtis, A., Pitts, J. and Irish, B. (2009) A 'mutually agreed statement of learning' in general practice trainer appraisal: the place of peer appraisal by experienced course members. *Education for Primary Care, 20*(2): 104–10.

Maitra, S. and Sangha, J. (2005) Intersecting realities: young women and call centre work in India and Canada. *Women and Environments*, Spring/Summer: 40–2.

Makin, K. (2007) Collective bargaining is a right, top court rules. *Globe and Mail*, 9 June, p. A4.

Makortoff, K. (2020) Diversity: How UK firms are failing to foster change. *The Guardian*, 13 June, p. 35.

Malik, K. (2020) 'White privilege' is a lazy distraction, leaving racism and power untouched. *The Observer*, 14 June, p. 35.

Mann, G. and O'Neil, C. (2016) Hiring Algorithms Are Not Neutral. *Harvard Business Review*, 9 December. Available at: https://hbr.org/2016/12/hiring-algorithms-are-not-neutral. Accessed 16 November 2020.

Manokha, I. (2017) Why the rise of wearable tech to monitor employees is worrying. *The Conversation*, 3 January online. Available at: https://theconversation.com/why-the-rise-of-wearable-tech-to-monitor-employees-is-worrying-70719. Accessed 4 October 2020.

Marchington, M. (2008) Employee voice systems. In P. Boxall, J. Purcell and P. Wright (eds) *The Oxford Handbook of Human Resource Management* (pp. 231–50). Oxford: Oxford University Press.

Marchington, M. (2015) Human resource management (HRM): too busy looking up to see where it is going longer term? *Human Resource Management Review*, *25*(2): 176–87.

Marchington, M. and Wilding, P. (1983) Employee involvement inaction? *Personnel Management*, December: 73–82.

Marchington, M. and Wilkinson, A. (2000) Direct participation. In S. Bach and K. Sisson (eds) *Personnel Management: A Comprehensive Guide to Theory and Practice* (Chapter 14). Oxford: Blackwell.

Marchington, M. and Wilkinson, A. (2008) *Human Resource Management at Work* (4th edn). London: CIPD.

Marchington, M. and Wilkinson, A. J. (1996) *Core Personnel and Development*. London: Institute of Personnel and Development.

Marchington, M. and Kynighou, A. (2012) The dynamics of employee involvement and participation during turbulent times. *International Journal of Human Resource Management*, 23(16): 3336–51.

Marchington, M., Cooke, F. I. and Hebson G. (2013) Human resource management across organizational boundaries. In A. Wilkinson, N. bacon, T. Redman and S. Snell (eds) *Sage Handbook of Human Resource Management* (pp. 460–74). London: Sage

Marginson, P and Meardi, G. (2010) Multinational companies: transforming national industrial relations? In T. Colling and M. Terry (eds) *Industrial Relations: Theory and Practice* (3rd edn) (pp. 207–30). Chichester: John Wiley & Sons.

Marginson, P., Armstrong, P., Edwards, P. K. and Purcell, J. (1995) Extending beyond borders: multinational companies and the international management of labour. *International Journal of Human Resource Management*, *6*(3): 702–19.

Marginson, P., Edwards, P., Edwards, T., Ferner, A. and Tregaskis, O. (2010) Employee representation and consultative voice in multinational companies operating in Britain. *British Journal of Industrial Relations*, *48*(1): 151–80.

Marin, S. (2014) Supreme Court of Canada: Wal-Mart must pay for closing unionized store. *Huffington Post/The Canadian Press*. 27 June. Available at: www.huffingtonpost.ca/2014/06/27/walmart-canada-supreme-court_n_5537051.html. Accessed 14 September 2016.

Markey, R. and McIvor, J. (2019) Environmental bargaining in Australia. *Journal of Industrial Relations*, *61*(1): 79–104. DOI:10.1177/0022185618814056

Markey, R., McIvor, J., O'Brien, M. and Wright, C. F. (2019) Reducing carbon emissions through employee participation: evidence from Australia. *Industrial Relations Journal*, *50*(1): 57–83.

Marler, J. H. and Fisher, S. (2013) An evidence-based review of e-HRM and strategic human resource management. *Human Resource Management Review*, *23*: 18–36.

Marowits, R. (2021) Ottawa should ban CEO bonuses at companies that receive wage subsidies, think-tank economists says. *Globe and Mail*, 5 January, p. B3.

Marr, B. (2018) What is Industry 4.0? Here's a Super Easy Explanation for Anyone. *Forbes* online. Available at: https://www.forbes.com/sites/bernardmarr/2018/09/02/what-is-industry-4-0-heres-a-super-easy-explanation-for-anyone/#54bb2ccd9788. Accessed 7 August 2020.

Martin, A. and Quick, A. (2020) *Unions Renewed*. Cambridge: Polity.

Martin, I. (2014) *Making It Happen*. London: Simon & Schuster.

Martin, J. N. and Nakayama, T. K. (2000) *Intercultural Communications in Context* (2nd edn). Mountain View, CA: Mayfield.

Martin, P. and Pope, J. (2008) Competency-based interviewing – has it gone too far? *Industrial and Commercial Training*, *40*(2): 81–6.

Martocchio, J. J. (2019) *Strategic Compensation: A Human Resource Management Approach* (10th edn). New York: Pearson Prentice-Hall.

Marx, K (1894/1972) *Capital, Volume 3*. London: Lawrence & Wishart.

Maslach, C., Schaufeli, W. B. and Leiter, M. P. (2001) Job burnout. *Annual Review of Psychology*, *52*: 397–422.

Maslow, A. (1954) *Motivation and Personality*. New York: Harper & Row.

Mason, P. (2016) *PostCapitalism: A Guide to our Future*. London: Penguin.

Matei, L., (2006) *Public Management* (2nd edn). Bucharest: Economic Publishing House.

Mathiason, N. (2008) Three weeks that changed the world. *The Guardian*, 28 December. Available at: https://www.theguardian.com/business/2008/dec/28/markets-credit-crunch-banking-2008. Accessed 9 December 2020.

Mathis, R. L., Jackson, J. H. and Valentine, S. R. (2014) *Human Resource Management*. Stamford: Cengage Learning.

Mattke, S., Liu, H., Caloyeras, J., Huang, C. Y., Van Busum, K. R., Khodyakov, D. and Shier, V. (2013) Workplace Wellness Programs Study: Final Report. *Rand Health Quarterly*, *3*(2): 7.

Maurice, M. and Sorge, A. (eds) (2000) *Embedding Organizations*. Amsterdam: John Benjamins Publishing.

May, D. R. and Flannery, B. L. (1995) Cutting waste with employee involvement teams. *Business Horizons*, *38*: 28–38.

Mayer, R. C. and Davis, J. H. (1999) The effect of the performance appraisal system on trust for management: A field quasi-experiment. *Journal of Applied Psychology*, *84*(1): 123–36.

Mayerhofer, H., Hartmann, L., Michelitsch-Riedl, G. and Kollinger, I. (2004) Flexpatriate assignments: a neglected issue in global staffing. *International Journal of Human Resource Management*, *15*(8): 1371–89.

Mayo, E. (1919) *Democracy and Freedom*. Melbourne: Macmillan.

McAllister, K. (2020) As we start to take steps out of lockdown, the Scottish space industry is stepping up. *BusinessHQ, 14*: 107–9.

McCann, L., Granter, E., Hyde, P. and Jeremy Aroles, J. (2020) 'Upon the gears and upon the wheels': terror convergence and total administration in the neoliberal university', *Management Learning, 51*(4): 431–45.

McCarthy, A. M. and Garavan, T. N. (2001) 360° feedback processes: performance improvement and employee career development. *Journal of European Industrial Training, 25*(1): 5–32.

McCauley, C. D. and Brutus, S. (1998) *Management Development through Job Experiences: An Annotated Bibliography*. Greensboro, NC: Centre for Creative Leadership.

McClean, B. (2017) How Wells Fargo's cutthroat corporate culture allegedly drove bankers to fraud. *Vanity Fair*, 31 May online. Available at: https://www.vanityfair.com/news/2017/05/wells-fargo-corporate-culture-fraud. Accessed 11 October 2020.

McCormack, N. and Cotter, C. (2013) *Managing Burnout in the Workplace: A guide for Information Professionals*. Whitney, Oxfordshire: Chandos Publishing.

McCulloch, M. and Turban, D. (2007) Using person–organization fit to select employees for high-turnover jobs. *International Journal of Selection and Assessment, 15*(1): 63–71.

McDonald, P. and Charlesworth, S. (2016) Workplace sexual harassment at the margins. *Work, Employment and Society, 30*(1): 118–34.

McDonald, P., Charlesworth, S. and Graham, T. (2016) Action or inaction: bystander intervention in workplace sexual harassment. *International Journal of Human Resource Management, 27*(5): 548–66.

McFarland, A. (2020) Shell Begins to Reskill Workers in Artificial Intelligence. *Unite AI*, 3 April online. Available at: https://www.unite.ai/shell-begins-to-reskill-workers-in-artificial-intelligence. Accessed 12 August 2020.

McGregor, D. (1960) *The Human Side of Enterprise*. New York: McGraw-Hill.

McGregor-Smith, R. (2017) *Race in the Workplace: The McGregor-Smith Review*, February. Available at: https://assets.publishing.service.gov.uk/government/uploads/system/uploads/attachment_data/file/594336/race-in-workplace-mcgregor-smith-review.pdf. Accessed 7 May 2021.

McGuire, D. and Kissack, H. (2015) Line managers and HRD. In R. F. Poell, T. S. Rocco and G. L. Roth (eds) *The Routledge Companion to Human Resource Development* (pp. 521–30). London: Routledge.

McIlroy, J. (1988) *Trade Unions in Britain Today*. Manchester: Manchester University Press.

McKinlay, A. and Starkey, K. (eds) (1998) *Foucault, Management and Organizational Theory*. London: Sage.

McKinsey & Company (2015) Why diversity matters. McKinsey & Company, 1 January online. Available at: https://www.mckinsey.com/business-functions/organization/our-insights/why-diversity-matters. Accessed 12 October 2020.

McKinsey (2017) Jobs lost, jobs gained: What the future of work will mean for jobs, skills, and wages. McKinsey Global Institute online. Available at: https://www.mckinsey.com/featured-insights/future-of-work/jobs-lost-jobs-gained-what-the-future-of-work-will-mean-for-jobs-skills-and-wages#automation. Accessed 7 August 2020.

McLean, G. N. (2004) National human resource development: what in the world is it? *Advances in Developing Human Resources, 6*(3): 269–75.

McLoughlin, I. and Clark, J. (1988) *Technological Change at Work*. Milton Keynes: Open University Press.

McMurray, S. (2020) The Impact of Covid-19 on the Health and Social Care Workforce. Northern Ireland Assembly Research and Information Service Briefing Paper, No. 34/20. Available at: http://www.niassembly.gov.uk/globalassets/documents/raise/publications/2017-2022/2020/health/3420.pdf. Accessed 9 August 2020.

McShane, S. L. (1990) Two tests of direct gender bias in job evaluation ratings. *Journal of Occupational Psychology, 63*: 129–40.

Meadows, D. H., Meadows, D. L., Randers, J. and Behrens, W. W. (1972) *The Limits to Growth*. Universe Books: New York.

Medros, A. (2019) Reskilling workers is a central part of Corporate Social Responsibility. *Harvard Business Review*, 1 October.

Mehrotra, K. and Keller, L. J. (2017) Wells Fargo's fake accounts grow to 3.5 million in suit. *Bloomberg*, 12 May online. Available at: https://www.bloomberg.com/news/articles/2017-05-12/wells-fargo-bogus-account-estimate-in-suit-grows-to-3-5-million. Accessed 11 October 2020.

Meijerink, J., Boons, M., Keegan, A. and Marler, J. (2018) Special issue of the *International Journal of Human Resource Management*: Digitization and the transformation of human resource management. *International Journal of Human Resource Management*. DOI: 10.1080/09585192.2018.1503845

Meinert, D. (2015) Is it time to put the performance review on a PIP? Society for Human Resource Management. 1 April. Available at: https://www.shrm.org/hr-today/news/hr-magazine/pages/0415-qualitative-performance-reviews.aspx. Accessed 7 July 2020.

Mello, J. A. (2005) *Strategic Human Resource Management* (2nd edn). London: Thomson South-Western.

Mencl, J. and Lester, S. (2014) More alike than different: what generations value and how the values affect employee workplace perceptions. *Journal of Leadership & Organizational Studies. 21*: 257–72. 10.1177/1548051814529825.

Mensi-Klarbach, H. and Risberg, A. (2019) *Diversity in Organisations – Concepts and Practices* (2nd edn). London: Red Globe Press.

Mensi-Klarbach, H. and Seierstad, C. (2020) Gender quotas on corporate boards: similarities and differences in quota scenarios. *European Management Review*.

Mercer (2013) *Global Performance Management Survey Report*. Available at: https://www.uk.mercer.com/newsroom/few-organisations-have-confidence-in-the-effectiveness-of-their-performance-management-programs.html. Accessed 26 June 2020.

Messenger, J. and Ghosheh, N. (2013) *Work Sharing During the Great Recession: New Developments and Beyond*. Cheltenham: Edward Elgar Publishing.

Messersmith, J. G., Patel, P. C. and Lepak, D. P. (2011) Unlocking the black box: exploring the link between high-performance work systems and performance. *Journal of Applied Psychology, 96*(6): 1105–18.

Messick Svare, G. Miller, L. and Ames, G. (2004) Social climate and workplace drinking among women in a male-dominated occupation. *Addictive Behaviours*, 29(8): 1691–8.

Meyer, H. H., Kay, E. and French, J. R. P. (1965) Split roles in performance appraisal. *Harvard Business Review, 43*: 123–29.

Mezirow, J. (1991) *Transformative Dimensions of Adult Learning*. San Francisco, CA: Jossey-Bass.

Miliband, E. (2021) It's now clear this government wants UK workers to have as little power as possible. *The Guardian*, January 15. Available at: https://www.theguardian.com/commentisfree/2021/jan/15/government-uk-workers-power-conservatives-britain-rights. Accessed 15 January 2021.

Miller, L., Rankin, N. and Neathey, F. (2001) *Competency Frameworks in UK Organizations*. London: Chartered Institute of Personnel and Development.

Miller, S. J., Hickson, D. J. and Wilson, D. C. (1999) Decision-making in organizations. In S. R. Clegg, C. Hardy and W. R. Nord (eds) *Managing Organizations: Current Issues* (pp. 43–62). London: Sage.

Milliman, J. and Clair, J. (1996) Best environmental HRM practices in the US. In W. Wehrmeyer (ed.) *Greening People: Human Resources and Environmental Management* (Chapter 2). Sheffield. Greenleaf.

Milliman, J., Nason, S., Zhu, C. and De Cieri, H. (2002) An exploratory assessment of the purposes of performance appraisals in North and Central America and the Pacific Rim. *Asia Pacific Journal of Human Resources, 40*(1): 78–101.

Mills, C. W. (1959/2000) *The Sociological Imagination* (Fortieth Anniversary Edition). New York: Oxford University Press.

Millward, N., Bryson, A. and Forth, J. (2000) *All Change at Work: British Employee Relations 1980–1998*. London: Routledge.

Milman, O. (2017) Trump's alarming environmental rollback: what's been scrapped so far. *The Guardian*, 4 July 2017.

Milmo, D. (2010) BA told to hit union 'where it hurts'. *The Guardian*, 27 March, pp. 1–2.

Minbaeva, D and Andersen, T. J. (2012) *The Role of Human Resource Management in Strategy Making*. Working Paper. Copenhagen: Copenhagen Business School.

Mind (2014) We've got work to do. MIND. Available at: https://www.mind.org.uk/media-a/2683/back-to-work-report_2015_web.pdf. Accessed 29 May 2021.

Mind (2020) Mental health facts and statistics. *Mind* online. Available at: https://www.mind.org.uk/information-support/types-of-mental-health-problems/statistics-and-facts-about-mental-health/how-common-are-mental-health-problems/#collapsedfe6e. Accessed 2 September 2020.

Miner-Rubino, K. and Cortina, L. M. (2004) Working in a context of hostility towards women: implications for employees' well-being. *Journal of Occupational Health Psychology, 9*(2): 107–22.

Mintzberg, H. (1978) Patterns in strategy formation. *Management Science, 24*(9): 934–48.

Mintzberg, H. (1987) Crafting strategy. *Harvard Business Review*, July/August: 66–75.

Mintzberg, H. (1989) *Mintzberg on Management*. New York: Collier/Hamilton.

Mintzberg, H. (2009) America's monumental failure of management. *Globe and Mail*, 16 March, p. A11.

Mittelstadt, B. D., Allo, P., Taddeo, M., Wacher, S. and Floridi, L. (2016) The ethics of algorithms: mapping the debate. *Big Data and Society*, July–December: 1–21.

Monbiot, G. (2017) *How Did We Get into this Mess?* London: Verso.

Monbiot, G. (2020) Tory privatisation is at the heart of the UK's disastrous coronavirus response, The Guardian, 27 May. Available at: https://www.theguardian.com/commentisfree/2020/may/27/privatisation-uk-disatrous-coronavirus-response-ppe-care-homes-corporate-power-public-policy

Mone, E., Eisinger, C., Guggenheim, K., Price, B. and Stine, C. (2011) Performance management at the wheel: driving employee engagement in organizations. *Journal of Business and Psychology, 26*(2): 205–12.

Montabon, F., Morrow, P. C. and Cantor, D. E. (2016) Promoting environmental citizenship behaviour. *International Journal of Integrated Supply Management, 10*(1): 63–88.

Montgomery, J. and Kelloway, E. K. (2002) *Management of Occupational Health and Safety* (2nd edn). Scarborough, Ontario: Nelson Thomson Learning.

Moore, O. (2020) Future of cities: a better way. *Globe and Mail*, 14 November, p. A10.

Moore, S. (2017) It's not a perk when big employers offer egg-freezing – it's a bogus bribe. *The Guardian*, 26 April online. Available at: https://www.theguardian.com/society/commentisfree/2017/apr/26/its-not-a-perk-when-big-employers-offer-egg-freezing-its-a-bogus-bribe. Accessed 20 September 2020.

Moore, T. and Bokelberg, E. (2019) How IBM incorporates Artificial Intelligence into strategic workforce planning. *People & Strategy, 42*(4): 52–55.

Moore, K. and Lewis, D.(1999) *Birth of the Multinational: 2000 Years of Ancient Business History – from Ashur to Augustus*. Copenhagen: Copenhagen Business School Press.

Morgan, G. and Kristensen, P. (2006) The contested space of multinationals: varieties of institutionalism, varieties of capitalism. *Human Relations, 59*(11): 1467–90.

Morgan, J. (2019) Will we work in twenty-first century capitalism? A critique of the fourth industrial revolution literature. *Economy and Society*. Available at: https://doi.org/10.1080/03085147.2019.1620027.

Morgeson, F. P. and Humphrey, S. E. (2008) Job and team design: toward a more integrative conceptualization of work design. In J. Martocchio (ed.) *Research in Personnel and Human Resources Management* (pp. 39–91). Emerald Group Publishing Limited.

Morouney, K. (1991) The Social Construction of Leading: Formulating a Critique of the Methodology of Leadership. In *Proceedings of the Annual Conference of the*

Administrative Sciences Association of Canada, Women in Management, 12(11): 21–30.

Morrell, K. M., Loan-Clarke, J. and Wilkinson, A. J. (2001) Unweaving leaving: the use of models in the management of employee turnover. *International Journal of Management Reviews, 3*(1): 219–44.

Morrell, K. M., Loan-Clarke, J. and Wilkinson, A. J. (2004) Organisational change and employee turnover. *Personnel Review, 33*(2): 161–73.

Morris, J., Wilkinson, B. and Gamble, J. (2009) Strategic international human resource management or the 'bottom line'? The case of electronics and garments commodity chains in China. *International Journal of Human Resource Management, 20*(2): 348–71.

Morris, S. and Snell, S. (2013) The evolution of HR strategy: adaptations to increasing global complexity. In A. Wilkinson, N. Bacon, T. Redman, and S. Snell (eds) *The SAGE Handbook of Human Resource Management* (pp. 84–99). London: Sage.

Morrow, A. (2021) Biden wastes no time charting a new course for the US. *Globe and Mail*, 23 January, p. A16.

Morton, A. (2020) Australian businesses call for climate crisis and virus economic recovery to be tackled together. *The Guardian*, 4 May. Retrieved from https://www.theguardian.com/environment/2020/may/05/australian-businesses-call-for-climate-crisis-and-virus-economic-recovery-to-be-tackled-together.

Mousteri, V., Daly, M. and Delaney, L. (2020) Underemployment and psychological distress: propensity score and fixed estimates from two large UK samples. *Social Science and Medicine, 244*: 112641.

Moyer-Lee, J. (2021) After the Uber ruling, there's no excuse for government not to enforce workers' rights. *The Guardian,* 20 February. Available at: https://www.theguardian.com/commentisfree/2021/feb/20/uber-ruling-government-workers-rights-conservatives-employers. Accessed 20 February 2021.

Muir, H. (2017) We say we want a fairer Britain – but how serious are we? *The Guardian*, 31 July, p. 21.

Mujtaba, D. F. and. Mahapatra, N. R (2019) Ethical Considerations in AI-Based Recruitment. *2019 IEEE International Symposium on Technology and Society (ISTAS)*, Medford, MA, USA, pp. 1–7. DOI: 10.1109/ISTAS48451.2019.8937920

Munby, H., Versnel, J., Hutchinson, N. L., Chin, P. and Berg, D. H. (2003) Workplace learning and the metacognitive functions of routines. *Journal of Workplace Learning, 15*: 94–104.

Munro-Fraser, J. (1971) *Psychology: General, Industrial, Social*. London: Pitman.

Murphy, J. and Bratton, J. (2020) Power and leadership. In J. Bratton (ed.) *Organizational Leadership* (pp. 57–76). London: Sage.

Murray, J. (2020) Cross-party group urges chancellor to consider four-day week for UK. *The Guardian*, 20 June. Available at: https://www.theguardian.com/world/2020/jun/20/cross-party-group-urges-chancellor-to-consider-four-day-week. Accessed 29 June 2020.

Mwita, J. I. (2000) Performance management model. *International Journal of Public Sector Management, 13*(1): 19–37.

Nadler, L. and Nadler, Z. (1989) *Developing Human Resources*. San Francisco, CA: Jossey-Bass.

Nagendra, A. and Deshpande, M. (2014) Human resource information systems (HRIS) in HR planning and development in mid to large sized organizations. *Social and Behavioral Sciences, 133*: 61–7.

Naima McCloskey, H. (2020) Stop making the business case for diversity. *Sifted*, 2 August online. Available at: https://sifted.eu/articles/diversity-business-case. Accessed 12 October 2020.

Nakatsu, R. T., Grossman, E. B. and Iacovou, C. L. (2014) A taxonomy of crowdsourcing based on task complexity. *Journal of Information Science, 40*(6): 823–34.

Nankervis, A., Stanton, P. and Foley, P. (2012) Exploring the rhetoric and reality of performance management systems and organisational effectiveness-Evidence from Australia. *Research and Practice in Human Resource Management, 20*(1): 40–56.

National Institute on Drug Abuse (NIDA) (2020) Misuse of Prescription Drugs Research Report: Overview. *National Institute on Drug Abuse* online. Available at: https://www.drugabuse.gov/publications/research-reports/misuse-prescription-drugs/overview. Accessed 20 September 2020.

National Safety Council (NSC) (2020) Assaults fourth leading cause of workplace deaths. *National Safety Council* online. Available at: https://www.nsc.org/work-safety/safety-topics/workplace-violence#:~:text=Every%20year%2C%20millions%20of%20American,according%20to%20Injury%20Facts%C2%AE. Accessed 20 September 2020.

Neal-Barnett, A. (2020) How organizations can support the mental health of Black employees. *Harvard Business Review*, 11 June. Available at: https://hbr.org/2020/06/how-organizations-can-support-the-mental-health-of-black-employees. Accessed 30 June 2020.

Neate, R. (2020) Billionaires' wealth rises to $10.2 trillion amid Covid crisis. *The Guardian*, 7 October. Available at: https://www.theguardian.com/business/2020/oct/07/covid-19-crisis-boosts-the-fortunes-of-worlds-billionaires. Accessed 22 January 2021.

Neate, R. (2021) Elon Musk becomes world's richest person. *The Guardian*, 7 January. Available at: https://www.theguardian.com/business/2021/jan/07/elon-musk-overtakes-amazon-bezos-world-richest-person-tesla-bloomberg-billionare-index-blue-senate. Accessed 8 January 2021.

Nebeker, D. M. and Tatum, B. C. (1993) The Effects of computer monitoring, standards, and rewards on work performance, job satisfaction, and stress 1. *Journal of Applied Social Psychology, 23*(7): 508–36.

Nelson, D. L. and Simmons, B. L. (2011) Savoring eustress while coping with distress: the holistic model of stress. In J. C. Quick and L. E. Tetrick (eds) *Handbook of Occupational Health Psychology* (pp. 55–74). Washington, DC: American Psychological Association.

Newman, J., Gerhart, B. and Milkovich, G. (2016) *Compensation* (12th edn). New York: McGraw-Hill.

Newton, T. J. and Harte, G. (1997) Green business: technicist kitsch? *Journal of Management Studies, 34*(1): 75–98.

Nga Thi Thuy Ho, Pi-Shen Seet and Jones, J. (2016) Understanding re-expatriation intentions among overseas returnees – an emerging economy perspective. *International Journal of Human Resource Management, 27*(17): 1938–66.

Nguyen, J. (2018) Egg freezing, yacht parties and pet insurance: unusual company benefits. *Marketplace*, 6 September online. Available at: https://www.marketplace.org/2018/09/06/egg-freezing-yacht-parties-and-pet-insurance-some-unusual-company-benefits. Accessed 20 September 2020.

Nguyen, S. (2014) The critical role of research in diversity training: how research contributes to an evidence-based approach to diversity training. *Development and Learning in Organizations: An International Journal*, *28*(4): 15–17.

Nicastro, D. (2018) Examining the role of wearables technology in the workplace. *CMS Wire*, 27 August online. Available at: https://www.cmswire.com/digital-workplace/examining-the-role-of-wearables-technology-in-the-workplace. Accessed 4 October 2020.

Nickson, D., Warhurst, C. and Dutton, E. (2005) The importance of attitude and appearance in the service encounter in retail and hospitality. *Managing Service Quality*, *15*(2): 195–208.

Nijholt, J. J. and Benders, J. (2010) Measuring the prevalence of self-managing teams: taking account of defining characteristics. *Work, Employment and Society*, *24*(2): 375–85.

Nixon, D. (2009) 'I can't put a smiley face on': working-class masculinity, emotional labour and service work in the 'new economy'. *Gender, Work and Organization*, *16*(3): 300–22.

Noe, R. A. and Tews, M. J. (2018) Strategic training and development. In J. Storey, P. M. Wright and D. Ulrich (eds) *The Routledge Companion to Strategic Human Resource Management* (pp. 262–84). London: Routledge.

Nolan, H. (2020) It's time to kick police unions out of the labor movement. They aren't allies. *The Guardian*, 13 June. Available at: https://www.theguardian.com/commentisfree/2020/jun/13/police-unions-afl-cio-labor-movement. Accessed 29 June 2020.

Nonaka, I. and Takeuchi, H. (1995) *The knowledge-creating company: How Japanese companies create the dynamics of innovation*. Oxford: Oxford university Press.

Nonaka, I., Toyama, R. and Nagata, A. (2000) A firm as a knowledge creating entity: a new perspective on the theory of the firm. *Industrial and Corporate Change*, *9*(1): 1–20.

Noon, M. and Hoque, K. (2001) Ethnic minorities and equal treatment: the impact of gender, equal opportunities policies and trade unions. *National Institute Economic Review*, *176*: 105–16.

Noon, M., Blyton, P. and Morrell, K. (2013) *The Realities of Work* (4th edn). London: Palgrave Macmillan.

Norlander, P., Erickson, C., Kuruvilla, S. and Kannan-Narasimhan, R. (2015) India's outsourcing industry and the offshoring of skilled services work: a review essay. *E-Journal of International and Comparative Labours Studies*, *4*(1): 1–24.

Northouse, P. G. (2019) *Leadership: Theory and Practice*. New York: SAGE Publications.

Norton, T. A., Zacher, H. and Ashkanasy, N. M. (2015) Pro-environmental organizational culture and climate. In J. Robertson and J. Barling (eds) *The Psychology of Green Organizations* (pp. 322–48). Oxford: Oxford University Press.

Nyberg, A. J., Moliterno, T. P., Hale Jr, D. and Lepak, D. P. (2014) Resource-based perspectives on unit-level human capital: a review and integration. *Journal of Management*, *40*(1): 316–46.

O'Connor, S. (2018) Dark factories: labour exploitation in Britain's garment industry. *The Financial Times*, 17 May. Available at: https://www.ft.com/content/e427327e-5892-11e8-b8b2-d6ceb45fa9d0. Accessed 9 July 2020.

O'Moore M., Seigne E., McGuire, L. and Smith M. (1998) Victims of workplace bullying in Ireland. *Irish Journal of Psychology*, *19*(2–3): 345–57.

O'Riordan, T. (1988) Politics of sustainability. In Turner, R. K. (ed) *Sustainable Environmental Management: Principles and Practices* (pp. 29–50). London: Belhaven Press.

Obinger, H. and Schmitt, C. (2011) Guns and butter? Regime competition and the welfare state during the Cold War. *World Politics*, *63*(2): 246–70.

Observer, The (2020) Across the world, figures reveal horrific toll of care home deaths. *The Observer* online. Available at: https://www.theguardian.com/world/2020/may/16/across-the-world-figures-reveal-horrific-covid-19-toll-of-care-home-deaths. Accessed 9 August 2020.

Odense Robotics (2020) Global robotics footprint made in Odense. Odense Robotics Insight Report. Available at: https://www.odenserobotics.dk/wp-content/uploads/2020/01/Odense-Robotics-Insight-Report-2020_web.pdf. Accessed 1 July 2020.

OECD (1996) *The Knowledge-based Economy*. Paris: OECD.

OECD (2015) *In It Together: Why Less Inequality Benefits All*. Paris: OECD Publishing

OECD (2019) *OECD Employment Outlook 2019, The Future of Work*. Paris: OECD Publishing.

OECD (2020a) *Employment Outlook 2020: Facing the Job Crisis*. Paris: Organisation for Economic Cooperation and Development. Available at: http://www.oecd.org/employment-outlook/2020/. Accessed 12 January 2021.

OECD (2020b) *Employment Outlook: Gender wage gap*. Paris: Organisation for Economic Co-operation and Development.

OECD (2020c) Job retention schemes during the Covid-19 lockdown and beyond. Organisation for Economic Cooperation and Development, 3 August online. Available at: http://www.oecd.org/coronavirus/policy-responses/job-retention-schemes-during-the-covid-19-lockdown-and-beyond-0853ba1d/. Accessed 12 August 2020.

OECD Stat (2020) Trade Union. *OECD* online. Available at: https://stats.oecd.org/Index.aspx?DataSetCode=TUD. Accessed 11 October 2020.

Office for National Statistics (ONS) (2018a) Adult drinking habits in Great Britain: 2017. *Office for National Statistics*, 1 May online. Available at: https://www.ons.gov.uk/peoplepopulationandcommunity/healthandsocialcare/drugusealcoholandsmoking/bulletins/opinionsandlifestylesurveyadultdrinkinghabitsingreatbritain/2017. Accessed 20 September 2020.

Office for National Statistics (2018b) Contracts that do not guarantee a minimum number of hours: April 2018. Available at: file:///C:/Users/User/Downloads/Contracts%20that%20do%20not%20guarantee%20a%20minimum%20number%20of%20hours%20April%202018.pdf. Accessed 11 June 2020.

Office for National Statistics (2019) Labour market economic commentary: February 2019. Available at: https://www.ons.gov.uk/employmentandlabourmarket/peopleinwork/employmentandemployeetypes/articles/labourmarketeconomiccommentary/february2019#:~:text=The%20Organisation%20for%20Economic%20Co,than%20in%20the%20private%20sector. Accessed 14 June 2020.

Office for National Statistics (2020a) Coronavirus Deaths by Occupation. London: Office for National Statistics. Available at: https://www.ons.gov.uk/peoplepopulationandcommunity/healthandsocialcare/causesofdeath/bulletins/coronaviruscovid19relateddeathsbyoccupationenglandandwales/deathsregisteredbetween9marchand28december2020. Accessed January 26, 2021.

Office for National Statistics (2020b) Ethnicity facts and figures: Employment by occupation. Office for National Statistics. Available at: https://www.ethnicity-facts-figures.service.gov.uk/work-pay-and-benefits/employment/employment-by-occupation/latest. Accessed 8 May 2021.

Ogbonnaya, C., Daniels, K. and Nielsen, K. (January 2017) Does contingent pay encourage positive employee attitudes and intensify work? *Human Resource Management Journal*, *27*(1): 94–112.

Oliveira, O. J. and Pinheiro, C. R. (2009) Best practices of the implantation of ISO 14001 norms: a study of change management in two industrial companies in the Midwest region of the state of Sao Paulo, Brazil. *Journal of Cleaner Production*, *17*: 883–5.

Oliver, B. (2015) Redefining graduate employability and work-integrated learning: proposals for effective higher education in disrupted economies. *Journal of Teaching and Learning for Graduate Employability*, *6*(1): 56–65.

Oliver, N. and Wilkinson, B. (1988) *The Japanization of British Industry*. Oxford: Blackwell.

Olson B., McGuire C. and Crawford A. (2020) Improving the quality of work life: an interdisciplinary lens into the worker experience. In S. Dhiman (eds) *The Palgrave Handbook of Workplace Well-Being*. Palgrave Macmillan, Cham. Available at: https://doi.org/10.1007/978-3-030-02470-3_3-1.

Ones, D. S. and Dilchert, S. (2012) Environmental sustainability at work: a call to action. *Industrial and Organizational Psychology*, *5*: 444–66.

Onita, L. (2020) How Covid convinced M&S to cut another 7,000 staff. *The Telegraph*, 18 August. Available at: https://www.telegraph.co.uk/business/2020/08/18/covid-convinced-ms-cut-another-7000-staff/. Accessed 19 August 2020.

Op de Beeck, S., Wynen, J. and Hondeghem, A. (2015) HRM implementation by line managers: explaining the discrepancy in HR-line perceptions of HR devolution. *International Journal of Human Resource Management*, *27*(17): 1–19.

Ordóñez, L., Schweitzer, M., Galinsky, A. and Bazerman, M. (2009) Goals gone wild: the systematic side effects of over-prescribing goal setting. *Academy of Management Perspectives*, *23*. 10.2139/ssrn.1332071.

Organ, D. (1990) The motivational basis of organizational citizenship behavior. In L. Cummings and B. Staw (eds) *Research in Organizational Behavior*, Volume 12 (pp. 43–72). Greenwich, CT: JAI Press.

Örtenblad, A. (2004) The learning organization: towards an integrated model. *Learning Organization*, *11*(2): 129–44.

Ouchi, W. (1979) A conceptual framework for the design of organizational control mechanisms. *Management Science*, *25*(9): 833–48.

Ouchi, W. (1981) *Theory Z: How American Companies Can Meet the Japanese Challenge*. Reading, MA: Addison-Wesley.

Owen, J. (2020) Key workers at risk of losing jobs because of sick pay rules, REC warns. *People Management*, 11 November. Available at: https://www.peoplemanagement.co.uk/news/articles/key-workers-at-risk-of-losing-jobs-because-of-sick-pay-rules. Accessed 14 January 2021.

Oxford Economics (2019) *How Robots Change the World: What Automation Really Means for Jobs and Productivity*. Oxford Economics: Oxford, UK. Available at: http://resources.oxfordeconomics.com/how-robots-change-the-world?source=recent-releases. Accessed 7 August 2020.

Özkazanç-Pan, B. and Pullen, A. (2020) Reimagining value: a feminist commentary in the midst of the COVID-19 pandemic. *Gender, Work and Organization*, November. Available at: https://doi.org/10.1111/gwas.12591.

Öztürk, B. M. and Calás, M. B. (2017) From here to there and back again: transnational perspectives on diversity in organizations. In R. Bendle, I. Bleijenbergh, E. Henttonen and A. Mills (eds) *The Oxford Handbook of Diversity in Organizations*, (pp. 575–602). Oxford: Oxford University Press.

Öztürk, M. B. and Tatli, A. (2015) Gender identity inclusion in the workplace: broadening diversity management research and practice through the case of transgender employees in the UK. *International Journal of Human Resource Management*. Available at: doi.org/10.1080/09585192.2015.1042902.

Paauwe, J. and Boon, C. (2019) Strategic HRM: a critical review. In D. G. Collings, G. T. Wood and L. T. Szamosi (eds) *Human Resource Management: A Critical Approach* (2nd edn) (pp. 49–73). London: Routledge.

Paauwe, J. and Boselie, P. (2003) Challenging 'strategic HRM' and the relevance of the institutional setting. *Human Resource Management Journal*, *13*(3): 56–70.

Paauwe, J. and Boselie, P. (2008) HRM and social embeddedness. In P. Boxall, J. Purcell and P. Wright (eds) *The Oxford Handbook of Human Resource Management* (pp. 166–84). Oxford: Oxford University Press.

Paauwe, J., Guest, D. and Wright, P. (eds) (2013) *HRM and Performance: Achievements and Challenges.* Chichester: John Wiley & Sons.

Paik, Y., Vance, C. and Stage, H. (1996) The extent of divergence in human resource practice across three Chinese national cultures: Hong Kong, Taiwan and Singapore. *Human Resource Management Journal*, *6*(2): 20–31.

Paisley, V. and Yayar, M. (2016) Lesbian, gay, bisexual and transgender (LGBT) expatriates: an intersectionality perspective. *International Journal of Human Resource Management*, *27*(7): 766–80.

Palmer, S. (2019) 12 million working days lost to work-related mental health conditions last year. *People Management*, 20 November.

Palmer, S. (2020) Excess workloads and fear of redundancy driving presenteeism during lockdown, study finds. *People Management*, 2 June. Available at: https://www.peoplemanagement.co.uk/news/articles/excess-workloads-and-fear-of-redundancy-driving-presenteeism-during-lockdown. Accessed 19 June 2020.

Parker, B. and Caine, D. (1996) Holonic modelling: human resource planning and the two faces of Janus. *International Journal of Manpower*, *17*(8): 30–45.

Parker, S. K. and Wall, T. D. (1998) *Job and Work Design: Organizing Work to Promote Well-being and Effectiveness* (Vol. 4). Thousand Oaks, CA: Sage Publications.

Parker, M. (2018) *Shut Down the Business School*. Chicago: University of Chicago Press Economics Books.

Parker, O. and Wright, L. (2001) The missing link: pay and employee commitment. *Ivey Business Journal*, *65*(3): 70–79.

Parker, S. K. (2007) `That is my job': how employees' role orientation affects their job performance. *Human Relations*, *60*(3): 403–34. Available at: https://doi.org/10.1177/0018726707076684.

Parker, S. K. (2014) Beyond motivation: job and work design for development, health, ambidexterity, and more. *Annual Review of Psychology*, *65*: 661–9.

Parker, S. K. and Wall, T. D. (1998) *Job and Work Design: Organizing Work to Promote Well-being and Effectiveness* (Vol. 4). London: Sage.

Parker, S. K., Morgeson, F. P. and Johns, G. (2017) One hundred years of work design research: Looking back and looking forward. *Journal of Applied Psychology*, *102*(3): 403–20.

Parker, S. K., Andrei, D. and Van den Broeck, A. (2019) Why managers design jobs to be more boring than they need to be. *Harvard Business Review*, 5 June. Available at: https://hbr.org/2019/06/why-managers-design-jobs-to-be-more-boring-than-they-need-to-be Accessed 16 June 2020.

Parkes, L., Bochner, S. and Schneider, S. (2001) Person–organisation fit across cultures: an empirical investigation of individualism and collectivism. *Applied Psychology*, *50*(1): 81–108.

Parry, E. and Tyson, S. (2008) An analysis of the use and success of online recruitment methods in the UK. *Human Resource Management Journal*, *18*(3): 257–74.

Parsons, D. (2010) Medical-workforce planning: an art or science? *Human Resource Management International Digest*, *18*(5): 36–8.

Partington, R. (2015) UK minimum wage to rise by four times rate of inflation. *The Guardian*, 31 December. Available at: https://www.theguardian.com/society/2019/dec/31/boris-johnson-to-raise-minimum-wages-by-four-times-inflation. Accessed 14 June 2020.

Partington, R. (2018) Number of zero-hours contracts in UK rose by 100, 000 in 2017 – ONS. *The Guardian*, 23 April. Available: https://www.theguardian.com/uk-news/2018/apr/23/number-of-zero-hours-contracts-in-uk-rose-by-100000-in-2017-ons. Accessed 16 May 2020.

Partington, R. (2019) Rapid robot rollout risks UK workers being left behind, report says. *The Guardian*, 19 June. Available at: https://www.theguardian.com/technology/2019/jun/26/rapid-robot-rollout-risks-uk-workers-being-left-behind-reports-say. Accessed 12 August 2020.

Partington, R. (2020a) Covid-19: UK economy plunges into deepest recession since records began. *The Guardian*, 12 August online. Available at: https://www.theguardian.com/business/2020/aug/12/uk-economy-covid-19-plunges-into-deepest-slump-in-history. Accessed 20 September 2020.

Partington, R. (2020b) UK heading for worst recession in more than 300 years. *The Guardian*, 13 June, pp. 1 & 4.

Partington, R. (2020c) UK's lowest paid most at risk during Covid-19 crisis, report finds. *The Guardian*, April. Available at: https://www.theguardian.com/world/2020/apr/28/uks-lowest-paid-most-at-risk-during-covid-19-crisis-report-finds Accessed 16 June 2020.

Partington, R. (2021a) UK economy hit by record slump in 2020 but double-dip recession avoided. *The Guardian*, 12 February. Available at: https://www.theguardian.com/business/2021/feb/12/uk-avoided-double-dip-recession-despite-covid-slump-in-2020-ons-gdp. Accessed 23 February 2021.

Partington, R. (2021b) UK 'faces labour shortage' as Covid and Brexit fuel exodus of overseas workers. *The Guardian*, 17 May. Available at: https://www.theguardian.com/business/2021/may/17/uk-faces-labour-shortage-as-covid-and-brexit-fuel-exodus-of-overseas-workers. Accessed 18 May 2021.

Parveen, N. (2021) Covid job losses show structural racism of the UK labour market, say TUC. 28 February. Available at: https://www.theguardian.com/society/2021/feb/27/covid-job-losses-show-structural-racism-uk-labour-market-tuc. Accessed 8 May 2021.

Parzefall, M.-R. and Salin, D. (2010) Perceptions of and reactions to workplace bullying: a social exchange perspective. *Human Relations*, *63*(6): 761–80.

Patel, R. (2009) *The Value of Nothing*. Toronto, Ontario: HarperCollins.

Pattisson P. (2016) UK building firms accused of labour abuses in Qatar. *The Guardian*, 14 April, p. 14.

Payne, C. (2020) Research highlights: the decarbonisation divide. *Nature*, 16 March online. Available at: https://www.nature.com/articles/s41562-020-0843-8. Accessed 13 October 2020.

Payne, S. C., Horner, M. T., Boswell, W. R., Schroeder, A. N. and Stine-Cheyne, K. J. (2009) Comparison of online and traditional performance appraisal systems. *Journal of Managerial Psychology*, *24*(6): 526–44.

Peccie, R. (2004) *Human Resource Management and the Search for a Happy Workplace*. Rotterdam, Eramus Research Institute of Management (ERIM).

Peccei, R. and Van De Voorde, K. (2019) Human resource management – well-being – performance research revisited: past, present, and future. *Human Resource Management Journal*, *29*(4): 539–63.

Peccei, R., van deVoorde, K. and van Veldhoven, M. (2013) HRM, well-being and performance: a theoretical and empirical review. In J. Paauwe, D. Guest and P. Wright (eds) *HRM and Performance: Achievements and Challenges* (pp. 15– 45). Chichester: John Wiley & Sons.

Peck, J. (1996) *Work-place: The Social Regulation of Labor Markets*. Guilford Press.

Pedler, M., Boydell, T. and Burgoyne, J. (1988) *The Learning Company Project Report*. Sheffield: Manpower Services Commission.

Pedler, M., Burgoyne, J. and Boydell, T. (1991) *The Learning Company: A Strategy for Sustainable Development*. Maidenhead: McGraw-Hill.

Peiperl, M. A. (2001) Best practice: getting 360-degree feedback right. *Harvard Business Review*, January: 142–7.

Pendleton, A. (1997) What impact has privatization had on pay and employment? *Relations Industrielles/Industrial Relations*, *52*(3): 554–82.

Pendleton, A. and Robinson, A. (2017) The productivity effects of multiple pay incentives. *Economic and Industrial Democracy*, *38*(4): 588–608.

Pennycook, M., Cory, G. and Alakeson, V. (2013) *A Matter of Time: The Rise of Zero-hours Contracts*. London: Resolution Foundation.

Pereira, M.d.M. (2021) Researching gender inequalities in academic labour during the COVID-19 pandemic: avoiding common problems and asking different questions. *Gender, Work and Organization*. 10 January, Accepted Author Manuscript. Available at: https://doi.org/10.1111/gwao.12618.

Perkins Gilman, C. (1892/1973) *The Yellow Wallpaper*. New York: Feminist Press.

Perlmutter, H. V. (1969) The tortuous evolution of the multinational corporation. *Practicing Manager*, *17*: 13–18.

Perraudin, F. (2016) UN urges Tory rethink on trade union bill. *the Guardian*, 15 February, p. 6.

Perron, G. M., Raymond, P. C. and Duffy, J. F. (2006) Improving environmental awareness training in business. *Journal of Cleaner Production*, *14*: 551–62.

Peters, T. and Waterman, R. (1982) *In Search of Excellence*. New York: Harper & Row.

Petrone, F. (2019) BRICS, soft power and climate change: new challenges in global governance? *Ethics & Global Politics*, *12*(2): 19–30. DOI: 10.1080/16544951.2019.1611339

Pfeffer, J. (1994) *Competitive Advantage Through People: Understanding the Power of the Workforce*. Boston, MA: Houghton Mifflin.

Pfeffer, J. (1998) *The Human Equation: Building Profits by Putting People First*. Boston, MA: Harvard Business School Press.

Pham, D. D. T and Paillé, P. (2019) Green recruitment and selection: an insight into green patterns. *International Journal of Manpower*, *41*(2): 258–72.

Pham, N. T., Vo-Thanh, T., Shahbaz, M., Huynh, T. L. D. and Usman, M. (2020) Managing environmental challenges: training as a solution to improve employee green performance. *Journal of Environmental Management*, *269*: 110781.

Philips, L. (2007) Go green now to combat climate change. *People Management*. 23 August. Retrieved from http://www.cipd.co.uk/pm/peoplemanagement/b/weblog/archive/2013/01/29/gogreennowtocombatclimatechange-2006-11.aspx on 22 February 2014.

Phillips, J. M., Gully, S. M., McCarthy, J. E., Castellano, W. G. and Kim, M. S. (2014) Recruiting global travelers: the role of global travel recruitment messages and individual differences in perceived fit, attraction, and job pursuit intentions. *Personal Psychology*, *67*(1): 153–201.

Pickett, K. E. and Wilkinson, R. G. (2015) Income inequality and health: a causal review. *Social Science and Medicine*, *128*: 316–26.

Piketty, T. (2014) *Capital in the Twenty-First Century* (translated by A. Goldhammer). Cambridge, MA: Harvard University Press.

Piketty T. (2017) *Capital in the Twenty-First Century* (2nd edn). (translated by A. Goldhammer). Cambridge, MA: Harvard University Press. Available at: https://www.youtube.com/watch?v=7TLtXfZth5w&t=19s.

Pinkos Cobb, E. (2017) *Workplace Bullying and Harassment: New Developments in International Law*. Abingdon, Oxfordshire: Routledge.

Piore, M. and Sabel, C. (1984) *The Second Industrial Divide*. New York: Basic Books.

Pisano, S., Lepore, L. and Lamboglia, R. (2017) Corporate disclosure of human capital via LinkedIn and ownership structure. *Journal of Intellectual Capital*, *18* (1): 102–27.

Poell, R. (2014) Workplace learning theories and practices. In R. Walton and C. Valentin, C. (eds) *Human Resource Development: Practices and Orthodoxies*. London: Macmillan Higher Education.

Poell, R. F., Rocco, T. S. and Roth, G. L. (eds) (2015) *The Routledge Companion to Human Resource Development*. London: Routledge.

Pohler, D. and Luchak, A. (2015) Are unions good or bad for organizations? The moderating role of management's response. *British Journal of Industrial Relations*, *53*(3): 423–59.

Pollitt, D. (2005) E-recruitment gets the Nike tick of approval. *Human Resource Management International Digest*, *13*(2): 33–5.

Pondy, L. R. (1967) Organizational conflict: concepts and models. *Administrative Science Quarterly*, pp. 296–320.

Porter, M. (1980) *Competitive Strategy*. New York: Free Press.

Porter, M. (1985) *Competitive Advantage: Creating and Sustaining Superior Performance*. New York: Free Press.

Porter, M. E. and Kramer, M. R. (2011) The big idea: creating shared value. *Harvard Business Review*, *89*(1): 2.

Portugal, E. and Yukl, G. (1994) Perspectives on environmental leadership. *Leadership Quarterly*, *5*: 271–76.

Powell, J. H. and Wakeley, T. (2003) Evolutionary concepts and business economics: towards a normative approach. *Journal of Business Research*, *56*: 153–61.

Prahalad, C. K. and Doz, Y. L. (1987) *The Multinational Mission: Balancing Local Demands and Global Vision*. New York: Free Press.

Prasad, A. , Prasad, P., Mills, A. J. and Mills J. M. (2018) (eds) *The Routledge Companion to Critical Management Studies*. Abingdon: Routledge.

Preskill, H. (2008) Evaluation's second act: a spotlight on learning. *American Journal of Evaluation*, *29*(2): 127–38.

Probert, B. (1999) Gender workers and gendered work: implications for women's learning. In D. Boud and J. Garrick (eds) *Understanding Learning at Work* (pp. 98–116) London: Routledge.

Proença, M. T. and de Oliveira, E. T. (2009) From normative to tacit knowledge: CVs analysis in personnel selection. *Employee Relations*, *31*(4): 427–47.

Psacharopoulos, G. (1991) From manpower planning to labour market analysis. *International Labour Review*, *130*, 459. Available at: https://heinonline.org/HOL/LandingPage?handle=hein.journals/intlr130&div=44&id=&page=.

Public Health England (2020) Disparities in the risk and outcomes of COVID-19. June. PHE publications. Available at: https://assets.publishing.service.gov.uk/government/uploads/system/uploads/attachment_data/file/892085/disparities_review.pdf. Accessed 16 June 2020.

Public Health England (2019) Alcohol: applying All Our Health. *Public Health England*, 28 August online. Available at: https://www.gov.uk/government/publications/alcohol-applying-all-our-health/alcohol-applying-all-our-health. Accessed 20 September 2020.

Pucik, V., Evans, P., Björkman, I. and Morris, S. (2016) *The Global Challenge: Frameworks for International Human Resource Management*. Chicago, IL: Chicago Business Press.

Pulignano, V. and Stewart, P. (2006) Bureaucracy transcended? New patterns of employment regulation and labour control in the international automotive industry. *New Technology, Work and Employment*, *21*(2): 90–106.

Pun, K. F. and White, A. S. (2005) A performance measurement paradigm for integrating strategy formulation: a review of systems and frameworks. *International Journal of Management Reviews*, *7*(1): 49–71.

Purcell, J. (1989) The impact of corporate strategy on human resource management. In J. Storey (ed.) *New Perspectives on Human Resource Management* (pp. 67–91). London: Routledge.

Purcell, J. (1995) Corporate strategy and its link with human resource management strategy. In J. Storey (ed.) *Human Resource Management: A Critical Text* (pp. 63–86). London: Routledge.

Purcell, J. (1999) Best practice and best fit: chimera or cul-de-sac? *Human Resource Management Journal*, *9*(3). 26–41.

Purcell, J. and Ahlstrand, B. (1994) *Human Resource Management in the Multi-divisional Company*. Oxford: Oxford University Press.

Purcell, J. and Kinnie, N. (2008) HRM and business performance. In P. Boxall, J. Purcell and P. Wright (eds) *The Oxford Handbook of Human Resource Management* (pp. 533–51). Oxford: Oxford University Press.

Purcell, J. and Sisson, K. (1983) Strategies and practices in the management of industrial relations. In G. Bain (ed.) *Industrial Relations in Britain* (pp. 95–120). Oxford: Blackwell.

Purcell, J., Kinnie, N., Hutchinson, S., Rayton, B. and Swart, J. (2003) *Understanding the People and Performance Link: Unlocking the Black Box*. London: Chartered Institute of Personnel and Development.

Purcell, J., Kinnie, N., Swart, J., Rayton, B. and Hutchinson, S. (2009) *People Management and Performance*. London: Routledge.

PwC (2017) Magnet for talent: Managing diversity as a reputational risk and business opportunity. *PwC* online. Available at: https://www.pwc.co.uk/human-resource-services/assets/documents/diversity-and-inclusion-reputation-2017.pdf. Accessed 12 October 2020.

PwC (2019a) Talent Trends 2019. *PwC* online. Available at: https://www.pwc.com/talent-trends-ceo-survey. Accessed 12 August 2020

PwC (2019b) The Low Carbon Economy Index 2019. PwC online. Available at: https://www.pwc.co.uk/services/sustainability-climate-change/insights/low-carbon-economy-index.html. Accessed 13 October 2020.

PwC (2020) 2020 AI Predictions: Rethink Upskilling. *PwC* online. Available at: https://www.pwc.com/us/en/services/consulting/library/artificial-intelligence-predictions-2020/rethink-upskilling.html. Accessed 12 August 2020.

Pye, M., Cullinane, J. and Harcourt, M. (2001) The right to refuse unsafe work in New Zealand. *New Zealand Journal of Industrial Relations*, *26*(2): 199–216.

Rahman, H. A. (2021) The invisible cage: workers' reactivity to opaque algorithmic evaluations. *Administrative Science Quarterly*. Available at: https://doi.org/10.1177/00018392211010118.

Rai, A. and Agarwal, U. A. (2018) Workplace bullying: A review and future research directions. *South Asian Journal of Management*, *23*(3): 27–56.

Ramsay, H., Scholarios, D. and Harley, B. (2000) Employees and high-performance work systems: testing inside the black box. *British Journal of Industrial Relations*, *38*(4): 501–31.

Ramus, C. A. (2001) Organizational support for employees: encouraging creative ideas for environmental sustainability. *California Management Review*, *44*: 85–105.

Ramus, C. A. (2002) Encouraging innovative environmental actions: what companies and managers must do. *Journal of World Business*, *37*: 151–64.

Randell, G. (1994) Employee appraisal. In K. Sisson (ed.) *Personnel Management* (pp. 221–52). Oxford: Blackwell.

Ransom, J. (2020) Harvey Weinstein is found guilty of sex crimes in #MeToo watershed. *New York Times*, 24 February. Available at: https://www.nytimes.com/2020/02/24/nyregion/harvey-weinstein-trial-rape-verdict.html. Accessed 3 August 2020.

Rarick, C. A. and Baxter, G. (1986) Behaviourally anchored rating scales (bars): an effective performance appraisal approach. *SAM Advanced Management Journal*, Winter: 36–9.

Rashidi, R. (2015) A review of performance management system. *International Journal of Academic Research*, *7*(1): 210–14.

Rasmussen, E. and Høgedahl, L. (2020) Collectivism and employment relations in Denmark: underpinning economic and social success, *Labour & Industry*. DOI: 10.1080/10301763.2020.1856619

Rawnsley, A. (2021) The bad taste question about Covid that everyone in Westminster is asking. *The Observer*, 31 January. Available at: https://www.theguardian.com/commentisfree/2021/jan/31/the-bad-taste-question-about-covid-that-everyone-at-westminster-is-asking. Accessed 1 February 2021.

Rayner, C. and Adam-Smith, D. (eds) (2009) *Managing and leading people* (2nd edn). Chartered Institute of Personnel and Development.

Rayner, C. and Lewis, D. (2011) Managing workplace bullying: The role of policies. In S. Einarsen, H. Hoel, D. Zapf and C. L. Cooper (eds) *Bullying and Harassment in* the Workplace: Developments in Theory, Research, and Practice (2nd edn) (pp. 327–40). Boca Raton, FL: CRC Press.

Rayner, G. (2020) Campaign to get Britain back to work flounders. *The Telegraph*, 2 September. Available at: https://www.telegraph.co.uk/politics/2020/09/02/campaign-get-britain-back-work-flounders. Accessed 6 October 2020.

Rebelo, T. M. and Gomes, A. (2011) Conditioning factors of an organizational learning culture. *Journal of Workplace Learning, 23*(3): 173–94.

Reckard, E. S. (2013) Well's Fargo's pressure-cooker sales culture comes at a cost. *Los Angeles Times*, 21 December online. Available at: https://www.latimes.com/business/la-fi-wells-fargo-sale-pressure-20131222-story.html. Accessed 7 October 2020.

Redman, T. (2001) Performance appraisal. In T. Redman, and A. Wilkinson (eds) *Contemporary Human Resource Management* (pp. 57–95). Harlow: Pearson Education.

Reed, J. and Jung-A, S. (2020) Samsung flies parts to Vietnam after coronavirus disrupts supply chain. *Financial Times*, 17 February, p. 9.

Reed, J., Ruehl, M. and Parkin, B. (2020) Coronavirus: will call centre workers lost their 'voice' to AI? *The Financial Times*, 23 April online. Available at: https://www.ft.com/content/990e89de-83e9-11ea-b555-37a289098206. Accessed 30 September 2020.

Rees, T. (1998) *Mainstreaming Equality in the European Union: Education, Training and Labour Market Policies*. London: Routledge.

Reeves, M. and Deimler, M. (2011) Adaptability: the new competitive advantage. *Harvard Business Review*, July–August Issue. Available at: https://hbr.org/2011/07/adaptability-the-new-competitive-advantage. Accessed 23 October 2020.

Regencia, T., Alsaafin, L. and Najjar, F. (2020) Beirut explosion death toll rises to 135 as 5,000 wounded: Live. *Al Jazeera*, 6 August online. Available at: https://www.aljazeera.com/news/2020/08/lebanon-eyes-state-emergency-deadly-beirut-blast-live-200804234925493.html?. Accessed 2 September 2020.

Reguly, E. (2021) Norway's oil sands message: Clean up your act or suffer. *Globe and Mail*, 27 February, p. B3.

Reilly, B., Paci, P. and Holl, P. (1995) Unions, safety committees and workplace injuries. *British Journal of Industrial Relations, 33*(2): 275–87.

Reilly, P. (1996) *Human Resource Planning: An Introduction. Report 312*. Poole: BEBC Distribution.

Remler, D. K. and Van Ryzin, G. G. (2011) *Research Methods in Practice: Strategies for Description and Causation*. Los Angeles, CA: Sage.

Ren, F. and Zhang, J. (2015) Job stressors, organisational innovation climate, and employee's innovative behaviour. *Creativity Research Journal*, 27(1): 16–23.

Ren, S., Tang, G. and Jackson, S.E. (2020) Effects of Green HRM and CEO ethical leadership on organizations' environmental performance. *International Journal of Manpower*, Vol. ahead-of-print No. ahead-of-print. Available at: https://doi.org/10.1108/IJM-09-2019-0414. Accessed 29 May 2021.

Renwick, D. W. S., Jabbour, C., Muller-Camen, M, Redman, T. and Wilkinson, A. (2016) Contemporary developments in green (environmental) HRM scholarship. *International Journal of Human Resource Management, 27*(2): 114–28.

Resolution Foundation (2020) *One-in-five young people and over one-in-five BAME workers who were furloughed during lockdown have since lost their jobs*, 27 October. London: Resolution Foundation. Available at: https://www.resolutionfoundation.org/press-releases/one-in-five-young-people-and-over-one-in-five-bame-workers-who-were-furloughed-during-lockdown-have-since-lost-their-jobs/. Accessed 10 December 2020.

Reynolds, M. (1999) Grasping the nettle: possibilities and pitfalls of a critical management pedagogy. *British Journal of Management, 10*(2): 171–84.

Richardson, D. and Monro, S. (2013) Public duty and private prejudice: sexualities equalities and local government. *The Sociological Review, 61*(1): 131–52. Available at: https://doi.org/10.1111/1467-954X.12007.

Richbell, S. and Wood, G. T. (2019) Reward management. In D. Collings, G. Wood and L. Szamosi (eds) *Human Resource Management: A Critical Approach* (2nd edn) (pp. 280–94). London: Routledge.

Rigg, C., Stewart, J. and Trehan, K. (2007) *Critical Human Resource Development: Beyond Orthodoxy*. Harlow: FT/Prentice Hall.

Rijamampianina, R. and Carmichael, T. (2005) A pragmatic and holistic approach to managing diversity. *Problems and Perspectives in Management, 3*(1): 109–17.

Riley Chapman, C., Mehta, K. S., Parent, B. and Caplan, R. L. (2019) Genetic discrimination: emerging ethical challenges in the context of advancing technology. *Journal of Law and the Biosciences*: 1–23. DOI: 10.1093/jlb/lsz016

Ritzer, G. (2004) *The McDonaldization of Society* (Revised New Century edn). Thousand Oaks, CA: Pine Forge Press.

Ritzer, G. (2014) *The McDonaldization of Society* (8th edn). Thousand Oaks, CA: Pine Forge Press.

Robertson, C. and Gebeloff, R. (2020) How millions of women became the most essential workers in America. *New York Times*, 18 April. Available at: https://www.nytimes.com/2020/04/18/us/coronavirus-women-essential-workers.html?action=click&module=Spotlight&pgtype=Homepage. Accessed 18 April 2020.

Robertson, I. T., Baron, H., Gibbons, P., MacIver, R. and Nyfield, G. (2000) Conscientiousness and managerial performance. *Journal of Occupational and Organizational Psychology, 73*(2): 171–81.

Robertson, J. L. and Barling, J. (2015) The role of leadership in promoting workplace pro-environmental behaviors. In J. L. Robertson and J. Barling (eds) *The Psychology of Green Organizations* (pp. 164–86): New York: Oxford University Press.

Rockstuhl, T., Ang, S., Ng, K. Y., Lievens, F. and Van Dyne, L. (2015) Putting judging situations into situational judgment tests: evidence from intercultural multimedia SJTs. *Journal of Applied Psychology, 100*(2): 464–80.

Rodger, A. (1970) *The Seven Point Plan* (3rd edn). London: National Foundation for Educational Research.

Roepe, L. (2017) How your appearance impacts hiring decisions. *Forbes*, 1 November. Available at: https://www.forbes.com/sites/lisaroepe/2017/11/01/how-your-appearance-impacts-hiring-decisions/#6baa97f4153d. Accessed 29 June 2020.

Roethlisberger, F. J. and Dickson, W. J. (1939) *Management and the Worker*. Cambridge, MA: Harvard University Press.

Rogaly, B. (2008) Intensification of workplace regimes in British horticulture: the role of migrant workers. *Population, Space and Place*, *14*: 497–510.

Rollinson, D., Hook, C., Foot, M. and Handley, J. (1996) Supervisor and manager styles in handling discipline and grievance, Part 2: Approaches to handling discipline and grievance. *Personnel Review*, *25*(4): 38–55.

Romei, V. and Giles, C. (2021) UK suffers biggest drop in economic output in 300 years. *Financial Times*, 12 February. Available at: https://www.ft.com/content/96e19afd-88b3-4e8d-bc3e-a72bd1f60d3c. Accessed 23 February 2021.

Roper, C. (2020) Union membership rises for third year running to 6.4 million. London: Trades Union Congress. Available at: https://www.tuc.org.uk/blogs/union-membership-rises-third-year-running-64-million#:~:text=There%20are%20now%206.44%20million%20union%20members%20in%20the%20UK.&text=Union%20membership%20increased%20in%20both,increased%20to%2023.5%20per%20cent. Accessed 19 August 2020.

Roscoe, S., Subramanian, N., Jabbour, C. J. and Chong, T. (2019) Green human resource management and the enablers of green organisational culture: enhancing a firm's environmental performance for sustainable development. *Business Strategy and the Environment*, *28*(5): 737–49.

Rose, M. (1988) *Industrial Behaviour: Research and Control*. London: Penguin.

Rose, M. (1990) *Industrial Behaviour: Research and Control*. London: Penguin.

Roser, D. (2016) A responsibility to innovate: the ethics of energy innovation. *Oxford Martin School, University of Oxford*, 14 October online. Available at: https://www.oxfordmartin.ox.ac.uk/blog/a-responsibility-to-innovate-the-ethics-of-energy-innovation. Accessed 13 October 2020.

Ross, I. and MacDonald, G. (1997) Scars from stress cut deep in workplace. *Globe and Mail*, 9 October, p. B16.

Rothwell, S. (1995) Human resource planning. In J. Storey (ed.) *Human Resource Management: A Critical Text* (pp. 167–201). London: Routledge.

Roubini, N. (2020) Coronavirus pandemic has delivered the fastest, deepest economic shock in history. *The Guardian*, 25 March. Available at: https://www.theguardian.com/business/2020/mar/25/coronavirus-pandemic-has-delivered-the-fastest-deepest-economic-shock-in-history. Accessed 10 December 2020.

Rouiller, J. Z. and Goldstein, I. L. (1993) The relationship between organizational transfer climate and positive transfer of training. *Human Resource Development Quarterly*, *4*(4): 377–90.

Rousseau, D. and Greller, M. (1994) Human resource practices: administrative contract makers. *Human Resource Management*, *33*(3): 385–401.

Rousseau, D. M. (1995) *Psychological Contracts in Organizations: Understanding Written and Unwritten Agreements*. Thousand Oaks, CA: Sage.

Rousseau, D. M. (2004) Psychological contracts in the workplace: Understanding the ties that motivate. *Academy of Management Perspectives*, *18*(1): 120–27.

Rowley, C. and Bae, J. (2002) Globalization and transformation of human resource management in South Korea. *International Journal of Human Resource Management*, *13*(3): 522–49.

Roy, D. F. (1980) Repression and incorporation. fear stuff, sweet stuff and evil stuff: management's defences against unionization in the South. In T. Nichols (ed.) *Capital and Labour: A Marxist Primer*. Glasgow: Fontana.

Roy, E. (2020) Jacinda Ardern flags four-day working week as way to rebuild New Zealand after Covid-19. *The Guardian*, 20 May. Available at: https://www.theguardian.com/world/2020/may/20/jacinda-ardern-flags-four-day-working-week-as-way-to-rebuild-new-zealand-after-covid-19. Accessed 29 June 2020.

Royal College of Obstetricians and Gynaecologists (RCOG) (2018) RCOG suggests caution over social egg freezing. *Royal College of Obstetricians and Gynaecologists*, 8 August online. Available at: https://www.rcog.org.uk/en/news/rcog-suggests-caution-over-social-egg-freezing. Accessed 20 September 2020.

Royal Society (2017) *Machine Learning: The Power and Promise af Computers that Learn by Example*. London.

Rubery, J. and Johnson, M. (2019) HRM in crisis. In D. G. Collings, G. T. Wood and L. T. Szamosi (eds) *Human Resource Management: A Critical Approach* (pp. 396–411). London: Routledge.

Rubery, J., Grimshaw, D. and Rubery, J. (2003) *The Organization of Employment: An International Perspective* (pp. 26–50). Basingstoke: Palgrave Macmillan.

Rubin, J. (2020) *The Expendables: How the Middle Class Got Screwed by Globalisation*. Scribe Publications.

Rupp, D. E., Shao, R., Thornton, M. A. and Skarlicki, D. P. (2013) Applicants' and employees' reactions to corporate social responsibility: the moderating effects of first-party justice perceptions and moral identity. *Personnel Psychology*, *66*: 895–933.

Rupp, D. E., Shao, R., Thornton, M. A. and Skarlicki, D. P. (2013) Applicants' and employees' reactions to corporate social responsibility: the moderating effects of first-party justice perceptions and moral identity. *Personnel Psychology*, *66*: 895–933.

Rushe, D. (2016) JP Morgan Chase to pay $264m over Chinese 'princelings' bribery scheme. *The Guardian*, 17 November.

Rushe, D. (2018) Employee rights: has Trump made America great for its working class? *The Guardian*, 26 January.

Rushe, D. (2019) Top bosses earn 278 times more than their employees. *The Guardian*, 14 August. Available at: https://www.theguardian.com/us-news/2019/aug/14/ceo-worker-pay-gap. Accessed 27 April 2020.

Russell, S. V. and McIntosh, M. (2011) Changing organizational culture for sustainability. In *The Handbook of Organizational Culture and Climate* (pp. 393–411). London: Sage.

Ryan, A. M and Ployhart, R. E. (2014) A century of selection. *Annual Review of Psychology*, *65*: 693–717.

Ryan, J. C. and Tipu, S. A. (2009) An instrument for the self-appraisal of scientific research performance. *International Journal of Productivity and Performance Management*, *58*(7): 632–44.

Saavedra, R. and Kwun, S. K. (1993) Peer evaluation in self-managing work groups. *Journal of Applied Psychology*, *78*(3): 450–62.

Sadler-Smith, E. (2006) *Learning and Development for Managers*. Oxford: Blackwell.

Saeed, B. B., Afsar, B., Hafeez, S., Khan, I., Tahir, M. and Afridi, M. A. (2019) Promoting employee's proenvironmental behavior through green human resource management practices. *Corporate Social Responsibility and Environmental Management*, *26*(2): 424–38.

Sagie, A. and Aycan, Z. (2003) A cross-cultural analysis of participative decision-making in organizations. *Human Relations*, *56*(4): 453–73.

Said, E. (1993) *Culture and Imperialism*. New York: Alfred A. Knopf.

Saifulina, N. and Carballo-Penela, A. (2017) Promoting sustainable development at an organizational level: an analysis of the drivers of workplace environmentally friendly behaviour of employees. *Sustainable Development*, *25*(4): 299–310.

Saint-Onge, H. and Wallace, D. (2012) *Leveraging Communities of Practice for Strategic Advantage*. Burlington, MA: Elsevier.

Salaman, G. (2016) The new corporate leadership. In J. Storey (ed.) *Leadership in Organisations* (pp. 54–69). London: Routledge.

Salas, E., Tannenbaum, S., Kraiger, K. and Smith-Jentsch, K. (2012) The science of training and development in organizations: what matters in practice. *Psychological Science in the Public Interest*, *13*(2): 74–101. Availabole at: www.jstor.org/stable/23484697. Accessed 1 July 2020.

Sammalisto, K. and Brorson, T. (2008) Training and communication in the implementation of environmental management system (ISO 14001): a case study at the University of Gavle, Sweden. *Journal of Cleaner Production*, *16*: 299–309.

Sanchiz, M., Chevalier, A. and Amadieu, F. (2017) How do older and young adults start searching for information? Impact of age, domain knowledge and problem complexity on the different steps of information searching. *Computers in Human Behavior*, *72*: 67–78.

Sanders, K. and Frenkel, S. (2011) HR-line management relations: characteristics and effects. *Journal of Human Resource Management*, *22*(8): 1611–17.

Santos, J. F. and Colón-Acevedo, S. E. (2020) Puerto Rico becomes first jurisdiction to adopt law against workplace bullying. *The National Law Review*, X (264). Available at: https://www.natlawreview.com/article/puerto-rico-becomes-first-jurisdiction-to-adopt-law-against-workplace-bullying. Accessed 20 September 2020.

Saul, J. R. (2005) *The Collapse of Globalism*. Toronto, Ontario: Viking.

Saunders, M. N. K. and Thornhill, A. (2006) Forced employment contract change and the psychological contract. *Employee Relations*, *28*(5): 449–67.

Savage, M. (2015) *Social Class in the 21st Century*. London: Pelican.

Savage, M. (2021) 'Fire and rehire' should be banned, say three-quarters of UK public. *The Guardian*, 9 May. Available at: https://www.theguardian.com/law/2021/may/09/fire-and-rehire-should-be-banned-say-three-quarters-of-uk-public. Accessed 12 May 2021.

Saville, P. (2016) *From Obscurity to Clarity in Psychometric Testing: Selected Works of Professor Peter Saville*. London: Routledge.

Sayer, A. (2000) *Realism and Social Science*. London: Sage.

Sayer, D. (1991) *Capitalism and Modernity: Excursus on Marx and Weber*. London: Routledge.

Sayre, G. M. and Dahling, J. J. (2016) Surveillance 2.0: How personality qualifies reactions to social media monitoring policies. *Differences*, *90*: 254–59.

Sayim, K. Z. (2010) Pushed or pulled? Transfer of reward management policies in MNCs. *International Journal of Human Resource Management*, *21*(14): 2631–58.

Scarbrough, H. (2000) The HR implications of supply chain relationships. *Human Resource Management Journal*, *10*(1): 5–17.

Schatsky, D. and Kumar, N. (2018) Workforce superpowers: wearables are augmenting employees' abilities. *Deloitte*, 25 July online. Available at: https://www2.deloitte.com/us/en/insights/focus/signals-for-strategists/wearable-devices-in-the-workplace.html. Accessed 4 October 2020.

Schein, E. H. and Schein, P. (2017) *Organizational Culture and Leadership* (5th edn). San Francisco, CA: Jossey-Bass.

Schein, V. E., Mueller, R., Lituchy, T. and Liu, J. (1996) Think manager – think male: a global phenomenon? *Journal of Organizational Behavior*, *17*(1): 33–41.

Schied, F., Carter, V., Preston, J. and Howell, S. (1997) The HRD factory: an historical inquiry into the production of control in the workplace. Crossing boarders breaking boundaries. *Research in the education of adults: An International Conference* (pp. 404–8). London: Birkbeck College, University of London.

Schlosberg, D. (2013) Theorising environmental justice: the expanding sphere of a discourse. *Environmental Politics*, *22*(1): 37–55.

Schmidt, F. L. and Hunter, J. E. (1998) The validity and utility of selection methods in personnel psychology: practical and theoretical implications of 85 years of research findings. *Psychological Bulletin*, *124*(2): 262.

Schmidt, F. L., Oh, I. S. and Shaffer, J. A. (2016) The *Validity and Utility of Selection Methods in Personnel Psychology: Practical and theoretical implications of 100 years of research findings*. Philadelphia, PA: Temple University, Fox School of Business Research Paper.

Schnabel, C. (2003) Determinants of trade union membership. In J. T. Addison and C. Schnabel (eds) *International Handbook of Trade Unions* (pp. 13–43). Cheltenham: Edward Elgar.

Schneider, B., Goldstiein, H. W. and Smith, D. B. (1995) The ASA framework: An update. *Personnel Psychology*, *48*(4): 747–73.

Schneider, R. (2001) Variety performance. *People Management*, *7*(9): 26–31.

Schön, D. A. (1983) *The Reflective Practitioner: How Professionals Think in Action*. London: Maurice Temple Smith.

Schonberger, R. and Schonberger, R. T. (1982) *Japanese Manufacturing Techniques: Nine Hidden Lessons in Simplicity*. New York: Simon and Schuster.

Schuler, R. S. (1992) Strategic human resources management: linking the people with the strategic needs of the business. *Organizational Dynamics*, *21*(1): 18–32.

Schuler, R. and Jackson, S. E. (2014) Human resource management and organizational effectiveness: yesterday and today. *Journal of Organizational Effectiveness: People and Performance*, *1*(1): 35–55.

Schuler, R. S. and Jackson, S. (1987) Linking competitive strategies and human resource management practices. *Academy of Management Executive*, *1*(3): 209–13.

Schuler, R., Dowling, P. and De Cieri, H. (1993) An integrative framework of strategic international human resource management. *Journal of Management*, *19*(2): 419–59.

Schuler, R. S., Jackson, S. and Storey, J. (2001) HRM and its links with strategic management. In J. Storey (ed.) *Human Resource Management: A Critical Text* (2nd edn) (pp. 114–30). London: Thompson Learning.

Schultz, T. W. (1961) Investment in human capital. *The American Economic Review*, 1–17.

Schultz, T. W. (1972) Human capital: policy issues and research opportunities. In *Economic Research: Retrospect and Prospect, Volume 6, Human Resources* (pp. 1–84). NBER.

Schultz, T. W. (1981) *Investing in People: The Economics of Population Quality*. Berkeley, CA: University of California Press.

Schwab, K. (2017) *The Fourth Industrial Revolution*. Switzerland: World Economic Forum.

Schwab, K. and Davis, N. (2018) *Shaping the Future of the Fourth Industrial Revolution*. London: Penguin.

Schwellnus, C., Geva, A., Pak, M. and Veiel, R. (2019) Gig economy platforms: boon or bane? Economics Department Working Papers, No. 1550. *OECD*, 15 May online. Available at: https://www.oecd.org/officialdocuments/publicdisplaydocumentpdf/?cote=ECO/WKP(2019)19&docLanguage=En. Accessed 3 October 2020.

Scott, B. (2020) Performance management and leadership. In J. Bratton (ed.) *Organizational Leadership* (pp. 245–65). London: Sage.

Scott, J. and Marshall, G. (2009) *Oxford Dictionary of Sociology*. Oxford: Oxford University Press.

Scullen, S. E., Mount, M. K. and Goff, M. (2000) Understanding the latent structure of job performance ratings. *Journal of Applied Psychology*, *85*(6): 956–70.

Scullion, H. (1995) International human resource management. In J. Storey (ed.) *Human Resource Management: A Critical Text* (pp. 388–313). London: Thompson.

Scullion, H. and Linehan, M. (eds) (2005) *International Human Resource Management: A Critical Text* (2nd edn). Basingstoke: Palgrave Macmillan.

Searle, R. H. (2003) *Selection and Recruitment: A Critical Text*. Milton Keynes: Open University & London: Palgrave.

Seierstad, C., Healy, G., Sønju Le Bruyn Goldeng, E. and Fjellvær, H. (2020) A 'quota silo' or positive equality reach? The equality impact of gender quotas on corporate boards in Norway. *Human Resource Management Journal*, *31*(1): 165–86.

Seijts, G., Crossan, M. and Carleton, E. (2017) Embedding leader character into HR practices to achieve sustained excellence. *Organizational Dynamics*, *46*(1): 30–39.

Selznick, P. (1957) *Leadership and Administration*. New York: Harper & Row.

Senge, P. (1990) *The Fifth Discipline*. New York: Doubleday.

Sennett, R. (1998) *The Corrosion of Character*. New York: Norton.

Sennett, R. (2012) *Together: The Rituals, Pleasures and Politics of Cooperation*. New Haven, CT: Yale University Press.

Sevastopulo, D. and Clark, P. (2015) Paris climate deal will not be a legally binding treaty. *Financial Times*, 11 November. Available at: http://www.ft.com/cms/s/0/79daf872-8894-11e5-90de-f44762bf9896.html#axzz3zrC2bCk3. Accessed 7 December 2015.

Sewell, G. (1998) The discipline of teams: the control of team-based industrial work through electronic and peer surveillance. *Administrative Science Quarterly*, *43*: 397–428.

Sharma, S. (2020) The importance of mentoring through a crisis. *People Management*, 9 June. Available at: https://www.peoplemanagement.co.uk/voices/comment/the-importance-of-mentoring-through-a-crisis. Accessed 19 June 2020.

Shaw, J. D. and Gupta, N. (2001) Pair fairness and employee outcomes: exacerbation and attenuation effects of financial need. *Journal of Occupational and Organizational Psychology*, *74*(3): 299–320.

Shortall, J. (2019) Why many businesses are becoming more vocal in support of LGBTQ rights. *Harvard Business Review*, 7 March. Available at: https://hbr.org/2019/03/why-many-businesses-are-becoming-more-vocal-in-support-of-lgbtq-rights. Accessed 2 July 2020.

Shrivastava, P. (1995) The role of corporations in achieving ecological sustainability. *Academy of Management Journal*, *20*(4): 936–60.

Siddique, H. (2020) Samira Ahmed verdict further damages BBC's reputation on equal pay. *The Guardian*, 10 January. Available at: https://www.theguardian.com/media/2020/jan/10/samira-ahmed-verdict-further-damages-bbc-reputation-on-equal-pay. Accessed 22 January 2021.

Sikka, P. (2020) Money begets money: how the Tories helped the rich get richer during the COVID-19 crisis. *Scottish Left Review*, *118*, July/August, pp. 5–6.

Sikka, P., Hudson, A., Hadden, T., Willmott, H., Christensen, J., Cooper, C., ... and Pettifor, A. (2018) *A Better Future for Corporate Governance: Democratising Corporations for Their Long-Term Success*. Technical report. Available at: http://www. researchgate. net/publication/327861085. Accessed 4 January 2021.

Sikora, D. M. and Ferris, G. R. (2014) Strategic human resource practice implementation: the critical role of line management. *Human Resource Management Review*, *24*(3): 271–81.

Sillup, G. P. and Klimberg, R. (2010) Assessing the ethics of implementing performance appraisal systems. *Journal of Management Development*, *29*(1): 38–55.

Simon, H. A. (1960) *The New Science of Management Decision*. New York: Harper & Row.

Sinclair A (2007) Teaching leadership critically to MBAs: experiences from heaven and hell. *Management Learning*, *38*(4): 461–75.

Sinclair, C., O'Shea, N., Allwood, L. and Durcan, G. (2020) Covid-19 and the nation's mental health - Forecasting needs and risks in the UK: July 2020. *Centre for Mental Health* online. Available at: https://www.centreformentalhealth.org.uk/sites/default/files/2020-07/CentreforMentalHealth_COVID_MH_Forecasting2_Jul20_0.pdf. Accessed 20 September 2020.

Singer, A. E. (2010) Integrating ethics and strategy. *Journal of Business Ethics*, *92*: 479–91.

Sisodia, R., Sheth, J. and Wolfe, D. (2014) *Firms of Endearment: How World-class Companies Profit from Passion and Purpose* (2nd edn). Upper Saddle River, NJ: Pearson Education.

Skidelsky, R. (2020) The future of work. In R. Skidelsky and N. Craig (eds) *Work in the Future*. Cham, Switzerland: Palgrave Macmillan. Available at: https://doi.org/10.1007/978-3-030-21134-9_2. Accessed 27 April 2021.

Skinner, B. F. (1954) The science of learning and the art of teaching. *Harvard Educational Review, 24*: 86–97.

Slocum, J., Lei, D. and Buller, P. (2014) Executing business strategies through human resource management practices. *Organizational Dynamics, 43*: 73–87.

Sloman, M. (2005) *Training to Learning*. London: Chartered Institute of Personnel and Development.

Smith, A. (1776/1982) *The Wealth of Nations*. Harmondsworth: Penguin.

Smith, K. J. (2015) Conducting thorough job analyses and drafting lawful job descriptions. *Employment Relations Today*, (Winter): 95–9.

Smith M. (2020) Most workers want to work from home after Covid-19, *YouGov*. 22 September. Available at: https://yougov.co.uk/topics/economy/articles-reports/2020/09/22/most-workers-want-work-home-after-covid-19. Accessed 18 November 2020.

Smith, P. and Morton, G. (2006) Nine years of New Labour: neoliberalism and workers' rights. *British Journal of Industrial Relations, 44*(3): 401–20.

Smyth, J. (2017) *The Toxic University: Zombie Leadership, Academic Rock Stars and Neoliberal Ideology*. Basingstoke: Palgrave Macmillan.

Snell, S. A., Youndt, M. A. and Wright, P. M. (1996) Establishing a framework for research in strategic human resource management: merging source theory and organizational learning. *Research in Personnel and Human Resources Management, 14*: 61–90.

Sobolewska, M. and Ford, R. (2020) *Brexitland: Identity, Diversity and the Reshaping of British Politics*, Cambridge: Cambridge University Press.

Solomon, N. (1999) Culture and difference in workplace learning. In Boud, D., Garrick, J. and Greenfield, K. (eds) *Understanding Learning at Work*, (pp. 119–31). London: Routledge.

Solon, O. (2017) Big Brother isn't just watching: workplace surveillance can track your every move. *The Guardian*, 6 November online. Available at: https://www.theguardian.com/world/2017/nov/06/workplace-surveillance-big-brother-technology. Accessed 29 September 2020.

Song, Z. and Baicker, K. (2019) Effect of a workplace wellness program on employee health and economic outcomes: A randomized clinical trial. *JAMA, 321*(15): 1491–501.

Soper, K. (2020) The pandemic is an opportunity to reconsider what makes a good life. *The Guardian*, 8 September. Available at: https://www.theguardian.com/commentisfree/2020/sep/08/pandemic-covid-19-work-society. Accessed 4 March 2021.

Sovacool, B., Martiskainen, M., Hook, A. and Baker, L. (2019) Decarbonization and its discontents: a critical energy justice perspective on four low carbon transitions. *Climatic Change, 155*: 581–619.

Sovacool, B. K., Hook, A., Martiskainen, M., Brock, A. and Turnheim, B. (2020) The decarbonisation divide: Contextualizing landscapes of low-carbon exploitation and toxicity in Africa. *Global Environmental Change, 60*: 1–19.

Soylu, S. and Sheehy-Skeffington, J. (2015) Asymmetric intergroup bullying: the enactment and maintenance of societal inequality at work. *Human Relations, 68*(7): 1099–129.

Sparrow, P., Brewster, C. and Harris, H. (2004) *Globalizing Human Resource Management*. London: Routledge.

Sparrow, P., Scullion, H. and Farndale, E. (2011) Global talent management: new roles for the corporate HR function? In H. Scullion and D. Collings (eds) *Global Talent Management* (pp. 39–55). New York: Routledge.

Spencer, B. (1998) *Purposes of Adult Education: A Guide for Students*. Toronto: Thompson Educational Pub.

Spicer, A. (2015) The flaw in Amazon's management fad. *The Guardian*. 17 August. Available at: https://www.theguardian.com/commentisfree/2015/aug/17/amazon-management-fad-rank-yank-jeff-bezos. Accessed October 2016.

Squires, G. (2001) Management as a professional discipline. *Journal of Management Studies, 38*(4): 473–87.

Stahl, G. K. and Björkman, I. (eds) (2006) *Handbook of Research in International Human Resource Management*. Cheltenham: Edward Elgar.

Stahl, G. K., Brewster, C. J., Collings, D. G. and Hajro, A. (2020) Enhancing the role of human resource management in corporate sustainability and social responsibility: a multi-stakeholder, multidimensional approach to HRM. *Human Resource Management Review, 30*(3): 100708.

Stainer, G. (1971) *Manpower Planning*. London: Heinemann.

Standing, G. (2011) *The Precariat: The New Dangerous Class*. London: Bloomsbury Academic.

Stanton, P. and Nankervis, A. (2011) Linking strategic HRM, performance management and organizational effectiveness: perceptions of managers in Singapore. *Asia Pacific Business Review, 17*(1): 67–84.

Starik, M. and Rands, G. P. (1995) Weaving an integrated web: multilevel and multisystem perspectives of ecologically sustainable organizations. *Academy of Management Review, 20*: 908–35.

Statista (2020) Number of monthly active Facebook users worldwide, as of 1st quarter 2020. Available at: https://www.statista.com/statistics/264810/number-of-monthly-active-facebook-users-worldwide/#:~:text=With%20over%202.6%20billion%20monthly,the%20biggest%20social%20network%20worldwide. Accessed 20 July 2020.

Stevenson, P. and Farmer, D. (2017) Thriving at work: The Stevenson/Farmer review of mental health and employers. Great Britain, Department for Work and Pensions and Department for Health and Social Care. Available at: https://assets.publishing.service.gov.uk/government/uploads/system/uploads/attachment_data/file/658145/thriving-at-work-stevenson-farmer-review.pdf. Accessed 2 September 2020.

Stewart, H. (2015) The great wages crash. *The Guardian*, 30 January, p. 1.

Stewart, J. (2007) The ethics of HRD. In C. Rigg, J. Stewart and K. Trehan (eds) *Critical Human Resource Development: Beyond Orthodoxy* (pp. 59–78). Harlow: Prentice Hall.

Stewart, J., Beardwell, J., Gold, J. Iles, P. and Holden, R. (2013) The Scope of HRD and national HRD policies & practices. In J. Gold, R. Holden, P. Iles, J. Stewart, and J. Beardwell (eds) *Human Resource Development: Theory and Practice* (2nd edn) (pp. 3–24). Basingstoke: Palgrave Macmillan.

Steyaert, C. and Janssens, M. (1999) Human and inhuman resource management: saving the subject of HRM. *Organization*, *6*(2): 181–98.

St-Hilaire, F., Gilbert, M-H. and Brun, J-P. (2019) What if subordinates took care of managers' mental health at work? *International Journal of Human Resource Management*, *30*(2): 337–59.

Stiglitz, J. (2020) Invest in the green economy and we'll recover from the Covid-19 crisis. *The Guardian,* 2 July. Available: https://www.theguardian.com/business/2020/jul/02/invest-in-the-green-economy-and-well-recover-from-the-covid-19-crisis. Accessed 4 March 2021.

Stiglitz, J. E. (2013) *The Price of Inequality*. London: Penguin.

Stiglitz, J. E. (2015) *The Great Divide*. London: Allen Lane.

Stohl, C. and Cheney, G. (2001) Participatory processes/paradoxical practices. *Management Communications Quarterly*, *14*(3): 349–407.

Stojanovic, A. (2020) Trade: rules of origin. London: Institute of Government. Available at: https://www.instituteforgovernment.org.uk/explainers/trade-rules-origin. Accessed 7 January 2021.

Stone, D., Deadrick, D. L., Lukaszewski, K. M. and Johson, R. (2015) The influence of technology on the future of human resource management. *Human Resource Management Review*, *25*(2): 216–31.

Stone, J. (2020) UK trade union membership reversing historic decline thanks to women workers, official figures show. *The Independent*, 27 May online. Available at: https://www.independent.co.uk/news/uk/politics/trade-union-members-women-tuc-coronavirus-worker-rights-wages-a9535651.html. Accessed 11 October 2020.

Stoner, J. S. and Gallagher, V. C. (2010) Who cares? The role of job involvement in psychological contract violation. *Journal of Applied Social Psychology*, *40*(6): 1490–514.

Storey, J. (2001) Human resource management today: an assessment. In J. Storey (ed.) *Human Resource Management: A Critical Text* (2nd edn) (pp. 3–20). London: Thompson Learning.

Storey, J. (2018) New organizational structures and forms. In J. Storey, P.M. Wright and D. Ulrich (eds) *The Routledge Companion to Strategic Management*, (pp. 90–105). London: Routledge.

Storey, J. (ed.) (1989) *New Perspectives on Human Resource Management*. London: Routledge.

Storey, J. (ed.) (1995) *Human Resource Management: A Critical Text*. London: Routledge.

Storey, J. (ed.) (2007) Human resource management today: an assessment. In J. Storey (ed.) *Human Resource Management: A Critical Text* (pp. 3–20). London: Thompson Learning.

Storey, J., Ulrich, D., Welbourne, T. M. and P. M. Wright (2018) Employee engagement. In J. Storey, P. M. Wright and D. Ulrich (eds) *The Routledge Companion to Strategic Human Resource Management* (pp. 299-315). London: Routledge.

Stouten, J., Baillien, E., Van den Broeck, A., Camps, J., De Witte, H. and Euwema, M. (2010) Discouraging bullying: The role of ethical leadership and its effects on the work environment. *Journal of Business Ethics*, *95*(1): 17–27.

Strauss, D. (2020) UK unemployment rate rises to 4.9% in 3 months to October. *Financial Times*, 15 December. Available at: https://www.ft.com/content/5bf2aaf5-c3ad-4a9a-9083-feccd8becac6. Accessed 11 January 2021.

Strauss, G. (1998) An overview. In F. Heller, E. Pusic, G. Strauss and B. Wilpert (eds) *Organizational Participation: Myth and Reality* (pp. 8–39). Oxford: Oxford University Press.

Strauss, G. (2006) Worker participation: some under-considered issues. *Industrial Relations*, *45*(4): 778–803.

Sullivan, R. (2009) Density matters: the union density bias and its implications for labor movement revitalization. *Mobilization*, *14*(2): 239–60.

Sullivan, R. (2010) Labour market or labour movement? The union density bias as barrier to labour renewal. *Work, Employment and Society*, *24*(1): 145–56.

Summers, L. (2001) Web technologies for administering multisource feedback programs. In D. W. Bracken, C. W. Timmreck, and A. H. Church (eds) *The Handbook of Multisource Feedback* (pp. 165–80). San Francisco: Jossey-Bass.

Sumner, J. (2005) *Sustainability and the Civil Commons: Rural Communities in the Age of Globalization*. Toronto, Ontario: University of Toronto Press.

Susskind, D. (2020) *A Work Without Work*. London: Allen Lane.

Suutari, V. and Brewster, C. (2003) Repatriation: empirical evidence from a longitudinal study of careers and expectations among Finnish expatriates. *International Journal of Human Resource Management*, *14*(7): 1132–51.

Swinburne, P. (2001) How to use feedback to improve performance. *People Management*, *7*(11): 46–7.

Tahvanainen, M. and Suutari, V. (2005) Expatriate performance management in MNCs. In H. Scullion and M. Linehan (eds) *International Human Resource Management* (pp. 91–113). Basingstoke: Palgrave Macmillan.

Tan, J.-S. (1998) Communication, cross-cultural. In M. Poole and M. Warner (eds) *Handbook of Human Resource Management* (pp. 492–97). London: Thomson Business.

Tannenbaum, S. (2002) A strategic view of organizational training and learning. In K. Kraiger (ed.) *Creating, Implementing, and Managing Effective Training and Development* (pp. 10–52). San Francisco, CA: Jossey-Bass.

Tapper, J. (2021) Low-paid shun Covid tests because the cost of self-isolating is too high. *The Guardian*, 16 January. Available at: https://www.theguardian.com/society/2021/jan/16/low-paid-shun-covid-tests-cost-of-self-isolating-too-high. Accessed 24 January 2021.

Tarr, T. (2018) How Icelandic women really feel about the new equal pay law. *Forbes*, 8 January. Available at: https://www.forbes.com/sites/tanyatarr/2018/01/08/how-icelandic-women-really-feel-about-the-new-equal-pay-law/#17be9bf14f13. Accessed 6 July 2020.

Taylor, F. W. (1911) *The Principles of Scientific Management*. New York: Harper.

Taylor, H. (1991) The systematic training model: corn circles in search of a spaceship? *Management Education and Development*, *22*(4): 258–78.

Taylor, P. (2010) The globalization of service work: analysing the transnational call centre value chain. In P. Thompson and C. Smith (eds) *Working Life* (pp. 244–68). Basingstoke: Palgrave Macmillan.

Taylor, P. and Bain, P. (1998) An assembly line in the head: the call centre labour process. *Industrial Relations Journal*, *30*(2): 101–17.

Taylor, P. J. and Pierce, J. L. (1999) Effects of introducing a performance management system on employees' subsequent attitudes and effort. *Public Personnel Management*, *28*(3): 423–45.

Taylor, S. and Napier, N. (1996) Working in Japan: lessons from women expatriates. *Sloan Management Review, 37*: 125–44.

Taylor, S., Beechler, S. and Napier, N. (1996) Toward an integrative model of strategic international human resource management. *Academy of Management Review, 21*(4): 959–85.

Teece, D. J. (2007) Explicating dynamic capabilities: the nature and microfoundations of (sustainable) enterprise performance. *Strategic Management Journal, 28*(13): 1319–50.

Teece, D. J. (2011) Achieving integration of the business school curriculum using the dynamic capabilities framework. *Journal of Management Development, 30*(5): 499–518.

Teece, D. J. (2016) Dynamic capabilities and entrepreneurial management in large organizations: toward a theory of the (entrepreneurial) firm, *European Economic Review, 86*: 202–16.

Teece, D., Pisano, G. and Shuen, A. (1997) Dynamic capabilities and strategic management. *Strategic Management Journal, 18*(7): 509–33.

Tett, G. (2009) *Fool's Gold: How Unrestrained Greed Corrupted a Dream, Shattered Global Markets and Unleashed a Catastrophe*. London: Little, Brown.

Teviño, L. K. and Nelson, K. A (2014) *Managing Business Ethics: Straight Talk about How to Do It Right* (6th edn). Hoboken, NJ: John Wiley & Sons.

Tews, M. J. and Stafford, K. (2020) Tattoos and perceptions of employment suitability in the hospitality industry. *Journal of Human Resources in Hospitality & Tourism, 19*(2): 148–67.

Tharenou, P. (2005) Does mentor support increase women's career advancement more than men's? The differential effects of career and psychosocial support. *Australian Journal of Management, 30*(1): 77–109.

Thelen, K. (2004) *How Institutions Evolve: The Political Economy of Skills in Germany, Britain, The United States, and Japan*. Cambridge University Press.

Thomas, D. (2020) Top UK chiefs paid 117 times more than the average worker in 2018. *Financial Times*, 5 January, online. Available at: https://www.ft.com/content/9d971c48-2fa5-11ea-a329-0bcf87a328f2. Accessed 21 August 2020.

Thompson, E. P. (1967) Time, work discipline and industrial capitalism. *Past and Present, 38*: 56–97.

Thompson, I. (2017) Force employees to take DNA tests for bosses? We've got a new law to make that happen, beam House Republicans. The Register online. Available at: https://www.theregister.com/2017/03/10/us_legislation_forcing_employees_genetic_info. Accessed 7 August 2020.

Thompson, M. and Ponak, A. (2005) The management of industrial relations. In M. Gunderson, A. Ponak and Taras, D. (eds) *Union–Management Relations in Canada* (5th edn) (pp. 112–33). Toronto, Ontario: Pearson.

Thompson, L. F., Surface, E. A., Martin, D. L. and Sanders, M. G. (2003) From paper to pixels: moving personnel surveys to the web. *Personnel Psychology, 56*(1): 197–227.

Thompson, P. (1989) *The Nature of Work* (2nd edn). Basingstoke: Palgrave Macmillan.

Thompson, P. (2013) Financialization and the workplace: extending and applying the disconnected capitalism thesis. *Work, Employment and Society, 27*(3): 472–88.

Thompson, P. and Ackroyd S (1995) All quiet on the workplace front? *Sociology*, 29(4): 19–33.

Thompson, P. and Harley, B. (2008) HRM and the worker: labour process perspectives. In P. Boxall, J. Purcell and P. Wright (eds) *The Oxford Handbook of Human Resource Management* (pp. 147–65). Oxford: Oxford University Press.

Thompson, P. and McHugh, D. (2009) *Work Organisations: A Critical Approach* (4th edn). Basingstoke: Palgrave Macmillan.

Thompson, P. and van den Broek, D. (2010) Managerial control and workplace regimes. *Work, Employment and Society, 24*(3): 1–12.

Thornhill, A., Saunders, M. N. K. and Stead, J. (1997) Downsizing, delayering – but where's the commitment. *Personnel Review, 26*(1): 81–98.

Thornthwaite, L., Balnave, N. and Barnes, A. (2018) Unions and social media: Prospects for gender inclusion. *Gender, Work & Organization, 25*(4): 401–17.

Tjosvold, D. (2008) The conflict-positive organization: it depends on us. *Journal of Organizational Behaviour, 29*(1): 19–28.

Tjosvold, D., Wong, A. S. and Feng Chen, N. Y. (2014) Constructively managing conflicts in organizations. *Annual Review of Organizational Psychology and Organizational Behaviour, 1*(1): 545–68.

Ton, Z. (2014) *The Good Jobs Strategy: How the Smartest Companies Invest in Employees to Lower Costs and Boost Profits*. New York: Houghton Mifflin Harcourt.

Topcic, M., Baum, M. and Kabst, R. (2016) Are high-performance work practices related to individually perceived stress? A job demands-resources perspective. *International Journal of Human Resource Management, 27*(1): 45–66.

Topham, G. (2020) BA tells longest-serving cabin crew to take 20% pay cut or lose jobs. *The Guardian*, 25 June. Available at: https://www.theguardian.com/business/2020/jun/25/ba-tells-longest-serving-cabin-crew-to-take-20-pay-cut-or-lose-jobs. Accessed 17 August 2020.

Toplis, J., Dulvicz, V. and Fletcher, C. (2005) *Psychological Testing* (4th edn). London: Chartered Institute of Personnel and Development.

Torbiörn, I. (2005) Staffing policies and practices in European MNCs: strategic sophistication, culture-bound policies or ad hoc reactivity? In H. Scullion and M. Linehan (eds) *International Human Resource Management* (pp. 47–68). Basingstoke: Palgrave Macmillan.

Torka, N., van Woerkom, M. and Looise, J. K. (2008) Direct employee involvement quality. *Creativity and Innovation Management, 7*(2): 147–54.

Torres, R., Fenwick, C., Tobin, S., Horne, R. and Rafferty, J. (2015) *OECD Report, World Employment and Social Outlook 2015: The Changing Nature of Jobs?* Geneva: International Labour Organization.

Torrington, D. (1998) Discipline and dismissals. In M. Poole and M. Warner (eds) *The Handbook of Human Resource Management* (pp. 498–506). London: International Thomson Business Press.

Toubøl, J. and Jensen C. (2014) Why do people join trade unions? The impact of workplace union density on union recruitment. *Transfer*, *20*(1): 135–54.

Townley, B. (1993) Performance appraisal and the emergence of management. *Journal of Management Studies*, *30*(2): 221–38.

Townley, B. (1994) *Reframing Human Resource Management*. London: SAGE.

Toynbee, P. and Walker, D. (2020) The lost decade: the hidden story of how austerity broke Britain. *The Guardian*, 3 March. Available at: https://www.theguardian.com/society/2020/mar/03/lost-decade-hidden-story-how-austerity-broke-britain Accessed 16 May 2020.

Trades Union Congress and New Economics Foundation (2015) *Outsourcing Public Services*. London: TUC.

Trapp, R. (2005) The mirror has two faces. *People Management*, May *19*: 40–2.

Travaglione, A. and Cross, B. (2006) Diminishing the social network in organizations: does there need to be such a phenomenon as 'survivor syndrome' after downsizing? *Strategic Change*, *15*: 1–13.

Travis, A. (2011) Probation officers spend 75% of time on red tape, report finds. *The Guardian*, 27 July, p. 7.

Travis, A. (2016) G4S suspended police control-room employees over 'bogus' 999 calls. *The Guardian*, 24 May, p. 11.

Treanor, J. (2015a) Workers demotivated by high executive pay, survey reveals. *The Guardian*, 18 December, p. 35.

Treanor, J. (2015b) Mark Carney calls on businesses to disclose carbon footprints. *The Guardian*, 26 June. Available at: https://www.theguardian.com/business/2015/jun/26/mark-carney-calls-on-businesses-to-disclose-carbon footprints. Accessed 12 December 2016.

Trehan, K. and Pedler, M. (2009) Animating critical action learning: process-based leadership and management development. *Action Learning: Research and Practice*, *6*(1): 35–49.

Tremblay, D.-G. (2003) Telework: a new mode of gendered segmentation? Results from a study in Canada. *Canadian Journal of Communication*, *28*(4): 461–78.

Trevino, L. and Nelson, K (2011) *Managing Business Ethics: Straight Talk About How To Do It Right* (5th edn). Hoboken, NJ: John Wiley & Sons.

Trevor, J. (2009) Can pay be strategic? In S. Corby, S. Palmer and E. Lindop (eds) *Rethinking Reward* (pp. 21–40). Basingstoke: Palgrave Macmillan.

Trompenaars, F. and Hampden-Turner, C. (2012) *Riding the Waves of Culture: Understanding Diversity in Global Business* (3rd edn). London: Nicholas Brealey Publishing.

Truss, C. (2001) Complexities and controversies in linking HRM with organizational outcomes. *Journal of Management Studies*, *38*(8): 1121–49.

Tsaur, S. H. and Tang, W. H. (2013) The burden of esthetic labor on front-line employees in hospitality industry. *International Journal of Hospitality Management*, *35*: 19–27.

Tsoukas, H. (2000) Knowledge as action, organization as theory. *Emergence*, *2*(4): 104–12.

TUC (2010) *One Million Climate Jobs*. London: TUC.

TUC (2016) Still just a bit of banter? Sexual harassment in the workplace 2016. TUC online. Available at: https://www.tuc.org.uk/sites/default/files/SexualHarassmentreport2016.pdf. Accessed 20 September 2020.

TUC (2018) I'll be watching you: A report on workplace monitoring. TUC, 17 August online. Available at: https://www.tuc.org.uk/research-analysis/reports/ill-be-watching-you. Accessed 29 September 2020.

TUC (2019a) Disability pay gap day: disabled people work 2 months of the year for free, says TUC. TUC, 4 November online. Available at: <https://www.tuc.org.uk/news/disability-pay-gap-day-disabled-people-work-2-months-year-free-says-tuc> Accessed 15 October 2020.

TUC (2019b) Sexual harassment of LGBT people in the workplace: A TUC report. TUC online. Available at: https://www.tuc.org.uk/sites/default/files/LGBT_Sexual_Harassment_Report_0.pdf. Accessed 20 September 2020.

TUC (2020a) *A Green Recovery and a Just Transition*. The Wales Trades Union Congress.

TUC (2020b) Amazon warehouse worker takes eight weeks to earn what Bezos makes in a second, says TUC. 18 December. London: TUC. Available at: https://www.tuc.org.uk/news/amazon-warehouse-worker-takes-eight-weeks-earn-what-bezos-makes-second-says-tuc. Accessed 7 January 2021.

TUC (2020c) Brazil: Meat giant in 'brutal' attack on its workers. Report 25, 28 March. London: TUC. Available at: https://www.tuc.org.uk/news/risks-940-28-march-2020. Accessed 21 July 2020.

TUC (2020d) Lack of PPE for health and social care staff is 'a crisis within a crisis' unions warn ministers. London: TUC. Available at: https://www.tuc.org.uk/news/lack-ppe-health-and-social-care-staff-crisis-within-crisis-unions-warn-ministers. Accessed 12 April 2020.

TUC (2020e) New approach to trade advisory groups will exclude workers' voices, warn TUC. 26 August. Available at: https://www.tuc.org.uk/news/new-approach-trade-advisory-groups-will-exclude-workers-voices-warns-tuc. Accessed 26 August 2020.

TUC (2020f) More than 4 in 10 workers would be plunged into financial hardship if forced to self-isolate, 10 September. Available at: https://www.tuc.org.uk/news/tuc-more-4-10-workers-would-be-plunged-financial-hardship-if-forced-self-isolate. Accessed 14 January 2021.

TUC (2020g) Zero-hours contracts – ban them now. 17 February. London: Trades Union Congress. Available at: https://www.tuc.org.uk/blogs/zero-hours-contracts-ban-them-now. Accessed 16 May 2020.

TUC (2021) Government has 'rowed back on promise' to boost workers' rights. 11 May. London: Trades Union Congress. Available at: https://www.tuc.org.uk/news/tuc-government-has-rowed-back-promise-boost-workers-rights. Accessed 12 May 2021.

Tucker, E. (2019) How to modernize workforce planning. *People & Strategy*, *42*(4): 14–19.

Turner, P. (2010) From manpower planning to capacity planning – why we need workforce planning. In CIPD (ed.) *Reflections on Workforce Planning*. London: Chartered Institute of Personnel and Development (CIPD).

Turner, T., Ryan, L. and O'Sullivan, M. (2019) Does union membership matter? Political participation, attachment to democracy and generational change. *European*

Journal of Industrial Relations. Available at: https://doi.org/10.1177/0959680119844926.

Tynan, R. J., Considine, R., Wiggers, J., Lewin, T. J., James, C., Inder, K., Kay-Lambkin, F., Baker, A. L., Skehan, J., Perkins, D. and Kelly, B. J. (2017) Alcohol consumption in the Australian coal mining industry. *Occupational and Environmental Medicine*, *74*: 259–67.

Tyrrell, J., Jones, S. E., Beaumont, R., Astley, C. M., Lovell, R., Yaghootkar, H. and Wood, A. R. (2016) Height, body mass index, and socioeconomic status: mendelian randomisation study in UK Biobank. *British Medical Journal Online*, *352*: i582.

Tyson, S. (1995) *Human Resource Strategy*. London: Pitman.

Tziner, A., Murphy, K. R. and Cleveland, J. N. (2005) Contextual and rater factors affecting rating behavior. *Group & Organization Management*, *30*(1): 89–98.

Tziner, A., Murphy, K. R., Cleveland, J. N., Beaudin, G. and Marchand, S. (1998) Impact of rater beliefs regarding performance appraisal and its organizational context on appraisal quality. *Journal of Business and Psychology*, *12*(4): 457–67.

Uen, J. F., Ahistrom, D., Chen, S. and Liu, S. (2015) Employer brand management, organizational prestige and employees' word-of-mouth referrals in Taiwan. *Asia Pacific Journal of Human Resources*, *53*(1): 104–23.

Uhl-Bien, M. (2003) Relationship development as a key ingredient for leadership development. In S. Murphy and R. Riggio (eds) *The Future of Leadership Development* (pp. 129–47). Mahwah, NJ: Lawrence Erlbaum.

Uhl-Bien, M., Riggio, R. E., Lowe, K. B. and Carsten, M. K. (2014) Followership theory: a review and research agenda. *The Leadership Quarterly*, *25*(1): 83–104.

Ulrich, D. (1997) *Human Resource Champions. The Next Agenda for Adding Value and Delivering Results*. Boston, MA: Harvard Business School Press.

Ulrich, D. (1998) A new mandate for human resources. *Harvard Business Review*, *76*: 124–34.

Ulrich, D., Younger, J., Brockbank, W. and Ulrich, M. (2012) *HR from the Outside In: Six Competencies for the Future of Human Resources*. New York: McGraw-Hill.

Ulrich, L. and Trumbo, D. (1965) The selection interview since 1949. *Psychological Bulletin*, *63*: 100–16.

UN (2018) *Emissions Gap Report 2018*. Geneva: United Nations Environment. Available at: https://wedocs.unep.org/bitstream/handle/20.500.11822/26895/EGR2018_FullReport_EN.pdf?sequence=1&isAllowed=y. Accessed 28 May 2021.

UNISON (2020) UNISON welcomes NI pledge on COVID sick pay. 4 June. Available at: https://www.unison.org.uk/news/article/2020/06/unison-welcomes-ni-pledge-covid-sick-pay. Accessed 9 August 2020.

United Nations General Assembly (2018a) Human Rights Council 39th Session; Report of the Special Rapporteur on the implications for human rights of the environmentally sound management and disposal of hazardous substances and waste. United Nations General Assembly. Available at: https://undocs.org/A/HRC/39/48/Corr.1. Accessed 29 May 2021.

United Nations General Assembly (2018b) Human Rights Council 39th Session; Report of the Special Rapporteur on the implications for human rights of the environmentally sound management and disposal of hazardous substances and waste: Note by the Secretariat. United Nations General Assembly. Available: https://undocs.org/A/HRC/39/48. Accessed 29 May 2021

United States National Library of Medicine (2020a) What does it mean to have a genetic predisposition to a disease? *National Library of Medicine* online. Available at: https://ghr.nlm.nih.gov/primer/mutationsanddisorders/predisposition. Accessed 7 August 2020.

United States National Library of Medicine (2020b) What is genetic discrimination? *National Library of Medicine* online. Available at: https://ghr.nlm.nih.gov/primer/testing/discrimination. Accessed 7 August 2020.

University of Bristol (2020) *Gender and Ethnicity Pay Gap*. Bristol: University of Bristol. Available at: http://www.bristol.ac.uk/medialibrary/sites/equality/documents/Gender%20&%20Ethnicity%20Pay%20Gap%20Report%20 2020.pdf. Accessed 22 January 2021.

Usher, R. (2000) Flexible learning, postmodernity and the contemporary workplace. In V. Jakupec and J. Garrick (eds) *Flexible Learning, Human Resource and Organizational Development* (pp. 225–38). London: Routledge.

Vachon, T. E., Wallace, M. and Hyde, A. (2016) Union decline in a neoliberal age: globalization, financialization, european integration, and union density in 18 affluent democracies. *Socius: Sociological Research for a Dynamic World*, *2*: 1–22. DOI: 10.1177/2378023116656847

Van Buren III, H. J. (2020) The value of including employees: a pluralist perspective on sustainable HRM", *Employee Relations*, Vol. ahead-of-print No. ahead-of-print. Available at: https://doi.org/10.1108/ER-01-2019-0041. Accessed 29 May 2021.

VandeWalle, D., Brown, S. P., Cron, W. L. and Slocum Jr, J. W. (1999) The influence of goal orientation and self-regulation tactics on sales performance: a longitudinal field test. *Journal of Applied Psychology*, *84*(2): 249.

Van den Heuvel, S. and Bondarouk, T. (2017) The rise (and fall?) of HR analytics: a study into the future application, value, structure, and system support. *Journal of Organizational Effectiveness: People and Performance*, *4*(2): 157–78.

Van Der Heijden, B. I., Peters, P. and Kelliher, C. (2015) New ways of working and employability. In R. F. Poell, T. S. Rocco and G. L. Roth (eds) *The Routledge Companion to Human Resource Development* (pp. 542–51). London: Routledge.

Van der Locht, M., Van Dam, K. and Chiaburu, D. (2013) Getting the most of management training: the role of identical elements for training transfer. *Personnel Review*, *42*(4): 422–39.

van der Zwan, N. (2014) Making sense of financialization. *Socio-Economic Review*, 12(1): 99–129.

Van Dyne, L., Ang, S. and Botero, I. C. (2003) Conceptualising employee silence and employee voice as multidimensional constructs. *Journal of Management Studies*, *40*(6): 1359–92.

Van Ewijk, A. R. (2011) Diversity and diversity policy: diving into fundamental differences. *Journal of Organizational Change Management*, *24*(5): 680–94.

Van Greuningen, M., Batenburg, R. S. and Van der Velden, L. F. J. (2012) Ten years of health workforce planning in the Netherlands: a tentative evaluation of GP planning as an example. *Human Resources for Health*, *10*(21). DOI: 10.1186/1478-4491-10-21

Van Hoye, G. (2013) Recruiting through employee referrals: an examination of employees' motives. *Human Performance*, *26*: 451–64.

van Wanrooy, B., Bewley, H., Bryson, A., Forth, J., Freeth, S., Stokes, L. and Wood, S. (2013a) *Employment Relations in the Shadow of Recession: Findings from the 2011 Workplace Employment Relations Study*. Basingstoke: Palgrave Macmillan.

van Wanrooy, B., Bewley, H. and Bryson, A. (2013b) *The 2011 Workplace Employment Relations Study: first findings*. Available at: https://www.gov.uk/government/uploads/system/uploads/attachment_data/file/336651/bis-14-1008-WERS-first-findings-report-fourth-edition-july-2014.pdf. Accessed October 2016.

Vanajan, A., Bültmann, U. and Henkens, K. (2019) Health-related work limitations among older workers – the role of flexible work arrangements and organisational climate. *The Gerontologist*, *60*(3): 450–9.

Vandaele, K. (2019) *Bleak Prospects: Mapping Trade Union Membership in Europe Since 2000*. Brussels: European Trade Union Institute. Available at: https://www.researchgate.net/publication/332511266_Bleak_prospects_mapping_trade_union_membership_in_Europe_since_2000. Accessed 17 August 2020.

Varma, A., Pichler, S. and Budhwar, P. (2011) The relationship between expatriate job level and host country national categorization: an investigation in the UK. *International Journal of Human Resource Management*, *22*(1): 103–20.

Varma, A., Zilic, I., Katou, A., Blajic, B. and Jukic, N. (2020) Supervisor-subordinate relationships and employee performance appraisals: a multi-source investigation in Croatia. *Employee Relations: The International Journal*, *43*(1): 45–62.

Varoufakis, Y. and Adler, D. (2020) The EU's green deal is a colossal exercise in greenwashing. *The Guardian*, 7 February. Available at: https://www.theguardian.com/commentisfree/2020/feb/07/eu-green-deal-greenwash-ursula-von-der-leyen-climate. Accessed 22 June 2020.

Veldman, A. (2017) Pay Transparency in the EU: A legal analysis of the situation in the EU Member States, Iceland, Liechtenstein and Norway. *European Commission Directorate General for Justice and Consumers*. Available at: https://ec.europa.eu/newsroom/just/document.cfm?action=display&doc_id=44501. Accessed 15 October 2020.

Verbeke A. (2013) *International Business Strategy* (2nd edn). Cambridge: Cambridge University Press.

Verma, A. (1995) Employee involvement in the workplace. In M. Gunderson and A. Ponak (eds) *Union–Management Relations in Canada* (3rd edn) (pp. 281–308). Don Mills, Ontario: Addison-Wesley.

Verma, A. (2005) What do unions do to the workplace? Union effects on management and HRM policies. *Journal of Labor Research*, *26*: 421–55.

Verma, A. and Taras, D. (2001) Employee involvement in the workplace. In M. Gunderson, A. Ponak and D. Taras (eds) *Union–Management Relations in Canada* (4th edn) (pp. 447–85). Don Mills, Ontario: Addison-Wesley.

Vesala, H. and Tuomivaara, S. (2015) Slowing work down by teleworking periodically in rural settings? *Personnel Review*, *44*(4): 511–28.

Vince, R. and Reynolds, M. (2010) Leading reflection: developing the relationship between leadership and reflection. In J. Gold, R. Thorpe and A. Mumford (eds) *The Gower Handbook of Leadership and Management Development* (pp. 331–46). Aldershot: Gower Press.

Visser, J. (2002) Why fewer workers join unions in Europe: a social custom explanation of membership trends. *British Journal of Industrial Relations*, *40*(3): 403–30.

Visser, J. (2006) Union membership statistics in 24 countries. *Monthly Labor Review*, *129*(1): 38–49.

Visser, J. (2019) *Trade Unions in the Balance*. Geneva, ILO.

Visser, J. and Waddington, J. (1996) Industrialization and politics: a century of union structural developments in three European countries. *European Journal of Industrial Relations*, *2*(1): 21–53.

Volini, E., Occean, P., Stephan, M. and Walsh, B. (2017) Digital HR: platforms, people, and work. *Deloitte*, 28 February online. Available at: https://www2.deloitte.com/us/en/insights/focus/human-capital-trends/2017/digital-transformation-in-hr.html. Accessed 7 May 2021.

Vroom, V. H. (1964) *Work and Motivation*. New York: John Wiley & Sons.

Vygotsky, L. S. (1978) *Mind and Society: The Development of Higher Mental Process*. Cambridge, MA: Harvard University Press.

Wach, B. A., Wehner, M. C. & Kabst, R. (2021) Performance implications of the HR business partner model and the mediating role of internal efficiency: a comparison between Germany and the United Kingdom. *The International Journal of Human Resource Management*. DOI: 10.1080/09585192.2021.1943490

Wackernagel, M., Schulz, N. B., Deumling, D., Linares, A.C., Jenkins, M., Kapos, V., Monfreda, C., Loh, J., Myers, N., Norgaard, R. and Randers, J., (2002) Tracking the ecological overshoot of the human economy. *Proceedings of the National Academy of Sciences*, *99*(14): 9266–71.

Waddington, J. and Whitston, C. (1994) The politics of restructuring: trade unions on the defensive in Britain since 1979. *Relations Industrielles/Industrial Relations*, *49*(4): 794–817.

Waddington, J. and Whitston, C. (1997) Why do people join unions in a period of membership decline? *British Journal of Industrial Relations*, *35*(4): 515–46.

Wagner, R. F. (1949) The employment interview: a critical summary. *Personnel Psychology*, *2*: 17–46.

Wajcman, J. (1998) *Managing Like a Man*. University Park, PA: Pennsylvania State University Press.

Wakabayashi, D., Griffith, E., Tsang., A. and Conger, K. (2018) Google walkout: employees stage protest over handling of sexual harassment. *New York Times*, 1 November. Available at: https://www.nytimes.com/2018/11/01/technology/google-walkout-sexual-harassment.html. Accessed 23 June 2020.

Wakeling, A. (2014) *Give and Take? Unravelling the true nature of zero-hours contracts*. ACAS Policy Discussion Papers. London: Advisory, Conciliation and Arbitration Service.

Walker, H, Sisto, L, and McBain, D., (2008) Drivers and barriers to environmental supply chain management practices: lessons from the public and private sectors. *Journal of Purchasing and Supply Management*, *14*(1): 69–85.

Walker, J. T. (1996) *The Psychology of Learning*. Englewood Cliffs, NJ: Prentice Hall.

Walker, S. (2008) The neglect of police unions: exploring one of the most important areas of American policing. *Police Practice and Research: An International Journal*, *9*(2): 95–112.

Wall, T. (2021) 'Fire and rehire' tactics rife at firms that are in profit and claiming Covid cash'. *The Guardian*, 18 April. Available at: https://www.theguardian.com/law/2021/apr/18/fire-and-rehire-tactics-rife-at-firms-that-are-in-profit-and-claiming-covid-cash. Accessed 26 April 2021.

Wall, T. D., Wood, S. J. and Leach, D. J. (2004) Empowerment and performance. *International Review of Industrial and Organizational Psychology*, *19*: 1–46.

Wallace, H. M. L., Hoover, K. F. and Pepper, M. B. (2014) Multicultural ethics and diversity discourse. *Equality, Diversity and Inclusion*, *33*(4): 318–33.

Walters, D. and Frick, K. (2000) Worker participation and the management of occupational health and safety: reinforcing or conflicting strategies. *Systematic Occupational Health and Safety Management: Perspectives on an International Development*, 43–65.

Walton, R. (1974) Improving the quality of working life. *Harvard Business Review*, *54*(3): 12–16.

Walton, R. (1985) From control to commitment in the workplace. *Harvard Business Review*, March/April: 77–84.

Walton, R. E. and McKersie, R. B. (1991) *A Behavioral Theory of Labor Negotiations: An Analysis of a Social Interaction System*. Ithaca, NY: Cornell University Press.

Wang, C. (2020) The business case for 'diversity and inclusion' is flawed. it's time to try a new framing. Kennedy School Review, 11 July online. Available at: https://ksr.hkspublications.org/2020/07/11/the-business-case-for-diversity-and-inclusion-is-flawed-its-time-to-try-a-new-framing-2/#_ftn16. Accessed 12 October 2020.

Wang, C. H. and Varma, A (2019) Supervisor-subordinate relationships. In A. Varma and P. Budhwar (eds) *Performance Management Systems: An Experiential Approach* (pp. 135–52). London: Sage.

Wang, L., Cheng, M. Y. and Wang, S. (2018) Carrot or stick? The role of in-group/out-group on the multilevel relationship between authoritarian and differential leadership and employee turnover intention. *Journal of Business Ethics*, *152*(4): 1069–84.

Warhurst, C. and Findlay, P. (2012) *More Effective Skills Utilisation: Shifting the Terrain of Skills Policy in Scotland*. SKOPE Research Paper No. 107. Cardiff: Cardiff University.

Warhurst, C. and Nickson, D. (2007) Employee experience of aesthetic labour in retail and hospitality. *Work, Employment and Society*, *21*(1): 103–20.

Warhurst, C., Eikhof, D. R. and Haunschild, A. (2008) *Work Less, Live More? Critical Analysis of the Work–Life Boundary*. Basingstoke: Palgrave Macmillan.

Waring, M. (1999) *Counting for Nothing: What Men Value and What Women are Worth* (2nd edn). Toronto: University of Toronto Press.

Warr, P. (1987) *Work, Unemployment and Mental Health*. Oxford: Clarendon Press.

Warr, P. (2008) Work values: some demographic and cultural correlates. *Journal of Occupational and Organizational Psychology*, *81*: 751–75.

Warren, D. I. (1969) The effects of power bases and peer groups on conformity in formal organizations. *Administrative Science Quarterly*, *14*:544–56.

Warren, T. (2015) Work-time underemployment and financial hardship: class inequalities and recession in the UK. *Work, Employment and Society*, *29*(2): 191–212.

Waterson, J. (2019a) BBC racism row: Naga Munchetty complaint was also about co-host Dan Walker. *The Guardian*, 30 September. Available at: www.theguardian.com/media/2019/sep/30/bbc-racism-row-naga-munchetty-complaintwas-also-about-dan-walker.

Waterfield, S. (2019) How Denmark became the unlikely home of the robotics industry. Institution of Mechanical Engineers, 7 August. Available at: https://www.imeche.org/news/news-article/feature-how-denmark-became-the-unlikely-home-of-the-robotics-industry. Accessed 1 July 2020.

Watson, S. and Harmel-Law, A. (2010) Exploring the contribution of workplace learning to an HRD strategy in the Scottish legal profession. *Journal of European Industrial Training*, *34*(1): 7–22.

Watson, T. (1999) Human resourcing strategies. In J. Leopold, L. Harris and T. Watson (eds) *Strategic Human Resourcing* (pp. 17–38). London: Pitman.

Watson, T. (2004) HRM and critical social sciences. *Journal of Management Studies*, *41*(3): 447–67.

Watson, T. (2010) Critical social science, pragmatism and the realities of HRM. *International Journal of Human Resource Management Studies*, *21*(6): 915–31.

Watson, T. J. (2008) *Sociology, Work and Industry*. London: Routledge.

Watt, P., Boak, G. and Gold, J. (2020) Leadership Development. In J. Bratton (ed.) *Organisational Leadership*, (pp. 267–85). London: Sage.

Watts, R. (2020) Super-rich lose billions to virus. *The Sunday Times*, 17 May, p. 1.

Weale, S. (2019) 25% of teachers in England work more than 60 hours a week – study. *The Guardian*, 18 September. Available at: https://www.theguardian.com/education/2019/sep/18/25-of-teachers-in-england-work-more-than-60-hours-a-week-study. Accessed 16 June 2020.

Webb, S. and Webb, B. (1911) *Industrial Democracy*. London: Longmans.

Weber, M. (1922/1968) *Economy and Society*. New York: Bedminster.

Weber, M., Parsons, T. and Tawney, R. H. (1930) *The Protestant Ethic and the Spirit of Capitalism*. London: George Allen & Unwin Lt.

Webster, F. (2014) *Theories of the Information Society* (4th edn). London: Routledge.

Wedderburn, Lord (1986) *The Worker and the Law* (3rd edn). Harmondsworth: Penguin.

Wedekind, S. (2020) Covid-19 catapults indoor air quality to top of the list. *Forbes*, 10 June online. Available at: www.forbes.com/sites/pikeresearch/2020/06/10/covid-19-catapults-indoor-air-quality-to-top-of-the-list/#77583352cdb1. Accessed 20 September 2020.

WEF (2020) Global gender gap report 2020. World Economic Forum, 16 December. Available at: http://www3.weforum.org/docs/WEF_GGGR_2020.pdf. Accessed 6 July 2020.

Weiss, T. B. and Hartle, F. (1997) *Reengineering Performance Management: Breakthroughs in achieving strategy through people*. Boca Raton, Fl.: St. Lucie Press.

Welbourne, T. and Trevor, C. (2000) The roles of departmental and position power in job evaluation. *Academy of Management Journal*, *43*(4): 761–71.

Wells, D. (1993) Are strong unions compatible with the new model of human resource management? *Relations Industrielles/Industrial Relations*, *48*(1): 56–84.

Wells, G. (1999) *Dialogic Inquiry: Towards a Sociocultural Practice and Theory of Education*. New York: Cambridge University Press.

Wells, J. (2020) The CIPD signs open letter committing to prioritise employee mental health during return to work. CIPD online. Available at: https://www.cipd.co.uk/news-views/news-articles/cipd-letter-mental-health-return-work. Accessed 2 September 2020.

West, M. A., Borrill, C., Dawson, J., Scully, J., Carter, M., Anelay, S., Patterson, M. and Waring, J. (2002) The link between the management of employees and patient mortality in acute hospitals. *International Journal of Human Resource Management*, *13*(8): 1299–310.

West, M. A., Guthrie, J. P., Dawson, J. F., Borrill, C. S. and Carter, M. (2006) Reducing patient mortality in hospitals: the role of human resource management. *Journal of Organizational Behavior*, *27*(7): 983–1002.

Wheelen, T. L. and Hunger, J. D. (2014) *Strategic Management and Business Policy* (14th edn). New York: Pearson.

White, C. and Avoubkhani, D. (2020) Updating ethnic contrasts in deaths involving the coronavirus (COVID-19). Office for National Statistics, 16 October. Available at: https://www.ons.gov.uk/peoplepopulationandcommunity/birthsdeathsandmarriages/deaths/articles/updatingethniccontrastsindeathsinvolvingthecoronaviruscovid19englandandwales/deathsoccurring2marchto28july2020#main-points. Accessed 11 January 2021.

Whitfield, D. (2012) *In Place of Austerity: Reconstructing the Economy, State and Public Services*. Nottingham: Spokesman Books.

Whitford, C. M. and Coetsee, W. J. (2006) A model of the underlying philosophy and criteria for effective implementation of performance management. *SA Journal of Human Resource Management*, *4*(1): 63–73. Available at: https://www.researchgate.net/publication/47727821_A_Model_Of_The_Underlying_Philosophy_And_Criteria_For_Effective_Implementation_Of_Performance_Management. Accessed 26 June 2020.

Whiting, K. (2020) How the world can 'reset' itself after COVID-19-according to these experts. World Economic Forum, 3 June. Available at: https://www.weforum.org/agenda/2020/06/covid19-great-reset-gita-gopinath-jennifer-morgan-sharan-burrow-climate/. Accessed 22 June 2020.

Whiting, K. (2020) New Zealand Prime Minister opens door to 4-day working week. World Economic Forum, 20 May. Available at: https://www.weforum.org/agenda/2020/05/new-zealand-jacinda-ardern-4-day-week-pandemic-productivity/. Accessed 29 June 2020.

Whitmore, J. (2002) *Coaching for Performance: Growing People, Performance and Purpose* (3rd edn). London: Nicholas Brealey.

Whittington, R. (1993) *What is Strategy and Does it Matter?* London: Routledge.

Wholey, J. S. (1996) Formative and summative evaluation: Related issues in performance measurement. *Evaluation practice*, *17*(2): 145–49.

Wickens, P. (1987) *The Road to Nissan*. London: Palgrave Macmillan.

Wiek, A., Withycombe, L. and Redman C. L. (2011) Key competencies in sustainability: a reference framework for academic program development. *Sustainability Science*, *6*(2): 203–18. Available at: http://dx.doi.org/10.1007/s11625-011-0132-6.

Wiggins, J. S. (ed.) (1996) *The Five-factor Model of Personality*. New York: Guildford Publications.

Wilk, S. and Cappelli, P. (2003) Understanding the determinants of employer use of selection methods. *Personnel Psychology*, *57*: 103–24.

Wilkinson, A., Gollan, P. J., Marchington, M. and Lewin, D. (2010) *The Oxford Handbook of Participation in Organizations*. Oxford: Oxford University Press.

Wilkinson, A., Donaghey, J., Dundon, T. and Freeman, R. B. (2014) Employee voice: charting new terrain. In A. Wilkinson, J. Donaghey, T. Dundon and R. Freeman (eds) *The Handbook of Research on Employee Voice: Participation and Involvement in the Workplace* (pp. 1–16). Cheltenham: Edward Elgar.

Wilkinson, A., Gollan, P. J., Kalfa, S. and Zu, Y. (2018) Voices unheard: employee voice in the new century. *International Journal of Human Resource Management*, *29*(5): 711–24.

Wilkinson, R. and Pickett, K. (2018) *The Inner Level*. London: Allen Lane.

Williams, M. (2020) Coronavirus – what now: unions' grand green plan for Scottish jobs and economy. *The Herald*, 24 May. Available at: https://www.heraldscotland.com/news/18471822.coronavirus-now-unions-grand-plan-reboot-battered-economy/. Accessed 22 June 2020.

Williams, S. (2008) Strategy and objectives. In F. Neale (ed.) *Handbook of Performance Management* (pp. 7–24). Mumbai: Jaico Publishing.

Willmott, H. (1995a) Managing the academics: commodification and control in the development of university education in the UK. *Human Relations*, *48*: 993–1027.

Willmott, H. (1995b) The odd couple?: re-engineering business processes; managing human relations. *New Technology, Work and Employment*, *10*(2): 89–97.

Wilmers, N. (2020) Job turf or variety: task structure as a source of organizational inequality. *Administrative Science Quarterly*. Available at: https://doi.org/10.1177/0001839220909101.

Wilson, H. J. and Daugherty, P. R. (2018) Collaborative intelligence: humans and AI are joining forces. *Harvard Business Review*, July–August.

Wilson, J. P. and Western, S. (2000) Performance appraisal: an obstacle to training and development. *Journal of European Industrial Training*, *24*(7): 384–90.

Wilson, R. and Hogarth, T. (2003) *Tackling the Low Skills Equilibrium: A Review of Issues and Some New Evidence*. London: Department of Trade and Industry.

Winstanley, D. and Woodall, J. (eds) (2000) *Ethical Issues in Contemporary Human Resource Management*. Basingstoke: Palgrave Macmillan.

Witherspoon, P. D. (1997) *Communicating Leadership*. Boston: Allyn & Bacon.

Wollstonecraft, M. (1792/2004) *A Vindication of the Rights of Woman* (ed. M. Brody). London: Penguin Classics.

Womack, J., Jones, D. and Roos, D. (1990) *The Machine that Changed the World*. New York: Rawson Associates.

Wood, G. (2013) Institutional diversity: current contestations and emerging issues. *Journal of Comparative Economic Studies, 8*(1): 7–20.

Wood, P. (2020) Employee monitoring software surges as companies send staff home. *ABC News*, 21 May online. Available at: https://www.abc.net.au/news/2020-05-22/working-from-home-employee-monitoring-software-boom-coronavirus/12258198. Accessed: 29 September 2020.

Wood, S. (2019) HRM and organizational performance. In D. G. Collings, Wood, G. T. and Szamosi, L. T. (eds) *Human Resource Management: A Critical Approach* (2nd edn) (pp. 74–97). London: Routledge.

Wood, S. (2000) The BJIR and industrial relations in the new millennium. *British Journal of Industrial Relations, 38*(1): 1–5.

Woodall, J. and Douglas, D. (2000) Winning hearts and minds: ethical issues in human resource development. In D. Winstanley and J. Woodall (eds) *Ethical Issues in Contemporary Human Resource Management* (pp. 116–36). Basingstoke: Macmillan.

Woodall, J., Scott-Jackson, W., Newham, T. and Gurney, M. (2009) Making the decision to outsource human resources. *Personnel Review, 38*(3): 236–52.

Woodhams, C., Lupton, B. and Cowling, M. (2015) The snowballing penalty effect: multiple disadvantage and pay. *British Journal of Management, 26*(1): 63–77.

Woods, S. A. and West, M. A. (2020) *The Psychology of Work and Organizations* (3rd edn). Andver: Cengage Learning EMEA.

World Commission on Environment and Development (1987) *Our Common Future*. New York: Oxford University Press.

World Economic Forum (2019) Progress towards gender equality in wages, where do we stand? *World Economic Forum* online. Available at: https://reports.weforum.org/global-gender-gap-report-2020/the-global-gender-gap-index-2020/box-1. Accessed 15 October 2020.

World Health Organization (2016) WHO definition of health. Available at: www.who.int/about/definition/en/print.html. Accessed 14 September 2016.

World Health Organization (2019) Mental health in the workplace. *World Health Organization* online. Available at: https://www.who.int/mental_health/in_the_workplace/en. Accessed 2 September 2020.

World Health Organization (2020) Who we are. *World Health Organization* online. Available at: https://www.who.int/about/who-we-are/constitution. Accessed 2 September 2020.

Wright, M. (1996) The collapse of compulsory unionism? Collective organization in highly unionized British companies, 1979–1991. *British Journal of Industrial Relations, 34*(4): 497–513.

Wright, P. and Gardner, T. (2003) The human resource–firm performance relationship. Methodological and theoretical challenges. In D. Holman, T. Hall, C. Clegg, P. Sparrow and A. Howard (eds) *The New Workplace: A Guide to the Human Impact of Modern Work Practices* (pp. 311–29). London: John Wiley & Sons.

Wright, P. M. and McMahan, G. C. (1992) Theoretical perspectives for strategic human resource management. *Journal of Management, 18*(2): 295–320.

Wylie, B. (2020) *Bandit Capitalism*. Edinburgh: Birlinn.

Xenikou, A. and Furnham, A. (2013) *Group Dynamics and Organizational Culture*. London: Red Globe Press.

Xie, X., Zhu, Q. and Qi, G. (2020) How can green training promote employee career growth? *Journal of Cleaner Production, 259*: 1–11.

Yang, C.-M., Shin, N.-Y., Weng, M.-W. and Hsu, C.-H. (2014) Using a two-dimensional mean value matrix (TDMVM) to improve users' satisfaction with government e-recruitment website. *Journal of Software, 10*(1): 82–93.

Yang, J. and Arthur, J. B. (2021) Implementing commitment HR practices: line manager attributions and employee reactions. *The International Journal of Human Resource Management, 32*(16): 3339–3369, DOI: 10.1080/09585192.2019.1629986.

Yap, M. H. T. and Ineson, E. M. (2012) Diversity management: the treatment of HIV-positive employees. *AIDS Care, 24*(11): 1349–58.

Yin, M., Shaewitz, D. and Megra, M. (2014) An uneven playing field: the lack of equal pay for people with disabilities. *Washington: American Institutes for Research*.

York, R. (2020) Bermuda: Bermuda welcomes new residents. *Mondaq*, 1 September online. Available at: https://www.mondaq.com/operational-impacts-and-strategy/980116/bermuda-welcomes-new-residents. Accessed 30 September 2020.

Yorke, M. (2006) *Employability in Higher Education: What It Is – What It Is Not*. York: The Higher Education Academy.

Young, W., Davis, M., McNeill, I. M., Malhotra, B., Russell, S., Unsworth, K. and Clegg, C. W. (2015) Changing behaviour: successful environmental programmes in the workplace. *Business Strategy and the Environment, 24*(8): 689–703.

Yu, G. and Park, J. (2006) The effect of downsizing on the financial performance and employee productivity of Korean firms. *International Journal of Manpower, 27*: 230–50.

Yuriev, A., Boiral, O., Francoeur, V. and Paille, P. (2018) Overcoming the barriers to pro-environmental behaviors in the workplace: A systematic review. *Journal of Cleaner Production, 182*: 379–94.

Zapf, D. (2002) Emotion work and psychological well-being: a review of the literature and some conceptual considerations. *Human Resource Management Review, 12*(2): 237–68.

Zedeck, S. (1986) A process analysis of the assessment center method. N. B. Staw and L. L. Cummings (eds) *Research in Organizational Behavior* (Vol. 8: pp. 259-6). Greenwich, CT: JAI Press.

Zenger, T. (2016) The case against pay transparency. *Harvard Business Review*, 30 September. Available at: https://hbr.org/2016/09/the-case-against-pay-transparency. Accessed 15 October 2020.

Zeytinoglu, I. U., Denton, M., Plenderleith, J. and Chowhan, J. (2015) Associations between workers' health, and non-standard hours and insecurity: the case of home care workers in Ontario, Canada. *International Journal of Human Resource Management, 26*(19): 2503–22.

Zhang, Y. and Albrecht, C. (2010) The role of cultural values on a firm's strategic human resource management development: a comparative study of Spanish firms in China. *International Journal of Human Resource Management, 21*(11): 1911–30.

Zheng, C., Kashi, K., Fan, D., Molineux, J. and Shan Ee, M. (2016) Impact of individual coping strategies and organisational work–life balance programmes on Australian employee well-being. *International Journal of Human Resource Management, 27*(5): 501–26.

Zhu, C. J., Cooper, B. K., Fan, D. and De Cieri, H. (2013) HR practices from the perspective of managers and employees in multinational enterprises in China: alignment issues and implications. *Journal of World Business 48*: 241–50.

Zibarras, L. and Ballinger, C. (2011) *Promoting Environmental Behaviour in the Workplace: A Survey of UK Organisations. A report produced by the Department of Psychology, City University, London for British Psychological Society Division of Occupational Psychology Green Working Group*. Leicester: British Psychological Society.

Zielinski, D. (2019) Get smarter about people analytics: success in using people depends more on people than technology. *HR Technology*, Winter: 24–9.

Zilahy, G. (2003) Organizational factors determining the implementation of cleaner production in the corporate sector. *Journal of Cleaner Production, 12*: 311–19.

Zink, K. J. (2014) Social sustainability and quality of working life. In *Sustainability and Human Resource Management* (pp. 35–55). Berlin: Springer.

Zottoli, M. A. and Wanous, J. P. (2000) Recruitment source research: current status and future directions. *Human Resource Management Review, 10*(4): 353–82.

Zuboff, S. (2015) Big other: surveillance capitalism and the prospects of an information civilization. *Journal of Information Technology, 30*(1): 75–89.

Zuboff, S. (2019) *The Age of Surveillance Capitalism*. London: Profile Books.

Zutshi, A. and Sohal, A. (2004) Environmental management system adoption by Australian organizations, Part 1: Reasons, benefits and impediments. *Technovation, 24*: 335–57.

NAME INDEX

A
Abma, T., 128
Acikgoz, Y., 158
Acker, J., 106
Ackers, P., 294, 306, 307, 373
Ackroyd, S., 9, 10, 298, 301
Adams, J. S., 180, 238, 242
Adams, R. J., 286
Adam-Smith, D., 216
Addison, J., 312
Adler, D., 271
Adler, N. J., 403
Afridi, M. A., 358
Afsar, B., 358, 364
Agarwal, P., 153
Agarwal, U. A., 337
Agashae, Z., 30
Aguinis, H., 192
Agyeman, J., 355
Ahistrom, D., 158
Ahlstrand, B., 58
Ahlvik, C., 387
Ahmad, R., 250
Ahmad, S., 70
Ahmed, I. Z., 148, 154
Ahmed, S., 158
Akerjordet, K., 161
Alagaraja, M., 203
Alakeson, V., 129
Albizu, E., 102
Albrecht, C., 393
Aldred, J., 402
Alis, D., 129
Allas, T., 134
Allen, B., xxvi
Allen, D., 158
Allen, J. B., 54
Allo, P., 207
Allwood, L., 332
Almeida, S., 394
Alpin, C., 273
Alsaafin, L., 325
Al-Sharif, R., 154
Alvesson, M., 13, 41, 42, 61, 76, 77, 181
Amadeo, K., 412
Amadieu, F., 162
Amadxarif, Z., 253
Ambrose, J., 265
Ames, G., 341
Anand, N., 93
Anderlucci, J., 359
Andersen, T. J., 67
Anderson, B. A., 394
Anderson, C., 188
Anderson, D., 130
Anderson, N., 155, 161
Anderson, V., 223
Andolšek, D. M., 30
Andrei, D., 94
Anelay, S., 9
Ang, S., 163, 316
Angeli, M., 253
Angrave, D., 120, 250
Anseel, F., 186
Antai, I., 132
Antonacopoulou, E. P., 13, 211
Antoni, C. H., 262
Antonioli, D., 371
Apaydin, M., 194
Apedoe-Dzidza, D. Y., 122
Apouey, B., 335
Appelbaum, E., 38, 64, 74, 98
Ardiç, K., 329
Aries, E., 315
Aritzeta, A., 71
Armenakis, A. A., 22
Armstrong, M., 54, 69, 71, 74–75, 175, 179, 180, 192, 211, 212, 224, 234, 242
Armstrong, P., 389
Armstrong, S. J., 213
Arnett, D., 208
Arnold, J., 250
Arnold, M, 145
Arthur, J. B., 9, 70, 71, 74
Arvey, R. D., 163
Ash, T. G., 413
Ashcroft, K., xxvi
Ashford, S. J., 189
Ashikali, T., 128
Ashkanasy, N. M., 70, 177, 353, 355, 364, 365
Ashley, L., 126, 136
Astley, C. M., 167
Astor, M., 285
Atkin, D. J., 162
Atkinson, J. S., 129
Audia, P., 186
Auflick, P., 191
Aust, I., 355, 356
Avoubkhani, D., 414
Aycan, Z., 316
Ayestarán, S., 71
Aylott, E., 296
Azasu, S., 234

B
Bacon, N., 21, 274
Badri, A., 344, 345
Bae, J., 399, 400
Bagilhole, B., 126, 127
Baicker, K., 344
Bailey, C., 51, 67
Bailey, T., 38, 64, 74, 98
Baillien, E., 338
Bain, G. S., 281
Bain, P., 106, 341
Baird, L., 8, 74
Bajorek, Z., 40, 41
Baker, A. L., 341
Baker, D. T., 127, 130, 131, 135, 136
Baker, L., 359
Baker, M., 253
Bal, P. M., 27, 130
Balabanova, E., 27
Baldamus, W., 236
Baldauf, B., 116–118
Baldry, C., 341
Baldwin, T. T., 221
Ballantyne, I., 178
Ballard, A., 196, 200
Balnave, N., 303
Bamber, G., 386
Bamberger, P., 62, 67, 75
Bandura, A., 180, 213, 218
Bangerter, A., 156
Banister, D., 355
Banks, K., 209, 210
Baran, P. A., 42
Barber, A. E., 240
Barber, B., 319
Barbier, E. B., 414

Barclay, J., 163
Barker-Scott, B., 251
Barling, J., xvi, 364, 421
Barlow, C. Y., 80
Barlow, G., 192
Barnes, A., 303
Barnett, N., 203
Barney, J. B., 8, 61, 65, 74, 205
Baron, A., 115, 175, 193
Baron, H., 162
Barrington, L., 124
Barry, J., 359
Barry, M., 316
Bartholomew, D. J., 115
Bartlett, C. A., 380–383, 388, 390–391, 395, 402
Bartoletti, I., 47
Bartsch, S., 320
Bassett, P., 273
Basuil, D., 133
Batenburg, R. S., 122
Bates, R. A., 221
Battisti, M., 135
Batty, R., 154
Baum, M., 108, 157
Baumgartner, R. J., 360
Baxter, G., 184
Bazerman, M., 179
Beal, B. D., 385
Beardwell, I., 306
Beardwell, J., 5, 29
Beaton, A., 271
Beatty, C. A., 251
Beaudin, G., 195
Beaumont, R., 167
Beauvais, L. L., 238
Beck, U., 130, 380
Beckett, D., 212, 213
Beechler, S., 386, 388, 390, 391, 403
Beer, M., 8, 13, 19, 20, 31, 34, 35, 64, 67, 74, 92, 103, 205, 235, 310, 330
Beevers, K., 206
Beevers-Cowling, F., 161
Begum, H., 253
Behnam, M., 55
Behrens, W. W., 353
Beioley, K., 168
Bélanger, J., 107, 389
Bell, D., 218
Bell, D. N. F., 131
Belt, V., 103
Beltrán-Martín, I., 72, 73
Benda, J., 11
Bendal, S. E., 27
Benders, J., 103
Bendle, R., 124
Bengio, Y., 226
Benn, S., 373
Bennett, C. V., 165, 393
Bennion, Y., 132
Benoliel, B., 150
Benschop, Y., 189, 227
Benson, J., 186
Berg, D. H., 207
Berg, J., 398
Berg, P., 38, 64, 74, 98
Bergman, S. M., 158
Berkes, F., 373
Berkhout, E., 254
Bernadin, H. J., 187
Berridge, J., 409
Berrone, P., 238, 242, 249
Berthold, A., 128
Bertrand, M., 384
Bertua, C., 161
Betcherman, G., 72
Betsill, M. M., 373
Betz, A., 262
Bevan, G., 181
Bewley, H., 19, 175, 252, 266, 273
Beynon, H., 98
Bhave, D. P., 24, 26, 272
Bhuiyan, F., 116
Bianchini, A., 328
Biazzo, S., 176
Bibby, J., 254
Bierema, L., 209
Bierly, P. E., 71
Biggane, J. E., 158
Bilge, S., 42
Billett, S., 211
Bini Smaghi, L., 115
Bishop, J., 372
Biswas, S., 206
Bititci, U., 176
Bittman, M., 334
Bjarnason, E., 246
Björkman, I., 387, 390, 394
Black, C., 326
Black, S. E., 384
Blackstock, K. L., 354
Blaize, N., 225
Blajic, B., 187
Blakeley, G., 258, 259
Blanchflower, D. G., 131, 268
Blaney, D., 190
Blanton, H., 162
Blatt, R., 189
Blau, P., 20
Blaze Baum, K., 357
Blevins, D., 348, 349
Blomme, R. J., 27
Bloom, M., 241
Bloom, N., 104, 220
Blyton, P., 241, 266
Boak, G., 224, 225, 233
Bochner, S., 155
Boffey, D., 235, 257, 275, 389
Bogen, M., 153
Boiral, O., 357, 358
Bokelberg, E., 125
Boltanski, L., 6, 30, 43, 44, 58, 90, 93, 96, 129, 132, 195, 233, 252, 259, 266, 272, 282, 286
Bolton, S. C., 20, 22, 41, 86, 105, 111, 183, 238, 345
Bonache, J., 395
Bondarouk, T., 23, 69, 182
Bonnin, D., 135, 402, 411, 415, 420
Bookter, A. I., 221
Boon, C., 38, 72, 73, 75
Boons, M., 23
Boot, K., 359
Booth, R., 348
Borman, W. C., 190
Borrill, C. S., 9, 70, 71
Boselie, P., 13, 35, 38, 72–74, 76, 393
Boswell, W. R., 190
Bosworth, D. L., 116–118
Botero, I. C., 316
Bottomley, C. R., 27
Boudreau, J. W., 356
Boudreau-Trudel, B., 344, 345
Bou-Llusar, J. C., 72, 73
Bowles, K., 10
Bowley, R., 154
Bowling, N.A., 301, 303
Boxall, P., xxvi, 20, 29, 31, 34, 35, 41, 58, 62–65, 67, 68, 72, 74, 76, 90, 104, 107, 135, 176, 181, 195, 219, 238, 307, 356, 366, 380
Boyatzis, R. E., 224, 225
Boydell, T., 208
Bradbury, H., 179
Bradley, A., 161
Bradshaw, J., 357
Bratton, A., 30, 31, 39, 41, 51, 53, 60, 66, 77, 85, 88, 93, 94, 96, 123, 126, 134, 145, 150, 181, 186, 191, 195, 199, 210, 216, 224, 242, 247, 272, 277, 287, 291, 303, 306, 313, 332, 343, 357, 363–365, 367, 368, 372, 377, 385, 393, 407
Bratton, J., xxvi, 3, 5, 7, 13, 14, 23, 25–27, 30, 32, 35, 42, 44, 72, 85, 88, 90, 92, 97, 100, 101, 107, 109, 156, 161, 165, 179, 181, 183, 190, 191, 193–195, 204–207, 209, 211–214, 218, 224, 227, 233, 238, 246, 250, 257, 273, 277, 307, 313,

315, 354, 357, 363, 365, 367, 372, 379, 380, 403, 407, 411, 414, 423
Braverman, H., 97
Breaugh, J., 160
Brecher, J., 363
Bresser-Pereira, L. C., 411
Bretz, R., 240
Brewster, C. J., 13, 35, 74, 353, 356, 373, 385, 393, 396, 397, 399, 403, 407, 421
Brey, P., 207
Bridger, E., 104, 307
Bridgman, T., 13
Broadbridge, A., 154
Brock, A., 401
Brockbank, W., 30, 37, 68
Brocker, J., 195
Brodbeck, F., 218
Broschak, J. P., 93
Brosse, M., 372
Brown, B., 59
Brown, D. J., 26, 54, 69, 71, 74–75, 234, 251, 284
Brown, J., 334
Brown, J. N., 159
Brown, J. S., 208
Brown, M., 173, 175, 186, 187, 311
Brown, R., 24
Brown, S. P., 180
Brown, V. R., 159
Brown, W., 7, 236, 240, 266, 282, 284
Brumbach, G. B., 182
Brun, J. -P., 333
Brunow, S. B. U., 128
Brunsden, J., 13, 420
Brutus, S., 224
Bryan, M., 196
Bryman, A., 154
Brynjolfsson, E., 101
Bryson, A., 19, 175, 196, 252, 266, 268, 273, 274, 280, 284, 287, 293, 326, 330
Bryson, J., 240, 266
Buch, R., 262
Buckingham, M., 188, 193
Buckley, R., 216
Budd, J. W., 24, 26, 27, 272
Budhwar, P., 385, 393
Bullard, R. D., 355
Buller, P., 209
Bullock, Lord, 309, 418
Bültmann, U., 327
Bunglawala, Z., 210
Burawoy, M., 21
Burchill, F., 265, 266, 282
Burgess, J., 157
Burgoyne, J., 208, 224
Busby, E., 305, 306
Busby, M., 238
Butler, P., 13, 274, 309
Butler, S., 5, 51, 53
Büttgen, M., 320
Byers, P. Y., 313
Byram, M., 329

C

Cable, D. M., 156, 196
Caffarella, R., 214
Cafferkey, K., 38, 70, 98, 106
Caine, D., 115, 121
Calás, M. B., 42, 157, 166
Caligiuri, P. M., 394, 396, 403
Callaghan, G., 106
Callahan, J., 209
Callesen, J., 216
Callinicos, A., 10, 204
Caloyeras, J., 343
Cameron, C., 233
Cameron, N., 190
Caminiti, S., 222
Campbell, D., 31, 43, 134, 330
Campion, J. E., 163
Campion, M. A., 163, 164
Camps, J., 338
Canal, M., 134
Cantor, D. E., 371
Caplan, R. L., 328
Caple, J., 216
Cappelli, P., 165
Cappotto, C., 162
Carabantes, M., 207
Carballo-Penela, A., 360
Carless, S. A., 154
Carleton, E., 224
Carlsson, L., 373
Carmichael, T., 170
Carollo, L., 42
Caron, C., 72
Carr, H., 3
Carroll, B., 225
Carroll, L., 414
Carroll, S. A., 157
Carsten, M. K., 51, 66, 191, 373
Carter, M. Z., 9, 22, 70, 71
Carter, V., 209
Caruth, D., 238
Cascio, W. F., 21, 76
Case, A., 3, 4, 6
Castellano, W. G., 155, 367
Castellanos, S., 222
Castells, M., 130, 380
Castka, P., 360
Cawley, B. D., 189
Celik, H., 128
Ceplenski, C., 337
Cha, M., 363
Chakrabortty, A., 414
Chakravarty, D., 291
Champy, J., 102, 103
Chance, P., 213
Chand, M., 71
Chang, C. W., 360, 365
Chapman, D. S., 157, 163
Charlesworth, S., 302, 336
Charlwood, A., 120, 250
Chaudhary, R., 366, 367
Cheatham, B., 226
Checchi, D., 277
Chen, H. G., 226
Chen, L., 23
Chen, S., 158
Chen, T., 189
Chen, Y. S., 360, 365, 367
Cheney, G., 317
Cheng, M. Y., 317
Cheung, S. Y., 188
Chevalier, A., 162
Chiaburu, D., 218, 219, 223
Chiapello, E., 6, 30, 43, 44, 58, 90, 93, 96, 129, 132, 195, 233, 252, 259, 266, 272, 282, 286
Child, J., 54, 58, 93, 360
Chin, P., 207
Chinander, K. R., 369
Choi, S., 136
Chomsky, N., 78
Chong, T., 365
Chou, B. K., 397
Chou, T., 46, 47
Chouhan, V. S., 147
Chow, I. H. S., 366
Chowdhury, M. M., 116
Chowhan, J., 335
Christensen, J., 420
Christophers, B., 6
Chui, C., 101
Chun, J., 195
Churchill, F., 210
Ciby, M., 338
Clair, J., 369
Clake, R., 115
Clark, D., xxvi, 282, 310
Clark, J., 58
Clark, T., 399
Clarke, I., 213
Clarke, N., 104
Claxton, J., 178
Clayton, T., 317
Clegg, C. W., 60
Clegg, H., 4, 277
Clegg, R., 298
Clegg, S. R., 19, 25, 43, 208, 266, 399

Cleveland, J. N., 181, 195, 389
Cleverly, P. M., 27
Clifford, B., 184
Coan, P., 365
Coates, D., 4, 115
Coates, J., 315
Cockburn, C., 42
Coens, T., 186
Coetsee, W. J., 174
Colling, T., 266
Collings, C. J., 143
Collings, D. G., 353, 356, 373, 379, 389–391, 394, 402, 407, 421
Collington, R., 52
Collins, H. M., 208
Collins, J. M., 243
Collins, P. H., 42
Collinson, D., 299
Colón-Acevedo, S. E., 339
Colquitt, J. A., 254
Colthart, I., 190
Colville, I. D., 5
Conger, K., 273, 278
Conlon, D. E., 254
Connell, J., 157
Connelly, C. E., 111
Considine, R., 341
Contractor, F. J., 132
Conway, N., 9, 26, 27, 104, 220
Cook, M., 163
Cooke, F. I., 131
Cooke, W. N., 382
Cools, E., 213
Coombs, J. E., 71
Cooper, B. K., 166
Cooper, C. L., 334, 337, 338, 420
Corby, S., 240, 245, 251, 257, 259
Corritore, M., 136
Corstjens, J., 162
Cortina, L. M., 301
Cory, G., 129
Cotter, C., 334, 335
Cotton, C., 252
Courville, A., 226
Cousins, S., 122, 123
Cowan, R. L., 338, 350
Cowling, A., 116
Cowling, M, 126
Cox, A., 357, 362, 367
Cox, J., 160
Crabbe, S., 224
Craig, A. W. J., 301
Crane, A., 26, 28, 96, 366
Crane, D., 391
Craven, L., 355
Crawford A., 105
Cregan, C., 311
Cridland, M., 319
Crifo, P., 356
Crockett, G., 135, 402, 411, 415, 420
Croft, J., 26
Cron, W. L., 180
Crossan, M. M., 194, 208, 224
Croucher, R., 419
Cruz, E., 154
Cuevas, M., 210
Cullen, J., 135, 402, 411, 415, 420
Cullinane, J., 348
Cullinane, N., 6
Curran, D., 379, 391
Currie, G., 11
Curson, J. A., 116–118, 122
Curtis, A., 190
Cushen, J., 281, 421
Czerny, A., 162

D

Dacin, M. T., 385
Daft, R. L., 90, 93
Dahling, J. J., 296
Daily, B. F., 199, 368, 369, 372
Daly, M., 335
Danford, A., 64, 65, 105, 107
Daniel, W. W., 311
Daniels, C., 106
Daniels, K., 91, 262, 343
Darlington, R., 10
Das, S. C., 148, 154
Datta, D., 133
Datta, N., 96
Daugherty, P. R., 101, 102
Davey, R., 133
Davies, P., 283
Davies, R., 162, 290
Davis, A., 162
Davis, C., 162, 401
Davis, G. F., 75, 93, 266, 267, 281, 385
Davis, J. H., 186
Davis, M. C., 60, 365
Davis, N., 226
Davis-Blake, A., 93
Dawson, J. F., 9, 70, 71
De Cieri, H., 166, 181, 362, 385, 387–390
De Cremer, D., 195
De Dreu, C. K. W., 299
De Gieter, S., 237, 238
De Oliveira, E. T., 160
De Stefano, V., 130, 259, 398
De Vries, G., 316
De Winne, S., 20, 40, 61
De Witte, H., 24, 74, 338
Deadrick, D. L., 158
Deakin, R., 339
Deakin, S., 7, 282
Dean, J., 162
Deat, F., 196, 200
Deaton, A., 3, 4, 6
Debono, J., 302
Deci, E. L., 238
Deegan, P., 421
Dehghan, S. K., 123
Deimler, M., 75
Del Brio, J. A., 123
Delaney, L., 335
Delbridge, R., 9, 10, 41
Delery, J. E., 64–66, 71
Dell, M. E., 116–118
Dellanna, A., 413
Den Hartog, D. N., 64, 65
Denham, D., 7, 23, 25, 35, 42, 85, 92, 97, 156, 165, 181, 246, 257, 379, 380, 411
DeNisi, A. S., 186, 188
Denti, L., 194
Denton, D. K., 369
Denton, M., 335
Depolo, M., 135
Derlien, H. U., 196
Deshpande, M., 116
Deumling, D., 354
Devanna, M., 8, 33, 143, 175, 192
Devanna, M. A., 8, 19, 20, 33, 54, 61, 74, 173, 393
Devine, T. M., 379
Dhar, R. L., 368
Dharmage, S. C., 394
Dharmapala, D., 276, 277
Dibben, P., 135, 402, 411, 415, 420
Dickens, L., 270
Dickinson, J., 242
Dickson, W. J., 95
Diekma, A. B., 189
Dietz, G., 38, 72, 73
Dijk, H., 127, 128
Dilchert, S., 354, 358
Disney, R., 281
Dix, G., 273
Dobbins, A., 108
Dobbins, T., 133
Docherty, P., 353, 355, 362
Dodd, V., 330
Doellgast, V., 312
Doeringer, P., 240
Doherty, N., 330
Dominguez, A., 162
Donaghey, J., 306
Donini, F., 328
Donkin, R., 86
Donovan, L., 283, 418
Doolittle, R., 257

Doorewaard, H., 189
Doran, T., 184
Dorenbosch, L., 130
Dorsey, D. W., 190
Doty, H. D., 64
Douglas, D., 64, 227
Doward, J., 165
Dowling, P., 195, 385, 387–391, 393, 397, 407
Downey, M., 225
Downey, S. N., 126, 127
Drohan, M., 346
Drucker, P., 8, 173
Drucker, P. F., 203
Du Gay, P., 92
Duberley, J., 126, 136
Duffy, J. F., 368, 371
Duggan, K., 187
Duguid, P., 208
Dulewicz, V., 161
Dulvicz, V., 161, 162
Duncan, R. B., 360
Dundon, T., 3, 5, 6, 70, 268, 306, 307
Dunkerley, D., 266
Dunkley, E., 146
Dunphy, D., 373
Durand, R., 356
Durcan, G., 332
Dutta, A., 262
Dutton, E., 149
Duxbury, L., 131
Dweck, C. S., 180
Dwelly, T., 132
Dyck, D. E., 328
Dyer, L., 9, 63
Dyllick, T., 356
Dysvik, A., 262

E

Eads, G. C., 70
Eady, J., 270
Eagle, S., 195, 390, 391, 393, 397, 407
Eagly, A. H., 189
Ebbinghaus, B., 282, 283
Edgell, S., 24, 29, 85, 111, 130, 131, 226, 233, 259, 379, 380, 402
Edmondson, A. C., 104
Edwards, G., 382, 389, 407
Edwards, H., 329
Edwards, K., 69
Edwards, M. R., 69
Edwards, P. K., 24, 107, 267, 294, 309, 382, 389
Edwards, R., 357
Edwards, T., 266, 309, 382, 385, 388, 389
Efendiev, A., 27
Egan, J., 243
Egan, M., 176
Egan, T., 225
Egri, C. P., 364
Ehnert, I., 370
Ehrke, F., 128
Ehrnrooth, M., 27
Eichinger, R. W., 190
Eikhof, D. R., 42
Einarsen, S., 337, 338
Eisenbaum, J., 162
Eisinger, C., 178
Elena-Iuliana, I., 182, 183
Elenkov, D., 399
Elger, T., 5
Ellinger, A. D., 30
Elliott, C., 382, 389, 407
Elliott, L., 96, 413
Elorza, U., 71
Emir, A., 269, 284, 305
Emmott, M., 306
Engen, M., 127, 128
Engert, S., 360
Epitropaki, O., 191
Epstein, G., 76, 81
Eraut, M., 208
Erdal, D., 317
Erickson, C., 133
Eronen, J. T., 115
Escrig-Tena, A. B., 72, 73
Eswaran, V., 118
Etzioni, A., 106
Eubanks, B., 226
Euwema, M., 338
Evans, B., 355
Evans, P., 394
Evans, R., 37
Evans, S., 80
Everett, C., 40, 41
Ewart, C., 419, 420
Ewing, K. D. E., 287

F

Fairclough, N., 196
Fairholm, G. W., 238
Fan, D., 166
Fang, H., 341
Fang, M., 193
Faragher, J., 303
Farazmand, A., 387, 403
Farina, E., 96
Farmer, D., 333
Farndale, E., 29, 407
Farnham, D., 30, 175, 176, 196, 265, 272, 273, 293, 297, 298, 307, 372
Farnhill, T., 371, 377
Farr, C., 327
Farrell, A., 59
Farrell, D., 132
Fasol, R., 135
Fearon, C., 133
Feild, H. S., 22, 180
Felstead, A., 90, 93, 111, 220
Feng Chen, N. Y., 297
Fenwick, C., 135
Fenwick, T., 207
Ferdous, F., 116
Ferguson, D., 208
Ferlie, E., 52, 54, 66
Fernandez Campbell, A., 255
Fernandez, E., 123
Fernández, Z. V., 395
Fernando, M., 394
Ferner, A., 309, 382, 388, 389, 393
Ferrant, G., 257
Ferris, D. L., 26
Ferris, G. R., 225
Ferris, P., 339
Festing, M., 195, 390, 391, 393, 397, 407
Festner, D., 219
Field, L., 209
Field, T., 338
Fieschi, C., 259
Figueres, C., 353
Findlay, P., 105, 173, 194, 195, 200, 283, 284, 291
Findley, H. M., 180
Fine, B., 24, 25
Fine, C., 246, 247
Fine, S., 168
Fineman, S., 366
Finkelstein, L. M., 157
Fischer, A. M., 401
Fischlmayr, I., 397
Fisher, C. D., 189
Fisher, S., 23
Fishman, C., 51
Fishman, J., 412
Fjellvær, H., 384
Flanders, A., 8
Flannery, B. L., 369
Flassbeck, H., 286
Fletcher, C., 161, 162
Flood, P., 61
Floridi, L., 207
Foley, B., 357, 362, 367
Foley, P., 23
Follett, M. P., 95
Fombrun, C. J., 8, 19, 20, 33, 54, 61, 74, 143, 173, 175, 192, 393
Foot, M., 305
Ford, H., 97
Ford, J. K., 221
Ford, R., 7

Forde, C., 133
Forth, J., 19, 252, 266, 273, 274, 280, 284, 287, 326, 330
Fortson, D., 189
Foster, P., 13, 420
Foucault M., 26
Fox, A., 23, 298, 310
Fox, S., 338, 350
Fraccaroli, F., 135
Francis, H., 37, 191, 217, 224, 313, 372
Francis, R., 163
Francoeur, V., 358
Franco-Santos, M., 238, 242, 249
Freedland, M., 283
Freedman, S., 242
Freeman, R. B., 306
Freeth, S., 19, 252, 266
Frege, C. M., 312
Freiberger, G., 191
French, J. Jr., 26
French, J. R. P., 187
French, M. T., 341
Frenkel, M., 403
Frenkel, S., 68
Frese, M., 218
Frick, K., 371
Friedan, B., 42
Friedberg, B. A., 121
Friedman, A., 21, 106
Friedman, G., 130
Fröbel, P., 102
Frost, A., 277
Frost, C., 104, 220
Frost, D., 326
Froud, J., 281
Fry, H., 226
Frye, K., 160
Fryer, M., 308
Fullwood, C., 184
Furnham, A., 162, 298
Furrer, M., 398
Furtmueller, E., 182
Fyfe, J., 121

G

Gabris, G. T., 186
Gabzdylova, B., 360
Gager, S., 154
Gagliardi, D., 325, 326
Galasso, N., 254
Galin, A., 150
Galinsky, A., 179
Gall, G., 274, 280, 282, 418–420, 424
Gallacher, G., 111
Gallagher, P., 121
Gallagher, V. C., 133
Gallie, D., 90, 93
Gallo, A., 334, 350
Gamble, J., 380, 383, 394, 401
Garavan, T. N., 29, 51, 67, 190, 208, 230, 369
Gardiner, J., 133
Gardner, M. T., 354
Gardner, T., 72, 73
Garengo, P., 176
Garvey, R., 179, 225
Geary, J. F., 108
Gebeloff, R., 22, 31, 32
Gedikli, C., 91
Gegenfurtner, A., 219
Gennard, J., 301
Gentle, S., 181
Georgiou, S., 329
Gerhart, B., 9, 73, 193, 233–235, 239, 241, 242, 262
Gershgorn, D., 153
Geva, A., 398
Gheyoh Ndzi, E., 96
Ghoshal, S., 380–383, 388, 390–391, 395, 402
Ghosheh, N., 410
Gibb, S., 211
Gibbons, P., 162
Giddens, A., 299, 317
Gilbert, C., 20, 40, 61
Gilbert, M. -H., 333
Giles, A., 346
Giles, C., 2, 242
Giles, L., 103
Giles, W. F., 180
Gillborn, D., 124
Gillinsky, A., 80
Gilman, M., 312
Ginsberg, B., 10
Giupponi, G., 96
Glaister, A., 133
Glasbeek, H., 346
Gloster, R., 357, 362, 367
Glowinkowski, S. P., 334
Glozer, S., 28, 96
Godard, J., 6, 9, 10, 12, 13, 27, 42, 107, 112, 266
Goff, M., 151
Gold, J., xxvi, 3, 13, 14, 29, 44, 176, 178, 194, 204, 206, 214, 224–226, 230, 233, 354
Goldberg, A., 136
Goldstein, I. L., 219
Goldstiein, H. W., 155
Goleman, D., 161
Gollan, P. J., 316, 372
Gomes, A., 66
Gomez-Mejia, L. R., 238, 242, 249
Gond, J. P., 356
Gong, Y., 188, 241
Gonsalves, L., 108
Gonzales, P. M., 162
Goodfellow, I., 226
Goodhart, D., 414, 424
Goods, C., 363
Goodstein, E. S., 59
Gopal, P., 126
Gopinath, M., 55
Gordon, M., 199
Gordon, T. J., 218
Gore, E., 134
Gorz, A., 85, 95
Gospel, H. F., 8, 272
Gottfredson, R. K., 192
Gould, A., 106
Gould, E., 162
Gourlay, S., 208
Govindarajulu, N., 199, 369
Graeber, D., 7, 11, 68, 85, 105, 112, 243, 250, 257, 258, 409, 412, 422
Graham, T., 302
Grant, K., 103
Grant, M., 204
Grant, R. M., 54
Granter, E., 10, 11, 24, 29, 51, 85, 111, 130, 131, 226, 233, 259, 379, 380, 402
Gravelle, H., 184
Green, C., 96
Green, F., 90, 93
Green, N., 281
Greene, A., 128
Greenhouse, S., 276, 277
Greenwood, I., 133
Greenwood, M., 28
Greenwood, R. G., 173
Greller, M., 24
Grey, C., 97, 100
Griffith, E., 303
Grimshaw, D., 13, 25, 204, 240
Grint, K., 85, 90, 95, 96, 106
Groeneveld, S., 128
Grossman, E. B., 23
Grossman, R., 218
Grote, R., 189
Gruber, H., 219
Grugulis, I., 227
Guba, E. G., 223
Guerci, M., 42, 360, 368
Guest, D. E., 4, 5, 9, 22, 24, 26, 27, 33, 35, 37, 40, 41, 64, 65, 68, 71, 72, 74, 76, 266, 273, 275, 293, 306, 307, 330, 346
Guggenheim, K., 178
Gül, H., 341
Gulati, R., 108

Gully, S. M., 155, 367
Gumbrell-McCormick R., 278
Gunderson, M., 265, 266
Gunnigle, P., 175, 389
Gupta, N., 71, 242
Gurney, M, 133
Guthrie, J. P., 61, 70, 71, 133, 238–240, 258

H

Habraken, M., 23
Hackman, J. R., 41, 95, 100
Hadden, T., 420
Haddock-Millar, J., 199
Hadikin, R., 335
Hafeez, S., 358
Hager, E., 277
Hager, P., 212, 213
Haigh, M., 360
Ha-Joon Chang, 5
Hajro, A., 353, 356, 373, 421
Halberstam, Y., 253
Haldane, A. G., 253
Hale, D. Jr., 66, 74
Hales, C. P., 75
Haligah, R. D., 122
Hall, D. T., 205
Hall, M., 270
Hall, P. A., 21, 67, 272, 386, 399, 415
Hall, R., 10
Hallock, K. F., 124
Hamel, G., 205
Hammer, M., 102, 103, 176
Hampden-Turner, C., 68, 393
Hampton, P., 371
Han, J. H., 40
Han, K., 367
Hanappi-Egger, E., 126, 136
Hancké, B., 398, 399, 407
Hancock, A., 168
Handley, J., 305
Handlogten, G., 238
Hannif, Z., 394
Hanson, M., 59
Harcourt, M., 348, 419
Hardy, C., 25, 208, 399
Harland, C., 132
Harley, B., 12, 107
Harmel-Law, A., 3
Harmon, E., 398
Harney, B., 70
Harrabin, R., 356, 357
Harris, H., 396, 403
Harris, L. C., 366
Harris, M. M., 162
Harrison, P., 226, 230
Harrison, R., 211
Hart, S. M., 59, 325
Harte, G., 366
Hartle, F., 174
Hartmann, L., 397
Harvey, D., 7, 58, 401
Harvey, F., 271, 272, 353
Harvey, G., 64, 130, 131
Harvey, R., 209, 210
Harzing, A. W., 383
Haslam, C. S., 281
Hastings, R., 32
Haunschild, A., 42, 346
Hauser, C., 246
Hayes, J., 365
Hayter, S., 283, 289, 291
Healy, C., 176, 177
Healy, G., 256, 384
Heath, A., 165
Hebson G., 131
Heenan, D. A., 390
Heery, E., 273–275, 291, 317
Heffernan, M., 70
Heinbokel, T., 218
Heller, F., 310
Helms Mills, J., 194, 205, 209, 211, 214, 227
Hemlin, S., 194
Henderson, R., 58, 258, 417, 421, 424
Hendry, C., 7, 20, 381
Hendy, J., 287
Henkens, K., 157, 327
Henry, A. E., 51
Henseke, G., 93, 111
Heraty, N., 389
Herman, S., 364
Hern, A., 128
Herod, A., 86
Herriot, P., 156
Hershcovis, M. S., 301, 303
Hertz, N., 5, 402
Hertzberg, F., 100
Hesketh, A., 115
Hettinger, L. J., 285
Heyes, J., 421
Hickson, D. J., 208
Higgins, C., 131
Higgins, M. D., 422
Higgins, T., 357, 362, 367
Higgs, M., 161
Hill, C. W., 51, 161, 381, 383
Hillage, J., 270
Hinsliff, G., 136
Hirch, A., 338
Hirsh, W., 217, 224
Hirst, P., 380
Hochschild, A. R., 24, 86, 183
Hockerts, K., 356
Hodder, A., 303
Hodgkinson, G. P., 213
Hoel, H., 337, 338
Hofmann, R., 124
Hofmans, J., 237, 238
Hofstede, G., 338
Hogarth, T., 220
Høgedahl, L., 282
Holbeche, L., 103, 112
Holden, E., 355
Holden, R., 29
Holder, G., 9, 63
Holgado, M., 80
Holgersson, C., 227
Holl, P., 191
Holmes, J., 315
Holton, E. F., 221
Holtz, B. C., 162
Holzer, M., 196, 200
Hondeghem, A., 40, 68
Honeyball, S., 26
Hood, C., 181
Hoogvelt, A., 75
Hook, A., 359, 401
Hook, C., 305
Hoover, K. F., 128
Hoque, K., 21, 126
Horne, R., 135
Horner, M. T., 190
Horsey, B. L., 354
Hossain, I., 111
Houghton, D. J., 303
Houghton, E., 52, 366, 377, 421
Houlihan, M., 20, 41
House, K., 162
Howe, C. L., 191
Howell, S., 209
Howlett, E., 96, 185, 186
Hsu, C.-H., 158
Huang, C. W., 360, 365
Huang, C. Y., 343
Huang, J. C., 188
Huang, S., 368
Huang, Y-H., 285
Huber, A., 320
Hudson, A., 420
Hughes, E., 5
Hughes, J., 105, 145
Hughes, P., 204
Humphrey, S. E., 91, 100
Hung, S. T., 360, 365
Hunger, J. D., 57
Hunt, V., 134
Hunter, J. E., 160, 161
Hunter, S. T., 54
Hurst, B., 370
Hurst, D., 319

Huselid, M. A., 9, 61, 70, 71, 74, 135
Hutchinson, N. L., 207
Hutchinson, S., 9, 38, 39, 64, 68, 70, 74, 85
Hutchison, A., 107
Hutton, W., 13, 68, 76, 247, 253, 257, 283, 286, 402, 410, 411
Huws, U., 131
Huynh, T. L. D., 368
Hyatt, D., 186
Hyde, P., 10, 11, 51
Hyman, R., 7, 9, 26, 32, 236, 266, 267, 270, 272, 275, 278, 282–284, 297, 386
Hynie, M., 159

I

Iacovou, C. L., 23
Iain, H., 346
Iavicoli, S., 325, 326
Ichniowski, C., 9, 70, 71, 195
Iddekinge, C. H., 158
Ihrke, D. M., 186
Iles, P., 29, 116, 117, 166, 193
Ilgen, D. R., 189
Inanc, H., 90
Inder, K., 341
Inesi, M. E., 196
Ineson, E. M., 128
Inman, P., 242, 412
Ipek, G., 256
Iqbal, N., 240
Irish, B., 190
Isichei, M., 394, 407
Iskasson, K., 24, 74
Iszatt-White, M., 382, 389, 407

J

Jabbour, C. J. C., 353, 357, 358, 365, 368
Jack, G., 28
Jackson, J. H., 116
Jackson, S. E., 62, 63, 71, 237, 364
Jacobs, E., 253
Jacobs, J. V., 285
Jacobs, K., 188, 194
Jacobs, M., 305
Jacoby, S. M., 76, 272, 399
Jaeger, C. C., 354
Jaeger, J., 176
Jaffee, D., 107
Jäger, J., 354
James, C., 341
Jang, B., 64
Janssens, M., 41
Jansz, J., 341
Järvensivu, P., 115
Jarvis, H., 135
Jarvis, P., 218
Javanmardian, K., 226
Jayanetti, C., 4
Jeffries, S., 285
Jehn, K. A., 299, 316
Jenkins, M., 186, 354
Jenkins, S., 254
Jensen, C., 281, 282
Jensen, K., 159
Jensen, S., 384
Jeremy Aroles, J., 10, 11, 51
Jewson, N., 126
Jin, X., 124
Johal, S., 281
John, O. P., 161, 188
Johnny, M., 159
Johns, G., 88, 92, 94, 95
Johnson, C., 204
Johnson, E. M., 265, 274
Johnson, M., 402, 411, 415, 420
Johnson, P., 2, 135, 402, 411, 415, 420
Johnston, D., 204
Johnston, K. A., 370
Johnstone, S., 306, 373
Johson, R., 158
Jolly, J., 226
Jones, D. A., 101, 157, 343
Jones, G. R., 51, 381, 383
Jones, J., 397
Jones, M. T., 360
Jones, O., 22, 124, 252, 285, 295, 409
Jones, S. E., 167
Joo, H., 192
Jordan, A., 186
Jørgensen, H. H., 367
Joshi, G., 368
Joyce, R., 2
Judd, C. M., 124
Judge, T. A., 156
Jukic, N., 187
Junco, E., 158
Jung-A, S., 402
Junquera, B., 123

K

Kabst, R., 37, 108, 157
Kalev, A., 118
Kalfa, S., 316
Kalleberg, A., 38, 64, 74, 98
Kannan-Narasimhan, R., 133
Kantor, J., 32
Kaplan, R. S., 71
Kapoor, C., 129
Kapos, V., 354
Karasek, R. A., 100
Karlsson, J. C., 209, 297
Karp, P., 319
Karsten, L., 129
Kasemir, B., 354
Kashi, K., 336
Katou, A., 187
Katz, H. C., 70
Katzenbach, J. R., 93
Kaufman, B. E., 12, 13, 19, 41, 63, 64, 75, 76
Kay, E., 187
Kaye, L., 76
Kay-Lambkin, F., 341
Keefe, J. H., 70
Keegan, A., 23, 37, 217
Keenoy, T., 9, 10, 41
Keep, E., 206
Keeping, L. M., 26, 189
Kehoe, R. R., 40, 135, 143
Keith, M., 301, 302
Kelan, E.K., 127, 130, 131, 135, 136
Keller, L. J., 176
Kelliher, C., 30, 51, 67, 130
Kellner, A., 38, 98, 106
Kelloway, E. K., 337
Kelly, A., 290
Kelly, B. J., 341
Kelly, G. J., 354
Kelly, J. E., 75, 265, 301, 373
Keltner, D., 188
Kennedy, S., 354
Kerr, C., 11
Kersley, B., 273
Kessler, I., 238, 240, 252, 258
Kessler, S., 130
Khan, I., 358
Khodyakov, D., 343
Kim, A., 367
Kim, H., 241
Kim, J., 225, 309
Kim, M. S., 155, 196, 200
Kim, S., 75, 93, 266, 267, 281, 385
Kimball, W., 162
King, Z., 37, 330
Kinnie, N., 9, 38, 39, 64, 68, 70, 74, 85, 367
Kira, M., 353, 355, 362
Kirkpatrick, D. L., 222, 223
Kirkpatrick, I., 120, 250
Kirton, G., 128
Kispal-Vitai, Z., 135
Kissack, H., 37, 68
Klass, B. S., 304
Klein, N., 287, 346
Klerck, G., 266, 317
Klikauer, T., 10, 51
Klimberg, R., 189

Klinge, I., 128
Kluger, A. N., 186, 188, 193
Knight, L., 132
Knights, A., 42
Knights, D., 11, 42
Knowles, M., 214, 218
Kochan, T. A., 9, 70, 71, 195
Kolb, D. A., 214
Kollewe, J., 285
Kollinger, I., 397
König, C. J., 143, 156
Kotter, J., 56, 365
Koveshnikov, A., 27
Kowalski, T. H., 326
Krahé, B., 155
Kraiger, K., 210–212, 217–220, 223
Kramar, R., 403
Kramer, A., 111
Kramer, K.Z., 111
Kramer, M. R., 355
Krashinsky Robertson, S., 31, 32
Krause, K., 143
Krippner G. R., 75
Kristensen, P., 299
Kroft, K., 253
Krugman, P., 4–6, 412
Krumm, S., 162
Kuhl, J. S., 158
Kuhn, K. M., 237
Kultalahti, S., 154
Kumar, N., 285
Kumar, R.V., 132, 419
Kumhof, M., 286
Kundu, S. K., 132
Kuruvilla, S., 133, 266, 385
Kuvass, B., 262
Kwong, E., 348
Kwun, S. K., 190
Kynighou, A., 310

L

La Prade, A., 125
Labrador, J., 160
Lähde, V., 115
Lamboglia, R., 158
Lammers, V., 160
Lamming, R., 132
Lane, A. B., 370
Lane, H., 208
Lange, R., 162
Langer, M., 143
Lapavitsas, C., 286
Lash, S., 130
Latham, G. P., 163, 174, 180, 184, 192, 234, 251
Latimer, J., 10
Laud, R. L., 192
Lave, J., 208
Lavell, J., 175
Lawford-Smith, H., 246, 247
Lawler, E. E., 61, 180, 239, 251
Lawrence, F., 393
Lawrence, M., 120, 250
Lawrence, P. R., 8, 19, 20, 31, 34, 35, 64, 67, 74, 92, 103, 205, 235, 310, 330
Lawrence, T. B., 22
Lawson, M., 254
Lazarova, M., 387, 396
Lazear, E. P., 70, 252
Leach, D. J., 90
Leat, M., 293
Lebarz, C., 286
Leckie, N., 72
Lee, C. H., 289, 291
Lee, D., 160
Lee, M. Y., 104
Lefkowitz, J., 187
Legge, K., xxvi, 5, 8–10, 20, 31, 35, 41, 64, 76, 96, 108, 193
Lei, D., 209
Leiter, M. P., 334
Leonard, N. H., 238
Leonard-Barton, D., 65
Leopold, J., 129
Lepak, D. P., 66, 74, 105
Lepore, L., 158
Lesch, M. F., 285
Leslie, J., 252
Leslie, L. M., 123
Lester, S., 126
Leung, K., 189
Levashina, J., 164
Levin, K., 401
Levine, D., 9, 71, 195
Levine, L., 413
Levinson, R., 276, 277
Levitt, T., 393
Levy, P. E., 189
Lewin, D., 29, 372
Lewin, T. J., 341
Lewis, D., 339, 379
Li, W., 277
Lian, H., 26
Liang, L. H., 26
Lievens, F., 155, 162, 163, 186
Liff, S., 127, 128
Ligthart, P., 407
Lim, V. S., 173, 175, 186, 187
Lin, C. A., 162
Lin, C. Y., 360, 365
Lin, M. H., 226
Lin, S. H., 360, 365
Linares, A.C., 354
Lincoln, Y. S., 223
Lindop, E., 240, 245, 251, 257, 259
Linehan, M., 379, 387, 388, 390, 391, 394, 397, 403
Linhares, C., 135, 402, 411, 415, 420
Linnerud, K., 355
Little, P., 203
Littler, C. R., 97, 98, 106, 272
Lituchy, T., 403
Liu, H., 343
Liu, J., 403
Liu, S. S., 158, 366
Liu, W., 61
Liverman, D., 59
Livingstone, D. W., 207
Lleras-Muney, A., 384
Lloyd-Williams, H., 133
Lo Piano, S., 206
Loan-Clarke, J., 120
Locke, E. A., 180, 238
Logan, J., 268
Loh, J., 354
Lombardo, M. M., 190
London, M., 174
Long, R. D., 262
Long, R. J., 234, 235, 237, 239
Longoni, A., 360, 368
Looise, J. K., 316
Lopez-Cabrales, A., 80
Lorange, P., 61
Lorenz, C., 10, 12
Loretto, W., 326
Lovelace, J. B., 54
Lovell, R., 167
Lowe, K. B., 51, 66, 191, 373
Loya, M. A., 210
Lozano, R., 360
Lub, X. D., 27
Luchak, A., 273
Lukaszewski, K. M., 158
Lund, H, L., 353, 371, 373
Lupton, B., 126
Luxemburg, R., 380
Luzzini, D., 360, 368
Lynch, D., 145
Lynch, K., 421

M

Mabey, C., 75, 196, 310, 397
Mabon, L., 359
MacCurtain, S., 61
MacDonald, G., 336
MacDuffie, J. P., 309
Machin, S., 96
Macintosh, R., 51
MacIver, R., 162
MacKenzie, R., 133
Macky, K., 104

MacLean, D., 51
Maclean, J. C., 341
MacLeod, D., 104
Macwhirter, I., 2
Maes, J. D., 111
Mahajan, A., 395
Mahapatra, N. R., 226
Mahboubi, P., 410
Mahmood, M., 153
Mahoney, J., 168
Main, P., 190
Maitra, S., 382
Majava, A., 115
Makin, K., 286
Makortoff, K., 189
Malhotra, B., 60
Malik, K., 165
Mankin, D., 51, 67
Mann, G., 148
Manokha, I., 285
Manyika, J., 101
Marchand, S., 195
Marchington, M., 37, 41, 71, 102, 131, 293, 301, 306, 307, 309, 310, 371, 372
Marginson, P., 309, 312, 382, 389
Maria, C., 182, 183
Marin, S., 275
Markey, R., 371, 375
Marks, A., 283, 284, 291
Marler, J. H., 23
Marowits, R., 419
Marr, B., 344
Marshall, G., 297
Marshall, L., 318
Martin, A., 77, 227, 258, 267, 273, 281, 286, 373
Martin, D. L., 181
Martin, I., 58, 258
Martin, J. N., 313, 315
Martin, P., 164
Martin, R., 191
Martiskainen, M., 359, 401
Martocchio, J. J., 233
Mas, A., 253
Maslach, C., 334
Maslow, A., 238
Mason, D., 126
Mason, P., 226, 259
Mathiason, N., 411
Mathieson, S., 339
Mathis, R. L., 116
Matten, D., 26, 28, 96
Matthews, B., 355, 356
Matthews, C., 355
Mattke, S., 343
Maurice, M., 67, 393
Maxwell, G. A., 103, 154
May, D. R., 369
Mayer, R. C., 186
Mayerhofer, H., 397
Mayo, E., 331
Mayrhofer, W., 385, 397, 399
Mazzanti, M., 371
McAdams, R. H., 276, 277
McAfee, A., 101
McAllister, K., 226
McBain, D, 276, 360
McCann, L., 10, 11, 51
McCarthy, A. M., 190
McCarthy, J. E., 155
McCauley, C. D., 224
McClean, B., 176
McCormack, N., 334, 335
McCulloch, M., 156
McCurdy, C., 252
McDonald, P., 302, 336
McDonnell, A., 175
McFarland, A., 222
McGrath-Champ, S., 86
McGregor, D., 85, 100
McGregor-Smith, R., 124
McGuire C., 105
McGuire, D., 37, 68, 369
McGuire, L., 338
McHugh, D., 42, 76, 90, 100, 106, 237, 312
McIntosh, M., 365
McIvor, J., 371, 375
McKay, S., 274
McKersie, R. B., 300
McKinlay, A., 196, 283, 284, 291
McKinstry, B., 190
McLaughlin, H., 133
McLean, G. N., 203
McLoughlin, I., 58
McMahan, G. C., 63
McMullen, K., 72
McMurray, S., 348
McNeill, I. M., 60
McShane, S. L., 243
McVicar, D., 96
Meadows, D. H., 353
Meadows, D. L., 353
Meager, N., 129
Meardi, G., 309, 382
Medros, A., 222
Megginson, D., 179, 225
Megra, M., 124
Mehrotra, K., 176
Mehta, K. S., 328
Meijerink, J., 23
Meinert, D., 194
Meira, J., 135, 402, 411, 415, 420
Mello, J. A., 121
Mencl, J., 126
Mensah, D. K. D., 122
Mensi-Klarbach, H., 139, 384
Mercer, 175
Merceron, A., 162
Merideth, R., 59
Mertens, J., 125
Meshoulam, I., 8, 62, 67, 74, 75
Messacar, D., 253
Messenger, J., 410
Messersmith, J. G., 105
Messick Svare, G., 341
Metzer, J., 162
Meyer, E., 32
Meyer, H. H., 187
Mezirow, J., 214
Michelitsch-Riedl, G., 397
Michie, J., 9
Miliband, E., 13, 420
Milkovich, G., 239, 242
Milkovich, G. T., 241
Miller, B. I., 75, 76
Miller, L., 161, 341
Miller, S. J., 208
Milliman, J., 181, 369
Mills, A. J., 42
Mills, C. W., 3
Mills J. M., 42
Millward, N., 274, 280, 284, 287, 311
Milmo, D., 269, 270
Minbaeva, D., 67
Mind, 332, 333
Miner-Rubino, K., 301
Mintzberg, H., 9, 51, 54, 57
Miranda, L., 135, 402, 411, 415, 420
Miremadi, M., 101
Mislove, A., 23
Mitchum, A., 162
Mittelstadt, B. D., 207
Mol, A. P. J., 359
Mole, K., 104, 220
Molineux, J., 336
Moliterno, T. P., 66, 74
Molitor, D., 343
Moloney, M., 319
Monbiot, G., 52, 132, 402
Mone, E. M., 174, 178
Monfreda, C., 354
Monro, S., 136
Montabon, F., 371
Montgomery, J., 337
Moon, J., 26
Moore, K., 379
Moore, O., 409
Moore, S., 346
Moore, T., 125

Mooser, C., 218
Morgan, G., 299
Morgan, J., 226
Morgeson, F. P., 88, 91, 92, 94, 95, 100
Morley, M., 389
Morouney, K., 166
Morrell, K. M., 120, 241
Morris, J., 380, 383, 401
Morris, S., 67, 68, 394
Morrison, R., 26
Morrow, A., 422
Morrow, P. C., 371
Morton, A., 60
Morton, G., 269
Moslein, K., 104, 220
Mossholder, K. W., 22
Motraghi, N., 270
Mount, M. K., 151
Mousteri, V., 335
Moyer-Lee, J., 26
Muchinsky, P. M., 243
Mueller, R., 403
Muir, H., 165
Mujtaba, D. F., 226
Müller-Camen, M., 199, 353, 355–357, 370
Mumford, A., 194, 224
Munby, H., 207
Munro, M., 165
Munro-Fraser, J., 147
Murlis, H., 242
Murphy, D., 61
Murphy, J., 26, 165, 183
Murphy, K. R., 181, 195, 389
Murray, J., 87
Mwita, J. I., 176
Myers, N., 354

N

Nadler, L., 211
Nadler, Z., 211
Nagano, S. M., 358
Nagata, A., 194
Nagendra, A., 116
Naima McCloskey, H., 117
Nair, A., 55
Najjar, F., 325
Nakatsu, R. T., 23
Nakayama, T. K., 313, 315
Nankervis, A., 23, 157, 175
Napier, N., 386, 388, 390, 391, 403
Nash, D., 284
Nason, S., 181
Naumann, L. P., 161
Neal-Barnett, A., 331, 332
Neate, R., 252, 254
Neathey, F., 161
Nebeker, D. M., 100
Neely, A., 104, 220
Neely, B. H., 54
Nelson, D. L., 334
Nelson, K. A, 28
Neus, A., 367
Newham, T., 133
Newman, J., 239, 242
Newton, S. K., 80
Newton, T. J., 366
Ng, K. Y., 163, 254
Nga Thi Thuy Ho, 397
Nguyen, J., 343
Nguyen, S., 128
Nicastro, D., 285
Nichol, L., 226, 230
Nicholls, H., 162
Nickson, D., 24, 86, 149
Nielsen, K., 262
Nienaber, A. M., 154
Nijholt, J. J., 103
Nir, D., 188, 193
Niven, K., 176, 177
Nixon, D., 86
Noe, R. A., 203, 217, 219
Nolan, H., 276, 277
Nolan, P., 421
Nonaka, I., 183, 194
Noon, M., 126, 241
Nord, W., 25, 399
Norgaard, R., 354
Norlander, P., 133
Northouse, P. G., 39
Norton, C., 161
Norton, D. P., 71
Norton, T. A., 70, 177, 353, 355, 364, 365
Notelaers, G., 338
Nowacka, K., 257
Nyberg, A. J., 66, 74
Nyfield, G., 162

O

Obinger, H., 4
O'Brien, M., 371
Occean, P., 23
O'Connor, S., 291
O'Driscoll, M., 335
Ogbonnaya, C., 262
Ogden, S., 103
Ogden, S. M., 154
Oh, I. S., 152, 160–162
Olazaran, M., 102
Oldham, G. R., 41, 95, 100
Oliveira, O. J., 366
Oliver, B., 204
Oliver, N., 101
Olson, B., 105
Olson, C., 9, 71, 195
O'Moore M., 338
O'Neil, C., 148
Ones, D. S., 354, 358
Ongaro, E., 52, 54, 66
Onita, L., 275
Op de Beeck, S., 40, 68
Ordóñez, L., 179
O'Riordan, T., 373
Örtenblad, A., 209
Ortlieb, R., 126, 136
O'Shea, N., 332
Otondo, R., 158
Ouchi, W., 95, 193
Owen, J., 252, 420
Owen, L., 367
Oxenbridge, S., 273
Oz, Y. L., 382
Özkazanç-Pan, B., 256, 258
Öztürk, B. M., 157, 166, 256
Öztürk, M. B., 128

P

Paauwe, J., 71, 75, 76, 127, 128, 393
Paci, P., 191
Paik, Y., 399
Paillé, P., 357, 358, 367
Paisley, V., 399
Pak, M., 398
Palmer, S., 185, 240, 245, 251, 257, 259, 342
Pandey, A., 133
Parent, B., 328
Park, B., 124
Park, J., 133
Parker, B., 115, 121
Parker, G., 168
Parker, M., 11–13, 29, 51
Parker, O., 369
Parker, S. K., 88, 90–92, 94, 95, 100, 160
Parkes, L., 155
Parkin, B., 398
Parry, E., 182
Parsa, S., 370
Parsons, D., 122
Partington, R., 19, 131, 134, 241, 310, 338, 345, 414
Parveen, N., 165
Parzefall, M.-R., 338
Pass, S., 115
Patel, P. C., 105
Patel, R., 60
Patterson, M., 9
Pattisson P., 403
Payne, C., 401

Payne, S. C., 190
Peccei, R., 22, 71, 72
Peck, J., 267
Pedersen, T., 132
Pedler, M., 179, 208
Peeters, H., 162
Peiperl, M. A., 190
Pellegrini, M., 328
Pelopida, B., 161
Pendleton, A., 239, 262
Peng, S., 196, 200
Pennycook, M., 129
Pepermans, R., 237
Pepper, M. B., 128
Pereira, M.d.M., 257
Perett, R., 133
Perkins, D., 341
Perkins Gilman, C., 42
Perlmutter, H. V., 388, 390
Perraudin, F., 269
Perron, G. M., 368, 371
Pesando, L. M., 257
Peters, B. G., 196
Peters, P., 30
Peters, T., 5
Petrone, F., 380
Pettifor, A., 420
Pettigrew, A., 7
Pfeffer, J., 9, 64, 65, 205, 251, 313
Pham, D. D. T., 367
Pham, N. T., 368
Philips, L., 368
Phillips, B., 62
Phillips, J. M., 155, 367
Phillips, N., 22
Phipps, D., 159
Piasentin, K. A., 157
Pichler, P., 315
Pichler, S., 393
Pickard, J., 13, 420
Pickett, K. E., 203, 253, 326
Pierce, J. L., 186
Piketty, T., 12, 247, 253, 257, 286
Piketty T., 258
Pil, F., 309
Pinheiro, C. R., 366
Pinkos Cobb, E., 339
Piore, M. J., 108, 240
Pisano, G., 66
Pisano, S., 158
Pi-Shen Seet, 397
Pittis, M., 158
Pitts, J., 190
Platt, L., 2
Plaut, V. C., 126, 127
Plenderleith, J., 335
Plows, A., 133
Ployhart, R. E., 156, 162, 166
Poell, R. F., 31, 76, 211
Pohler, D., 273
Pollitt, D., 162, 165
Ponak, A., 265, 266, 272
Pondy, L. R., 297
Pope, J., 164
Poppleton, A., 42
Porter, C. O., 254
Porter, M. E., 8, 57, 237, 355
Poutsma, E., 407
Povah, N., 178
Powell, J. H., 75
Prahalad, C. K., 382
Prasad, A., 42
Prasad, P., 42
Pratt, A. C., 135
Preece, D., 193
Prennushi, G., 70
Preskill, H., 223
Preston, J., 209
Price, B., 178
Price, R., 281
Probert, B., 227
Proença, M. T., 160
Psacharopoulos, G., 115
Pucik, V., 394
Pugh, D., 399
Pulignano, V., 108
Pullen, A., 256, 258
Pun, K. F., 181
Purcell, J., xxvi, 9, 13, 20, 29, 31, 38, 39, 41, 58, 61–65, 67, 68, 70, 72, 74–76, 85, 90, 135, 176, 181, 195, 219, 238, 252, 258, 272, 273, 307, 356, 366, 367, 380, 389
Pursell, E. D., 163
Pusic, E., 310
Pye, M., 348
Pyrch, T., 194, 205, 209, 211, 214, 227

Q

Qi, G., 368
Quick, A., 77, 227, 258, 267, 273, 281, 286
Quigley, M., 161
Quinn Mills, D., 8, 19, 20, 31, 34, 35, 64, 67, 74, 92, 103, 205, 235, 310, 330
Quintanilla, J., 382, 389

R

Rabe, B. G., 373
Raffensperger, J. F., 360
Rafferty, A., 3
Rafferty, J., 135
Rahman, H. A., 196
Rai, A., 337
Raineri, N., 357, 358
Rainey, H. G., 136
Rainnie, A., 86
Ramsay, H., 107
Ramstad, P. M., 356
Ramus, C. A., 364, 368, 369
Rancière, R., 286
Randell, G., 192
Randers, J, 354
Randers, J., 353
Rands, G. P., 369
Rani, U., 398
Rankin, J., 271, 272
Rankin, N., 161
Ransom, J., 302
Rantanen, J., 325, 326
Rappaport, J., 276, 277
Rarick, C. A., 184
Rasche, A., 55
Rashidi, R., 178
Rasmussen, E., 282
Rauter, R., 360
Raven, B., 26
Rawnsley, A., 2
Raya, R. P., 338
Raymond, P. C., 368, 371
Rayner, C., 216, 339
Rayner, G., 28
Rayton, B., 9, 38, 39, 64, 68, 70, 74, 85
Rea, A., 206
Rebelo, T. M., 66
Reckard, E. S., 176
Redman C. L., 354
Redman, T., 353, 357
Reed, J., 398, 402
Rees, T., 315
Reeves, D., 184
Reeves, M., 75
Regencia, T., 325
Reguly, E., 59
Reif, J., 343
Reilly, B., 191
Reilly, P., 116
Remery, C., 157
Remler, D. K., 73
Ren, F., 334
Ren, S., 364
Renwick, D. W. S., 353, 357
Reynolds, M., 14, 224
Rhodes, C., 130
Richardson, D., 136
Richardson, M., 64, 65, 105, 107
Richardson-Owen, A., 329
Richbell, S., 235, 419
Richter, D. A., 286
Rigg, C., 211

Riggio, R. E., 51, 66, 191, 373
Rijamampianina, R., 170
Riley Chapman, C., 328
Risberg, A., 139
Ritzer, G., 92, 106
Rivero Morales, P. A., 254
Robertson, C., 22, 31, 32
Robertson, I. T., 162
Robertson, J. L., xvi, 364, 421
Robinson, A., 262
Roca-Puig, V., 72, 73
Rocco, T. S., 31, 76
Rockstuhl, T., 163
Rodger, A., 147
Roepe, L., 150
Roethlisberger, F. J., 95
Rogaly, B., 392
Roland, M., 184
Rollinson, D., 305
Romei, V., 2
Roos, D., 101
Roper, C., 280
Roper, I., 370
Roscoe, S., 365
Rose, M., 105, 166
Roser, D., 401
Ross, I., 336
Roth, G. L., 31, 76
Roth, P. L., 158
Rothwell, S., 120, 135
Roubini, N., 412
Rouiller, J. Z., 219
Roulin, N., 156
Roumpi, D., 65, 66
Rousseau, D. M., 24, 159
Rowley, C., 399, 400
Roy, D. F., 268
Roy, E., 87, 268
Rubery, J., 13, 25, 204, 240, 402, 411, 415, 420
Rubin, J., 3, 6, 7, 13, 253, 258, 278, 412, 414, 421
Ruehl, M., 398
Rupp, D. E., 367
Rushe, D., 2, 64, 145
Russell, S. V., 60, 365
Ryan, A. M., 155, 156, 166
Ryan, J. C., 190
Ryan, P., 7, 282
Ryan, R. M., 238
Ryan, S., 386

S

Saari, L. M., 163
Saavedra, R., 190
Sabel, C., 108
Saccani, C., 328
Sadler-Smith, E., 213
Saeed, B. B., 358
Sagie, A., 316
Said, E., 403
Saifulina, N., 360
Saint-Onge, H., 208
Salaman, G., 51, 58, 75, 97, 98, 106, 166, 181, 196, 397
Salas, E., 210–212, 217–220, 223
Salgado, J., 161
Salin, D., 338
Samandari, H., 226
Sanchiz, M., 162
Sanders, K., 68
Sanders, M. G., 181
Sangha, J., 382
Santos, F. C. A., 358, 368
Santos, J. F., 339
Sanyal, C., 199
Saul, J. R., 382
Saunders, M. N. K., 27, 133
Savage, M., 165, 252, 316
Saville, P., 154
Sawchuk, P., 194, 205, 207, 209, 211, 214, 227
Sayer, A., 73
Sayim, K. Z., 393, 395
Sayre, G. M., 296
Scarbrough, H., 108
Schafer, M., 157
Schalk, R., 27
Schapper, J., 28
Schatsky, D., 285
Schaufeli, W. B., 334
Schedlitzki, D., 382, 389, 407
Schein, E. H., 58
Schein, P., 58
Schein, V. E., 403
Schied, F., 209
Schilling, M. A., 51, 381, 383
Schippers, J., 157
Schleiffenbaum, E., 218
Schlosberg, D., 355
Schmidt, F. L., 152, 160–162
Schmitt, C., 4
Schnabel, C., 277
Schneider, B., 155
Schneider, R., 127
Schneider, S., 155
Scholarios, D., 107, 126, 136
Scholl, R. W., 238
Schollaert, E., 162
Schön, D. A., 208
Schonberger, R. T., 101
Schroeder, A. N., 190
Schroeder, R. G., 70
Schuler, R. S., 62, 63, 71, 237, 385, 387, 388, 390
Schultz, T. W., 66, 74, 203, 205
Schulz, N. B., 354
Schwab, K., 226
Schwanitz, V. J., 355
Schweitzer, M., 179
Schwellnus, C., 398
Scott, B., 181, 195
Scott, J., 297
Scott, N., 250
Scott-Jackson, W., 133
Scullen, S. E., 151
Scullian, H., 379, 391
Scullion, H., 29, 379, 387, 388, 390, 391, 394, 397
Scully, J., 9
Searle, R. H., 143, 147, 154, 166
Seierstad, C., 256, 384
Seigne E., 338
Seijts, G., 224
Sels, L., 20, 40, 61
Selznick, P., 65
Semkina, A., 91
Senge, P., 208
Sengupta, S., 294
Sennett, R., 25, 26, 133, 283, 296
Severinsson, E., 161
Sewell, G., 106
Shackley, S., 359
Shaewitz, D., 124
Shaffer, J. A., 152, 160–162
Shah, I., 364
Shahbaz, M., 368
Shahjehan, A., 364
Shan Ee, M, 336
Shani, A. B., 353, 355, 362
Shao, R., 367
Sharma, S., 185, 186
Shaw, J. D., 242
Shaw, K., 70
Sheehan, M. J., 9, 338
Sheehy-Skeffington, J., 337, 338
Sheth, J., 21, 238, 310
Shier, V., 343
Shin, N.-Y., 158
Shortall, J., 305, 306
Shrivastava, P., 367
Shuen, A., 66
Siddique, H., 256
Siebert, W., 312
Sikka, P., 233, 420
Sikora, D. M., 225
Silberman, M. S., 398
Sillup, G. P., 189
Silva, E. A., 80
Simmons, B. L., 334

Simmons, L. A., 285
Simms, M., 273–275, 291
Simon, H. A., 154
Sinclair A, 11, 14
Sinclair, C., 332
Sindelar, J. L., 341
Singer, A. E., 55
Singh, P., 234, 235, 237, 239
Sisodia, R., 21, 238, 310
Sisson, K., 272, 273
Sisto, L., 276, 360
Skarlicki, D. P., 367
Skeggs, B., 10
Skehan, J., 341
Skidelsky, R., 6
Skinner, B. F., 213
Skinner, D., 310
Slocum, J., 209
Slocum, J. W. Jr., 180, 209
Sloman, M., 216
Smale, A., 385
Smircich, L., 42
Smith, A., 422
Smith, C., 5
Smith, D. B., 155
Smith, D. K., 93
Smith, K. J., 93, 146
Smith M., 247, 338, 409
Smith, M. L., 225
Smith, P., 269
Smith-Jentsch, K., 210–212, 217–220, 223
Smyth, J., 124
Snell, S. A., 62, 67, 68
Sobolewska, M., 7
Sohal, A., 358, 370
Sojo, V., 246, 247
Solomon, N., 207, 301
Solon, O., 296
Sommerlad, H., 126, 136
Song, Z., 344
Sønju Le Bruyn Goldeng, E., 384
Soper, K., 51
Soraker, J. H., 207
Sorge, A., 67, 393
Soskice, D., 21, 67, 272, 386, 399, 415
Soto, C. J., 161
Souissi, A., 344, 345
Sovacool, B. K., 359, 401
Soylu, S., 337, 338
Sparrow, P., 29, 396, 403
Spector, B., 8, 19, 20, 31, 34, 35, 64, 67, 74, 92, 103, 205, 235, 310, 330
Spence, L., 28, 96
Spencer, B., 207
Spicer, A., 32
Squires, G., 29–31
Srivastava, S. B., 136, 147
Stabile, M., 335
Stafford, K., 149
Stage, H, 399
Stahl, G. K., 353, 356, 373, 387, 390, 421
Stainer, G., 115
Stallworth, L. E., 338
Standing, G., 129
Stanton, P., 23, 175
Starik, M., 369
Starkey, K., 11, 196
Statista, 5, 379
Stead, J., 133
Štebe, J., 30
Steffens, M. C., 128
Steiner R., 372
Stephan, M., 23
Stevenson, P., 333
Stewart, H., 63
Stewart, J., 29, 211
Stewart, P., 64, 65, 105, 107, 108
Steyaert, C., 41
St-Hilaire, F., 333
Stiglitz, J. E., 51, 247, 253, 286
Stine, C., 178
Stine-Cheyne, K. J., 190
Stohl, C., 317
Stojanovic, A., 413
Stokes, L., 19, 252, 266, 326, 330
Stokes, P., 179, 225
Stone, D., 158
Stone, J., 268
Stoner, J. S., 133
Storey, J., 8, 9, 20, 31, 35, 36, 41, 62, 75, 76, 108, 196, 236, 274, 397, 422
Stouten, J., 338
Strauss, D., 13, 168, 413, 420
Strauss, G., 9, 71, 195, 307, 310, 317
Streitfeld, D., 32
Stuart, M., 120, 133, 250
Subramanian, N., 365
Sullivan, R., 279, 284
Summers, L., 182
Sumner, J., 59, 353, 373
Surface, E. A., 181
Susskind, D., 6, 209
Suutari, V., 395, 397
Sveningsson, S., 181
Swart, J., 9, 38, 39, 64, 68, 70, 74, 85
Sweezy, P. A., 42
Swinburne, P., 189
Syed, J., 403

T

Taddeo, M., 207
Tahir, H., 158
Tahir, M., 358
Tahvanainen, M., 395
Tailby, S., 64, 65, 105, 107
Takeuchi, H., 183
Tamkin, P., 217
Tan, J.-S., 315
Taneja, A., 254
Tang, G., 364
Tang, W. H., 149
Tannenbaum, S., 210–212, 217–220, 223
Tapper, J., 233
Taras, D., 265, 266, 310, 312
Tarique, I., 396
Taris, D., 277
Tarr, T., 246, 247
Tatli, A., 128, 256
Tatum, B. C., 100
Taylor, F. W., 95
Taylor, H., 227
Taylor, M. S., 189
Taylor, P. J., 106, 186, 341
Taylor, S., 175, 179, 180, 192, 211, 212, 386, 388, 390, 391, 403
Teece, D. J., 66
Tekleab, A., 219, 223
Terry, M., 266
Tett, G., 12
Teviño, L. K., 28
Tews, M. J., 149, 203, 217, 219
Thangaraj, V., 55
Tharenou, P., 185, 272
Thelen, K., 204
Theorell, T., 100
Thiemann, P., 218
Thomas, D., 286
Thomas, G., 191
Thomas, K. M., 126, 127
Thompson, E. P., 24
Thompson, I., 173, 194, 195, 328
Thompson, L. F., 181
Thompson, M., 272
Thompson, P., 6, 9, 10, 12, 42, 51, 76, 77, 90, 100, 106, 173, 194, 195, 200, 237, 281, 283, 284, 291, 298, 301, 312, 380, 402, 421
Thomson, M., 329
Thornhill, A., 27, 133
Thornthwaite, L., 303
Thornton, M. A., 367
Thorpe, R., 176, 194, 224
Throckmorton, N., 286
Tichy, N. M., 8, 19, 20, 33, 54, 61, 74, 143, 173, 175, 192, 393
Tipu, S. A., 190
Tjosvold, D., 297, 299
Tobin, S., 135
Todorova, M., 218
Toivanen, T., 115

Tolson, H., 225
Ton, Z., 21
Topcic, M., 108
Topham, G., 265
Toplis, J., 161, 162
Torbiörn, I., 394
Torka, N., 316
Torres, R., 135
Torrington, D., 19
Toubøl, J., 281, 282
Townley, B., 9, 10, 24, 41, 162, 165, 166, 196, 346, 391
Townsend, K., 38, 98, 106
Toyama, R., 194
Toynbee, P., 133
Travis, A., 31
Treanor, J., 54
Tregaskis, O., 309, 382, 389
Trehan, K., 179, 211
Trevor, C., 243
Trompenaars, F., 68, 393
Trumbo, D., 163
Tsaur, S. H., 149
Tucker, E., 125, 126
Tung, R., 394, 403
Tuomivaara, S., 132
Turban, D., 156
Turel, O., 111
Turnbull, P., 64, 266
Turner, P., 115, 116
Turner, T., 175
Turnheim, B., 401
Tynan, R. J., 341
Tyrrell, J., 167
Tyson, S., 158, 330
Tziner, A., 181, 195

U

Uen, J. F., 158
Uggerslev, K. L., 157
Uhl-Bien, M., 51, 66, 191, 373
Ulrich, D., 30, 37, 62, 68, 217, 236
Ulrich, L., 163
Ulrich, M., 37, 68
Üngan, M. C., 329
Unsworth, K. L., 60
Upchurch, M., 64, 65, 105, 107
Usher, R., 227
Usman, M., 368

V

Vachhani, S. J., 130
Vadén, T., 115
Valenti, A., 325, 326
Valentine, S. R., 116
Valle-Cabrera, R., 80
van Buren, H. J., 356
van Busum, K. R., 343
van Dam, K., 155, 218
van De Voorde, K., 71
van de Werfhorst, H., 277
van den Brink, M., 227
van den Broeck, A., 94, 338
van den Broek, D., 106
van den Heuvel, S., 23, 69
van der Heijden, B. I., 30
van der Locht, M., 218
van der Velden, L. F. J., 122
van der Werff, L., 126, 127
van der Zwan, N., 51, 75
van deVoorde, K., 22
van Dyne, L., 163, 316
van Ewijk, A. R., 129
van Fossen, K., 80
van Greuningen, M., 122
van Hoye, G., 157
van., Lanivich, S. E., 158
van Ryzin, G. G., 73
van Scotter, J., 158
van Veldhoven, M., 22
van Wanrooy, B., 19, 175, 252, 266
van Woerkom, M., 316
Vanajan, A., 327
Vance, C., 399
Vandaele, K., 278, 279, 281, 282, 284
VandeWalle, D., 180, 189
Varma, A., 187, 191, 393
Varoufakis, Y., 271
Varul, M. Z., 389
Vaughn, E. D., 159
Vaughn, O., 91
Vázquez Pimentel, D.A., 254
Veermans, K., 219
Vega, R. F., 80
Veiel, R., 398
Veldman, A., 253
Venkataramakrishnan, S., 26, 168
Ventresca, M. J., 385
Verbeke A., 380
Verburg, R. M., 64, 65
Vercelli, S., 359
Verma, A., 273, 310, 312
Verma, S. K., 285
Versnel, J., 207
Vesala, H., 132
Vidican, S., 162
Viitala, R., 154
Villanova, P., 187
Vince, R., 224
Visser, J., 277, 279, 282, 283
Vladimirova, D., 80
Volini, E., 23
Vo-Thanh, T., 368
Vroom, V. H., 180, 238
Vygotsky, L. S., 214

W

Wach, B. A., 37
Wacher, S., 207
Wackernagel, M., 354
Waddington, J., 277, 282, 283
Wagner, J., 312
Wagner, M., 370
Wagner, R. F., 163
Wahl, A., 227
Wailes, N., 386
Wajcman, J., 31, 166, 334
Wakabayashi, D., 303
Wakeley, T., 75
Wakeling, A., 5, 53
Walker, D., 133
Walker, H., 132, 276, 360
Walker, J. T., 213
Walker, S., 276, 360
Wall, T. D., 13, 88, 90, 258
Wallace, D., 208
Wallace, H. M. L., 128
Walsh, B., 23
Walters, D., 371
Walters, M., 116
Walton, R. E., 8, 19, 20, 31, 34, 35, 41, 64, 67, 71, 74, 92, 103, 205, 235, 300, 310, 330
Wang, C. H., 118, 191, 257
Wang, G., 203
Wang, L., 317
Wang, M., 188
Wang, S., 317
Wanous, J. P, 157
Warhurst, C., 24, 42, 86, 105, 149
Waring, J., 9
Waring, M., 207
Warr, P., 29, 41, 71
Warren, D. I., 26
Warren, T., 133
Warsi, S. W., 158
Wassenaar, B., 107
Waterfield, S., 215, 216
Waterman, R. H., 5
Waterson, J., 126
Watson, D., 91
Watson, S., 3
Watson, T. J., 9–11, 13, 21, 42, 76, 236
Watt, P., 225, 233
Watts, R., 233
Weale, S., 93
Webb, B., 277
Webb, S., 277
Weber, E., 320
Weber, M., 195

Webster, F., 194
Wedderburn, L., 304
Wedekind, S., 342
Wedlock, J., 159
Wehner, M. C., 37
Wei, X., 312
Weick, K. E., 5
Weiss, T. B., 174
Welbourne, T. M., 236, 243
Weldy, T. G., 111
Wells, D., 101
Wells, G., 214
Wells, J., 334
Weng, M. -W., 158
Wenger, E., 208
Wesson, M. J., 254
West, M. A., 9, 70, 71, 296
Western, S., 193
Wexley, K. N., 184
Wheelen, T. L., 57
White, A. S., 181
White, C., 414
White, L. A., 190
White, R., 208
Whiteman, G., 354
Whitfield, D., 175, 196
Whitfield, K., 240, 266
Whitford, C. M., 174
Whiting, K., 88, 272
Whitmore, J., 225
Whitston, C., 277, 282
Wholey, J. S., 182
Wickens, P., 273
Widder, G., 128
Wiek, A., 354
Wierling, A., 355
Wiggers, J., 341
Wiggins, J. S., 161
Wilder, D.A., 262
Wilding, P., 310
Wilk, S., 165
Wilkinson, A. J., 120, 293, 294, 301, 306, 307, 309, 316, 353, 357, 372
Wilkinson, B., 101, 380, 383, 401
Wilkinson, R., 203, 253
Wilkinson, R. G., 203, 253, 326
Willcocks, L., 106
Willets, J. L., 285
Williams, A., 354
Williams, K. J., 130, 162, 281
Williams, M., 271
Williams, S., 173, 224
Willmott, H., 10, 13, 42, 102, 107, 204, 420
Wilmers, N., 106
Wilpert, B., 310
Wilson, C., 23
Wilson, D. C., 208
Wilson, H. J., 101, 102
Wilson, J. P., 193
Wilson, R. A., 116–118, 220
Winstanley, D., 64
Witherspoon, P. D., 313
Withycombe, L., 354
Wittman, M., 208
Wolfe, D., 21, 238, 310
Wollstonecraft, M., 42
Womack, J., 101
Wong, A. S., 297
Wood, A. R., 167
Wood, G. T., 21, 135, 235, 402, 411, 415, 419, 420
Wood, P., 265, 296
Wood, S. J., 19, 72, 90, 135, 235, 252, 265, 266, 419
Woodall, J., 64, 133, 227
Woodhams, C., 126
Woods, S. A., 148, 296
Wright, A., 71, 125
Wright, C. F., 371
Wright, L., 369
Wright, M., 107, 281
Wright, P., xxvi, 20, 29, 31, 41, 72, 73, 195, 356, 380
Wright, P. M., 62, 63, 135, 236
Wright, T., 256
Wu, P., 189
Wylie, B., 77, 258, 275, 286, 287, 416, 417, 419, 421
Wynen, J., 40, 68
Wynne, B., 130

X

Xenikou, A, 298
Xie, X., 368

Y

Yaghootkar, H., 167
Yamkovenko, 221
Yang, C.-M., 158
Yang, J., 74
Yang, M., 80
Yap, M. H. T., 128
Yayar, M., 399
Yeo, R., 214
Yin, M., 124
York, R., 398
Yorke, M., 10, 11, 204
Youndt, M. A., 62
Young, W., 60
Younger, J., 37, 68
Yu, G., 133
Yuriev, A., 358

Z

Zacher, H., 70, 177, 353, 355, 364, 365
Zapf, D., 100, 337
Zedeck, S., 154
Zemaityte, G., 253
Zenger, T., 253
Zeytinoglu, I. U., 335
Zhang, J., 334
Zhang, Y., 393
Zheng, C., 336
Zhu, C. J, 166, 181
Zhu, Q., 368
Zibarras, L., 362
Zielinski, D., 69
Zilahy, G., 368
Zilic, I., 187
Zink, K. J., 368
Zito, A. R., 359
Zottoli, M. A., 157
Zu, Y., 316
Zuboff, S., 409
Zutshi, A., 358, 370
Zweig, D. I., 163
Zycher, B., 353

SUBJECT INDEX

A

ability tests, 160, 161
affective engagement, 307
age, of neoliberalism, 3–7
agreeableness, 161
all-seeing eye, 295
the 'American Dream,' 4
Americanised HRM model, 282
analytical preference, 213
andragogy, 218
Anglo-American model, 403
'Anglo-American' model, 2
appraisal, 189–191
appraiser bias, 189
arbitration, 300
artificial intelligence (AI), 226
  reskilling workers for, 221–222
assessment centres (ACs), 164–165
attention-deficit hyperactivity disorder (ADHD), 340
autonomy, 100

B

Bandit Capitalism, 415
Basil Café, 261–262
Bath model, 38–40, 68
behavioural learning, 212
behavioural observation scales (BOSs), 184
behaviour-anchored rating scales (BARSs), 184
best-fit model, 64, 75
'best-practice' model, 64–65
Black, Asian and minority ethnic (BAME), 332, 412, 414
BlueGreen Alliance, 363
boundaryless structure, 93
Britain
  collective agreement in, 284
  labour relations in, 266
  trade unions in, 275
Britain's economy, 2
British Trades Union Congress, 356
British welfarism, 4
Bruntland Commission, 353
business case, 328, 345
business ethics, 28
business-level strategy, 57
business process re-engineering (BPR), 102–103, 106–107

C

'call-centre discourse,' 106
capitalism, 24
carbon emissions, 359, 363
Carillion, 415–417, 419, 421
causality, 73
causal model, 73
centralisation, 91
centralised and structured coaching approach, 225
chain of command, 91
Chartered Institute of Personnel and Development (CIPD), 11, 293, 294
Climate Change (Scotland) Act 2009, 360, 362
coaching, 225
cognitive learning, 212, 213
collective agreement, 284
collective bargaining, 269, 276, 279
  collective agreement, 284
  cumulative decline, 287
  definition, 283
  procedural rules, 283
  structure, 283–284
  substantive rules, 283
The Combination Acts of 1799 and 1800, 269
commitment behaviour, 237
community of practice (CoP), 208
competencies and leadership, 224
competency-based interviewing, 163
competency-oriented appraisal, 183
Conciliation and Arbitration Service (ACAS), 300
confessional device, 166
conflict, 236
conflict management, 299
  causes of, 298–299
  disciplinary procedure, 300
  employee relations, 296
  grievance procedure, 300
  negotiation, 299–300
  types of, 297–298
conscientiousness, 161
Conservative government's Wages Act 1986, 5
contested terrain, 357
continuous reinforcement, 213
control approach, 181
convergence/divergence debate, 399–400
cooperation, 236
coordinated market economies (CMEs), 272, 414, 415, 419
coronavirus, *see* Covid-19
Coronavirus Job Retention Scheme (CJRS), 233
corporate environmental performance, 354
corporate-level strategy, 57
  corporate social responsibility, 61
  ethics, 60–61
  ideology, 57–58
  sustainable strategy, 58–60
corporate manslaughter, 329
corporate-oriented sustainability, 373

corporate social responsibility (CSR), 60–61, 353, 354
corporate strategy, for reward, 237
corrective discipline, 304
country-of-origin effects, 389
Covid-19, 108, 178, 181, 317, 330
  catastrophic effects of, 209
  crisis, 6, 13, 28
  and earnings of working-class women, 256
  economic crisis, 2020-21, 412
  effects on workers' pay, 233
  ground zero, 348
  health-care professionals, 353
  HRMS, 409–411
  4IR technologies, 226
  job lose, 403
  learning and development during, 212
  mental health work, 332
  MNCs, 397
  multiple workplace injustices, 409
  pandemic, 3, 203, 252, 254, 257, 261, 265, 290
  pay issues in Britain during, 247
  post-pandemic capitalism, 411–414
  surveillance software demand, 295
  swab robot, 216
  trade unions during, 278
  work-integrated learning during, 204
  work-life balance during, 185
  work-related stress, 342
criterion-related validity, 151
critical discourse analysis (CDA), 195, 196
critical feedback, 188
critical HRM, 22
critical management studies (CMS), 9–10
critiquing employee relations, 316–317
critiquing international HRM, 401–403
critiquing workplace health, 345–355
curriculum vitae (CV), 160
customer-oriented approach, to performance management, 176

D

data-driven algorithms, 148
Data Mining, 226
Davos Agenda, 254
Decent Work, 326
Deep Learning, 226
demand forecasting
  qualitative approaches, 120
  quantitative approaches, 118–120
Denmark, robotics industry, 215–216
departmentalisation, 91
de-recognition strategy, 274
'destandardization of work,' 130
detriment, sexual harassment, 301
de-unionisation phenomenon, 195
development, 211
'developmental humanism' model, 193, 206
dialogic communication, 313
differentiation strategy, 57
digital cage, 295–296
digital technologies, 23
disciplinary procedure, 295
disconnected capitalism thesis (DCT), 77, 286
distributive bargaining, 300
distributive justice, 287
distributive negotiation, 300
divergence debate, 399–400
diversity, 126–127
Diversity at DigitalArt*, 46–47
diversity management at Kore, 229–230
Donovan Commission, 283
downsizing, 133
downward communication, 313
dual-role syndrome, workplace stress, 335–336
dyadic conflict, 299
dyadic relations and feedback, 191
dysfunctional conflict, 299
dysfunctional organisational behaviour, 337

E

education, 211
effective voice, 418
efficient market theory, 412
egalitarian pay structure, 258
embedding sustainability strategies, 360–362
emotional stability, 161
Employee Assistance Programme (EAP), 334, 344
employee communication, 313–315
employee discipline, 304–305
employee discord, 297
employee engagement, 306–307, 371
employee flow analysis, 120–121
employee genetic testing, 327–328
employee grievance, sexual harassment, 301–303
employee involvement and participation (EIP), 306
employee pay types, 239
employee relations (ER), 293
  case study, 319–320
  communication, 313–315
  conflict management, 296–300
  critiquing employee relations, 316–317
  employee discipline, 304–305
  employee grievance, 301–303
  employee voice, 306–312
  important dimensions of, 294
  nature of, 293–295
employee silence, 316
employees' pro-environmental behaviours, 357–358, 364
employee voice (EV), 294
  employee engagement, 307
  employee involvement and participation, 306
  environmental sustainability, 371–382

European Works Councils, 312
forms of, 309
framework, 308
indirect, 311
Joint Consultative Committees, 311–312
theory of, 310–311
employers, working hours, 129–130
employment contract features, 236
employment relations, 385–386
Employment Relations Act 1999, 289
employment relationship, characteristics of, 266
environmental analysis, 54
environmental justice, 355
environmental leadership, 364–365
performance management and sustainability, 369
pro-environmental behaviours, 369
pro-environmental learning, 368
recruitment and selection, 367–368
reframing organisational culture, 365–366
environmental management system (EMS), 354, 358, 370
environmental sustainability
case study, 375–377
critiquing corporate, 373
embedding sustainability strategies, 360–362
employee voice, 371–382
leadership and culture, 364–366
low-carbon workplace, 366–369
management systems, 358
nature of, 353–356
workers' pro-environmental behaviours, 357–358
The Equality Act 2010, 197
equality, defined, 254
equal opportunities legislation, 126
ethics, 60–61
eudemonic well-being, 326
European Agency for Safety and Health at Work, 328
European Green Deal, 271
European Parliament, 301
European Trade Union Confederation, 356
European Union, 389
European Works Councils (EWCs), 312
exchange, 20
executive burnout, 335
experiential learning, 210, 214
external equity, *see* pay levels
external flexibility, 93
extravagant CEO pay phenomenon, 258
extrinsic reward, 233, 237, 238
extrinsic rewards, 192
extroversion, 161

F

Fair Work Framework (FWF), 104–105, 417–419, 421
fast-food work, 106
feedback, 100
acceptance, 186
critical, 188
dyadic relations and, 191
employee reactions to, 186
response to, 186
feedforward approach, 188
financialisation, 75
Financial Services Modernization Act of 1999, 412
financial technology (FinTech) sector, 138
First Industrial Revolution, 344
first-line managers (FLMs), 74
flat structures, 92
flexibility
downsizing, 133
'neo-villeiny,' 130
non-standard contracts, 129–130
outsourcing and offshoring, 132–133
precarity, 131
teleworking, 131–132
types of, 129
zero-hours contracts, 131
flexibility paradox, 108
focused goal-centred development, 205
focus strategy, 57
foreign direct investment (FDI), 380
formal and informal employee relations, 294
formal appraisal, 187, 188
formal communication process, 294
formal conflict, 297
formalisation, 91
formal job evaluation, *see* job evaluation
Fourth Industrial Revolution, 226
functional conflict, 299
functional-level strategy, 57
future performance, 193
planning, 179
Futures and Foresight Learning (FFL), 218

G

gender pay gap (GPG), 255–258
General Data Protection Regulations, 295
genetic discrimination, 328
Gini coefficient, 254
Global Britain, 413
global business strategy
integration-responsiveness grid, 382–383
overview, 380–382
global capitalism, economic crises, 411
global financial crisis (GFC), 6, 411
global integration, 389
globalisation, 5, 67
critical scholars, 380
and HRM model, 400
and typologies, 379–380
work and employment, 398
global pandemic crisis (GPC), 402
global strategy, 383

Good Health and Well-being, 326
G&Q Manufacturing, 110–111
Gramm-Leach-Bliley Act, 412
grapevine, 294, 295
green economic recovery, 271
green economy, 366
Green HRM (GHRM), 357
Greening People: Human Resources and Environmental Management, 366
Green New Deal, 372
grievance, 300
gross domestic product (GDP), 412
ground zero, 348

H

Harvard model, 34–35
Health and Safety at Work (HASAW) Act 1974, 8, 329
Health and Safety Executive, 334
healthier workplace, 330
Health & Safety Act (HASAWA) 1974, 229
health, safety and wellness
  case study, 348–349
  critiquing workplace, 345–355
  economic considerations, 328–329
  ethical considerations, 330–331
  legal considerations, 329–330
  psychological considerations, 330
hedonic well-being, 326
hierarchy, 91
high-performance work systems (HPWS), 103–105, 309, 367, 418
'horizontal integration,' 61
host country national (HCN), 390, 394
hot-stove rule metaphor, 304
human capital theory (HCT), 65
human resource black box, 313
human resource development (HRD), definition, 211
human resource management (HRM)
  ascendency, 8–10
  Bath model, 38–40
  case study, 46–47
  crisis, 12–14
  definition, 19, 20
  effect of critique, 43–44
  employment relationship, 23–27
  global, 384–385
  globalisation and, 400
  goals, 31
  Harvard model, 34–35
  international, 385
  management education, 10–12
  Michigan model, 33
  pre-Covid-19, 409–411
  role of critique, 41–42
  scope, 29–31
  Storey model, 35–37
  theorising, 32–33
  transformative changes to, 14
  Ulrich Human Resource Business Partner model, 37
human resource (HR) strategy, 272
Human Rights Act 1998, 270

I

Iceland, equal pay law, 246–247
identification of vision, 54
IHRM, *see* international human resource management
IKAN, 405–407
income inequality, 4, 252–255
indeterminacy, 21
indeterminate, 24
India Trades Union Act in 1926, 289
individual-based pay, 239
individualism and performance management, 194–195
industrial democracy, 309
industrial relations, 265, 293
Industrial Revolution, 345
Industry 4.0, 344–345
informal appraisal, 187
informal communication, 294
informal conflict, 297
information and communications technology (ICT), 380
in-group relationships, 191
inputs-oriented appraisal, 183
insightful learning, 213
Institute of Personnel Management (IPM), 19
institutionalising process, 208
integrating process, 208
integration-responsiveness grid, 382–383
integrative bargaining, 300
integrative negotiation, 300
intellectual engagement, 307
interactionism, 298
internal equity, *see* job evaluation
internal flexibility, 93
International Energy Agency (IEA), 198
international human resource management (IHRM), 379, 401–403
  case study, 405–407
  implementation, 400
  internalisation, 400
  orientation, global business strategies, 390
  SIHRM, 386–387
International Labour Organization (ILO), 19, 268, 269, 339, 356
international management, 379
International Monetary Fund, 301
international performance appraisal, 396–397
international staff, 394
internet, 158–159
interpreting process, 208
interventionism *vs.* voluntarism, in L&D, 204, 205
intrinsic reward, 192, 233, 237
intuiting process, 208
intuitive preference, 213
inventories, 161
iron cage, 296

J

Japanese-based MNCs, 309
Japanese management work design, 100–101
'Japanization,' 5
job analysis, 239

job-based reward, 238
job description format, 146
job design, *see* work and job design
job enlargement, 99
job enrichment, 99
job evaluation, 239
  characteristics of, 243
  compensable factors, selection of, 243
  definition, 242
  goal of, 242
  job analysis data gathering, 243
  point method, 244–245
  pricing the pay structure, 245
  ranking method, 244
job rotation, 98, 99
joint consultation, 311
Joint Consultative Committees (JCC), 311–312, 376
Joint Consultative Councils, 309
judgements, and diversity, 188–189

K

'Keynesian economic doctrine,' 4
knowing-how, 207–208
knowing-that, 207–208
kob-related stress, 334
Kolb's learning model, 214, 215
Køre, 138–139, 168–169
'Kurzarbeit', 2

L

Labour administration, 4, 5
labour law, 269
labour market, 240
'labour market flexibility,' 6
labour process theory (LPT), 10
labour relations (LR), 388
  case study, 289–291
  critiquing, 286–287
  definition, 267
  HRM and, 272–275
  legal context of, 269–270
  nature of, 265–267
  technological advancements impact, 285
  see also trade unions
Lagan Meadows Care Home, 348–349
latent skills gap, 220
leader-member exchange (LMX) theory, 191
leadership development (LD), 223–225
leadership, role in performance management systems, 181
learning
  adult, 210–215
  and competitive advantage, 205–206
  in dealing racism issues, 209–210
  definition of, 210–211
  theories, 212–214
  workplace, 207–209
learning and development (L&D), 203
  case study, 229–230
  definition of, 211–212
  evaluation of, 222–223
  interventionist strategy, 204, 205
  voluntarist/market-oriented approach, 204, 205
learning and development needs analysis (LDNA)
  individual analysis, 220–221
  job analysis, 220
  organisational analysis, 219
  outcome of, 219
learning organisation (LO), 208, 317
learning-oriented practice, 194
learning transfer model, 221
Learning Transfer System Inventory, 221
leitmotiv, 20
lesbian, gay, bisexual and transgender (LGBTQ+), 332, 337
LGBT+, 399
LGBTQ, 305–306
liberal market economies (LMEs), 415
line managers (LMs), 68, 70
line managers' support activities, 219
Long-Term Incentive Plans (LTIPs), 419
low-carbon economy, 359
low-carbon workplace (LCW), 353
  sustainable HRM, 366–367
low-carbon work system (LCWS), 367
low-cost leadership strategy, 57

M

machine-learning (ML) algorithms, 206–207, 226
management by objective (MBO) approach, 173–174
managerial ideology, 272
'managerialist plates,' 11
Mandla Winery*, 79–80
Markov modelling, 121
Maternity Benefit Act in 1961, 290
matrix structures, 92
maximising shareholder value (MSV), 75, 227, 258, 266–267, 281, 286, 385, 416, 418, 419
'McJob,' 106
means and outcomes, 193
mediation, 300
membership behaviour, 237
mental health of Black employees, 331–332
mental health work, 332–334
mentorship, benefits during crisis, 185–186
meritocratic extremism, 257
methyl isocyanate (MIC), 346
MeToo movement, 302
Michigan model, 33
misbehaviour in organisations, 298
monetary reward, 233
motivation to learn, 218
multidomestic strategy, 383
multinational corporations (MNCs), 67, 309, 379
  employment relations, 385–386
  global integration effects, 389
  HR strategy, 393

IHRM orientation, global business strategies, 390
international learning and development, 395–396
international performance appraisal, 396–397
international reward, 394–395
international staffing, 394
national culture and institutional structures, 395
national infrastructure, 381
repatriation, 397
multisource feedback (MSF), 190–191
Munro-Fraser's fivefold grading system, 147

N

nanodegree, 222
national living wage, 241–242
National Minimum Wage, 349, 420
natural justice, 305
the Neo-Human Relations School, 98
neoliberalism, 3–7, 58
neoliberal market economies (NMEs), 272
neoliberal theories, 241
Netflix, 31–32
network society, 380
The New Labour government's Employment Relations Act 1999, 269
new managerialism, 176
new pay agenda, 251–252
new public management (NPM), 51, 175, 176
Nikefication, 93, 267, 385, 402
non-monetary reward, 233
non-union strategy, 273
non-verbal communication, 314
Nordic-based MNCs, 309

O

occupational health and safety (OHS), 325, 330
well-being in Industry 4.0, 344–345
offshoring, 132–133
One Million Climate Jobs, 363
online activism, 303
online appraisal systems, 181–182
online testing, 162
openness to experience, 161
organic and emergent coaching approach, 225
organisational behaviour (OB), 299
organisational culture and practice, 240
organisational learning (OL), 208–209
organisational pay, 239
organisational structure, 90
organisation communication, 314–315
Organisation for Economic Cooperation and Development (OECD), 414
organised conflict, 300
organizational conflict, 297
out-group relationships, 191
outsourcing, 132–133

P

paradox, 107
parent country nationals (PCNs), 379, 394
Paris Accord, 421
pay dispersion, 247
pay-for-environmental performance (PEP), 376
pay gap, 253
pay inequality, 254
pay levels
construction of, 248, 249
determination, 248
payment system, 234
pay structures, 247, 249
pay transparency, 253
peer-appraisal, 190
Pension Regulator, 421
Pensions Act, 415, 421
perceived psychological contracts (PPCs), 27
perceptual biases, 150–151
performance
appraisal instruments for assessment, 183–184
defined, 182–183
future, 193
judgements and feedback, 186–194
and rewards, 192–193
as transformation process, 193
performance appraisal (PA), 180, 239, 369, 396–397
process, 173
as a strategic control, 192
performance appraisal system (PAS), 175, 199, 376
performance-based pay, 239
performance behaviour, 237
performance management (PM)
activities, 177
antecedents of, 181
case study, 198–199
criticism, 195–196
customer-oriented approach to, 176
cycle, 177–180
definitions of, 174
monitor performance, 179
nature and development of, 173–176
objective setting in, 176–177
performance appraisal, 180
planning future performance, 179
review performance plan, 177–179
theories guiding, 179, 180
in the US, 194–195
performance management systems (PMSs), 175, 369
and organisational performance, 188
in SMEs, 176
performance-related pay (PRP), 192, 193, 196, 252, 258
personality testing, 161
personal protection equipment (PPE), 6, 330, 348
pluralist perspective, organisations, 298

point method, 244–245
police unions, 276–277
police *vs.* corporate brutality, 209
Pollution Prevention Pays (3Ps) programme, 368
post-Brexit labour markets, 413
post-Covid-19 world, 225
post-L&D intervention stage, 218–219
post-pandemic capitalism, 411–414
post-pandemic labour markets, future of, 259
Post Traumatic Stress Disorder (PTSD), 348
power, 26
pre-Covid-19, 221
predictive validity, *see* criterion-related validity
pre-L&D intervention stage, 218
Preserving Employee Wellness Programs Act, 328
procedural rules, 283
process conflict, 299
product market, 24, 240
pro-environmental behaviours, 369
pro-environmental learning, 368
profit-related pay, 252
proportionality test, 270
pseudo-employee voice, 316
psychological contract, 26, 27
psychological contract breach (PCB), 27
psychologisation, 13
psychometric paradigm, 154–155
psychometric testing, 160–162
public health crisis (PHC), 411
public limited companies (PLCs), 384
public sector organisations, 51, 52

Q

Qatar, domestic workers in, 122–123
quadruple bottom line, 354

R

race to the bottom, 420
radical perspective, organisations, 298
RailCo, 375–377
Rajah Apparel Co., 289–291
ranking method, 244
reaganomics, 6
recruitment
  advertising, 157
  agencies, 157
  algorithmic bias, 153
  assessment, 159
  assessment centres, 164–165
  attraction, 153–154
  case study, 168–169
  channels, 156–157
  critiquing, 165–166
  curriculum vitae, 160
  employee referrals, 157
  internet and social networking, 158–159
  internships, 159
  interviews, 163–164
  person organisation fit paradigm, 155–156
  psychometric paradigm, 154–155
  psychometric testing, 160–162
  reliability, 151
  selection criteria, 146–148
  selection process, 143–144
  situational judgement tests, 162–163
  social process paradigm, 156
  validity, 151–152
  workforce action plan, 144, 146
Reimagining Capitalism, 422
reliability, 151
rentier capitalists, 6
repatriation, 397
'resource-based' model, 65–66
resource-based view (RBV), 65–66, 76
results-oriented appraisal, 183
review performance plan, 177–179
rewards, 234
  behavioural outcomes of, 234
  case study, 261–262
  choices, 238–239
  competitiveness, 240
  corporate strategy, 237
  definition, 233, 234
  and employment relationship, 236
  evaluation, 240–241
  extrinsic, 233, 237
  for front-line workers, 235
  individualisation of, 237
  intrinsic, 233, 237
  monetary, 233
  motivation theories, 237
  non-monetary, 233
  objectives, 237
  and performance, 192–193
  strategic framework for, 236–241
  techniques, 239
rightsizing, *see* downsizing
right to manage, 312
Rodger's seven-point plan, 147
Royal Bank of Canada (RBC), 357
rules of origin, 413

S

'Search of Excellence,' 5
self-appraisal, 189–190
self-directed learning, 214
self-efficacy, 218
self-negative feedback, 188
self-positive feedback, 188
sexual acts, 305
sexual harassment
  employee grievance, 301–303
  European code on, 302
sick building syndrome (SBS), 332, 341–342
SIHRM, *see* strategic international human resource management
Singapore, hospitality industry, 149–150
Single Europe Act of 1986, 381
situational judgement tests (SJT), 162–163
skills, defined, 220
skills inventories, 120

skill variety, 100
small and medium-sized enterprises (SMEs), 21, 328
SMART objectives, 179
smart rewards, 252
  see also rewards
social engagement, 307
social exchange theory (SET), 20
social learning, 214
social networking, 158–159
social process paradigm, 156
social stigma, 333
social triangle, 26
sociological imagination, 3
Solas Resort and Spa, 319–320
span of control, 91
state influences, 24
statutory sick pay (SSP), 420
Storey model, 35–37
strategic formulation, 54
strategic HRM, 61
  'best-fit' model, 64
  'best-practice' model, 64–65
  critical perspectives and analysis, 75–77
  defined, 62–63
  line managers, 68, 70
  and organisational dynamics, 67–68
  performance, 70–75
  'resource-based' model, 65–66
  theorising, 63
strategic international human resource management (SIHRM), 385, 389
  endogenous factors, 389
  ethnocentric orientation, 390–391
  exogenous factors, 389
  geocentric orientation, 391
  IHRM, 386–387
  integrated framework, 388
  orientation, 390
  polycentric orientation, 391
  pressures and goals, 390
  regiocentric orientation, 391
strategic learning and development
  delivery stage, 218
  discourse, 227
  human capital theory, 203–205
  learning and competitive advantage, 205–206
  post-L&D intervention stage, 218–219
  pre-L&D intervention stage, 218
  process, 216–219
strategic management
  definitions, 51
  five-step process, 54
  hierarchy of strategy, 56
  three traditional poles, 52
strategic rewards
  critiquing, 258–259
  framework, 236–241 (*see also* rewards)
strategy implementation, 54
substantive rules, 283
succession planning, 121
surveillance capitalism, 409
sustainability science, 354
sustainable Covid-19 recovery, 271–272
Sustainable Development Goals (SDGs), 326
sustainable health and safety, 325–327
sustainable strategy, 58–60
Sustaintricity Co., 198–199
systematic training cycle (STC) model, 216

T

tacit knowledge, 194, 208
tailored middle ground coaching approach, 225
task conflict, 299
task identity, 100
task significance, 100
team pay, 239
teleworking, 131–132
third-country national (TCN), 394
third-party intervention, 295, 296, 300
360-degree appraisal, 190, 191
total-quality-control (TQC) system, 195
Trades Union Congress (TUC), 372
Trade Union Act 2016, 269
Trade Union and Labour Relations (Consolidation) Act, 269, 289
trade union law, 298
trade unions, 363
  in action, 278
  in Britain, 275
  decline in unionisation, 281–282
  membership, 278–281
  reasons for joining, 277
  structure, 282–283
training, 211
training and learning needs analysis (TLNA), 218
training needs, assessment and analysis of, 220
transfer of learning, 218–219
transfer of training, 221
transnational corporation (TNC), 383
transnational strategy, 383
triple bottom line, 354
TUC-affiliated super-unions, 283

U

UK Equality Act 2010, 229
UK Health and Safety Executive (HSE), 327, 332
UK statute law, 197
Ulrich Human Resource Business Partner model, 37
unilateral regulation, 272
union-acceptance strategy, 272–273
union-avoidance, 268, 275
unionisation levels, 282
union learning representative (ULR), 229
union membership, 278–281
union-replacement strategy, 274
union-resistance strategy, 273
union voice, 294
unitarist perspective, organisations, 298
United kingdom
  average union density, 280, 281

average union membership, 280
Covid-19 recovery, 271
salaries for selective occupations and CEOs, 247
trade union density, private sector collective bargaining and rising income inequality, 287
United Nations Conference on the Human Environment, 353
United Nations Development Index (HDI), 203
United States, performance management in, 194–195
unit labour costs (ULC), 250
unit of analysis, 72
unorganizational conflict, 297
UN Sustainable Development Goals (SDGs), 326, 370
UN's World Commission on Environment and Development (WCED), 353

V

validity, 151–152
values-based interviewing, 163
variable pay scheme (VPS), 252
varieties of capitalism approach, 272
verbal communication, 314
'vertical integration,' 61
voluntarism *vs.* interventionism, in L&D, 204, 205

W

wage-bargaining, *see* collective bargaining
well-being
Industry 4.0, 344–345
at work, 326
wildcat strike, 297, 298
work and job design
business process re-engineering, 102–103
case study, 110–111
classical work systems, 97–99
critiquing job, 105–108
definition, 88–93
development, 94–96
high-performance work systems, 103–105
Japanese management, 100–101
job characteristic model, 100
job enlargement, 99
job enrichment, 99
job rotation, 99
nature of, 85–86
Taylorism, 99–100
workers
employment and psychological contract, 27
laying off, 133
workers' pro-environmental behaviours, 357–358
work ethic, 392
workforce planning
case study, 138–139
critiquing, 135–136
definition, 115
demand forecasting, 117–120
diversity management, 123–129
nature of, 115–117
organisational responses to forecasts, 121–122
scope of, 115–117
supply forecasting, 120–121
see also flexibility
work-integrated learning (WIL), 204
work-life balance (WLB), 336
workplace
bullying, 337–339
communication issues, 314
employers, 13
individualising reward in, 252
violence, 336–337
wellness, 343–344
Workplace Employment Relations Survey (WERS), 252
workplace health and safety issues
alcohol and drug abuse, 340–341
mental health at work, 332–334
sick building syndrome, 341–342
workplace bullying, 337–339
workplace stress and burnout, 334–336
workplace violence, 336–337
workplace learning
analysis, 227
and knowledge creation, 207–209
workplace pro-environmental behaviour (WPEB), 354, 355, 365
workplace sexual harassment, 301–303
workplace stress
and burnout, 334–336
employee perceptions of, 342–343
work-related accidents, 329
Works Councils, 311
work specialisation, 91
work-wage bargain, 24
World Economic Forum (WEF), 246
World Health Organization (WHO), 325, 332, 341
written communication, 314

Z

zero-hours contracts (ZHCs), 3, 5, 53, 96, 131